I0216613

# THE ETERNAL COVENANT

*Living With God*

## WILLEM J. OUWENEEL

AN EVANGELICAL INTRODUCTION TO
REFORMATIONAL THEOLOGY
VOL IV/2

PART IV: CONSUMMATION:
THE LIVED SHAPE OF THEOLOGY

# AN EVANGELICAL INTRODUCTION TO REFORMATIONAL THEOLOGY

*Part I: Scripture: The Revealed Source For Theology*
    I/1 *The Eternal Word*: God Speaking To Us
    I/2 *The Eternal Torah*: Living Under God

*Part II: God: The Personal Source Behind Theology*
    II/1 *The Eternal God*: God Revealing Himself To Us
    II/2 *The Eternal Christ*: God With Us
    II/3 *The Eternal Spirit*: God Living In Us

*Part III: Redemption: The Christ-Centered Heart of Theology*
    III/1 *The Eternal Purpose*: Living In Christ
    III/2 *Eternal Righteousness*: Living Before God
    III/3 *Eternal Salvation*: Christ Dying For Us
    III/4 *Eternal Life*: Christ Living In Us

*Part IV: Consummation: The Lived Shape of Theology*
    IV/1a *The Eternal People*: God in Relation To Israel: Israel in the Tanakh and the New Testament
    IV/1b *The Eternal People*: God in Relation To Israel: Post-New Testament Israel
    IV/2 *The Eternal Covenant*: Living With God
    IV/3 *The Eternal Kingdom*: Living Under Christ

*Part V: Method: The Comprehensive Foundation of Theology*
    V/1 *Eternal Truth*: The Prolegomena of Theology

# THE ETERNAL COVENANT

*Living With God*

WILLEM J. OUWENEEL

*The Eternal Covenant: Living With God*

This English edition is a publication of Paideia Press (P.O. Box 500, Jordan Station, Ontario, Canada L0R 1S0). Copyright © 2023 by Paideia Press. All rights reserved. Except for brief quotations in critical publications or reviews, no part of this book may be reproduced in any manner without prior written permission from Paideia Press at the address above.

Unless otherwise indicated, Scripture quotations are from the ESV® Bible (The Holy Bible, English Standard Version®). Copyright © 2001 by Crossway, a publishing ministry of Good News Publishers. Used by permission. All rights reserved.

Scripture quotations or references marked as NKJV are taken from the New King James Version®. Copyright © 1982 by Thomas Nelson, Inc. Used by permission. All rights reserved.

Scripture quotations or references marked as NIV are taken from the Holy Bible, New International Version®, NIV®. Copyright © 1973, 1978, 1984, 2011 by Biblica, Inc.™ Used by permission of Zonderan. All rights reserved worldwide. **www.zonderan.com**. The "NIV" and "New International Version" are trademarks registered in the United States Patent and Trademark Office by Biblica, Inc.™

Book Design By: Michael Wagner (Interior), Steven Martins (Exterior)

ISBN 978-0-88815-350-0

Printed in the United States of America

*I will faithfully give them their recompense, and I will make an **everlasting covenant** with them. Their offspring shall be known among the nations, and their descendants in the midst of the peoples; all who see them shall acknowledge them, that they are an offspring the Lord has blessed.*
Isaiah 61:8–9

*They shall be my people, and I will be their God. I will give them one heart and one way, that they may fear me forever, for their own good and the good of their children after them. I will make with them an **everlasting covenant**, that I will not turn away from doing good to them. And I will put the fear of me in their hearts, that they may not turn from me.*
Jeremiah 32:38–40

*May the God of peace who brought again from the dead our Lord Jesus, the great shepherd of the sheep, by the blood of the **eternal covenant**, equip you with everything good that you may do his will, working in us that which is pleasing in his sight, through Jesus Christ, to whom be glory forever and ever. Amen.*
Hebrews 13:20–21

# Table of Contents

| | | |
|---|---|---|
| Table of Contents (Expanded) | | |
| Series Preface | | i |
| Author's Preface | | v |
| Chapter 1 | The Covenant—What Is It? | 1 |
| Chapter 2 | The Old Testament Covenants | 47 |
| Chapter 3 | The Old Covenant According to the Old Testament | 99 |
| Chapter 4 | Reformed Covenant Theology: Principles | 151 |
| Chapter 5 | Reformed Covenant Theology: History | 205 |
| Chapter 6 | The New Covenant in the New Testament | 249 |
| Chapter 7 | Israel and the Church | 305 |
| Chapter 8 | Some Recent Developments in Covenant Theology | 363 |
| Chapter 9 | An Evangelical Covenant Theology | 415 |
| Appendix 1 | Infant Baptism and "the" Covenant | 465 |
| Appendix 2 | Traveling and Destination | 485 |
| Appendix 3 | Some Notes on the Sovereignty of God | 497 |
| Appendix 4 | Spiritualization | 503 |
| Bibliography | | 521 |
| Scripture Index | | 549 |
| Subject Index | | 571 |

# Table of Contents Expanded

| | |
|---|---|
| Series Preface | i |
| Author's Preface | v |
| 1 The Covenant—What Is It? | 1 |
|   1.1 Introduction | 2 |
|     1.1.1 Three "Projects" | 2 |
|     1.1.2 Israel and the Covenant | 4 |
|     1.1.3 A Dispensationalist Approach? | 7 |
|     1.1.4 Similarities | 9 |
|   1.2 The Character of the Covenant | 10 |
|     1.2.1 What Is a Covenant? | 10 |
|     1.2.2 Duties and Promises | 12 |
|     1.2.3 The New Covenant | 15 |
|   1.3 Torah, Covenant, Righteousness, Kingdom | 18 |
|     1.3.1 Covenant and Torah | 18 |
|     1.3.2 Covenant and Righteousness | 19 |
|     1.3.3 Covenant and Kingdom | 21 |
|   1.4 Terminology | 23 |
|     1.4.1 *Berit* | 23 |
|     1.4.2 *Synthēkē* and *diathēkē* | 25 |
|     1.4.3 *Testamentum* | 26 |
|     1.4.4 Types of Covenants | 27 |
|   1.5 The God-Givenness of the Covenant | 31 |

|  |  | 1.5.1 The God-Given Guarantor | 31 |
|---|---|---|---|
|  |  | 1.5.2 Offices of Christ | 32 |
|  | 1.6 | Ancient Examples of Covenants | 34 |
|  |  | 1.6.1 Characteristics | 34 |
|  |  | 1.6.2 Metaphors | 36 |
|  |  | 1.6.3 Examples of Covenantalism | 37 |
|  | 1.7 | No Paradigms? | 39 |
|  |  | 1.7.1 Not Paradigm but "Truth"? | 39 |
|  |  | 1.7.2 "No Paradigm Needed" | 42 |
| 2 | The Old Testament Covenants | | 47 |
|  | 2.1 | Introduction | 48 |
|  |  | 2.1.1 Different Covenants — In What Sense? | 48 |
|  |  | 2.1.2 Covenants Initiated by Leaders | 50 |
|  |  | 2.1.3 Single-Purpose Covenants | 52 |
|  |  | 2.1.4 Human Covenants | 53 |
|  | 2.2 | Covenants Involving the Whole World | 56 |
|  |  | 2.2.1 The Covenant with the Celestial Bodies (Wider: with Creation) | 56 |
|  |  | 2.2.2 The Covenant with Adam | 59 |
|  |  | 2.2.3 The Covenant with Noah | 64 |
|  | 2.3 | Three Individual Covenants | 68 |
|  |  | 2.3.1 The Covenant with Abr(ah)am | 69 |
|  |  | 2.3.2 The Covenant with Levi | 74 |
|  |  | 2.3.3 The Covenant with David | 78 |
|  | 2.4 | Three Covenants with Israel | 82 |
|  |  | 2.4.1 The Sinaitic Covenant with Israel | 82 |
|  |  | 2.4.2 The Palestinian Covenant with | |

|   |     | Israel | 89 |
|---|---|---|---|

|   |     | 2.4.3 The New Covenant with Israel | 91 |
|---|---|---|---|
| 3 | The Old Covenant According to the Old Testament | | 99 |
|   | 3.1 | Its Matrimonial Character | 100 |
|   |     | 3.1.1 Israel's Wedding Vow | 100 |
|   |     | 3.1.2 More on Wedding Vows | 103 |
|   | 3.2 | Love and Loyalty | 105 |
|   |     | 3.2.1 A Relationship of Steadfast Love | 105 |
|   |     | 3.2.2 Covenant Loyalty | 107 |
|   |     | 3.2.3 Love and Counter-Love | 108 |
|   | 3.3 | The Wedding at Sinai | 111 |
|   |     | 3.3.1 Some Prophetic Words | 111 |
|   |     | 3.3.2 A Jewish Wedding | 112 |
|   | 3.4 | Kinds of Covenant Partners | 116 |
|   |     | 3.4.1 Two Groups | 116 |
|   |     | 3.4.2 Three Groups | 119 |
|   | 3.5 | Conditional Versus Unconditional | 122 |
|   |     | 3.5.1 An Alleged Covenant of Works | 122 |
|   |     | 3.5.2 A Covenant of Works at Sinai? | 125 |
|   |     | 3.5.3 No Works Without Redemption and Faith | 127 |
|   | 3.6. | Was There a Covenant of Works in Eden? | 129 |
|   |     | 3.6.1 Misunderstanding Grace | 129 |
|   |     | 3.6.2 A Supra-Logical State of Affairs | 131 |
|   |     | 3.6.3 Reformed Corrections | 133 |
|   | 3.7 | Old and New Covenant | 135 |

|  |  | 3.7.1 Pointing to Christ | 135 |
|---|---|---|---|
|  |  | 3.7.2 The Ten Words Again | 137 |
|  | 3.8 | Responsibility and Grace | 139 |
|  |  | 3.8.1 The Demanding and the Giving God | 139 |
|  |  | 3.8.2 Two Viewpoints | 142 |
|  | 3.9 | Once Again: the Old and the New Covenant | 145 |
|  |  | 3.9.1 The Two Are One | 145 |
|  |  | 3.9.2 The Conditionality of the Abrahamic Covenant | 147 |
|  |  | 3.9.3 The Conditionality of the New Covenant | 149 |
| 4 | Reformed Covenant Theology: Principles | | 151 |
|  | 4.1 | Reformed Faith | 152 |
|  |  | 4.1.1 TULIP | 152 |
|  |  | 4.1.2 Pervasive Covenantalizing and Inferentialism | 155 |
|  | 4.2 | Presbyterian Faith | 157 |
|  |  | 4.2.1 The Westminster Standards | 157 |
|  |  | 4.2.2 The Westminster Confession | 159 |
|  | 4.3 | Differences Between Reformed and Presbyterian | 161 |
|  |  | 4.3.1 Early Development | 161 |
|  |  | 4.3.2 No Innate Law | 164 |
|  |  | 4.3.3 A Case Study | 167 |
|  | 4.4 | Covenant and Baptism | 171 |
|  |  | 4.4.1 The Reformed Connection | 171 |

|     |     | 4.4.2 The Connection Loosened | 173 |
|     |     | 4.4.3 The Covenants in Reformed Forms | 176 |
|     | 4.5 | Theologizing About the Covenant | 179 |
|     |     | 4.5.1 The Federalist Paradigm | 179 |
|     |     | 4.5.2 Birth of the Paradigm | 183 |
|     |     | 4.5.3 Graafland's Analysis | 186 |
|     | 4.6 | Covenant Faith and Covenant Theory | 190 |
|     |     | 4.6.1 Jonker on the Covenant | 190 |
|     |     | 4.6.2 Objections | 191 |
|     | 4.7 | Other Metaphors | 194 |
|     |     | 4.7.1 Juridical Metaphors | 194 |
|     |     | 4.7.2 A Juridical and a Social-Economic Metaphor | 197 |
|     |     | 4.7.3 An Ethical Metaphor: Father–Child | 199 |
|     |     | 4.7.4 Another Ethical Metaphor: Husband–Wife | 203 |
| 5   | Reformed Covenant Theology: History | | 205 |
|     | 5.1 | "Covenant Glasses" | 206 |
|     |     | 5.1.1 Introduction | 206 |
|     |     | 5.1.2 Herman Bavinck | 207 |
|     |     | 5.1.3 Herman Ridderbos | 210 |
|     |     | 5.1.4 Johan Heyns | 212 |
|     |     | 5.1.5 Other Voices | 214 |
|     | 5.2 | "Type of Piety" | 215 |
|     |     | 5.2.1 What Was First? | 215 |
|     |     | 5.2.2 Three "-isms" | 217 |

|  |  |  |  |
|---|---|---|---|
| | 5.3 | Older Reformed Theologians | 218 |
| | | 5.3.1 John Calvin | 218 |
| | | 5.3.2 Johannes Cocceius | 222 |
| | | 5.3.3 Alexander Comrie | 224 |
| | 5.4 | Works *Versus* Grace | 228 |
| | | 5.4.1 Again: the Sinaitic Covenant | 228 |
| | | 5.4.2 Circumcision of the Heart | 231 |
| | | 5.4.3 Children of Abraham | 234 |
| | 5.5 | Other Ways | 236 |
| | | 5.5.1 Recapitulation | 236 |
| | | 5.5.2 Wisdom | 238 |
| | | 5.5.3 "Evangelical Reformed" | 239 |
| | 5.6 | Some Exceptional Authors | 242 |
| | | 5.6.1 Philipp van Limborch | 242 |
| | | 5.6.2 Jean de Labadie | 245 |
| 6 | The New Covenant in the New Testament | | 249 |
| | 6.1 | The New Covenant Today | 250 |
| | | 6.1.1 The New Covenant in Old and New Testaments | 250 |
| | | 6.1.2 New Covenant and Federalism | 253 |
| | | 6.1.3 Significance for Today | 255 |
| | | 6.1.4 Continuity | 257 |
| | 6.2 | The Mosaic and the Messianic Torah | 259 |
| | | 6.2.1 Righteousness in Paul's Writings | 259 |
| | | 6.2.2 Righteousness in James' Writings | 262 |
| | | 6.2.3 Similarities | 264 |
| | 6.3 | Various New Testament Passages | 265 |
| | | 6.3.1 Being Like Christ | 265 |

|  |  |  |
|---|---|---|
| | 6.3.2 Passages in Luke's Writings | 267 |
| | 6.3.3 Passages in Paul's Writings | 270 |
| 6.4 | The Covenant in Galatians 3 | 272 |
| | 6.4.1 No Annulment of the Promise | 272 |
| | 6.4.2 The Torah as Guardian: Correct Approach | 275 |
| | 6.4.3 The Torah as Guardian: Incorrect Approach | 278 |
| 6.5 | The Covenant in Galatians 4 | 280 |
| | 6.5.1 Introduction | 280 |
| | 6.5.2 The Two Women | 281 |
| | 6.5.3 Application | 284 |
| 6.6 | The New Covenant in Hebrews: Israel | 286 |
| | 6.6.1 Israel and the Messianic Kingdom | 286 |
| | 6.6.2 Again: Supersessionism | 289 |
| | 6.6.3 The Promises of the New Covenant | 291 |
| 6.7 | The New Covenant in Hebrews: the Church | 293 |
| | 6.7.1 No Spiritualizing the Covenant | 293 |
| | 6.7.2 Characteristics of the New Covenant | 295 |
| | 6.7.3 Jesus As Example and Essence | 296 |
| 6.8 | The Old and New Covenants Again | 298 |
| | 6.8.1 The Ark and Its Covering | 298 |
| | 6.8.2 The Need for a New Polity | 299 |
| | 6.8.3 The Blood of the Covenant | 301 |

| | | |
|---|---|---|
| 7 | Israel and the Church | 305 |
| | 7.1 Introductory Remarks | 306 |
| |     7.1.1 The Central Question | 306 |
| |     7.1.2 Reformed Creeds and Catechisms | 309 |
| |     7.1.3 An Old Testament Church? | 311 |
| | 7.2 The Church Born at Pentecost | 314 |
| |     7.2.1 The Unity of the Church | 314 |
| |     7.2.2 The Mystery of the Church | 317 |
| |     7.2.3 The Church and the Spirit | 320 |
| | 7.3 Similarities Between Old and New Testament Saints | 324 |
| |     7.3.1 Chafer's "Contrasts" | 324 |
| |     7.3.2 More Similarities | 326 |
| |     7.3.3 Metaphors | 330 |
| | 7.4 Differences Between Old and New Testament Saints | 333 |
| |     7.4.1 The People of God | 333 |
| |     7.4.2 The Family of God | 336 |
| |     7.4.3 The Body of Christ | 338 |
| |     7.4.4 The House or Temple of God | 340 |
| | 7.5 The "Spiritual Israel" | 342 |
| |     7.5.1 An Old Testament "Church"? | 342 |
| |     7.5.2 Supersessionism | 345 |
| |     7.5.3 Incorporated into Israel? | 348 |
| |     7.5.4 God's People, Abraham's Offspring, New Covenant | 352 |
| | 7.6 The Olive Tree of Romans 11 | 355 |
| |     7.6.1 Not Israel | 355 |

|  |  |  |  |
|---|---|---|---|
|  | 7.6.2 The Covenant Tree | | 358 |
| 8 | Some Recent Developments in Covenant Theology | | 363 |
|  | 8.1 | Newer Covenant Theories | 364 |
|  |  | 8.1.1 One Covenant of Grace? | 364 |
|  |  | 8.1.2 A Covenant of Redemption? | 367 |
|  |  | 8.1.3 Internal Speculations | 370 |
|  |  | 8.1.4 A Prelapsarian Covenant? | 372 |
|  | 8.2 | Further Developments | 375 |
|  |  | 8.2.1 Theology and Truth | 375 |
|  |  | 8.2.2 Theology and Church Divisions | 377 |
|  |  | 8.2.3 Examples | 379 |
|  | 8.3 | The Covenant Governed by Election | 382 |
|  |  | 8.3.1 Baptized Children | 382 |
|  |  | 8.3.2 A Well-Meant Offer | 383 |
|  | 8.4 | The Covenant Governed by Faith | 386 |
|  |  | 8.4.1 Federal Vision | 386 |
|  |  | 8.4.2 Disappointment | 389 |
|  |  | 8.4.3 Confusion | 391 |
|  |  | 8.4.4 Karl Barth | 394 |
|  | 8.5 | Different Views | 396 |
|  |  | 8.5.1 A "Static" View | 396 |
|  |  | 8.5.2 Nationalistic Supersessionism | 397 |
|  |  | 8.5.3 Natural *Versus* Spiritual | 401 |
|  |  | 8.5.4 Circumcision | 406 |
|  | 8.6 | Final Questions | 408 |
|  |  | 8.6.1 Practical Aspects | 408 |
|  |  | 8.6.2 Covenant and Torah | 411 |

| 9 | An Evangelical Covenant Theology | 415 |
|---|---|---|
| | 9.1 Federalism Evaluated | 416 |
| |     9.1.1 Misunderstandings | 416 |
| |     9.1.2 Goal and Means | 419 |
| | 9.2 Covenant and Kingdom | 421 |
| |     9.2.1 The Earlier Covenants and the Kingdom | 421 |
| |     9.2.2 The Later Covenants and the Kingdom | 424 |
| | 9.3 Christianity Is Not Federalist | 427 |
| |     9.3.1 Problems of Federalism | 427 |
| |     9.3.2 Six "-isms" | 431 |
| | 9.4 Again, the Abrahamic Covenant | 433 |
| |     9.4.1 Two Promises | 433 |
| |     9.4.2 Continuity and Discontinuity | 436 |
| | 9.5 Again, the New Covenant | 438 |
| |     9.5.1 Hebrews 7–12 | 438 |
| |     9.5.2 Second Corinthians 3 | 440 |
| | 9.6 More Than Justification | 442 |
| |     9.6.1 Quintessentially Christian | 442 |
| |     9.6.2 Justification | 443 |
| | 9.7 *Theosis* | 446 |
| |     9.7.1 Conform to the Image | 446 |
| |     9.7.2 Two Central Questions | 448 |
| |     9.7.3 The Eastern Approach | 451 |
| |     9.7.4 Some Highlights in the Epistles | 453 |
| |     9.7.5 Conclusion | 456 |
| | 9.8 Quintessential Christian Blessings | 457 |

|  |  |  |
|---|---|---|
| | 9.8.1 Individual Blessings | 457 |
| | 9.8.2 Collective Blessings | 460 |
| Appendix 1 | Infant Baptism and "the" Covenant | 465 |
| 1 | Exegesis of Colossians 2:11–12 | 465 |
| | 1.1 Figurative Circumcision | 465 |
| | 1.2 The "Circumcision of Christ" | 467 |
| 2 | How Some Federalists Handle Colossians 2 | 470 |
| | 2.1 A Parallel? | 470 |
| | 2.2 Reformed Arguments | 473 |
| 3 | The Context of Colossians 2 | 476 |
| | 3.1 Credobaptism | 476 |
| | 3.2 Leaving the World Behind | 477 |
| 4 | Further Arguments | 479 |
| | 4.1 No Replacement of Circumcision | 479 |
| | 4.2 Natural and Spiritual Progeny | 482 |
| Appendix 2 | Traveling and Destination | 485 |
| 1 | The Traveling Concept | 485 |
| | 1.1 Traveling in the Covenants | 485 |
| | 1.2 Traveling in Luke | 487 |
| 2 | The Altar Concept | 490 |
| | 2.1 The Destination of Traveling | 490 |
| | 2.2 The Altar of the Old Covenant | 492 |
| | 2.3 The Altar of the New Covenant | 494 |
| Appendix 3 | Some Notes on the Sovereignty of God | 497 |
| 1 | Theological Imagination | 497 |
| 2 | God's Counsel and God's Ways | 499 |

| | | | |
|---|---|---|---|
| Appendix 4 | | Spiritualization | 503 |
| 1 | | Spiritualizing Prophecy Away | 503 |
| | 1.1 | Romans 9–11 | 503 |
| | 1.2 | Matthew 24 | 504 |
| 2 | | Examples of Spiritualization | 506 |
| | 2.1 | Israel: Physical Aspects | 506 |
| | 2.2 | Israel: Spiritual Aspects | 508 |
| 3 | | The Kingdom of God | 510 |
| | 3.1 | Passages | 510 |
| | 3.2 | Approaches | 512 |
| 4 | | Federalism and Spiritualism | 514 |
| | 4.1 | The Promised Land and the Covenant of Grace | 514 |
| | 4.2 | Irrevocable Promises | 516 |
| Bibliography | | | 521 |
| Scripture Index | | | 549 |
| Subject Index | | | 571 |

# Series Preface

BY MEANS OF THIS PREFACE, the editor and publisher of this series wish to help the reader both understand and process the content of these volumes.

The capacities and erudition of Dr. Willem Ouweneel need no demonstration or defense from us. His voluminous work and prodigious writing stand as a testimony of his love for the Lord Jesus Christ, God's Word, and God's people.

But these volumes present ideas that will surprise some, anger others, and possibly confuse still others. Both the editor and publisher disagree with some of Dr. Ouweneel's assertions and conclusions, but this is not the place for offering our counter-arguments. That requires an altogether different venue. Nevertheless, discerning readers will legitimately wonder why this editor and publisher invested effort and resources in putting these volumes into print.

At least three reasons justify that investment. Each of them is very sensitive.

The first reason is: *self-examination*. Some of our readers may conclude that, in presenting his exegetical, doctrinal, and historical case, Dr. Ouweneel is "coloring outside the lines" of what they have come to believe. He challenges deeply and firmly held convictions and beliefs, like those associated with Israel, with the law of God, with election and reprobation, with infant baptism, with covenant theology, and with justification. At each point, his challenges call us readers to self-examination, regarding our love for Scripture, for the God of Scripture, and for the Truth revealed and incarnated personally in Jesus Christ. One of Ouweneel's challenges is for us believers in Jesus Christ who are Reformed and Presbyterian church members to recognize that there are millions, even billions, of Jesus-believers who disagree with us *and are nevertheless genuine Christians.* And they ought to be acknowledged as such.

The second reason is: *repentance.* Coming, as they do, from one who lives and teaches outside the orbit of many of our readers, Dr. Ouweneel's observations about the state of our (numerous) churches and of our (interminable) doctrinal squabbles ought to embarrass us Reformed and Presbyterian church members. Our incessant polemicizing, our cantankerous stridency, and our offenses against the unity of Christ's church seriously compromise the gospel's witness to the watching world. Brothers and sisters, we must repent of these, for the sake of the gospel, for the sake of the church's witness, and for the sake of our children.

The third reason is: *ecumenicity.* This reason may indeed strike you as strange, but one of the salutary outcomes of reading Dr. Ouweneel's arguments can be this: *not* that you surrender your commitments and convictions that are being challenged, but instead that you come to *respect* and *love* those Jesus-believers who don't share them with you. These Christians are those whose spiritual pilgrimage and gospel-guided history have not brought them to the same place on the road, but who nonetheless are walking the same road as we.

You may well be asking: How, then, is this different from advocating doctrinal relativism? If these distinctive features of Reformed confession and theology are biblical, then why is Dr. Ouweneel being given a microphone for proclaiming his criticisms and rejections of these distinctive emphases of Reformed teaching? The short answer is this: So that from this brother in Christ, this close cousin in the faith, this fellow pilgrim-soldier, we may learn how to lock arms with other Jesus-believers as we face unbelief in our day, even if we can't hold hands. So that we may learn what it means to be Jesus-believers *first*, Reformed or Presbyterian confessors *second*, and only then, *thirdly*, *theological advocates*.

So we leave you with this challenge: Why do you believe what you believe? What is your biblical warrant? Dr. Ouweneel presents the various positions prevalent in Christendom fairly. The reader will learn why others believe what they believe, and why they don't emphasize certain teachings in the same way that we do.

These books, then, are *not* for the faint of faith. But they *are* for those wanting to grow up and mature into the unity of faith in our Lord Jesus Christ (John 17: 20-23; Eph. 4:13).

Nelson D. Kloosterman, editor
John Hultink, publisher

# Author's Preface

THIS BOOK IS A RE-WORKING and expansion of part of Volume 9 of my *Evangelical Dogmatic Series*, which was published by Medema, Heerenveen [the Netherlands] and comprises a total of twelve volumes.[1] Part of it was already introduced in the first volume of the present series, *The Eternal Torah*.[2] I have discussed virtually every part of this present book far more extensively in this Dogmatic Series, which is available only in Dutch, however.

In the present series, the next volume will be *Eternal Righteousness*, dealing with the doctrine of righteousness and justification. Because I would like all the volumes in this series to be largely independent of each other, a certain overlap between them is inevitable.

In Volume 7 of the *Evangelical Dogmatic Series* just mentioned, *De Kerk van God I*,[3] I pointed to God's three great "projects," (a) the church of God, (b) the covenant of God, and (c) the kingdom of God, and the relationships between them. For theologians, it is of special interest to notice that dispensationalists emphasize the church as well as the kingdom (viewed too one-sidedly in relation to Israel), at the expense of

---
1. Ouweneel (2011, chapters 1–4; also see 2010a, e.g., 91–92, 204–205, 210–16).
2. Ouweneel (2015a).
3. Ouweneel (2010b).

the covenant. By contrast, federalists emphasize the covenant too much, at the expense of the church and the kingdom. Or rather, they subsume the church and the kingdom under the overarching heading of the covenant. They "covenantalize" Scripture, as someone has put it, just as dispensationalists see all Scripture in the light of the alleged sharp distinction between the church and Israel. As a theologian, but also as a philosopher with great interest in the formation of scholarly theories and paradigms, I find it highly fascinating to investigate how federalist covenant theology came to full blossoming — with all the positive as well as negative sides of such a development.

In the present book, the term *Evangelical* means little more than orthodox Protestant (in which "orthodox" refers to Protestants rooted in the Apostolic and Nicene Creeds, as well as in the sixteenth-century Reformation). I use the term Evangelical to indicate that I am neither a classical dispensationalist, nor a classical federalist, and that I feel more at home with pre-scholastic Christianity. This Christianity apparently did not yet feel constrained to develop what I call an "inferential theology": an elaborate thought system built upon inferences from inferences from inferences (inferentialism). All of these matters will be explained in this book.

I have written the present volume with essentially two purposes in mind. On the one hand, I wanted to emphasize the importance of God's covenant in Scripture — a fact that is often too little appreciated by Roman Catholics, Anglicans, Lutherans, and Free Church Evangelicals. On the other hand, I wished to point out that some federalists (Reformed and Presbyterian theologians) have stretched the notion of the covenant too far. They did so, not only in "covenantalizing" all Scripture, but also in their "inferential-theological" approach, in which they have invented and imagined the most subtle distinctions in their covenant doctrine that go way beyond Scripture and about which they have been quarreling from the seventeenth century onward until this very day, even creating church divisions over their distinctions. We learn from federalists about the importance of the biblical covenant(s); I am tremendously grateful to them for that. However, we also learn from them the consequences of not remaining as close to Scripture as possible.

Part of this book was written in the Holy Land of Israel, where a nation is living that still claims to be *the* covenant people of God. During my writing, I noticed how all the quarrels between federalists and other Christians, or even among federalists themselves, were far removed from this place. In this land, thinking about the covenant occurs on a very different level. Throughout the years (since 1983), I have met here with orthodox Jews, liberal Jews, Messianic Jews, traditional Christian Palestinians, and Evangelical Palestinians (not to mention Muslims, of course). The people most interested in the subject of "the" covenant seemed to be Jews of all stripes. The Christians—again: of whatever stripe—seemed to have very different things on their minds. I would recommend that all my Reformed friends, in the Netherlands, in North America, and in South Africa, live here for awhile and have their horizon broadened through conversations with all the movements mentioned. It might heal them from the insularity that I find so characteristic of the Reformed intramural debates on the covenant.

Bible quotations in this book are usually from the English Standard Version. When other translations are used, this is indicated. Quotations from deuterocanonical books are from the Good News Translation. I have taken the liberty of occasionally substituting "Torah" for "law," or "Messiah" for "Christ," or capitalizing the word "covenant" in these quotations. For quotations from the Talmud, I have used the Soncino edition.

I thank Dr. Nelson D. Kloosterman again very warmly for his expert editorial work on the manuscript of this book. And I am again deeply thankful to my publisher, John Hultink, for his constant encouragement in this entire project.

Willem J. Ouweneel
Huis ter Heide, Netherlands
Fall, 2014

# Chapter 1
# The Covenant — What Is It?

*Then the* L*ord* *spoke to you*
  *out of the midst of the fire.*
*You heard the sound of words,*
  *but saw no form;*
    *there was only a voice.*
*And he declared to you his covenant,*
  *which he commanded you to perform,*
  *that is, the Ten Commandments,*
*and he wrote them*
  *on two tablets of stone. . . .*
*Take care, lest you forget the covenant of the*
L*ord* *your God,*
  *which he made with you,*
*and make a carved image,*
  *the form of anything that the* L*ord* *your*
*God has forbidden you.*
*For the* L*ord* *your God is a consuming fire,*
  *a jealous God. . . .*
*For the* L*ord* *your God is a merciful God.*
  *He will not leave you or destroy you*
*or forget the covenant with your fathers*
  *that he swore to them.*
        Deuteronomy 4:12–13, 23–24, 31

**Summary:** *The covenant is one of three great divine "projects," the other two being the church and the kingdom. Christ in relation to Israel is the center of all three projects. This chapter introduces the notion of the covenant, and describes its main characteristics in regard to both Human–Human and God–Human covenants. Most important are the so-called Old Covenant and New Covenant. The covenant concept is briefly compared with the related concepts of the Torah and of righteousness (see the other two volumes in this series). Terms for, and types of, covenant are briefly discussed. Christ is presented as the Guarantor, Mediator, Executor, and Testator of the New Covenant. A brief comparison with ancient covenants is made, and a brief initial comment on federalism (Reformed covenant theology) is given.*

## 1.1 Introduction
### 1.1.1 Three "Projects"

THIS BOOK IS ABOUT THE biblical notion of the covenant. It is not easy to speak about this notion as such, because it is linked with many theological subjects. For instance, there is the continuity question: What is the relationship and the distinction between (Old Testament) Israel and the (New Testament) church, and thus between the Old Covenant and the New Covenant? Is the church the universal covenant people of God from converted Adam until the last day, or is the church (the *Ekklesia*) the New Testament Body of Christ, unified with its glorified Head at the right hand of God, and the Temple of the Holy Spirit, and as such emphatically distinct from Old Testament Israel? What are the implications of our answers to these questions for the doctrine of the covenant? Did God make a covenant with the Body of Christ? How can we prove this from Scripture if we wish to avoid the supersessionist view that the church is the "new Israel" (or "spiritual Israel"), which has *replaced* Israel as God's people on earth?

Consider another issue dividing so many Christians: water baptism. Many theologians agree that baptism is an initiatory rite. But to what is it the initiation? To the covenant, is the federalist reply (because of how they read Col. 2:11–12). To the Body of Christ, is the claim of many Baptists (because of how they read 1 Cor. 12:12–13). To the kingdom of God, is what many other theologians would argue (because of how they read Matt. 28:18–19). The real controversy about baptism is not so much the choice between infant baptism (paedobaptism) or believers' baptism (credobaptism[1]), but primarily about whether baptism is a covenantal, an ecclesiastical, or a kingdom matter. All other questions concerning baptism follow from this one.

Thank God, apart from these and many other questions, there are many points on which all orthodox (say, "Nicene") Christians will easily agree. First, we have to note that Jesus Christ is, of necessity, the very center of all three "projects" that we may distinguish within God's ways with the world: (a) the *church* of God, (b) the *covenant* of God, and (c) the *kingdom* of God. That is, Jesus is (a) the Head of the Body (Eph. 4:15; 5:23; Col. 1:18; 2:10, 19), the Bridegroom of the bridal church (2 Cor. 11:2; Eph. 5:25–32; Rev. 19:7–9), (b) he is the Guarantor and Mediator of the New Covenant (Heb. 7:22; 8:6; 9:15; 12:24), and (c) he is the Lord and King of God's kingdom (Matt. 28:18; Phil. 2:9–11; Rev. 19:11–16).

Second, the Holy Spirit is of eminent importance as well: the *church* is the dwelling place of the Holy Spirit (Eph. 2:22; cf. 1 Cor. 3:16), and the *covenant* as well as the *kingdom* are, so to speak, the spheres wherein the Spirit works (see, e.g., Isa. 59:21; Hag. 2:4–5; 2 Cor. 3:6; Heb. 10:29).

Third, there is a clear eschatological dimension in all three "projects": the New *Covenant* is fully realized in the coming *kingdom* of God (e.g., Jer. 30:36–41),[2] in which the *church* will be, so to speak, the "last Eve" at the side of the "last Adam" (cf. 1 Cor. 15:45–49; Eph. 5:25–32). We will return in chapter 7 to discuss the latter point extensively.

---

1. An ugly word, because paedo- and baptism are Greek, while credo- is Latin (though *baptismus* is a loanword in the Vulgate).
2. Cf. the title of Gentry and Wellum (2012).

Fourth, I mention the question concerning the Lord's Supper. There is a clear *covenantal* aspect to it, because Jesus said at its institution: "[T]his is my blood of the covenant, which is poured out for many for the forgiveness of sins" (Matt. 26:28). There is a clear *ecclesiastical* aspect to it, as Paul explained to the Corinthians: "The bread that we break, is it not a participation in the body of Christ? Because there is one bread, we who are many are one body, for we all partake of the one bread" (1 Cor. 10:16-17). There is a clear *kingdom* aspect to it, because Jesus said after he had handed out the cup: "Truly, I say to you, I will not drink again of the fruit of the vine until that day when I drink it new in the kingdom of God" (Mark 14:25); and Paul wrote: "For as often as you eat this bread and drink the cup, you proclaim the Lord's death until he comes" (1 Cor. 11:26; notice how Paul uses the typical kingdom term "the Lord" seven times in vv. 17-32).

## 1.1.2 Israel and the Covenant

I have written several books on two of the "projects" mentioned: on the church of God and the kingdom of God.[3] The present volume is on the covenant of God. I do not consider Israel as such to be a separate main "project" of God in world history *apart from* the covenant, the church, and the kingdom, because Israel is the very pivot of all these three "projects." First, the Abrahamic covenant was in view of Israel ("in your offspring [i.e., Israel] shall all the nations of the earth be blessed," Gen. 22:18; cf. John 4:22, "salvation is from the Jews"), the Sinaitic covenant was established with Israel (Exod. 24), and the New Covenant is established with "the house of Israel and the house of Judah" (Jer. 31:31-34). The apostle Paul even says, "to them [i.e., Israel] belong . . . the covenants" (Rom. 9:4).

Second, in the early part of its existence, the New Testament church consisted exclusively of Israelites (Acts 4-8). The (half-Jewish) Samaritans of Acts 8 were the first newcomers.

---

3. See especially Ouweneel (2010b; 2010c; 2011, chapters 9-14).

Moreover, the apostles and prophets who laid its foundation (Eph. 2:20) were all Jews. (If we may reckon Luke to be among these [New Testament] prophets, he was of non-Jewish descent, but presumably a Jewish proselyte even before he heard the Christian gospel.)

Third, Israel will be the center of the kingdom in its future glorious form: "It shall come to pass in the latter days that the mountain of the house of the LORD shall be established as the highest of the mountains, and shall be lifted up above the hills; and all the nations shall flow to it, and many peoples shall come, and say: 'Come, let us go up to the mountain of the LORD, to the house of the God of Jacob, that he may teach us his ways and that we may walk in his paths.' For out of Zion shall go the Torah, and the word of the LORD from Jerusalem. He shall judge between the nations, and shall decide disputes for many peoples; and they shall beat their swords into plowshares, and their spears into pruning hooks; nation shall not lift up sword against nation, neither shall they learn war anymore" (Isa. 2:1–4; cf., e.g., 9:6–7; Zech. 14).

For a biblical understanding of the covenant(s), a biblical view of the people Israel is indispensible. Christian theology badly needs what Arnold Fruchtenbaum has called "Israelology."[4] In federalism (that is, Reformed and Presbyterian covenant theology), the view of the covenant is usually connected with some—moderate or severe—form of supersessionism (or substitutionalism, or replacement theology). Each of these refers to the view that to some extent the church has taken the place of Israel as God's people on earth, assigning the blessings to the church and the curses to Israel. Among other things, this leads to a very different view of eschatology (the doctrine of the future things of God). As dispensationalist Dwight Pentecost put it: "God's eschatological program is determined and prescribed by these covenants [mentioned in Scripture] and one's eschatological system is determined

---

4. Fruchtenbaum (1992).

and limited by the interpretation of them."[5] To this he added his view that the biblical covenants strongly differ from the theological covenants as postulated by federalist theologians. Of course, we will enter into this question extensively in the following chapters.

One could speak of a (Reformed/Presbyterian) paradigm in which the covenant is made *the* central notion of the Bible (federalism; see the Foreword to the present book: Scripture is "covenantalized"). I do not believe that such a federalism is the correct approach; the church and kingdom cannot be subsumed under the covenant, just as, for that matter, the church and the covenant cannot be subsumed under the kingdom, or the covenant and the kingdom subsumed under the church. But I do believe that the doctrine of the covenant is more important than what many non-Reformed theologians (Catholics, Anglicans, Lutherans, Free Church Evangelicals) have made of it—as long as we view the covenants in their proper biblical context.

In this respect, I have learned much from Reformed theologians. However, I have never felt the inclination to subscribe to federalism myself; I prefer a "CCK paradigm," in which the church (C), the covenant (C), and the kingdom (K) of God are treated as distinct "projects" of God, which come together in Jesus Christ. If I were forced to choose between the three, I would suggest that the kingdom is the most overarching concept of the three (if properly understood; see on this, §1.3.3). Fortunately, I am *not* forced to choose which of the three—church, covenant, or kingdom—is the leading principle in the Bible. I prefer to live with these three "projects" placed alongside each other on equal footing as three different ways to describe God's decrees concerning, and ways with, the world or, if you like, three different aspects of these divine decrees and ways.

In this book, I will concentrate on the covenant, without

---

5. Pentecost (1964, 65).

for one moment losing sight of the other two "projects." And I will strongly concentrate on Israel because the Israelites are the primary partners and beneficiaries of most of the covenants. It cannot even be proven from Scripture that the New Covenant was ever, or will ever be, *established* with the church as such — unless, in a typically suppersessionist way, one views the church as the "spiritual Israel." Therefore, any theological treatment of covenant theology presupposes a certain view of the relationship between Israel and the church, as I hope to elucidate in the course of this book.

### 1.1.3 A Dispensationalist Approach

Let me add, however, that there *is* a clear relationship between the covenant and the church. This cannot be denied, as classic dispensationalists have often done: Jesus referred to the New Covenant at the institution of the Lord's Supper (Luke 22:20; 1 Cor. 11:25), and the apostles are called "ministers of a new covenant" (2 Cor. 3:6). I will come back to this often and extensively. I wish to underscore, then, that the present book is *not* a classic dispensationalist approach to covenant theology in the line of John N. Darby, the *Scofield Reference Bible*, and the systematic theology of Lewis Sperry Chafer.[6] Others may judge whether this book is part of what is called "revised"[7] or "progressive" dispensationalism.[8] I do not enter into this question here, because dispensationalism is not my subject at the moment.[9]

There is one thing that all the varieties of dispensationalism have in common, and that is the view of the fundamental differences between Israel and the church (see chapter 7). This is the view that I myself take; in this sense, the present book definitely belongs more to the dispensationalist tradition than to any other tradition. For an evaluation of federalism this

---

6. See the prophetic volumes in Darby (n.d.-a); Scofield (1909); Chafer (1983).
7. See, e.g., Ryrie (1953; 1986); Pentecost (1964); Walvoord (1999).
8. See especially Saucy (1993); Blaising and Bock (2000).
9. See Ouweneel (2012a, especially chapters 5 and 9).

means, as I will explain later in more detail, that the church has *not* replaced ethnic Israel in God's ways with the world, as federalism teaches. None of the promises that God has made with the nation of Israel specifically, particularly in view of the promised land, has anything to do with God's plan of salvation for the nations. The church is the Body of the glorified Christ and the Temple of the Holy Spirit that was poured out on the day of Pentecost, and as such is essentially different from ethnic Israel. However, in opposition to classic dispensationalists, I maintain that there *is* a connection between the salvation of Israel and that of the nations, which lies in the promises made to Abraham: "In you all families of the earth shall be blessed" (Gen. 12:3; cf. 18:18; 22:18; 26:4; 28:14). This is not just a reference to the nations in the Messianic kingdom. The faith of Abraham (Gen. 15:6) made him the father of all believers (Rom. 4:11), and is used by Paul as the model for justification by faith (Rom. 4:3; Gal. 3:6; cf. James 2:23).

The two most important differences between dispensationalism and federalism, then, lie within ecclesiology and eschatology.[10] They lie in ecclesiology because of dispensationalism emphasizing the discontinuity, and federalism the continuity, between Israel and the church. They lie in eschatology because of the realization of the New Covenant: primarily in the restored ethnic Israel or primarily in the church, respectively. One of the practical consequences of this difference is the view of baptism. Dispensationalists are usually credobaptists (with John N. Darby and some other Exclusive Brethren leaders as a striking exception), federalists are usually paedobaptists (with Reformed Baptists as striking exceptions) (see Appendix I). Another consequence is that dispensationalists are invariably premillennialists (the view that Christ will return before his millennial reign), whereas federalists are usually amillennialists (the view that there is no future millennial reign) or postmillennialists (the view that Christ returns after

---

10. Cf. Wellum (2012, 42–43, 58–59).

the future millennial reign).[11]

### 1.1.4 Similarities

Instead of emphasizing only the differences between dispensationalism and federalism, we must also point to certain similarities. I limit myself to a simple summary.

(1) The "dispensation of innocence," as dispensationalists call it, that is, the alleged dispensation before the fall of Adam, is characterized by the alleged "covenant of works" that God made with prelapsarian Adam (see chapters 2 and 3).

(2) The alleged "dispensation of conscience," extending from postlapsarian Adam to Noah, is characterized by the alleged "covenant of grace" that God, in its earliest form, made with postlapsarian Adam.

(3) The alleged "dispensation of human government," extending from Noah to Abraham, is characterized by the Noahic covenant.

(4) The alleged "dispensation of promise," or "of patriarchal rule," extending from Abraham to Moses, is characterized by the Abrahamic covenant.

(5) The alleged "dispensation of the (Mosaic) Torah," extending from Moses to Christ, is characterized by the Mosaic or Sinaitic covenant (which was further specified in the Palestinian covenant; also the Levitical and the Davidic covenants belong to this "dispensation").

(6) The alleged "dispensation of grace," or "of the church," extending from the first to the second coming of Christ, is characterized by the New Covenant in its present, preliminary fulfillment.

(7) The alleged "dispensation of the kingdom," or "of the Millennium," extending from the second coming of Christ to the "eternal state" (the new heavens and the new earth), is characterized by the definitive establishment of the New Cov-

---

11. See Ouweneel (2012a, chapter 9); *millennium* ("thousand years") may be taken literally or figuratively here.

enant with Israel.

The main difference is probably this: these dispensations do not overlap. A new one begins when the previous one ends, each of these eras being characterized by a specific test of God, and ending in judgment, after which God makes an entirely new beginning. The biblical covenants, however, do overlap to a certain extent. The Noahic, the Abrahamic, the New Covenant (as the renewal of the Old Covenant), the Levitical and the Davidic covenants, all retain their validity as long as the present earth lasts, or even longer. One covenant was added to the previous ones, as Paul says of the Sinaitic Torah that it was "added" to the Abrahamic promise: "For if the inheritance comes by the law, it no longer comes by promise; but God gave it to Abraham by a promise. Why then the law? It was added because of transgressions, until the offspring should come to whom the promise had been made, and it was put in place through angels by an intermediary" (Gal. 3:18–19).

## 1.2 The Character of the Covenant
### 1.2.1. What Is a Covenant?[12]

In a covenant viewed in its biblical meaning, at least the following seven features can be identified.[13]

(a) *Two parties*. A covenant is a relationship, arrangement,

---

12. For introductions to the subject, especially from a Reformed or related point of view, see the following works in English language: Kline (1963; 1967; 2006a; 2006b); Pentecost (1964, 65–128); Fensham (1967); Hillers (1969); McCarthy (1972; 1978); Jewett (1978); Kaiser (1978); Robertson (1980); Dumbrell (1984); Nicholson (1986); Kaufmann (1988); Strehle (1988); Lehne (1990); Van der Waal (1990); Weir (1990); Lohfink (1991); Wright (1991); Christiansen (1995); Schouls (1996); Stam (1999); Shepherd (2000); Lillback (2001); McKay (2001); Horton (2002; 2006; 2007; 2009; 2011); Smith (2003); Strawbridge (2003); Golding (2004); Wilkins and Garner (2004); Grant and Wilson (2005); Gräbe (2006); Schreiner and Wright (2006); Waters (2006); Clark (2007); Estelle et al. (2009); Hahn (2009); Jeon (2009); Frame (2011); Nichols (2011); Brown and Keele (2012); Gentry and Wellum (2012); Elam et al. (2014); Ouweneel (2015a).
13. See earlier Ouweneel (1982, I, 106).

characterized by a treaty (pact, union, league, alliance, agreement, contract), which always involves at least two parties. There are many earthly covenants in the Bible, between people, that give us an idea of such formal agreements, such as the covenant of Abram with Aner, Eshcol, and Mamre (Gen. 14), between Abraham and Abimelech (Gen. 21), between Abimelech and Isaac (Gen. 26), between Laban and Jacob (Gen. 31), between Joshua and Gibeon (Josh. 9), between Nahash and Jabesh (1 Sam. 11), between Solomon and Hiram (1 Kgs 5), between Ahab and Ben-hadad (1 Kgs 20), and between Nebuchadnezzar and Zedekiah (as implied in 2 Chron. 36:13; see Ezek. 17:13–16).[14]

(b) *God and people*. In the divine covenants, the one party is God, the other party is a certain person (invariably together with his offspring), or a certain group of people linked together by blood bonds (a family such as the family of Abraham, Levi, or David; a nation, namely, the nation of Israel). This fact that there are always two partners in the divine covenants is sometimes referred to as the *dipleuric* character of the divine covenants. They are never rooted in a subject–object scheme, in which God would be the subject, and a human or humans the object. Rather, we speak of intersubjectivity: it is God who actively institutes and keeps the covenant, it is people who actively keep or break the covenant.

(c) *Unilateral initiative*. Nevertheless, in the biblical covenants, it is always God who unilaterally takes the initiative in establishing a covenant, never people; therefore, he calls each of them "*my* covenant" (Gen. 6:18; 9:9–15; 17:2–21; Exod. 6:4–5; Lev. 26:15, 42–44; etc.). Therefore, we also speak of the *monopleuric* character of the divine covenants. God invites a certain person (with his offspring), or a certain group of people (a family or nation) to enter into a covenant relationship with him. Such an invitation is often called a "calling": "out of Israel I called my son" (Hos. 11:1; cf. Exod. 4:22), which

---

14. See Van der Waal (1990, chapter 1).

already implied God's covenantal wishes concerning Israel. There are cases in which people do take the initiative, namely, when a godly leader, together with his people, decides to *renew* an extant covenant between God and his people (see §2.1.2).

The unilateral character of the divine covenants is depicted in some of the earthly covenants mentioned under (a). Many of these covenants were two-sided in that the two parties were more or less equal ("parity covenants"). In other examples, one party — the one who took the initiative — was clearly above the other one (suzerainty covenants): the superior party dictated the terms to the other party, no matter how friendly the dominating party behaved. Examples: the covenant between Joshua and Gibeon, between Nahash and Jabesh, and between Nebuchadnezzar and Zedekiah (see further in §1.4.4).

## 1.2.2 Duties and Promises

(d) *Duties*. In a covenant, both parties take certain *duties* upon themselves that they have to fulfill. Because the two parties in a divine covenant are always unequal (cf. [c] above), God assumes his "duties" *voluntarily* (see [f] below). On humanity, however, he *imposes* the latter's duties (cf. [c] above). Usually, both parties accept their duties with a solemn *oath* (e.g., Gen. 21:31; 26:3; Deut. 7:8; 2 Kgs 11:4; 2 Chron. 15:12-14; Ezek. 16:59; 17:16-19; Heb. 6:17). Sometimes, such oaths have a positive form ("as the LORD lives . . . ," e.g., Ruth 3:13; 1 Sam. 14:39, 45; 19:6; etc.). Sometimes, however, they take the form of a *curse* that people invoke upon themselves in case they do not keep the covenant (Gen. 17:14; Deut. 27; Josh. 8:30-34). A striking example is the well-known phrase: "God [or, the gods] do so to me and more if . . .," through which a person curses himself in case he would not keep his promises (e.g., Ruth 1:17; 2 Sam. 3:35; 19:13; 1 Kgs 2:23; 20:10; 2 Kgs 6:31).

By the way, this does *not* mean that "oath" is a synonym

for "covenant."[15] The oath by king Saul with respect to his son Jonathan (1 Sam. 14:39), and the counter-oath of the people (v. 45), did not constitute a covenant at all. The oath taken by Paul's enemies in order to kill him (Acts 23:12, 14, 21) had nothing to do with covenants either — unless one follows a circular argument and claims that every swearing by definition constitutes some form of a covenant. Then Shimei's cursing constituted a covenant, too (2 Sam. 16:5-13), which, of course, is nonsense.

(e) *God's commandments*. People's duties, which they must fulfill, are the terms on which they can have continual communion with God within the covenant. These stipulations or conditions are God's *commandments*. As we will see, there is no biblical covenant without commandments and prohibitions from God. The general character of such commandments is this: "If you wish to remain within the sphere of the covenant, with all its blessings and promises of blessings (see [f] below), then you have to do this and this. . . ." It is the *quid pro quo* principle: "I will do P for you, if you do Q for me."

(f) *God's promises*. The duties that God has voluntarily assumed have the form of *promises* that he makes in regard to the covenant partner: promises of communion with people, support for people, blessings for people. As we will see, there is no biblical covenant without promises from God, which he always perfectly fulfills. As Paul puts it: "[T]he gifts and the calling of God are irrevocable" (Rom. 11:9); and "[A]ll the promises of God find their Yes in him [i.e., Christ]" (2 Cor. 1:20).

Incidentally, this does not mean that "God's promise and his covenant are two words for the same matter."[16] We just saw that the word *oath* was asserted to be a covenant term, and the same has happened to the word *promise*. However, the "promise of the Spirit" (Acts 2:33; cf. John 14:16-17, 26) or the promise of eternal life (Titus 1:2; 1 John 2:25) cannot

---
15. *Contra* Brown and Keele (2012, 19).
16. Hoek and Verboom (2010, 62).

reasonably be called covenantal, unless one starts with the presupposition—which of course cannot be proven—that everything in the Bible is covenantal. The danger of a circular argument is always lurking in such arguments. For instance, several Reformed expositors have taken for granted that "the promise" in Acts 2:39 ("the promise is for you and for your children and for all who are far off, everyone whom the Lord our God calls to himself") is the Abrahamic promise,[17] whereas the reference is clearly and exclusively to the promise of the Spirit (v. 33). Even more clearly, the promise of eternal life in the Johannine sense (cf. John 17:3; 1 John 5:20) has nothing to do with any covenant whatsoever (see §9.7.4).

(g) *Judgment and grace.* If the human covenant partners do not fulfill their covenantal duties, God brings judgment upon them. Sometimes, this judgment was already implied in the *curses* that God announced in advance upon those who would fail to keep the covenant (e.g., Lev. 26; Deut. 28; 2 Sam. 7:14). Yet, he always faithfully keeps his promises, namely, in regard to a "remnant according to the election of grace" (Rom. 11:5 NKJV), even if he has to bring judgment on the wicked majority of the people. Reformed theologians sometimes speak here of "promise and demand," in which, in the well-chosen formulation by Jan van Genderen, God's demand "as demand of the covenant of grace is preceded and followed, supported and surrounded by the promise. Within this covenant, all is grace, including the demand of faith and repentance."[18]

In addition to these seven features relating to the content of a covenant, there are also features pertaining to the outward form: sacrifices, meals, tokens, salt, written documents,

---

17. E.g., the marginal note in the Dutch Statenvertaling; Grosheide (1962, 43–44); Horton (2011, 795); Joel R. Beeke and Ray B. Lanning (www.paedobaptism.com/files/beeke.htm); Thomas Miersma (www.reformedspokane.org/homepages/What's_New_folder/The_Promise_Ad/The_Promise_Ad2.html).
18. Van Genderen (2008, 561; see 560–62).

etc. We will return to this especially in chapter 2.

### 1.2.3 The New Covenant

Generally speaking, we may say that a biblical covenant is a set of conditions instituted by God, on the basis of which people can have communion with him, and God can bless them. Under the Old (Mosaic, Sinaitic) Covenant these conditions consisted of the Mosaic (or Sinaitic) Torah. Under the New Covenant, matters are a little different but—as I showed in the previous volume[19]—not essentially different; here we could speak of conditions in three ways.

(1) God's conditions contain the requirement of an atonement of the "transgressions committed under the first [or, old] covenant" (Heb. 9:15). There can be no New Covenant if there is no repair of what went wrong under the Old Covenant. Jesus Christ fulfilled this condition for his people through his propitiatory work on the cross.

(2) God's conditions also contain the requirement of a righteous foundation for the blessings of the New Covenant.[20] Through this same sacrifice on the cross, Jesus fulfilled this condition for his people, too, that is, for those who take refuge in this propitiatory work of Christ, in the "blood of the covenant" (Heb. 9:20; 10:29; 13:20; cf. Matt. 26:28).[21]

(3) The New Covenant contains its own form of the Torah—the one essential Torah as such is everlasting—namely, the Torah in its Messianic form (see the first volume of this series). This Messianic Torah is imposed upon the beneficiaries of the New Covenant. However, the Messianic commandments are "not burdensome" (1 John 5:3; cf. Deut. 30:11), for Jesus (a) is the great Example for the observation thereof, and he also (b) gives the power of the Holy Spirit to this end.

Other than in the case of the previous two conditions,

---

19. Ouweneel (2015a).
20. See Ouweneel (2009, chapters 7–9).
21. Interestingly, in the Talmud (Yebamoth 71a), the blood flowing at circumcision is also called "blood of the covenant."

Jesus fulfills this third condition not *for* us (on the cross) but *in* us, namely, through his Holy Spirit (Rom. 8:4). The first two conditions are objective, the third is subjective. In the case of the first two conditions, people are entirely passive, but not in the case of the third condition; saying that Jesus fulfills this condition in believers is the same as saying that *believers* fulfill this condition, but then by God's grace, in the power of Jesus, through his Holy Spirit.

Under the Old Covenant, the explicitly granted promises were essentially always earthly and temporary; they referred to an earthly country and an earthly nation, and to all kinds of additional material blessings (see especially Lev. 26:3-13; Deut. 7:12-24; 11:13-15; 28:1-14). But of course, the spiritual blessings (communion with, mutual love between God and his people) were even more important: "For you are a people holy to the LORD your God. The LORD your God has chosen you to be a people for his treasured possession, out of all the peoples who are on the face of the earth. It was not because you were more in number than any other people that the LORD set his love on you and chose you, for you were the fewest of all peoples, but it is because the LORD loves you and is keeping the oath that he swore to your fathers, that the LORD has brought you out with a mighty hand and redeemed you from the house of slavery, from the hand of Pharaoh king of Egypt. Know therefore that the LORD your God is God, the faithful God who keeps covenant and steadfast love with those who love him and keep his commandments, to a thousand generations, and repays to their face those who hate him, by destroying them. He will not be slack with one who hates him. He will repay him to his face" (Deut. 7:6-10).

Under the New Covenant there are also material blessings: Israel—which is still a thoroughly earthly nation—will be restored in the thoroughly earthly land of Israel; there Israel will see "every man under his vine and under his fig tree" (Micah 4:4; Zech. 3:10), they will have abundance of "the grain, the wine, and the oil" and "the young of the flock and the herd" (Jer. 31:12), "the mountains shall drip sweet wine, and the hills shall flow with milk" (Joel 3:18; cf. Amos 9:13). But again, the spiritual blessings (communion, mutual love) will be far more important: "For this is the covenant that I will make with the house of Israel after those days . . .: I will put my law within them, and I will write it on their hearts. And I will be their God, and they shall be my people. And no longer shall each one teach his neighbor and each his brother, saying, 'Know the LORD,' for they shall all know me, from the least of them to the greatest. For I will forgive their iniquity, and I will remember their sin no more" (Jer. 31:33-34).

These will be *eternal* blessings: the promises refer to an "eternal inheritance" (Heb. 9:15), and the covenant will be an "eternal covenant" (13:20; cf. Isa. 55:3; 61:8; Jer. 32:40; 50:5; Ezek. 37:26, *berit 'olâm*, literally "covenant of the [coming] age" or "world"). In the book of Hebrews the word "eternal" must be linked especially with the Messianic kingdom (cf. "the world to come," 2:5; "the age to come," 6:5; "the good things to come," 10:1; "the city to come," 13:14; cf. the "Sabbath rest" in 4:9, and the "kingdom that cannot be shaken" in 12:28). It is on the basis not of the Old Covenant but of the New Covenant that God's people will eventually share in the blessings of that kingdom. This will be explained in chapter 6.

Please note that the contrasts mentioned here must be formulated in a proper way: "earthly" contrasts with "heavenly," but not with "spiritual." As I have emphasized in the first volume of this series, and as we will see more extensively in the present volume, also under (the conditions of) the Old Covenant, true believers in fact always lived by the grace of God, in communion with God, received life from God and forgiveness of sins through (the blood of) the New Covenant, the blood of Christ, and were justified by faith. In opposition to certain Reformed theologians, we will see that this was not *in spite of* the terms of the Old Covenant, but that it was *part and parcel* thereof.

## 1.3 Torah, Covenant, Righteousness, Kingdom
### 1.3.1 Covenant and Torah

In the present series, the Torah is the subject of the first volume, and the covenant the subject of the present, second volume. There is a close relationship between the Torah and the covenant; sometimes, the words even seem almost interchangeable. In the Mishnah, Rabbi Eleazar of Modin spoke of "nullifying the covenant," apparently meaning, "trespassing the Torah."[22] Sifre to Numbers 15:22 explicitly identifies the covenant with the Torah.[23] Scripture speaks several times of "breaking the covenant" in the sense of trespassing the Torah (e.g., Gen. 17:14; Lev. 26:15; Deut. 31:16, 20; Isa. 24:5; Jer. 11:10; Ezek. 16:59; 44:7). When trespasses will have heaped up, God himself "breaks" his covenant with Israel (Lev. 26:44; Jer. 14:21). However, this is only for a time; therefore, it can be said as well: "I will never break my covenant with you" (Judg. 2:1).

In the volume on the Torah, I distinguished a number of "Torahs," or rather, several forms (manifestations) of the Eternal Torah, which may each be considered to be associated with a certain covenant.

(a) The *Adamic Torah* may be viewed in the light of a covenant that God (allegedly) made with prelapsarian Adam, although Scripture does not explicitly speak of such a covenant (I will discuss this point later, together with Hos. 6:7).

(b) The *Noahic Torah* is explicitly associated with the Noahic covenant in Genesis 9. This is the first clear indication in Scripture that there is no Torah without a covenant linked to it, and no covenant without a Torah linked to it.

(c) The *Abrahamic Torah* is explicitly associated with the Abrahamic covenant in Genesis 17. One of the commands of that Torah was circumcision; refusing to obey this command

---

22. Aboth III, 11.
23. Sifre Numbers (ed. Friedman, §III, 31b) (see footnote to Aboth III, 11 in the Soncino edition of the Babylonian Talmud).

is the same as "breaking the covenant" (v. 17). Sometimes, "covenant" and "circumcision" (the sign of the Abrahamic covenant) are treated as interchangeable.[24]

(d) The *Mosaic Torah* is explicitly associated with the Sinaitic covenant in Exodus 19–24. Compare the poetic parallelism in the following passages: Psalm 78:10 ("They did not keep God's *covenant*, but refused to walk according to his *law*"); Isaiah 24:5 ("The earth lies defiled under its inhabitants; for they have transgressed the *laws*, violated the statutes, broken the everlasting *covenant*"); Hosea 8:1 ("[T]hey have transgressed my *covenant* and rebelled against my *law*").

(e) The *Messianic Torah* and the *Millennial Torah* are both associated with the New Covenant, in the "present age" and in the "age to come," respectively: "For this is the *covenant* that I will make with the house of Israel after those days, declares the LORD: I will put my *Torah* within them, and I will write it on their hearts" (Jer. 31:33; cf. Heb. 8:10; 10:16).

See the next chapter for a further treatment of the various Old Testament covenants.

## 1.3.2 Covenant and Righteousness

Justification by faith is the great subject of the third volume of the present series. After the "eternal Torah" (first volume) and the "eternal covenant" (present volume), I will deal with what Daniel 9:24 calls "everlasting righteousness" (cf. Ps. 119:142, "Your righteousness is righteous forever"; Isa. 51:8, "my righteousness will be forever"). Clarence Stam made the interesting observation that "[t]he element of righteousness by faith is never lacking in the covenant relationship. . . . The covenant has always been built on the justification that comes by faith. . . . In the covenant we live by faith alone, publicly show forth the fruits of faith, and all this results from a close,

---

24. E.g., Talmud: Niddah 24b: ". . . a child that is fit for the covenant of the eight days"; in Jewish parlance, "circumcision" is called *berit milah*, "covenant of circumcision" (cf. Acts 7:8, "he [= God] gave him [= Abraham] the covenant of circumcision").

deeply personal fellowship with the LORD himself. This is *in all ages* the profile of a true covenant child."[25] And later he adds:"Faith becomes evident in works, but Abraham's justification was not achieved by his works. It was granted out of grace through faith. This is the bottom line in all covenantal thinking."[26] He observes that, when it comes to walking by faith alone, "the old covenant is not different from the new."[27]

Just as there is no covenant without its own specific form of the Eternal Torah, there is no covenant without its own emphasis on faith and righteousness. Under the (alleged) covenant that God made with postlapsarian Adam and Eve, their son Abel seems to be the prototype of the righteous: he is called the "righteous Abel" (Matt. 23:35), and Hebrews 11:4 tells us: "By faith Abel offered to God a more acceptable sacrifice than Cain, through which he was commended as righteous, God commending him by accepting his gifts."

Regarding Noah, we have a threefold testimony. Genesis 6:9 tells us that he "was a righteous man, blameless in his generation. Noah walked with God." Peter calls Noah "a herald of righteousness" (2 Pet. 2:5), and Hebrews 11:7 calls him "an heir of the righteousness that comes by faith."

Abraham "believed the LORD, and he counted it to him as righteousness" (Gen. 15:6; cf. Rom. 4:3–22; Gal. 3:6; James 2:23). "I have chosen [lit., known] him, that he may command his children and his household after him to keep the way of the Lord by doing righteousness and justice, so that the LORD may bring to Abraham what he has promised him" (Gen. 18:19). "Abraham obeyed my voice and kept my charge, my commandments, my statutes, and my laws" (26:5).

Under the Sinaitic covenant, David is an excellent example (in spite of his failures!): "[H]e walked before you [i.e., God] in faithfulness, in righteousness, and in uprightness of heart toward you" (1 Kgs 3:6). "David . . . walked, with in-

---

25. Stam (1999, 73–74).
26. Ibid., 83.
27. Ibid., 85.

tegrity of heart and uprightness, doing according to all that I have commanded you [i.e., Solomon], and keeping my statutes and my rules" (9:4). Zechariah and Elizabeth stand as New Testament models: "[T]hey were both righteous before God, walking blamelessly in all the commandments and statutes of the Lord" (Luke 1:6). God tells us that there are those "who know righteousness, the people in whose heart is my law" (Isa. 51:7); it is "the doers of the law who will be justified" (Rom. 2:13), says Paul. Walking in the Torah is walking in righteousness.

David wrote: "Blessed is the one whose transgression is forgiven, whose sin is covered. Blessed is the man against whom the LORD counts no iniquity, and in whose spirit there is no deceit. . . . Many are the sorrows of the wicked, but steadfast love [i.e., covenant loyalty! see §3.2] surrounds the one who trusts in the LORD. Be glad in the LORD, and rejoice, O righteous, and shout for joy, all you upright in heart!" (Ps. 32:1–2, 11).

Under the New Covenant it is said of Israel: "In the LORD all the offspring of Israel shall be justified and shall glory" (Isa. 45:25). "[B]y his knowledge shall the righteous one, my servant, make many to be accounted righteous, and he shall bear their iniquities" (Isa. 53:11). "Your people shall all be righteous; they shall possess the land forever, the branch of my planting, the work of my hands, that I might be glorified" (Isa. 60:21).

### 1.3.3 Covenant and Kingdom

Here I must add a note on the kingdom of God. In opposition to a "covenant theology" — a theology dominated by the covenant concept — I would rather plead for a "kingdom theology." This is not the place to elaborate on this,[28] but I must make one remark here. Reformed author Clarence Stam has taken issue with this emphasis on the kingdom instead of on the covenant: "Some people say that in the New Testament

---

28. See Ouweneel (2011, chapters 9–14).

the covenant receives little or no attention and that the focus is, instead, on the kingdom of heaven. . . . It is unfortunate that in this way the concepts of the covenant and the kingdom are placed over against each other, for God's kingdom has always existed. He is king over all the earth . . . (Ps 14:1). The kingdom of God had its earthly centre in Zion: . . . (Ps 24:7-10). It pleased God who is King over all to make his covenant of life with Israel, and to bring forth the Saviour of the world from that people. The line of the covenant is also the line of the kingdom."[29]

There is a lot of truth in this, yet Stam seems to miss an essential point. It is true, the kingdom of God has existed since creation. It was recognized by redeemed Israel (Exod. 15:18 NIV, "The LORD reigns [or, is King] for ever and ever"). But the point that Stam seems to overlook is one essential characteristic of the kingdom of God: *from the outset, it was God's plan and pleasure to place this kingdom under the feet of humanity*. Originally, this was the "first Adam" (Gen. 1:26-28), but he failed miserably. Since then, God is moving, together with his people, to the time when the "Second Man," the "Last Adam," will assume the dominion (cf. 1 Cor. 15:45-47). Since Genesis 3, everything in the Old and New Testaments occurs in preparation for "the kingdom of our God and the authority of his Christ" (Rev. 12:10). This kingdom is presented in the form (a) of Old and New Testament prophecies, (b) of the parables of Jesus, and (c) of many Old Testament types. When it comes to Jesus' kingship, the most important types are Adam, Joseph, Moses, David, Solomon, and further, the Davidic kings. They underscore the fact that in the kingdom of *God* it will be *humans* who will have the dominion.

Of course, Stam is right in emphasizing that "[c]ovenant and kingdom are not two separate entities," and that they "find their unity in Christ."[30] The two are closely interwoven. Yet, the accents in the two are quite different. It is no wonder

---

29. Stam (1999, 105).
30. Ibid., 106.

that Reformed theology was always more interested in "the" covenant, for this could be linked with well-known Reformational themes, such as forgiveness of sins and justification by faith. The interest in the kingdom of God was always more limited and, as I just quoted from Stam, linked more strongly with themes such as God's universal rule (cf. Heidelberg Catechism, Q&A 123: "'Your kingdom come' means: Rule us by your Word and Spirit in such a way that more and more we submit to you [i.e., God]"). In the Synoptic Gospels, however, especially in Matthew, the kingdom is linked far more closely with discipleship and servanthood, with following Christ, with dedication, and elsewhere with the power of the Spirit (e.g., Matt. 12:28; Acts 1:6–8; 1 Cor. 4:20). These are subjects that, on the whole, have received too little attention in the Reformed tradition.

## 1.4 Terminology
### 1.4.1 *Berit*

The Old Testament word for "covenant" is transcribed as *berit* or *brit*,[31] derived from *b-r-h*, a root that seems to have two very different meanings: either "eating" (2 Sam. 12:17; 13:6, 10), or "choosing" (1 Sam. 17:8; 1 Kgs 18:25). Perhaps we need to think here of the first meaning because making a covenant always seems to involve eating (see §2.1.1). Or we have to think of a meaning, preserved in the Akkadian word *burru*, which refers to an agreement established by testimony with an oath (cf. Gen. 26:28; Deut. 29:12–14; 2 Kgs 11:4; 1 Chron. 16:16; Ps. 105:9; Ezek. 16:59; 17:13, 16–19; Heb. 6:16–17; 7:20–21, 28). Generally speaking, a *berit* is an agreement connected with some form of a solemn ceremony to underscore its significance.

(a) The *oath* just mentioned; sometimes, it takes the form of a *curse* that people invoke upon themselves in case they do not keep the covenant (see §1.2.1).

---

31. See extensively Hillers (1969); McCarthy (1978); Harris *et al.* (1980, I, 128–30); VanGemeren (1996, I, 747–55).

(b) *Eating*, having a meal together (see the next chapter, with its references to many covenant meals); meals are also essential at weddings (cf. Laban in Gen. 29:22; Samson in Judg. 14:10), which is of interest because marriage has a covenantal character (cf. Prov. 2:17; Ezek. 16:8; Mal. 2:14).

(c) Shaking *hands* ("He despised the oath in breaking the covenant, and behold, he gave his hand and did all these things," Ezek. 17:18).

(d) The use of *salt* ("It is a covenant of salt forever before the LORD for you and for your offspring with you," Num. 18:19; "[T]he LORD God of Israel gave the kingship over Israel forever to David and his sons by a covenant of salt," 2 Chron. 13:5).

(e) Bringing *sacrifices* that were cut up; hence the Hebrew expression *karat berit*, "to make [literally, cut] a covenant," namely, by cutting up the sacrifices (cf. Gen. 15:18; Jer. 34:18).

(f) Setting up a *stone*, or a *heap of stones*, as a sign that a covenant had been made (Jacob and Laban in Gen. 31:44–47; cf. Jacob in 28:18; 35:14; Moses in Exod. 24:4; Joshua in Josh. 4:3, 8–9, 20; 24:26–27).

(g) Sometimes, when a covenant was made between two royal houses, it was sealed by a *marriage* between two members of these respective houses (e.g., Solomon and Pharaoh's daughter, 1 Kgs 9:16).

(h) The most important ceremony was *writing a document* that contained the promises and duties of the covenant; the clearest example is the "Book of the covenant" (Exod. 24:7; ultimately, the entire written Torah was the Book of the Sinaitic covenant). Other examples are the documents written by Joshua (24:26) and Nehemiah (9:38), to formalize the covenants they established (see §2.1.2).

For more details on the establishment of covenants between people, and covenants between God and his people, I refer the reader to the next chapter.

## 1.4.2 Synthēkē and diathēkē

The New Testament word for "covenant" is not the common Greek word *synthēkē*, which involves an agreement between two equal partners, but *diathēkē*, an arrangement made by one party for the benefit of another party, such as a will or testament. *Synthēkē* does not even appear in the New Testament, and appears only twice in the Septuagint (Isa. 30:1; Dan. 11:6). Apparently, in the New Testament the Holy Spirit prefers the word *diathēkē* to emphasize the fact that the biblical covenants always proceeded from God. The word is derived from *dia* (here something like "between") and *tithēmi* ("to place"), and means something like "that which is placed (arranged) between two parties."

In classical Greek, the word meant "arrangement concerning property through a will," or in short, "will (testament), arrangement, agreement, treaty, covenant." In the *koinē* Greek of the New Testament, the word actually still meant only "testament, last will."[32] This meaning is clearly visible in Hebrews 9:16-17, "For where a will is involved, the death of the one who made it must be established. For a will takes effect only at death, since it is not in force as long as the one who made it is alive." This meaning is also implied in Galatians 3:15, "even with a man-made covenant, no one annuls it or adds to it once it has been ratified"; this is a reference not to a contract between two equal partners, but to a *diathēkē* that is ratified by one party, and thus has become inviolable, namely, a will.

When the Septuagint translators rendered the Hebrew word *berit* as *diathēkē*, they apparently did so because they realized that a biblical covenant is *never* a mutual agreement between two parties, but rather always a will of one party, God, in regard to another party, namely, a certain group of people (cf. Gal. 3:15, 17). It is therefore always *God's* covenant (see, e.g., Gen. 6:18; 9:9-15; 17:2-21; Exod. 2:24; 6:4-5; Lev. 26:15, 42-44; Deut. 17:2; 2 Kgs 13:23; Ps. 25:10, 14; Luke 1:72; Rev.

---

32. Kittel and Friedrich (1964, 2.106-34); Brown (1992, 365-76).

11:1), never humanity's covenant, or Israel's covenant, or our covenant. Naturally, the Septuagint could not honor the second element in the meaning of *diathēkē*, namely, the bringing it into effect by the death of the testator ("the one who made it [i.e., the will]," Heb. 9:16–17). This is precisely what the book of Hebrews *could* do, for the New Covenant has come into force through the death of Christ, who, as God (the Son), is also the one who had established the covenant.

### 1.4.3 *Testamentum*

Following the Septuagint, the Vetus Latina, the earliest tradition of the Bible in Latin translation, consistently renders *berit* as *testamentum*. However, in the Vugate, the definitive Latin Bible translation, we find besides *testamentum* also *foedus* and *pactum*.

Reformed writer Hendrik J. de Bie described how church father Jerome in this respect followed the Greek translations by the Jews Aquila and Symmachus, "probably under the influence of the Jewish scholars with whom he was in contact. In Judaism of that time the emphasis was rather put on the two-sided character of the covenant. This suggests a shift in accent from the sovereignty of God toward the work-holiness of humans."[33] In other words, the more that the dipleuric character of the covenant is emphasized at the expense of its monopleuric character, the more the sovereignty of God is jeopardized. In the course of this book, I will explain to what extent I can agree with this (see §5.5).

The King James Version sometimes renders the word *diathēkē* as "testament" (Matt. 26:28 and parallels; 2 Cor. 3:6, 14; Heb. 7:22; 9:15–20; Rev. 11:19), whereas the New King James Version and many other modern translations usually prefer the term "covenant." In 2 Corinthians 3:14, the NKJV retains the translation "Old Testament," where other modern translations have "old covenant." This phrase "Old Testament" has become the common Christian name for the Tana-

---

33. H. J. de Bie in Hagoort (1999, 9).

kh (the Hebrew Bible), and concomitantly gave rise to the (non-biblical but useful) phrase "New Testament." Thus, the first part of the Christian Bible is considered to be the Book of the Old Covenant, and the second part is the Book of the New Covenant. These names are sometimes used by Reformed theologians to underscore their view that everything in the Bible is covenantal (see §1.6.2).

### 1.4.4 Types of Covenants

Through the study of ancient Near Eastern covenants, we have learned to distinguish between several types of covenants. This holds both for covenants between people and for covenants between God and people (see the next chapter for a treatment of the various Old Testament covenants).

(a) *Succession covenant.* This is a covenant that is made in view of the posterity of the people with whom, or between whom, the covenant is made. Among the covenants made between people, we may think of the covenant between David and Jonathan (1 Sam. 18:3-4; 20:8). Jonathan said to David, "'If I am still alive, show me the steadfast love [Heb. *hesed*,[34] covenant loyalty] of the LORD, that I may not die; and do not cut off your steadfast love [or, covenant loyalty] *from my house* forever, when the LORD cuts off every one of the enemies of David from the face of the earth.'[35] And Jonathan made a covenant *with the house* of David, saying, 'May the LORD take vengeance on David's enemies'" (20:14-15). Many inter-personal covenants contain this succession element because covenants have consequences for the offspring of the people involved. For instance, in the covenant between Abraham and Abimelech, the former asked the latter: "[S]wear to me here by God that you will not deal falsely with me or with my descendants or with my posterity" (Gen. 21:23).

As far as the divine covenants are concerned, if they were

---

34. The sound of the *h* in Hebrew words such as *(c)hokmah, (c)hesed* and *(c)huppah* is somewhere between the common *h* and the *ch* as in Loch Ness.
35. Gentry (2012, 131) calls this a "loyalty agreement."

made with individuals (Noah, Abraham, Levi, David), they are always established with a view to the progeny of these men: Noah (all humanity, even all creation), Abraham (his physical as well as his spiritual offspring), Levi (the Levites, with a blessing for all Israel), David (the royal house of David, again with a blessing for all Israel). If we may speak of a covenant with Adam, then this one, too, had Adam as well as his offspring in view: his breaking the covenant had dramatic effects upon his descendants (Rom. 5:12-21).

(b) *Parity covenant.* This is a covenant between two parties who are more or less equal in standing, such as the covenants between Abraham and the Amorites Mamre, Eshcol, and Aner (Gen. 14:13),[36] Abraham and Abimelech (Gen. 21:22-33), Isaac and Abimelech (Gen. 26:26-30), Jacob and Laban (Gen. 31:22-55), Jonathan and David (1 Sam. 18:3; 20:8, 16; 22:8; 23:18; 2 Sam. 21:7), David and Nahash (implied in 2 Sam. 10:2), Asa and Ben-hadad (1 Kgs 15:19), Ahab and Ben-hadad (1 Kgs 20:34), Jehoshaphath and Ahaziah (2 Chron. 20:35). In a parity covenant, it is not uncommon that the two partners call each other "brother" (1 Kgs 9:13; 20:32-33) (see §4.7.3). Such a covenant is sometimes even called a "covenant of brotherhood" (Amos 1:9).

Of course, the divine covenants are never parity covenants but always belong to the next category.

(c) *Suzerainty covenant.* This is a covenant between a king and his vassals, or more generally, between a leader and a party subject to him. Among the covenants in the Bible that were made between people, the covenant between Joshua, as representing Israel, and the men of Gibeon (Josh. 9) constitutes a good example. Actually, suzerainty covenants with the Canaanite cities and tribes were strictly forbidden (Deut. 7:2), but the Gibeonites deceived Joshua and managed to impose a vassal covenant upon him. In 2 Samuel 10:19, the vassals of Hadadezer became vassals of David ("made peace with

---

36. The Hebrew phrase in this text for "allies" (confederates) is *ba'alê berit*, "covenant partners."

Israel and became subject to them"). The proposed covenant between Jabesh and king Nahash (1 Sam. 11:1-2) is another example of an intended suzerainty covenant. In the case of such a covenant, the partners were not "brothers" but "servants" of the king.

Of a special character is the covenant that king Zedekiah made "with all the people in Jerusalem to make a proclamation of liberty to them, that everyone should set free his Hebrew slaves, male and female, so that no one should enslave a Jew, his brother" (Jer. 34:8-9). This covenant has a special place among the covenants that earlier leaders (Joshua, Nehemiah) or kings (David, Asa, Joash, Hezekiah, Josiah) made *together with* their people *before God* (see §§2.1.2 and 2.1.3).

The divine covenants in the Bible generally have this character of a suzerainty or vassal covenant, in which God unilaterally stipulates the conditions of a covenant.

(d) *Royal grant covenant.* This type of covenant, especially in comparison with the previous one, has been explained by Moshe Weinfeld.[37] It involves a grant in the broadest sense (land property, a high office) given as a favor by a god or a king. Whereas the suzerainty covenant emphasizes the obligation of the vassal to the suzerain, the grant covenant emphasizes the obligation of the suzerain to the vassal. But the other side is always present as well: the suzerain promises to protect the vassal, while the vassal receives the grant because of his previous loyalty to the suzerain. Peter Gentry presumes "that a covenant in the Old Testament has features of both types" of covenants: the suzerainty and the grant covenants.[38] In the facts that in both the Abrahamic and the Sinaitic covenants, God promises to his people a special land, and he elevates them to be a "kingdom of priests" (Exod. 19:6), we see typical features of the royal grant covenant coming to light.

(e) *Connubium (intermarriage covenant).* The intended cov-

---
37. Weinfeld (1970).
38. Gentry (2012, 135).

enant between Jacob's sons and Hamor and his men (Gen. 34) — although the word "covenant" is not mentioned here — was made especially with a view to intermarriage, at least ostensibly: "Hamor spoke with them [i.e., Jacob's sons], saying, 'The soul of my son Shechem longs for your daughter [i.e., Dinah]. Please give her to him to be his wife. Make marriages with us. Give your daughters to us, and take our daughters for yourselves'" (Gen. 34:8–9).

This is not applicable to divine covenants. The Sinaitic covenant clearly had a marriage character (see §§3.1–3.3), but that is a different matter.

(f) *Commercium (trade covenant)*. The covenant between king Solomon and Tyre's king Hiram had this specific purpose: "So Hiram supplied Solomon with all the timber of cedar and cypress that he desired, while Solomon gave Hiram 20,000 cors of wheat as food for his household, and 20,000 cors of beaten oil. Solomon gave this to Hiram year by year. And the LORD gave Solomon wisdom, as he promised him. And there was peace between Hiram and Solomon, and the two of them made a treaty [*berit*, covenant]" (1 Kgs 5:10–12). Here, the phrases "making peace" and "making a treaty" are virtually synonymous (cf. Deut. 20:10–12; Josh. 9:15; 2 Sam. 10:19).

This type of covenant is not applicable to divine covenants, apart from the element of peace. Several times, the Bible uses the term "covenant of peace," namely, in reference to the Levitic covenant (Num. 25:12) and the New Covenant (Isa. 54:1, 10; Ezek. 34:25; 37:26). "I know the thoughts that I think toward you ... thoughts of peace and not of evil, to give you a future and a hope" (Jer. 29:11).

(g) More designations could be mentioned, which are specific products of federalist reasoning, such as *law covenant* and *promise covenant*, or *covenant of works* and *covenant of grace*, and *covenant of redemption*. These designations will be discussed in following chapters.

## 1.5 The God-Givenness of the Covenant
### 1.5.1 The God-Given Guarantor

The primary meaning of *diathēkē*, which in the Septuagint is the common rendering of *berit*, is "will, testament" (cf. Gal. 3:15; Heb. 9:16-17). As Stephen put it: God *"gave* him [i.e., Abraham] the *diathēkē* of circumcision" (Acts 7:8), as his will for Abraham and his children. In accordance with this meaning, Galatians 3:17 speaks of "a *diathēkē* previously ratified by God"; (N)KJV, ESV, NIV, and others render *diathēkē* here as "covenant," CEB and NCV as "agreement," Phillips as "contract," MSG as "will."[39] Here, as in Hebrews 9, the covenant has the character of a will because the authors are referring to an inheritance (Gal. 3:18; Heb. 9:15). Just as by means of a will one makes arrangements for others (usually offspring), by means of a covenant that he establishes God makes arrangements for his people.

Moreover, just as a human *diathēkē* is effectuated only by the death of a testator, God's *diathēkē* is effectuated only by the death of Christ, who is both Testator and Heir, both High Priest and sacrifice (see Heb. 9:16-17). Even in the Old Testament, a *diathēkē* comes into effect only by the death of one or more animal sacrifices (e.g., Gen. 8:20-9:17; 15:7-21; Exod. 24:1-11; 2 Sam. 6:17; 24:24-25; cf. Heb. 9:18).

Especially in the book of Hebrews the meaning of *diathēkē* becomes clearer. The word occurs first in Hebrews 7:22, which states that Jesus has become "the guarantor [(N)KJV, surety] of a better covenant." A "guarantor" (Greek *engyos*) is someone who accepts legal liability for the maintenance of an agreement between two parties, just as, for instance, Judah did in regard to Benjamin (Gen. 43:9).[40] The guarantor agrees to become accountable for one of the parties, or for both parties, in case one party fails to fulfill its duties, especially financially. The guarantor then assumes these duties and fulfills

---
39. Guthrie (1983) and Lane (1991) plead for rendering *diathēkē* also in the book of Hebrews consistently as "covenant."
40. See Ouweneel (1982, I, 95–96).

them. Someone can become a guarantor only if he can prove that, should it become necessary, he is *able* to fulfill the duties of the failing party. The word occurs frequently in the papyri.[41]

In some cases, the guarantor had to vouch for someone else even with his own life. An example of this we find in Sirach 29:14-15, "A good man is willing to guarantee his neighbor's debts.... If someone does this favor for you, don't forget it; he has risked his good name for you." Of course, this has New Testament significance: Jesus as the Guarantor of the New Covenant has vouched with, and even given, his own life with a view to fulfilling this covenant.

## 1.5.2 Offices of Christ

Thus, Jesus has become the Guarantor of the covenant. In the Old Covenant of Sinai, God assigned duties to the people through the Torah, but the sinful nation failed hopelessly, and squandered its right to all the promised blessings. Insofar as a part of the nation will yet receive these blessings, this will be on the basis of divine grace and human repentance (cf. the notion of the "remnant" in, e.g., Isa. 10:20-22; 11:11, 16; Rom. 11:5). The New Covenant is "better," for here Jesus himself has assumed all of its duties as its Guarantor. That is, he not only fulfilled the Torah but also took upon himself the hopeless case of the people by giving his own life for them. Therefore it is an entirely "new" covenant (Heb. 8:8; 9:15; 12:24), an "eternal covenant" (13:20), founded upon Jesus' blood, the "blood of the covenant" (Matt. 26:28; Heb. 9:20; 10:29; cf. Exod. 24:8).

Lutheran and Reformed expositors usually claim that Jesus has become Guarantor for people toward God,[42] and I think they are right: as High Priest on the cross, he has made atonement for the sins of the people, and thus fulfilled all God's demands in regard to sinful humanity (Heb. 2:17); moreover, he gives them the power of the Holy Spirit in order to fulfill

---

41. Brown (1992, 124–25); Moulton and Milligan (1930, 148–49).
42. See, e.g., Grosheide (1955, 176–77).

the new, Messianic Torah.[43]

Other expositors believe that Jesus has become Guarantor for God toward people,[44] and I think they are right, too: as High Priest in heaven he is the warrant that now all the blessings of the New Covenant that God has promised will indeed flow to God's people. For the *present* this means drawing near to God in the heavenly sanctuary (Heb. 7:19–25; 10:19–22); to this end, Jesus is the "minister [Greek *leitourgos*, "liturgist"] in the holy places" (Heb. 8:2). For the *future* Jesus' Guarantorship implies the complete fulfillment of God's promises. This contains the promise of entering the "Sabbath rest" of the Messianic kingdom (Heb. 4:1, 9), of receiving the fulfillment, of our "hope" (Heb. 6:11–12, 17–18, that is, the Messianic kingdom), the "eternal inheritance" (Heb. 9:15, that is, the Messianic kingdom). All guarantees of the New Covenant on which Hebrews 8 focuses are embodied in the heavenly High Priest, glorified at God's right hand.

Jesus has become both Guarantor as well as Mediator (Greek *mesitēs*, Heb. 8:6; 9:15; 12:24) of that covenant. The *Guarantor* assumes the duties of the covenant, the *Mediator* forges or restores the relationship between the two parties. Thus, in the first place, Christ safeguarded the "interests" of humanity by assuming the latter's duties as Guarantor, and as Mediator, by undergoing sacrificial death for humanity, eliminating the failures in performing these duties. Compare the words of the Canons of Dort (II.2): "Since, however, we ourselves cannot give this satisfaction or deliver ourselves from God's wrath, God in boundless mercy has given us as a guarantee his only begotten Son, who was made to be sin and a curse for us, in our place, on the cross, in order that he might give satisfaction for us." Secondly, Christ safeguarded the "interests" of God by furnishing him with a holy and perfect foundation on which God can bless people, and can have communion with them.

---

43. See Ouweneel (2010c, chapter 13).
44. E.g., Grotius (1646); James Peirce (1727); see Dods (1979, 315–16).

If we consider the primary meaning of *diathēkē*, namely "will, testament," then Christ is also the Executor, who brings this will of God in regard to humanity into effect. At the same time he is the Testator, who through his death makes the execution of God's will possible. These are his four offices with respect to the covenant: Christ is the New Covenant's . . .

(a) *Guarantor*, that is, the guarantee that the covenant will be effectuated and maintained at all costs;

(b) *Mediator*, that is, the one who mediates between the two parties: God and his people;

(c) *Executor*, that is, the one who, through his work on the cross and today through the work of the Holy Spirit, executes the will of God with respect to humanity; and

(d) *Testator*, that is, the one who makes a certain will, and does everything that is needed to make its effectuation possible.

## 1.6 Ancient Examples of Covenants
### 1.6.1 Characteristics

Much light has been shed on ancient treaties that kings have made with their vassals, and that exhibit similarities to the Mosaic covenant.[45] The essence of such treaties is that the king promises certain privileges and support to his vassals on the condition that they submit to him, serve him, and support him in war. A biblical example is the covenant that the mighty king Nebuchadnezzar established with king Zedekiah, who had been downgraded to the status of a vassal (Ezek. 17:13–15). We may also think of the covenants that Israel established with Egypt or Assyria in order to submit itself to these countries, or to expect support from them (Isa. 28:15, 18; Hos. 12:2). In such covenants, we are generally dealing with six fixed elements.[46]

(a) *The king who takes the initiative*. In the biblical covenants

---

45. Mendenhall (1955); Kline (1963; 1967); H. J. de Bie in Hagoort (1999, 8–9).
46. Cf. Heyns (1988, 201).

it is always God who takes the initiative in making a covenant, just as a suzerain takes the initiative in establishing a covenant with his vassals. The vassals themselves are not in a position to make any proposals of their own. This divine prerogative comes to light especially in the fact that God often refers to the covenants that he makes with his people as "*my covenant*" (Gen. 6:18; 9:9, 11; 17:2-21 [nine times]; etc.).

(b) *The historical relationship between the king and his vassal.* In the Sinaitic covenant, this comes to light in the way that God had dealt with his people up to this point. See especially the prologue of the Ten Commandments—actually, "Ten Words";[47] Exod. 34:28; Deut. 4:13; 10:4—which in the Jewish enumeration actually constitutes the first of the Ten Words: "I am the LORD your God, who brought you out of the land of Egypt, out of the house of slavery" (Exod. 20:2; Deut. 5:6).

(c) *Duties that the vassal must fulfill.* In the Sinaitic covenant, these are especially the Ten Words, but they also entail the entire Torah. In the first volume of the present series, we have seen that these Words do not form the conditions for *entering* the covenant, but for *remaining* in the covenant and for continually enjoying the blessings of the covenant. Therefore, the prologue of the Ten Words (see [b] above) is so important: God addresses Israel as a *redeemed* nation.

(d) *Blessings for those who keep the covenant, and curses for those who break it.* In the Sinaitic covenant, Leviticus 26 and Deuteronomy 28-29 must be mentioned; these chapters form the most extensive and comprehensive treatise on the conditions of the covenant and of the reprisals that, as God threatens, will follow if the covenant is violated (cf. Josh. 8:30-35).

(e) *A command that a copy of the agreement must be kept in the sanctuary.* At the establishment of the Sinaitic covenant, the tablets of stone were laid in the Ark of the covenant as a lasting "testimony" of the established covenant (Deut. 10:5; 1 Kgs 8:9; Heb. 9:4). They are therefore called the "tablets

---

47. Heb. ᶜaseret haddebarim; in Rabbinical tradition: ᶜaseret haddibrot.

of the testimony" (Exod. 31:18; 32:15; 34:29) and the "ark of the testimony" (e.g., Exod. 25:22; 26:33-34), respectively. The Bible even speaks of the "tabernacle of the testimony" (Exod. 38:21; Num. 1:50, 53; 10:11), and the "tent of the testimony" (Num. 9:15; 17:7-8; 18:2), which is the same. Everything in Israel's worship revolved around the "testimony," which is the same as saying that it revolved around the covenant that God had established with them.

Usually, in an ancient Near Eastern covenant two identical copies of the treaty were made—for instance, two clay tablets or two stone tablets, one for each party. It has been suggested that the two stone "tablets of the covenant" (Deut. 9:9, 11, 15; Heb. 9:4) were two identical copies as well: one for God and one for the people.[48] Indeed, the Bible nowhere says that the Ten Commandments were divided across the two tablets, as traditional representations suggest.

(f) *Enumeration of the witnesses.* As far as the Sinaitic covenant is concerned, we may think here of the role of the angels (Acts 7:38, 53; Gal. 3:19; Heb. 2:2). There has been much discussion on their role;[49] I mention only Flavius Josephus,[50] who quotes Herod as saying that the Jewish laws had been taught by God through angels (Heb. *mal'akhim*, "messengers," but this might also refer to prophets). For the rest, see especially the rabbinical traditions.[51]

## 1.6.2 Metaphors

We will always have to consider that, as far as the divine covenants are concerned, we are dealing with metaphors. That is, what is literally true when it comes to covenants between people receives a metaphorical character as soon as the term "covenant" is applied to the relationship between God and people. It is therefore a little bit strange to see how Dwight

---

48. M. J. Paul in Hagoort (1999, 27).
49. See Ouweneel (1997, 210, 218); also cf. Bruce (1988, 153n99).
50. *Jewish Antiquities* 15.136.
51. Jub. 1:29; Sifre Num. 102 (on Num. 12:5); Mechilta Exod. 20:18; Pesiqta rabbati 21 (Bruce [1985, 28n3]).

Pentecost emphasizes that the biblical covenants are "*literal* covenants and have to be interpreted literally."[52] I suppose I understand his intention—if you take "covenants" too figuratively, you can easily get rid of them, and they lose their expressiveness—but that does not change their basic metaphorical character.

Sometimes we see in Reformed thinking that the argument is turned upside down, as if the divine covenants are the "real thing," whereas the human covenants are only earthly reflections of it. In this view, it is in fact not the divine covenants that are metaphors, but the human covenants. According to this view, the humans making covenants with each other still had some vague idea of the divine covenants, and imitated these in their earthly covenants. Of course, there is not a trace of evidence for this idea in the Bible. This idea is nothing but a consequence of the pre-theoretical premise of all covenant thinking: "everything is covenantal" in the divine sense of the word, that is, all relationships between God and his people, even Father–child and Bridegroom–bride relationships (see §§4.5.3, 4.5.4), are of a basically covenantal nature. Along these lines, even the human covenants are just shadows of the divine covenants.

I repeat: this is nothing but a self-chosen premise. It cannot be proven, or even made plausible, from the Scriptures—but once (Reformed) theologians put on covenantal glasses, they are not surprised that everything in the Bible looks divinely covenantal. We will encounter many Reformed examples of this way of thinking.

### 1.6.3 Examples of Covenantalism

At this point let me limit myself to two examples. Clarence Stam opens his book on the covenant as follows: "One cannot capture the riches of the Bible in a single word. But if one word merits consideration as a key concept in the Holy Scriptures, it is the word *covenant*. With this term I refer to the whole rev-

---

52. Pentecost (1964, 69).

elation of the covenant which God in his love establishes and maintains with his children. Throughout Scripture the theme of God's covenant faithfulness keeps recurring as a dominant theme."[53] Let me offer three comments on this.

(a) *The* key word of the Bible is, of course, God, or Jesus Christ. Apart from divine persons, it is my impression that *kingdom* is a more comprehensive concept in the Bible than *covenant*.

(b) "Covenant" and "children" are terms that point to very different relationships between God and his people; a father-child relationship is as such never covenantal (see §4.5.3). We should not mix biblical metaphors.

(c) In post-Pentecost New Testament times, the concept of the covenant plays only a secondary role (unless one reads the covenant into many other New Testament subjects, as we will see).

The second example is Cornelis van der Waal, who opens his — otherwise valuable — book by saying, "In ignoring the covenant, we oppose that which the *Novum Testamentum* [New Covenant!] itself claims to be."[54] We ask, where does the New Testament do so? The *name* "New Testament (= New Covenant)" may suggest this, but this name was only modeled after 2 Corinthians 3:14 ("Old Testament = Old Covenant") and is not an inspired name at all. A bit later, Van der Waal says, "[T]his book [i.e., his own volume] will seek to prove that the gospel is covenant-oriented from A to Z."[55] To be sure, his book does not prove anything of the kind; it shows what the gospel looks like only if one looks at it through covenantal glasses. This is what I myself will "seek to prove" in the present book.

Let me add here, however, that I do not wish to belittle the significance of the biblical covenant concept through such

---

53. Stam (1999, 7).
54. Van der Waal (1990, 2).
55. Ibid., 3.

criticisms. On the contrary, this pivotal biblical idea is of the utmost importance. As an illustration, I quote three non-Reformed authors who have stressed this point. One is Rabbi Richard E. Friedman, who wrote: "If we could delete [from the Tanakh] all references to covenant—which we cannot do, precisely because it is regularly integral to its contexts—we would have an anthology of stories. As it is we have a structure that can house a plot."[56] The second one is Evangelical Paul R. Williamson: "Covenant is without a doubt one of the most important motifs in biblical theology . . . while 'biblical' and 'covenant theology' must certainly not be confused as synonymous, covenant is indisputably one of the Bible's core theological themes."[57] And thirdly, Baptist Peter J. Gendry wrote: "[T]he covenants constitute the framework of the larger story. They are the backbone of the biblical narrative . . . the *covenants* adequately account for the literary or plot structure of the Bible as a text."[58]

## 1.7  No Paradigms?
### 1.7.1  Not Paradigm but "Truth"?

Such Reformed statements as just quoted (from appreciated theologians Stam and Van der Waal) show the power of any theological paradigm, so much so that the covenantal thinker cannot imagine that other serious readers of the Bible do not equally "see" that everything is covenantal. Indeed, Eastern Orthodox, Roman Catholic, Anglican, Lutheran, and Free Church Evangelicals do not see what Reformed Christians see in the Bible. They are wearing different glasses—and from their own various paradigmatic points of view they see that "all is X" or "all is Y," but *not* necessarily covenantal. They may certainly accept the importance of the covenant concept in the Bible, as I do myself. But they do not assign it as prominent and paradigmatic a place as Reformed Christians do.

---

56. Friedman (1987, 215).
57. Williamson (2007, 29–30).
58. Gentry (2012, 138–39).

The paradigm concept was developed in the 1960s by Thomas S. Kuhn.[59] It was first applied within the natural sciences, and it took some time before it also began to influence the humanities. In theology it took much longer.[60] We cannot blame any of the older theologians for not having imbibed this concept. However, take this post-Kuhn statement by Michael Horton, who claims that the biblical covenants are "the architectural structure that we believe the Scriptures themselves to yield."[61] That is, in his thinking there is no question of any paradigm that is imposed upon the Bible; no, the Scriptures themselves teach us to read them covenantally.

In even stronger terms this viewpoint is expressed by Michael G. Brown and Zach Keele. How is it possible that they can still write: "This introduction [i.e., to their book] should also help us understand that *covenant theology* is not an abstract system imposed on the Bible, but the very structure and framework that naturally arises from Scripture itself as the drama of redemptive history unfolds from Genesis to Revelation. Covenant theology is the Bible's prescribed method of helping us interpret the Scriptures properly."[62] And a bit later: "Reformed theology is covenant theology because it is exegetical theology, that is to say, it is based on and rooted in the exegesis of Scripture. Reformed theology teaches the covenant of works because it is found in God's Word."[63]

These are quite amazing statements. Covenant *theology* "naturally arises" from the Bible! The Bible *prescribes* covenant theology! Such statements betray a fundamental lack

---

59. Kuhn (1962).
60. See extensively Ouweneel (2013, chapter 13; 2014b, chapters 8–9), and many references there.
61. Horton (2006, 13; cf. 2011, 46: "this biblical paradigm").
62. Brown and Keele (2012, 21).
63. Ibid., 46; cf. Horton (2006, 11): "*Reformed* theology is synonymous with *covenant* theology." But Baptist Wellum (2012, 22n4) adds: "All Christian theology has rightly viewed the covenants as central to how the Scriptures unfold and how we think of what our Lord Jesus has accomplished as our new covenant head."

of understanding of what (academic) theology and scholarly theory-building actually are. This is not a present-day view of theology, but a "modernist" (Enlightenment) or even pre-modern idea of theological scholarship. The Bible contains not one single droplet of theology in any academic sense of the word. Therefore, theology cannot "arise" from the Bible. Even if the authors actually meant covenant *doctrine*, this does not change the picture all that much. The Bible does not even present us with "doctrines"; doctrines are designed and constructed by theologians in order to explain what they find in Scripture.

It is even less valid to say that the Bible prescribes any (theological or doctrinal) method. Again, such statements involve a basic lack of understanding of the paradigmatic nature of all science and scholarship. Covenant theology is precisely what the authors deny: "an abstract system imposed on the Bible" — not necessarily wrong, but not necessarily right either, just like Roman Catholic ecclesiasticalism or Evangelical dispensationalism are. People *choose* to read the Bible covenantally, just as Catholics *choose* to read it ecclesiastically, or dispensationalists *choose* to read it dispensationally.[64] The Bible does not prescribe for us anything in this direction; theological theories are the free products of theological minds.

It is even less valid to claim that covenant theory follows from pure exegesis as such. Exegesis does not yield a covenant of works, a covenant of redemption, or a covenant of grace. These concepts are products not of Old Testament or New Testament exegesis, but of systematic theology. They have been designed in order to *account for* certain states of affairs that are encountered in Scripture. They are *dogmatic theories*, which are not necessarily false, but it is quite misleading to suggest that they are the conclusions of exegesis as

---

64. Baptists Gentry and Wellum (2012) have tried to find a middle way between federalism and dispensationalism; but their approach is spoiled by the adoption of spiritualism in their interpretation of Old Testament prophecies (see their summary: 709–16).

such. They are not.

Interestingly, the authors make these statements: it is "true that covenant theology *is* Reformed theology," and "Reformed theology is covenant theology."[65] This seems to me perfectly correct. Radical covenantal thinking—seeing Scripture through covenantal glasses—is thoroughly Reformed, and Reformed theologians read the Bible in a thoroughly covenantal way. It is just as true as saying that ecclesiasticalism *is* Roman Catholic theology, and that dispensationalism characterizes a considerable part of Evangelical theology. In itself there is nothing wrong with such a state of affairs. This is how systematic theology works, designing concepts and theories all the time. But asserting that ecclesiasticalism or dispensationalism *follows* from pure exegesis is just as false as claiming that federalism follows from pure exegesis.

### 1.7.2 "No Paradigm Needed"

In the midst of all paradigmatic confusion, there have always been voices exclaiming that we should throw all paradigmatic or other theological prejudices overboard, and listen only to the Bible. A recent work that takes this viewpoint was written by Blake White.[66] It presents so-called "New Covenant Theology," that is, a developing system of theology that allegedly seeks to let the Bible inform our theology. White endeavors to show that New Covenant Theology is the system of theology that allows the Bible to have the final say most consistently. He claims that dispensationalism rests on presuppositions provided by its beloved Scofield Bible, and that covenant theology rests on presuppositions provided by its cherished Westminster Confession. In opposition to this, New Covenant Theology allegedly does not have any outside document that must be imposed on the text of Scripture. It strives to let the Sacred Text speak on its own terms.

With all due respect, this is nonsense. Dispensational-

---

65. Brown and Keele (2012, 21, 46).
66. White (2012).

ism does *not* rest on presuppositions provided by the *Scofield Reference Bible* because it had been developed already in the century before that Bible was published. Dispensationalists never appeal to the Scofield Bible as an authority for their views. With the Westminster Confession it is a bit different, as we will see (§4.2), because it is an official church confession. Yet, federal theology was developed before the Westminster Standards were written, otherwise these could not have been written. Federalists may appeal to the Westminster Standards — and this is sometimes a hindrance in an open theological discussion — but their final authority is Holy Scripture. Both dispensationalists and federalists strive to let the Sacred Text speak on its own terms, though perhaps not in the same way as New Covenant theologians.

Meanwhile, New Covenant Theology amazingly has its own "New Covenant Confession of Faith,"[67] which is full of theologisms from the past. How could it be otherwise? New Covenant theologians may not realize it, but they have simply endeavored to develop a new paradigm. There is nothing wrong with this, but let them simply admit this instead of acting as if they have invented biblical theology anew. Article 9 of this Confession deals with the covenants; in it, we find many misunderstandings that are familiar to us from federalism: the emphasis on salvation ("The Abrahamic covenant is a picture of God's plan of salvation"; "The New Covenant is a description of the saving work of Jesus Christ"), the denial that the Noahic covenant is a salvation covenant, the denial that the Sinaitic covenant is a gracious covenant. (All these points will be extensively dealt with in the present study.) So what is the advantage of this so-called New Covenant Theology with respect to federalism? In what respects is it more biblical?

Every generation invents theologies that are designed because all other theologies allegedly have failed, and be-

---

67. See ncbf.net/pdf/confession.pdf.

cause their designers want again, in all simplicity, to listen to the Bible alone. This form of biblicism is rather dangerous, since it seems godly and scriptural but in reality is neither. No theologians can bypass the many approaches to Scripture that church history has yielded, and in one or several of which they have been socialized. Asserting that one rejects all theological presuppositions can mean only that one is not conscious of one's own presuppositions. A striking older example of this is found with Norman L. Geisler, who edited an entire book on the philosophical presuppositions of his opponents,[68] called "errantists," whereas, when it came to his own "inerrantism," he appealed to "factual evidence."[69] This is not only biblicism; it is theological hybris.

Let me make very clear that I do not intend to speak in a deprecating way about a "simple reading" of Scripture, or of a listening to what it "actually says." On the contrary, the believingly prayerful and humble reading of Scripture to hear God's voice in it, to have communion with the Christ of the Scriptures, to "eat" his Word as food for the soul, precedes and surpasses all theologizing and all constructing of dogmatics. In this existential fellowship with God's Word, it is not believers who interrogate *Scripture*, but it is God who interrogates *them* through his Word and Spirit. This way of interacting with the Bible is more important than all theology — *but such interacting is itself no theology*. Eating bread is more important than, but at the same time something very different from, providing a chemical analysis of the bread. The chemist is doing with bread what the theologian is doing with Scripture. In theology, humans speak about the Bible; in their believing listening to the Bible, it is God's Word that speaks about and to *them*.

There is no theology without certain theological as well as philosophical prejudices.[70] Generally speaking, dispensa-

---
68. Geisler (1981).
69. Geisler (1979, 333–34); see extensively Ouweneel (2012b, 328–30).
70. See extensively Ouweneel (2014b).

tionalists and federalists are not ashamed to admit this. All theologians who embark upon the praiseworthy enterprise of finding a middle road between dispensationalism and federalism should not be ashamed of this either. This is how theology works, just as all other forms of science and scholarship. The only thing to be ashamed of is the kind of biblicism that seeks to re-invent the theological wheel and fire. This is either naïve, or a form of deceit, as if this biblicism guarantees a more scriptural look at dispensations and covenants than dispensationalism and federalism have tried to offer so far.

There is always room for newer theological models, which ultimately might even supersede both dispensationalism and federalism. This is how things go in science. But there can be very little appreciation for those who pretend to come up with theological truth by simply throwing aside all theological craftsmanship. Non-theology can never lead to good theology.

# Chapter 2
# The Old Testament Covenants

> *"Come now, let us make a covenant, you and I.*
>    *And let it be a witness between you and me."*
> *So Jacob took a stone*
>    *and set it up as a pillar.*
> *And Jacob said to his kinsmen,*
>    *"Gather stones."*
> *And they took stones and made a heap,*
>    *and they ate there by the heap. . . .*
> *Laban said, "This heap is a witness*
>    *between you and me today. . . .*
> *The* L<small>ORD</small> *watch between you and me,*
>    *when we are out of one another's sight.*
> *If you oppress my daughters,*
>    *or if you take wives besides my daughters*
> *although no one is with us,*
>    *see, God is witness between you and me."*
>                                 Genesis 31:44–50

**Summary:** *In addition to many inter-human covenants as well as the renewals of the divine covenant at the initiative of Israel's leaders, we may distinguish nine covenants that God established. There are three with the whole world: the cosmic, the Adamic, and* *the Noahic covenants. Three with individuals (but with significance for their offspring, and for all Israel): the Abrahamic, the Levitical, and the Davidic covenants. And three with Israel: the Sinaitic, the Palestinian, and the New Covenants. For each covenant we try to describe the antecedent evil, the covenant partner(s) involved, the way God's love is expressed in it, its sacrificial basis, its form of Torah, its covenant sign, its covenant meal, the way "sonship" comes to light in it, the "garden" involved, its present blessing, and its eschatological meaning.*

## 2.1  Introduction
### 2.1.1  Different Covenants — In What Sense?

INTERESTINGLY, JOHAN HEYNS WRITES: "There are theologians who believe that they can distinguish in Scripture two, three, and even four covenants."[1] To me as an Evangelical, this sounds rather strange, for I find in the Old Testament at least nine divine covenants, with at least seven or eight covenant partners. But this is not at all what a federalist like Heyns is talking about; he is referring to the covenant of works, the covenant of redemption, the covenant of grace, terms that we do not encounter in Scripture but that relate to concepts that are the fruits of federalist theory building (see chapters 4, 5, and 7).

The Bible speaks in a very different way about a number of various covenants. Dwight Pentecost speaks of five major covenants: the Abrahamic, the Palestinian, the Sinaitic, the Davidic, and the New Covenant.[2] The reason why Reformed theologians count the covenants in their own way is because, to them, all the covenants just mentioned are nothing but varieties of one and the same divine covenant, which they usually call the "covenant of grace." Later we will discuss this Reformed notion extensively, but at this point I can say that I cannot go along with this idea of just one covenant because the biblical covenants differ essentially in many respects, as we will see in the present chapter.

---

1. Heyns (1988, 200).
2. Pentecost (1964, 67).

For instance, in order to properly grasp the bearing of a biblical covenant, it is essential to consider accurately who are the covenant partners; therefore, I define these partners explicitly in the following summary of the covenants. I will also indicate, wherever applicable, which is the special "covenant sign" belonging to each covenant, and what specific Torah belongs to it. The existence of such covenant signs is a phenomenon well known from ancient Near Eastern covenants.[3] Such visible and tangible signs in biblical non-divine covenants include Abraham's seven lambs commemorating his covenant with king Abimelech (Gen. 21:28-32), Jacob's heap of stones commemorating his covenant with his father-in-law Laban (31:43-53), and Joshua's big stone commemorating his covenant with Israel (Josh. 24:25-27).

Wherever relevant, I refer in the following discussion to the sacrifice(s) on which a certain covenant was based, to the specific character of the Torah under each covenant, and to the sacrificial meal that often occurred when divine covenants were made. For the latter, too, we find examples in non-divine covenants: the meal of Isaac and Abimelech (Gen. 26:26-30), and that of Jacob and Laban (31:44, 51-54). We will also see that usually the covenants have a specific preceding history, especially an antecedent evil, to which the covenant in view is to a certain extent God's answer. Likewise, God's love expresses itself differently in the various covenants. We will also look at the way sonship often comes to light in it, whether a specific garden is involved that has sanctuary features (or a sanctuary that has garden features), what is the present blessing that flows from a specific covenant, and what will be its eschatological meaning.

In a general way, the nine divine, biblical covenants may be divided into three groups of three each:

(a) Three covenants that involve the whole world.

---

3. Cf. Berkhof (1991, 232-33); Berkowitz (1999, 20–21). Wentsel (1998b, 51–59) speaks here of Old Testament "sacraments" because of the general sign-character of sacraments.

(b) Three covenants that involve individual persons with their progeny, but are significant for all the people of God.

(c) Three covenants that involve the people of Israel, but in fact also have significance for the whole world.

## 2.1.2   Covenants Initiated by Leaders

The group (c) just mentioned contains in its wider sense also a group of covenants that we encounter at later times among Israel and that were made at the initiative of the spiritual leader or king of the nation, or of Judah, and in which all Israel or all Judah was involved. These covenants seem to be of a very different nature than the covenants mentioned above, because here the initiative does not proceed from the LORD, but from the leader or king. However, in fact these covenants usually involve nothing but renewals of the covenant that existed from early times between God and Israel. They involved especially a renewed dedication of the people to Yahweh and his Torah after a period of decline. I count seven of them (not including 1 Sam. 12, where Samuel renewed the covenant but without mentioning the word).

(1) *Joshua:* "So Joshua made a covenant with the people that day, and put in place statutes and rules for them at Shechem. And Joshua wrote these words in the Book of the Torah of God. And he took a large stone and set it up there under the terebinth that was by the sanctuary of the LORD. And Joshua said to all the people, 'Behold, this stone shall be a witness against us, for it has heard all the words of the LORD that he spoke to us. Therefore it shall be a witness against you, lest you deal falsely with your God'" (Josh. 24:25–27). This looks like a "horizontal" covenant, that is, one between Joshua and the people. But at a deeper level this involved (a renewal of) the "vertical" (Sinaitic/Palestinian) covenant between God and his people (see below).

(2) *David:* "So all the elders of Israel came to the king at Hebron, and David made a covenant with them at Hebron before the LORD. And they anointed David king over Israel,

according to the word of the Lord by Samuel" (1 Chron. 11:3). This too is a "horizontal" covenant subservient to the "vertical" covenant between God and David, and between God and Israel.

(3) *Asa:* "And he [i.e., king Asa] gathered all Judah and Benjamin. . . . They were gathered at Jerusalem in the third month of the fifteenth year of the reign of Asa. They sacrificed to the Lord on that day from the spoil that they had brought. . . . And they entered into a covenant to seek the Lord, the God of their fathers, with all their heart and with all their soul, but that whoever would not seek the Lord, the God of Israel, should be put to death, whether young or old, man or woman. They swore an oath to the Lord with a loud voice and with shouting and with trumpets and with horns. And all Judah rejoiced over the oath, for they had sworn with all their heart and had sought him with their whole desire, and he was found by them, and the Lord gave them rest all around" (2 Chron. 15:9–15). Here, the "vertical" aspect comes more to the fore.

(4) *Joash:* "And all the assembly made a covenant with the king [i.e., Joash] in the house of God. And Jehoiada said to them, 'Behold, the king's son [i.e., Joash, son of king Ahaziah]! Let him reign, as the Lord spoke concerning the sons of David'" (2 Chron. 23:3). This is a "horizontal" covenant, but subservient to the "vertical" Davidic covenant (see below).

(5) *Hezekiah:* "Now it is in my heart to make a covenant with the Lord, the God of Israel, in order that his fierce anger may turn away from us. My sons [i.e., priests and Levites], do not now be negligent, for the Lord has chosen you to stand in his presence, to minister to him and to be his ministers and make offerings to him" (2 Chron. 29:10–11). This is a "horizontal" covenant subservient to the "vertical" Levitical covenant.

(6) *Josiah:* "And the king went up to the house of the Lord, and with him all the men of Judah and all the inhabitants of

Jerusalem and the priests and the prophets, all the people, both small and great. And he read in their hearing all the words of the Book of the covenant that had been found in the house of the LORD. And the king stood by the pillar and made a covenant before the LORD, to walk after the LORD and to keep his commandments and his testimonies and his statutes with all his heart and all his soul, to perform the words of this covenant that were written in this book. And all the people joined in the covenant" (2 Kgs 23:2-3). The emphasis here is on the "vertical."

(7) *Nehemiah:* "Because of all this [i.e., the sins of the past and their punishment] we make a firm covenant [i.e., a formal promise to serve God by observing his Torah] in writing [i.e., put it down in a document]; on the sealed document are the names of our princes, our Levites, and our priests" (Neh. 9:38). Again, the emphasis here is on the "vertical."

## 2.1.3 Single-Purpose Covenants

There are a few covenants mentioned in the Bible that could be called single-purpose covenants.

(1) *Zedekiah:* "King Zedekiah had made a covenant with all the people in Jerusalem to make a proclamation of liberty to them, that everyone should set free his Hebrew slaves, male and female, so that no one should enslave a Jew, his brother. And they obeyed, all the officials and all the people who had entered into the covenant that everyone would set free his slave, male or female, so that they would not be enslaved again. They obeyed and set them free" (Jer. 34:8-10).

This covenant involved only one specific intention, namely, setting free the slaves of Israelite origin that some Judeans possessed. After Judah had broken this covenant (v. 11), the prophet Jeremiah came to rebuke the people, placing this single-purpose covenant in the broader context of the Sinaitic covenant, which they had broken as well, with all due consequences (vv. 12-22).

(2) *Ezra:* "Shecaniah the son of Jehiel, of the sons of Elam,

addressed Ezra: 'We have broken faith with our God and have married foreign women from the peoples of the land, but even now there is hope for Israel in spite of this. Therefore let us make a covenant with our God to put away all these wives and their children, according to the counsel of my lord and of those who tremble at the commandment of our God, and let it be done according to the Torah. Arise, for it is your task, and we are with you; be strong and do it.' Then Ezra arose and made the leading priests and Levites and all Israel take an oath that they would do as had been said. So they took the oath" (Ezra 10:2-5).

This covenant similarly involved only one specific intention, namely, putting away foreign wives with their children, which the Judeans did (see the remainder of Ezra 10).

### 2.1.4 Human Covenants

In addition to these, there are of course all kinds of other covenants in the Old Testament that are not divine covenants (i.e., made by God with humans). They may generally help us to understand how the concept of covenant functions in the Old Testament. Striking examples (positive and negative) are the following covenants (some were already mentioned in chapter 1).[4]

1. *Positive parity covenants (i.e., made with good intentions and good results) between:*

(a) *Abraham and Abimelech* (Gen. 21:22-33). Striking features: it had an element of succession covenant in it (v. 23), and presumably also a sacrificial element (cf. the sheep and oxen in v. 27); oaths were sworn (v. 31).

(b) *Isaac and Abimelech* (Gen. 26:26-30). Striking features: mainly a non-aggression pact (vv. 28-29); a meal was attached to it (v. 30); oaths were exchanged (v. 31).

(c) *Jacob and Laban* (Gen. 31:22-55). Striking features: it had

---
4. Cf. Van der Waal (1990, 5-17).

a visible sign (v. 45), a meal was held (v. 46), Jacob took an oath (v. 53) and brought a sacrifice (v. 54).

(d) *Jonathan and David* (1 Sam. 18:3; 20:8, 16; 22:8; 23:18; 2 Sam. 21:7). This was not a purely personal covenant, but was also in view of the descendants (succession covenant): David promised that he would protect the *house* of Jonathan (1 Sam. 20:14-15), which indeed he did (see, e.g., 2 Sam. 9; cf. 21:7).

(e) *David and Nahash* (2 Sam. 10:2); the word "covenant" is not mentioned here, but the covenant terminology is used: "I will show kindness [*hesed*, covenant loyalty] to Hanun the son of Nahash, as his father showed kindness [idem] to me."

(f) *Solomon and Hiram* (1 Kgs 5:12, "treaty" in this verse is *berit*, "covenant").

(g) A very special category: *marriage* ("the adulteress . . . who forsakes the companion of her youth and forgets the covenant of her God," Prov. 2:16-17; "the wife of your youth . . . she is your companion and your wife by covenant," Mal. 2:14). God's covenant with Jerusalem—though not a parity covenant but a suzerainty covenant—had a marriage character (cf. §§3.1-3.3): "When I passed by you again and saw you, behold, you were at the age for love, and I spread the corner of my garment over you and covered your nakedness; I made my vow to you and entered into a covenant with you, declares the Lord God, and you became mine" (Ezek. 16:8; cf. vv. 59-63).

2. *Negative parity covenants (i.e., made with bad intentions and bad results*[5]*) between:*

(a) *Jacob's sons and Hamor and his men* (Gen. 34, an intended covenant): the word "covenant" is not found here, but the expression "in peace" (*shalem*, Gen. 33:18; *shelēmim*, 34:21) points to the willingness to come to a covenantal agreement, especially in view of intermarriage (v. 9; cf. "seek peace"

---

5. Compare the prohibition of false covenants: Exod. 23:32; 34:12, 14.

[Deut. 23:6] means "make a covenant"). In reality, Jacob's sons wanted to do harm to Hamor and his men.

(b) *Joshua/Israel and Gibeon* (Josh. 9). Striking features: the common meal (v. 14), oaths (v. 15), promises of mutual help (10:6).

(c) *King Asa and king Ben-hadad* (1 Kgs 15:19), in continuation of the covenant between Asa's father Abijam and Ben-hadad's father Tabrimmon (not mentioned elsewhere in the Bible).

(d) *King Ahab and king Ben-hadad* (1 Kgs 20:34). Notice the reference to the (prospective) covenant partner as "my brother" (vv. 32–33).

3. *Negative suzerainty covenants (cf. 2.) between:*

(a) *The proposed covenant between Jabesh and king Nahash* (1 Sam. 11:1–2). A typical example of an (intended) suzerainty or vassal covenant. Interestingly, king Saul's counteraction had some typical features of a covenant as well: "He took a yoke of oxen and cut them in pieces and sent them throughout all the territory of Israel by the hand of the messengers, saying, 'Whoever does not come out after Saul and Samuel, so shall it be done to his oxen!'" (v. 7).

(b) *Jerusalem and "death/Sheol"* (Isa. 28): "We have made a covenant with death, and with Sheol we have an agreement" (v. 15). "Then your covenant with death will be annulled, and your agreement with Sheol will not stand" (v. 18). The reference is probably to Egypt (cf. 30:1–7; 36:6–9); according to others: Assyria (cf. Hos. 12:1, "they make a covenant with Assyria, and oil is carried to Egypt"). This is a suzerainty covenant in that Israel placed itself under the protection of a foreign (pagan) power, and thus declared itself prepared to pay tribute for that protection.

(c) *The "coming prince" and Israel* (Dan. 9:27). I follow here the common dispensational interpretation of the prophecy of the Seventy Weeks (Dan. 9:24–27), which I have explained extensively elsewhere.[6] In this interpretation, the "he" of verse 27 is the last-mentioned person in verse 26, that is, "the prince who is to come." His people have destroyed "the city and the sanctuary" (AD 70), so this prince will be a Roman. The seventieth week is the seven years just before the great eschatological restoration described in verse 24, connected with the second coming of Christ and his establishment of the Messianic kingdom. The covenant, then, is a covenant that the restored Roman Empire will make with (the unbelieving majority of) Israel. A totally different interpretation, recently extensively defended by Peter Gentry,[7] is that this covenant is the New Covenant made by the Messiah, mentioned in verses 25–26 (see §2.4.3).

## 2.2 Covenants Involving the Whole World
### 2.2.1 The Covenant with the Celestial Bodies (Wider: with Creation)

We find this covenant in Jeremiah 33:20–21 and 25–26: "If you can break my covenant with the day and my covenant with the night, so that day and night will not come at their appointed time, then also my covenant with David my servant may be broken. . . . If I have not established my covenant with day and night and the fixed order of heaven and earth, then I will reject the offspring of Jacob and David my servant. . . ." This "fixed order of heaven and earth" refers to the sun, the moon and the stars and their regular, predictable orbits.

Psalm 89:3–4 says, "I have made a covenant with my chosen one; I have sworn to David my servant: 'I will establish your offspring forever, and build your throne for all generations'"; and verses 36–37, "His [i.e., David's] offspring shall endure forever, his throne as long as the sun before me. Like the moon it shall be established forever, a faithful witness in the skies." Here, a parallel is drawn between God's faithfulness as it comes to light in the fixed order of the celestial bod-

---

6. See Ouweneel (2012a, §6.5).
7. Gentry (2012, 531–64).

ies and his faithfulness to his covenant with David (see §2.3.3).

This shows that actually it is humanity who is the real object of this cosmic covenant: God's faithfulness to the firmament is a guarantee for his promise of faithfulness to people on earth. God freely makes use of the celestial bodies: ". . . who commands the sun, and it does not rise; who seals up the stars" (Job 9:7); "he makes his sun rise on the evil and on the good" (Matt. 5:45). In the same vein, he is powerful to keep his promises to Israel. Even apart from his promises, God is faithful toward humanity, and shows this in the celestial bodies, and other natural phenomena: "In past generations he allowed all the nations to walk in their own ways. Yet he did not leave himself without witness, for he did good by giving you rains from heaven and fruitful seasons, satisfying your hearts with food and gladness" (Acts 14:16–17).

This undeserved and sovereign grace that God bestows upon all humanity is often called "common grace,"[8] or "general, universal grace," allegedly bestowed upon humanity because of God's goodness, apart from salvation and apart from Christ's redemptive work. Others have combated this notion, and have claimed that grace by definition is always particular, which means God's grace is exhibited only in the salvation of sinners (see §3.6.1).

*Antecedent evil:* according to several expositors, even creation as we know it today, since the six days of Genesis 1, was God's work in opposition to apparent evil: "The earth was without form and void, and darkness was over the face of the deep" (v. 2; cf. Isa. 45:18; Jer. 4:23; 2 Cor. 4:3–6, passages that point to the negative meaning of "form and void," and of darkness).

*Partner:* in a limited sense, this was Israel, especially the house of David, but in a wider sense this covenant involves all humanity, even all creation.

---

8. See especially Abraham Kuyper (2011; 2013); other parts of his Dutch work (*De Gemeene Gratie*) are still to appear in English translation. A fair summary of it was given by Louis Berkhof (1979, 432–36).

*God's love:* it is God's love that "he makes his sun rise on the evil and on the good, and sends rain on the just and on the unjust" (Matt. 5:45; cf. Acts 14:16–17, just quoted). Postlapsarian humanity is an "unlikely candidate"[9] for God's covenant love; the ground for this love lies in God himself, not in sinful humanity (cf. with respect to the patriarchs and Israel, Deut. 4:37; 7:7–8; 10:15).

*Sacrificial basis:* Common grace is a highly controversial subject.[10] Does it exist at all? In what sense does it exist? This controversial subject has even led to church divisions (in 1924, what was to become the Protestant Reformed Churches in America broke away from the Christian Reformed Churches because of this controversy; the former committed the "error" of limiting God's grace to the elect; cf. §3.6.1). I simply mention here the question as to whether common grace is based upon the atoning work of Christ or not. Some have argued that common grace cannot be viewed apart from the work of Christ on the cross; others have called this an outright heresy. Within the scope of our present subject, any further elaboration of this subject would carry us too far afield.

*Torah:* The cosmic Torah is the wisdom of God that is reflected in the cosmos that he created: "The LORD by wisdom founded the earth; by understanding he established the heavens; by his knowledge the deeps broke open, and the clouds drop down the dew" (Prov. 3:19–20). The book of Proverbs presents us with God's wisdom in the midst of a world of foolishness, confusion, and wickedness. God's creational wisdom as wonderfully exhibited in the cosmos is to be displayed, too, in the smallest details of human life. Elsewhere, I have discussed in detail the relationship between *Hokmah* (Wisdom) and Torah.[11]

*Covenant sign:* there is something ambiguous in this covenant, for it is a covenant *with* the celestial bodies, but intended

---

9. I borrow this phrase from Stam (1999, 17).
10. See Reformed introductions by Douma (1976) and Van Til (1977).
11. Ouweneel (2015a, especially chapter 3).

*for* humanity. Seen from this viewpoint, one might say that sun, moon, and stars are here covenantal signs of God's faithfulness toward humanity (cf. Gen. 1:14).

*Covenant meal* and *Sonship:* not applicable.

*Garden:* the world was planned to be a garden for God (see §2.4.3).

*Present blessing:* evidence of the fixedness of God's promises, intended to strengthen our faith in them.

*Eschatological meaning:* God's faithfulness toward David as well as his house, as well as to all Israel, as well as to all creation, finds its fulfillment in the Messianic kingdom.

This covenant with the celestial bodies reminds us of some other references to covenants made with natural elements in creation. Eliphaz says to Job, "For you shall be in league with the stones of the field, and the beasts of the field shall be at peace with you" (Job 5:23). Job says, "I have made a covenant with my eyes; how then could I gaze at a virgin?" (31:1). God says to Job, "Will he [i.e., Leviathan] make a covenant with you to take him for your servant forever?" (41:4). Through Ezekiel he says, "I will make with them [i.e., Israel] a covenant of peace and banish wild beasts from the land, so that they may dwell securely in the wilderness and sleep in the woods" (Ezek. 45:25; cf. Zech. 11:10). And through Hosea he says, "I will make for them a covenant on that day with the beasts of the field, the birds of the heavens, and the creeping things of the ground" (Hos. 2:18; see §2.2.3). The latter, too, is a reference to the Messianic kingdom.

It is unhelpful to ask when precisely this covenant was established, except in very general terms: at creation. Therefore, there is no reason to equate this covenant with either some Adamic covenant (§2.2.3) or the Noahic covenant (§2.2.3).[12]

## 2.2.2 The Covenant with Adam

The covenant with Adam is, through him, at the same time a

---

12. Cf. Gentry (2012, 220–21).

covenant with all humanity (at that time still future). In Genesis 1–5, there is no explicit reference to a covenant.[13] The only suggestion in this respect is adopted from Hosea 6:7, "But like Adam they transgressed the covenant; there they dealt faithlessly with me" (ESV; thus also ASV, CEB [note: "Or *at Adam*," i.e., a town]; cf. [N]KJV, "like men"; NIV, "at Adam" [note: "*Like Adam*; or *Like human beings*"[14]]; GNV, "like men" [note: "That is, like light and weak persons"]; The Message: "You broke the covenant—just like Adam!").[15] Brown and Keele presume that the "prophet is actually making a play off of Adam. He is pointing to two entities named Adam: the first man Adam, and a town named Adam. Both referents characterize the severe nature of Israel's sin."[16]

It is not at all clear whether the reference in Hosea 6:7 is really to a covenant that God had made with Adam. Moreover, if there was anything like an (implicit) covenant between God and Adam (and Eve), what character did it have? We will come back to this question when we discuss the Reformed hypothesis of the "covenant of works" (§3.5).

Cornelis Van der Waal has an interesting, though speculative argument for the existence of some Adamic covenant: "We have already seen that Gen. 6:18 ["I will confirm (hiphil of *qum*) my covenant with you"] concerns the *confirmation* of an *existing* covenant, even though the word 'covenant' does not occur in the preceding part of the Scripture. The LORD, who does not change, speaks about the covenant with Noah as 'My covenant.' That covenant, in other words, was already functioning in the time of Noah's youth, and even before, in the days of Enoch and of Adam."[17] In his view, this is why God's covenantal name, YHWH, is present already at the beginning of Genesis (from chapter 2:4 onward). Others have

---

13. Willamson (2007, 72) concludes that there was no covenant before Gen. 6.
14. So, e.g., Heyns (1988, 207).
15. See the discussion by Gentry (2012, 217–20).
16. Brown and Keele (2012, 53–54).
17. Van der Waal (1990, 48); cf. Dumbrell (1984, i.l.).

strongly combated this view that Genesis 6:18 refers to an existing covenant that is here confirmed,[18] but recently Gentry has again defended this view.[19]

Perhaps the most compelling reasons to speak of an Adamic covenant are implicit ones.[20]

(1) If there was an Adamic Torah, as I argued in the previous volume, then there was also an Adamic covenant, because all forms of the Eternal Torah seem to demand a covenantal context, just as, conversely, there is no covenant without some form of Torah.

(2) If there was not only an Adamic Torah — which was broken — but also a divine promise which marked Adam's restoration after his fall (Eve's offspring would one day bruise the serpent's head, Gen. 3:15; cf. Rev. 12:9; 20:2), then two of the principal characteristics of a covenantal relationship — demands and promises — are found here.

(3) In Romans 5:12–19 and 1 Corinthians 15:21–22, 45–49, Adam and Christ (the "second man," the "last Adam") are placed in juxtaposition, each as head/Head of a corresponding human family. From there, it seems to be an obvious step to argue that, if Christ is covenantal Head under the New Covenant, that is, of the new humanity according to the Spirit, likewise prelapsarian Adam was the covenantal head of humanity according to the flesh.[21]

(4) I may add here the summary by Peter Gentry: Genesis 1–3 "speaks of man's relationship to God as son and his [i.e., man's] relationship to creation as servant king. In the ancient Near East, both the context of the family and the relationship of king and people is covenantal, requiring loyal love, obedience, and trust."[22]

Also compare what is said in §2.2.3 about Isaiah 24:5 with

---

18. Williamson (2007, 190–91).
19. Gentry (2012, 266–68).
20. Cf., e.g., arguments by Robertson (1980, i.l.) and Dumbrell (1984, i.l.).
21. Cf. Wellum (2012, 616–18).
22. Gentry (2012, 217).

respect to the Noahic covenant, and possibly to the Adamic covenant.

*Antecedent evil:* the (presumed) covenant that God made with postlapsarian Adam came after the disaster of humanity's fall into sin. It seems that God's promises are always given after evil has entered; they involve a return to God's blessings that were lost through the evil committed.

*Partner:* Adam (and Eve), and in him (them) their entire offspring, that is, humanity.

*God's love:* there is only one ground for God's (presumed) covenant with postlapsarian Adam and Eve, and that is his love. In a sense, they were the most "unlikely candidates" for a covenant, having just revolted against God.

*Sacrificial basis*: of course, for the prelapsarian Adam and Eve no sacrifice was necessary. If a covenant with Adam also implies the alleged beginning of a new covenant after Adam's fall and conversion, one may see in the "garments of skins" (Gen. 3:21), for which the death of animals seems to have been indispensable, the first (vague) hint at the sacrifice as the foundation for God's covenants.[23]

*Torah*: The five commandments of the Adamic Torah:[24]

(a) "Be fruitful and multiply and fill the earth" (Gen. 1:28a).

(b) "Subdue [the earth], and have dominion over the fish of the sea and over the birds of the heavens and over every living thing that moves on the earth" (v. 28b).

(c) "Every plant yielding seed . . . and every tree with seed in its fruit . . . [you] shall have them for food" (v. 29).

(d) Work the Garden of Eden and keep it (implicit in Gen. 2:15).

(e) "You may surely eat of every tree of the garden, but of the tree of the knowledge of good and evil you shall not eat, for in the day that you eat of it you shall surely die" (2:16–17).

---

23. Cf. Ouweneel (2008a, 175, 178, 184; 2009, 147).
24. Cf. Ouweneel (2015a, §2.3.1).

*Covenant sign:* if we can distinguish here such a sign at all, it could—if we think of a covenant with the *pre*lapsarian Adam—only be the tree of life. This tree was God's guarantee for everlasting blissful life on earth, as long as people would observe their side of the covenant (cf. Gen. 3:22, "Behold, the man has become like one of us in knowing good and evil. Now, lest he reach out his hand and take also of the tree of life and eat, and live forever").[25] As to the *post*lapsarian Adam, I think again of the "garments of skins."

*Covenant meal:* in a certain sense, we could think of the tree of life here again; breaking the covenant implies that humanity is barred from this tree, and cannot eat from it anymore.

*Sonship:* In the genealogy of Luke 3, Adam is called "son of God" (v. 38). Actually, the word "son" is not in the Greek text; it has to be carried forward all the way from verse 23.

*Garden:* "And the LORD God planted a garden in Eden, in the east, and there he put the man whom he had formed. And out of the ground the LORD God made to spring up every tree that is pleasant to the sight and good for food. The tree of life was in the midst of the garden, and the tree of the knowledge of good and evil. A river flowed out of Eden to water the garden, and there it divided and became four rivers.... The LORD God took the man and put him in the garden of Eden to work it and keep it" (Gen. 2:8-10, 15). This garden had features of a sanctuary because God walked there in the cool of the day (Gen. 3:8), just as, conversely, the sanctuaries of later days would have garden features (see §2.3.2).

*Present blessing:* the blessing for prelapsarian Adam consisted of the tree of life (Gen. 1:28), and the blessing for postlapsarian Adam consisted of the "mother promise" (or *protevangelium*): "I will put enmity between you and the woman, and between your offspring and her offspring; he shall bruise your head, and you shall bruise his heel" (Gen. 3:15). All blessings of the New Covenant are essentially a renewal,

---

25. Cf. Ouweneel (2008a, §9.1.1).

extension, and deepening of the Edenic promise.

*Eschatological meaning:* the tree of life finds its fulfillment in Christ and in the Messianic kingdom: "To the one who conquers I will grant to eat of the tree of life, which is in the paradise of God" (Rev. 2:7b). "Then the angel showed me the river of the water of life, bright as crystal, flowing from the throne of God and of the Lamb through the middle of the street of the city; also, on either side of the river, the tree of life with its twelve kinds of fruit, yielding its fruit each month. The leaves of the tree were for the healing of the nations" (22:1-2).

### 2.2.3 The Covenant with Noah

In fact, this is a covenant with the whole of humanity after the flood, and even with "every living creature of all flesh that is on the earth" (Gen. 6:18; 9:9-17). God promises that he will never again destroy his creatures through a worldwide flood. It is an "everlasting covenant" (v. 16), that is, a covenant that remains valid as long as the present earth continues to exist, that is, including the future Messianic kingdom.

As we saw (§2.2.2), Van der Waal argued that this Noahic covenant did not begin in Genesis 9 but in Genesis 6; he wanted to translate Genesis 6:18 as follows: "I will *confirm* [or *uphold*; Heb. *qum*, cf. the same verb in Lev. 26:9, "confirm"] my covenant with you," and saw such a translation supported by the covenant context in Genesis 6: "Noah found favor in the eyes of the LORD. . . . Noah was a righteous man, blameless in his generation. Noah walked with God" (vv. 8-9).[26] This is taken to imply that a covenant relationship between God and Noah already existed. We saw that others have rejected this interpretation.

Of special interest is Isaiah 24:5, "The earth lies defiled under its inhabitants; for they have transgressed the laws, violated the statutes, broken the everlasting covenant." To which covenant does the prophet refer here? The great Me-

---

26. Van der Waal (1990, 25–29); the same holds for Gen. 9:9; 17:7. Also see Wellum (2012, 612–13).

dieval Jewish expositor Rashi thought here of the Sinaitic Torah; other rabbis thought of the Noahic covenant, under which "every member of the human race is subject to certain moral laws, one of which is the prohibition of murder" (Gen. 9:5-6).[27] John Oswalt, too, presumed that the reference here is primarily "to the Noahic covenant in Gen. 9:1-17 with its prohibition of bloodshed," but assumes that "its broader reference is to the implicit covenant between Creator and creature, in which the Creator promises abundant life in return for the creature's living according to the norms laid down at Creation."[28] Geoffrey Grogan also thought of the Noahic covenant but added: "It is possible too that the prophet had Genesis 3 in mind, particularly in view of his reference to the curse in v. 6. The world as a whole did not possess the moral commandments of God in written form as in the Mosaic Law; but those laws nevertheless represent the will of God for mankind, and mankind is under judgment for their violation. The word 'disobeyed' [ESV: 'transgressed'] implies at least some awareness of these moral requirements in the human conscience (cf. Rom 1:18-32; 2:11-16), thus an element of deliberateness in sin."[29]

*Antecedent evil:* this covenant was made (or renewed?) after the disaster of the flood, which was God's punishment for humanity's universal sin.

*Partner:* Noah, and in him all living creatures; it is a universal covenant. Some expositors have presumed that this is the same as "the covenant that I had made with all the peoples" (Zech. 11:10).[30] Others have thought here of God's "covenant of security and restraint, by which he had been apparently holding back the nations from his people (cf. Ezek 34:25; Hos 2:18)."[31]

---

27. Slotki (1983, 111).
28. Oswalt (1986, 446); cf. Brown and Keele (2012, 53).
29. Grogan (1986, 152).
30. So Ridderbos (1935, 158).
31. Barker (1985, 677); rejected by Ridderbos (see previous note).

*God's love* comes to light here in at least three respects: (a) his *long-suffering* ("My Spirit shall not abide in man forever, for he is flesh: his days shall be 120 years," being the time God gave humanity for repentance, Gen. 6:3); (b) the fact that he spared Noah and his house ("Noah found favor in the eyes of the LORD," v. 8); and (c) it is quite amazing that the argument that God used to bring a water flood over humanity (Gen. 6:5) was virtually the same as the argument he used after the flood henceforth to spare humanity (8:21). In his (justified) anger, he brought judgment; but in his love, he spared humanity on the basis of Noah's sacrifice (see next point).

*Sacrificial basis:* the burnt offering that Noah brought from all clean animals, and of which the "pleasing aroma" was smelled by God (Gen. 8:20-21). This foundation shows that this was not a covenant of *common* grace, as has sometimes been asserted,[32] but of *redemptive* grace.[33] Ever since the flood, God would deal with the earth, not according to humanity's sinful works but according to the sacrifice of Christ that is anticipated here. Even what some Reformed theologians have called "common grace" is based on the cross, including those temporary favors bestowed upon unbelieving humanity (cf. Matt. 5:45; Acts 14:17).

*Torah:* the four commandments of the Noahic Torah, of which the third and the fourth were new:[34]

(a) "Be fruitful and multiply and fill the earth" (9:1; cf. v. 7).

(b) Rule over "every beast of the earth and upon every bird of the heavens, upon everything that creeps on the ground

---

32. Cf. Bavinck (2006, 3.216–19); Van der Waal (1990, 28); Brown and Keele (2012, 74–75).
33. Though he hardly refers to the sacrifice, Gentry (2012, 175) underscores the redemptive nature of this covenant: "The unmerited favour and kindness of God in preserving his world in the covenant with Noah creates a firm stage of history where God can work out his plan for rescuing his fallen world. It also points ahead to the coming deliverance in Jesus Christ."
34. Ouweneel (2015a, §2.3.2); not to be confused with the seven "Noahide Commandments" distinguished in Judaism (see ibid., §8.3.3).

and all the fish of the sea. Into your hand they are delivered" (v. 2).

(c) "Every moving thing that lives shall be food for you. And as I gave you the green plants, I give you everything. But you shall not eat flesh with its life, that is, its blood" (vv. 3–4).

(d) "And for your lifeblood I will require a reckoning: from every beast I will require it and from man. From his fellow man I will require a reckoning for the life of man. Whoever sheds the blood of man, by man shall his blood be shed, for God made man in his own image" (vv. 5–6).

*Covenant sign:* The sign of the Noahic covenant is the rainbow: "This is the sign of the covenant that I make between me and you and every living creature that is with you, for all future generations: I have set my bow in the cloud, and it shall be a sign of the covenant between me and the earth" (Gen. 9:12–13). Also see Ezekiel 1:28; Revelation 4:3; 10:1, where the rainbow is connected with the glory of God.

*Covenant meal:* Noah's eating from his own vines (Gen. 9:20) could have had covenantal significance if it had been done in thankfulness and moderation. In fact, Noah's drunkenness implied his personal violation of God's covenant. It was the "wrong" meal, just as was Adam and Eve's eating from the forbidden fruit. These were anti-covenantal meals.

*Sonship:* no reference.

*Garden:* Just as after creation, Adam fell in the Garden of Eden by eating of the forbidden fruit, after the flood Noah fell too, in a new garden (a vineyard), by abusing the fruit thereof. In both cases this had consequences for their descendants (Gen. 3:15–16; 9:25).

*Present blessing:* the promise that God will not again destroy the earth through a flood (Gen. 9:14–15); the promise of blessing for the "Japhethites" (read, Western Gentiles) in the "tents of Shem" (read, Israel, Shem's most important offspring; v. 27).

*Eschatological meaning:* God's faithfulness toward his creation will last as long as the present earth will last. Never again has God destroyed the earth through a universal flood, although the following is true: "For they [i.e., the scoffers] deliberately overlook this fact, that the heavens existed long ago, and the earth was formed out of water and through water by the word of God, and that by means of these the world that then existed was deluged with water and perished. But by the same word the heavens and earth that now exist are stored up for fire, being kept until the day of judgment and destruction of the ungodly . . . the day of the Lord will come like a thief, and then the heavens will pass away with a roar, and the heavenly bodies will be burned up and dissolved, and the earth and the works that are done on it will be exposed . . . the coming of the day of God, because of which the heavens will be set on fire and dissolved, and the heavenly bodies will melt as they burn! But according to his promise we are waiting for new heavens and a new earth in which righteousness dwells" (2 Pet. 3:5-13). In the future, though there will not be a water judgment, there *will* be a fire judgment.

## 2.3   Three Individual Covenants

Of course, artificial divisions like this (§§2.2-2.4) have only relative value. In a certain sense, the covenants with Adam and Noah were also individual but nevertheless—because Adam and Noah were heads of the whole human race—had significance for all humanity. The covenants to be mentioned now were made with individuals, too, far more personally with them even than those with Adam and Noah. However, the covenant with Abraham was significant not only for himself but also for his entire (physical as well as spiritual) progeny, even for "all the families of the earth." The covenants with Levi and David, too, had a strongly personal character, yet they were intended for the whole people of Israel, and the covenant with David—through Israel and the great Son of David—even for the entire world.

## 2.3.1 The Covenant with Abr(ah)am

The covenant with Abram in Genesis 15 contained a promise involving a numerous offspring, which one day would possess the land of Canaan (v. 18). This covenant was elaborated in Genesis 17. Abram (*Av-ram*, i.e., "lofty father") was now called Abraham (*Abir-hamôn*, i.e., "father of a multitude"), a name linked with the promise that a multitude of nations would come forth from him (Gen. 17:1-21; 28:3; 35:11; 48:4; Deut. 33:3 [lit. "peoples," i.e., (the tribes of) Israel]; 1 Chron. 16:17; Ps. 105:8-11). According to Romans 4:11-12, this also implies a spiritual offspring, consisting of all those who walk in the same faith as did their father Abraham (cf. Gen. 15:6). In a wider sense, it is the covenant with "the fathers" (Rom. 9:5): Abraham, Isaac, and Jacob (Exod. 2:24; 6:3-4; Lev. 26:42; Deut. 4:31; 7:12; 8:18; 1 Kgs 8:21; 2 Kgs 17:15; Jer. 11:10; 31:32; Micah 7:20). See the (or our, or your) "fathers" in the New Testament (Luke 1:55, 72-73; Acts 3:13, 25; 7:32; 13:32; 26:6; Rom. 9:5; 11:28; 15:8), although "fathers" usually means "ancestors" in the broad sense.

Many theologians have discussed whether Genesis 15 and 17 describe two different covenants between God and Abr(ah)am, or whether they are basically one covenant. One argument for the latter view is that the Bible never speaks of covenants (plural) with Abraham, but only of the one covenant with him (Exod. 2:24; Lev. 26:42; 2 Kgs 13:23; 1 Chron. 16:16; Ps. 105:9). Some have defended the position that Genesis 15 and 17 represent two different covenants,[35] but others have combated their arguments.[36] I myself deal with just one covenant with Abraham, although the emphases in Genesis 15 and 17 are clearly different. Genesis 15 deals more with the natural-temporal aspects, Genesis 17 more with the spiritual-eternal aspects of God's relationships with Abraham and his offspring.

Notice how God twice introduces himself to Abr(ah)am,

---
35. E.g., Williamson (2007, 89).
36. E.g., Gentry (2012, 275–80).

namely, with an "I am" preamble: "Fear not, Abram, I am your shield; your reward shall be very great" (Gen. 15:1). "I am God Almighty" (17:1). Compare the reiteration of the covenant with Jacob: "I am the Lord, the God of Abraham your father and the God of Isaac" (28:13; cf. 35:11). Such an "I am" preamble is also found in other covenants: in the Sinaitic covenant, and in the preparation for it (Exod. 3:6, 14; 6:2, 6-8, 29; 7:5; etc. ["I am YHWH"]; 20:2; 29:46 ["I am YHWH their God"]), and in the New Covenant (Jer. 32:27, "I am the YHWH, the God of all flesh").

Another typical feature we find in several covenants is that the duties that either one party or both parties assume are underscored with an oath. In Abraham's case, this does not happen in Genesis 15 or 17, but in Genesis 22:16-18, "By myself I have sworn . . . because you have done this and have not withheld your son, your only son, I will surely bless you, and I will surely multiply your offspring as the stars of heaven and as the sand that is on the seashore. And your offspring shall possess the gate of his enemies, and in your offspring shall all the nations of the earth be blessed, because you have obeyed my voice" (cf. 26:3; Ps. 105:8-11).

The importance of this solemn oath is strongly emphasized in Hebrews 6:13-18, "For when God made a promise to Abraham, since he had no one greater by whom to swear, he swore by himself, saying, 'Surely I will bless you and multiply you.' And thus Abraham, having patiently waited, obtained the promise. For people swear by something greater than themselves, and in all their disputes an oath is final for confirmation. So when God desired to show more convincingly to the heirs of the promise the unchangeable character of his purpose, he guaranteed it with an oath, so that by two unchangeable things [i.e., promise and oath], in which it is impossible for God to lie, we who have fled for refuge might have strong encouragement to hold fast to the hope set before us."

*Antecedent evil:* the calling of Abram came after humanity's rebellion as it expressed itself in building the tower of Babel (Gen. 11:1-9). God dispersed the people over the face of all the earth, and now began to follow an entirely new course: the election of one single man, in whom he would realize his counsels (cf. Isa. 51:2, "Look to Abraham your father and to Sarah who bore you; for he was but one when I called him, that I might bless him and multiply him").

*Partner:* Abraham and all his progeny, both bodily (sign: physical circumcision) and spiritual (sign: not baptism, but spiritual circumcision; see Appendix I). Objectively, it is a universal covenant—"in you all families of the earth shall be blessed" (Gen. 12:3; cf. 18:18; 22:18; 26:4; 28:14; Gal. 3:8)—but subjectively, it is a particular covenant, that is, effectuated only in the believing part of humanity.[37]

*God's love:* in the calling of Abraham, and in the promise of blessing to all families of the earth, God's love comes to light in an entirely new way. God loves to act through "unlikely candidates," as we saw before: "If you are going to build a great nation, would you choose an old man with a barren wife, such as Abraham (Gen. 11:30)?"[38] God's *long-suffering* comes to light in the fact that Abraham's progeny would have to "be afflicted for four hundred years" before they would obtain the promised land, "for the iniquity of the Amorites is not yet complete" (Gen. 15:13-16). God would rather have his people suffer in the "iron furnace" of Egypt (Deut. 4:20; 1 Kgs 8:51; Jer. 11:4) than not show enough patience to the Amorites.

*Sacrificial basis:* the sacrifice brought by Abram, cutting the sacrificial animals into halves.[39] These halves were laid

---

37. J. Hoek in Hoek and Verboom (2010, 23): "It is a particular covenant, yet with a universal bearing." H. J. de Bie in Hagoort (1999, 12) speaks of the "particularist [read, particular] period."
38. Stam (1999, 17).
39. It has been presumed that this act is the basis for the expression *karat berit*: "making [lit., cutting] a covenant."

opposite each other, so that a "blood street"[40] emerged (Gen. 15:9-11, 17-21). Passing through such a blood street apparently meant: if I do not keep my covenantal duties, may I be killed just like these animals (cf. Jer. 34:18-20).[41] Amazingly, however, it was not Abram who had to pass through the blood street, but God himself did so under the tokens of a smoking fire pot and a flaming torch (v. 17). God is thereby emphasizing his own "duties" (promises) rather than those of Abram and his progeny.

One may wonder whether this was a true "sacrifice";[42] indeed, the curse aspect prevailed. I see a parallel, however, with Exodus 24, where the curse aspect is also prominent (vv. 6-8), whereas the sacrificial aspect cannot be denied: ". . . young men of the people of Israel, who offered burnt offerings and sacrificed peace offerings of oxen to the LORD" (v. 5).

*Torah*: the three commandments of the Abrahamic Torah:[43]

(a) "Walk before me, and be blameless" (Gen. 17:1).

(b) "Every male among you shall be circumcised . . . and it shall be a sign of the covenant between me and you" (vv. 10-11; see further vv. 12-14).

(c) "Command your children and your household after you to keep the way of the LORD by doing righteousness and justice" (this command is implied in 18:19; of course, indirectly this was also a command for Abraham himself: "[K]eep the way of the LORD by doing righteousness and justice").

To Isaac God declares (Gen. 26:5): "Abraham obeyed my voice and kept my charge, my commandments [Heb. *mitzwot*], my statutes [*chukkot*], and my laws [*torot*]."

*Covenant sign*: the sign of this covenant is circumcision,

---

40. See for this expression Schilder (1957, 97, etc.).
41. C. B. Elsinga in Hagoort (1999, 20–21).
42. It is denied by Brown and Keele (2012, 91), for example.
43. Ouweneel (2015a, §2.3.1).

which in Genesis 17 is administered to all men in Abraham's household, and after Genesis 17 to all the sons of the covenant partners, wherewith these sons themselves become covenant partners (vv. 11, 14: "You shall be circumcised in the flesh of your foreskins, and it shall be a sign of the covenant between me and you. . . . Any uncircumcised male who is not circumcised in the flesh of his foreskin shall be cut off from his people; he has broken my covenant"). In Acts 7:8, Stephen therefore speaks of "the covenant of [i.e., characterized by] circumcision."[44]

*Covenant meal:* the meal that Abraham enjoyed with the three persons who visited him, of whom one became known as YHWH—or if one so wishes: YHWH revealed himself in particular through one of these three angels—and that confirmed the covenantal promise of a physical son (Gen. 18:1-15).

*Sonship:* Abraham is nowhere referred to as son of God. However, in Galatians 3, "sons of Abraham" (v. 7) is almost equivalent to "sons of God" (v. 26), which makes Abraham part of the family of God, too (cf. Matt. 1:1, the Son of God is Son of Abraham).

*Garden:* the precious land that God promised to Abraham was compared with the "garden of the LORD" (Gen. 13:10; cf. §2.4.3), thus establishing a direct link between Eden (Paradise) and Canaan (the promised land; cf. Isa. 51:3; Ezek. 36:35).[45]

*Present blessing:* the Abrahamic blessing for the nations (Gal. 3:8-9, 14) contains every spiritual blessing that Jesus-believers enjoy today, *except* the quintessential blessings of the church, which surpass the latter (see chapters 7 and 9). More specifically, this Abrahamic blessing consists of justification by faith (vv. 6-9; Rom. 4).

---

44. J. Hoek commits a minor error in Hoek and Verboom (2010, 35), when he writes: "In the book of Acts, the term 'covenant' is not used" (see, however, Acts 3:25; 7:8).
45. See more extensively Wright (1991, 21–23).

*Eschatological meaning:* the Abrahamic covenant, though not identical with all subsequent covenants, is certainly the foundation and starting point for them. Therefore, in connection with the Messianic kingdom and the restoration of Israel it is said, for instance: "He will again have compassion on us; he will tread our iniquities underfoot. You will cast all our sins into the depths of the sea. You will show faithfulness to Jacob and steadfast love to Abraham, as you have sworn to our fathers from the days of old" (Micah 7:19–20).

I just emphasized that *not* all the spiritual blessings enjoyed by the Ekklesia are also fruits of the Abrahamic promises. Paul makes a careful distinction in Galatians 3: believers receive "the blessing of Abraham" (v. 14a), which, as the context shows, is here specifically justification by faith. But they also receive "the promised Spirit through faith" (v. 14b), which was *not* part of the promises made to Abraham. When therefore Michael Horton says that the Abrahamic covenant "establishes the basis for the everlasting inheritance of the heavenly Jerusalem,"[46] he is mistaken. Abraham "was looking forward to the city that has foundations, whose designer and builder is God" (Heb. 11:10), but that does not mean that this city was part of God's explicit promises made to him. In looking forward to this heavenly city, Abraham's faith *rose above* what God had explicitly promised to him. It is the same in John 8, where Jesus said, "Your father Abraham rejoiced that he would see my day. He saw it and was glad" (v. 56). There was nothing in the Abrahamic covenant about seeing the "day" of Jesus. Horton's statement is nothing but an unfortunate fruit of supersessionism.

## 2.3.2 The Covenant with Levi

---

46. Horton (2006, 105); cf. Brown and Keele (2012, 86): "God's promise [to Abraham] of a land looks forward to the greater fulfillment of the new heavens and new earth"; and: "The promised land of Canaan was temporary, not permanent. The permanent Promised Land is the heavenly country that still awaits us" (95). In this way, the irrevocable, everlasting significance of the "land promise" for Israel is spiritualized away (see Appendix IV).

This covenant was made with all the descendants of Levi, the Levites, and especially with the Aaronic family ("my covenant with Levi," Mal. 2:4-5; "the covenant of Levi," v. 8); more specifically with Phinehas, Aaron's grandson: "Phinehas . . . has turned back my wrath from the people of Israel, in that he was jealous with my jealousy among them, so that I did not consume the people of Israel in my jealousy. Therefore say, 'Behold, I give to him my covenant of peace, and it shall be to him and to his descendants after him the covenant of a perpetual priesthood, because he was jealous for his God and made atonement for the people of Israel'" (Num. 25:11-13). Please note here the interesting expression "covenant of peace" (cf. Isa. 54:10; Ezek. 34:25; 37:26). Ultimately, "peace" (Heb. *shalôm*) is the fullness of Messianic blessing.

More generally, with respect to the Levites, we may consider here Moses' prayer to God: "Give to Levi your Thummim, and your Urim to your godly one, whom you tested at Massah, with whom you quarreled at the waters of Meribah [see Exod. 17:7]; who said of his father and mother, 'I regard them not'; he disowned his brothers and ignored his children [see Exod. 32:26-29]. For they observed your word and kept your covenant. They shall teach Jacob your rules and Israel your law; they shall put incense before you and whole burnt offerings on your altar. Bless, O Lord, his substance, and accept the work of his hands; crush the loins of his adversaries, of those who hate him, that they rise not again" (Deut. 33:8-11). This shows the importance of this Levitical covenant: it is the guarantee of an everlasting Levitical priesthood for Israel (see below).

*Antecedent evil:* initially the firstborn sons of Israel had been chosen to minister to the Lord (cf. Exod. 13:2; 22:29; 34:19; Num. 3:13; 8:17). However, after Israel had worshiped the golden calf, while the Levites had remained faithful (Exod. 32:26; Deut. 33:8-9), God decided to have the firstborn replaced by the loyal Levites (Num. 3:12; 8:15-18). Every firstborn was carefully exchanged for a Levite (3:15-51).

*Partner:* Levi, and in him the Levites, more specifically the house of Aaron (see above), and in the end, the house of Zadok (see below).

*God's love* comes to light in the fact that, in spite of his faithfulness at Mount Sinai, Levi still was an "unlikely candidate": "Simeon and Levi are brothers; weapons of violence are their swords. Let my soul come not into their council; O my glory, be not joined to their company. For in their anger they killed men, and in their willfulness they hamstrung oxen. Cursed be their anger, for it is fierce, and their wrath, for it is cruel! I will divide them in Jacob and scatter them in Israel" (Gen. 49:5–7; cf. 34:25–30). The latter phrase sounds like a punishment, but eventually it came to mean that the God-serving Levites lived in their own sacred cities among the Israelites.

*Sacrificial basis:* the consecration of the priests, as described in Exodus 29 and Leviticus 8–9, was based on a bull for a sin offering, a ram for a burnt offering, and a ram for a consecration offering (Exod. 29:22, 26, 27, 31, "ram of ordination"). The consecration of the Levites, as described in Numbers 8:5–26, was based on two bulls, one sacrificed as a burnt offering, and one as a sin offering.

*Torah:* the two essential commandments of the Levitical Torah (especially for the Aaronic priests) were these:

(a) The ministry of the tabernacle: "I have given the Levites as a gift to Aaron and his sons from among the people of Israel, to do the service for the people of Israel at the tent of meeting and to make atonement for the people of Israel, that there may be no plague among the people of Israel when the people of Israel come near the sanctuary" (Num. 8:19; cf. 1:50–53; 1 Chron. 6:48).

(b) The teaching of the Mosaic Torah: "They shall teach Jacob your rules and Israel your law; they shall put incense before you and whole burnt offerings on your altar" (Deut. 33:10).

In addition, there were many specific regulations for the

purity of the priests (Lev. 21:1–22:16), and for them and the Levites (Num. 18; cf. Ezek. 44).

*Covenant sign:* perhaps we may say that the sign of the Levitical covenant is the Levitical (high) priest himself (see something similar in the next covenant).

*Covenant meal:* at their consecration, the priests had to solemnly eat the breast and the right thigh from the "ram of ordination" (Exod. 29:26–33; Lev. 8:29–32).

*Sonship:* there is only a very indirect, but interesting reference: Jesus is priest "after the order of Melchizedek" (Ps. 110:4), although on earth, and at present in heaven, the priestly work he carried and carries out is obviously "after the order of Levi," so to speak: sacrifice and intercession (Heb. 2:17; 4:15; 7:23–28; 9:11–14). Practically speaking, he is a Levite priest, though formally he is a Melchizedekian priest. Now notice Hebrews 7: "For this Melchizedek, king of Salem, priest of the Most High God, . . . is . . . resembling the Son of God" (vv. 1–3).

*Garden:* in a certain sense, the Garden of Eden had been a sanctuary, in which God dwelt (Gen. 3:8). In this respect, Eden points to the tabernacle and the temple of Solomon with their clear Paradise motifs: flowers and trees (cf. the lampstand: Exod. 25:31–36; 37:17–22; also see 1 Kgs 6:18, 29, 32, 35; 7:18, 20, 22, 24; cf. Ezek. 41:18–20), and a river of life (Ps. 36:7–9; Jer. 17:13; Ezek. 47:1–12; cf. Rev. 22:1).

*Present blessing:* Jesus is called the High Priest according to the order of Melchizedek (Heb. 5:6, 10; 6:20; 7:1, 10–11, 15, 17; cf. Gen. 14:17–18; Ps. 110:4), but the actual priestly ministry he is performing today for his people is typically Aaronic (carrying out the work of atonement, intercession in the heavenly sanctuary, ministry in the holy places; Heb. 2:17; 4:14–16; 7:25; 8:1–2). This ministry of Jesus is in fact a blessed result of the Levitical covenant.

*Eschatological meaning:* the descendants of Phinehas, more specifically, of the priest Zadok, living in David's lifetime, will serve in the temple of the Messianic kingdom (Ezek. 40:46; 43:19; 44:15; 48:11; cf. 2 Sam. 8:17; 15:24-36). At the same time, Christ himself will be the King-Priest on the throne: "Yes, He shall build the temple of the LORD. He shall bear the glory, and shall sit and rule on His throne; so He shall be a priest on His throne, and the counsel of peace shall be between them both" (Zech. 6:13 NKJV). See the model for this in Melchizedek: "king of Salem . . . the priest of God Most High" (Gen. 14:18). This double office will be in line with David and Solomon, who both acted as king-priests (2 Sam. 6:17-18; 24:25; 1 Kgs 3:4, 15; 8:62-63; 9:25).

### 2.3.3 The Covenant with David

David said, God "has made with me an everlasting covenant, ordered in all things and secure. For will he not cause to prosper all my help and my desire?" (2 Sam. 23:5; cf. 7:12; 1 Kgs 8:25; 2 Chron. 6:16; 21:7; Jer. 33:21; also see Isa. 55:3; Ezek. 37:25). The importance of this covenant is the guarantee of an "everlasting" kingship to Israel, an eternal bond between the chosen people, the promised land, the chosen city (Jerusalem, Zion), and the chosen royal family. This kingship finds its ultimate fulfillment in Messiah Jesus, *the* Son of David *par excellence* (cf. Ps. 89:3-4; Jer. 30:9; 33:22, 25-26; Ezek. 34:23-24; 37:24-25; Luke 1:32-33, 69).

It is quite amazing that Clarence Stam can say that this Davidic "covenant, too, is not different from the one made with Abraham, Isaac, and Jacob."[47] He could make such a statement only under the power of the federalist paradigm, which prescribes that all postlapsarian covenants be lumped together in the one "covenant of grace." In reality, everyone can see that the Abrahamic and the Davidic covenants involve different covenant partners, different forms of the Torah, different covenant signs, different blessings, and different accents in their eschatological meaning. Stam's claim boils down to this: A is not different from B—except that all the characteristics of

---

47. Stam (1999, 101).

A and B are different.

*Antecedent evil:* David was the "man after God's own heart" (1 Sam. 13:14), who succeeded Saul, the man after the people's heart (cf. 1 Sam. 8). The natural is first, then the spiritual, as stated in the rule of 1 Corinthians 15:46. Saul's kingship ended in disaster (1 Sam. 31), David's kingship will debouch into the Messianic kingdom. The apostle Paul said in Pisidian Antioch: "Then they asked for a king, and God gave them Saul the son of Kish, a man of the tribe of Benjamin, for forty years. And when he had removed him, he raised up David to be their king, of whom he testified and said, 'I have found in David the son of Jesse a man after my heart, who will do all my will'" (Acts 13:21).

*Partner:* David and his "house," specifically his royal successors, the kings of Judah. Of this royal line, Christ is the point of culmination; in the prophetic Books he himself is sometimes called "David" (Jer. 30:9; Ezek. 34:23-24; 37:24-25; Hos. 3:5). In the New Testament, "Son of David" is one of Jesus' important titles, especially in Matthew (1:1; 9:27; 12:23; 15:22; 20:30-31; 21:9, 15).

*God's love* is, through David, shown to all Israel, the people who benefit from this covenant, but concerns first David in person: God "rejected the tent of Joseph; he did not choose the tribe of Ephraim, but he chose the tribe of Judah, Mount Zion, which he loves. He built his sanctuary like the high heavens, like the earth, which he has founded forever. He chose David his servant and took him from the sheepfolds; from following the nursing ewes he brought him to shepherd Jacob his people, Israel his inheritance" (Ps. 78:67-71). David was an "unlikely candidate": God did not choose one of the impressive elder sons of Jesse, but the youngest, still a boy, who tended the sheep and who had almost been forgotten (1 Sam. 16:6-13). Isaiah 55:3 (NKJV) speaks of the "sure mercies of David," that is, the sure tokens of God's steadfast love (Heb. *hesed*, covenant loyalty), which he will grant to his people through the great Son of David (cf. Acts 13:34). God's *long-suffering* came to light in the fact that David had to be persecuted under king Saul for many years—from his boyhood until his thirtieth year (2 Sam. 5:4)—before God's patience with Saul was finally finished (after forty years, Acts 13:21), and even then he had to wait for seven years until he was anointed king over all Israel (2 Sam. 5:1-5).[48]

*Sacrificial basis:* (a) the sacrifices that David brought when he took the ark of the covenant to Mount Zion (2 Sam. 6:17); (b) his sacrifices on the threshing floor of Araunah, the subsequent location of the temple (24:24-25); (c) the sacrifices that king Solomon brought at the consecration of the temple (1 Kgs 8:62-64). In short, the Davidic covenant is closely related with the election of the city of Jerusalem ("Zion") and the temple; these three form forever an unbreakable triad: royal throne, city, and temple. Jerusalem is the "city of David" (2 Sam. 5:7, 9; 6:10, 12, 16; etc.; exception: in Luke 2:4 and 11, Bethlehem, David's native city, is called the "city of David").

*Torah:* the Davidic Torah: "I will be to him [i.e., David's son] a father, and he shall be to me a son. When he commits iniquity, I will discipline him with the rod of men, with the stripes of the sons of men" (2 Sam. 7:14). "[I]f his children forsake my law and do not walk according to my rules, if they violate my statutes and do not keep my commandments, then I will punish their transgression with the rod and their iniquity with stripes" (Ps. 89:30-32; see already the law of the king in Deut. 17:14-20).

*Covenant sign:* perhaps we may say that the sign of the Davidic covenant is the Davidic king himself, who will never fail on the throne of David (cf. 2 Sam. 7:13, 16; 1 Kgs 9:5; 1 Chron. 17:12, 14; 22:10; 2 Chron. 6:16; 9:8; Ps. 89:4, 29, 36; 132:11-12; Isa. 9:7; Jer. 33:17, 20-21).[49] As long as there is no

---

48. Cf. ibid., 103: "How long did not Abraham have to wait before Isaac was born? And how long did it not take until David was undisputed king over Israel?"
49. Cf. Brown and Keele (2012, 128): "Due to the unconditional nature of the

Davidic king on the throne, the (now invisible) throne itself is, as it were, the covenant sign. This throne never moved to heaven, as some Reformed expositors seem to think; it is still the Davidic throne in Jerusalem, which is even called the "throne of the LORD" (1 Chron. 29:23; cf. Jer. 3:17; also see Rev. 3:21, where Jesus carefully distinguished between the throne of the *Father*, where he is sitting now, and *his own* throne, where he will sit in the future).

*Covenant meal:* I am thinking here of the "cake of bread," the "portion of meat," and the "cake of raisins" that David "distributed among all the people, the whole multitude of Israel, both men and women" (2 Sam. 6:19) on the occasion of bringing the ark to Mount Zion, thus forever forging the bond between his kingship, the nation of Israel, Mount Zion, and the future temple.

*Sonship:* God prophesied of David's son (Solomon): "He shall build a house for my name, and I will establish the throne of his kingdom forever. I will be to him a father, and he shall be to me a son" (2 Sam. 7:13-14; cf. Ps. 89:26; in Heb. 1:5 this is applied to the Son of God). In 2 Samuel 12 God claimed his fatherhood with respect to Solomon by giving him a name of himself: "Bathsheba . . . bore a son, and he [i.e., David] called his name Solomon. And the LORD loved him [i.e., the boy] and sent a message by Nathan the prophet. So he called his name Jedidiah [i.e., 'beloved of the LORD'], because of the LORD" (vv. 24-25).[50]

*Garden:* see §2.3.2 (temple of Solomon) and §2.4.3.

*Present blessing:* it is always good for Christians to remember that "their" Jesus is none other than *Israel's* Messiah, *Israel's* anointed King, *Israel's* true David. "[S]alvation is from the Jews" (John 4:22). We have the privilege of having a share in the kingdom of God, already in its present (largely concealed) form (cf. Rom. 14:17-18; Col. 1:12-13), but we should

---

[Davidic] covenant, a Davidic son will always be on the throne, but only the obedient son [i.e., the Messiah] will get an everlasting throne."

50. Cf. Wellum (2012, 640–41).

never forget that our King is and remains none other than the Son of David. Even some Gentiles appealed to him as "Son of David" (Matt. 15:22).

*Eschatological meaning:* as the Son of David, Christ will receive the throne of his father David (Luke 1:32). "The LORD swore to David a sure oath from which he will not turn back: 'One of the sons of your body I will set on your throne. . . .' For the LORD has chosen Zion; he has desired it for his dwelling place: 'This is my resting place forever; here I will dwell, for I have desired it. . . . There I will make a horn to sprout for David; I have prepared a lamp for my anointed. His enemies I will clothe with shame, but on him his crown will shine" (Ps. 132:11-18). "For to us a child is born, to us a son is given; and the government shall be upon his shoulder, and his name shall be called Wonderful Counselor, Mighty God, Everlasting Father, Prince of Peace. Of the increase of his government and of peace there will be no end, on the throne of David and over his kingdom, to establish it and to uphold it with justice and with righteousness from this time forth and forevermore. The zeal of the LORD of hosts will do this" (Isa. 9:6-7).

## 2.4  Three Covenants with Israel

Of course, it is perfectly true that the following three covenants form a continuum: the Palestinian covenant is a renewal of the Sinaitic covenant, and the New Covenant is the renewal of the previous two. Yet the Palestinian covenant is more than the Sinaitic covenant in that in the former, the Sabbath does not occupy the central place, as it does in the latter, but rather the promised land of Canaan is central. Therefore, the Palestinian covenant is exclusively Israelite, whereas the New Covenant, though formally made with Israel, has significance for the entire (renewed) humanity.

### 2.4.1  The Sinaitic Covenant with Israel

This is a covenant that is made no longer with a single individual (and possibly many people comprised in him), but with an entire nation, in its quality as "people of God," a covenant people (Exod. 19:5-6; 24:7-8; 34:10, 27-28; Deut. 28:1-14, 15-68). It is an "everlasting" or "eternal" covenant, that is, a covenant whose validity lasts forever (Exod. 31:16; cf. Lev. 24:8; Isa. 24:5). Of course, this can be understood only if we recognize that this Old Covenant ultimately merges into the New Covenant.

There is no contrast between, but rather a smooth transition from, the Sinaitic or Old Covenant to the New Covenant. Likewise, there is no contrast between, but rather a smooth transition from, the Abrahamic covenant to the Sinaitic covenant. We see this in Psalm 105:8-11, where it is declared that the covenant that God made with Abraham "was confirmed to Jacob as a statute, to Israel as an everlasting covenant." The psalmist speaks as if there were only one covenant, given first to the patriarchs, then confirmed to Israel. It is important to emphasize this over against those who describe the Abrahamic covenant as an (unconditional) "promise covenant," and the Sinaitic covenant as a (conditional) "law covenant." They see primarily contrast, whereas Scripture sees primarily continuity. This has led to the conflict within Reformed theology as to whether the Sinaitic covenant is a "covenant of works" or a "covenant of grace," or includes something of each. Later, we will see in what sense this entire distinction is based on false premises (§3.5).

Of course, the Abraham and Sinaitic covenants are not identical; otherwise, Moses could not have said: "The LORD our God made a covenant with us in Horeb. Not with our fathers did the LORD make this covenant, but with us" (Deut. 5:2-3). Yet, the continuity between the two covenants is just as certain as the difference between them. Presumably, this continuity is the reason why we do not hear of a new oath that God swore at the establishment of the Sinaitic Covenant; it was enough simply to remind the people of the oaths he had already sworn to the patriarchs (Exod. 6:8; 13:5, 11; 32:13; 33:1; etc.). The people in turn made a triple declaration to God that clearly had the character of an oath: "All the people answered together and said, 'All that the LORD has spoken we will do'" (Exod. 19:8). "And all the people answered with one voice and said, 'All the words that the LORD has spoken we will do. . . . All that the LORD has spoken we will do, and we will be obedient'" (24:3, 7).

It is rather exaggerated to say, as does Hendrikus Berkhof, that Israel "precisely through the covenant with God became a nation."[51] Before this covenant was made, God had called Israel not only a "nation" but "*his (my)* people" (Exod. 3:7, 10; 5:1; 7:4, 16; etc.). Apparently, this was simply because they were the offspring of the patriarchs, the bearers of the promise. This is parallel to what happened with Adam. Some have presumed that God did not necessarily create Adam in order subsequently to enter with him into a covenant relationship, but rather that this relationship was already given with God's creation of Adam as such. So too with Israel. From the moment they manifested themselves as a nation (people) — let us say, since Exodus 1 — they were "God's people." See Exodus 2:25, "God saw the people of Israel — and God knew [them]" (NIV, "God looked on the Israelites and was concerned about them"). The factual establishment of the Sinaitic covenant (Exod. 19–24) was just the formal confirmation of this. It is like the young man who speaks of "my girl" long before he is able to say "my wife."

Incidentally, in the entire Bible, the expression "Old Covenant" occurs only in 2 Corinthians 3:14, where several translations render the phrase as "Old Testament." See further Hebrews 8:13 ("In speaking of a new covenant, he makes the first one obsolete. And what is becoming obsolete and growing old is ready to vanish away"). The term "old" is also implied in Jeremiah 31:31–32, "Behold, the days are coming, . . . when I will make a new covenant with the house of Israel and the house of Judah, not like the covenant that I made with their

---

51. Berkhof (1991, 339).

fathers on the day when I took them by the hand to bring them out of the land of Egypt, my covenant that they broke, though I was their husband."

The Sinaitic covenant, too, begins with the (by now well-known) preamble: "I am the LORD." God had first presented himself this way to Moses (Exod. 6:2), then through him to the whole people of Israel (Exod. 6:6–8; 29:46; especially in 6:8 in an explicitly covenantal way), and then at the beginning of the Ten Commandments: "I am the LORD your God, who brought you out of the land of Egypt, out of the house of slavery" (Exod. 20:2; cf. 29:46; Lev. 11:45; 19:36; 22:33, 43; 25:38, 55; 26:13, 45; Num. 15:41; Deut. 5:6; Ps. 81:10). In Leviticus this phrase is repeated many times to underscore the importance of certain statutes.

*Antecedent evil:* in the establishment of this covenant, time and again the people are reminded of their slavery in Egypt, and their glorious exodus from there: "I am the LORD, and I will bring you out from under the burdens of the Egyptians, and I will deliver you from slavery to them, and I will redeem you with an outstretched arm and with great acts of judgment. I will take you to be my people, and I will be your God, and you shall know that I am the LORD your God, who has brought you out from under the burdens of the Egyptians" (Exod. 6:6–7). "I am the LORD your God, who brought you out of the land of Egypt, out of the house of slavery.... You shall remember that you were a slave in the land of Egypt, and the LORD your God brought you out from there with a mighty hand and an outstretched arm. Therefore the LORD your God commanded you to keep the Sabbath day [the covenant sign; see below]" (Deut. 5:6, 15; also see 4:20, 34; 6:12, 21–22; 7:8, 15; 8:14; 10:19; 13:5, 10, 15; 16:12; 24:22; 26:6). "I myself made a covenant with your fathers when I brought them out of the land of Egypt, out of the house of slavery" (Jer. 34:13).

*Partner:* the twelve tribes of Israel, and no one else. The intimate relationship into which God entered with Israel is brought out beautifully in Exodus 19:4, "You yourselves have seen what I did to the Egyptians, and how I bore you on eagles' wings and *brought you to myself.*" God did not just want to take the nation to a mighty mountain and a wonderful land, but *to himself.* That was the essence of his covenant relationship with them: his self-revelation to the people was the basis for his relationship with them.

*God's love:* Moses was an "unlikely candidate": "[W]ould you choose a fugitive like Moses, a man who does not even want the job anymore and offers many excuses?"[52] Israel itself was an "unlikely candidate": "It was not because you were more in number than any other people that the LORD set his love on you and chose you, for you were the fewest of all peoples, but it is because the LORD loves you" (Deut. 7:7-8).[53] God's *long-suffering* came to light in several forty-year periods of testing. First, Moses had to keep his father-in-law's flock for forty years (Acts 7:23) until God's patience with Egypt was exhausted (cf. Exod. 2:24-25; 3:7-9). The next forty years Moses spent with Israel in the wilderness (first mentioned in Exod. 16:35), during which time God showed them constantly that he is "slow to anger" (Exod. 34:6; Num. 14:18).

*Sacrificial basis:* the burnt and peace offerings that the young men of Israel (as precursors of the priests; cf. Num. 3:11-13, 40-51) brought, from which came the "blood of the covenant that the LORD has made with you" that was sprinkled on the people (Exod. 24:4-8).

*Torah:* the Mosaic or Sinaitic Torah, summarized especially in the Ten Words (Exod. 20:1-17), together with the announcement of reprisals in case the people would break the covenant (Lev. 26:14-39). Torah and covenant are closely con-

---

52. Stam (1999, 17).
53. *Contra* Rabbi Nachmanides, who claims that among all people God found Israel worthy of becoming his chosen, and that their qualification for this selection was their determined will to endure whatever trials would come upon them; see Cohen (1983, 1027). The ground for Israel's election was God's love, not Israel's worthiness.

nected but they should not be identified.[54] The Torah is the set of divine stipulations of the covenant, not the covenant as such.

*Covenant sign*: the Sabbath; as Exodus 31:13-17 says, "Above all you shall keep my Sabbaths, for this is a sign between me and you throughout your generations, that you may know that I, the LORD, sanctify you. You shall keep the Sabbath, because it is holy for you. . . . Therefore the people of Israel shall keep the Sabbath, observing the Sabbath throughout their generations, as a covenant forever. It is a sign forever between me and the people of Israel that in six days the LORD made heaven and earth, and on the seventh day he rested and was refreshed." Compare this with Ezekiel 20:12, 20: "I gave them my Sabbaths, as a sign between me and them, that they might know that I am the LORD who sanctifies them . . . keep my Sabbaths holy that they may be a sign between me and you, that you may know that I am the LORD your God." It is striking how often the Sabbath commandment is mentioned in the Sinaitic Torah, also without any mention of the word "sign" (Exod. 16:23-29 [already before Sinai!]; 20:8-11; 31:13-16; 35:2-3; Lev. 19:30; 23:3; 26:2; Deut. 5:12-15; cf. Num. 15:32-36).[55]

*Covenant meal:* here we think of the remarkable words in Exodus 24:8-11, "And Moses took the blood and threw it on the people and said, 'Behold the blood of the covenant that the LORD has made with you in accordance with all these words.' Then Moses and Aaron, Nadab, and Abihu, and seventy of the elders of Israel went up, and they saw the God of Israel. There was under his feet as it were a pavement of sapphire stone, like the very heaven for clearness. And he did not lay his hand on the chief men of the people of Israel; they

---

54. As does, e.g., Gentry (2012, 304); a bit later (387), he implicitly recognizes the difference.
55. In federalist thinking, Sabbath has moved to Sunday (without any biblical warrant; see Ouweneel [2015a, App. III]): "The Sunday is still a sign of the covenant," says Stam (1999, 150).

beheld God, and ate and drank." It should also be considered that every peace offering in Israel had the character of a covenant meal, in which God had his share (Lev. 3:11, 16), the priest had his (7:14, 32–35), and the people were allowed to eat the rest of the peace offering's meat (v. 19). Already at the establishment of the covenant, peace offerings are mentioned (Exod. 20:24; 24:5).

*Sonship:* God's covenant people, Israel, were called a son, or sons, of God in three respects:

(a) in anticipation already in Egypt: "Israel is my firstborn son, and I say to you, 'Let my son go that he may serve me'" (Exod. 4:22–23; cf. Ps. 80:15; Hos. 11:1);

(b) ". . . in the wilderness, where you have seen how the LORD your God carried you, as a man carries his son, all the way that you went" (Deut. 1:31); "[y]our clothing did not wear out on you and your foot did not swell these forty years. Know then in your heart that, as a man disciplines his son, the LORD your God disciplines you" (8:4–5);

(c) in view of the promised land: "You are the sons of the LORD your God. You . . . are a people holy to the LORD your God, and the LORD has chosen you to be a people for his treasured possession, out of all the peoples who are on the face of the earth" (14:1–2).

*Garden:* at Israel's exodus, the people themselves were a "vine [brought] out of Egypt" (Ps. 80:8; cf. Hos. 10:1): "You will bring them in and plant them on your own mountain" (Exod. 15:17; cf. 2 Sam. 7:10; Ps. 44:2; Isa. 17:11; 60:12). Israel was a "vineyard on a very fertile hill" (Isa. 5:1–2). It belonged to the essence of the Old Covenant that God "looked for it to yield grapes, but it yielded wild grapes" (v. 2), that is, "bloodshed . . . outcry" (v. 7). "I made you flourish like a plant of the field" (Ezek. 16:7). "I planted you a choice vine, wholly of pure seed. How then have you turned degenerate and become a wild vine?" (Jer. 2:21; cf. 11:17; 24:6; 32:41; 42:10). In the *eschaton* they will "be called oaks of righteousness, the planting of the LORD, that he may be glorified" (Isa. 61:3; cf. Amos 9:15). Notice how in Exodus 15:17 the notions of "planting" and "sanctuary" are linked; thus, the promised land is garden and sanctuary alike (cf. §§2.2.2 and 2.3.2).

*Present blessing:* this becomes visible in the New Covenant, which is nothing but the renewal and extension of the Sinaitic covenant (see below).

*Eschatological meaning:* idem.

### 2.4.2 The Palestinian Covenant with Israel

This is the renewal of the previous covenant, now especially in view of the promised land, Canaan, which Israel was about to enter (Deut. 29:1, 9, 12, 14) (the Sinaitic covenant had been established about forty years earlier).

*Antecedent evil:* in Deuteronomy, a "new Israel," as it were, stood before Moses because all the men older than twenty had died in the wilderness after their rebellion against God (Num. 14:29; 32:11). Abraham Ibn Ezra said that Deuteronomy was necessary to teach the "new Israel" God's commandments, and to renew the covenant with them.[56]

*Partner:* the twelve tribes of Israel, viewed as if they had already taken possession of the promised land.

*God's love* and *long-suffering* came to light in the fact that not all of Israel had died in the wilderness. The people could apply to themselves these words: "Because of the steadfast love [*hesed*, covenant loyalty] of the LORD, we are not cut off" (Lam. 3:22, margin). "And you shall remember the whole way that the LORD your God has led you these forty years in the wilderness, that he might humble you, testing you to know what was in your heart, whether you would keep his commandments or not. And he humbled you and let you hunger and fed you with manna, which you did not know, nor did your fathers know, that he might make you know that man does not live by bread alone, but man lives by every word

---

56. Cohen (1983, 1016).

that comes from the mouth of the LORD. Your clothing did not wear out on you and your foot did not swell these forty years. Know then in your heart that, as a man disciplines his son [whom he loves!; cf. Prov. 3:12], the LORD your God disciplines you" (Deut. 8:2-5).

*Sacrificial basis:* no special offerings; Israel existed before the LORD on the basis of the "pleasing aroma" of the daily burnt offerings (Exod. 29:38-46) and the annual sin offering of Yom Kippur (Lev. 16).

*Torah:* the reiteration of the Ten Words (Deut. 5:6-21), and thus of the entire Mosaic Torah, together with the announcement of reprisals for breaking the covenant (Deut. 28:15-68).

*Covenant sign:* although this is never explicitly said, we may argue that the sign of this covenant was in fact nothing other than the land itself: as long as it belongs to Israel — and this is "forever,"[57] even though Israel because of its sins was driven out of it several times — that is how long this covenant will last. Thus God had promised it already to Abram: "[A]ll the land that you see I will give to you and to your offspring *forever*" (Gen. 13:15), and to Abraham: "I will give to you and to your offspring after you the land of your sojournings, all the land of Canaan, for an *everlasting* possession" (Gen. 17:8; cf. 48:4; Exod. 32:13; Josh. 14:9; Ps. 37:18; Isa. 60:21). David told his son Solomon: "[O]bserve and seek out all the commandments of the LORD your God, that you may possess this good land and leave it for an inheritance to your children after you *forever*" (1 Chron. 28:8).

*Covenant meal:* not applicable.

*Sonship:* see what was said in §2.4.1 about Israel's sonship in view of the promised land.

*Garden:* in the Palestinian covenant, the prospect of the promised land was central (cf. §§2.3.1 and 2.4.3).

---

57. In such cases as these, "forever" (Heb. *'ad-'olâm*) in fact always means: as long as the present earth lasts, that is, until the end of the "age/world (*'olâm*) to come," when a new heaven and a new earth will come.

*Present blessing:* this becomes visible in the New Covenant, which is the renewal and extension of both the Sinaitic and the Palestinian covenants (see §2.4.3). Already today, a part of Israel possesses part of the promised land again, as a harbinger of the full realization of God's promises concerning the Holy Land.

*Eschatological meaning:* with the latter, the significance of the Palestinian covenant for the Messianic covenant also becomes visible: the promise of the land has an "everlasting" validity. There can be no Messianic kingdom in glory and power without a restored Israel living in its own land (see the next covenant).

### 2.4.3 The New Covenant with Israel

"Behold, the days are coming . . ., when I will make a new covenant with the house of Israel and the house of Judah. . . . For this is the covenant that I will make with the house of Israel after those days . . . : I will put my Torah within them, and I will write it on their hearts. And I will be their God, and they shall be my people. And no longer shall each one teach his neighbor and each his brother, saying, 'Know the LORD,' for they shall all know me, from the least of them to the greatest. . . . For I will forgive their iniquity, and I will remember their sin no more" (Jer. 31:31–34; cf. Isa. 59:21). In connection with the Messianic kingdom, this New Covenant is called an "everlasting covenant" (Jer. 32:36–41; 50:2–5; Isa. 55:1–5; 61:8–9; Ezek. 16:59–63; 37:15–28; see note 57) and a "covenant of peace" (Isa. 54:9–10; Ezek. 34:20–31; 37:15–28).

Although in principle the New Covenant is made with Israel, it is relevant for all nations (cf. Isa. 56:4–7; Matt. 26:28; 1 Cor. 11:25; 2 Cor. 3:6). However, this is something very different from the allegation that the covenant partner in the New Covenant would be a "new people of God," whose bond with God is "purely internal."[58] The actual covenant partner is not some "spiritual Israel" but ethnic Israel; at best we may say

---

58. Aalders (1939, 158).

that the believing Gentiles are admitted under the umbrella or into the courtyard of this covenant (see chapters 7 and 9).[59]

Since Jesus Christ himself is the Mediator of the New Covenant (Heb. 9:15; 12:24; cf. 1 Tim. 2:5), it is striking that he himself is called a "covenant," as if he is the personification of the New Covenant. God says to his Servant: "I will give you as a covenant for the people, a light for the nations" (Isa. 42:6; cf. 49:8). Other typically covenantal terms are applied in a personal way to God or Christ as well: "God is our salvation" (Ps. 68:19), "he [i.e., Christ] himself is our peace" (Eph. 2:14); ". . . Christ Jesus, who became to us wisdom from God, righteousness and sanctification and redemption" (1 Cor. 1:30). In other words, Christ is the embodiment of all covenant blessings.

*Antecedent evil:* Israel's history was for a large part a history of wickedness. Under the Old Covenant, all was lost because of its unfaithfulness, under the New Covenant all is regained by the grace and the power of God: "And when all these things come upon you, the blessing and the curse, and you . . . return to the LORD your God, . . . with all your heart and with all your soul, then the LORD your God will restore your fortunes and have mercy on you, and he will gather you again from all the peoples where the LORD your God has scattered you. . . . And the LORD your God will bring you into the land that your fathers possessed, that you may possess it. And he will make you more prosperous and numerous than your fathers. And the LORD your God will circumcise your heart and the heart of your offspring, so that you will love the LORD your God with all your heart and with all your soul, that you may live" (Deut. 30:1–6).

*Partner:* strictly speaking this would be only the twelve tribes of Israel, but the blessings of the covenant extend to all nations: "And the foreigners who join themselves to the LORD, to minister to him, to love the name of the LORD, and to be his

---

59. See extensively Ouweneel (2010b, chapter 3).

servants, everyone who keeps the Sabbath and does not profane it, and holds fast my covenant—these I will bring to my holy mountain, and make them joyful in my house of prayer; their burnt offerings and their sacrifices will be accepted on my altar; for my house shall be called a house of prayer for all peoples" (Isa. 56:6–7).

*God's love* comes to light nowhere more clearly than in the New Covenant. Shortly before its announcement, God says, "I have loved you with an everlasting love; therefore I have continued my faithfulness to you. Again I will build you, and you shall be built, O virgin Israel!" (Jer. 31:3-4). This time God's *long-suffering* has lasted for thousands of years: "The LORD is not slow to fulfill his promise as some count slowness, but is patient toward you, not wishing that any should perish, but that all should reach repentance" (2 Pet. 3:9). "Many years you bore with them and warned them by your Spirit through your prophets. Yet they would not give ear. Therefore you gave them into the hand of the peoples of the lands. Nevertheless, in your great mercies you did not make an end of them or forsake them, for you are a gracious and merciful God" (Neh. 9:30–31).

*Sacrificial basis:* the one and only sacrifice of Christ: "Therefore he is the mediator of a new covenant, so that those who are called may receive the promised eternal inheritance, since a death has occurred that redeems them from the transgressions committed under the first covenant. . . . Indeed, . . . without the shedding of blood there is no forgiveness of sins . . . Christ has entered . . . into heaven itself, now to appear in the presence of God on our behalf . . . he has appeared once for all at the end of the ages to put away sin by the sacrifice of himself" (Heb. 9:15, 22–26).

*Torah*: the Messianic Torah (Matt. 5–7 and other passages)[60] and the Millennial Torah (Ezek. 44–46).[61]

---

60. See Ouweneel (2015a).
61. Ibid., chapter 6.

*Covenant sign:* just as one could call the Levitical priest and the Davidic king himself the sign of the Levitical and the Davidic covenants, respectively, Christ, the Guarantor and Mediator of the New Covenant (Heb. 7:22; 8:6; 9:15; 12:24; cf. Matt. 26:28), is himself the "sign" of this covenant. In this context, we notice that *all* the covenant signs mentioned have eschatological significance in view of the Messianic kingdom: the judicial glory of God is compared to the rainbow (Ezek. 1:28; Rev. 4:3; 10:1), circumcision and the Sabbath will be continued in the Messianic kingdom (Isa. 52:1; 56:1–7; 66:23; Ezek. 44:9, 24; 46:1, 3–4, 6), and the Davidic Messiah will reign on David's throne in Jerusalem; he will even be King-Priest on his throne (Isa. 9:6–7; Jer. 30:9; 33:15–22; Ezek. 34:23–24; 37:24–25; Hos. 3:5; Amos 9:11; Zech. 6:13).

In a sense, also the elements used in the Lord's Supper could be called covenant "signs": "This cup . . . *is* the new covenant in my blood" (Luke 22:20). It goes too far, however, to claim that baptism is the "covenant sign of inclusion in the new covenant."[62] In the Bible, baptism is never a sign of inclusion in the New Covenant, but in the kingdom of God (e.g., Matt. 28:18–19) (see further Appendix I). The New Covenant parallel with the sign of the Abrahamic covenant (circumcision) is not baptism but spiritual circumcision (§2.3.1).

*Covenant meal:* in the present epoch, we think here of the Lord's Supper: "In the same way also he took the cup, after supper, saying, 'This cup is the new covenant in my blood. Do this, as often as you drink it, in remembrance of me'" (1 Cor. 11:25). With a view to the Messianic kingdom, the prophet said: "On this mountain the LORD of hosts will make for all peoples a feast of rich food, a feast of well-aged wine, of rich food full of marrow, of aged wine well refined. And he will swallow up on this mountain the covering that is cast over all peoples, the veil that is spread over all nations. He will swallow up death forever; and the LORD God will wipe away

---

62. *Contra*, e.g., Brown and Keele (2012, 89).

tears from all faces, and the reproach of his people he will take away from all the earth, for the Lord has spoken. It will be said on that day, 'Behold, this is our God; we have waited for him, that he might save us. This is the Lord; we have waited for him; let us be glad and rejoice in his salvation'" (Isa. 25:6–9).

*Sonship:* with respect to Israel: "Yet the number of the children of Israel shall be like the sand of the sea, which cannot be measured or numbered. And in the place where it was said to them, 'You are not my people,' it shall be said to them, 'Children [or, Sons] of the living God'" (Hos. 1:10). With respect to New Testament believers, there are many references to their sonship (Luke 6:35; 20:36; Rom. 8:14–15, 19, 23; 2 Cor. 6:18; Gal. 3:26; 4:5–6; Eph. 1:5; Hebr. 12:5–8; Rev. 21:7).

*Garden:* "For the Lord comforts Zion; he comforts all her waste places and makes her wilderness like Eden, her desert like the garden of the Lord; joy and gladness will be found in her, thanksgiving and the voice of song" (Isa. 51:3). "And they will say, 'This land that was desolate has become like the garden of Eden, and the waste and desolate and ruined cities are now fortified and inhabited'" (Ezek. 36:35). Also compare: "I will put in the wilderness the cedar, the acacia, the myrtle, and the olive. I will set in the desert the cypress, the plane and the pine together, that they may see and know, may consider and understand together, that the hand of the Lord has done this, the Holy One of Israel has created it" (Isa. 41:19–20). "For you shall go out in joy and be led forth in peace; the mountains and the hills before you shall break forth into singing, and all the trees of the field shall clap their hands. Instead of the thorn shall come up the cypress; instead of the brier shall come up the myrtle; and it shall make a name for the Lord, an everlasting sign that shall not be cut off" (Isa. 55:12–13). "The glory of Lebanon shall come to you, the cypress, the plane, and the pine, to beautify the place of my sanctuary, and I will make the place of my feet glorious" (Isa. 60:13).

*Present blessing*: all the spiritual blessings that Jesus-believers today have received and enjoy in Christ, apart from certain, specifically Christian blessings that surpass the New Covenant (the Father's house, "eternal life" in the sense used in John's writings, the church as the Body of Christ and the bride of the Lamb, the *theōsis*). As we will see in chapters 7 and 9, this distinction is not grasped by Christians who hold to the "everything is covenantal" view.[63]

*Eschatological meaning:* the New Covenant is in fact totally eschatological. It concerns the "times [Greek *kairoi*] of refreshing," that is, the "times [Greek *chronoi*] of restoration of all things" (Acts 3:19, 21 NKJV), "the dispensation of the fullness of the times [*kairoi*]" (Eph. 1:10 NKJV).[64] This involves Israel's restoration to its own land, and in this nation there will be blessing for all nations of the earth (cf. Gen. 22:18), peace and righteousness: "It shall come to pass in the latter days that the mountain of the house of the Lord shall be established as the highest of the mountains, and shall be lifted up above the hills; and all the nations shall flow to it, and many peoples shall come, and say: 'Come, let us go up to the mountain of the Lord, to the house of the God of Jacob, that he may teach us his ways and that we may walk in his paths.' For out of Zion shall go the law, and the word of the Lord from Jerusalem. He shall judge between the nations and shall decide disputes for many peoples; and they shall beat their swords into plowshares, and their spears into pruning hooks; nation shall not lift up sword against nation, neither shall they learn war anymore. O house of Jacob, come, let us walk in the light of the Lord" (Isa. 2:2-5; cf. Micah 4:1-5).

In the summary of Dwight Pentecost: "When the covenants are studied analytically we find seven great features which are determinative: (1) a nation forever, (2) a land forever, (3) a king forever, (4) a throne forever, (5) a kingdom

---

63. See Ouweneel (2010a, §§4.1-4.3 and chapter 14 on *theōsis*).
64. Very briefly, *kairos* refers more to the qualitative aspect of time, while *chronos* refers more to its quantitative aspect (length of time).

forever, (6) a new covenant, and (7) abiding blessings."[65] As far as the eschatological dimension is concerned—that is, *in concreto*, the Messianic kingdom—this means respectively:

(1) *Israel* converted and restored, and in or with it (believers from) all nations blessed;

(2) in the promised *land*, the land of Israel;

(3) under the dominion of the *Messiah*, the Son of David;

(4) who will be sitting on the *throne* of David;

(5) as the supreme ruler over an everlasting *kingdom*;

(6) under the conditions of the *New Covenant*; and

(7) in the possession and enjoyment of God's everlasting *blessings*.

Actually, we should add at least these:

(8) a *city*: Jerusalem, which will be the earthly capital of the "world to come";

(9) a *mountain*: Zion, seat of throne and temple; and

(10) the new *temple* (Ezek. 40-44).

---

65. Pentecost (1964, 128), with reference to Chafer (1983, IV, 315).

# Chapter 3
# The Old Covenant According to the Old Testament

*When I passed by you again and saw you,*
  *behold, you were at the age for love,*
*and I spread the corner of my garment over you*
  *and covered your nakedness;*
*I made my vow to you*
  *and entered into a covenant with you . . .*
  *and you became mine.*
*Then I bathed you with water*
  *and washed off your blood from you*
  *and anointed you with oil.*
*I clothed you also with embroidered cloth*
  *and shod you with fine leather.*
*I wrapped you in fine linen*
  *and covered you with silk . . .*
*You grew exceedingly beautiful*
  *and advanced to royalty.*
*And your renown went forth among the nations*
  *because of your beauty,*
*for it was perfect*
  *through the splendor that I had bestowed on*
  *you.*
Ezekiel 16:8–14

***Summary:*** *In God's view, marriage is a covenant, and the Old Covenant was a marriage, with all the well-known characteristics of a (Jewish) wedding: love, fidelity, the* mikweh, *the* (c)huppa, *the* ketubbah. *However, the Old Covenant also illustrates how among the covenant partners there are very different people: the true lovers of the* LORD, *the haters of the* LORD, *and the hypocrites. For some theologians one vital question is whether the Old Covenant was a conditional covenant (of works) or an unconditional covenant (of grace). I show that this is a false choice: no grace exists without works, and no works occur without grace. In this sense, the phrases "covenant of works" and "covenant of grace" are misnomers. There was no covenant of works in Eden, and even less was there a republication of such a covenant at Mount Sinai. This also means that there is no essential contrast between the Old Covenant and the New Covenant: both contain the elements of grace and of works. The real difference between the Old Covenant and the New Covenant is only this: under the former, Christ had not yet come.*

## 3.1 Its Matrimonial Character
### 3.1.1 Israel's Wedding Vow

WHAT EXACTLY WAS THE CHARACTER of the Old Covenant, the covenant that God made with Israel at Mount Sinai? The book of Hebrews tells us that the Old Covenant was not "faultless" (Heb. 8:7), and that it was "becoming obsolete and growing old," and therefore "ready to vanish away" (v. 13).[1] In other words, is the Old Covenant at all relevant to Christians today, and if so, what is its relevance?

In each covenant there are two parties, each of which must fulfill certain duties. God took upon himself to bless the people with all kinds of blessings (Deut. 7:11–20; 11:26–27; 15:45; 28:1–14; 30:15–16); Israel took upon itself to keep the Torah: "All that the LORD has spoken we will do" (Exod. 19:8). "All

---

1. Incidentally, the latter verse is the only one in which this covenant is called "old"; 2 Cor. 3:14 refers to what we call the "Old Testament," although "covenant" and "Testament" are two renderings of the same Greek word *diathēkē*; see §1.4.2.

the words that the Lord has spoken we will do" (24:3). "All that the Lord has spoken we will do, and we will be obedient" (v. 7). The opinion of Cyrus Scofield that the "Dispensation of Promise" ended when Israel precipitously (!) accepted the Torah[2] may contain some truth, but is weakened by the fact of God's own apparent joy over these words of Israel. The people said to Moses, "'Go near and hear all that the Lord our God will say, and speak to us all that the Lord our God will speak to you, and *we will hear and do it.*' And the Lord heard your words, when you spoke to me. And the Lord said to me, 'I have heard the words of this people, which they have spoken to you. They are right in all that they have spoken. Oh that they had such a heart as this always, to fear me and to keep all my commandments, that it might go well with them and with their descendants forever!'" (Deut. 5:27–29).

Of course, God knew the weakness of the people, their continual inclination to sin. Yet he accepted their vow in which they pledged to keep all his commandments. Israel was God's son (Exod. 4:22; Deut. 1:31; 8:5; Hos. 11:1; plural: Deut. 14:1, *banim attem, l'YHWH Elohekem*, lit. "sons are you, [namely,] of the Lord your God"). As a good father, God assumed his son's loyalty until the opposite turned out to be true. The most beautiful comparison with this in the Old Testament is the way in which the *torah* (from *y-r-h*, "to teach": "law," but literally "teaching") in the book of Proverbs functions between parent and son(s) (Prov. 3:1; 4:1–2; 6:20; 7:1–2; 28:7). The father (or mother) is teaching the son, and the son willingly places himself under this teaching.

The Sinaitic covenant is also compared to the matrimonial covenant.[3] In this context, Israel's covenant vow to submit to the Lord obtains the character of a wedding vow. In the Old Testament, marriage in general is called a "covenant" between a husband and a wife. Proverbs 2:17 speaks of the adulteress who "forgets the covenant of her God" — not the cove-

---
2. Scofield (1909, 20).
3. Ouweneel (2015a, §7.3.4).

nant *with* her God but the covenant *with* her husband that was brought about when she made vows to her husband *before* God. Malachi 2:14 tells the husband: "she is your companion and your wife by covenant" (NIV: "the wife of your marriage covenant"). Likewise, God said to Jerusalem, "When I passed by you again and saw you, behold, you were at the age for love, and I spread the corner of my garment over you and covered your nakedness; I made my vow to you and entered into a covenant with you, . . . and you became mine" (Ezek. 16:8).

Israel's love for the LORD during its wilderness journey is compared to bridal love: "I remember the devotion of your youth, your love as a bride, how you followed me in the wilderness, in a land not sown" (Jer. 2:2). This love came to expression in the people's observance of the Torah. In such a prophecy God deliberately overlooks Israel's failures in the wilderness, just as he did with David's failures when he described him as one "who kept my commandments and followed me with all his heart, doing only that which was right in my eyes" (1 Kgs 14:8). This is the way a loving husband loves to think of his honeymoon that he enjoyed with his now divorced wife.

Other prophecies, though not mentioning the word "covenant," also compare God's relationship with Israel to a marriage: "'For your Maker is your husband, the LORD of hosts is his name. . . . For the LORD has called you like a wife deserted and grieved in spirit, like a wife of youth when she is cast off, says your God. For a brief moment I deserted you, but with great compassion I will gather you. In overflowing anger for a moment I hid my face from you, but with everlasting love I will have compassion on you,' says the LORD, your Redeemer" (Isa. 54:5-8; cf. 62:5). "I will betroth you to me forever. I will betroth you to me in righteousness and in justice, in steadfast love and in mercy. I will betroth you to me in faithfulness. And you shall know the LORD" (Hos. 2:19-20). In such passages, the (re)marriage metaphor functions as just another term for the New Covenant.

### 3.1.2 More on Wedding Vows

Since the Sinaitic covenant is compared to a matrimonial relationship, the fact that God did not contradict the people after their threefold vow, but took their words seriously, reminds us of Numbers 30. This is the chapter on vows. If a woman is still living with her father and pledges a vow, or pledges a vow as an engaged or married woman, this is the rule: if such a woman pledges a vow "or any thoughtless utterance of her lips by which she has bound herself" (v. 6), and her father or fiancé/husband, respectively, hears it but remains silent to her, then her vows and pledges shall stand (vv. 3-4, 6-7). Also when the woman becomes a widow or is divorced, her vows will stand (v. 9; cf. Isa. 50:1; 54:4-8).

The wife's vow is described in verses 10-11 and 14: "[I]f she vowed in her husband's house or bound herself by a pledge with an oath, and her husband heard of it and said nothing to her and did not oppose her, then all her vows shall stand, and every pledge by which she bound herself shall stand . . . if her husband says nothing to her from day to day, then he establishes all her vows or all her pledges that are upon her. He has established them, because he said nothing to her on the day that he heard of them." Such a typological interpretation of these verses fits the marriage metaphor that Scripture uses for the Sinaitic covenant. Israel's triple vow to observe the Torah was accepted by her husband, and therefore she was bound to it.

In his providential ways with his people, God acts with Israel according to what it has vowed when the covenant was made, and what it has repeatedly pledged as the covenant was renewed, as happened under Joshua (Josh. 24:16-17, 21), king Asa (2 Chron. 15:12-13), and king Josiah (2 Kgs 23:3). Time and again, this entailed God's judgments over his people when they failed to comply with their own vows and pledges. For his part, however, God always kept *his* vows and pledges. Even though he could not, and cannot, fulfill them with regard to the majority of the people of Israel, he fulfilled them, and will fulfill them, with regard to a "remnant, chosen by grace" (Rom. 11:5). It is as Isaiah had said already a long time before: "In that day the remnant of Israel and the survivors of the house of Jacob will no more lean on him who struck them, but will lean on the LORD, the Holy One of Israel, in truth. A remnant will return, the remnant of Jacob, to the mighty God. For though your people Israel be as the sand of the sea, only a remnant of them will return. Destruction is decreed, overflowing with righteousness. For the LORD God of hosts will make a full end, as decreed, in the midst of all the earth" (Isa. 10:20-23).

Because God will keep his promises under all circumstances, the Sinaitic covenant will never end, just as the marital bond lasts as long as both partners are alive (Rom. 7:2). The LORD told his people, "I will never break my covenant with you" (Judg. 2:1). Not only the New Covenant but also the Sinaitic covenant as such is an *"everlasting* covenant" (Exod. 31:16; Lev. 24:8; Isa. 24:5), just as the Abrahamic (Gen. 17:7, 13, 19; cf. 1 Chron. 16:15-18; Ps. 105:8-11) and the Davidic covenant (2 Sam. 23:5) (see §3.6.3). The LORD "remembers his covenant forever . . . he has commanded his covenant forever" (Ps. 111:5, 9). This "everlasting" covenant is "broken" each time the people sin (Isa. 24:5). However, "broken" never means "abolished," just as adultery as such never really abolishes a marriage. Rather, the covenant is "renewed," as it was under king Joash (2 Kgs 11:17), king Josiah (13:23; 23:3), king Asa (2 Chron. 15:12), king Hezekiah (29:10), and under the scribe Ezra (Ezra 10:3). Each time this happens, the renewed covenant is called an "everlasting covenant" again.

Our conclusion must be that the New Covenant (Jer. 31:31-32) is not the replacement of, but the renewal of, the Old Covenant, just as when husband and wife have separated for a while but come together again, this is a renewal of their marital covenant (cf. Isa. 54:4-8). It is true, Jeremiah 31:32-33 suggests a certain contrast: "*not* like the covenant that I made with their fathers on the day when I took them by the hand to bring them out of the land of Egypt, my covenant that they broke, though I was their husband. . . . *For this* is the covenant that I will make with the house of Israel after those days. . . ." Yet, it is not the differences but the correspondences between the two covenants that stand out.

In the New Covenant, the Torah again occupies its central place—and this is essentially no other Torah than that of Mount Sinai (v. 33). Therefore, the establishment of the New Covenant has the character of a *mattan torah*, a lawgiving, as we read literally in Hebrews 8:10b (Greek *didous nomous mou*, lit. "giving my laws"). And because the Millennial Torah, the Torah of the Messianic kingdom to come,[4] will be essentially the same as the Mosaic Torah, the establishment of the New Covenant is essentially again a *z'man mattan toratênu*, a "time of the giving or our law," the renewal of the lawgiving at Sinai. "[T]his is the *covenant* that I will make with the house of Israel after those days . . .: I will put my *Torah* within them, and I will write it on their hearts" (Jer. 31:33). "I will remember my covenant with you in the days of your youth, and I will establish for you an everlasting covenant" (Ezek. 16:60).[5] The word "establish" might indeed suggest replacement, but the word "remember" points to continuity and renewal.

## 3.2  Love and Loyalty
### 3.2.1  A Relationship of Steadfast Love

If one insists on finding one common term for all the covenants that God made with postlapsarian humanity, the term "covenant of love" would be an excellent one.[6] It is a much broader, and therefore better, description than "covenant

---

4. Ouweneel (2015a, §5.2 and passim).
5. Brown and Keele (2012, 142) are mistaken in asserting that the covenant in v. 60 is the Abrahamic covenant; it is the Sinaitic covenant (cf. "the days of your youth" with Jer. 2:2).
6. Cf. Stam (1999, book title: *The Covenant of Love*; 30: "the covenant is a relationship of love between God and his people"; also see 52–53).

of grace." There may be many reasons why a ruler bestows grace on certain subjects, one reason being self-interest. But love is something that points to the deeper motive behind all the tokens of God's grace. This further underscores the deep meaning of marriage as a metaphor for the relationship between God and his people. As Clarence Stam put it: "It is love that gives all and therefore demands all. So we see that the covenant is a total *commitment of love*, from God to man and from man to God. It is all this, or it is nothing."[7]

A matrimonial covenant is a contract in which both parties take duties upon themselves. But they do this out of love, according to the saying, "Your wish is my command." Thus, the Torah, too, that bond between God and his people, can be understood only within the framework of the love between God and his people (Deut. 7:7-9, 13). Without that love, which is possible only in regenerate hearts through the power of the Holy Spirit, the Torah is nothing but an unbearable yoke (cf. Acts 15:10), just as marriage is for two married people who do not love each other (anymore): ". . . because lawlessness [Torah-lessness] will be increased, the love of many will grow cold" (Matt. 24:12). And one could say as well: because the love of many will grow cold, Torah-lessness will be increased.

The more Torah-keeping, the more love; but also: the more love, the more Torah-keeping: "Blessed is the man . . . [whose] delight is in the Torah of the LORD, and on his Torah he meditates day and night" (Ps. 1:1-2). "Oh how I love your Torah! It is my meditation all the day" (Ps. 119:97). The psalmist loves the Torah because he loves the LORD. In the words of Jesus, "If you love me, you will keep my commandments. . . . Whoever has my commandments and keeps them, he it is who loves me. . . . If anyone loves me, he will keep my word. . . . Whoever does not love me does not keep my words" (John 14:15, 21, 23-24). "If you keep my commandments, you will abide in my love, just as I have kept my Father's commandments and

---

7. Stam (1999, 53).

abide in his love" (John 15:10).

## 3.2.2 Covenant Loyalty

The NIV uses the phrase "covenant of love" at seven places (Deut. 7:9, 12; 1 Kgs 8:23; 2 Chron. 6:14; Neh. 1:5; 9:32; Dan. 9:4) where the Hebrew says, *(hab)berit w'(ha)hesed*, "covenant and steadfast love" (ESV). This word *(c)hesed* ("steadfast love") is a genuine *terminus technicus* that beautifully expresses this mutual love relationship in the covenant. *Hesed*, if used for people, means something close to "piety, godliness," but if used for God, it means something close to "loving-kindness, indulgence, favor."[8] Related to this is the word *(c)hasid*, which we know from the Jewish movement of the (C)has(s)idim. *Hasid* means either "pious, holy" (this is a characteristic of the *hasid* himself), or the object of God's favor (this is a characteristic of God).[9] The *hasid* is the godly person who is favorable toward the LORD, as well as the one who enjoys the LORD being favorable toward *him*. Both aspects are unbreakably linked together.

In the seven passages mentioned above, covenant (*berit*) and steadfast love (*hesed*) are closely linked together. Apparently, the NIV views the coupling as a hendiadys in rendering *berit w'hesed* as "covenant of love." Indeed, with *hesed/hasid* we are always dealing with the special covenant relationship between God and his people, such that God's *hesed* and human *hesed* both refer to their *faithfulness* toward that covenant, and thus to each other. In somewhat modern terms: *hesed* is the *solidarity* or *loyalty* of two parties in a relationship with each other motivated by mutual love.[10] God is *hasid* in that out of love, he bestows upon humanity all the favors involved in his covenant promises. A human being is *hasid* in that, out of love and in answer to God's favors, one faithfully observes the To-

---

8. Ibid.; see extensively Glueck (1967).
9. This meaning of *hasid* is expressed in the Dutch translation *gunstgenoot* ("object of favor"; NBG-transl., e.g., in Ps. 16:10 [ESV: "holy one"]; 30:5 [ESV: v. 4, "saints"]; etc.).
10. Van der Waal (1990, 6) translates *hesed* as "covenant fidelity."

rah. God is loyal to his people by keeping his promises, his people are loyal to him by observing the Torah. And both are loyal out of love. These two elements of loyalty and love are expressed in the ESV's rendering of *hesed* as "steadfast love."

*Hesed* is often linked with *emeth*, "faithfulness" (rendered in [N]KJV as "truth," which apparently has the sense here of "truthfulness"). In a covenantal context the two terms are more or less synonymous: ". . . a God merciful and gracious, slow to anger, and abounding in steadfast love and faithfulness" (Exod. 34:6; cf. Gen. 24:27, 49; 32:10; 2 Sam. 2:6; 15:20; Prov. 3:3; 14:2; 16:6; 20:38; and many times in the Psalms).

If *hesed* plays an essential role in the covenant, then it does so also in marriage. In Genesis 20:13, Abraham speaks of Sarah's *hesed* ("loyalty," CEB, GNT) to him as her husband ("kindness," NKJV, RSV, WEB, ESV; "love," NIV; "favor," MSG, NCV, NLT). God remembers the bridal *hesed* ("devotion") that Israel showed him when they were still traveling through the wilderness (Jer. 2:2). Two friends who have made a covenant together also experience this *hesed* (1 Sam. 20:8, 14–15, "steadfast love," i.e., covenant loyalty). We have seen that God's covenant is like the covenant between a king and his vassals; thus, the vassal shows *hesed* ("steadfast love") to his king (2 Sam. 3:8), and the king shows solidarity with his subjects when they are being threatened.

An earthly king can also show *hesed* ("mercy") to his enemies (1 Kgs 20:31); in this case, the meaning is not "loyalty" but "mercy." The root meaning in these two words is something like "benevolence," namely, to a party that does not deserve it, but is in misery ("mercy"), or to a party that is entitled to it on the basis of an existing covenant between the two ("loyalty").

### 3.2.3 Love and Counter-Love

Interestingly, in connection with the covenant we find God's love in two opposite senses. On the one hand, God's love was his starting point for his attitude toward his people. He loved them first, and *then* he asked for their love in return, which they could show him by obeying his Torah: "[I]t is because the LORD loves you and is keeping the oath that he swore to your fathers, that the LORD has brought you out with a mighty hand and redeemed you from the house of slavery, from the hand of Pharaoh king of Egypt" (Deut. 7:8). The Sinaitic covenant was rooted in God's prior unconditional love.

On the other hand, only a few verses later, Moses says about God: "And because you listen to these rules and keep and do them, the LORD your God will keep with you the covenant and the steadfast love that he swore to your fathers. He will love you, bless you, and multiply you. He will also bless the fruit of your womb and the fruit of your ground, your grain and your wine and your oil, the increase of your herds and the young of your flock, in the land that he swore to your fathers to give you" (vv. 12-13). Here, God's love toward Israel is the *consequence* of their faithfulness toward him. There is no real contradiction here. A love that is not answered is doomed to fade away; a love that *is* answered is strengthened. God initiated his covenant with Israel out of pure love; but his love is intensified by the counter-love of Israel.

Love is a keyword in God's covenant relationships. The Hebrew name of the synagogal blessing referring to the Torah-giving, *Ahabah*, means "love" and expresses the fullness of God's love, which he bestowed upon Israel in giving the Torah. Israel in turn must show this love to Israel's neighbors: to strangers (Lev. 19:34), widows and orphans (Exod. 22:21-22; 23:9; Lev. 19:33; Deut. 14:29; 16:11, 14; 24:17-21; 26:12-13; 27:19), to the deaf and the blind (Lev. 19:14; Deut. 27:18), and to poor people (Exod. 22:25; 23:6, 11; Lev. 19:10, 15; 23:22; Deut. 15:7-11; 24:14).[11]

God himself is Israel's example here: "[T]he LORD set his heart in love on your fathers and chose their offspring after them, you above all peoples, as you are this day. Circumcise

---

11. Ouweneel (2010c, chapter 12).

therefore the foreskin of your heart, and be no longer stubborn. For the LORD your God is God of gods and LORD of lords, the great, the mighty, and the awesome God, who is not partial and takes no bribe. He executes justice for the fatherless and the widow, and loves the sojourner, giving him food and clothing. Love the sojourner, therefore, for you were sojourners in the land of Egypt" (Deut. 10:15-19).

The Medieval Jewish expositor Rashi (i.e., Rabbi Shlomo Yitschaqi) told Israel to obey God's commands from love and not from fear.[12] And the orthodox Jew, Pinchas Lapide (1922-1997), who was a New Testament scholar, once wrote of the Talmud: "Basically, the entire Talmud, as it is called, is nothing but one commentary on charity, with no other goal than the perfect realization of this love to one's neighbor — also in such prosaic matters as protection of tenants, reparation for damage, compensation, crop failure or suspension of payment because of sudden illness."[13]

All true covenant loyalty rests in love; therefore, in chapter 2, I tried to indicate how God's love functioned in each of the nine covenants. Specifically, I mention two forms of love that play a role in the covenants:

(a) *Matrimonial love:* this love is perhaps nowhere expressed in a more lovely way than in Ezekiel 16: "I made you flourish like a plant of the field. And you grew up and became tall and arrived at full adornment. Your breasts were formed, and your hair had grown; yet you were naked and bare. When I passed by you again and saw you, behold, you were at the age for love, and I spread the corner of my garment over you and covered your nakedness; I made my vow to you and entered into a covenant with you, . . . and you became mine" (vv. 7-8; cf. vv. 59-63).

(b) *Amiable love (friendship):* the great example here is the covenant between David and Jonathan: "Then Jonathan made

---

12. Quoted by Cohen (1983, 1022).
13. Lapide (1983, 88).

a covenant with David, because he loved him as his own soul. And Jonathan stripped himself of the robe that was on him and gave it to David, and his armor, and even his sword and his bow and his belt" (1 Sam. 18:3-4). "And Jonathan made a covenant with the house of David, saying, 'May the LORD take vengeance on David's enemies.' And Jonathan made David swear again by his love for him, for he loved him as he loved his own soul" (20:16-17). "Saul and Jonathan, beloved and lovely! . . . my brother Jonathan . . . your love to me was extraordinary, surpassing the love of women" (2 Sam. 1:23, 26).

## 3.3 The Wedding at Sinai
### 3.3.1 Some Prophetic Words

If the Sinaitic covenant had the character of a marriage, the lawgiving at Mount Sinai had the character of a wedding. In Jewish tradition, this is one of the aspects of the meaning of *Shavu'ot*, the Feast of Weeks or Pentecost, which Israel celebrates in the third month of the religious year (Lev. 23:16-22; cf. Exod. 19:1).[14] In Jeremiah 2:2-3, the LORD tells Israel, "I remember the devotion of your youth, your love as a bride, how you followed me in the wilderness, in a land not sown. Israel was holy to the LORD, the firstfruits of his harvest. All who ate of it incurred guilt; disaster came upon them." We find here, though in a concealed form, a double hint of Pentecost. First, God reminds the people of their sojourning in the wilderness, where Israel as a bride devotedly followed her Bridegroom, that is, since the wedding at Mount Sinai. Second, Israel is described here in terms relating to harvest, Pentecost being the feast of the barley and wheat harvest: "firstfruits of his harvest," such as the two loaves of bread of the Pentecost wave offering (Lev. 23:17, 20; "You shall observe the Feast of Weeks, the firstfruits of wheat harvest," Exod. 34:22).

As indicated earlier, the parallel between a covenant and a marriage is also seen in Malachi 2, where God points to his ancient covenant with Israel (v. 10, "the covenant of [i.e., es-

---
14. See Ouweneel (2001, §§4.2 and especially 4.3.3).

tablished with] our fathers"), but also calls marriage a covenant: "the LORD was witness between you and the wife of your youth, to whom you have been faithless, though she is your companion and your wife by covenant" (v. 14).

As we saw, in Ezekiel 16 Israel is compared to a woman with whom the LORD enters into marriage, that is, makes a covenant: "When I passed by you again and saw you, behold, you were at the age for love, and I spread the corner of my garment over you and covered your nakedness; I made my vow to you and entered into a covenant with you . . ., and you became mine" (v. 8). And after Israel has committed spiritual adultery by falling into idolatry, and has thus broken the covenant, the LORD promises: "I will deal with you as you have done, you who have despised the oath in breaking the covenant, yet I will remember my covenant with you in the days of your youth, and I will establish for you an everlasting covenant. . . . I will establish my covenant with you, and you shall know that I am the LORD, that you may remember and be confounded, and never open your mouth again because of your shame, when I atone for you for all that you have done" (vv. 59–63).

God's covenant with Israel at Mount Sinai was a marital covenant. Therefore, Israel is so often called the "bride" or "wife" of God (Isa. 49:18; 50:1; 54:5-8; 61:10; 62:4-5; Jer. 2:32; Ezek. 16 and 23; Hos. 2:19-20). In these passages, phrases such as "I will betroth you (again)," that is, I will accept you again as my bride, mean the same as "I will again enter into a covenant with you" or "I will renew the covenant with you" (cf. Isa. 55:3; 56:4-7; 59:21; 61:8).

### 3.3.2 A Jewish Wedding

At Mount Sinai, the five most typical characteristics of a Jewish wedding were clearly exhibited.

(a) The *mikweh*, which is the ritual bath that the bride undergoes before her wedding.[15] The *mikweh* is not mentioned

---
15. Cf. Ouweneel (2011, §5.1.2).

explicitly in the Old Testament, but the rabbis found a hint of it in Exodus 19:10, where the people receive the command to wash their clothes: if the clothes, then certainly the body.[16] Another argument is the one based on Exodus 24:8, where Moses sprinkled blood on the people. The rabbis argued that they had a tradition that there can be no sprinkling without ritual washing; therefore, they were convinced that at Sinai Israel had literally undergone the *mikweh*.[17]

New Testament parallel: Incidentally, it seems that Ephesians 5:25–26 ("Christ loved the church and gave himself up for her, that he might sanctify her, having cleansed her by the washing of water with the word") is also a reference to the *mikweh*, now in regard to Christ and his New Testament Bride, the Ekklesia.

(b) The *(c)huppah*, which is literally "canopy" (Isa. 4:5), and from there also the bridegroom's or bridal "chamber" (Ps. 19:5; Joel 2:16). During a Jewish wedding, the *huppah* is a baldachin, under which the wedding takes place. At Sinai, the mountain itself formed as it were a baldachin over the people—they stood "under the mountain," so to speak—or perhaps instead under the "thick cloud" that covered the mountain (Exod. 19:9, 16–17; 24:15–16).

New Testament parallel: Although not in direct reference to the Ekklesia, there is a remarkable parallel in Luke 9:34–35 (the account of the transfiguration of Jesus on the mountain): "As he [i.e., Peter] was saying these things, a cloud came and overshadowed them, and they were afraid as they entered the cloud. And a voice came out of the cloud, saying, 'This is my Son, my Chosen One; listen to him!'"

(c) The *witnesses*, also called the "friends of the bridegroom" (cf. John 3:29; we would call them "groomsmen"), who had mediated in the formation of the marital contract (see [d]). At the "wedding" at Sinai, Moses was *the* witness, or

---

16. This is an *a fortiori* argument, or in rabbinical vernacular, a *kal v'chomer* argument.
17. Bab. Talmud: Yebamot 46a–b.

rather, mediator, between God and his people.

New Testament parallel: Moses was the mediator of the Old, like Jesus was the Mediator of the New Covenant (Gal. 3:19; Heb. 8:6; 9:15; 12:24). The difference is that Jesus is not only Mediator between God and his people, but also the Bridegroom of the Ekklesia (cf. 2 Cor. 11:2; Eph. 5:21–31; Rev. 19:6–9; 21:2, 9; 22:17).

(d) The *ketubbah*, which is the marital act or contract, in which the mutual duties of bridegroom and bride have been stipulated. At Sinai, these were, on the one hand, the promises that God made to his people, and on the other hand, the Torah, which the people voluntarily took upon themselves (Exod. 19:8; 24:3, 7); more specifically: "And Moses wrote down all the words of the LORD. . . . Then he took the Book of the Covenant and read it in the hearing of the people' (24:4, 7).

New Testament parallel: Likewise, the Messianic Torah as contained in the New Testament may be viewed as a *ketubbah* regulating the relationship between Christ and his followers: "If you love me, you will keep my commandments" (John 14:15; cf. 15:10; 1 John 5:3). In a certain sense, the *entire* New Testament (or Covenant!) is the *ketubbah* of the New Covenant (although, as we will see, the specific blessings of the Ekklesia surpass the New Covenant).

(e) The *marriage supper*, of which Exodus 24:9–11 might be a hint: "Then Moses and Aaron, Nadab, and Abihu, and seventy of the elders of Israel went up, and they saw the God of Israel. There was under his feet as it were a pavement of sapphire stone, like the very heaven for clearness. And he did not lay his hand on the chief men of the people of Israel; they beheld God, and ate and drank."

New Testament parallel: Similarly, among the many characteristics of the Lord's Supper is the love bond between Christ and his Body/Bride (1 Cor. 10:16–17, "The bread that we break, is it not a participation in the body of Christ? Because there is one bread, we who are many are one body, for we all partake of the one bread"), while the remembrance aspect (Luke 22:19; 1 Cor. 11:24) is like remembering a dearly beloved who has died (cf. Jer. 16:7, "No one shall break bread for the mourner, to comfort him for the dead, nor shall anyone give him the cup of consolation to drink for his father or his mother").

Just as for Israel the matrimonial bond with the LORD God began with the lawgiving at Mount Sinai, for the church the matrimonial bond with the Lord Jesus began with the outpouring of the Holy Spirit on Mount Zion. Interestingly, Pentecost refers to both occasions![18] Paul wrote to the Corinthians: "I feel a divine jealousy for you, since I betrothed you to one husband, to present you as a pure virgin to Christ" (2 Cor. 11:2). And for the Ephesians, he compared the bond between Christ and his Body, the church, to the matrimonial bond: "Husbands, love your wives, as Christ loved the church and gave himself up for her, that he might sanctify her, having cleansed her by the washing of water with the word, so that he might present the church to himself in splendor, without spot or wrinkle or any such thing, that she might be holy and without blemish" (Eph. 5:25-27; also see vv. 28-33).

In the book of Revelation, the "bride" or "wife" of the Lamb (Rev. 19:7; 21:2, 9; 22:17) is the church, which is clear from the parallel between the true and the false church (cf. 17:1-3 with 21:9-10). This does not change the fact that Israel in the Messianic kingdom will be the bride of the Messiah. I see an example of these two brides in connection with Jacob's two wives, Leah and Rachel. In this image, as I see it, Leah does not represent Israel, and Rachel the church, as various church fathers believed, due especially to their supersessionist views ("the church is spiritual Israel"). No, the Messiah came for Israel (Rachel), and got Leah (the church), but in the end he will also have his Rachel.[19]

---

18. See Ouweneel (2001, 114–27).
19. See Ouweneel (2007, 258). By the way, if Rachel (Israel) is the more beloved and Leah (the church) is the less beloved wife, in Deut. 21:15–17 the imagery

Pentecost is traditionally the Jewish flower festival. It is, as it were, one large bridal bouquet, which refers back to the covenant wedding as it took place at Mount Sinai. But it also points forward to the great wedding at the start of the Messianic kingdom, which will be a recapitulation of the exodus from Egypt and the wedding at Sinai: "Therefore, behold, I will allure her, and bring her into the wilderness, and speak tenderly to her. And there I will give her her vineyards and make the Valley of Achor a door of hope. And there she shall answer as in the days of her youth, as at the time when she came out of the land of Egypt. And in that day, . . . you will call me 'My Husband,' and no longer will you call me 'My Baal.' . . . And I will betroth you to me forever. I will betroth you to me in righteousness and in justice, in steadfast love and in mercy. I will betroth you to me in faithfulness. And you shall know the LORD . . . I will sow her for myself in the land. And I will have mercy on No Mercy [*Lo Ruchamah*], and I will say to Not My People [*Lo Ammi*], 'You are my people'; and he shall say, 'You are my God'" (Hos. 2:14-23; cf. 1:6-10).

## 3.4 Kinds of Covenant Partners
### 3.4.1 Two Groups

Already in the Old Testament, it is obvious that, on the side of the people, there are two kinds of partners in the covenant. There are those who wholeheartedly love the LORD, and therefore also the covenant, and therefore also God's Torah, even if they, from time to time, trespass the Torah. However, there are also partners who are foreign to the s/Spirit of the covenant. Therefore, from the outset the Torah had a *double function*: it shows to those who love God how they can remain in the sphere of the covenant, and it shows to those who do not truly love God that, according to the letter, they belong to the covenant, but not at all according to its s/Spirit. The Torah is the joy of the true people of God, but it is an annoying burden and a curse for the wicked, for by breaking the Torah they

---

is the reverse: Jesus is the Firstborn through the less beloved wife (Israel).

break the covenant, and in this way they forfeit all the blessings of the covenant (cf. Lev. 26; Deut. 11:26–28; 27:11; 28:68).

God's (presumed) covenant with postlapsarian Adam was made in view of his posterity too. However, immediately two types of covenant members became visible: Cain and Abel (Gen. 14). "By faith Abel offered to God a more acceptable sacrifice than Cain, through which he was commended as righteous" (Heb. 11:4; cf. Matt. 23:35, "righteous Abel"). "We should not be like Cain, who was of the evil one and murdered his brother. And why did he murder him? Because his own deeds were evil and his brother's righteous" (1 John 3:12). "Woe to them [i.e., the backsliders]! For they walked in the way of Cain" (Jude 11). In three of these passages the word "righteous" (*tsaddiq*) is mentioned. The true members of any covenant are the real *tsaddiqim*; the others are "of the evil one."

Similarly, God made a covenant with Noah, including his posterity. However, Noah's son Ham manifested himself in a wicked way (Gen. 9:22), and the other two sons, Shem and Japheth, in a righteous way (v. 23). This was not just a temporary failure of Ham; the event revealed what was in the *hearts* of these three men. Hence Noah's prophecy, in which he cursed Ham's son Canaan, and blessed his other two sons (vv. 25–27). Under the Noahic covenant, again, there are the righteous and the wicked.

History repeats itself: among Abraham's sons—both of whom were circumcised, that is, both included in the Abrahamic covenant—Ishmael was "a wild donkey of a man, his hand against everyone, and everyone's hand against him" (Gen. 16:12), whereas of Isaac it was said, "We see plainly that the Lord has been with you.... You are now the blessed of the Lord" (26:28–29).

Isaac's sons, too, both had the sign of the Abrahamic covenant in their flesh, namely, circumcision. But after looking back over 1,400 years of their respective histories, God says, "I have loved Jacob, but Esau I have hated" (Mal. 1:2-3; cf. Rom. 9:13). "See to it that . . . no one is sexually immoral or unholy like Esau, who sold his birthright for a single meal. For you know that afterward, when he desired to inherit the blessing, he was rejected, for he found no chance to repent, though he sought it with tears" (Heb. 12:15-17). Under the Abrahamic covenant, again, there are the righteous and the wicked.

It was the same with later Israel under the Sinaitic covenant: God loved the nation as a whole, but he loathed the wicked among them (Ps. 95:10). Compare the comment of Hebrews 3:16-19: "For who were those who heard and yet rebelled? Was it not all those who left Egypt led by Moses? And with whom was he provoked for forty years? Was it not with those who sinned, whose bodies fell in the wilderness? And to whom did he swear that they would not enter his rest, but to those who were disobedient? So we see that they were unable to enter because of unbelief." As Paul put it: "[O]ur fathers were all under the cloud, and all passed through the sea, and all were baptized into Moses in the cloud and in the sea. . . . Nevertheless, with most of them God was not pleased, for they were overthrown in the wilderness" (1 Cor. 10:1-5).

The judgment that befell the wicked was not the Torah's fault: "[W]hat great nation is there, that has statutes and rules so righteous as all this Torah that I set before you today?" (Deut. 4:8); the word of the Torah is "your very life" (Deut. 32:47; cf. Rom. 7:12, "the Torah is holy, and the commandment is holy and righteous and good"). No, it is the fault of the wicked themselves, who prefer death to life: "I call heaven and earth to witness against you today, that *I have set before you life and death*, blessing and curse. Therefore *choose life*, that you and your offspring may live, loving the LORD your God, obeying his voice and holding fast to him, for *he is your life* and length of days, that you may dwell in the land that the LORD swore to your fathers, to Abraham, to Isaac, and to Jacob, to give them" (Deut. 30:19-20).

Shortly before this passage, Moses had told the people that one day curses might come upon them, "because you did not obey the voice of the LORD your God, to keep his commandments and his statutes that he commanded you.... Because you did not serve the LORD your God with joyfulness and gladness of heart, because of the abundance of all things" (Deut. 28:45-47). This is a negative statement, but in its reversed form, it is one of the loveliest descriptions of what observing the Torah involves. It means *serving the LORD your God with joyfulness and gladness of heart*. Genuine observance of the Torah is not just obedience, even less is it blind submission — it is *serving with joy*. This is true life: loving and joyful dedication. For the true believer, the Torah is not a heavy yoke, but a light and happy burden — the "yoke of iron" is precisely what a person gets on his neck by *no longer* observing the Torah with joy (v. 48). I refer here again to Peter's reference to the "yoke" in Acts 15:10, and John's expression "not burdensome" in 1 John 5:3 (cf. Deut. 30:11; Matt. 11:30).

A wonderful New Testament example of those who loved the Lord, and therefore loved the Torah, was the pious Jewish couple Zechariah and Elizabeth (the future parents of John the Baptist): "[T]hey were both righteous before God, walking blamelessly in all the commandments and statutes of the LORD" (Luke 1:6). In Hebrew, they might be called true *hasidim* ("holy/pious/faithful ones") or *tsaddiqim* ("righteous ones").

### 3.4.2 Three Groups

To put it a little more precisely, with respect to the Torah we distinguish three groups within Israel.[20]

(a) The *lovers* of the LORD, who are also lovers of the Torah; these are the true Israel (cf. "the Israel of God," Gal. 6:16). Israel is God's chosen people, but the true Israel are the elect among these chosen people (Rom. 11:7). To them he says: I am the LORD "showing steadfast love [Heb. *hesed*] to thousands of

---

20. Cf. here what I have said elsewhere about the double function of the Torah: Ouweneel (2015a, §§1.3, 3.2.2, and 3.3).

those who love me and keep my commandments" (Exod. 20:6; Deut. 5:10). "Know therefore that the LORD your God is God, the faithful God who keeps covenant and steadfast love [*hesed*] with those who love him and keep his commandments, to a thousand generations" (Deut. 7:9). "And now, Israel, what does the LORD your God require of you, but to fear the LORD your God, to walk in all his ways, to love him, to serve the LORD your God with all your heart and with all your soul, and to keep the commandments and statutes of the LORD, which I am commanding you today for your good?" (10:12-13; cf. 11:1, 13, 22; 13:3; 19:9; 30:6, 16, 20). Already in the Sinai wilderness, then, many followed the LORD with a loving heart: "I remember the devotion [*hesed*] of your youth, your love [*ahabah*] as a bride, how you followed me in the wilderness, in a land not sown" (Jer. 2:2).

(b) The *haters* of the LORD, who are also haters of the Torah (cf. Exod. 20:5; Deut. 5:9): the LORD "repays to their face those who hate him, by destroying them. He will not be slack with one who hates him. He will repay him to his face. You shall therefore be careful to do the commandment and the statutes and the rules that I command you today" (Deut. 7:10-11; cf. 32:40-43). These are those who openly break the LORD's Torah in a spirit of rebellion: "with a high hand" (Num. 15:30), that is, "defiantly" (NIV). Please note, these are not the "haters of God" who are found among the Gentiles (Rom. 1:30; cf. Num. 10:35; Deut. 33:11). On the contrary, these are God's haters *in Israel*, belonging to the chosen people but having no personal relationship with him.

(c) The third group has not been mentioned so far. These are the *hypocrites*, who pretend to keep the Torah but are not really sincere in doing so, those who observe the Torah only outwardly, who deny the spirit of the Torah in an attitude of legalism, ritualism, and ethnocentric arrogance. We do not yet clearly find them in the Pentateuch, but in the prophetic books and in the Gospels they can be easily discerned (see, e.g., Matt. 6:2, 5, 16; 7:5; 15:7; 22:18; 23:13-29; 24:51). The original meaning of the Greek word *hypocritēs* is "actor"; especially in Matthew 6:2, 5, and 16 this meaning is still clearly visible. They are those in Israel who *play* at being the godly and righteous ones, but their hearts are far away from God ("Woe to you, scribes and Pharisees, hypocrites! For you are like whitewashed tombs, which outwardly appear beautiful, but within are full of dead people's bones and all uncleanness," Matt. 23:27).

Sometimes the Old Testament prophets speak of the hypocrites in a way that suggests that they (the prophets) have no high regard for the Temple's sacrificial ministry (e.g., Isa. 1:11, 13; 66:3; Jer. 6:20; Hos. 9:4; Micah 6:6–8; Mal. 1:10, 13; 2:13; cf. Matt. 9:13; 12:7). But what they are really fighting against is the spirit of hypocrisy. What the prophets emphasize is that the LORD seeks the true love of people's hearts. They never speak derogatorily of Torah observance as such: "For I desire steadfast love [covenant loyalty!] and not sacrifice, the knowledge of God rather than burnt offerings" (Hos. 6:6–7). "Were I to write for him my laws by the ten thousands, they would be regarded as a strange thing. As for my sacrificial offerings, they sacrifice meat and eat it, but the LORD does not accept them" (8:12–13). "I hate, I despise your feasts, and I take no delight in your solemn assemblies. Even though you offer me your burnt offerings and grain offerings, I will not accept them; and the peace offerings of your fattened animals, I will not look upon them. Take away from me the noise of your songs; to the melody of your harps I will not listen. But let justice roll down like waters, and righteousness like an ever-flowing stream" (Amos 5:21–24).[21]

In Psalm 40:6–8 — aside from its prophetic application to Christ (Heb. 10:5-10) — the loving self-surrender of the protagonist stands in contrast to the many Sinaitic animal sacrific-

---

21. Also cf. Bab. Talmud: Shabbath 30a, where God says to David, "better is to Me the one day that thou sittest and engagest in learning than the thousand burnt-offerings which thy son Solomon is destined to sacrifice before Me on the altar."

es: "In sacrifice and offering you have not delighted, but you have given me an open ear. Burnt offering and sin offering you have not required. Then I said, 'Behold, I have come; in the scroll of the book it is written of me: I delight to do your will, O my God; your Torah is within my heart [lit., my bowels, as the seat of deepest feelings; cf. Jer. 4:19 KJV]'."

We might refine our grouping even further by dividing this third group into those who *know* they are hypocrites (group 3a), and those who in good faith deceive themselves by believing that they faithfully observe the Torah (group 3b). The apostle Paul seems to have belonged to the latter group; he could say of his former life: "[A]s to righteousness under the law, [I was] blameless" (Phil. 3:6) — until he met Jesus. It is difficult to say whether the Pharisee in Luke 18:11-12 deceived others, or in the first place deceived himself in boasting: "God, I thank you that I am not like other men, extortioners, unjust, adulterers, or even like this tax collector. I fast twice a week; I give tithes of all that I get." Presumably he belonged to the second group because he even involved God in his naïve bombast. When a person is alone with God, he can hardly be imagined as acting. However, when Jesus referred many times to the "hypocrites," he was apparently thinking especially of group 3a.

## 3.5 Conditional Versus Unconditional
### 3.5.1 An Alleged Covenant of Works

Basically there are only *two* covenants that have been made specifically with Israel, though with a view to all humanity. These are the "Old (Sinaitic) Covenant" and the "New Covenant" of Jeremiah 31:31-34, which is nothing but a renewal of the Old Covenant. The New Testament speaks implicitly or explicitly of a "first" and a "second covenant," the good and the "better covenant," the "Old" and "New Covenant," that is, the Sinaitic covenant and the eschatological New Covenant (Heb. 8:7, 13; 9:1, 15, 18; 7:22; 8:6; 13:20; 8:8, 13; 9:15; 12:24; cf. Luke 22:20; 2 Cor. 3:14). *Both* are called an "everlasting" covenant because the Old Covenant was never annulled (cf. Matt. 5:17) but merges into the New Covenant.[22]

This corresponds generally to the federalist terminological inventions of the "covenant of works" (allegedly first made with prelapsarian Adam, but "republished" — as the expression goes[23] — at Mount Sinai) and the "covenant of grace," both of them appearing in all kinds of variations (see more extensively chapters 4 and 5). I apologize for the word "inventions"; I am merely following the anonymous opponent of Reformed theologian Alexander Comrie (seventeenth century), who claimed that the covenant of works was "newly invented" and in that time was "held to be the Shibboleth and slogan of Orthodoxy" (see §5.3.3). Comrie defended himself against these accusations, not so much with biblical arguments — that would have been difficult, because Scripture does not know the term "covenant of works" — but by appealing to former theologians: Johannes Cocceius, Johannes Cloppenburg, and Johannes Piscator.[24]

In the broadest sense, the covenant of works is the name for any divine covenant in which God's demands of obedience are the alleged condition for receiving true life. As evidence for such a covenant, advocates point to Leviticus 18:5; Deuteronomy 6:24–25; Nehemiah 9:29; Ezekiel 18:9; 20:11–13; Amos 5:4, 6, 14 (cf. Luke 10:28; Rom. 10:5; Gal. 3:12).[25] The proponents of this idea believe that this covenant existed already before the fall, but some Reformed theologians believe that it received its form particularly in the Sinaitic covenant. They speak, then, of the "republication" of the covenant of works at Mount Sinai. In the covenant of works, the gift of life is made to depend on human good works, whereas in the

---

22. See Ouweneel (2015a, chapter 4).
23. Or "re-enacted"; cf. Hodge (1998, 433): "[T]he law of Moses was a re-enactment of the covenant of works." Cf. Owen (1991, 70–78): the Mosaic covenant "is no other but the covenant of works revived. . . . Yea, in sundry things it re-enforced, established, and confirmed that covenant."
24. Graafland (1996, 363–64).
25. See Van der Zwaag (2003, 107–111).

covenant of grace it is thought to depend purely on God's grace. Thus, the Old and the New Covenants are contrasted as the covenants in which everything depended on human beings, or everything depended on God, respectively.

According to more recent investigations, in which especially the Jewish explanation of the Sinaitic covenant has been investigated and better understood, such a view of the Sinaitic covenant as a covenant of works can now be considered to be largely mistaken. However, I must say that only very few Reformed theologians seem to be prepared to accept this. Apparently, the terms "covenant of works" and "covenant of grace" are too deeply embedded in the Reformed mindset; moreover, they have been forever solidified in the Westminster Standards.

To begin with an obvious but vital consideration: the twofold character described before—promises on God's side, duties on the human side—holds for *all* divine covenants, including both the Old and the New Covenants. The (seeming) difference between the two covenants lies especially in this question: what is first, the divine promises or the human duties? Where is the emphasis? That is, must people first fulfill certain duties before God fulfills his promises? Under the Old Covenant, God's blessing did indeed *formally* depend on the observance of the Torah. See (in addition to the passages mentioned above) this example: "And because [or, if; Heb. ᶜéqeb] you listen to these rules and keep and do them, the LORD your God will keep with you the covenant and the steadfast love that he swore to your fathers" (Deut. 7:12). If Israel would keep the Torah, God would bless the people (Exod. 23:25; Deut. 29:2, 8, 12). Under the New Covenant, the situation seems to be essentially different. Here, all God's holy demands have been fulfilled *a priori* in and through Jesus and his work. No wonder that the Old Covenant has often been called a "law covenant" (or "conditional covenant"), and the New Covenant a "grace covenant" (or "unconditional covenant").[26] The question that naturally arises here is whether such a construal is corroborated in Scripture. For our further considerations, this question is of essential importance.

### 3.5.2 A Covenant of Works at Sinai?

The presentation just given must be viewed as one-sided, if not simply wrong. In a certain sense, the Old Covenant is both a conditional and an unconditional covenant, and precisely the same holds for the New Covenant.[27] On the one hand, the Old Covenant, too, was rooted in God's redeeming grace. This becomes visible already in the prologue (Jewish counting: First Word) of the Ten Words: "I am the LORD your God, who brought you out of the land of Egypt, out of the house of slavery" (Exod. 20:2; Deut. 5:6). All of the subsequent nine Words must be seen in this light: they belong to a nation already delivered. The grace character also becomes visible in the mercy that God bestowed upon his people after they had broken the covenant, immediately after its establishment (Exod. 32-34). The Old Covenant was primarily a covenant of grace, with love that basically came from one side only.[28]

This grace manifested itself most clearly in the sacrificial ministry: Israel stood before God on the basis not of its good works, but of the pleasing aroma of the daily burnt offerings: "Now this is what you shall offer on the altar: two lambs a year old day by day regularly. One lamb you shall offer in the morning, and the other lamb you shall offer at twilight. . . . for a pleasing aroma, a food offering to the LORD. . . . at the entrance of the tent of meeting before the LORD, where I will meet with you, to speak to you there. There I will meet

---

26. See, e.g., Chafer (1983, IV, 313–28); Pentecost (1964, 65–128); Walvoord (1999, chapters 4, 5, 9, 21); Fruchtenbaum (1992, 334–73, 570–87); Hays et al. (2007, 11). Cf. Hughes (1977, 300): the Old Covenant is one of works, the New Covenant is one of grace.
27. Cf. Wellum (2012, 608): "Viewing the biblical covenants as either unconditional or conditional is not quite right."
28. H. D. Leuner in Kac (1986, 177); cf. Niell (2003, 133–36).

with the people of Israel, and it shall be sanctified by my glory. . . . I will dwell among the people of Israel and will be their God. And they shall know that I am the LORD their God, who brought them out of the land of Egypt that I might dwell among them. I am the LORD their God" (Exod. 29:38-46).

If the Ten Words had been trespassed, the people could be restored to communion with God through the sin offerings, which God himself had instituted as the way of restoration (Lev. 4-5). See especially Leviticus 16 (*Yom Kippur*, the "Day of Atonement"): "Then he [i.e., Aaron] shall kill the goat of the sin offering that is for the people and bring its blood inside the veil . . . sprinkling it over the mercy seat and in front of the mercy seat. Thus he shall make atonement for the Holy Place, because of the uncleannesses of the people of Israel and because of their transgressions, all their sins" (vv. 15-16). This was the essence of the tabernacle (Exod. 25-27): it was God's dwelling place in the midst of Israel, as well as the place where the people could come near to him on the basis of the sacrifices, *not* on the basis of their good works. It was a "tent of *meeting*" between God and his people, which functioned on the only possible basis for people standing before him: the sacrifice. Under the Old Covenant, Israel *never* stood before God on the basis of their own good works, but only on the basis of God's grace. In other words, the *allegedly conditional* (Sinaitic) "covenant of works" is based on God's *unconditional* grace.

Conversely, the *New* Covenant is not *just* a covenant of grace; that is, it is *not* without responsible obedience. At a minimum, entering the New Covenant demands obedience to God's call for repentance: "[W]hen all these things come upon you, the blessing and the curse, which I have set before you, and you call them to mind among all the nations where the LORD your God has driven you, and *return to the* LORD *your God*, you and your children, and *obey* his voice in all that I command you today, *with all your heart and with all your soul*, then the LORD your God will restore your fortunes and have mercy on you. . . . And the LORD your God will circumcise your heart and the heart of your offspring, so that you will love the LORD your God with all your heart and with all your soul, that you may live. . . . And you shall again obey the voice of the LORD and keep all his commandments that I command you today. The LORD . . . will again take delight in prospering you, as he took delight in your fathers, when you obey the voice of the LORD your God, to keep his commandments and his statutes that are written in this Book of the Law, *when you turn to the LORD your God with all your heart and with all your soul*" (Deut. 30:1–10).

"I will take you from the nations and gather you from all the countries and bring you into your own land. I will sprinkle clean water on you, and you shall be clean from all your uncleannesses. . . . And I will give you a new heart, and a new spirit I will put within you. . . . And I will put my Spirit within you, and cause you to walk in my statutes and be careful to obey my rules. You shall dwell in the land that I gave to your fathers, and you shall be my people, and I will be your God. . . . Then you will remember your evil ways, and your deeds that were not good, and you will loathe yourselves for your iniquities and your abominations" (Ezek. 36:24–31). In other words, the *allegedly unconditional* New Covenant involves the *conditions* of repentance and true faith, as well as the fruits of this faith. Even if we readily admit that these conditions can be fulfilled only by the power of the Holy Spirit, this does not change their character as conditions.

### 3.5.3 No Works Without Redemption and Faith

Without repentance and conversion, there is no possibility whatsoever of entering the New Covenant. There is no room for universalism here: although in Abraham, in principle all nations are blessed, in effect this becomes true only for those from the Gentiles who come with confession of sins, and with faith in Christ's finished work of atonement. The kingdom of God is for the *righteous* only, those who in faith entrust themselves to God on the basis of the true sacrifice, and are thus *declared* righteous (i.e., are justified), and *whose faith bears the fruit of righteousness* (Phil. 1:11; Heb. 12:11; James 3:17–18; cf. Isa. 45:8; Amos 6:12).

However, this differs in no way from the situation under the Old Covenant. The following principle *always* remains true, under both the Old and the New Covenants: "O Lord, who shall sojourn in your tent? Who shall dwell on your holy hill? He who walks blamelessly and does what is right and speaks truth in his heart; who does not slander with his tongue and does no evil to his neighbor, nor takes up a reproach against his friend; in whose eyes a vile person is despised, but who honors those who fear the Lord; who swears to his own hurt and does not change; who does not put out his money at interest and does not take a bribe against the innocent. He who does these things shall never be moved" (Ps. 15).

"Who among us can dwell with the consuming fire? Who among us can dwell with everlasting burnings? He who walks righteously and speaks uprightly, who despises the gain of oppressions, who shakes his hands, lest they hold a bribe, who stops his ears from hearing of bloodshed and shuts his eyes from looking on evil, he will dwell on the heights; his place of defense will be the fortresses of rocks; his bread will be given him; his water will be sure" (Isa. 33:14–16).

Under both the Old and the New Covenants, the true *tsaddiqim* have always understood that such practical righteousness before God is possible only through faith, through the grace of God, in the power of the Holy Spirit (see extensively the third volume of the present series, dealing with justification). In this sense, there never was a "covenant of works" in which God's blessings were made dependent on human works, *apart from faith, grace, and redemption*. Under the New Covenant, God puts his Torah in the *hearts* of his people (Jer. 31:33), but it was no different under the Old Covenant: "You shall love the LORD your God with all your *heart* and with all your soul and with all your might. And these words that I command you today shall be on your *heart*" (Deut. 6:5–6). "[T]he word is very near you. It is in your mouth and in your *heart, so that you can do it*" (30:14). Who placed it there? God himself. It is God who "circumcises" hearts and turns them to himself (Deut. 30:6; cf. Ezek. 36:25–27), but that does not exclude human responsibility: "Circumcise . . . the foreskin of your heart, and be no longer stubborn" (Deut. 10:16). This is a true act of *faith*, in pure dependence on God, who alone can perform the actual "circumcision" of the heart.

## 3.6 Was There a Covenant of Works in Eden?
### 3.6.1 Misunderstanding Grace

I repeat: I fundamentally reject the scheme of a "covenant of works" and a "covenant of grace" because there are no divine conditions—demanding works—without God's grace accompanying that demand. And there is no divine grace without God simultaneously appealing to human responsibility. There *is* no specific "covenant of works" because never in history did God demand works apart from a framework of grace, and there *is* no specific "covenant of grace" because there is no bestowal of divine grace without God demanding obedience to some manifestation of the Torah. I will come back extensively to this important subject; I limit myself right now to some introductory remarks.

In the Garden of Eden, the first humans lived by pure grace. It is a typically Reformed mistake to link divine grace specifically and exclusively with the problem of sin, whereas in the Bible, grace is a much wider notion. *Every gift of God is always a gift of pure grace*, including everything that God gave to the first humans in Paradise.[29] Paul spoke of God's "grace, which he gave us in Christ Jesus before the ages began" (2 Tim. 1:9). Here, all God's blessings that he prepared for be-

---

29. *Contra* Brown and Keele (2012, 18): "*[A]ll* divine covenants are legal, though not all are gracious."

lievers before the foundation of the world are summarized as "grace," without any reference to the problem of sin.

Fortunately, this element of grace in Eden has been clearly discerned by several Reformed theologians. They preferred the term "covenant of nature" or "covenant of creation" to bring out that this covenant was not just about works but also about grace; there is no relationship between God and humanity without grace, even before the fall. Reformed theologian O. Palmer Robertson is one of several such theologians.[30]

Cornelis van der Waal, though thoroughly Reformed, was another of the happy exceptions who discerned the gracious character of God's relationship with prelapsarian Adam: "True, we cannot yet speak about [prelapsarian] Adam as living in grace by which his trespasses were forgiven. But he was called to acknowledge God in everything, and to be totally dependent on Him. Today we call this: living by grace."[31] He goes on to mention all kinds of examples from the Old Testament in which God's grace or favor was *not* linked to forgiveness and redemption, such as Laban asking favor from Jacob (Gen. 30:27), Jacob asking favor from Esau (32:5), or from Joseph (47:29), Joseph asking favor from Pharaoh (50:4). In Paradise Adam lived by the favor of God, totally apart from the problem of sin (which had not yet arisen).

Grace is simply the opposite of merit, and neither concept is necessarily linked with sin. People receive grace from earthly kings, apart from sin (Esther 2:17; 5:8). Paul called his apostleship a gift of grace, which had nothing to do with the problem of sin (Rom. 1:5). It is the "merciful" who receive "mercy," again apart from sin, because the reference is to the righteous (Matt. 5:7). The two blind men and the father of the epileptic asked for the "mercy" of healing, and the Canaanite woman for the "mercy" of deliverance of demons, apart from any sins (9:27; 15:22; 17:15; 20:30). Perhaps the clearest example of grace that has no reference whatsoever to sin is

---

30. Robertson (1980, 56); cf. Murray (1977, 47–59); Wellum (2012, 61).
31. Van der Waal (1990, 55).

Luke 2:40, where it is said of the young Jesus that "the grace of God" was upon him (NKJV).

Mercy (Latin *misericordia*) is God's benevolence toward those in misery (*miseria*), apart from sin. Of course, in a general sense all misery is a consequence of the fall, but that is not the point here. The point is that in his grace and mercy, God bestows blessings upon humanity that humanity has not deserved. To put it more strongly: People, fallen or not, do not deserve anything anyway. Both before and after the fall, people lived and live by grace. The only difference is that, after the fall, God's grace also included forgiveness and redemption. But that does not change the general rule: Human beings cannot live before God in any other way than by grace.

### 3.6.2 A Supra-Logical State of Affairs

This is why I have said that there are no demands of God apart from his grace. Adam and Eve lived out of pure grace, and all God's demands must be viewed within this framework. At the same time, there is no grace of God apart from certain demands. That is, there is no covenant of grace without divine conditions accompanying such grace, conditions that people have to fulfill in order to remain within the blessings of the covenant (see §3.5). Therefore, already before the fall, Adam lived under what I have called the "Adamic Torah."[32] There is no alleged covenant of works without grace, and there is no alleged covenant of grace without works. Prelapsarian Adam lived by grace without needing any forgiveness of sins; postlapsarian saved humankind lives by grace, including the forgiveness of sins. *Every covenant is a covenant of both grace* (divine favor, divine blessings, divine promises) *and works* (people's response of keeping the Torah characteristic of the covenant concerned).

Certainly, true works—works that are pleasing to God— are always brought about by God's grace and by the power of the Holy Spirit; but that does not detract in any way from hu-

---
32. See Ouweneel (2015a, §2.3.1).

man responsibility. There is no sovereign divine grace without human responsibility, and no human responsibility without sovereign divine grace, as Paul brings out so beautifully in Philippians 2:12-13: "Therefore, my beloved, as you have always obeyed, so now, not only as in my presence but much more in my absence, work out your own salvation with fear and trembling [*human responsibility*], for it is God who works in you, both to will and to work for his good pleasure [*divine sovereign grace*]."

If the covenant of works is rooted in a mistaken view of the relationship between works and grace, it concomitantly also misunderstands the meaning of merit or earning. For instance, Brown and Keele mentioned the following aspect of the covenant of works: "[T]he promise of life everlasting is based on Adam's obedience. His works were the means of obtaining the promise. Adam's righteous deeds would have earned him the reward."[33] And a bit later: "Eternal life was merited by Adam's obedience." And: "Had Adam obeyed, he would have earned eternal life. . . . Adam would merit life by his obedience to the terms of the covenant."[34] This is all utterly unbiblical. Scripture does not breathe a word suggesting that Adam could *earn* everlasting life through his righteous deeds. Eternal life, as well as all other blessings from God, is a gift of God's pure *grace*. There was no earning involved at all.

The alleged Adamic covenant was not about the way Adam and Eve could *earn* eternal life, but about the way they could *lose* it. If they would receive it, this would be on the basis not of merit but of God's grace. If they would lose it, this would be entirely due to their own failure. Of course, there is a tension here, which is always encountered where we consider the relationship between God's sovereign grace and human responsibility. It is the tension that we also encounter in the Canons of Dort (chapter III/IV), a tension of which the Dort divines were certainly aware, but with which they right-

---

33. Brown and Keele (2012, 43).
34. Ibid., 44-46.

ly chose to live: the fact that some sinners accept the gospel is *entirely* due to the grace of God; the fact that some sinners reject the gospel is *entirely* their own fault. This surpasses our human logic and must nevertheless be believed.

### 3.6.3 Reformed Corrections

Reformed writer Clarence Stam rightly described the prelapsarian situation as follows: "The suggestion that man in paradise by perfect, personal obedience would *merit* eternal life is unsubstantiated and quite problematic. There is no biblical proof for the idea that Adam would have earned eternal life if only he had shown himself to be faithful and obedient. Adam and Eve . . . were *given* life and abundance by the gracious and kind provisions of God in the covenant that he made with them. They did not have to earn these gifts or attain some higher degree of perfection. . . . Man's fall into sin is not a matter of his failing to do the required works; it is, rather, a matter of rebellion and unfaithfulness, a *breaking of the covenant* which God in his goodness had made with man."[35]

Indeed, Adam could *lose* the blessings through disobedience, but in no way can it be concluded from this that, were he to have remained faithful, he would have *earned* the blessings. We are dealing here with purely human reasoning — logically flawed at that — without any biblical basis. As Stam continues: "If one wishes to maintain the idea of a covenant of works, one needs to hold to the position that man at creation was imperfect, and had still to earn, attain and achieve perfection and eternal life. Then Adam at this time was on his own quest for glory, in which he needed to demonstrate his worthiness. But where does the Word if God state such things?"[36]

Interestingly, Reformed theologian Herman Bavinck wrote: "[Religion] is not work by which we bring advantage to God, make a contribution to him, and have a right to re-

---

35. Stam (1999, 48–49).
36. Ibid., 49.

ward. It is grace for us to be allowed to serve him."[37] Yet he wrote a few pages earlier: "The doctrine of the covenant of works rests on a scriptural foundation and is of excellent value."[38] So, on the basis of his own reasoning, the very first form of religion that God would have given to humanity was one of "work by which we bring advantage or profit to God and have a right to a reward"!?[39] Apparently, he was not aware of this contradiction in his own considerations.

I think Reformed theologian Klaas Schilder was much closer to the truth on this point: "Many think that in the covenant of works people earned their own salvation, and that now [i.e., in the new dispensation] Christ does this for us. But the contrasting of work and grace has caused much confusion. Ursinus saw it correctly. No human being can ever earn anything with God," not even before the fall, that is.[40] Stam comments: "What Schilder is saying is that everything depends—before and after the fall—upon God's (sovereign) grace. He uses two terms, however: *grace and favour*. 'There was favour in Paradise; grace in a strict sense after the fall.'"[41] Stam rightly thinks that grace and favor must not be distinguished: God's favor before the fall was his grace: "The point is that we can never earn anything with God but are always dependent on his grace or favour," that is, even before the fall.

Stam also refers to Reformed theologian Simon G. de Graaf, who was of the same opinion: "[I]n Adam's case we cannot speak of earning: God granted him his full favor, and the only thing that God asked of him was to choose that favor and to show through his obedience that he wanted to remain in that favor."[42] And elsewhere: "[W]e should not take this name [i.e., covenant of works] to mean that man was expect-

---

37. Bavinck (2004, 2.571).
38. Ibid., 529–30.
39. Cf. Stam (1999, 49).
40. Schilder (n.d., 13).
41. Stam (1999, 51).
42. De Graaf (1940, 61).

ed to earn eternal life as a reward for doing good works, as though eternal life was man's payment for services rendered . . . it might be wiser to speak of the covenant of God's favour."[43] Stam observes: "Man deserved or merited nothing [in Eden], but was given everything, even a position of honour and glory in creation."[44] One can only be very happy with such (Reformed) considerations.

In passing I mention here another well-known mistake. Brown and Keele assert, "The Lord made Adam righteous, so that he was naturally inclined to obedience," and, "Being in the image of God, Adam had a righteous and holy nature, wherein he was able to earn the reward by works."[45] Unfortunately, this idea of prelapsarian Adam being "righteous and holy" is also found in the Heidelberg Catechism (Q&A 6): "God created them good and in his own image, that is, in true righteousness and holiness." For the latter phrase, the Catechism points to Ephesians 4:24, but Paul is evidently speaking here not of the prelapsarian Adam but of the "new man"![46] The difference is enormous: Adam was innocent; he did not yet "know good and evil," because it was precisely this that he would obtain through eating from the forbidden tree (Gen. 2:9). Therefore, Adam could obey the LORD, but he was also capable of sinning. However, the new man *as such* "does not sin," and even "*cannot* sin" (1 John 3:6, 9; 5:18 NKJV; if the believer sins, it is the flesh in him that sins).

I will come back to the problem of the "covenant of works" several times, especially in §§4.3.3, 5.3.3, and 5.4.

## 3.7 Old and New Covenant
### 3.7.1 Pointing to Christ

Under the New Covenant, everything revolves around Jesus Christ (by the way, this is basically the case in *all* covenants).

---

43. De Graaf (1977, I, 37).
44. Stam (1999, 51).
45. Brown and Keele (2012, 44–45); cf. Stam (1999, 49).
46. *Contra* Horton (2011, 420–21): "Adam was not created merely in a state of innocence, but in a state of positive righteousness."

On the one hand, he bore the curse for the trespasses committed by his people under the Mosaic Torah; on the other hand, he laid the right foundation for the positive blessings of the covenant. God is free to grant his blessings to all those who place themselves on the foundation of Jesus' sacrifice, that is, the "blood of the covenant" (cf. Exod. 24:8; Heb. 9:20; 10:29). In his *person*, Jesus is the Guarantor and Mediator of this New Covenant (Heb. 7:22; 8:6; 12:24), that is, the Executor of this covenant (or testament, will). His *work* is that he fulfilled God's holy demands, and leads people to God (cf. 1 Tim. 2:5-6; 1 Pet. 3:18), through his blood (Matt. 26:28; Mark 14:24; Luke 22:20; 1 Cor. 11:25; Heb. 9:14-15; 10:29; 12:24; 13:20), that is, through his sacrificial death (Heb. 9:14-15, 26-28; 10:10, 14).

At the same time, we must consider that, as a matter of principle, *all* these elements were present already in the Old Covenant; otherwise, no one could have been saved under the Old Covenant. To be sure, these elements were present then in the form of foreshadowing only because Christ had not yet come. But this does not diminish the concrete value of this foreshadowing. They were not just a matter of typology. That is, sins *were* forgiven on the basis of animal sacrifices, *not* on the basis of any atoning value these sacrifices might have in themselves — which they did not — but in anticipation of the true and only sacrifice of Christ. The Torah is quite explicit in this regard: for instance, ". . . Thus shall he [i.e., the priest] do with the bull. As he did with the bull of the sin offering, so shall he do with this. And the priest shall make atonement for them [i.e., sins], and they shall be forgiven. . . . And all its fat he shall burn on the altar, like the fat of the sacrifice of peace offerings. So the priest shall make atonement for him for his sin, and he shall be forgiven" (Lev. 4:20, 26; cf. vv. 31, 35).

The same book of Hebrews that says, "[I]t is impossible for the blood of bulls and goats to take away sins" (10:4), also says, "For if the blood of goats and bulls, and the sprinkling of defiled persons with the ashes of a heifer, sanctify for the purification of the flesh, how much more will the blood of

Christ ... purify our conscience from dead works" (9:13–14), and: "Indeed, under the Torah almost everything is purified with blood, and without the shedding of blood there is no forgiveness of sins" (v. 22). So animal blood does sanctify and purify! If we take these three statements together, their meaning is clear. Animal blood *in itself* can do nothing for the sinner; animal blood *as referring to the true sacrifice of Christ* does sanctify and purify. This is more than just typology; animal blood can sanctify and purify *in anticipation*. However, this emphatically means that sanctification and purification *were enjoyed* under the Old Covenant.

Again, under the Old Covenant everything revolves around *pointing forward* to Christ. People were saved through repentance, through trusting God's grace, as well as through the vicarious sacrifices, which he had made available *a priori*. In their subjective sense, the Old Testament sacrifices were just as efficacious as the New Testament sacrifice of Jesus; in their objective sense, the former derived their significance from the latter.[47] In essence, there is no difference in the way people are saved under the Old and New Covenants because the animal sacrifices had meaning only insofar as they pointed forward to the true and only sacrifice: that of Jesus (cf. Rom. 3:25; Heb. 9:13-14, 22). In other words, under both the Old and the New Covenants, people are saved only in and through Jesus Christ, by God's grace. Therefore, there is an element of truth in what the Westminster Confession of Faith says (Art. VII.6): "There are not therefore two covenants of grace, differing in substance [viz., the Old and the New Covenants], but one and the same, under various dispensations."[48]

### 3.7.2 The Ten Words Again

The rabbinical enumeration of the Ten Words begins not with

---

47. Cf. Freeman (1962).
48. I would add only that this Confession, like federalists in general, does not distinguish that the Old and the New Covenants were/are made with *Israel*, *not* with the church—or rather, it claims that these two are the same—and ignores all typical Israelite elements in the two covenants.

an imperative but with an indicative: "I am the LORD your God, who brought you out of the land of Egypt, out of the house of slavery" (Exod. 20:2; Deut. 5:6; cf. Lev. 11:45; 22:32-33). This Word places the Decalogue in the context of the covenant by first pointing to the Redeemer-God of the covenant. Even his name illustrates this. Moses said to God, "If I come to the people of Israel and say to them, 'The God of your fathers has sent me to you,' and they ask me, 'What is his name?' what shall I say to them?" God replied to Moses, "'I am who I am' [Heb. *ehyeh asher ehyeh*, from *h-y-h*, "to be"] ... Say this to the people of Israel, '"I am" has sent me to you. ... The LORD [YHWH, probably also from *h-y-h*, "to be"], the God of your fathers, the God of Abraham, the God of Isaac, and the God of Jacob, has sent me to you.' This is my name forever, and thus I am to be remembered throughout all generations" (Exod. 3:13-15).

The expression *ehyeh asher ehyeh* has been rendered in several ways: "I will be who/what I will be," "I am the one who [always] is/will be," "I am the one who will be there [for you]," that is, as the one on whom you can always count. The name, then, is probably an expression of God's covenant love and faithfulness. Therefore, we call the name YHWH God's covenant name.

A midrash explains why the Ten Words were not placed at the start of the Torah, in Genesis 1, or possibly in Exodus 4: a nation readily accepts a man as king if he first grants them all kinds of benefits.[49] Thus, God first led the Israelites out of Egypt, divided the sea for them, caused manna and quail to rain down for them, opened a well for them, and made war for them against Amalek (Exod. 13-17). After that, he told them, "I will be your king" (cf. Exod. 15:18; Num. 23:21), and the people readily accepted him (cf. Exod. 19:8; 24:3, 7; Deut. 5:27). Another Jewish tradition compares the Ten Words one by one with the ten statements by God ("and God said ... ") that he made during the creation of the world (Gen. 1:3-29).

---

49. Mekhilta of Rabbi Ishmael, Bachodesh 5; see Ginzberg (1968, 104-106).

In this case, the Decalogue *would* indeed stand at the beginning of the Torah, although in a concealed form.

The Ten Words are addressed explicitly to a *redeemed* nation, if not in the full spiritual sense (cf. 1 Cor. 10:1-5), then at least in the typological sense (vv. 6-12). Even the famous words, "[I]f a person does them [i.e., my laws], he shall live by them" (Lev. 18:5), do not literally answer the question as to how one can *receive* eternal life—in spite of Paul's apparent application of this verse in Romans 10:5 and Galatians 3:12—but the question as to *how one, as a covenant partner, can maintain a truly blessed life*—not in eternity, that is, but in the promised land (Deut. 4:40; 5:33; 8:1; 11:9; 16:20; 25:15; 30:16; cf. v. 18). Please note that the phrase in Leviticus 18:5, just mentioned, is preceded by the declaration, "I am the LORD your God," and by the implicit reminder of the deliverance out of Egypt (vv. 1-3). Israel is being addressed as a redeemed and holy nation (Exod. 19:4-6). The phrase in Leviticus 18:15 explains not how one can *become* holy but how one can *remain* holy; that is, not how one can *obtain* a share in the covenant but how one can *retain* his share. Giving heed to the commandments is "remaining with the Redeemer."[50]

## 3.8 Responsibility and Grace
### 3.8.1 The Demanding and the Giving God

The whole problem of the conditional (works) versus the unconditional (grace) models of the covenant can be investigated meaningfully only in the light of two seemingly contradictory truths. Since the tree of life and the tree of knowledge,[51] we encounter these two truths so often in Scripture. They are God's *unconditional* electing, redeeming, atoning, and preserving grace, on the one hand (exemplified in the tree of life), and humanity's responsibility to obey as *condition* for whatever divine blessing (exemplified in the tree of

---

50. Cf. the book title by Becking (1986): *Blijf bij uw bevrijder* ("Remain With Your Redeemer").
51. See Ouweneel (2008a, 152–64).

knowledge).⁵² The tension between the two has plagued the entire history of Christian theology; we need only think of Augustine *versus* Pelagius, Luther *versus* Erasmus, Gomarus *versus* Arminius. In some of these cases, one may easily feel unhappy with *both* of the contending parties. Denominations can almost be aligned according to the two sides: more emphasis on sovereign grace (at the expense of human responsibility, as in hyper-Calvinism), or more emphasis on human responsibility (at the expense of sovereign grace, as in much of Evangelicalism).

Again, one may feel uncomfortable with *both* of the contending parties. One example: Walter C. Kaiser accuses Andrew A. Bonar (1810–1892) of a one-sided, dispensationalist interpretation ("Torah-keeping leads to eternal life"), while he himself falls into the opposite one-sidedness of federalism ("Torah-keeping always presupposes eternal life").⁵³

Do we dare to seek for a middle way here? At any rate, again, there are no unconditional promises without a specified obedience demanded from people—even if it is perfectly true that this obedience is worked by God's grace—just as there are no conditional promises without God's grace giving the strength to satisfy the conditions, and intervening whenever people break the conditions *and* truly repent of this. In this sense the entire distinction between conditional and unconditional covenants—or between a covenant of works and a covenant of grace—is mistaken in quite a fundamental way. Scripture *always* speaks with two words, that is, both conditionally (i.e., from the viewpoint of human responsibility, that is, of the *demanding* God) and unconditionally (i.e., from the viewpoint of God's sovereign grace, that is, of the *giving* God).

In conclusion, it is utterly wrong to depict the entire Sinaitic covenant, or even the relationship between God and

---

52. See extensively Ouweneel (2008b); cf. Berkhof (1966, 16): the covenant "dangles by the silk thread of obedience."
53. Kaiser (1978, 111–12).

prelapsarian Adam, as a system of works righteousness.[54] It is therefore refreshing that federalist Willem Verboom writes: "The term 'covenant of works' with which this relationship is described is in our view less appropriate. It suggests too much that there was some contract that both parties had to keep. Is the covenant at creation not far more a spontaneous, loving relationship between God and humanity? People often use the term covenant of works to distinguish this covenant from the covenant of grace, instituted after the fall. But is this distinction so sharp? Is the covenant between God and humanity not from the outset full of grace, favor and love?"[55]

The same holds, *mutatis mutandis*, for the Sinaitic covenant, as federalist Mart-Jan Paul says: "[H]e who reads the book of Exodus notices that grace and atonement belong to the covenant from the start."[56] It is a basic error to suggest that God would really submit his newly delivered people to conditions they could not possibly keep. First, this would not be in line with the character of the *redeeming* God. Second, if God indeed made life dependent on works, no single Israelite could have been saved under the Old Covenant. The New as well as the Old Covenants are each a system of human responsibility as well as of divine grace, and of the perfect divine equilibrium between the two.

Jewish New Testament scholar Pinchas Lapide emphasizes that "law and grace, Gospel and Torah, are merely two aspects of one and the same love of God, aspects that Torah-keeping Jews never have viewed other than as an unbreakable unity."[57] To which he adds: "[N]o rabbi has ever asserted that the Torah is a redemptive path leading to heaven. On the contrary! No world record in the domain of

---

54. See the quoted allegations by Christian theologians in Lapide (1984, 41–42).
55. W. Verboom in Hoek and Verboom (2010, 124–25); cf. H. J. de Bie in Hagoort (1999, 10): the term "covenant of works" "has been sharply criticized as if the stay in paradise had been an achievement of Man, and not a favor of God." Also see De Vries (2001, 26).
56. M. J. Paul in Hagoort (1999, 28).
57. Lapide (1984, 53).

Torah-keeping can take away the least from God's sovereign, loving grace.... The Torah is not about self-justification but about the connection between freedom and voluntary obedience, between independence and duty; a free decision of faith leads to believing responsibility."[58] I wish many Reformed theologians would listen more to such Jewish voices. The Rabbis have thought about the Old Covenant for many centuries longer than have the Reformed theologians!

### 3.8.2 Two Viewpoints

One could put it this way: seen from the conditional viewpoint, Israel would be God's "treasured possession," "a kingdom of priests and a holy nation," "*if* you will indeed obey my voice and keep my covenant" (Exod. 19:5-6). Seen from the unconditional viewpoint, Israel was encouraged to keep God's Torah *because* it was God's redeemed and holy nation (Deut. 7:6-11; 14:1-2, 21).

Seen from the conditional viewpoint, Israel would lose every blessing if it would disobey God's Torah and thus break the covenant. Seen from the unconditional viewpoint, God would always keep for himself a "remnant, chosen by grace" (cf. Rom. 11:5), even after the gravest failures. Under *all* the covenants, on the basis of human responsibility *all* is lost, but on the basis of God's sovereign grace, rooted in the vicarious sacrifice prescribed by him, in the end *all* will be restored.

Seen from the conditional viewpoint, Torah-keeping is a means to *obtain* God's favor, if this is done with a humble heart, not trusting oneself but God's goodness. Seen from the unconditional viewpoint, Torah-keeping is a means to *praise* God's favor through a dedicated life as an answer to the fact that one *has* obtained God's favor. In the latter meaning, redemption is presupposed. In other words, redemption is not the issue; the central question is how the redeemed may live blissfully. The answer is: through walking according to God's Torah (cf. Lev. 26:3-13; Deut. 10:12-22; 28:1-14). In the words

---

58. Ibid., 54.

of Walter Gutbrod: "Observing the Law does not *create* the relation to God; it *keeps* the people in this continuing relation" (italics added), with a reference to 2 Chronicles 33:8, "I will no more remove the foot of Israel from the land that I appointed for your fathers, if only they will be careful to do all that I have commanded them, all the law, the statutes, and the rules given through Moses."[59] (Interestingly, Gutbrod is also of the opinion that, after the Babylonian exile, "the emphasis and concern rest increasingly on the second aspect [i.e., Israel had to obey God's Law to live], so that everything depends on observance of the Law."[60])

All this is not just about earthly blessing; the question of eternal life is certainly not left out. One who lives with the LORD on earth will live with him in eternity. Where his people live together in peace and harmony, there the LORD commands "life forevermore" (Ps. 133:3). Those whose names are written in the "book of life" (cf. Exod. 33:32-33; Ps. 69:29; Phil. 4:3; Rev. 3:5; 13:8; 17:8; 20:15; 21:27; 22:19), shall one day "awake to everlasting life" (cf. Dan. 12:2). A Jewish man who was about to be executed could say, "You may kill us, but the king of the universe will raise us from the dead and give us eternal life, because we have obeyed his laws" (2 Macc. 7:9; cf. v. 36). The New Testament underscores this eternal aspect as well; Jesus said, "If you would enter life, keep the commandments" (Matt. 19:17), and "[I]f anyone keeps my word, he will never see death" (John 8:51).

Seen from the conditional viewpoint, no one will ever enter eternal divine bliss who has not done good works, that is, acts of obedience to the (Mosaic or Messianic) Torah. This principle remains valid, even though we know that such good works can be done only by a regenerate and humble heart, as a fruit of new life, in the power of the Holy Spirit (cf. Eph. 2:8-10; Titus 3:4-8; Rom. 8:4; James 2:14-26). In other words, a person is not justified by faith *per se* but by *true* faith, that is,

---

59. In Kittel and Friedrich (1964, 4.1043).
60. Ibid.; cf. Ouweneel (2015a, Appendix II).

"faith working through love" (Gal. 5:6).[61] "What good is it, my brothers, if someone says he has faith but does not have works? Can that faith save him? ... So also faith by itself, if it does not have works, is dead" (James 2:14, 17).[62]

Seen from the unconditional viewpoint, no one will ever enter into eternal divine bliss other than through God's sovereign, electing grace, which leads to regeneration and good works — even though this never excludes the human responsibility to come to repentance, to believe in Christ, and to develop the Spirit-worked desire to do good works (John 6:44; Rom. 2:4; Titus 2:14; cf. Matt. 24:22; Phil. 2:12-13; 1 Pet. 4:18). As the tension contained in Philippians 2:12-13 indicates, if you love God, you must "work out your own salvation with fear and trembling," because your faithfulness is a *condition* for your salvation; and at the same time you have to know that your salvation totally depends on God's *unconditional* faithfulness: "... for it is God who works in you, both to will and to work for his good pleasure."[63]

We should take heed not to play off these two sides of the coin against each other, as has been done so many times in the history of theology. Nor must we downplay one of them in order to save our own logically consistent paradigm, in which there allegedly can be no place for any (seeming) contradictions. Arminianism tended to downplay God's sovereign electing grace, (hyper-)Calvinism tended to downplay human responsibility. It is time we begin to recognize that both "-isms" fell victim to precisely the same rationalistic temptation, namely, to construct a paradigm that would not contain any logical inconsistencies.

---

61. Cf. Stam (1999, 8): "We are saved by faith, through grace, and this faith must be evident in works."
62. See extensively Ouweneel (2010a, chapters 8–10); also see the third volume in this series.
63. Ouweneel (2008b, 225, 250, 282, 292, 294).

## 3.9 Once Again: the Old and the New Covenants
### 3.9.1 The Two Are One

Perhaps there is nothing that illustrates more clearly that the Old and the New Covenants are essentially one than the fact that the Old Covenant is also called an everlasting covenant (Heb. *b'rît ʿôlâm*; Exod. 31:16; Lev. 24:8). In Judges 2:1, the LORD says, "'I will never break my covenant with you"; literally, "not break in eternity" (*l'ʿôlâm*). If the Old Covenant is not abolished in eternity, this can only mean that the New Covenant is nothing but a renewal and extension of the Old Covenant. "New" does not imply a fundamentally *different* covenant, which would definitely be the case if the Old Covenant had only been strictly conditional (a covenant of works) and the New Covenant were strictly unconditional (a covenant of grace). No, here "new" must mean "renewed." A covenant of grace and works is renewed, but still remains what it always was: a covenant of grace and works. Later, we will see what then is really *new* in the New Covenant (chapter 6).

Isaiah 24:5 says, "The earth lies defiled under its inhabitants; for they have transgressed the laws, violated the statutes, broken the everlasting covenant," which Rashi applies to the Sinaitic covenant; others think of the Noahic covenant (cf. §2.2.3). At any rate, the latter is also called an "everlasting covenant" (Gen. 9:16).

The Abrahamic covenant, too, was an eternal covenant: "I will establish my covenant between me and you and your offspring after you throughout their generations for an everlasting covenant, to be God to you and to your offspring after you . . . both he who is born in your house and he who is bought with your money, shall surely be circumcised. So shall my covenant be in your flesh an everlasting covenant. . . . Sarah your wife shall bear you a son, and you shall call his name Isaac. I will establish my covenant with him as an everlasting covenant for his offspring after him" (Gen. 17:7, 13, 19). Also see 1 Chronicles 16:14–18 (more or less identical with

Ps. 105:7–11): "He is the LORD our God; his judgments are in all the earth. Remember his covenant forever, the word that he commanded, for a thousand generations, the covenant that he made with Abraham, his sworn promise to Isaac, which he confirmed to Jacob as a statute, to Israel as an everlasting covenant, saying, 'To you I will give the land of Canaan, as your portion for an inheritance [Gen. 28:13].'"

The fact that the Noahic, the Abrahamic, the Old, and the New Covenants are all called "everlasting," does not mean that in Scripture there is essentially only one covenant, which then in federalism is called the "covenant of grace." The covenants form a unity, but it would go too far to say they are basically identical. Even less should we speak one-sidedly of a covenant of grace; it is *always* a covenant of grace *as well as works*. Only a theology that drives a wedge between divine grace and human responsibility can arrive at the misleading idea of assuming a distinct covenant of works and a distinct covenant of grace. Again, all covenants are covenants of works as well as of grace, are conditional as well as unconditional, form a fine balance of divine grace and human responsibility. There can be no grace apart from human responsibility, but also: there can be no works apart from the divine grace through which alone they can be realized.

It is a relief to see how, for example, Stephen Wellum recently broke through the false conditional-unconditional dilemma: "[D]ividing up the biblical covenants in terms of unconditional versus conditional is not correct. Instead, the Old Testament covenants blend both aspects."[64] Exactly! *All* the covenants have an unconditional aspect, coming to light in God's unbreakable promises, which he will fulfill at all costs, though perhaps only to a penitent remnant of his people. And *all* the covenants have a conditional aspect, coming to light in the duties that are assigned to the human covenant partners (see the next two §§). Even if these conditions can be fulfilled

---

64. Wellum (2012, 120; cf. 608–11, 634–35).

only by God's grace, through the power of the Holy Spirit, this does not change their conditional character.

### 3.9.2   The Conditionality of the Abrahamic Covenant

We see this in a beautiful way in that exemplary unconditional covenant: the Abrahamic covenant. Here all the promises arise purely from God's sovereign grace. Nonetheless, God said as an introduction to the covenant of Genesis 17: "I am God Almighty; *walk before me, and be blameless*, that I may make my covenant between me and you, and may multiply you greatly" (vv. 1–2).[65] In Genesis 18, God says, "I have chosen [lit., known] him, that he may command his children and his household after him to keep the way of the LORD by doing righteousness and justice, so that the LORD may bring to Abraham what he has promised him" (v. 19). Notice especially the last "so that" (Heb. *lemaᶜan*): the LORD can fulfill his promises to Abraham only if the latter will command his house to go the way of righteousness. The *conditional* aspect of the Abraham covenant could not be expressed any more clearly.

In Genesis 26:4–5, God said to Isaac: "I will multiply your offspring as the stars of heaven and will give to your offspring all these lands. And in your offspring all the nations of the earth shall be blessed, *because* Abraham obeyed my voice and kept my charge, my commandments [Heb. *Mitswot*], my statutes [*chuqqot*], and my laws [*torot*, plural of *torah*]." Here again, God's promises—no matter how unconditional they are in many respects—are explicitly linked with Abraham's obedience. In conclusion, the Abrahamic covenant, too, exhibits both the conditional and the unconditional aspects that we have postulated for all biblical covenants.

Of course, the New Covenant is the everlasting covenant

---

65. Heb. *tamim*, CEB: "trustworthy"; CEV: "always do right"; ERV: "live the right way"; MSG: "live to the hilt"; cf. Gen. 6:9; Job 12:4; Ps. 37:18; 101:6; 119:1 (in connection with the Torah); Prov. 2:21b ("those with integrity"); 11:5, 20; 28:10.

*par excellence*; it is the form of the covenant in which all the previous forms find their purpose and significance. Moreover, the passages I am going to quote illustrate that this covenant is made strictly with ethnic Israel, and stands in an unbreakable connection with the promise of the Holy Land: "Instead of your shame there shall be a double portion; instead of dishonor they shall rejoice in their lot; therefore *in their land* they shall possess a double portion; they shall have everlasting joy. For I the LORD love justice; I hate robbery and wrong; I will faithfully give them their recompense, and I will make an *everlasting covenant* with them. Their offspring shall be known among the nations, and their descendants in the midst of the peoples; all who see them shall acknowledge them, that they are an offspring the LORD has blessed" (Isa. 61:7–9, italics added; cf. 24:5; 55:3; 56:4; 59:21; also see 42:6 and 49:8 in connection with the LORD's Servant).

"Behold, I will gather them from all the countries to which I drove them in my anger and my wrath and in great indignation. I will bring them back *to this place* [i.e., the Holy Land], and I will make them dwell in safety. And they shall be my people, and I will be their God. I will give them one heart and one way, that they may fear me forever, for their own good and the good of their children after them. I will make with them an *everlasting covenant*, that I will not turn away from doing good to them. And I will put the fear of me in their hearts, that they may not turn from me. I will rejoice in doing them good, and I will plant them *in this land* in faithfulness, with all my heart and all my soul" (Jer. 32:37–41). "In those days and in that time, . . . the people of Israel and the people of Judah shall come together, weeping as they come, and they shall seek the LORD their God. They shall ask the way to *Zion*, with faces turned toward it, saying, 'Come, let us join ourselves to the LORD in an *everlasting covenant* that will never be forgotten'" (Jer. 50:4–5, italics added).

"My servant David shall be king over them, and they shall all have one shepherd. They shall walk in my rules and be careful to obey my statutes. They shall dwell *in the land* that I gave to my servant Jacob, where your fathers lived. They and their children and their children's children shall dwell there *forever*, and David my servant shall be their prince forever. I will make a covenant of peace with them. It shall be an *everlasting covenant* with them. And I will set them in their land and multiply them, and will set my sanctuary in their midst *forevermore*. My dwelling place shall be with them, and I will be their God, and they shall be my people. Then the nations will know that I am the LORD who sanctifies Israel, when my sanctuary is in their midst *forevermore*" (Ezek. 37:24-28, italics added).

### 3.9.3 The Conditionality of the New Covenant

The New Covenant might seem to be the unconditional covenant *par excellence*. Yet, there are clear elements of conditionality even in this ultimate covenant of God. I mention three conditional aspects (partially alluded to before).[66]

(a) There could never be a realized New Covenant if Christ had not obeyed the Father in coming into this world, in perfectly fulfilling the Mosaic Torah (whether he did this as our substitute is to be investigated in the third volume of this series), and in going to the cross in order to fulfill the work of atonement for believers.

(b) No person could ever share in the blessings of the New Covenant without personal repentance and faith. These obligations are not meritorious grounds for the believers' salvation; rather they are "necessary responses to the covenant's promises," and as such are "instrumental to the enjoyment of the covenant's blessings."[67]

(c) Moreover, true faith is "faith working through love" (Gal. 5:6), a faith producing works of righteousness (James 2:14-26). No true faith without the perseverance of faith. Thus, for example, Michael Horton emphasizes that, for fi-

---

66. Cf. for the first two, see Wellum (2012, 66–67).
67. Venema (2003, 211).

nal salvation, not only initial repentance and faith are needed, but perseverance in repentance and faith, as well as holiness of life. But he hastens to add, quite correctly, that "everything that God *required* in this covenant is also *given* by God!"[68]

In federalism, this point (c) is often connected with infant baptism (about this, see Appendix I). All those who have received baptism are members (or "children") of the covenant. But if they do not live up to it they become "covenant breakers." Even under the New Covenant, the covenant community is allegedly a circle that includes covenant keepers and breakers, and is thus wider than the circle including the elect. We will see that other Reformed theologians do not agree with this, and identify the true circle of the covenant with the circle of election. In the course of this book, I will try to make clear why I cannot agree with the idea held by the former group of theologians, namely, concerning "covenant breakers," because the New Covenant apparently only comprises truly born again believers.

Yet, I maintain the notion of the conditionality of the New Covenant in the sense that the true covenant members are believers who produce works of righteousness. Such works are nothing but the fruit of the Holy Spirit in them: "the righteous requirement of the law" is "fulfilled in us, who walk not according to the flesh but according to the Spirit" (Rom. 8:4). But such works can never be separated from the believers' own responsibility. To produce fruits of righteousness is a condition *they* have to fulfill, albeit in the power of the Holy Spirit: "by the Spirit you put to death the deeds of the body" (v. 13). It is "you" who do this, albeit "by the Spirit." "[W]alk by the Spirit, and you will not gratify the desires of the flesh" (Gal. 5:16). This latter thing is accomplished by the Spirit in the believer — but it is the believer who receives the command: "*Walk* by the Spirit."

---

68. Horton (2006, 184).

# Chapter 4
# Reformed Covenant Theology: Principles

*Therefore [Jesus] is the mediator of a new covenant,*
>   *so that those who are called*
>   *may receive the promised eternal inheritance,*
*since a death has occurred*
>   *that redeems them from the transgressions*
>   *committed under the first covenant . . .*
*Therefore not even the first covenant*
>   *was inaugurated without blood.*
*For when every commandment of the Torah*
>   *had been declared by Moses to all the people,*
*he took the blood of calves and goats,*
>   *with water and scarlet wool and hyssop,*
*and sprinkled both the book itself*
>   *and all the people, saying,*
*"This is the blood of the covenant*
>   *that God commanded for you."*
>                         Hebrews 9:15–20

**Summary:** No theology of the covenant can get around the Reformed/Presbyterian tradition because this tradition has analyzed the biblical idea of the covenant the most intensively of all. This can *easily be illustrated by their basic confessions and catechisms. At the outset, Reformed covenant theology was designed to combat the Anabaptists' doctrine of believers' baptism, and to undergird infant baptism. The doctrines of covenant and predestination became the two most central and distinctive doctrines of Reformed theology. The rise of this theology forms a striking example of how a theological paradigm develops, until it becomes* the *explanatory principle for understanding Scripture. Ultimately, Reformed/Presbyterian thinkers were no longer able to read the Bible in any other way than in a thoroughly covenantal way. This development is compared with that of other theological paradigms, which incidentally tend to look at Scripture in an equally one-sided and universal way.*

## 4.1 Reformed Faith
### 4.1.1 TULIP

LET US NOW ENTER INTO some of the elements in the historical development of Reformed/Presbyterian covenant theology (federalism). To begin with, it is good to point out that terms like "covenant doctrine" and "covenant theology" are ambiguous. They may refer to that part of systematic theology that is occupied with the biblical notion of "the covenant"; as such, the term "covenant" is strictly neutral. However, these may also refer to a certain theological school that makes the biblical notion of "the covenant" the foundation of its theology; in this case the term is *not* neutral. In the first case, one could speak of federology (from the Latin *foedus*,[1] "covenant," and the Greek *logia*, say, the doctrine of the covenant); in the second case, one could speak of federalism (covenant theology in the stricter, more ideological sense).

The situation is a bit similar to that of the term "theology" in general, which may refer to an academic discipline, but also to a certain school ("the theology of Calvin," etc.). The same holds for the term "philosophy." In the present book, the term "covenant theology" usually has the first meaning. If the second meaning is intended, I use the term "federalism,"

---

1. Not *foederus*, as Wellum (2012, 57) has it.

or I specify: Reformed or Presbyterian covenant theology.

We have to distinguish between Reformed and Reformational. I call myself a Reformational theologian but not a Reformed theologian. The term "Reformational" refers in a general way to the Protestant Reformation of the sixteenth century; it includes the Lutherans, Calvinists, Zwinglians, Anglicans, Anabaptists, and Mennonites of the sixteenth century. The term "Reformed" is usually identified with "Calvinist," that is, that type of theology that is characterized by and rooted in the writings of John Calvin (1509–1564). Reformed people often prefer much wider definitions, such as this one by Cornelius Plantinga: "Our accents lie more on the sovereignty of God, on the authority of Scripture, on the need for disciplined holiness in personal Christian life, and finally, on Christianity as a religion of the kingdom."[2] Apparently, this is far too wide a description, for I wholeheartedly subscribe to it—yet I do not call myself "Reformed."

Another example is Robert De Moor, who wrote an entire book on the question about what is "Reformed."[3] For instance, he points out in what respects Calvin differed from Martin Luther and Ulrich Zwingli, especially in the matters of the Lord's Supper and of civil government. With many other Evangelical Christians, on all these points I agree more with Calvin than with Luther and Zwingli. Yet, I do not call myself "Reformed." Or let us look at the well-known Five Points of Calvinism (according to the popular acronym of TULIP).

(a) **T**otal Depravity (also known as Total Inability: People are by nature totally corrupted by sin) (cf. Gen. 6:5; 8:21; Job 15:14–16; John 3:6; Rom. 3:19–20, 23);

(b) **U**nconditional Election (that is, God's election of believers is not based on any foreknowledge of their future choices but entirely on his own sovereign choice) (cf. Rom. 8:29; 9:23; Eph. 1:3–5);

---

2. Plantinga (2001, 281).
3. De Moor (2001); see a summary on www.crcna.org/welcome/beliefs/reformed-accent/what-reformed.

(c) **L**imited Atonement (also known as Particular Atonement; that is, though Jesus' sacrifice was sufficient for all, it is efficacious only for the believers) ("for our sake," 2 Cor. 5:21; "our sins," 1 Cor. 15:3; Gal. 1:4; 1 Pet. 2:24; 1 John 4:10; Rev. 1:5);[4]

(d) **I**rresistible Grace (when God calls people to salvation, they cannot resist; he offers to all people the gospel message — the external call — but to the elect, God extends an internal call that cannot be resisted) (cf. John 6:44; Gal. 5:13; Eph. 4:4; 1 Thess. 2:12; 1 Tim. 6:12);

(e) **P**erseverance of the Saints (also known as Once Saved Always Saved; if someone is truly born again through the Spirit of God, this regeneration can never be undone) (cf. John 10:27–29; Phil. 1:6; 2 Thess. 3:3; 2 Tim. 1:12).

With many other Evangelical Christians, I agree wholeheartedly with all these five points — yet, I do not call myself "Reformed." In other words, I consider these five points not to be distinctive enough. In fact, I can see only two main points in which Reformed Christians differ from all other orthodox Christians.

(a) "Everything is covenantal" in the Bible, that is, the relationships between God and people are always basically covenantal. This belief touches the subject of the present book. I cannot accept this Reformed thesis because the Bible does not speak this way.[5] For instance, two of the most vital relationships between God and believers are not covenantal at all, namely, the relationship between the Father and his children, and the relationship between the Bridegroom Jesus Christ and the bridal church. (There is a covenantal aspect to marriage,

---

4. It is not "He is the propitiation for our sins, and not for ours only but also for *the sins of* the whole world" (1 John 2:2 ESV, etc.), but "He is the propitiation for our sins, and not for ours only but also for the whole world" (Darby, NKJV, WEB, YLT, etc.), that is, sufficient for the sins of the whole world, but efficacious only for the sins of believers.
5. One simple counter-argument against the Reformed view is that God already had relationships with Noah, Abram, Israel, Levi, and David before he made covenants with them; cf. Niehaus (2009, 237–38).

but this does not express the essence of marriage, as I hope to explain.) A covenantal relationship is basically juridical, a father-child relationship, or a husband-wife relationship, is basically ethical. To call these relationships also "covenantal" is precisely what must be demonstrated; Reformed theologians call them "covenantal" not because Scripture does so—it does not—but because of their covenantal premise: "everything is covenantal." As the seventeenth century Reformed theologian Francis Turretin put it: covenant is "as it were the center and bond of all religion."[6]

(b) The doctrine of what is called "double predestination": as a corollary of eternal unconditional election, genuine Calvinists also believe in eternal unconditional reprobation. That is, already before the foundation of the world, the non-elect have been destined to hell, *not* because of their foreseen unbelief but because of a sovereign decision of God's will. This latter doctrine is not in the Bible; it is only an inference from the doctrine of unconditional election.[7] As the Westminster Confession declares in chapter III.7, after stating the doctrine of election: "The rest of mankind, God was pleased, according to the inscrutable counsel of His own will, whereby He extendeth or withholdeth mercy as He pleaseth, for the glory of His sovereign power over His creatures, to pass by, and to ordain them to dishonor and wrath for their sin, to the praise of His glorious justice."

### 4.1.2 Pervasive Covenantalizing and Inferentialism

Perhaps one could view me this way: I am Reformed because I attach great importance to the biblical notion of the covenant, and because I firmly believe in the sovereign divine election of the saints from eternity. I am *not* Reformed to the extent that I reject pervasive covenantalizing—more specifically, I consider the notion of the kingdom to be more central

---

6. Turretin (1994, II, 169).
7. See on the subject of election and reprobation extensively Ouweneel (2008b, especially chapters 9–14).

than that of the covenant (§5.5.1) — and I reject the doctrine of sovereign divine reprobation of the wicked from eternity. I will explain why.

Under (a) (see the previous §) we are dealing with the logical flaw of *pervasive covenantalizing*: one biblical element is universalized in a way that subsumes all other biblical notions under this single one. This form of covenantalizing is just as unwarranted as those in which the church, or the kingdom, or the spiritual (charismatic), or atonement, or salvation, or the Eastern Orthodox idea of *theosis*, or what have you, is universalized. Pervasive covenantalizing is not properly recognized as such: one who wears "covenant glasses" *sees* everything "covenantally,"[8] and cannot understand that others do *not* "see" everything that way.

Under (b) above, we are dealing with the logical flaw of *inferentialism*: certain inferences are drawn as though a term like election were a plain logical concept from which plain logical conclusions can be drawn.[9] For instance, from the concept of "father" we may conclude that a person who is "father" is masculine and has procreated one or more children through one or more women. But from the theological *idea* of a "father," as in the case of God's Fatherhood, we *cannot* draw such conclusions: God is neither masculine, nor has he had intercourse with women, as we know from the rest of Scripture. Likewise, from the *idea* of divine election we may draw only such conclusions as are explicitly drawn in Scripture itself.[10]

In the Bible, there is not a trace of an unconditional reprobation of the non-elect *before the foundation of the world*. It is a

---

8. E.g., De Graaf (1940, 61): "[A]ll religion, all fellowship with God is from the beginning rooted in the covenant."
9. Cf. the Westminster Confession of Faith, I–VI: "The whole counsel of God, concerning all things necessary for his own glory, man's salvation, faith, and life, is either expressly set down in Scripture, or *by good and necessary consequence* may be deduced from Scripture" (ital. added). See on this, McGraw (2012) for a defense of such "inferentialism."
10. See on this important distinction between "concept" and "idea," Ouweneel (2013, §1.5).

"consequence," allegedly "deduced from Scripture," but one that is *not* "good and necessary" because it is based on the confusion of concepts and ideas (see note 10). God does reprobate the wicked, but only *after* they have stubbornly continued in their wickedness. This is the sense of Proverbs 16:4, for instance: "The LORD has made everything for its purpose, even the wicked for the day of trouble." Also notice carefully the difference between the "vessels of wrath prepared for destruction," namely *by themselves* (cf. 2 Pet. 2:1, "bringing upon themselves swift destruction"), and the "vessels of mercy, which *he* [i.e., God] has prepared beforehand for glory" (Rom. 9:22–23). Scripture knows of an election of the saints before the world began; it does not know of a reprobation of the wicked before the world began.

Incidentally, the reproach of inferentialism is usually met with the reproach of biblicism ("you wish to believe only what is explicitly stated in the Bible"). People point to terms like "Trinity" and "substitution," which do not occur in the Bible and are yet embraced by all orthodox Christians. This is so because the *content* of these notions is taught in the Bible. However, this is not necessarily the case with infant baptism, covenant of works, covenant of redemption, covenant of grace, eternal reprobation, etc. Opponents of these subjects are not quibbling over terms as such; they are taking issue with the *content* of these terms. The point is not that they cannot find the *term* "covenant of works" or the *term* "eternal reprobation" in the Bible, but that they cannot find the *content* of these notions in the Bible. We will return to this subject extensively.

## 4.2   Presbyterian Faith
### 4.2.1   The Westminster Standards

Reformed and Presbyterian Christians call themselves Calvinists. Sometimes, "Reformed" is identified with "Calvinist," and Presbyterianism is then called a special branch of Reformed Christianity. But often the name "Reformed" is reserved for continental European, especially Dutch, Calvinists

(Dutch: *gereformeerd*, German: *reformiert*), whereas the name "Presbyterian" is reserved for Scottish and English Calvinists. The term "Reformed" refers back to the (Protestant) Reformation of the sixteenth century, while the term "Presbyterian" refers to a specific form of church government, namely, one in which congregations are governed by representative assemblies of *presbyters* (elders).

We must also mention here the *Puritans*, a mainly Reformed movement of sixteenth- and seventeenth-century English Calvinists, who were *not* always Presbyterian in their views on church government. The Church of England never was a Presbyterian church, unlike the Church of Scotland. However, in later times, Anglo-Saxon Puritanism and Presbyterianism largely coincided.

To be sure, Reformed Christians also have a presbyterial form of church government, and Presbyterian Christians also identify by and large with the Reformed theological tradition. They differ mainly historically, as I just explained. However, there are also theological differences. To discern these, we do not point to all kinds of Reformed and Presbyterian theologians, respectively—for the two groups often differ greatly among themselves—but to their formal confessions. Reformed Christians generally hold to the Three Forms of Unity, that is, the Belgic Confession (1561; of Walloon origin), the Heidelberg Catechism (1563; of Palatinate-German origin), and the Canons of Dort (1619; of Dutch origin) (see §4.3). Presbyterians generally also hold to the Westminster Standards, all three of which are named according to the Westminster Assembly of Divines (i.e., English and Scottish theologians), which began in 1643 and ended somewhere in the 1650s. Around 1647, this Assembly produced the Westminster Confession of Faith, the Westminster Larger Catechism, and the Westminster Shorter Catechism.

It is quite remarkable that all Three Forms of Unity speak of the covenant mainly in the context of infant baptism. This is in line with John Calvin, who explicitly refers to the covenant only when he speaks of infant baptism.[11] The few references to the covenant in the Forms of Unity would make it impossible to build a full-fledged covenant theology on them (see §4.3). This is very different in the Westminster Standards, probably because they originated in a much later period—the Westminster Confession is about eighty-six years younger than the Belgic Confession—at which point Presbyterian/Reformed federalism was at a much later stage of theological development.

### 4.2.2 The Westminster Confession

In the Westminster Confession of Faith, the covenant is discussed in a separate chapter, Chapter VII, *On God's covenant with Man*, the essence of which is (original version):

"II. The first covenant made with man was a covenant of works, wherein life was promised to Adam; and in him to his posterity, upon condition of perfect and personal obedience. [See on the covenant of works more extensively, Chapter XIX, *Of the law of God*.]

"III. Man, by his fall, having made himself incapable of life by that covenant, the Lord was pleased to make a second, commonly called the covenant of grace; wherein He freely offereth unto sinners life and salvation by Jesus Christ; requiring of them faith in Him, that they may be saved, and promising to give unto all those that are ordained unto eternal life His Holy Spirit, to make them willing, and able to believe....

"V. This covenant was differently administered in the time of the law, and in the time of the gospel: under the law, it was administered by promises, prophecies, sacrifices, circumcision, the paschal lamb, and other types and ordinances delivered to the people of the Jews, all foresignifying Christ to come; which were, for that time, sufficient and efficacious, through the operation of the Spirit, to instruct and build up

---

11. See Graafland (1992, 186); see on this subject, J. van Genderen in Hagoort (1999, 85–92).

the elect in faith in the promised Messiah, by whom they had full remission of sins, and eternal salvation; and is called the old Testament.

"VI. Under the gospel, when Christ, the substance, was exhibited, the ordinances in which this covenant is dispensed are the preaching of the Word, and the administration of the sacraments of Baptism and the Lord's Supper: which, though fewer in number, and administered with more simplicity, and less outward glory, yet, in them, it is held forth in more fullness, evidence, and spiritual efficacy, to all nations, both Jews and Gentiles; and is called the new Testament. There are not therefore two covenants of grace, differing in substance, but one and the same, under various dispensations."

In this chapter, there is no reference to infant baptism; the latter is found only in Chapter XXVIII: "Baptism is a sacrament of the new testament, ordained by Jesus Christ, not only for the solemn admission of the party baptized into the visible church; but also, to be unto him a sign and seal of the covenant of grace, of his ingrafting into Christ, of regeneration, of remission of sins, and of his giving up unto God, through Jesus Christ, to walk in newness of life.... Not only those that do actually profess faith in and obedience unto Christ, but also the infants of one, or both, believing parents, are to be baptized." Please notice how several matters are associated with baptism here that are never directly and unequivocally associated with baptism in the New Testament: admission to the (visible) church[12] and regeneration.[13]

The *Westminster Larger Catechism* and the *Westminster Shorter Catechism*, together with the comments of especially Isaac Chauncy, James Fisher, and the brothers Ebenezer and Ralph Erskine (seventeenth and eighteenth centuries), give a

---

12. Many expositors believe that in 1 Cor. 12:12–13 Paul is referring to Spirit baptism, not water baptism; see §7.2.2 and Ouweneel (2007a, 209–11).
13. Many expositors believe that John 3:5 ("water") and Titus 3:5 ("washing") do not refer to (water) baptism at all (people are *not* regenerated through water baptism, with or without the Spirit); see Ouweneel (2007a, 197–99).

good picture of the Presbyterian view of the covenant.[14] The Catechisms, too, tell us about the two postulated covenants: the covenant of works and the covenant of grace, and claim that the latter was made in eternity with Christ, and in him with the elect. (The Westminster Confession of Faith rather suggests that the covenant of grace refers to all people.) Apparently, the well-meant offer of (redemptive) grace to sinners—not only to the elect, as one might expect—is viewed as falling outside the covenant as such. That is, God's grace is preached to all, not only to covenant members.

It is all the more remarkable that the two Catechisms speak with such emphasis about the alleged connection between the covenant and (infant) baptism, as if to assume that the children of believing parents belong to the elect. In fact, there are three concentric circles here: the inner circle of the elect, the middle circle of the covenant members, and the outer circle of all those who are reached by the preaching of the gospel (not to mention the still wider circle of all humanity). The relationship between the inner and the middle circle leads to a theological tension because it is obvious that *not* all baptized church members will ultimately be saved. As we will see later, this tension—arising every time people try to bring the covenant and predestination together in one conceptual system—permeates all Reformed/Presbyterian theology.

## 4.3 Differences Between Reformed and Presbyterian
### 4.3.1 Early Development

The length of time between the Belgic Confession (1561) and the Heidelberg Catechism (1563), on the one hand, and the Westminster Standards (c. 1647) is probably significant. The two greatest minds behind the Heidelberg Catechism, Zacharias Ursinus and Caspar Olevianus, have both written things in which the influence of scholastic and humanistic thinking was clearly discerniable, but which, thank God, *did not make it into the Heidelberg Catechism*. In the *Maior*, the draft of the

---

14. See extensively Graafland (1994, 265–309).

Heidelberg Catechism that Ursinus wrote, he said in answer 36: "The law contains the covenant of nature, made by God with the people in creation. This is [the covenant] which is *known to men by nature*. It *demands* from us perfect obedience towards God, and *promises* all those who indeed perform it, life everlasting. However, it *threatens* with everlasting punishments those who do not render this [obedience]."[15] In answer 158 he claimed that the Ten Commandments were not given for the first time at Mount Sinai but that, at Sinai, that law was repeated and proclaimed to Israel *ad quid omnes creaturae rationales sint conditae* ("to which all rational creatures are enabled"). In his Larger Catechism of 1562, Ursinus wrote that the covenant of works "requires our perfect obedience to God" and "promises eternal life to those who keep it."[16]

This entire notion of a covenant "known to men by nature" is a product of scholastic thinking (in Ursinus' case, due probably to Philip Melanchton), and is contrary to Scripture. None of this made it into the Heidelberg Catechism because wise men objected to it.

Something similar we see with Olevianus, in his treatise on the Apostolic Creed: "The law is a doctrine, which God has innately implanted in man and which He has summarized and renewed in His commandments."[17] He called this implantation a matter of "human nature." Again, Scripture does not teach anything about some natural or moral law that was instilled in people at creation. Reformed theologian Van der Waal observes: "Adam did not have to live by an inner light, but he received his instructions from his Great King. Adam did not live as the image of God because of a natural theology and natural ethics or morals. Neither did he live by a double standard: his inbred morals plus the revealed test-commandment. Similarly, he did not subscribe to a doctrine of dual source: his own heart and God's mouth. . . . In retaining the

---

15. See Lang (1907); Diemer (1933); quoted by Van der Waal (1990, 53).
16. Cf. Bierma et al. (2005, 168–69).
17. Olevianus (1995; orig.: 1567); quoted by Van der Waal (1990, 57).

doctrine of the inbred law of nature, a lump of natural theology and humanism was hauled into the church. The remnants of this still wreak their vengeance to the present day."[18]

In this context, we must pay attention to Romans 2:14–15: "For when Gentiles, who do not have the law, by nature do what the law requires, they are a law to themselves, even though they do not have the law. They show that the work of the law is written on their hearts, while their conscience also bears witness." This statement by the apostle Paul must be handled carefully: Torah-abiding Gentiles followed their conscience, not some natural law. These are different things. Moreover, it is not some *law*, but the *work* of the law, that was written on their hearts. These are different things, too.

Again, we note with joy that this opinion of Olevianus did not make it into the Heidelberg Catechism. Neither the concept of an "innate law," nor that of a "covenant of works" is found in any of the Three Forms of Unity. I may add that the word "covenant" is even totally lacking in the (Calvinist) French Confession of 1559, and in the Thirty-Nine Articles of 1562. The Scots Confession of 1560 mentions the word only once (chapter 21), in connection with the sacraments, and the Second Helvetic Confession of 1566 mentions it four times, once very generally, and three times in connection with (infant) baptism. In none of these older Reformed confessions is there any reference to a "covenant of works" or a "covenant of grace." These terms are products of later scholastic developments within the Reformed and Presbyterian world, and have introduced a lot of contention into it, until this very day.

Around the middle of the seventeenth century, Protestant scholasticism had made great progress. Whereas there is no "covenant of works" in the Three Forms of Unity, it *is* found in the Westminster Larger Catechism, answer 30: "God doth not leave all men to perish in the estate of sin and misery, into which they fell by the breach of the first covenant, commonly

---

18. Van der Waal (1990, 57).

called the *covenant of works*; but of his mere love and mercy delivereth his elect out of it, and bringeth them into an estate of salvation by the second covenant, commonly called the *covenant of grace*."

### 4.3.2 No Innate Law

The idea of an "innate law" did not make it into the Three Forms of Unity, but it did make it into the Westminster Standards. In the Westminster Larger Catechism we read in answer 92: "The rule of obedience revealed to Adam in the estate of innocence, and to all mankind in him, besides a special command not to eat of the fruit of the tree knowledge of good and evil, was the moral law." And in answer 93: "The moral law is the declaration of the will of God to mankind, directing and binding every one to personal, perfect, and perpetual conformity and obedience thereunto, in the frame and disposition of the whole man, soul and body, and in performance of all those duties of holiness and righteousness which he oweth to God and man: promising life upon the fulfilling, and threatening death upon the breach of it." Please notice that this "moral law" allegedly existed already in the Garden of Eden, in the heart of human beings; but answer 98 adds: "The moral law is summarily comprehended in the ten commandments." In both cases—Eden and Sinai—the nature of the alleged "covenant of works" is thought to be the same: obedience to it would bring righteousness (justification) by works.

The Westminster Confession of Faith says: "After God had made all other creatures, He created man, male and female, with reasonable and immortal souls, endued with knowledge, righteousness, and true holiness, after His own image; having the law of God written in their hearts" (IV.2). Notice the errors in such a short statement:

(a) The idea of a "reasonable soul" (*anima rationalis*) as well as an "immortal soul" is purely Greek-Roman (going back to Aristotle), and has nothing to do with biblical revelation. (The WCF refers to Gen. 2:7 here, which teaches nothing of the kind; on the contrary, the verse does not speak about a "soul" that a person *has*, but about what a person *is*.)[19] God "alone has immortality" (1 Tim. 6:16); believers receive it only in resurrection (1 Cor. 15:53).

(b) Scripture nowhere says that at creation, people were righteous and holy. (The WCF refers here to Col. 3:10 and Eph. 4:24, which explicitly speak of the "new man" in Christ.) Prelapsarian Adam and Eve were innocent, which is something very different.

(c) Scripture nowhere says that Adam and Eve had "the law of God written in their hearts." (The WCF refers here to Rom. 2:14, which, first, does not speak of Adam and Eve, but of pagans; and second, does not say that the pagans have the *law* of God written in their hearts, but the *work* of the law.)

This whole idea of an innate law that allegedly came to Israel in the form of the Ten Commandments is basically nonsense. At best, one can imagine that non-fallen people — and even some fallen people — may have a natural idea that it is wrong to kill or to steal, and even to commit adultery, because this is not in their own interest. If I were allowed to kill, to steal, or to commit adultery, then others are equally allowed to kill *me*, to steal from *me*, to touch *my wife*. It is also in people's own interest to honor their parents because (a) children are dependent on their parents — so you had better show them respect — and (b) if we honor our parents, our children will honor *us*.

However, what innate law could ever teach a person that he has to observe the seventh day of the week? At best, intelligent people might come up with the idea that it would be wise to have a day of rest once in a while. But why every *seventh* day? And why such a comprehensive rest that includes household members, servants, and even cattle? Moreover, this was not for health reasons at all, but because "in six days the

---

19. See extensively, Ouweneel (2008a, chapters 6–8).

Lord made heaven and earth, the sea, and all that is in them, and rested on the seventh day" (Exod. 20:11), and because "you were a slave in the land of Egypt, and the Lord your God brought you out from there with a mighty hand and an outstretched arm" (Deut. 5:15). Certainly no innate law could ever have told us that. This is precisely why the Sabbath commandment is repeated so often (Exod. 16:23-29; 31:13-16; 35:2-3; Lev. 19:3, 30; 23:3; 26:2). Even the greatest sinners have a minimal sense that stealing and killing are wrong—at least among themselves—but there is nothing obvious or self-evident about the Sabbath commandment. That is why it has been repeated time and again. Israel had to observe it, not because it was self-evident, or even because it was healthy, but because God told them to, for redemptive-historical reasons.

But then, does the same not hold for the first of the Ten Commandments? Theologians have often discussed to what degree there is some innate sense of God in every human, also after the fall. Even if there is such a sense of divinity (*sensus divinitatis*, as Calvin called it, or *semen religionis* ["seed of religion"]), why would it require that there be only one God ("You shall have no other gods before me")? The large majority of pagan nations worshiped many gods. Besides, what innate law would tell people, even non-fallen people, that you are not supposed to make a "carved image, or any likeness of anything" in heaven or on earth, be it of the one God or of the false gods? We know all these things because God revealed them to us. There is no such thing as an innate law that could have taught them to us.

The Reformed (!) theologian Cornelis Van der Waal concludes: "[T]he fact that seventeenth century Puritans have actually made Adam into just such a rational creature, who with the innate divine and legal knowledge could work out his own salvation, has played into the hands of [secular philosopher René] Descartes and of rationalism, as well as of workholiness and of a perfectionism, but in fact it has strained the *gospel."*[20]

In §§3.5 and 3.6 above, I have undertaken to refute the entire notion of a "covenant of works" and of its alleged "republication" at Mount Sinai, and I will come back to this in §5.4. The point I wish to make right now is this: *it is very difficult to convince people of wrong theological theories if these theories have made it even into their cherished creeds and catechisms.* Reformed Christians who adhere to the Three Forms of Unity are blessed. They may have their own reasons for defending notions such as the "covenant of works" and the "natural law," but at least they do not have to defend their creeds and catechisms in this regard. For Presbyterian Christians, the situation is far more difficult because a refutation of the ideas mentioned affects the confessional ground on which they stand. For many Christians, who often are not unwilling to consider new ideas, this is almost unthinkable when it comes to ideas that fundamentally deviate from their creeds and catechisms.

### 4.3.3 A Case Study

A practical example of the impact of the Westminster Standards may be appropriate; especially at the present time, this exemplary case is playing quite some role in the North American Presbyterian and Reformed world. At the heart of the controversy is Westminster Seminary in California. The name of the institution signals its theological "color": it teaches and studies within the boundaries of the Westminster Standards, but also those of the Three Forms of Unity. It is therefore truly both a Presbyterian and Reformed theological academy. Yet, the controversy I am briefly summarizing here involves especially the Westminster Standards, to such an extent that I wonder whether such a controversy could have had such a devastating effect if people had been living by the light of the Three Forms of Unity only.

However this may be, the controversy is of such a nature that, "it is claimed, the very integrity of the gospel is at

---

20. Ibid., 54–55.

stake."[21] The two sides of the present conflict have recently been described in two publications, one publication from both sides.[22] The basic nature of the controversy is the interpretation not so much of Scripture but of the Westminster Standards: one party speaks of "The Faithful Plumb Line of the Westminster Confession of Faith,"[23] and the other party would probably agree. It is not the Westminster Standards that are at stake, but some interpretations of it and inferences that some draw from it.

Central to the controversy is the "covenant of works." Please remember that this notion does not appear in the Three Forms of Unity, but it does appear in the Westminster Standards. In §3.4 above, I have tried to explain why I cannot accept the notion of a "covenant of works"; it is basically unscriptural, and I am thankful that there are also Reformed theologians who have come to the same conclusion. But for Westminster Standards confessionalists this is of course unacceptable, because the "covenant of works" is taught in the Westminster Standards, and these are "a faithful summary of the teaching of Scripture."[24] What happened at Westminster Theological Seminary in Philadelphia was that several of its professors, such as John Murray, Norman Shepherd, and Meredith Kline,[25] deviated from the Westminster Standards in the eyes of their opponents. Their teachings "all need to be evaluated in light of, and measured against, the standard of this plumb line."[26]

Now I can imagine that Westminster Standards confessionalists have great difficulty with the teachings of those who not only hold to the "covenant of works" — that is what all

---

21. W. Shishko in Elam et al. (2014, viii).
22. Estelle et al. (2009); Elam et al. (2014).
23. Elam et al. (2014, 38; cf. 39: "This plumb line has served as a faithful standard for faith and life for hundreds of years").
24. Ibid., 19.
25. Some relevant publications: Murray (1954); Shepherd (2000); Kline (2006a; 2006b).
26. Elam et al. (2014, 19).

Westminster Standards loyalists do—but also teach that this covenant was "republished" (or reaffirmed) at Mount Sinai, so that the Sinaitic covenant, at least partly, had the character of a "covenant of works"; one version of this idea was propagated by Meredith Kline. The idea of a "covenant of works" is to be rejected, but this "republication" theory is even worse (see §3.5). However, what Kline's opponents do not see is that this erroneous teaching of Kline and others comes from the same root that his opponents also adhere to: the doctrine of the "covenant of works."

What is even more shocking is the way the two parties accuse each other of jeopardizing the gospel. The followers of Kline claim that a rejection of the "republication" theory "will only leave us necessarily impoverished in our faith. We will see in only a thin manner the work of our Savior."[27] The opponents of Kline's approach use similar strong language: "Ironically, the republication teaching, which was intended to preserve and protect the doctrine of justification, may (when consistently worked out) actually undercut this doctrine—the very doctrine by which the church stands or falls."[28] Not only is the gospel allegedly at stake, but, according to both parties, so is Reformed doctrine. The Klineans tell us that the "republication" doctrine "is part of the warp and woof of Scripture and sound doctrine," that is, Reformed doctrine.[29]

I myself see a few positive elements in John Murray's teaching, and that is, first, his allowance for some grace in the covenant with prelapsarian Adam. His opponents cannot live with that; they prefer to limit the term "grace" to "specifically redemptive grace"—which is a mistake (see §3.6 above).[30] Second, Murray wondered whether one can at all use the term "covenant" for the prelapsarian situation. Yet, Murray maintained that prelapsarian Adam "was under obligation to

---

27. Estelle et al. (2009, 19).
28. Elam et al. (2014, 3–4).
29. Estelle et al. (2009, 6).
30. Elam et al. (2014, 18).

perform perfect, personal obedience to the commandments as the legal basis of his attainment of the reward of life."[31] This was viewed by Norman Shepherd as an error: he saw "no place at all left for a covenant of works or meritorious human obedience."[32] Meredith Kline disagreed with both Murray and Shepherd, and even described their views as an "encroachment of this radical renunciation of the Reformation, this subtle surrender to Rome."[33] To make it even more complicated, some opponents of Murray and Shepherd also disagree with Kline.

Throughout this entire debate, the central issue has been: which party best represents the Westminster Standards, or more broadly, the history of Reformed covenant theology? I will return to this issue in the third volume of the present series because it is closely linked with the traditional Reformed doctrine of justification by faith. But already now I emphasize how unhappy one can feel with such a controversy, where one can distinguish at least four parties, and where one cannot agree with any them *because they all operate within the same Westminster Standards paradigm*. It is the *roots* of this paradigm that we must take issue with; from wrong roots one can expect not only wrong fruits, but also heated controversies *between* these wrong fruits. The reason is that, if certain fruits are wrong, this is often discerned by other thinkers—but if these theologians work within the same paradigm, they necessarily combat these wrong weapons with other wrong weapons. The problem does not lie in Murray, Shepherd, Kline, or their opponents—but the basic problems lie in the Westminster Standards themselves (more than in the Three Forms of Unity). As long as these Standards as such are not questioned—and in the Presbyterian world this is virtually impossible to do without being thrown out—new controversies, sometimes followed by new church divisions, will keep emerging.

---

31. Ibid., 27.
32. Ibid., 30.
33. Ibid.

## 4.4 Covenant and Baptism
### 4.4.1 The Reformed Connection

In Appendix I, I will deal extensively with the remarkably close link between covenant and (infant) baptism in Reformed and Presbyterian theology. Here I will simply make some introductory remarks. In all Three Forms of Unity the covenant is mentioned mainly in connection with the baptism of the believers' children: because the covenant is for them, they must be baptized.[34] See especially the Belgic Confession, Article 34: "... For that reason we reject the error of the Anabaptists who are not content with a single baptism once received and also condemn the baptism of the children of believers. We believe our children ought to be baptized and sealed with the sign of the covenant, as little children were circumcised in Israel on the basis of the same." This one reference to the covenant in the Belgic Confession presupposes the self-evidentness of the claim that, whereas circumcision was the "sign of the covenant" in the Old Testament, baptism is that in the New Testament. This was the kernel of Calvin's doctrine of baptism,[35] and of that of many of his learned followers, as we will see.

This close connection between covenant and (infant) baptism goes back to Calvin and Zwingli. Thus, Zwingli's covenant view took its starting point in baptism and its alleged connection with the Abrahamic covenant.[36] However, there is a very important point to be made here. It is this: historically speaking, infant baptism was not derived from the doctrine of the covenant, but it was the other way around: *the doctrine of covenant was mainly developed to justify the unrelinquishable teaching and practice of infant baptism.* For some reason, infant baptism was rather uncritically taken over from Roman Catholicism, and all the more so in opposition to the detested Anabaptists. However, infant baptism could no longer be defended in the Roman Catholic way, that is, it was no longer

---

34. See note 5.
35. Cf. his *Institutes* 4.16.3; see the extensive discussion by Lillback (2001).
36. Van Genderen (2008, 540).

viewed as the entrance to the [Catholic] church, and regeneration was no longer viewed as accompanying baptism (which was based on a false appeal to John 3:5 and Titus 3:5). Therefore, a new foundation had to be sought. This was creatively found in federalism.

From a historical point of view, the course of this process is undeniable; but if one asks a Reformed theologian what is his main argument for infant baptism, he will invariably refer to the covenant doctrine. Of course, this does not work. If someone wishes to derive infant baptism from, or base it upon, the doctrine of the covenant, he has fallen into a circular argument: the Reformed baptism doctrine was already certain before the Reformed covenant doctrine was even developed. Nevertheless, Reformed infant baptism is continually defended on the basis of Reformed federalism. A few examples: Benjamin Warfield summarized his entire view of baptism in four "arguments": "God established his church [!] in the days of Abraham and put children into it. They must remain there until he puts them out. He has nowhere put them out. They are still then members of his church and as such entitled to its ordinances," including baptism.[37] This reasoning was summarized further by Cornelis Venema: "Who belongs to the church, that is, the covenantal community of God's people?" with the implication: not only believers but also their children, just as in the Old Testament.[38]

Louis Berkhof based infant baptism on five arguments, four of which referred to the Abrahamic covenant, and the fifth one to the "covenant of grace."[39] This is what I have been saying: the doctrine of the covenant was *expressis verbis* developed to legitimize infant baptism, and subsequently that same infant baptism came to be derived from the doctrine of the covenant. The doctrine of infant baptism must be true because the doctrine of the covenant is true; and the doctrine

---

37. Warfield (1932, 408).
38. Venema (2003, 201).
39. Berkhof (1979, 632–34).

of the covenant must be true because the doctrine of infant baptism is true.

To give some more recent examples of basing infant baptism upon the covenant: Randy Booth defended infant baptism with an appeal to (1) Reformed covenant theology, (2) the continuity of the covenant of grace, (3) the continuity of the people of God, (4) the continuity of the covenant signs (circumcision, baptism), and (5) the continuity of households.[40] Ben Wentsel saw four grounds for infant baptism: (1) the covenant of grace with the promises of God, (2) the fact that the progeny of the covenant partners is always included, (3) the parallel with Old Testament circumcision, (4) the fact that in Romans 5:12-21 and 6:1-4 the children implicitly share in original sin (race of Adam) or in the church (race of Christ), respectively.[41] Michael Horton referred to two well-known Baptist arguments ("in the New Testament baptism is a symbol of the believer's profession to be a follower of Jesus Christ" and "nowhere does it teach that children are to be baptized"), and replied: "At least from the Reformed perspective, both objections are best addressed by attending to the continuity of the covenant of grace."[42] Precisely. I cannot see any other way from the Reformed perspective.

### 4.4.2 The Connection Loosened

Stephen Wellum summarizes:[43] the entire (Reformed) argument for infant baptism is based on one central argument: the one, continuous "covenant of grace" in Old and New Testament.[44] This fact is recognized by Ben Wentsel: "The main ground [for infant baptism] is the covenant of God with

---

40. Booth (1995, 8; also see his contribution in Strawbridge [2003, 175–200]).
41. Wentsel (1995, 253–54; see the elaboration in 256–79).
42. Horton (2011, 794).
43. Wellum (2006, 97).
44. Cf. the title of Marcel (1958: "... *Infant Baptism: Sacrament of the covenant of grace*. He clearly says that it is the covenant [of Grace] that is the only basis for [infant] baptism" [219]). Cf. Voorberg (2007, 7: "From covenant to baptism is a small step.")

Abraham. . . . Infant baptism finds its strong ground in the covenant of grace, made with Abraham and his (pneumatic) progeny."[45] Cornelis Venema argued that the teaching of infant baptism is the fruit of a broad covenantal understanding of the Scriptures.[46] It is framed in a coherent collection of convictions concerning the substantial unity of the covenant of grace in the course of salvation history, and the nature of the sacraments as God-given signs and seals of the covenant promise. In other words, criticize the doctrine of the "covenant of grace," and infant baptism is entirely up in the air.

This is exactly the honest conclusion that federalist Willem Verboom drew: "[T]he covenant is the most important argument for infant baptism. He who abandons the covenant as biblical foundation has no real defense anymore against the rejection of infant baptism."[47]

The same link between infant baptism and covenant doctrine is found in many writings from Reformed authors who defend infant baptism. In our time, in which infant baptism comes under ever stronger Evangelical pressure, these writings are numerous. They usually suffer from the same weakness, namely, that they start from federalism, which for the authors is so evident that they no longer defend this starting point. However, they forget that for their opponents — and often for their own young people — federalism is not all that self-evident. No discussion about baptism can make any sense if Reformed authors themselves do not become conscious of their federalist presuppositions, which are not based on direct biblical statements but on inferentialism. In such a situation, the debate turns into shooting at each other from fortresses from where one cannot hit the other. Credobaptists can attempt to refute the view of infant baptism only by hitting at the underlying federalism. The reverse is true as well: if paedobaptists consider this federalism to be self-evident, and do

---

45. Wentsel (1995, 224–25).
46. Venema (2003, 228; cf. 204–17).
47. W. Verboom in Hoek and Verboom (2010, 75).

not take pains to defend the *basics* of it, their baptismal arguments will convince only their own people, as Wellum rightly remarks.[48] And unfortunately this is what we see happening all the time.

To make things even more complicated, this does not mean that federalism and infant baptism are inescapably linked together, for that matter. The same holds for dispensationalism and believers' baptism. Perhaps those who hold infant baptism can learn here from the *Strict Baptists*, such as John Bunyan (1628-1688) and Charles H. Spurgeon (1834-1892).[49] They adhered to federalism, that is, to the notions of the covenant of works in Adam and the covenant of grace in Christ, and at the same time advocated believers' baptism, not infant baptism. Apparently, these "Reformed Baptists" had no difficulty combining a Reformed theology with believers' baptism—which is all the more striking because the writings of these authors are highly regarded by many paedobaptists.

The reverse has also occurred: Roman Catholic and Eastern Orthodox theologians have never based infant baptism on some form of covenant theology. They had and have their own, very different grounds for it. And among Protestants, Martin Luther did not need the term "covenant" to defend infant baptism. For instance, his Large Catechism does speak extensively of baptism, but it contains no reference to the divine covenants. The father of classical dispensationalism, John N. Darby (nineteenth century),[50] was just like many Exclusive Brethren—for instance, Frederick W. Grant[51]—an adherent of infant baptism, or rather, household baptism, as it was called, but without basing it upon some covenant doctrine. Other leading early Brethren, however, such as Charles

---

48. Wellum (2006, 125).
49. See seven statements by Spurgeon about baptism quoted in Engle and Armstrong (2007, 194–95).
50. Darby wrote about it especially in his letters (e.g., n.d.-b, I, 296; II, 47–52, 228–30, 275–94, 446, 473–74; III, 204–205, 277–78, 418–19, 471–74).
51. Grant (n.d.-b.).

H. Mackintosh, William Kelly (Great Britain), Carl Brockhaus (Germany), and Herman C. Voorhoeve (the Netherlands), advocated believers' baptism.

Anglican theologian Alister McGrath supposes that it is not the New Testament itself that bases baptism upon covenant and circumcision, but that the early Christians invented infant baptism. He presumes that the existence of Jewish circumcision led to a desire among Christians to institute a corresponding *rite de passage* ("rite of transition").[52] He speaks of the pastoral need of Christian parents to celebrate the birth of a child in a believing family, and that infant baptism originated in part because of such needs. That is, an infant baptism that was not rooted *in* circumcision, but was invented *because of* circumcision.

### 4.4.3 The Covenants in Reformed Forms

In the Heidelberg Catechism, the covenant is — apart from Q&A 68: "the New Covenant or Testament" — mentioned four times in connection with baptism (Q&A 74), and once with the Lord's Supper (Q&A 82). I limit myself to Q&A 74: "Q. Should infants also be baptized? A. Yes. Infants as well as adults are included in God's covenant and people [Gen. 17:7; Matt. 19:14], and they, no less than adults, are promised deliverance from sin through Christ's blood and the Holy Spirit who produces faith [Luke 1:15; Ps. 22:10; Isa. 44:1-3; Acts 2:38-39; 16:31]. Therefore, by baptism, the sign of the covenant, they too should be incorporated into the Christian church and distinguished from the children of unbelievers [Acts 10:47; 1 Cor. 7:14]. This was done in the Old Testament by circumcision [Gen. 17:14], which was replaced in the New Testament by baptism [Col. 2:11-13]."

Two ideas strike us here. First, the idea of continuity: to prove that children are part of the church, the text points to Genesis 17:7, where the church is not mentioned at all (the church is the Body of the glorified Christ, the dwelling place of

---

52. McGrath (1997, 459).

the poured out Spirit, and thus could not exist before Acts 2[53]). Second, the idea that baptism has replaced circumcision[54] is based on Colossians 2:11–13, which does not say anything of the kind (see Appendix I): Paul speaks of the parallel between baptism and *spiritual* circumcision (i.e., regeneration), *not* of baptism having been substituted for *physical* circumcision.[55] This is all the more important because this passage is virtually the only biblical support for the alleged link between (infant) baptism and the covenant.

The Belgic Confession (Art. 34) speaks in a similar (erroneous) vein: "We believe our children ought to be baptized and sealed with the sign of the covenant, as little children were circumcised in Israel on the basis of the same promises made to our children."

In the Canons of Dort, the covenant is mentioned nine times, usually in a correct connection with the New Covenant, and once in connection with baptism (Head 1, Art. 17): "Since we must make judgments about God's will from his Word, which testifies that the children of believers are holy, not by nature but by virtue of the gracious covenant in which they together with their parents are included, godly parents ought not to doubt the election and salvation of their children whom God calls out of this life in infancy" (with reference to Gen. 17:7; Acts 2:39; 1 Cor. 7:14).[56] That is, ordinary believers must first be made familiar with a theological construct such

---

53. See extensively chapter 7 below, and Ouweneel (2010b). There *is* no "holy congregation of true Christian believers" (Belgic Confession, Art. 27) in the Old Testament; Israel's *ekklesia* in the wilderness (Acts 7:38) had as little to do with the church (*Ekklesia*) as the *ekklesia* in the city of Ephesus (Acts 19:32, 39, 41).
54. Cf. the neat formulation by Wentsel (1995, 224): "Baptism is the Christological and pneumatic fulfillment of circumcision."
55. See extensively, Ouweneel (2011, §§6.1.2 and 6.2).
56. Versteeg (1983, 133) makes the same connection: "Even though baptism is not mentioned in 1 Cor. 7:14, the children's being sanctified in the parents makes us recognize the same covenantal structure in the New Testament dispensation as that which was present in the Old Testament dispensation." Of course, this can be "recognized" only by federalists.

as the covenant of grace before they can understand why their infants have to be baptized. The same happens three times in the classical Reformed Form for the Celebration of the Lord's Supper. Ordinary believers should be kept close to the Word, and not burdened with theological theories, which are quite controversial at that.

As may be expected, the Form for the Administration of Baptism refers to the covenant (of grace) many times, for instance, in the following typically federalist statements: "[W]hen we are baptized in the name of the Father, God the Father witnesseth and sealeth unto us, that he doth make an eternal covenant of grace with us, and adopts us for his children and heirs . . . baptism is a seal and undoubted testimony, that we have an eternal covenant of grace with God. . . . Since then baptism is come in the place of circumcision, therefore infants are to be baptized as heirs of the kingdom of God, and of his covenant. . . . [Y]ou have heard that baptism is an ordinance of God, to seal unto us and to our seed his covenant." These are interesting statements, given the fact that in Scripture baptism, though "an ordinance of God," is *never and nowhere* linked with any covenant, not even in Colossians 2:11-13 (see Appendix I). Here again, some federalist "evidence" — which, according to millions of non-Reformed Christians, is not biblical evidence at all — is imposed upon ordinary believers.[57]

Let me conclude this section with some references to another important Reformed confession, the Second Helvetic [i.e., Swiss] Confession of 1562, written by Heinrich Bullinger (Chapter 20): "[T]o be baptized in the name of Christ is to be enrolled, entered, and received into the covenant and family, and so into the inheritance of the sons of God. . . . God, who is rich in mercy, freely cleanses us from our sins by the blood of his Son, and in him adopts us to be his sons, and by

---

57. Cf. Church Order of Dort, Art. 56: "God's covenant shall be sealed for the children of Christians by baptism as soon as its administration can take place."

a holy covenant joins us to himself, and enriches us with various gifts, that we might live a new life. All these things are assured by baptism." Against the Anabaptists, the Confession says: "[A]ccording to evangelical teaching, of such [i.e., newborn infants of the faithful] is the kingdom of God, and they are in the covenant of God. Why, then, should the sign of God's covenant not be given to them?"

These statements are eminently confusing: "evangelical" here means Reformed. Apparently, in this view the Anabaptists are not "evangelical" — although in some important historical respects they can be viewed as forerunners of present-day Evangelicalism.

## 4.5 Theologizing About the Covenant
### 4.5.1 The Federalist Paradigm

As we have seen, federalism (from Latin *foedus*, "covenant") is the theological school that has made the biblical concept of the covenant the starting point and the foundation of all its theological thinking. Just like, for instance, dispensationalism (from Latin *dispensatio*, here "dispensation" in the sense of a distinct redemptive-historical epoch; cf. Eph. 1:10 [N]KJV), federalism has the character of a *paradigm*, a broad theoretical frame of thought that for its adherents carries and encompasses all their theological theory building.[58] In this sense, federalism is necessarily one-sided and limited; of many possible glasses, it chooses those that make all biblical data look covenantal, just as for dispensationalists they all look dispensational. Both federalism and dispensationalism are striking examples of how a paradigm originates within theology, how it continually develops, and thus — due to inferentialism (see §4.1.2 above) — becomes increasingly a comprehensive and closed thought system, and thus increasingly independent from Scripture. The same holds — to mention a third example — for the Roman Catholic paradigm, in which the (institutional) church plays the central and foundational role (eccle-

---

58. Regarding theological paradigms, see Ouweneel (2013, chapter 13).

siasticalism).

Reformed theologians, like most other theologians, do not like to see their theology relativized by such speaking about a covenant *paradigm*. In §1.6.3, I quoted Brown and Keele, who asserted that covenant theology "is not an abstract system imposed on the Bible, but the very structure and framework that naturally arises from Scripture itself." No paradigms for them! They are simply representing biblical truth. If the word "paradigm" is used at all it is in reference to *other* Reformed theologians with whom they do not agree. Thus, Elam, Van Kooten, and Bergquist speak of the "republication paradigm" of their opponents.[59] It does not seem to occur to them that their own brand of Reformed thinking moves within the boundaries of a theological paradigm in exactly the same way.

A theological paradigm constantly refers to itself for the "evidences" desired; insofar as it refers to Bible passages, the "evidence" is convincing only for those who have *a priori* accepted the way these verses function within the thought system. One has only to look at the Bible passages to which the confessional documents refer that were quoted in the previous section. *None* of these passages says what those who quote them want to prove; they only "say" that within the framework of the federalist thought system. The Bible verses "prove" federalism only after federalism has told us how the verses are to be read. This is nothing to worry about: it works this way in *every* paradigm, for instance, in dispensationalism, so popular among many Evangelicals, or in Roman Catholic ecclesiasticalism. It becomes a problem only when people do not realize anymore that we are dealing here with theological paradigms, but begin to tell themselves and others that *this* is what Scripture "really" teaches. They have become prisoners of their own paradigm; recall what I just said about Brown and Keele.

Moreover, no paradigm is perfect; it is always defective

---

59. Elam et al. (2014, chapters 9–11).

because it is a human-deficient piece of work. The evidence for this is that the adherents of one and the same paradigm are often constantly fighting each other. Think, for instance, of all the fights within the Reformed/Presbyterian world about the covenant of works, or the relationship between the (alleged) "covenant of works" and the (alleged) "covenant of redemption" (see §5.3.3), from the outset until this very day. The battle is bitter; the most militant fighters are even prepared to create church divisions over them. Almost all intramural Reformed church divisions in the Netherlands—and there were quite a few—involved the covenant, in some way or another, sometimes in relation to predestination. Such fights will go on forever because the combatants are never prepared to ask themselves whether their fights might be due to *weaknesses within the federalist paradigm as such*. No, the paradigm in itself is unassailable—and so the battle goes on.

An Evangelical reader might respond: Why then bother about the federalist paradigm? In answer to this, I mention four reasons.

(1) The biblical idea of the covenant, neglected by many theological schools, is definitely of great importance.

(2) We can learn from Reformed and Presbyterian theologians, for they have investigated this idea by far the most intensively.

(3) Many Christians embrace federalism (the World Alliance of Reformed Churches contains about 75 million members).

(4) Other paradigms are not doing much better; if you are searching for a perfect paradigm, you will search in vain.

Evangelicals can learn from federalists how a theological paradigm functions in practical life; they can learn from this how they can more clearly distinguish their own paradigms, as well as the weaknesses in them.

The covenant concept already played a role in patristic theology. Among other things, this was related to the development of the terms "Old" and "New Covenants," especially as a reference to what we since then call the Old and the New Testaments. Already Irenaeus and Tertullian discussed the unity between the two, as well as the differences between them.[60] However, the covenant concept never acquired that central position that it obtained within Reformed and Presbyterian Protestantism. In Roman Catholic theology, the covenant never became a separate theological topic in systematic theology; at best, it was dealt with in exegesis. Only in the newer Roman Catholic theology has it received more attention, presumably especially under the influence of Karl Barth.[61] In Lutheran theology, the covenant concept did not acquire that central position which it has in Reformed theology,[62] to say nothing about its place in Eastern Orthodox or Evangelical theology.

This is a bad sign. Elsewhere, I have warned against the problem of unique doctrines that are found only in certain theological or ecclesiastical movements, because they give such movements a sectarian flavor.[63] Thus, Reformed Christians are the only ones who believe both in the universal centrality of the covenant and in double predestination.[64] It is my solid conviction that a view that is found exclusively in one ecclesiastical movement is always—I would almost say, by definition—wrong. I do not know of any genuine divine truth that has been properly grasped in only one ecclesiastical movement, no matter how lofty this movement may be. It is only "with all the saints" that we comprehend the truth (cf. Eph. 3:18); no part of it is ever entrusted to a tiny part of world Christianity. This is why the Apostolic and the Nicene Creeds are so important, because they link together by far the most Christians.

---

60. See Ferguson (2003, passim) for what the church fathers said on the covenant, and Duncan (1998) specifically on Irenaeus and the covenant.
61. Wentsel (1970, 325–44); cf. §8.4.4.
62. See on this Graafland (1992, 30–50).
63. See Ouweneel (2010b, 459–60).
64. See Ouweneel (2008b, chapters 12 and 14).

## 4.5.2 Birth of the Paradigm

When it comes to federalist theology, the pretenses of Reformed theologians run high. Herman Bavinck wrote, "The doctrine of the covenant was most fully developed in Reformed theology."[65] The theologian Philippus van Ronkel, of Jewish origin, called the doctrine of the covenant the peculiar and particularly characteristic feature of Dutch Reformed theology, and claimed that, when Reformed theology had seen and determined this doctrine in Scripture, it was at the summit of its greatness.[66] I would prefer not to say that Scripture *contains* a doctrine of covenants; rather, such a doctrine is *developed* by theologians. Only within Reformed theology has the covenant *concept* developed into a real covenant *paradigm*, which is something quite different. Yet, one can imagine how happy a man of Jewish descent was to discover how such a typically Jewish concept as the covenant had become central to the brand of Protestantism he found all around himself in the Netherlands.

As we stated earlier, this paradigm was born of a theological conflict, especially between, on the one hand, Ulrich Zwingli[67] and John Calvin (and others, such as Heinrich Bullinger,[68] Johannes Oecolampadius, Martin Bucer[69]), and, on the other hand, the Anabaptists.[70] In certain (not all) respects, Anabaptist theology was a precursor to nineteenth-century Evangelicalism in assuming, in addition to some correspondence, also a contrast between the Old and the New Covenants (cf. chapter 7). Whereas Zwingli and Calvin emphasized the continuity between the Old and New Testaments[71] (without overlooking the differences), the Anabaptists as well as the later Evangelicals emphasized the discontinuity between the two

---

65. Bavinck (2006, 3.209).
66. See Van Ronkel (1886).
67. Graafland (1992, 17–29).
68. Ibid., 51–67; see Bullinger (1923).
69. Graafland (1992, 217–20).
70. Jonker (1988, 80–81); cf. extensively Van 't Spijker (1986); Lillback (2001).
71. See, e.g., Van der Vegt (1938); Wolf (1958).

(without overlooking the similarities).⁷² One could argue, then, that the covenant paradigm originated from the early conflict with dispensationalism even before the latter was given that name. The conflict between those two daughters of the Reformation, Calvinism and Evangelicalism, began already in the sixteenth century.

According to the South African Reformed dogmatician Willie Jonker, covenant theology is called federalism "because it uses the covenant as an ordering principle for the entire theology."⁷³ Of course, Jonker means the *notion* of the covenant, and means this not in the sense of the biblical-practical covenant *idea*, but the independently developed, theological-theoretical-logical-analytical covenant *doctrine*.⁷⁴ But apart from this, Jonker in this way implicitly hints at what a paradigm is: a theoretical framework of thought for ordering and systematizing the results of theological investigation. In the view of Reformed writer R. Scott Clark: "Covenant theology structures all of biblical revelation. . . . Covenant [read, the covenant doctrine] is the most coherent explanation for biblical revelation and the nature and authority of the canon."⁷⁵ Of course, this is the same as what adherents of dispensationalism and ecclesiasticalism claim about *their* paradigms.

The development of the covenant paradigm—the covenant doctrine as the allegedly primary and central explanatory principle in the study of the biblical truth—is not based on a simple and straightforward study of the Bible, but is indeed a *theological* development. Some men who played an essential role in this development were the English theolo-

---

72. Wellum (2006, 125) argues that federalism does not properly understand the actual relationships between the biblical covenants and the measure of continuity and discontinuity between them.
73. Jonker (1988, 82).
74. Cf. ibid.: Wellum argues that the "covenant of grace" is a constitutive *theological* category, not a biblical one (126); (cf. 160: the question of baptism is a primary test case for one's entire theological system, since it tells much about how one views the entire canon).
75. http://rscottclark.org/2012/09/theses-on-covenant-theology/

gian William Perkins (1558–1602), the German-Dutch scholar Johannes Cocceius (1603–1679; §5.3.2), the Dutch theologian Herman Witsius (1636–1708),[76] the Scottish thinker Thomas Boston (1676–1732), and the Scottish-Dutch theologian Alexander Comrie (1706–1774; §5.3.3). They developed federalism — which is something very different from "finding" the covenant doctrine in the Bible. The Bible as such contains neither doctrines, "-isms," nor theologies; these are invariably developed by theologians.

This is a point of great importance. Scholarly theories are not *found* in reality (here, Scripture) (*contra* Van Ronkel, see above), but *designed* by — in this case — theologians to account for insights and connections that they believe to have found in reality. This holds not only for theological theories, but for *all* scientific and scholarly theories. Theologians, however, usually belong to those scholars who dislike the word "theory" most, at least when it comes to *their own* theories. This is because of the naïve idea that they have *adopted* their doctrines from Scripture.[77] It was *theologians* who worked out the doctrine of the covenant into its finest details (continually quarreling about these details, until today). Perhaps Johannes Cocceius must be mentioned as the one who was the first to develop a full-fledged redemptive-historical covenant theology.[78]

In this entire process, scholasticism played a major role.[79] By this we are referring to a medieval, strongly rationalistic analysis of theological problems, in which concepts and often even thought contents (though this latter is sometimes denied) were adopted from Greek philosophers.[80] In this

---

76. See Witsius (1990).
77. See on this important matter Ouweneel (2013a, chapters 11–14).
78. Jonker (1988, 82); see especially Cocceius' *Summa doctrinae de foedere et testamento Dei* (1648).
79. Graafland (1987b; 1987c); Van der Zwaag (2003, 134–36).
80. E.g., substantialism in the doctrine of God and Christology (see Ouweneel [2007, 74–78, 294–96]) and anthropological dichotomy (see Ouweneel [2008a, chapters 6–8]).

way, a considerable gap could originate between a meticulously refined logical-analytical covenant system, on the one hand, and the direct scriptural testimony, on the other. Theodore Beza, Hieronymus Zanchius, Gisbert Voetius, and in the twentieth century in the Netherlands, Valentijn Hepp and Cornelis Steenblok, and in North America, John Murray, are well-known examples of those who helped widen this gap by adding ever new intricacies.

The evaluation of these scholastic influences in Reformed circles has been very diverse, for that matter. According to some, Reformed theology would not have survived without this scholastic "codification."[81] There certainly may be some truth in this. Theology can hardly operate without any theory building. There is nothing wrong with this; such is part and parcel of the theological handiwork. Problems arise only when these theories are elevated to the status of absolute biblical truths.

### 4.5.3  Graafland's Analysis

The Reformed theologian Cornelis Graafland (1928–2004) has written an extensive and expert study on the development of covenant doctrine within Reformed theology.[82] In this study, it is striking that he hardly enters into the question (which for my purpose is so fascinating) about *why* the covenant doctrine acquired such a central position precisely in Reformed theology, and not somewhere else. Only naïve people, who do not understand philosophy of science, will reply that Reformed theologians read the Bible better, more accurately.

Graafland gives at best a negative reason: in classical Roman Catholic theology, the covenant can hardly be found, because, among other reasons, "Israel, and thus the Old Testament covenant testimony, has not occupied an integral place in Roman Catholic theology. Because it considered the (Roman Catholic) church as the fulfilled New Testament form

---

81. Van der Zwaag (2003, 135n745).
82. Graafland (1992; 1994; 1996).

of the Old Testament Israel, and made this datum the foundation of its entire theology, we see that salvation is almost entirely merged into, and thus submerged into, the church of office and sacrament, so that for Israel and the typically Old Testament contours of salvation, which have been brought together precisely in the covenant of God, no equivalent room was left any longer."[83]

This analysis cannot satisfy me very much because Graafland apparently does not see that, first, classical Reformed theology had embraced Augustinian supersessionism[84] just as wholeheartedly as classical Roman Catholicism had done. Therefore, this can hardly be the cause of the difference. The only difference that remains is that Reformed theologians apparently pay more attention to the Old Testament (or Old Testament theology) than Roman Catholic ones. *Why* this might be so is not elucidated by Graafland.

Second, Graafland does see clearly that "the church (of office and sacrament)" has become the central ordering principle in Roman Catholic theology, under which all other matters have been subsumed, without making this a correct paradigm. However, Graafland apparently does *not* see that exactly the same holds for the covenant paradigm. If as a general ordering principle for theology Catholics chose the church, and many Evangelicals chose the dispensation, then the Reformed chose the covenant. All three movements thought (and think) they derived their paradigm from the Bible, and all three were (and are) fundamentally wrong. All three paradigms have the power—just as the Lutheran law-gospel paradigm, or the Pentecostal second-blessing paradigm, etc.—to explain the entire content of the Bible in terms of these paradigms. But this does not make any of these paradigms correct. In principle, many paradigms can do the same

---

83. Graafland (1992, 15–16).
84. See Ouweneel (2010b, 99–100). Supersessionism (substitutionalism, "replacement theology") teaches that the church, as the "spiritual Israel," has superseded ethnic Israel as the present-day covenant people of God.

job, and do this so smoothly that the adherents think: This *must* be right. Yet, this is never necessarily the case.

A little later in his argument, Graafland brings up a deeper cause for the development of the Reformed covenant doctrine, one that we have already discussed briefly: Ulrich Zwingli, the first to write extensively about the covenant, needed the covenant concept in his conflict with the Anabaptists, as we mentioned earlier: "He [i.e., Zwingli] was particularly concerned with maintaining infant baptism.[85] Over against the Anabaptists, Zwingli was forced to show its biblical legitimacy. He believed that he could do this in the strongest way by emphasizing the unity of the Old and the New Testaments. In both Testaments, we are dealing with the same salvation, in which the same people are allowed to share. Especially this last point was based by Zwingli on the covenant. . . . In this way, Zwingli arrived at making the covenant central also in the understanding of the New Testament, and thus he made it one of the main elements of his theology."[86]

From the standpoint of philosophy of science—that is, in terms of the processes commonly taking place in theory building—this line of thought is highly fascinating. Zwingli had not primarily seen and determined (see again Van Ronkel) the central meaning of the covenant in Scripture, but he needed it in his conflict with the Anabaptists. Apparently, *the starting point of infant baptism was* a priori *unassailable*. Thus, the doctrine of infant baptism is not a result of the covenant doctrine, but it is the opposite: the covenant doctrine is a result of the doctrine of infant baptism (see §4.4). In other words, designing the covenant doctrine was necessary to legitimize infant baptism, which had been taken over from Roman Catholicism and apparently was not negotiable (because of its respectable age?). Because Reformed thinkers felt that infant baptism could no longer be defended on the basis of the Catholic ecclesiastical paradigm, they had to develop a

---

85. Graafland refers to Locher (1979, 254, etc.).
86. Graafland (1992, 18–19).

new paradigm in which infant baptism could find a new legitimate place. The Catholic ecclesiastical paradigm made room for the Reformed covenant paradigm, but the central element of these paradigms, infant baptism, remained the same. The covenant doctrine was an *a posteriori* argument for something that was unassailable from the outset.

Evangelicals often have hardly any understanding of this situation. They believe that believer's baptism is "so very clear in the Bible," and cannot understand why Reformed people cling so stubbornly to infant baptism. These Evangelicals do not understand, first, that their own view of baptism is no less debatable than the view of infant baptism.[87] Second, they do not see that infant baptism is the cornerstone undergirding all of Reformed theology; pull it away, and the whole building will collapse. This does not prove, of course, that infant baptism is right; but it does prove how strongly infant baptism is interwoven with the entirety of Reformed thinking. Young Reformed people who have themselves re-baptized in some Evangelical church, and yet wish to remain Reformed, do not seem to understand this inner contradiction either.

If this is the situation, it is difficult to claim that it is the covenant doctrine that *a priori* was well established, and that infant baptism followed from it. See, for instance, the self-evidence with which Reformed writer Aart Moerkerken states: "[I]n these few drops of [baptismal] water they are allowed to see something of the eternal firmness of God's covenant . . . the unshakable faithfulness of the covenant of grace."[88] No Bible reader will ever "see" such a reality in baptism unless he has first embraced federalism—an "-ism" that was designed for this very reason: to legitimize infant baptism. Here, a theological construct rules over the simple faith of the baptized and their parents.

---

87. See extensively Ouweneel (2011, chapters 5–8).
88. Moerkerken (2004, 361).

## 4.6 Covenant Faith and Covenant Theory
### 4.6.1 Jonker on the Covenant

The fact that in Reformed covenant theology we are dealing with the development of a real paradigm, in which pre-theoretical and theoretical aspects can hardly be distinguished anymore, is clearly illustrated by South African Reformed theologian Willie Jonker (1929–2006): "[A]lready at an early stage, the covenant concept occupied an essential place in the Reformed understanding of redemptive revelation, and actually from the outset formed the ground-pattern of Reformed religion. No doubt this fact is related with the Reformed type of piety with its love for the Old Testament, in which great emphasis is put on creation and law, the communal character of salvation, and the rule of God over all domains of existence. Especially through their view of the theocratic message of the Old Testament, the early Reformed theologians came to the joyful discovery of the covenant thinking of all Scripture. . . .

"Within Reformed thinking, the truth of the covenant imposed itself automatically as a counterpart to the confession of election. Therefore, in the course of time, many Reformed theologians have spoken of the covenant as the foundation and heart of all Holy Scripture.[89] The covenant concept was soon considered to be the hermeneutical key to understanding Scripture, and has contributed to finding the covenant message also at places in Scripture where this term does not occur.[90] The result was that an encompassing covenant doctrine could be developed, which was able to clarify the entire redemptive plan of God in Christ, and to express the conviction that the relationship between God and humanity as such cannot be understood any other way than covenantally."[91]

Such a surprising argumentation, similar to what we can find with so many other covenant theologians, calls for a crit-

---

89. Here, Jonker is referring to Heppe (1958, 34).
90. Cf. Wellum (2006, 126), who points out that paedobaptists have made the covenant into a crucial organizing principle of God's relationship to us.
91. Jonker (1988, 82–83).

ical analysis. This is not necessarily because Jonker has been the most important twentieth-century covenant theologian, but because his way of reasoning is a good example of how Reformed theory-building works with respect to the covenant. I have chosen Jonker's argument as an example in order to bring to light the factors that play a role in any paradigm building. (I could also have chosen a Dutch example, such as Jan Hoek and Willem Verboom,[92] or a North American example, such as Michael Brown and Zach Keele,[93] but they are quoted often enough in the present study.)

### 4.6.2 Objections

First, at the outset of his argument Jonker had told us that Cocceius designed an encompassing redemptive-historical covenant theology, whereas *now* he tells us that theologians "came to the joyful discovery of the covenant thinking of all Scripture."[94] The question is whether they designed their covenant theology, or discovered it (a question that, by the way, holds for *all* scholarly theories, including theological ones[95]). They did not discover the Bible passages that speak of the covenant, for theologians had been familiar with them already for centuries. Much less did they discover covenant *theology* in Scripture, for (1) the Bible neither contains nor teaches any theology in the Western-academic sense of that term, and (2) if the covenant concept possessed such a universal significance in Scripture, why did non-Reformed theologians *never* see this significance? This is not because they were blind or disobedient, but because they each happened to be working, and are still working, within the framework of a different paradigm. For this is always the essence of the matter: theological paradigms and theories are designed in order

---

92. Hoek and Verboom (2010).
93. Brown and Keele (2012).
94. Cf. Van Genderen (2008, 540): "It was not until after the Reformation, however, that the church discovered the richness of the covenant"; König (2006, 438): "[T]he covenant . . . runs like a thread of gold through the entire Bible."
95. See again Ouweneel (2013, chapter 13).

to place the scriptural data in a logically coherent system, but they are not discovered in Scripture.

What Reformed theologians "joyfully discovered" was that, as soon as their covenant *paradigm* (Jonker's "hermeneutical key") had been designed, it managed to bring the scriptural data together in a logical coherence. *But this does not prove that the paradigm is true.* It only shows that it is (to a certain extent) a logically consistent paradigm. However, several other logically consistent paradigms are *a priori* conceivable, such as Roman Catholic ecclesiasticalism or Evangelical dispensationalism, which place exactly the same scriptural data in another meaningful coherence.[96] Those who prefer an ecclesiastical or a dispensationalist paradigm discover with equal joy Scripture's ecclesiastical or dispensationalist way of thinking, respectively. That is, these paradigms also work. *But this does not prove that either of these paradigms is true.* The fact that through red or blue glasses, everything *looks* red or blue, respectively, does not prove that things *are* red or blue.

The *really* interesting question is, first, which of the competing paradigms—federalist, dispensationalist, ecclesiastical, to say nothing of Eastern Orthodox, Anglican, Lutheran, Baptist, Pentecostal approaches, etc.—explains the scriptural data in the smoothest, most efficient and elegant way, using as few auxiliary hypotheses as possible to iron out the wrinkles found in each thought system, and is left with as few data as possible that cannot be explained, or can be explained only in a forced way.[97] Unfortunately, *such* investigations are hardly ever carried out—apparently because there are no objective and unprejudiced investigators who *could* perhaps carry them out.

The second question is whether the covenant really is the "foundation and heart" of all Scripture.[98] In the New Testa-

---

96. See Ouweneel (2011, chapter 14).
97. See for the truth-value of scientific theories, Ouweneel (2013, chapter 14).
98. Or, according to Woelderink (1974), the essence of Christianity; Brown and Keele (2012, 11): "[C]ovenant is the very fabric of Scripture. It is God's cho-

ment, the term occurs only a few times, mostly in Hebrews 7–13, often in a purely Old Testament sense (see for a more New Testament sense, Matt. 26:28 par.; 2 Cor. 3:6; Heb. 7:22; 8:6, 8–10; 9:15; 10:16, 29; 12:24; 13:20).[99] Jonker should rather have said that the covenant *concept* is the foundation and heart of covenant *theology*. It is therefore not correct to say that this concept is *found* at places in Scripture where the term does not occur. Jonker should have said that the efficiency of the covenant paradigm is evident from the fact that it can account for such passages in terms of the covenant concept. That is something very different. Other paradigms might account for these passages in an equally efficient way, or even in a more efficient way. For instance, dispensationalism (or ecclesiasticalism) is just as (or as little) entitled to claim that "the dispensational (or ecclesiastical) message was found also at places in Scripture where the term 'dispensation' (or 'church') does not occur." Through the glasses of all three paradigms, all relevant passages look covenantal, or dispensational, or ecclesiastical, respectively.

As far as federalism is concerned, there is clearly a measure of theological incest to be noted. It is the earlier British and Dutch divines plus their spiritual — and often even physical — descendants (in the Netherlands, North America, and South Africa in particular) who carry on the debate, within quite a narrow *discourse*. In these countries, the discussion is often painfully introverted, without much consciousness of the fact that this internal federalist debate is totally irrelevant for two billion Christians, among whom hundreds of millions are Evangelicals. Within the boundaries of the federalist paradigm, people debate down to the dot and the comma, without realizing — and often apparently without being able to imagine — that the discussion is lost on so many other Christians, because these do not share the presuppositions of federalism.

---

sen framework for the Bible."
99. Nevertheless, Van der Waal (1990, 95) speaks of the "covenantal structure of the New Testament gospel."

In order for theology to become more ecumenical, it would be very wholesome if federalists would not only carry on the internal debate but also enter into discussions with other orthodox Christians about their respective presuppositions.

The same holds, of course, for internal debates on dispensationalism, or Roman Catholics discussions on the immaculate conception of the Virgin Mary (which was accepted by neither Eastern Orthodox nor Protestant Christians), or Evangelical discussions on pre-tribulationism, or Baptist debates on the relationship between baptism and church, or Pentecostal debates on the so-called second blessing, etc. All these matters are of interest only for those who share common presuppositions—but they are debated as if the highest truth of God is at stake. And this is precisely what many of their adherents indeed earnestly believe.

## 4.7 Other Metaphors
### 4.7.1 Juridical Metaphors

Abraham Kuyper wrote that all revelation presupposes the One who reveals himself, the one to whom he reveals himself, and the relationship between the two.[100] In his opinion, this relationship would by definition be covenantal, as Gordon Spykman elucidates.[101] Grant and Wilson write: "[C]ovenant presents God's desire to enter into relationship with men and women created in his image. . . . Covenant is all about relationship between the Creator and his creation."[102] Willem Verboom, too, believes "that the relationship into which God as Creator entered with humanity as his creature, may be referred to as a covenant."[103] As if all kinds of other relationships are inconceivable! Hendrikus Berkhof, who himself lived in the federalist world of thought, rightly remarked that in the encounter between God and Israel there is more involved

---

100. Kuyper (1965, 257); quoted in Spykman (1992, 92).
101. Spykman (1992, 92, etc.).
102. Grant and Wilson (2005, 12).
103. W. Verboom in Hoek and Verboom (2010, 124).

than can be expressed in the term covenant.[104] I wish more Reformed theologians would come to this elementary insight! Berkhof mentions some other metaphors for the relationship between God and Israel, which I will briefly elaborate here.

*A juridical metaphor: the covenant relationship.* Indeed, a covenant (treaty, contract, agreement, etc.) is a strictly *juridical* metaphor, which as such does not imply affection at all. This is brought out, for example, in the definition by Gordon Hugenberger: "A covenant, in its normal sense, is an elected, as opposed to natural, relationship of obligation under oath."[105] This definition does not include *each* type of relationship, as Reformed theologians often seem to do. In particular, it excludes natural relationships, apparently like the one between parents and children (§4.7.3). Moreover, notice the formal (juridical) character of a covenant: a "relationship of obligation under oath."

The word "elected" in the definition implies that the parties have chosen for each other. Especially in parity covenants, one party voluntarily takes the initiative, and the other voluntarily accepts the proposal. The true basis for human covenants is usually some form of self-interest ("you scratch my back, and I'll scratch yours"). Of course, there is affection in God's covenant with Israel (Deut. 7:9; Neh. 1:5; Isa. 56:6; Ezek. 16:8; Dan. 9:4), just as there is affection in the marriage covenant (Mal. 2:14). But with this difference: affection is proper to marriages as such, but not to covenants as such. I know no better way to describe this state of affairs than in Reformational-philosophical terms: a covenant is qualified by the juridical modality of cosmic reality—in other words: it finds its "destination" in the juridical modality—but also always functions in all other modalities, such as the ethical or love modality. However, according to its own nature, or internal destination function, it is juridical, not ethical. With marriage

---

104. Berkhof (1991, 230).
105. Hugenberger (1994, 11).

it is very different; see below (§4.7.4).[106]

Brown and Keele offer an excellent example of failing to understand these distinctions.[107] They are federalists, which means that they believe they can "see" the covenant everywhere in Scripture; they even "see" a "sinful covenant between Satan and the woman [Eve]."[108] This seems to me way over the top. There was hardly anything like a relationship between Eve and Satan, much less a covenant. Apparently for Brown and Keele, not just every relation, but even every conversation is covenantal.

Such a comprehensiveness is possible only by making the definition of covenant as wide as they can: "a covenant can be an agreement of just about any sort." Thus, Brown and Keele rightly describe a covenant as a formal agreement that creates a relationship with legal aspects, but they immediately include husband-wife and government-citizen relationships. Here is where they go wrong. They do not see that although all social relationships have legal aspects, *this does not make them all covenantal*. Only those relationships are covenantal that are *qualified* by the legal aspect, and even then such relationships are not always covenantal. For instance, the relationship between government and citizens has, of course, legal aspects, but it is rather absurd, or at least very unusual, to say that there is a covenant between the two. I will return to Brown and Keele's view in the next sections.

Reformed author Clarence Stam seems to follow another course: "Specific privileges and duties are *officially* acknowledged. It is important, when speaking of the covenant, to recognize this legal, official character. Sometimes the adjective *forensic* is used in connection with the covenant in order to show that it has been judicially (lawfully) established and is fully binding for all the partners."[109] So far so good. However,

---

106. See extensively Ouweneel (2014).
107. Brown and Keele (2012, 11–12).
108. Ibid., 61.
109. Stam (1999, 26).

a few pages later he says, "All this allows us to define the covenant which God makes with his people. It is not first of all a formal contract, but a *living relationship* in which two partners, God and his people, constantly interact."[110] What he had rightly emphasized earlier—the forensic, judicial character of a covenant—now disappears into the background. Another element, which does *not* strictly belong to the character of a covenant as such, comes to the fore: a covenant allegedly is a "living relationship."

In Scripture the covenants may *function* as living relationships between God and his people, but that is not part of the definition of a covenant. It only confuses the picture because it contributes to covenantalizing the Bible. Some—not all—covenants function as living relationships, but that does not mean that all living relationships are covenants. The living relationship between a man and his beloved dog is not covenantal. The living relationship between two friendly neighbors is not covenantal. The living relationship between children in the same school class is not covenantal. Federalists do not see that by labeling *all* relationships covenantal they turn the covenant into a hollow, empty concept. If everything is covenantal, then nothing is covenantal, because the term has no specific meaning anymore.

### 4.7.2 A Juridical and a Social-Economic Metaphor

In addition to the previous one, we may mention differently qualified relationships, which are just as important as the covenantal (juridically qualified) relationship, and in some cases perhaps even more important (compare this to the Reformed covenant view, which recognizes only the covenantal relationships, and subsumes all other possible relationships under this one.)

Let me first mention another juridical, but non-covenantal metaphor. It is that of people as God's *agents* or *representatives* on earth. God's people are by definition his representatives in

---
110. Ibid., 29.

this world: ". . . children of God without blemish in the midst of a crooked and twisted generation, among whom you shine as lights in the world" (Phil. 2:15). The relationship between the one who is representing and the one who is represented does not have to be covenantal (contractual) at all. Something of this resounds in Israel's calling as described in Romans 2:19-20, "[A] guide to the blind, a light to those who are in darkness, an instructor of the foolish, a teacher of children, having in the law the embodiment of knowledge and truth." Of course, these functions of Israel are related to the latter's covenant with God, but as such they are not covenantal at all, nor do they necessarily demand, or follow from, a covenantal relationship.

One social-economic metaphor is that of *master* and *servant*. Someone may make a covenant with his servant or slave, like a king may do with his vassals; but that does not mean that the master-servant/slave relationship *as such* possesses a covenantal character. God said to his people, "Israel, my servant, Jacob, whom I have chosen" (Isa. 41:8). "Remember these things, O Jacob, and Israel, for you are my servant; I formed you; you are my servant" (44:21; also see Isa. 44:1-2; 45:4; 48:20; 49:3; Jer. 30:10; 46:27-28; Ezek. 28:25; 37:25; Mal. 1:6). This Master-servant/slave relationship is as such not covenantal at all, nor does it necessarily demand, or follow from, a covenantal relationship.

"For just as you once presented your members as slaves to impurity and to lawlessness leading to more lawlessness, so now present your members as slaves to righteousness leading to sanctification. For when you were slaves of sin, you were free in regard to righteousness. . . . But now that you have been set free from sin and have become slaves of God, the fruit you get leads to sanctification and its end, eternal life" (Rom. 6:19-22). In such a description there is nothing that by itself is necessarily of a covenantal character.

### 4.7.3 An Ethical Metaphor: Father–Child

I turn now to discuss two ethical metaphors,[111] the first being the *father-child relationship*. This is the one that has the least in common with a covenantal relationship, since it is not based on contract but on birth.[112] Even before God made a covenant with Israel, he called the people his "firstborn son" (Exod. 4:22; cf. Deut. 1:31; 8:5). "When Israel was a child, I loved him, and out of Egypt I called my son" (Hos. 11:1). He also called the Israelites "sons" of the LORD, their God (Deut. 14:1); "in the place where it was said to them, 'You are not my people,' it shall be said to them, 'Children of the living God'" (Hos. 1:10). Of course, fathers may make covenants with their children, if they so wish. But the father-child relationship as such is not covenantal at all, nor does it necessarily arise from the covenantal relationship. It is a very different, in fact much deeper, relationship of filiation and affection. One may argue that wherever the covenantal relationship is overemphasized, the father–child relationship is neglected.[113]

Clarence Stam speaks of "the covenant which God in his love establishes and maintains with his children."[114] Of course, I understand his intention, yet this is a mixture of metaphors. The Bible does not know of fathers making covenants with their children. What comes closest is the covenant between Laban and Jacob—father-in-law and son-in-law—in Genesis 31:44-54, a covenant based on mistrust. The fact that the Israelites are sometimes called "children of God" does not mean that God made his covenant with the people in his role of Father. God is the King who made a covenant with his vassals or servants; he is a Father who entered into an intimate love relationship with his children. That is an utterly different matter.

Willem Verboom says: "The God of the covenant is the

---

111. See on both McCarthy (1978).
112. *Contra* Hahn (2009), who sees the Father-son bond between God and his people as characteristic of the covenant.
113. See about this Ouweneel (2010a, 112–16).
114. Stam (1999, 7).

God who promises much. God promises to fallen people his salvation, which consists in the adoption as children."[115] Here we see the overwhelming power of the covenant paradigm: in Scripture, the covenant as such is nowhere linked with such an adoption. I just argued that the covenantal relationship is even essentially different from the father–child relationship. Even if God calls his covenant partner Israel his "son," this does not mean that the two relationships are identical, nor that the one presupposes, or demands, or arises from, the other. One could even argue the reverse: the covenantal relationship is one of the many relationships that are all subsumed under the one father-child relationship.

With Cornelis van der Waal we encounter the same semantic problem, this time with respect to a consequence of the father-son relationship: the relationship between "brothers" (sons of the same father). Sometimes, covenant partners refer to each other as "brothers." For instance, king Hiram of Tyre called his covenant partner, king Solomon, "my brother" (1 Kgs 9:13). King Ahab did the same with respect to king Ben-hadad (20:32), Ben-hadad responded to this ("Yes, your brother Ben-hadad," v. 33), and the two made a covenant (v. 34). Now listen to Van der Waal's conclusion: "The word 'brother,' which also occurs in the same way in the New Testament, is not just a neutral term: it presumes a covenant relationship."[116]

There are two different logical fallacies here. First, "all covenant partners are brothers, therefore, brothers are covenant partners." For a comparison, consider this claim: birds can walk, so all walking organisms are birds (class A exhibits feature P, so those exhibiting P fall in class A). The fact that covenant partners are sometimes called brothers does not mean that all brothers are covenant partners.

The second fallacy is this. Under the New Covenant, believers are called each other's "brothers (and sisters)." But

---
115. Verboom (2009, 37).
116. Van der Waal (1990, 13).

they are not each other's covenant partners; on the contrary, together they form one covenant party. Two covenant partners may call each other "brothers," but if one of the partners is an entire people, it does not mean that the members of that people are now also brothers *of each other*. From the brotherhood of two covenant partners, Van der Waal smoothly moves to brotherhood *within* God's people, which is something totally different.

Moreover, "brotherhood" in the New Testament is *never* linked with a covenantal relationship. On the contrary, it is a typical *familial* relationship. There was no covenant between Shem, Ham, and Japheth, yet they were brothers, for they had the same father. There was no covenant between Abraham, Nahor, and Haran, yet they were brothers, for they had the same father. It is *not* true that brotherhood implies a covenantal relationship. Jesus-believers are called brothers and sisters because they are children of the same Father (John 20:17; Rom. 8:29); it is *the* Son of the Father who calls them "brothers and sisters" (Heb. 2:11, margin). Even if this were a facet of the New Covenant, this does not mean that on the basis of this covenant, New Testament Jesus-believers are covenant partners *of each other*. Under the New Covenant, God and his people are covenant partners, but that is something very different from a covenant between believers and believers. Just like Verboom, Van der Waal is a victim of pervasive covenantalizing: "seeing" covenants even where they do not exist.

Elsewhere, Van der Waal writes: "Also when we talk about the covenant in the New Testament, we will meet these same [covenantal] terms: oath, brother, servant/slave, evidence/witness, token, messengers/ambassadors/apostles, mercy/grace, peace. This gives us all the more reason to not only look for the use of the word 'covenant' where the New Testament is concerned, but to also pay attention to other terms, related to the covenant!"[117] It is the same logical flaw once again: sometimes these terms are associated with covenants, but this does not mean that wherever they occur they *always* imply a covenantal relationship. Not all witnesses, tokens, apostles, mercy, peace, etc. are *covenantal* witnesses, tokens, apostles, mercy, or peace. Just try to prove that every example of divine grace, mercy, or peace in the Bible is covenantal grace, mercy, or peace. This is true only for those who *a priori* have already adopted the covenant paradigm.

Brown and Keele, too, call the parent-child relationship covenantal, and again this is highly unusual.[118] Their argument is very simple. The parent-child relationship has legal aspects—which is undoubtedly true—and therefore this relationship is supposedly covenantal. It is the well-known logical flaw: all dogs are carnivores, all cats are carnivores, so dogs are cats (all A's are P, all B's are P, therefore all A's are B's). In this case: covenants have legal aspects, parent-child relationships have legal aspects, so the latter are covenants. The flaw is quite transparent; but because Brown and Keele are under strong pressure to see covenants everywhere, they do not perceive this flaw.

Even Baptist Peter Gentry, though no federalist, says: "There is a covenant relationship between father [Jacob] and son [Joseph], since family relationships are covenantal in the Old Testament."[119] I do not see where he supplies us with biblical evidence for this daring statement. His only argument is the presence of the key terms *hesed* and *emet* in Genesis 47:29–30. It is true that *hesed* is a quintessentially covenantal term; but this does not mean, of course, that wherever we find the term we are thereby dealing with a covenantal relationship. For instance, *hesed* may be a general term for love (Hos. 4:1; Zech. 7:9), or for loyalty between friends (2 Sam. 16:17; Job

---

117. Ibid., 17; he even calls "(to) sin," and "good" and "evil," covenantal terms (43, 49).
118. Brown and Keele (2012, 11–12).
119. Gentry (2012, 142).

6:14; unless one declares all friendships to be covenants), or the kindness of a righteous person (Ps. 141:5), or of a king toward subjects (2 Sam. 9:3; 1 Kgs 20:31; Esther 2:9; Dan. 1:9), or of a good man or woman (Prov. 11:17; 31:26), or of someone to his relatives (Gen. 24:49) or to a helper (Josh. 2:14). None of these examples of *hesed* necessarily presupposes a covenantal relationship.

### 4.7.4 Another Ethical Metaphor: Husband–Wife

The second ethical metaphor is the *husband–wife relationship*. It is true that marriage is sometimes compared with a covenant (Prov. 2:17; Ezek. 16:8; Mal. 2:14), and that the covenant is sometimes compared with a marriage (e.g., Isa. 54:6-10; Ezek. 16:8; cf. Hos. 1-3). But notice what I stated earlier: marriage has a juridical aspect—just like all things do—but as such it is *qualified* by the ethical modality; and a covenant has an ethical aspect—just like all things do—but as such it is *qualified* by the juridical modality. In other words, a marriage is a form of contract, but as a relationship of love it highly surpasses this contractual aspect. Likewise, God's love relationship with Israel is as such not covenantal, nor does it presuppose, or demand, or follow from, the covenantal relationship. God made a covenant with Israel because he loved it (Deut. 7), but that does not mean that a covenantal relationship as such is a love relationship. It is not. Federalism suffers from a pervasive confusion of metaphors.

Instead of the juridical covenant doctrine, one could imagine just as well that Reformed theology would have developed a very different, social-economic, or even better: an ethical paradigm, depending on the theological or ecclesiastical challenges it would have encountered, or on the inner dynamics of its own internal development. It may even be presumed that Reformed federalism developed especially because its greatest non-Catholic challenge happened to be the baptismal doctrine of the Anabaptists. How would Reformed theology have developed if it had been confronted with a very different challenge, for instance, a denial of the divine Father-child relationship? In that case, it might have become, not a covenant, but a Father-child theology, which in fact would have been loftier.

Only federalists could ever have invented the idea of making this husband-wife metaphor and other metaphors subservient to the covenant metaphor, which is fully arbitrary. Thus, for instance, Jan Hoek says, "The word 'covenant' is found only at a few places in the Gospels. However, we should add immediately that the New Testament notions of *koinonia* (fellowship), *basileia* (kingdom of royalty) and *ekklēsiai* (church) continue the notion of *berith*."[120] But according to what objective criteria is this a more correct statement than the one in which, for instance, the covenant is made subservient to the kingdom or the church? Hoek suggests that everything is covenant, including fellowship, kingdom, and church. I myself might suggest that everything is kingdom, including fellowship, church, and covenant; or that everything is church, including fellowship, kingdom, and covenant. This depends only on where people theologically choose their starting point. Such suggestions are plausible only for those who already work within the same paradigm.

---

120. J. Hoek in Hoek and Verboom (2010, 33), with reference to A. Houtepen in Noort et al. (1989, 148).

# Chapter 5
# Reformed Covenant Theology: History

*I will establish my covenant between me and you*
    *and your offspring after you*
        *throughout their generations*
*for an everlasting covenant,*
    *to be God to you*
        *and to your offspring after you.*
*And I will give to you*
    *and to your offspring after you*
*the land of your sojournings,*
    *all the land of Canaan,*
*for an everlasting possession,*
    *and I will be their God . . .*
*As for you, you shall keep my covenant,*
    *you and your offspring after you*
        *throughout their generations.*
                      Genesis 17:7–9

**Summary:** *The power of the covenant paradigm is great: many Reformed thinkers (Kuyper, Bavinck, Ridderbos, Heyns, Wentsel, Hoek, Verboom, and many others) have shown how the Scriptures look if you see them through covenantal glasses. Willie Jonker has described the development of the covenant paradigm in a fascinating* *way, in which he unconsciously showed how such a paradigmatic development takes place. For instance: what came first, Reformed covenant theology or the Reformed (covenantal) "type of piety"? This development is briefly compared with that of other theological paradigms, such as ecclesiasticalism, dispensationalism, and epangelicalism. Special attention is given to some early covenant thinkers (Calvin, Cocceius, Comrie, Van Limborch, de Labadie) and their views; for instance, are there two, or three, or even four covenants? What is the relationship between covenant and predestination? Or between divine sovereign grace and human responsibility? And how do non-Reformed Evangelicals feel about these matters?*

## 5.1 "Covenant Glasses"
### 5.1.1 Introduction

AS WE HAVE SEEN, according to federalists all covenants arising after the fall are nothing but distinct forms of the one covenant of grace, as it is called, that is, from the divine promise (*protoevangelium*) reaching from Genesis 3:15 to the New Covenant. Basically therefore, there is only one covenant people, which consists of all those who, from before the foundation of the world, have been elected by God for eternal salvation.[1] In this matter, federalists are divided over the question whether the covenant people consist of only the elect, or the elect with their children (some of whom later turn out to be non-elect). In other words: (a) are there two kinds of members of the covenant, elect and non-elect, or is there only one kind of member of the covenant, namely, *either* (b) all those to whom the covenantal promises have been made at infant baptism,[2] *or* (c) only the elect children? These are *three* different views initially; we will encounter more.

If federalists who hold opinion (c) were consistent, they would have to wait with baptism until it has become suffi-

---

1. Cf. Brown and Keele (2012, 58): "The covenant of grace is the one covenant through which all believers are saved." Hahn (2009, book title): God's covenants are about "God's Saving Purposes."
2. Cf. Van Genderen (2008, 542–44); cf. the fierce attack on this view by Kersten (1947, I, 311, etc.).

ciently probable from the faith of those who are to be baptized that they belong to the elect.[3] Those holding to believers' baptism are way beyond this kind of conflicting question because they do not link baptism with the covenant (but especially with the kingdom of God, which is a totally different line of thinking, although some federalists might deny that). Actually, those holding to believers' baptism have their own problems—there are no theological views without problems—such as: do the infants of the believers belong to the Body of Christ, or not? If yes, in what way and on what basis? If no, in what way do the not-yet-believing children of the believers belong to the community of believers?[4]

As we stated earlier, the enormous, and—humanly speaking—in every way respectable, construct of Reformed theology is like an ellipse with two focal points: predestination and the covenant. In this paradigm, with its strong idea of continuity and comprehensiveness, there is since the fall only one covenant of grace,[5] and therefore only one covenantal community: the church existing from Adam to the last day.[6] Federalism is therefore necessarily linked with the thought that the church is spiritual Israel, and thus with supersessionism, that is, the doctrine that the (New Testament) church has superseded ethnic Israel. The ecclesiological and eschatological consequences of this approach are gigantic, as we will see (especially in chapter 7).[7]

### 5.1.2 Herman Bavinck

Let me now give some striking examples of the covenantal

---

3. Cf. Wellum (2006, 107–109).
4. Cf. Ouweneel (2011, chapters 5–8).
5. Van Genderen (2008, 563): "... the covenant of grace is essentially the same covenant in all dispensations," an assertion that he uses as an argument for the unfounded claim that "the" covenant is always about believers *and* their children. See below in the text.
6. A clear introduction to this argumentation is found in Wentsel (1995, 224–31).
7. Also see Ouweneel (2010b; 2011; 2012).

glasses, which make the one wearing them see every Bible passage as covenantal. I already mentioned Abraham Kuyper as a first example (see §4.7.1). A second example of covenantal glasses is found with Herman Bavinck, who wrote for instance: "Among rational and moral creatures all higher life takes the form of a covenant. . . . Love, friendship, marriage, as well as all social cooperation in business, industry, science, art, and so forth, is ultimately grounded in a covenant, that is, in reciprocal fidelity and an assortment of generally recognized moral obligations. It should not surprise us, therefore, that also the highest and most richly textured life of human beings, namely, religion, bears this character. In Scripture 'covenant' is the fixed form in which the relation of God to his people is depicted and presented."[8]

In this quotation, the term covenant is generalized in such a way that it is declared to be applicable to every form of agreement that exist between people. The errors committed by Bavinck here are immediately obvious. First, *not* all human agreements are of a covenantal, and thus juridical, nature: many contracts, such as commercial and employment contracts, do not have a covenantal character at all—unless we fall into the circular argument mentioned earlier: covenantal is *a priori* declared to be identical with contractual, or even wider: relational. The argument then amounts to saying this: covenantal is the same as relational; therefore, all relationships are covenantal. Such reasoning does not help us at all.

Second, many human relationships (love, friendship, science, art) are not based on agreements at all. Of course, people who love each other, or work together, often come to agreements. But first, not all agreements are covenantal. And second, the proper nature of their love, their cooperation, their relationship, does not lie in these agreements, that is, is not juridically qualified. Again: Bavinck calls any conceivable relationship between people a covenant, and then concludes

---

8. Bavinck (2004, 2.568–69).

that covenants are a comprehensive matter.

What happens here is a well-known phenomenon: a concept that in itself is perhaps scientifically useful to a certain extent is absolutized and generalized. In this way, covenant theology became a true federal*ism*. Think again of the two most important vertical relationships that exist between God and believers: first, the Father–child relationship, and second, in the Body of Christ, the relationship between Head and Body, and between the members. Neither relationship is based on a contractual agreement, much less on a covenant. These very metaphors (parents and children, a body with a head and members) do not allow for the notion of contracts, treaties, agreements, in short: covenants.

We could take this one step further: by far the most frequently used metaphors for the church in the New Testament—a city, a house with stones, a family with members, a body with members, an army with soldiers, a chandler, a flock, a field, a vine or vineyard, a mother[9]—have nothing whatsoever to do with covenantal relationships. In the case of the church as bride or wife of Christ one could, by analogy with Israel, bring in the covenant metaphor, but I previously referred to a covenant as a *juridical* contract, and to marriage as an *ethical* relationship.

Even the relationship between God and the church as the people of God does not necessarily have to be covenantal. The kings of Israel or Judah could call Israel "my people" because they reigned over them (e.g., 2 Sam. 22:44; 1 Kgs 22:4; 2 Kgs 3:7; 1 Chron. 28:2; 29:14), but this does not necessarily imply a covenant between these kings and their subjects. To be sure, in §2.1.2 we found several examples of a covenant that was literally made between the leader (Joshua, David, Joash) and the people of Israel. But, first, such a covenant was not necessarily implied in the relationship as such between the leader and the people; the king could have said "my people" before

---

9. See extensively Ouweneel (2010b, chapters 4–5).

any such covenant was made. Second, in such cases it actually always concerned a covenant with the LORD; in §2.1.2, I called these "horizontal" covenants that were subservient to the "vertical" covenant between God and Israel. The point I want to make is that the fact that Israel was God's people did as such not necessarily presuppose a covenantal relationship. This is illustrated by the fact that God called them "my people" even before he had made any covenant with them (Exod. 3:7, 10; 5:1; 7:4, 16; etc.).

In summary, we conclude that it is simply *not* true that a covenant is the most characteristic metaphor to describe the relationship between God and his church. This idea follows neither from the scriptural data nor from any inner (theo) logical argumentation. It is based on nothing but these two "-isms" mentioned before: pervasive covenantalizing and inferentialism by federalists.

Another example from Bavinck is this one: "From the very first moment of its revelation, grace assumes the form of a covenant that arises not by a natural process, but by a historical act and hence gives rise to a rich history of grace. This covenant of grace already begins immediately after the fall."[10] For this claim, not a single proof is given, nor *can* any be given; Bavinck merely recognizes that the word "covenant" is not yet mentioned in Genesis 3.[11] The "covenant of grace" is a theological construction, which here is simply *a posteriori* read into the biblical text.

### 5.1.3 Herman Ridderbos

A third example of using covenantal glasses is found with Reformed theologian Herman Ridderbos, who wrote: "To be sure, he [i.e., Paul] speaks only in a few places explicitly of the New Covenant, namely, in 1 Corinthians 11:25 and 2 Corinthians 3:6ff., but it has frequently been pointed out rightly that the idea of the New Covenant in Paul's conception of the

---

10. Bavinck (2004, 2.197).
11. Ibid., 200.

New Testament church and the salvation given to it plays a much greater role than may be gathered from the sparing use of this datum of revelation and from the slight attention that has been paid to it in the history of [theological] interpretation."[12]

But this is precisely what is to be demonstrated! Federalists see "the" covenant everywhere in Scripture, including on every page of Paul's epistles. But that does not prove it *is* there. It is there only if one is wearing covenant glasses.

Moreover, Ridderbos' arguments are not valid. For instance, he points to Romans 2:28-29, where Paul says: "For no one is a Jew who is merely one outwardly, nor is circumcision outward and physical. But a Jew is one inwardly, and circumcision is a matter of the heart, by the Spirit, not by the letter." Ridderbos concludes from this statement that every true member of the covenant would be a "Jew."[13] This is mistaken. In the passage mentioned, Paul is dealing with the question what is a "true Jew," in contrast with someone who is of Jewish descent and has been circumcised, but has no renewed heart. The status of non-Jews is not at all Paul's subject here; therefore no conclusions as to the status of believing Gentiles can be drawn in this instance.[14] The well-known logical flaw in Ridderbos' argument is this: being spiritually circumcised is a property of both believing Jews and believing Gentiles; therefore, believing Gentiles are Jews. This is like arguing that since cats and dogs both have ears, therefore, cats are dogs (A is a property of both B and C, therefore B = C).

This does not work. The New Testament *never* calls Gentile Christians "Jews" or "Israel," as we will see extensively in chapter 7. The following is just a little foretaste.

(a) Spiritually, all Jesus-believers are circumcised (Phil. 3:3; Col. 2:11), but that does not give Gentile Christians the right

---

12. Ridderbos (1975, 335), with reference to Van Unnik (1960, 98, 118); thus, earlier, Ridderbos (1962, 192-94).
13. Ridderbos (1975, 334–36).
14. See Ouweneel (2010b, 102).

to call themselves Israel. It is exactly the same logical flaw as mentioned above: Jewish and Gentile believers are both spiritually circumcised, but that does not mean that Gentile believers are now Jewish.

(b) Ephesians 2:11-22 and 3:3-11 do *not* say that believing Gentiles have joined the "commonwealth of Israel," on the contrary: believing Gentiles and believing Jews now form something entirely new: the Body of Christ, unified with its glorified Head at the right hand of God.

(c) In Galatians 6:16, the "Israel of God" is *not* necessarily the church; on the contrary, they are distinguished from "all who walk by" the rule of the new creation, which according to the context must be the Gentile believers. For further discussion of this, see chapter 7 below.

### 5.1.4 Johan Heyns

A fourth striking example of looking through covenantal glasses is offered by South African Reformed theologian Johan Heyns: "The covenant is inclusive, that is to say: just about all aspects of God's dealings with humanity come, to a greater or lesser extent, in some way or another, within our purview whenever the covenant is discussed.... For the entire revelation is determined by the covenant, so that every subject or *locus* in dogmatics exhibits a covenantal perspective. If things are understood this way, we ought to have dealt with the covenant already in our doctrine of creation, for human beings, as God's image-bearing creatures, were created for covenantal communion. From the first moments of their existence on earth, they therefore were destined for and included in a covenantal relationship with God."[15]

It is scarcely possible to imagine a better example of the power of a paradigm: Heyns' eyes see the covenant in every Bible passage, whereas Genesis does not speak a word about a covenant relationship between God and the first pair of humans. It is not even true that the relationship between

---
15. Heyns (1988, 200).

God and humanity is above all covenantal; the Father–child relationship as well as the relationship between the glorified Head and his Body, are both different and in fact more elevated than any type of contract or agreement. Thus, the relationship between God and Israel is more than just covenantal.

In the alleged extension of the federalist paradigm, Heyns indeed goes very far: "It is here, in the covenant of grace, that the heart of the biblical message of atonement is beating."[16] And a bit later: "Even the intertrinitarian relationship of the three Persons" is "a federal [i.e., covenantal] relationship" — without even an attempt to undergird such a bold (and unwarranted) statement in a scriptural way.[17] There *is* no such argument, for the relationship between the three divine Persons is an ontic and a love relationship rather than a contractual relationship (John 3:35; 5:20; 10:17; 15:9–10; 17:24, 26; Rom. 15:30; Col. 1:13). Love and covenant do not have to exclude each other, but they are not identical either. Later, we will enter more deeply into this idea of a covenantal relationship between divine persons.

Several pages later, Heyns writes: "[I]t is obvious that each consideration of the church without the covenant degrades the church to a content-less historical form," and: the church is "the way the covenant is given an institutional, cultic-liturgical form" — whereas no single Bible passage provides an explicit link between church and covenant.[18] Imagine: according to Heyns, either the church is covenantal or church is a content-less notion! It is the covenant or nothing. This is the summit of inferential thinking. Heyns loses himself here in paradigmatic *hybris*.

One would not even *like* such statements to be true. I can very well imagine "the church without the covenant." This is because the New Testament never directly links the church as such — according to its collective aspect (Body of Christ,

---

16. Heyns (1988, 210).
17. Ibid., 216.
18. Heyns (1988, 226–27).

Temple of God, Bride of the Lamb) — with the (New) covenant. Even less does it identify the church with the New Covenant people of God; on the contrary, Hebrews 8:8, 10 quotes from Jeremiah 31:31 that the New Covenant is made with Israel. To be sure, the individual members of the church are under the blessed umbrella of the New Covenant through the blood of Jesus. However, viewed as *church*, the love relationship of the Bride to her heavenly Bridegroom, or of the Body to its glorified Head, is infinitely more lofty than any form of contract or agreement can express. See again chapter 7 for a more extensive treatment of this important subject.

### 5.1.5 Other Voices

Ben Wentsel calls the covenant a central concept in Scripture, one of the most fitting hermeneutical keys, perhaps even the only correct key, to open Scripture.[19] He believes concerning the covenant doctrine that "its breadth, bearing, dynamics, and strength are operative in every [Bible] text, just as the blood is pressed throughout the entire body, all the way to the fingertips. Therefore, the covenant may not become the slogan of one current in the church, or the characteristic of one modality, or the specialty of one group of churches: it is an essential-biblical, and thus an essential-catholic, ecumenical heritage granted to the church as a whole."

Wentsel exaggerates here even more strongly than Heyns did. Only Reformed Christians accept what Wentsel writes here, and they do not comprise even three percent of all Christians worldwide. It is therefore quite pretentious to call the Reformed covenant doctrine "essential-catholic" and "ecumenical." This is another typical example of how the theoretical, and necessarily tentative, character of a paradigm is not recognized but is elevated to the status of absolute truth, and leads to a measure of theological *hybris*.

To be sure, other Christian schools of thought have sometimes done precisely the same with *their* respective paradigms.

---
19. Wentsel (1987, 209).

If you are a Roman Catholic, all Bible verses are colored by your ecclesiastical paradigm; if you are a dispensationalist, all Bible verses look dispensational; and if you are an epangelicalist, all Bible verses look epangelical. (Epangelicalism is the "promise theology" of Walter Kaiser, Jr.[20]) In fact, there is not much wrong with such an attitude; a theology without a paradigmatic framework is hardly conceivable. The only problem is that so often this paradigmatic character is not recognized, so that covenantal thinking, or ecclesiastical thinking, or dispensationalist thinking, or epangelicalist thinking, is sold as "plain biblical truth," or even "essential-biblical, and thus essential-catholic, ecumenical" truth. Look through my glasses, and you will easily see that *I* am right.

Recently, Reformed theologians Jan Hoek and Willem Verboom, too, wrote that "the covenant takes up such an important place in Holy Scripture. The message of all Scripture can be characterized as covenantal. According to Reformed understanding, the covenant can even be called the basis for church and faith."[21] Here we encounter the covenantal glasses again: they see the covenant in *all* (!) Scripture. At the same time, Hoek and Verboom implicitly recognize that indeed we are dealing here with glasses when they add the words, "according to Reformed understanding." This is a wise and humble addition, from which other federalists, as well as ecclesiasticalists and dispensationalists, can learn. It implies that, in principle, other ways of understanding are conceivable, according to which the message of all Scripture can be characterized very differently — for instance, in a Catholic-ecclesiastical or dispensational or epangelical (or in a Lutheran, or a Baptist, or a Pentecostal) way.

## 5.2 "Type of Piety"
### 5.2.1 What Was First?

We come now to the third point in South African theologian

---

20. See Kaiser (1970; 1978; 1987).
21. Hoek and Verboom (2010, 7).

Willie Jonker's reasoning (see the previous chapter for the previous two points). Jonker has told us earlier that covenant theology originated from a *theological* conflict, namely, with the Anabaptists.[22] However, in the passage that I quoted from Jonker (in §4.6.1 above), he claimed that the covenant concept was primarily a *pre-theoretical* element in what I would call the Reformed worldview, and even "the ground-pattern of Reformed *religion*," related to the Reformed "type of piety." This suggests that there is a kind of Reformed *ground-motive* — a driving force, governing the heart and from there, all of human life[23] — of which the covenant idea would form an essential element.

However, the fundamental question is what came first. Was the Reformed covenant theology born of some Reformed worldview, or even of some Reformed ground-motive, *or* is covenant theology one of the theologies produced by the general ground-motive of the Reformation, and has this in its turn produced a kind of Reformed piety? What was first: the Reformed worldview and piety, *or* the Reformed covenant theology? By far the most likely answer is: the latter — or at best the two developed hand in hand. At any rate, there never was a Reformed piety that logically — or even chronologically — preceded Reformed federalism. To a certain extent, already John Calvin was a covenant theologian; federalism existed virtually from the Reformed beginnings. There was not *a priori* some Reformed piety that could be historically and theologically considered apart from covenant theology.

Moreover, is there not already too much "theology" present in Jonker's description of the Reformed "type of piety" (emphasis on creation, the law, the community, God's dominion)? Apart from this, when it is really a matter of the Christian ground-motive, of our piety, is there really something like a typically *Reformed* type of piety? Are we not dealing instead with a (Protestant-)Christian type of piety, which only

---

22. Jonker (1988, 80–81).
23. Ouweneel (2013, §13.3; 2014a, chapter 2).

secondarily receives its specific Reformed "form" through the Reformed covenant *theology*? It is obvious that theological theories leave their traces in the everyday life of faith, particularly in more educated circles. But that does not in the least change the fact that our faith—in its transcendent-religious meaning[24]—as well as our (pre-rational) Protestant-Christian ground-motive and our (rational, pre-theoretical) worldview have to be carefully distinguished from our theological-theoretical paradigms and theories.[25]

### 5.2.2 Three "-isms"

It seems obvious that a federalist (just like an ecclesiasticalist or a dispensationalist or an epangelicalist) paradigm is never a product of some "type of piety" or some "Reformed (or Catholic, or Evangelical) religion." Our pre-theoretical understanding of Scripture may certainly be a source of inspiration for designing theological theories. But scientific and scholarly theories as such are primarily—to speak with philosopher Karl Popper—"free creations of our own minds,"[26] though designed to account for such empirical facts. As such, theological theories are certainly designed to approximate the truth concerning the respective fields of investigation. But that does not change the fact that they are designed. I repeat this very important point: theological theories are not discovered in the Bible, for the simple reason that the Bible does not contain theological theories; they therefore cannot be drawn out of the Bible.

Reformed federalism, Roman Catholic ecclesiasticism, dispensationalism, and epangelicalism are human constructs, which as such are imposed on the Bible. In itself, this is not problematic; in scholarly (including theological) theory-building it always goes like this—we have no choice. It would be very naïve to plead—as often happens in certain Evangelical

---

24. Ouweneel (2014b, chapter 3).
25. Ouweneel (2013, chapters 12–14; 2014b, chapters 8–9).
26. Popper (1972, 192).

circles—for a "plain reading" of the Bible, forgetting all preceding theological models. That would be biblicism *par excellence*. None of us can begin reading the Bible with a blank mind, because we are all products of the Western, twenty-first-century, Protestant mindset, of our religious, ecclesiastical, and school education, etc.

There is nothing wrong with that, as long as we are *conscious* of it. However, from a historical point of view, theology belongs to the sciences that, generally speaking, are the least conscious of basic philosophical questions preceding all scholarly theory-building. Reformed federalism, Roman Catholic ecclesiasticism, dispensationalism, and epangelicalism have all turned out to be fruitful theoretical constructs in that they all managed to bring the scriptural data together in a meaningful synthesis, and have inspired theologians to new research. However, it would imply a total ignorance of the nature of scholarly theory-building if we were to elevate one of these "-isms," or any theological "ism," to the level of undoubted biblical truth, and would even be prepared to create church divisions for them (as has so often been done).[27]

## 5.3  Older Reformed Theologians
### 5.3.1  John Calvin

Before we continue with our description of, and confrontation with, the Reformed covenant doctrine, it is important first to pay some attention to John Calvin (1509–1564), theologically speaking certainly the greatest of the great Reformers of the sixteenth century.[28]

Whereas James Veninga speaks of a well-developed cov-

---

27. See extensively Ouweneel (2013, chapters 6–14).
28. See, e.g., Van den Bergh (1879); Hoekema (1967); Veninga (1974); Graafland (1978, 24–38; 1992, 71–220); Helm (1983); Osterhaven (1984); Loonstra (1987); Van Campen (1988); De Kroon (1996); M. van Campen in Hagoort (1999, 67–76); Lillback (2001); Van der Zwaag (2003, 115–28); Horton (2006); Balke et al. (2008); Jeon (2009); Verboom (2009); Van der Vegt (n.d.); see the summary by J. Hoek in Hoek and Verboom (2010, 47–48).

enant theology in Calvin,[29] other authors are more careful. Anthony Hoekema feels it is impossible to locate the central or fundamental principle of Calvin's theology in his covenant doctrine.[30] We might say that, in this respect, Calvin can hardly be called a Calvinist. Cornelis Harinck wrote: "For Calvin, the doctrine of predestination is more important than the doctrine of the covenants. . . . Calvin places the covenant of grace under the predestination doctrine. In Calvin's thinking, the covenant of grace is subservient to election, and resulted from it."[31] And according to Cornelis Graafland, the covenant does have an important place with Calvin, but it "receives in his theology not an equally central position as justification and election. Of the latter . . . the covenant is only one constitutive element."[32]

The terms *foedus*, *pactum*, and *testamentum*, all three as possible Latin renderings of "covenant" (and all three occurring in the Vulgate), occur in Calvin's *Institutes of the Christian Religion* hundreds of times. We therefore have to limit ourselves to some striking references. First, the covenant is dealt with in Calvin's treatment of, respectively, the similarity and the difference between Old and New Testaments.[33] He says, among other things: "The covenant made with all the patriarchs is so much like ours in substance and reality that the two are actually one and the same. Yet they differ in the mode of dispensation."[34]

Second, the covenant is dealt with in Calvin's treatment

---

29. Veninga (1974, 23); cf. Verboom (2009, 36 [also see 49]): "The covenant forms . . . an integral part of Calvin's theology. I would even like to call the covenant the supporting soil for the kernels in his theology." J. Hoek in Hoek and Verboom (2010, 47): "The covenant takes up a large part in the whole of Calvin's doctrine of faith. As an integrated part of Calvin's theology, the significance of the covenant is even its supporting soil."
30. Hoekema (1967, 134).
31. Harinck (1986, 41).
32. Graafland (1992, 71).
33. *Institutes* 2.10 and 2.11.
34. *Institutes* 2.10.2; the former is elaborated in *Institutes* 2.10, and the latter in 2.11.

of election, where he begins immediately by saying that "In actual fact, the covenant of life is not preached equally among all men, and among those to whom it is preached, it does not gain the same acceptance either constantly or in equal degree. In this diversity the wonderful depth of God's judgment is made known."[35] This turns out to mean that, with Calvin, the covenant comprises so-called *general* election. This is the election of Israel as a nation, of whom not all were elected for eternal salvation (cf. Rom. 11:7, "Israel failed to obtain what it was seeking. The *elect* obtained it, but the rest were hardened"). The expression also refers to the church as a whole, the so-called visible church, which includes non-regenerate confessors. Here we are dealing with the universal offer of salvation in Christ, that is, to both the elect and the non-elect. This is distinguished from *particular* election, which involves the assignment and appropriation of salvation through the Holy Spirit to the elect (2 Tim. 2:10, "the elect, that they also may obtain the salvation that is in Christ Jesus"). This concerns individual persons *within* Israel and the church, respectively.

The way Calvin deals with the covenant leads to a certain ambiguity. There is the covenant in a Christological, general, objective sense, as well as the covenant in a pneumatological, particular, subjective sense. This ambiguity has led to much discussion, in particular with respect to the question whether, in Calvin's view, the covenant includes all Israel or the whole (visible) church (so Gottlob Schrenk, Peter A. Lillback, Willem van 't Spijker), or is limited to the elect (so Andries D. R. Polman, Cornelis Harinck, Leonard J. Trinterud, Hans H. Wolf, James B. Torrance, J. Wayne Baker).[36] For our purpose, it suffices to establish the fact that, with Calvin, the covenant doctrine has not yet reached a mature and independent form.

Interesting is the suggestion by Willem Verboom that, for Calvin, the covenant is so important, among other things, be-

---
35. *Institutes* 3.21.1.
36. Graafland (1992, 79–81, 147–70), and more extensively Lillback (2001).

cause "Calvin considers the Anabaptist view of the covenant to be a heresy. . . . Therefore, the significance of infant baptism is the practical point of entrance for Calvin's treatment of the covenant. From there, this time and again becomes visible in his theology."[37] In this respect, it is with Calvin no different than with Ulrich Zwingli, Martin Luther, and Heinrich Bullinger: as we have seen, to a large extent, the covenant doctrine originated in the conflict with the Anabaptists.[38] In other words, the discussion about the covenant is determined by the discussion about baptism, not the other way around. I have stressed this before, but the point is so important that it is worth mentioning again (see further Appendix I).

The orthodox Reformed covenant doctrine was further elaborated by Theodore Beza and Hieronymus Zanchius, followed by Zacharias Ursinus and Caspar Olevianus (the men of the Heidelberg Catechism), by the Puritans William Perkins and Robert Rollock (all of them in the sixteenth century), and by Franciscus Gomarus (around 1600).[39] For the seventeenth century, we must mention, in addition to Richard Baxter,[40] Johannes Cocceius, and for the eighteenth century especially Alexander Comrie (see the next §§). In addition to discussing these men, Graafland deals with Dutchmen such as Jacobus Koelman, Petrus van Mastricht, Wilhelmus à Brakel, Friedrich Adolph Lampe (of German descent), Hillebrandus Janssonius, and Johannes Conradus Appelius (seventeenth/eighteenth century). Herman Witsius is hardly discussed by Graafland,[41] but he is reviewed by several other authors.[42] In what follows, I will limit myself to Cocceius and Comrie,

---

37. Verboom (2009, 36).
38. Also see M. van Campen in Hagoort (1999, 67–69).
39. Graafland (1994, 11–107, 134–95; 1996, 11–87); Van der Zwaag (2003, 130–34, 145–47); about Ursinus and Olevianus, see J. van Genderen in Hagoort (1999, 77–82); about Olevianus' covenant doctrine, see Bierma (1980); about Gomarus, see Ouweneel (2008b, 263, 266–67, 272).
40. Graafland (1994, 245–64).
41. See Graafland (1996, 281, 300, 302).
42. Van Genderen (1995); Kroneman (1987); Bakker (1991).

because, in the Netherlands, we find in the former a highlight and in the latter a (preliminary) endpoint in the development of the Reformed covenant theology.

### 5.3.2 Johannes Coccejus

There is no doubt that, in the development of the Reformed covenant doctrine, Johannes Coccejus (1603–1669) played a crucial role.[43] It was he, more than anyone, who gave the covenant doctrine its central place in Reformed theology. We have to add, though, that his covenant doctrine has been interpreted in rather different ways, and especially in hyper-Calvinist circles his views have been judged rather negatively. However, it is of interest that Alexander Comrie (see next §), who is highly regarded by hyper-Calvinists, himself spoke of Coccejus' covenant doctrine in a positive way.[44]

Coccejus moved along orthodox Reformed lines by emphasizing the powerlessness of the sinner, the unilateral character of God's grace and double predestination, and by fiercely combating the Arminians. In addition to this emphasis on God's counsel, he wanted to provide more room for God's concrete covenantal dealings in history. In this way, a tension arose between Coccejus' emphasis on God's counsel, which is from eternity, and concrete salvation history, which is in time.[45] According to some interpreters, we are dealing here with a real interaction between the two[46] — which in the eyes of some Reformed thinkers would be essentially un-Reformed — whereas others believe that Coccejus was referring only to a realization within time of what had been decided from eternity.[47]

---

43. See Coccejus (1990); see about him, e.g., Schrenk (1967); Faulenbach (1973); Weir (1990); Graafland (1996, 279–324); Van Asselt (1997; 2008).
44. Cf. C. Graafland in Brienen et al. (1986, 343–44).
45. I also see this with J. W. Maris in Hagoort (1999, 103–104), and W. Verboom in Hoek and Verboom (2010, 92), who I think too simplistically connect election with eternity, and the covenant with time or history.
46. Van Asselt (1988, 106).
47. Graafland (1996, 283).

Cocceius is one of the theologians who developed a "three covenant" doctrine. He described it in this form: there is

(a) the "covenant (*testamentum*) of peace,"[48] which allegedly existed from eternity between the three Persons of the Trinity (also called "counsel of peace"; the expression comes from Zech. 6:13, but stands there in a totally different context);

(b) the supposed treaty (*pactum*) between the Father and the Son, which constitutes the main contents of the covenant of peace;

(c) the covenant (*foedus*) of grace with humanity.

In addition to this comes the thoroughly Reformed question as to how double predestination is to be connected with these covenants. According to Cocceius, within the eternal counsel of God, predestination precedes the *pactum* between the Father and the Son.[49] This question becomes even more complicated when, within this scheme, the thoroughly Reformed distinction between the covenant of works and the covenant of grace must also be interwoven (see below).

Again, we are dealing here with a striking example of controversial theological theory-building within the framework of an already chosen paradigm. Although this is a typically modern consideration of mine—the philosophy of science is little more than a century old—we cannot get around applying such distinctions to earlier theology as well, in order to evaluate the measure of truth in its statements. Through the method of inferential theology (see §4.1.2 above), one conclusion is built upon the other at the whims of the investigators—necessarily leading to ever more varieties in covenant theology, fiercely combating each other.

Cocceius got entangled in his own reasoning in such a way that his interpreters have arrived at very different conclusions about what precisely he taught and intended. In particular,

---

48. The expression is derived from Num. 25:12; Isa. 54:10; Ezek. 34:25; 37:26, although it has a very different meaning there.
49. See on this problem extensively Ouweneel (2008b, especially chapters 10–12).

this involved the relationship between God's eternal counsel and its concrete realization in time. For an Evangelical theology this is of importance because, in spite of all the confusion, one gets the impression that Cocceius has shifted here to a more biblical position, in which he approximated more accurately the relationship between God's sovereign counsel and human responsibility. It is therefore no wonder that some have doubted whether Cocceius, in spite of his fierce opposition to the Arminians, can still be called orthodox Reformed. (As is usual in such cases, orthodox Reformed means here either mainstream Reformed, or most clearly in line with Reformed creeds and catechisms, or both.)

### 5.3.3  Alexander Comrie

Franciscus Gomarus, Johannes Cocceius, and Alexander Comrie have all worked in the (Northern) Netherlands, but by origin the first was Flemish (from Bruges), the second German (from Bremen), and the third Scottish (from Perth). J. W. ("Hans") Maris called Comrie "undoubtedly one of the most able Reformed theologians of the eighteenth century."[50] In the work of Alexander Comrie (1706–1774), we meet with a (preliminary) endpoint in the development of the Reformed covenant doctrine.[51] In the scheme of the covenant of works *versus* the covenant of grace, Comrie believed that the former did not only exist in the Garden of Eden but, following Olevianus, he encountered it everywhere in Scripture where God's demands form the (supposed) condition for obtaining life and salvation, especially at Mount Sinai. The covenant of works is supposed to be conditional, whereas the covenant of grace is viewed as unconditional (see my comments in §§3.5 and 3.6 above).

Only on the basis of this false dilemma between a cove-

---

50. J. W. Maris in Hagoort (1999, 102).
51. See Kersten (1947, I, 263–79) on the covenant of works in Comrie's writings; Leurdijk and Moerkerken (1986); Honig (1991); Graafland (1996, 362–77); J. W. Maris in Hagoort (1999, 102–109).

nant of works and a covenant of grace could the battle arise about whether there are two or three covenants, not now in the sense of Cocceius (§5.3.2), but in a somewhat different sense. Comrie points to those who teach three covenants: the covenant of works (*foedus operum*), the covenant of redemption (*pactum salutis*, or *pactum pacis*, "covenant of peace"), and the covenant of grace (*foedus gratiae*). The covenant of redemption would then be the agreement from eternity between the divine Persons concerning the redemption of the elect. According to Comrie's opponents, this would have to be distinguished from the covenant of grace, which is made with both baptized believers and their baptized (but not necessarily elect) children. Thus, the covenant of grace is wider than the covenant of redemption, which applies only to the elect.[52] Through the covenant of grace, the covenant of redemption is realized within time; such is the idea of those who wish to distinguish between the two.

Comrie rejects making a distinction between some covenant of redemption and the covenant of grace, although he considers those who do make the distinction to be orthodox. However, he does consider the distinction to be doubtful because, in his opinion, the idea of a covenant of redemption, which was first launched by Jacob Arminius—which for many orthodox Reformed was reason enough to be suspicious of the very idea—does open the door to the doctrine of universal atonement (Christ died for all people, or at least for those with whom the covenant is made, elect or not).[53]

This difference of opinion still exists in our own day. Among other things, it was the reason why around 1919 any rapprochement became impossible between the Netherlands Reformed Congregations, who in their two-covenants doctrine entirely followed Comrie, and the Christian Reformed Churches in the Netherlands, who held the three-covenants

---

52. See, e.g., Heerma (1951, 20, etc.); Van der Schuit (1982); Van Genderen (1995); cf. Van der Zwaag (2003, 112–14).
53. See Ouweneel (2009, 256–65).

doctrine, without teaching universal atonement. Dutch theologians in other Reformed denominations, such as Klaas Schilder and Jan Gerrit Woelderink, also made a distinction between the covenant of redemption and the covenant of grace.[54]

Basically, the discussion involves the question as to whether in the covenant of grace the (well-meant) promise of salvation comes to all those with whom the covenant is made, that is, believers and their children (elect or not), or only to the elect. In this respect, the Netherlands Reformed Congregations wholeheartedly followed Comrie.[55] Others, such as Schilder and Woelderink, put great emphasis on the covenantal promises, which come to all the baptized (covenant of redemption), but which have to be accepted in faith in order to factually receive salvation (covenant of grace).

One reason why we call Comrie and certain other Reformed theologians hyper-Calvinists is because Comrie removed the covenant of grace from time (salvation history) to eternity (God's eternal counsel), and limited it emphatically to the elect. If the gospel may yet be preached to all people, or at least to all the baptized, then he viewed this fact fully apart from the covenant of grace (which for Comrie was identical with the covenant of redemption), for that is limited to the elect. As a consequence, the baptized person can never appeal to the covenantal promises — just because he was baptized — for those covenantal promises are exclusively for the elect. In other words, there surely is a broad *administration* of the covenant of grace, in the sense that non-elect children are baptized as well; to *both* groups, the sign of the covenant is granted. However, in baptism the *seal* of the covenant is granted in baptism to the elect children alone.

On this point, there is a wide gap within the Reformed world. It is fascinating to see that, in fact, Comrie and his spiritual descendants, such as G. H. Kersten, come to the same

---

54. See Schilder (1946); Woelderink (1974).
55. See, e.g., Kersten (1947, I, 308–21); Moerkerken (1979, 47–86).

view as, for instance, Klaas Schilder and his spiritual descendants: there is only one kind of covenant member.[56] The huge difference is this:

(a) According to Alexander Comrie, as well as, for instance, William Perkins, Herman Witsius, and Thomas Boston, the covenant members are identical with the elect. This is sometimes called the hyper-Calvinist view; here, the doctrine of the covenant is entirely subservient to the doctrine of double predestination.

(b) According to Klaas Schilder, following Heinrich Bullinger and (presumably) John Calvin, covenant members are identical with believers *and* their children, elect or non-elect. This is a wider circle than (a) because *all* baptized children of believers are viewed as *genuine* covenant members, whether they come to faith or not. Here, the doctrine of predestination is subservient to, or even separated from, the doctrine of the covenant.

(c) Naturally, a third standpoint is conceivable, namely, among those who wish to find some balance between predestination and the covenant. This leads to the view that there are *two kinds* of covenant members, the elect and the non-elect, within the covenant of grace (see further in chapter 8). This is the way Jan Hoek describes the view of Calvin: "All church members are children of the covenant. But there are two kinds of children. Apart from those who answer to the covenant in faith there are also covenant members who break the covenant through unbelief, and change the covenant blessing into covenant revenge."[57] Notice here the term "church members": they can be equally described as the total-

---

56. See Los et al. (1943): "We believe . . ., second, that God in Christ has established his covenant of grace with believers and their offspring [Gen. 17:7; Gal. 3:14, 29); third, that therefore all children of believers are covenant members [Acts 3:25]; . . . fifth, that therefore the redemptive promise of that covenant belongs to all those children [2:39]; sixth, that therefore for all those children the ministry of baptism is a signifying and sealing to them, namely, of the covenant of grace or that redemptive promise [Gen. 17:11, 13–14]."
57. J. Hoek in Hoek and Verboom (2010, 48).

ity of the baptized, and as the members of the *visible* church; at any rate, they are a wider term than members of the Ekklesia, that is, true members of the Body of Christ. The first "church" is the totality of all the baptized; the second "church" is the totality of the elect.

The ardent Comrian, G. H. Kersten, fiercely opposed the adherents of the "three covenants" doctrine. He called this a "covenant uprooting doctrine," which is "dishonoring to God" and "soul-corrupting."[58] This bitterness has to be viewed against the background of the conflict with the Christian Reformed Churches in the Netherlands of those days. With this kind of sharp language the conflict was hardened and the gap widened. This is the more remarkable because the Netherlands Reformed Congregations in 1953, in spite of their "two covenants" doctrine, maintained the doctrine of the "well-meant offer of God's grace" to all the baptized, or even to all people, in opposition to Cornelis Steenblok and his adherents, who afterwards formed the "Reformed Congregations in the Netherlands."

Incidentally, I may note here that we will nowhere find a broader offer of divine grace as well as an appeal to human responsibility than with the Scottish brothers Ebenezer and Ralph Erskine (eighteenth century, a generation older than Comrie). Yet, they still fully adhered to the "two covenants" doctrine. This is one example of the virtual impossibility of coming up with a variety of federalism that has not been defended at some time and some place by some theologians.

## 5.4  Works *Versus* Grace
### 5.4.1  Again: the Sinaitic Covenant

All these considerations amount to saying that *the Reformed distinction between the covenant of works and the covenant of grace is invalid*. Perhaps we see this most clearly in all the senseless discussions on the question whether the Sinaitic covenant was a covenant of works or a covenant of grace, or in a sense

---
58. G. H. Kersten in his foreword to Boston (1931, 8).

both at the same time, and whether the Sinaitic covenant involved a republication of the covenant of works, or not. Or even worse: "the covenant of redemption . . . was for Christ a covenant of works rather than a covenant of grace"[59] — as if there was a covenant between God and Jesus, and as if Jesus has obtained salvation (for himself or others) through his good works. There is a complex reasoning behind this in Reformed theology, namely, the doctrine of imputed righteousness. See, for instance, the Heidelberg Catechism (Q&A 60): "God grants and credits to me the perfect . . . righteousness . . . of Christ," or the Westminster Confession of Faith (XI.1): "God . . . justifies . . . by imputing the obedience . . . of Christ unto them." See about this question extensively the third volume in this series.

Such questions — was first prelapsarian Adam, then Israel, then Christ, under some covenant of works? — are senseless because they are rooted in wrong presuppositions. But it is very difficult to attack the distinctions between conditional and unconditional covenants, law and promise covenants, covenants of works and covenants of grace, *because they are contained in Presbyterian creeds and catechisms.* Fighting theological theories is one thing, but once these theories have crept into confessions they become sacrosanct and are therefore far more difficult to combat. For many, it feels as if one is combating Scripture itself.

Here we see the damaging consequences of all theologies that do not properly maintain the balance between God's sovereign grace and human responsibility; the mere mention of the latter is sometimes seen as a sign of Arminianism. From the outset, Reformed theology has badly suffered under this lack of balance, not only in its doctrine of predestination,[60] but also in its covenant doctrine. And this lack became even worse in and through the debate with the Arminians (at the beginning of the seventeenth century).

---

59. Berkhof (1979, 268); cf. Brown and Keele (2012, 59).
60. See extensively Ouweneel (2008b, chapters 10–14).

Perhaps, the tension surrounding the two notions, covenant of works and covenant of grace, is felt nowhere more painfully than in treatments of the Sinaitic covenant, which allegedly has aspects of both. Reformed (!) theologian Gerhard C. Aalders has rightly said about this: "How can one say that the one God of the one covenant forced his people [at Mount Sinai] into the harness of a works covenant, thus ordering them to strive for merit, while that same God revealed himself in His grace, and commanded them to live out of that grace only? How can one maintain, as a watered-down derivative of this, that the covenant of Sinai is given in a form that is strongly reminiscent of a covenant of works?"[61] What a relief that there are also Reformed opinions like this one!

According to this view, the Sinaitic covenant is, in Aalders' terms, "a covenant of grace wrapped up as a covenant of works," which he rejects. A theologian who is equally Reformed, Cornelis Van der Waal, adds: "Does one not sin against God, by ascribing to Him 'evil,' disloyalty to His one covenant administration?"[62] That is harsh language—but understandable over against those who impose a works–grace dualism upon the Sinaitic covenant. I have argued earlier, with special reference to Psalm 105 and Galatians 3, that in fact the Sinaitic covenant was—if not identical with, at least—a direct continuation and elaboration of the Abrahamic covenant. It is the same God of grace with his covenantal loyalty who revealed himself to Adam before the fall, to Adam after the fall, to Noah, to Abraham, and to Israel at Mount Sinai.

Listen, for instance, to Deuteronomy 7:7-8, and ask whether this is the austere language of a covenant of works, or whether this is the language of grace and love: "The LORD your God has chosen you to be a people for his treasured possession, out of all the peoples who are on the face of the earth. It was not because you were more in number than any other people that the LORD set his love on you and chose you, for

---

61. Aalders (1939, 179).
62. Van der Waal (1990, 59).

you were the fewest of all peoples, but it is because the LORD loves you and is keeping the oath that he swore to your fathers, that the LORD has brought you out with a mighty hand and redeemed you from the house of slavery, from the hand of Pharaoh king of Egypt. Know therefore that the LORD your God is God, the faithful God who keeps covenant and steadfast love [*hesed*] with those who love him and keep his commandments, to a thousand generations."

I know the next sentences (vv. 10–11) are: ". . . and repays to their face those who hate him, by destroying them. He will not be slack with one who hates him. He will repay him to his face. You shall therefore be careful to do the commandment and the statutes and the rules that I command you today." That is a necessary counterpart of God's love: covenantal vengeance upon those who consistently and rebelliously break the covenant. But that does not alter its basic character: this is a God of love and *hesed* (covenant loyalty) who enters into a relationship with a redeemed people, into a true covenant of love, in which every blessing is based—not on works-holiness but—on God's being "merciful and gracious, slow to anger, and abounding in steadfast love and faithfulness, keeping steadfast love for thousands, forgiving iniquity and transgression and sin" (Exod. 34:6–7).

## 5.4.2 Circumcision of the Heart

There is yet another important reason why the Old Covenant is not a covenant of works, which comes to light in the eschatological restoration of Israel: "And the LORD your God will circumcise your heart and the heart of your offspring, so that you will love the LORD your God with all your heart and with all your soul, that you may live" (Deut. 30:6). That is, here life is not something that is earned through merit, but is a consequence of *God's* gracious circumcision of Israel's hearts. In other words: here works are not a *condition* for life, but an *effect* of God's gracious work in the soul—exactly like under the New Covenant.

What then is the meaning of God's emphatic statement in Leviticus 18:5: Observe the Torah, and you shall live? This is the key verse for all those who want to see in the Sinaitic covenant a covenant of works, especially because of the way Paul seems to apply this verse. However, if we consider these statements in their contexts, we get a different view. Such verses, which seem to make life dependent on Torah observance, have to be explained *within the entire framework of the Mosaic Torah*. Moses could never have meant that a mere doing of good works will provide a person with (eternal) life, for at least four reasons.

(1) Such a rule would contradict God's own being, which is "merciful and gracious, slow to anger, and abounding in steadfast love and faithfulness." God forgives the trespasses committed against the Torah on the basis of the sacrifices (Exod. 34:6-7). (Those who come under God's vengeance are not all those who turned out to be unable to keep the Torah—because then *all* would be lost—but they are the rebellious haters of God.) This is why so many were saved under (not, in spite of!) the Old Covenant: they lived by the grace and mercy of God, and their good works were the fruit thereof (cf. Luke 1:6, "righteous before God, walking blamelessly in all the commandments and statutes of the LORD").

(2) This rule—"do this and live"—must be seen in its covenant context: God is constantly addressing an *already redeemed people* (Exod. 13:3, 9, 14, 16; 20:2; Lev. 11:45; 19:36; etc.). Of course, the redemption out of Egypt did not imply eternal redemption, but the principle remains the same: there is never a divine demand for good works outside a framework of love, grace, and redemption. A Torah apart from its covenant context is a *nuda lex* ("naked law"), that is, a law separated from the grace and Spirit of Christ.[63] Such a Torah, if it comes from God, simply cannot exist: the Noahic Torah functioned in the context of the Noahic covenant, the Abrahamic Torah func-

---

63. Cf. Wolf (1958, 44).

tioned in the context of the Abrahamic covenant, the Messianic and the Millennial Torah function in the context of the New Covenant.

(3) The rule—"do this and live"—can be applied only in the light of this principle: no good works without first a divine circumcision of the heart. Sometimes, this is demanded of the people as a matter of their own responsibility (Lev. 26:41; Deut. 10:16; Jer. 4:4), but other places make clear that in fact this is God's own doing (Deut. 30:6; cf. Jer. 32:39; Ezek. 11:19; 36:26). Again, the balance between God's sovereign grace and human responsibility has to be carefully maintained here.

(4) The unity of, and continuity between, the Abrahamic and the Sinaitic covenants, as well as between the Old and the New Covenants, make it perfectly clear that the Old Covenant cannot possibly have a fundamentally different character ("covenant of works") than the Abrahamic and the New Covenant ("covenant of grace"). This unity and continuity prevents us from arguing, for instance, as follows: under the Old Covenant Israel had to circumcise their own hearts, in the *eschaton* it is God doing that within them. In the Torah, too, as well as in the Sinaitic covenant as a whole, everything revolves around God's grace and mercy, from the beginning to the end: "[The Israelites] refused to obey and were not mindful of the wonders that you [i.e., the Lord] performed among them, but they stiffened their neck and appointed a leader to return to their slavery in Egypt [Num. 14:4]. But you are a God ready to forgive, gracious and merciful, slow to anger and abounding in steadfast love, and did not forsake them" (Neh. 9:17; cf. v. 31; Num. 14:18).

"He made known his ways to Moses, his acts to the people of Israel. The Lord is merciful and gracious, slow to anger and abounding in steadfast love. He will not always chide, nor will he keep his anger forever. He does not deal with us according to our sins, nor repay us according to our iniquities" (Ps. 103:7–10). In the end it is never the people's evil works that have the last say, but always God's mercy — even if always to a remnant only. Even under the Sinaitic covenant, it is not human works but God's grace that will triumph.

### 5.4.3 Children of Abraham

Many Reformed theologians hold the view that there is only one kind of covenant member, but they strongly differ about what this entails. Comrie said that the covenant members are the elect; Kuyper said that the covenant members are the baptized. Those who hold that there are two kinds of covenant members say that there are true covenant members, namely, the elect baptized (or, if preferred, those who believe), and the non-elect baptized (those who do not believe). Which of these three views is the correct one?

Psalm 105:6, "O offspring of Abraham, his servant, children of Jacob, his chosen ones," does not really help here, because in this case "chosen" refers not to the eternal election of individuals (cf. Eph. 1:4–5) but to the election of Israel as a "chosen people." There is a fundamental difference between these two elections, as is made clear in Romans 11:7, "Israel failed to obtain what it was seeking. The elect obtained it, but the rest were hardened." Here, the elect are those destined for eternal bliss, living in the midst of a chosen nation, many of whom are hardened. Quite a different example, but based on the same principle, is this: "Did I not *choose* you twelve, and one of you is a devil?" (John 6:70). Twelve had been chosen, only eleven were saved.

The expression, "children of Abraham" contains a certain tension, because there are the physical descendants of Abraham who are not necessarily his spiritual children, and there are the spiritual children of Abraham who are not necessarily his physical descendants. In Matthew 3, the Jewish leaders boasted that they had "Abraham as our father," but John the Baptist denied that they were (true) children of Abraham: "God is able from these stones to raise up children for Abraham," that is, instead of you (v. 9; cf. Luke 3:8).

In John 8, it is the Lord himself who discussed with the Jewish leaders whether they were children of Abraham. They told him: "We are offspring of Abraham" (v. 33). Jesus of course did not deny that, but he accused them of not acting accordingly (v. 37). "They answered him, 'Abraham is our father.' Jesus said to them, 'If you were Abraham's children, you would be doing the works Abraham did, but now you seek to kill me, a man who has told you the truth that I heard from God. This is not what Abraham did. You are doing the works your father [i.e., the devil; v. 44] did'" (vv. 39–41). The true children of Abraham are the true children of the covenant.

We find something similar in Romans 4: "The purpose [of circumcision] was to make him [i.e., Abraham] the father of all who believe without being circumcised, so that righteousness would be counted to them as well, and to make him the father of the circumcised who are not merely circumcised but who also walk in the footsteps of the faith that our father Abraham had before he was circumcised" (vv. 11–12). The children of Abraham—the true children of the covenant—are those who walk in the faith of their spiritual father, whether they are his physical descendants or not. This corresponds with what Paul wrote to the Galatian Christians: "Know then that it is those of faith who are the sons of Abraham" (Gal. 3:7); "those who are of faith are blessed along with Abraham, the man of faith" (v. 9); "if you are Christ's, then you are Abraham's offspring, heirs according to promise" (v. 29).

In Romans 9 Paul writes, "For not all who are descended from Israel belong to Israel, and not all are children of Abraham because they are his offspring" (vv. 6–7). Here, the same point is being made in different words: the fact that someone is a physical descendant of Abraham does not mean that he is also his true child. This is illustrated by the examples of Ishmael and Esau: they were descendants of Abraham, but not children in the spiritual sense of the word.

Today, all the Gentile Jesus-believers have come to belong to the New Covenant, although they do not belong to the "house of Israel" or the "house of Judah" (Jer. 31:31; Heb. 8:8). Therefore, they are all children (or sons) of Abraham in the spiritual sense of the word. However, in a wider sense one could argue that the *whole* of baptized Christendom has come to belong to the New Covenant, although many so-called Christians are unregenerate. Within Christianity there are true and false children of Abraham. In *this* sense, if we see things from the viewpoint of human responsibility, there are two kinds of covenant members: regenerate and unregenerate. But if we see things from the viewpoint of divine sovereign grace, there can be only one kind of covenant member: regenerate believers. In this light, the battle between those who see only one and those who see two kinds of covenant members is useless and fruitless. From the viewpoint of divine sovereign grace, the former are right; from the viewpoint of human responsibility, the latter are right.

## 5.5   Other Ways
### 5.5.1   Recapitulation

It is sad when church denominations are divided, or remain divided, over purely theoretical-theological distinctions, which can hardly be explained to many common church members (and perhaps one should not even want to try this). *If* people wish to theorize in such a way about two or three covenants, we might listen to the wisdom of Herman Bavinck: "Indeed, there is a difference between the pact of salvation [i.e., covenant of redemption] and the covenant of grace. In the former, Christ is the guarantor and head; in the latter, he is the mediator. The first remains restricted to Christ and demands from him that he bear the punishment and fulfill the law[64] in the place of the elect; the second is extended to and through

---

64. See on this misunderstanding Ouweneel (2010a, 255–62). Scripture never says that Christ fulfilled the law *for us*, as our substitute; it does say that he bore the punishment for our trespasses of the law as our substitute, which is something very different. (See extensively the third volume in this series.)

Christ to humans and demands from them the faith and repentance that Christ has not, and could not, accomplish in their place.[65] The first concerns the acquisition of salvation, is eternal, and knows no history; the second deals with the application of salvation, begins in time, and passes through several dispensations. Still, given this distinction, we must not overlook the connection between them and their unity. In Scripture there are only two covenants, two ways to heaven for human beings, the covenant of works and the covenant of grace. The covenant of works is the way to heaven for the unfallen, the covenant of grace is that for fallen humans. The covenant of works was made with humankind in Adam; the covenant of grace was made with humankind in Christ. He, and he alone, is the substitutionary and representative head of humankind."[66]

We see here how Bavinck chose a middle position. On the one hand, he distinguished between the covenant of grace and the covenant of redemption. But on the other hand, in the end he turns out to have been an adherent of the "two covenants" doctrine. Also notice how Bavinck differed from Comrie, who extended the covenant of works to the Sinaitic covenant (see above), whereas Bavinck and many others limit it to the (alleged) covenant with prelapsarian Adam. In this way, room is created for distinguishing in the Sinaitic covenant the grace of God as well.

As I argued earlier (§3.5), the Sinaitic covenant is not a variety, or, as it is sometimes called, a "republication," of the covenant of works.[67] No, it is a variety of the covenant of grace (if one insists on using this term; see the last chapters of this book). Of course, there are Reformed theologians who argue that the Sinaitic covenant had a double character: it had features of both the covenant of works and the covenant of grace.

---

65. That is, Christ has not believed or repented as humanity's substitute.
66. Bavinck (2006, 3.227–28).
67. See extensively Estelle et al. (2009).

### 5.5.2 Wisdom

Wisdom is something we especially need here, wisdom in the sense of balance, harmony, and equilibrium. The covenant is an important notion in the Bible—more important than many Evangelicals seem to realize—but not necessarily the most important. As I have said elsewhere, I see the notion of the kingdom of God as far more encompassing in both the Old and the New Testament.[68] There is no wisdom in overemphasizing the covenant, and certainly not in speaking of the covenant in what one could almost call a romanticized way. To give a small example by Willem Verboom: "In the time of the Reformation, the movement of the Anabaptists strived for a pure congregation of only believers. Among them were people of integrity, such as Menno Simons (1496-1561).[69] However, the gap that arose as a consequence of the loss of the covenant of grace[70] could easily be filled by ruthless dictators."[71]

With all due respect, this strikes me as nonsense. Let me work this out a bit, because it is a typical example of federalist *hybris*.

(a) I have always found it strange that Christians could object to such striving for pure congregations of believers only. Unbelievers are heartily welcomed in church services, but that does not change the fact that the church as such is the "holy congregation and gathering of true Christian believers" (Belgic Confession, Art. 27), and that church meetings there-

---

68. See Ouweneel (2011, chapters 9–14). As to the Old Testament: "The idea of the rule of God over creation, over all creatures, over the kingdoms of the world, and in a unique and special way, over his chosen and redeemed people, is the very heart of the message of the Hebrew scriptures" (Goldsworthy in Rosner at al. [2000, 618]). As to the New Testament: the kingdom is God "is of prime importance in NT theology" (Schreiner [2008, 41]); cf. Wellum (2012, 591–92).
69. Menno Simons was the spiritual father of the Mennonites, who were named after him; they formed the movement of moderate (pacifist) Anabaptists.
70. Of course, Verboom means to say "the *notion* (or *doctrine*) of the covenant of grace."
71. W. Verboom in Hoek and Verboom (2010, 119).

fore are basically gatherings of believers.

(b) The doctrine of the covenant of grace has never stopped authoritarian leaders. The Reformed, especially the hyper-Calvinist, world has known many pastors who had an almost unassailable authority in "their" congregations. With regard to the Netherlands, I mention only Abraham Kuyper (Reformed Churches in the Netherlands), Klaas Schilder (Reformed Churches Liberated), G. H. Kersten (Netherlands Reformed Congregations), Frans Mallan (Reformed Congregations in the Netherlands), and Adriaan Wink (Reformed Congregations in the Netherlands seceded). I will refrain from giving examples of pastors who are still alive, especially in North America.

(c) Notice the imprecise formulation: Verboom speaks of "the loss of the covenant of grace," but what he means is the refusal to accept the *doctrine* of the covenant of grace—apart from the fact that in the lifetime of Menno Simons, this Reformed doctrine had hardly achieved any development.

(d) Abandoning the Reformed doctrine of the covenant of grace is no license for dictators at all; it is even difficult to see what kind of connection there might be between these two matters. The Mennonites were, and are, the most peaceful Christians one could imagine, in spite of their rejection of the Reformed covenant doctrine. They usually are even anti-militarists, whereas many Reformed leaders were and are staunch militarists.

In Verboom's comment, I see an alarming overestimation of the significance of the covenant doctrine, leading to silly comparisons with non-Reformed views. Such derailments do not help to further the credibility of Reformed theology.

### 5.5.3 "Evangelical Reformed"

In several important ways, Evangelical theology is more closely related to the theology of the Mennonites of the sixteenth century, and in their wake to the first Baptists of the seventeenth century, as well as related to the theology of the

Arminians (seventeenth century), rather than that of the Lutheran and Reformed Protestants. (Of course, I am referring here to collateral issues, not to the fundamentals of the faith as they have been formulated, for example, in the ecumenical creeds.) In this context, it hurts a little that Cornelis Graafland distinguished between "orthodox Reformed" and "humanist Reformed" covenantal theologians.[72] This is a rather biased distinction, for who decides which of the two groups is orthodox (i.e., doctrinally right)? It is always the (allegedly) orthodox themselves who decide this; they make themselves to be the yardstick of the right doctrine.[73]

However this may be, most of those whom Graafland called "humanist Reformed" have always considered themselves to be fully Reformed, and thus fully orthodox according to common Reformed standards. Among other things, this is apparent from the great attention they paid to the covenant doctrine.[74] They were federalists just like the other Reformed theologians.

Graafland gave the "humanist Reformed" this label because he believed he saw in them an Erasmian humanist influence,[75] or he believed that they took a path different from the one Calvin and Beza (apparently *the* standards for Reformed orthodoxy) had pointed out.[76] Because of the negative connotation that the word "humanist" has for many — especially in contrast with "orthodox" — I prefer to speak of "Evangelical Reformed" *avant la lettre*. Graafland dealt with Dirk Volkertszoon Coornhert (who, by the way, remained a Roman Catholic, just like Desiderius Erasmus), Joannes Anastasius Veluanus, Gellius Snecanus, Cornelis Wiggertszoon and Jacobus Arminius, the father of the Remonstrants (Arminianism)

---

72. Graafland (1996, 9–210).
73. See Ouweneel (2010b, chapters 13–14). This is why denominational names like "Orthodox Reformed" and "Orthodox Presbyterian" are so objectionable.
74. Ibid., 209.
75. Ibid., 88.
76. Ibid., 98.

(all sixteenth century). Their most important common characteristics are their rejection of the doctrine of eternal reprobation (from before the foundation of the world), and thus also of the doctrine of *double* predestination, and their much larger emphasis on human responsibility. In this sense, they may be called forerunners of Evangelical theology, even if they sometimes moved too far away from the divine side of sovereign grace to the human side of responsibility (something which some Evangelical theologians do as well).[77]

For the Evangelical Reformed covenant doctrine, this means specifically that it does emphasize divine grace, but never at the expense of human responsibility, especially a person's faithful acceptance of the gospel.[78] Important is also the Evangelical Reformed view that Christ died "for all" (2 Cor. 5:14-15; cf. 1 Tim. 2:6; 1 John 2:2) or "everyone" (Heb. 2:9), and thus objectively made justification and salvation available for all (Rom. 5:18; Titus 2:11). Personally, I take an intermediate position as to this so-called "universal atonement": Jesus did die for all people—that is, his blood is *sufficient* for all people—so that salvation can be offered to all people in a full and well-meant way, but one cannot say that he bore the sins of all people, for in that case no human could ever be lost; Christ's blood is *efficacious* only for the elect.[79] Evangelical Reformed Protestants, too, believe that salvation is for all people, but only those have a share in it who accept it in faith (which group coincides with those who were elected from eternity).

There is a striking correspondence between the Evangelical Reformed and Calvin in that both seem to recognize only one covenant, namely, the covenant of grace.[80] Only starting with William Perkins do we encounter the notion of the covenant of works. One could therefore divide Reformed thinkers

---

77. See extensively Ouweneel (2008b, chapters 10–14).
78. Graafland (1996, 209–10).
79. See Ouweneel (2009, 256–65).
80. Cf. Van der Zwaag (2003, 109–10).

in terms of those who recognize:

(a) only one covenant: the covenant of grace,

(b) two covenants (cf. Comrie): the covenants of works and of grace,

(c) three covenants: the covenants of works, of redemption, and of grace,

(d) four covenants (R. Scott Clark; see §8.1.3).

## 5.6 Some Exceptional Authors
### 5.6.1 Philipp van Limborch

Perhaps the most important Evangelical Reformed theologian of the seventeenth century was Philipp van Limborch (1633–1712).[81] Van Limborch was an Arminian, but we have to keep in mind that the early Arminians all insisted on being called Reformed, even if they were rejected by the self-designated orthodox (i.e., anti-Arminian) Reformed. Arminians could call themselves Reformed insofar as they too emphasized the importance and comprehensiveness of the covenant of grace. This is why Reformed theologian William Den Boer even called Arminius himself a Reformed theologian,[82] which caused a little stir in hyper-Calvinist circles in the Netherlands.

Van Limborch, too, recognized only one covenant of God with humanity, of which all postlapsarian covenants are just varieties. According to him, Scripture knows of no covenant with the prelapsarian Adam (cf. §3.6). After the fallen Adam had been restored, God made the covenant of grace with all humankind, but this was made historically concrete in the Abrahamic covenant. Through the Sinaitic covenant, this covenant developed further into the New Covenant, which is established in Jesus Christ. All these are views that are closer to Scripture than any of the complex views we have discussed so far. It would go too far to call Van Limborch an Evangelical

---

81. Barnouw (1963); Hicks (1985); Graafland (1996, 213–42).
82. Den Boer (2008).

in the modern sense of the term. Yet, he is of great importance for Evangelical theology in that he pointed to the moral-rational character of the covenant throughout the ages. This implies that what matters is not only people's (once for all) surrender in faith to Christ, but also their submission to what I have called the Messianic Torah.[83]

Graafland calls this a "humanization and moralization of the covenant,"[84] but this is a prejudiced and erroneous characterization. Using my own terminology: what matters is not only the mere act of faith and justification by faith, but also sanctification, and even more: discipleship in the kingdom of God under the Messianic Torah.[85] One is justified by faith, but then "faith working though love" (Gal. 5:6). Such a walk is never one's own merit; it is divine *grace* that is constantly "training us to renounce ungodliness and worldly passions, and to live self-controlled, upright, and godly lives in the present age" (Titus 2:12).

What Graafland rejects here is precisely what I deeply appreciate: "The fact that Van Limborch nevertheless even then keeps speaking of grace is possible only due to his Arminian description of this grace as grace 'coming in between,' namely, between the divine demand and human, voluntary obedience." As in so many cases, the word Arminian (or Remonstrant) is used here because the strictly Reformed author wants to express his disgust in regard to another—also Reformed—author with whom he wholeheartedly disagrees. Especially when the matter of human responsibility is brought up, the accusation of Arminianism is always very easily—and often cheaply—made by the hardline Reformed. As if we have to *choose* between human responsibility (the Remonstrant approach) and divine sovereign grace (the Contra-Remonstrant approach). Even the (Evangelical) appeal to find a biblical balance between the two is often countered with the accusation

---

83. See Ouweneel (2015a, chapter 6).
84. Graafland (1996, 242).
85. See extensively Ouweneel (2011, chapters 9–14).

of Arminianism.

We do mention with respect, however, that Graafland shows some understanding of the humanist Reformed. Their covenant doctrine was a reaction to that of Reformed orthodoxy, first, because of "the concern that they had for the concrete congregation and its individual members. In their view, the congregation was pushed by the orthodox Reformed election doctrine into a passive corner, so that people's own responsibility was lost. In their view, this had dramatic consequences in that also the humanity of persons was threatened. People have the possibility, and also the calling, to decide themselves about that which by God, due to his grace, is promised to him, and to the acceptance of which they are called by him. [The humanist Reformed theologians] saw how the orthodox Reformed [theologians] downplayed the congregation's own responsibility, and basically human responsibility as genuinely human."[86]

Second, Graafland showed understanding of the scriptural hermeneutical arguments of the humanist Reformed. They believed that the orthodox were not faithful to their own *sola Scriptura* (Scripture alone), for indeed the covenant is central in Scripture, but eternal election is mentioned very infrequently, and eternal reprobation not at all, in Scripture: "Therefore, their reproach was that the orthodox Reformed claimed Scripture for what in fact they wanted to see introduced on the basis of their theological system. In contrast with this dogmatism, the humanists placed their own 'purely biblical' way of believing."[87]

This, then, is Graafland's view of the humanist Reformed. I wholeheartedly agree with the latter, though with the marginal note that theologically it is rather naïve and biblicistic—though it has happened often—to place over against the theological system of the opponents one's own "purely bib-

---

86. Graafland (1996, 398–99).
87. Ibid., 399.

lical way of believing."⁸⁸ In reality, here the one theological system necessarily stands in opposition to the other system. However, at the time, this kind of philosophical insight into scholarship and theory-building did not yet exist.

In a certain sense, I also agree with Graafland's conclusion: "In fact, what was involved was a profound contrast [between orthodox- and humanist-Reformed], which has to do with the heart of salvation, and thus of faith."⁸⁹ It seems rather excessive to speak here of the *heart* of faith — this almost seems to imply that the opponent could not be saved — but theologically there are indeed wide gaps here. If we apply this to our own time, we may say that also the ways of the (orthodox) Reformed and the Evangelicals part here. However, this concerns only the theoretical-theological level — fortunately not necessarily the existential level of the heart and of saving faith.

### 5.6.2 Jean de Labadie

It is interesting that in this context Graafland points to the church view of the French-Dutch Reformed theologian Jean de Labadie (1610–1674), which he described as a "radicalization": "If the covenant comprises only the elect [as many orthodox Reformed taught and teach], then also the Christian congregation must consist of elect persons only, and all church life, including the administration of the sacraments, must be placed under this norm."⁹⁰ De Labadie could point here to ecclesiastical forerunners like Theodore Beza and Hieronymus Zanchius, who had already spoken in this vein; he was merely giving concrete ecclesiastical form to this view. It must be added, though, that his followers, the Labadists, did not maintain their ecclesiastical separation for a very long time, as has happened so often with secession movements. However, the basic idea remains fascinating: if the church is

---

88. Cf. Ouweneel (2010b, 458–60).
89. Graafland (1996, 399).
90. Ibid., 400.

the "holy congregation and gathering of true Christian believers" (Belgic Confession, Art. 27), why does she not strive for a concrete ecclesiastical form of this in "assemblies of believers (*with* their children)" (see §5.5.2 point [a])?

In spite of his unrealistic idealism, de Labadie did not aim at anything different than what so many seceded Protestants, including the Evangelicals, have sought in their fundamental resistance to the national church (*volkskerk*) or the state church. As a matter of principle, the church in a given country does not encompass that nation or that state but only the believers in that country. At the same time, it is fascinating to see how few Reformed thinkers followed de Labadie in this, even those who emphasized that it was not some institution but the heart and the devoted Christian life that was at stake. The reason for this was pastoral rather than theological: they were unable to resign themselves to writing off from the church in this way those who were not yet believers.[91] Reformed secessionists as well as Evangelicals cannot agree with this, because in *their* church services all those who are not yet believers are also welcome — Evangelical services are often even far more accessible than many Reformed services — whereas the actual congregation is a "holy congregation of true Christian believers" (see above).

It is a typically Reformed fear that both modernists and Evangelicals put too much emphasis on the mutuality in the covenant, in which God is thought to assign to humanity an independent, and often even decisive, role in history.[92] Elsewhere, I have endeavored to explain this mutuality more extensively, and to distinguish it from a rigid predestination doctrine, without getting into Arminian or Open Theist waters.[93]

In this respect, Reformed theologians will never be easily satisfied. Hendrikus Berkhof, himself of Reformed origins,

---

91. Ibid.
92. See, e.g., Van Genderen (1995).
93. Ouweneel (2008b, 86–89 and passim).

struggled with this mutuality for a long time,[94] and wrote, among other things: "We may not (in extreme Protestant fashion) speak of the 'sole activity' of God; then we are in danger of eliminating man and his responsibility. . . . This is how we must see it: God creates for himself a partner and allows himself to be limited and resisted by the freedom of that partner. But all of salvation history guarantees that ultimately he will not lose his grip on the world and will not rest until he has—no, not conquered and subjugated but—led his human opponent to the true freedom of the sons of God."[95]

I find this a splendid—I would almost say, Evangelical—statement. However, on the one hand, there were theologians who believe that Berkhof had not gone far enough here, such as Ellen Flesseman-van Leer.[96] On the other hand, Berkhof's view could not find favor in Reformed eyes. Both Cornelis Graafland and Jan Hoek found that in this statement, Berkhof "is belittling the absolute sovereignty of God's grace."[97] In opposition to this allegation I would ask: in their view, would even the smallest human contribution belittle God's sovereignty? I consider this to be a basic mistake (see more extensively Appendix III). There would be some truth in it if humans could actually disrupt or impede some of God's plans. But if it is God himself who has *sovereignly decided* to leave room for human contribution, I fail to see how this could ever be interpreted as belittling the absolute sovereignty of God's grace. Elsewhere, I have extensively discussed this entire tension between divine sovereignty and human responsibility.[98]

---

94. See Berkhof (1966).
95. Berkhof (1991, 217–18).
96. See Flesseman-van Leer (1974).
97. J. Hoek in Hagoort (1999, 97); cf. J. Hoek in Hoek and Verboom (2010, 59–60).
98. Ouweneel (2008b).

# Chapter 6
# The New Covenant in the New Testament

*And he took bread, and when he had given thanks,*
    *he broke it and gave it to them, saying,*
*"This is my body, which is given for you.*
    *Do this in remembrance of me."*
*And likewise the cup after they had eaten, saying,*
    *"This cup that is poured out for you*
    *is the New Covenant in my blood."*
                              Luke 22:19–20

*Such is the confidence that we have*
    *through Christ toward God.*
*Not that we are sufficient in ourselves*
    *to claim anything as coming from us,*
*but our sufficiency is from God,*
    *who has made us sufficient*
    *to be ministers of a New Covenant,*
*not of the letter*
    *but of the Spirit.*
*For the letter kills,*

> *but the Spirit gives life.*
> 2 Corinthians 3:4–6

**Summary**: *To understand the Eternal Covenant it is of great importance to study what the New Testament has to say about the New Covenant. Jesus spoke about it when instituting the last supper, Paul speaks of the apostles as "ministers of the New Covenant," James speaks of the "Torah of freedom" and the "royal Torah." The New Covenant is closely linked with the Messianic Torah, as the Old Covenant is with the Mosaic Torah (see the previous volume in this series), just as the concept of covenant is linked with the concept of righteousness (see the next volume in this series). The New Covenant is not a replacement of the Old Covenant, but a renewal of it. Paul's most extensive treatment of the covenant is in Galatians, where he argues that the Sinaitic covenant could in no way annul the unconditional promise of the Abrahamic covenant (Gal. 3), and where he extensively compares the Old Covenant (Hagar-Ishmael-Sinai-earthly Jerusalem) and the New Covenant (Sarah-Isaac-Zion-heavenly Jerusalem). In opposition to the Judaizers, he argues that the two polities cannot be intermingled in any way. The book of Hebrews adds to this in a unique way. It explains why the Old Covenant had to be replaced by a new one, and what are the characteristics of this New Covenant. It shows how this covenant is made with restored Israel, but how the blessings of it are already granted to the Jesus-believers today. There is no room here for any supersessionism or spiritualization.*

## 6.1 The New Covenant Today
### 6.1.1 The New Covenant in Old and New Testaments

ACCORDING TO JEREMIAH 31 AND HEBREWS 8, the New Covenant is formally established with the twelve tribes of Israel (see §2.4.3): "'Behold, the days are coming,' declares the LORD, 'when I will make a New Covenant with the house of Israel and the house of Judah'" (Jer. 31:31; cf. Heb. 8:8). In Jeremiah 31, the nations are nothing other than witnesses of the renewed covenant that God makes with the ten and the two tribes (v. 10, "Hear the word of the Lord, O nations, and declare it in the coastlands far away; say, 'He who scattered Israel will gather him, and will keep him as a shepherd keeps his flock'"). Also in Jeremiah 33:9 the distinction is clearly maintained: "And this city [i.e., Jerusalem] shall be to me a name of joy, a praise and a glory before all the nations of the earth who shall hear of all the good that I do for them [i.e., Israel]. They shall fear and tremble because of all the good and all the prosperity I provide for it."

Only a few times, the nations enter the picture as beneficiaries of the New Covenant, and, as far as the Old Testament is concerned, only in Isaiah. God tells the Servant of the Lord: "I am the Lord; I have called you in righteousness; I will take you by the hand and keep you; I will give you as a covenant for the people, a light for the nations" (Isa. 42:6). This verse does not explicitly say that the covenant, which is for "the people" (i.e., Israel), will also be a blessing for the nations, but the parallelism does suggest such a connection. In Jesus, who is the embodiment of the New Covenant, there is blessing for all the nations. More concrete is Isaiah 56:6-7: "And the foreigners who join themselves to the Lord, to minister to him, to love the name of the Lord, and to be his servants, everyone who keeps the Sabbath and does not profane it, and holds fast my covenant—these I will bring to my holy mountain, and make them joyful in my house of prayer; their burnt offerings and their sacrifices will be accepted on my altar; for my house shall be called a house of prayer for all peoples."

In the New Testament, at first only Israel is in the picture; in the words of the priest Zechariah: "Blessed be the Lord God of Israel, . . . as he spoke by the mouth of his holy prophets from of old, . . . to show the mercy promised to our fathers and to remember his holy covenant, the oath that he swore to our father Abraham" (Luke 1:68-73). Peter told the Jews, "You are the sons of the prophets and of the covenant that God made with your fathers, saying to Abraham, 'And in your offspring shall all the families of the earth be blessed'" (Acts 3:25).

The Gentile nations enter the picture only gradually. Jesus said, "the Son of Man came not to be served but to serve, and to give his life as a ransom *for many*" (Matt. 20:28; cf. Mark 10:45). And later, "[T]his is my blood of the covenant, which is poured out *for many* for the forgiveness of sins" (Matt. 26:28; cf. Mark 14:24; Luke 22:20; 1 Cor. 11:25). Note here the word "many," which suggests a much wider circle than that of the disciples, and even than that of Israel. They are the "many" of Matthew 8:11–12: "[M]any will come from east and west and recline at table with Abraham, Isaac, and Jacob in the kingdom of heaven, while the sons of the kingdom [i.e., non-repenting Jews[1]] will be thrown into the outer darkness" (cf. Luke 13:29).

This meaning of the word "many" is entirely fitting within Matthew's Gospel, because from the outset he wants to show why and how the gospel of Jesus was rejected by the majority of Israel but was accepted by many outside Israel (cf. Matt. 24:14, "[T]his gospel of the kingdom will be proclaimed throughout the whole world as a testimony to all nations"; 28:19, "Go therefore and make disciples of all nations"). Of course, Matthew uses the word also with different meanings (cf. 7:13, 22; 22:14; 24:5, 10, 12; 27:53).

In John 10:16, Jesus said, "I have other sheep [i.e., Gentiles] that are not of this fold [i.e., Israel]. I must bring them also, and they will listen to my voice. So there will be one flock [i.e., that which Paul calls the *Ekklesia*], one shepherd." In all these cases, believers from the Gentiles are brought near to take part in the blessings of the New Covenant, together with believing Israel (cf. Eph. 2:11–22). More explicitly, this is what Jesus said as he instituted the Lord's Supper: *many* will be included under the blessings of the New Covenant, namely, all those believing Gentiles who, just like believing Jews, receive

---

1. Cf. the difference with Matt. 13:38 ("The field is the world, and the good seed is the sons of the kingdom"), where the "sons of the kingdom" are *true* disciples, coming primarily from the *Gentile* world.

forgiveness of sins through Jesus' blood.[2]

We get the same picture in 2 Corinthians 3, where the apostles are called "ministers of a New Covenant." That is, they administer the New Covenant by preaching the gospel and thus leading people to repentance and salvation. This is described in verse 3 in a peculiar way (NKJV): "[Y]ou are an epistle of Christ, ministered by us, written not with ink but by the Spirit of the living God, not on tablets of stone but on tablets of flesh, [that is,] of the heart." Note the clear allusion to Jeremiah 31:33, "I will put my Torah within them, and I will write it on their hearts." Please carefully note the comparison Paul is making here. Under the Old Covenant, God wrote "with ink" the Torah on tablets of stone (Exod. 31:18; 34:1; Deut. 10:2). Under the New Covenant, by the Spirit and through the "ministers of the New Covenant," God writes Christ on tablets of flesh, namely, on the hearts of all those who believe in him, both Jews and Gentiles. (Also Gentiles, because Paul writes here to Corinthians believers, who were mostly of Gentile origin.)

I also point here to Galatians 4:24 and 28, but this passage will be dealt with later (see §6.5).

## 6.1.2 New Covenant and Federalism

In the discussion with federalists, the identity of the actual covenant partner in the New Covenant is of essential importance. The main reason is that federalists acknowledge only one covenantal people: the "church" from Adam (or Abraham) until the "last day," that is, "spiritual Israel," the "Israel of God," or whatever it is called. For instance, see the Heidelberg Catechism (Q&A 54): "Q. What do you believe concerning 'the holy catholic church'? A. I believe that the Son of God through his Spirit and Word, out of the entire human race, from the beginning of the world to its end, gathers, protects, and preserves for himself a community chosen for eternal life and united in true faith."

---

2. See extensively Ouweneel (2010c, chapters 8–9).

Please note that this "community chosen for eternal life" apparently is identical with what in the question is identified as "the holy catholic [i.e., universal] church." The "church" is here simply the collective term for *all* believers, indiscriminately, from *all* dispensations ("from the beginning of the world to its end"). If the New Covenant is made with "Israel," this is no problem at all for federalists, since the church is "(spiritual) Israel."³

As an example, let me quote here the comments of John Gill (1697–1771), who was a Baptist pastor, but thoroughly Calvinistic in much of his theology. In connection with Hebrews 8:8 he wrote: "The persons with whom this covenant is promised to be made, are the houses of Israel and Judah; which being literally taken, had its fulfilment in the first times of the Gospel, through the ministry of John the Baptist, Christ, and his apostles, by whom this covenant was made known to God's elect among the twelve tribes; but being mystically understood, includes both Jews and Gentiles, the whole Israel of God; Israel not after the flesh, but after the Spirit; such as were Jews inwardly; God's elect of every nation."⁴ In a very concise form, all the supposed evidence for the idea that the church is the "Israel of God" or "Israel after the Spirit" is put together here. See for an extensive refutation, chapter 7 below.

Federalists see this New Covenant realized in the present dispensation. However, according to Jeremiah 31 and many other Old Testament passages, viewed in the light of the New Testament, this covenant will be established at the second coming of Christ, namely, at the beginning of the Messianic kingdom (Heb. ᶜolâm habba, the "age [or, world] to come"). To limit myself to Jeremiah 30–31: the New Covenant will be

---

3. E.g., Brown and Keele (2012, 18): "The new covenant is the constitution for the church, the kingdom of heaven on earth." That is a double mistake. The New Covenant is made with Israel, and the kingdom of heaven is a much wider and different concept than the church; see Ouweneel (2011, chapters 9–14).
4. http://biblehub.com/commentaries/gill/hebrews/8.htm.

established when Israel and Judah, "in the latter days" (cf. Isa. 2:2), will have been restored in the promised land (cf. Deut. 4:30; Ezek. 38:16) under "David their king/prince/ruler," that is, the Messiah (cf. Hos. 3:5), the hostile nations will be judged, and "the city" (i.e., Jerusalem) will be repaired (Jer. 30, especially vv. 9, 11, 18, 20–21, 24).

Jeremiah 31 adds concrete geographical references, thus underscoring its literal fulfillment: the "hill country of Ephraim" (ancient home of the principal of the ten tribes), Zion (ancient home of the two tribes), Ramah (vv. 6, 15), the Tower of Hananel, the Corner Gate, Gareb, Goath, the brook Kidron, the Horse Gate, all in Jerusalem (vv. 38–40). It is absurd to spiritualize all such precise geographical references. There cannot be the slightest doubt where and when the New Covenant will be made: with the united twelve tribes, in the promised land, at or after the second coming of the Messiah.

### 6.1.3 Significance for Today

Of course, I am not denying that the New Covenant has great significance already today. To be sure, it has not yet been formally established, or at least it has not yet been formally effectuated. However, the believers of the (New Testament) Ekklesia of Christ—though never called "Jews" or "Israel" (see chapter 7)—have already been introduced, so to speak, under the umbrella of the New Covenant. They have been brought under the Mediator of the New Covenant, who is their life, and whose blood, upon which the New Covenant is founded, has cleansed them (Heb. 8:6; 12:24; Luke 22:20; 1 Cor. 11:25). However, except for a few Jews who by faith have joined the Ekklesia, *the actual covenant partner, that is, the restored ethnic Israel, is not yet in the picture*. This is a pivotal point: the New Covenant will be effectuated only at the coming of the Messianic kingdom, the center of which will be the converted and restored Israel.[5]

In the meantime, one could argue that the realization of the

---

5. See extensively Ouweneel (2012, especially chapters 12–13).

New Covenant in the present age is God's program for God's kingdom.[6] The two are closely linked together. We have the kingdom of God today in a hidden form—because the King is still hidden (cf. Col. 3:3)—and in the "age to come" (Heb. 6:5) and the "world to come" (2:5) he will appear in a visible form. Likewise, we might argue that we have the New Covenant today in a hidden form, and in the "age to come" and the "world to come" in a visible form. In the well-known Old Testament passages on the New Covenant, Jeremiah 30–31 and Ezekiel 37,[7] the Messiah occupies the central position. We saw this already in Jeremiah 30:9 and verses 21–22. See also Ezekiel 37:24–26, "My servant David shall be king over them, and they shall all have one shepherd. They shall walk in my rules and be careful to obey my statutes. They shall dwell in the land that I gave to my servant Jacob, where your fathers lived. They and their children and their children's children shall dwell there forever, and David my servant shall be their prince forever. I will make a covenant of peace with them. It shall be an everlasting covenant with them. And I will set them in their land and multiply them, and will set my sanctuary in their midst forevermore."

When the King himself institutes the Lord's Supper for his disciples, he does so in an eschatological context in that he refers to both the kingdom of God and the New Covenant: "'For I tell you that from now on I will not drink of the fruit of the vine until the kingdom of God comes.' And he took bread, and when he had given thanks, he broke it and gave it to them, saying, 'This is my body, which is given for you. Do this in remembrance of me.' And likewise the cup after they had eaten, saying, 'This cup that is poured out for you is the New Covenant in my blood'" (Luke 22:18–20). It is in this context that Christians celebrate the Lord's Supper: they not only look back to the cross by eating and drinking "in

---

6. See extensively Ouweneel (2011, chapters 9–14).
7. Also cf. Isa. 54:10; 55:3; 59:21; 61:8; for a special reference to the Messiah, see 42:6; 49:8.

remembrance of him," but they also look forward to the appearance of the King in glory and majesty in that they eat and drink "until he comes" (1 Cor. 11:24-26), that is, until both God's kingdom and the New Covenant will find their perfect fulfillment.[8]

## 6.1.4 Continuity

There is far more continuity between the Old and the New Covenants than real dispensationalists have ever realized. Likewise, there is continuity between the pre-Mosaic covenants: the Noahic promises are still in force under the Abrahamic covenant, the Abrahamic promises are still in force under the Mosaic covenant, the Mosaic promises are still in force under the New Covenant. *All* these covenants are rooted in God's gracious and unconditional promises. Thus, in Galatians 3:15-4:7, the terms "covenant" (Gr. *diathēkē*) and "promise" (*epangelia*) are used more or less interchangeably. The covenant that God made with Abraham (Gen. 15 and 17) consisted of unilateral and unconditional ("irrevocable," Rom. 11:29) promises that God had made to him. These promises are for those believers who, in the present dispensation, are called "sons," "offspring," and "heirs" (Gal. 3:7, 29). This includes the Jesus-believers from the Gentiles, who are fully included in the Abrahamic covenant by belonging to the nations that would be blessed in Abraham (vv. 8, 14).

At the same time, I repeat that none of these covenants was only unconditional. We have seen this earlier: no covenant between God and humans existed without some form of Torah connected with it, which the covenant partners had to observe. On the one hand, every covenant between God and humans was based on unconditional grace, including the covenant that God allegedly made with the prelapsarian Adam (cf. §3.6). On the other hand, it is equally true that no bestowal of covenantal grace occurred without God prescribing a way of obedience connected with it, in order to show how people

---
8. See Ouweneel (2010c, chapters 8–9).

are to live under that grace.

The very same grace that brings us salvation—as a free, sovereign gift of God—is the grace that is "training us to renounce ungodliness and worldly passions, and to live self-controlled, upright, and godly lives in the present age, waiting for our blessed hope, the appearing of the glory of our great God and Savior Jesus Christ, who gave himself for us to redeem us from all lawlessness and to purify for himself a people for his own possession who are zealous for good works" (Titus 2:11-14). In a double way, Paul teaches us here both sides of the truth: (a) grace leads us to salvation, but also to a self-controlled, upright, and godly walk; (b) Christ redeemed us from our sins, but this was in order that we would be a people "zealous for good works."

This is in full agreement with Jesus' own doctrine. In the Great Commandment, he gave the order that "repentance and forgiveness of sins should be proclaimed in his [i.e., Christ's] name to all nations" (Luke 24:47), but also: "Go therefore and make disciples of all nations" (Matt. 28:19). The two go together: no forgiveness without this leading to discipleship (dedication to the Master), and *vice versa*. "My sheep hear my voice, and I know them, and they follow me. I give them eternal life, and they will never perish" (John 10:27-28). Again, the two go together: following Jesus and receiving eternal life; the two are inseparable. To be sure, for *both* elements, God's grace and the work of the Holy Spirit are indispensable. But that does not alter the appeal to human responsibility: salvation *through* Messiah brings people under the Torah *of* Messiah.

If there is no self-controlled, upright, and godly walk, no elementary obedience to the Torah of Christ, why should we assume that the person concerned is really saved? If we do not see in him any "zeal for good works," why should we assume that he has been redeemed from his sins? If we do not see any evidence of following the Good Shepherd, why should we assume that the sheep will receive eternal life? If there are no *signs* of life (breath, pulse, warmth), why should we assume that the person is alive?

We have seen that from Adam to eternity, no manifestation of the Torah of God is unaccompanied by a certain measure of sovereign and saving grace. But neither is there any covenantal grace without some form of the Torah under which the partners are placed. Since, or perhaps even from before, the fall, every manifestation of the one, eternal Torah was associated with a certain covenant. Conversely, every covenant was associated with a certain Torah, which always was the delight of those who had truly learned to live out of divine grace: the righteous man's "delight is in the Torah of the Lord, and on his Torah he meditates day and night" (Ps. 1:2). "[T]he precepts of the Lord are right, rejoicing the heart," that is, the heart of the righteous (Ps. 19:8). "Your testimonies are my delight. . . . Lead me in the path of your commandments, for I delight in it . . . your Torah is my delight. . . . If your Torah had not been my delight, I would have perished in my affliction" (Ps. 119:24, 35, 77, 92, 174; also cf. vv. 14, 16, 47, 70, 143).[9]

## 6.2   The Mosaic and the Messianic Torah
### 6.2.1   Righteousness in Paul's Writings

The New Testament view of the Sinaitic covenant corresponds precisely with the Old Testament view described above (§6.1). If we pay attention to the connection that exists, according to the New Testament, between the Mosaic and the Messianic Torah (see the previous volume in this series), we will also better understand the coherence of the Old and the New Covenants.

Paul refers to the Torah as the basic rule for the true people of God: the Torah as the great Love Command (Rom. 13:8–10), the "Torah of Messiah" (Gal. 6:2). The purpose of our salvation is "that the righteous requirement of the Torah

---

9.  Cf. Messianic Jew L. R. Dewitz in Kac (1986, 173): law and grace are never to be severed; no law without grace, no grace without law.

might be fulfilled in us, who walk not according to the flesh but according to the Spirit" (Rom. 8:4).[10] In the expression, "law [Gr. *nomos*] of faith" (Rom. 3:27), *nomos* can have the sense of "principle" (here, faith principle), but *nomos* might also refer to the (Messianic) Torah as it is known in and by faith.[11] Likewise, the "law of righteousness" (Rom. 9:31, margin) could mean the principle of someone's own (alleged) righteousness, but it could also refer to the Torah as a means of attaining or maintaining righteousness.[12] For a Christian, this implies putting aside one's own strength and entrusting oneself to God in Christ; otherwise, one will not "reach" that Torah, as our verse says.

In this sense, for Paul the Torah is still fully in force. In Romans 9:31, we see that he is definitely interested in how one can "reach" the Torah, that is, the true righteousness that the Torah is all about. Paul knew of himself that he was "under the Torah of Christ" (1 Cor. 9:21). In Greek the expression is *ennomos Christou*, which means something close to being "in-lawed of Christ," that is, "placed under (ruled by, bound by) the Torah of Messiah," or even, "living within (the polity determined by) the Messianic Torah." Paul calls the commandments of the Mosaic Torah "holy," and the commandment "holy and righteous and good" (Rom. 7:12), "spiritual" (v. 14), "good" (v. 16). Therefore, *as such* there can be nothing wrong with a "righteousness" that is "through the Torah" (Gal. 2:1; cf. 3:21), or a "righteousness [that is rooted] in the Torah" (Phil 3:6); Paul even tells us emphatically that "the doers of the Torah will be justified" (Rom. 2:13), without any "buts" and "howevers." As such, it is perfectly true: he who faithfully observes the Torah will be justified (that is, declared righteous).

---

10. See Ouweneel (2010c, 13). Regarding the various Pauline passages concerning the Torah of Love, see Söding (1995, 187–267), especially on Galatians and Romans.
11. See the discussion in Moo (1996, 247–50, incl. note 14).
12. Ibid., 622–27.

My point here is not that there is no human who, *by and of himself,* can keep the Torah, and thus can be declared righteous (although it is perfectly true that there is no such human). My point is rather that even the righteousness of believers, though objectively rooted in God's grace and (subjectively) conditioned by human faith, in the end can be no other righteousness than one that satisfies the demands of the Messianic Torah. There is no true righteousness that does not, in some way or another, answer to God's Torah.[13]

A "righteousness that is through the Torah" could be faulty, however, if one tries to attain it in one's own strength, apart from the work of Christ and the power of the Holy Spirit (traditional view), and/or if one finds in the Torah a ground for ethnocentric arrogance by claiming that those who wish to receive the covenant blessing have to join Israel through circumcision (newer view).[14] In these senses, *and in these senses alone,* the *alleged* "righteousness that is through the Torah" stands in opposition to the *genuine* "righteousness that is through the Torah" (Rom. 10:6; cf. Gal. 3:11-12). The true righteousness that is through faith is exactly identical with what genuinely satisfies the commands of the Messianic Torah. Thus, the righteousness that is through faith is *not* in opposition to the righteousness that is through the Torah, for it is itself a righteousness that agrees with the Messianic Torah. No, it stands in opposition only to the righteousness that is allegedly through the Torah *alone,* and implicitly or explicitly rejects the work of Christ and the power of the Holy Spirit.

---

13. See Ouweneel (2010a, chapters 7–8); see more extensively the third and last volume in the present series.
14. See especially Dunn (1998, 128–61, 354–71, 631–58), and his references to earlier literature. Dunn's interpretation of expressions like "under the law," "works of the law," "released from the law" in the light of his view concerning Israel's ethnocentric arrogance is clarifying and fruitful, but seems to me just as one-sided as the traditional view (the law as a means of self-justification); see Ouweneel (2015a, App. II).

## 6.2.2 Righteousness in James' Writings

We meet the same positive meaning of the Torah in the epistle of James, which refers to the "law of liberty" (James 1:25; 2:12) and the "royal law" (2:8). Perhaps in this respect James was familiar with an ancient Jewish tradition. Exodus 32:16 says, "The tablets were the work of God, and the writing was the writing of God, engraved on the tablets." The Hebrew word for "engraved" is *harut*, but the Midrash Rabbah on this verse says that we should read it as *herut*, "freedom." The idea then is that God's Torah implies true freedom, not slavery.

The expression, "royal law," could be rendered as "Torah (law, constitution) of the kingdom," that is, the kingdom of God in Christ;[15] what Paul calls the "Torah of Messiah," that is, the anointed King (Gal. 6:2). Jesus saw this Torah summarized in the Love Command: "'You shall love the LORD your God with all your heart and with all your soul and with all your mind' [Deut. 6:5]. This is the great and first commandment. And a second is like it: 'You shall love your neighbor as yourself' [Lev. 19:18]. On these two commandments depend all the Torah and the Prophets" (Matt. 22:37-40). "A new commandment I give to you, that you love one another: just as I have loved you, you also are to love one another. By this all people will know that you are my disciples, if you have love for one another" (John 13:34-35).

The apostle Paul expressed the same thought, while at the same time highlighting the close relationship between the Mosaic Torah and the Messianic Torah by quoting several of the Ten Words: "Owe no one anything, except to love each other, for the one who loves another has fulfilled the Torah. For the commandments, 'You shall not commit adultery,' 'You shall not murder,' 'You shall not steal,' 'You shall not covet,' and any other commandment, are summed up in this word: 'You shall love your neighbor as yourself.' Love does no wrong to a neighbor; therefore love is the fulfilling of

---

15. Cf. Ouweneel (2011, §12.3.2; 2015a, §§1.3.2, 3.2.1, 4.3.1, 8.2.1).

the Torah" (Rom. 13:8–10). "For you were called to freedom, brothers. Only do not use your freedom as an opportunity for the flesh, but through love serve one another. For the whole Torah is fulfilled in one word: 'You shall love your neighbor as yourself'" (Gal. 5:13–14).

The apostle James, too, saw this Torah concentrated in the Love Command: "If you really fulfill the royal Torah according to the Scripture, 'You shall love your neighbor as yourself,' you are doing well. But if you show partiality, you are committing sin and are convicted by the law as transgressors. For whoever keeps the whole Torah but fails in one point has become accountable for all of it. For he who said, 'Do not commit adultery,' also said, 'Do not murder.' If you do not commit adultery but do murder, you have become a transgressor of the law. So speak and so act as those who are to be judged under the Torah of liberty" (2:8–12).

Earlier in the epistle, James had written, "But the one who looks into the perfect Torah, the Torah of liberty, and perseveres, being no hearer who forgets but a doer who acts, he will be blessed in his doing" (1:25). In itself, the Torah is indeed always perfect, simply because it has been given by God. And those who live by God's grace, whether under the Old or under the New Covenants, have always known the Torah as a "Torah of liberty." This is a Torah that is valid for the person who has been genuinely set free by faith in God, and (since the coming of Christ) by faith in Christ: "For freedom Christ has set us free; stand firm therefore, and do not submit again to a yoke of slavery" (Gal. 5:1). A law of slavery constantly demands of those under it to do the things that they do not like to do, things that are against their will. In this sense, the Torah is a heavy "yoke" (Acts 15:10). A law of liberty, however, is not opposed to our freedom but guarantees it. It is a law that demands of us the very things that our new nature in the power of the Holy Spirit desires to do.

### 6.2.3 Similarities

There are more similarities between the Mosaic Torah and the Messianic Torah, and therefore between the Old and the New Covenants. Thus, the Messianic Torah, too, knows its sacred times (Heb. *mo'adim*). I am not referring to the Sunday, for the New Testament does not know a consecration of the Sunday as an obligatory day of rest, no particular sacred day, as the Shabbat was (see the first volume in this series). A better example of a sacred time is the celebration of the Lord's Supper, no matter how frequently, possibly even daily (cf. Acts 2:42, 46).[16] I cannot see anything wrong with taking Jesus' word, "Do this in remembrance of me" (Luke 22:19; 1 Cor. 11:24–25), as a command in the sense of the Messianic Torah, just as thanking God (Gr. *eucharisteite*, from which the word Eucharist was derived) is an imperative (1 Thess. 5:18; cf. Eph. 5:20, *eucharistountes* ["giving thanks"]; Col. 4:2, *grēgorountes en eucharistíai*, ["being watchful in thanksgiving"], participles functioning here as imperatives). These are only some of the many commandments of the Messianic Torah—and some of the loveliest commandments at that—each of which are expressions of the love for God and for Christ.

Another example of the similarity between the Mosaic Torah and the Messianic Torah, and thus between the Old and the New Covenants, is that, in the New Testament, too, the people of God are "a chosen race, a royal priesthood, a holy nation, a people for his own possession" (1 Pet. 2:9). These words remind us of God's words to the people of Israel: "[T]herefore, if you will indeed obey my voice and keep my covenant, you shall be my treasured possession among all peoples, for all the earth is mine; and you shall be to me a kingdom of priests and a holy nation" (Exod. 19:5–6).

As such, living under the Messianic Torah, believers must be a people devoted to God, distinguishing itself from all other people as far as their eating and clothing are concerned, their

---

16. See ibid., §11.7.3.

partaking in sexual, social, economic, and political life, and living out their religion (Rom. 12:1; 1 Cor. 8:37; 10:31; 1 Thess. 4:3-8; 1 Tim. 2:9; Heb. 13:14-16; 1 Pet. 2:5; 3:3). Today, the "dividing wall of hostility," namely, between Jews and Gentiles, has been broken down, *not* by abolishing the Torah as such, as certain translations and commentaries might suggest, but by breaking down the hostility between Jews and Gentiles that the Torah—inadvertently, against its own nature—had brought about. A good example of a correct rendering is the translation by David Stern: "[H]e has made us both [i.e., Jewish believers and Gentile believers] one and has broken down the *m'chitzah* [dividing wall] which divides us by destroying in his own body the enmity occasioned by the Torah, with its commands set forth in the form of ordinances."[17]

For instance, circumcision in terms of its dividing significance, keeping Jews and Gentiles apart, has no use anymore (Rom. 3:30; 1 Cor. 7:19; Gal. 5:6; 6:15). This issue must be distinguished from the question whether it is useful for Messianic Jews to be circumcised and have their little sons circumcised (see again the previous volume). At the same time, the Messianic Torah creates necessarily a new "dividing wall," namely, between the circumcised and uncircumcised *of heart* (cf. Acts 7:51; Rom. 2:28-29; 4:12; Phil. 3:3; Col. 2:11; 3:11; in the Old Testament: Lev. 26:41; Deut. 10:16; 30:6; Isa. 52:1; Jer. 4:4; 6:10; 9:25; Ezek. 44:7, 9).[18] This is a "dividing wall" that God is *not* going to remove; it involves the deep cleft in all of humanity: the cleft between the righteous and the wicked, whether they are Jews or Gentiles.

## 6.3 Various New Testament Passages
### 6.3.1 Being Like Christ

Of course, the Messianic Torah is indirectly a revelation of who the Messiah is in himself. *He* loved God with all his heart, soul, and mind. *He* loved his people to the very end

---

17. Stern (1989, 259).
18. See Ouweneel (2011, §6.1.2).

(John 13:1; Eph. 5:2, 25). *He* honored his parents (Luke 2:51), *he* honored the Sabbath (Matt. 12:8), *he* testified to the truth (John 18:37), etc. In the first volume of the present series, I tried to show that Jesus not only *observed* the Torah — he lived it out. He *was* the Torah.[19] The believers' observance of the Torah with a circumcised heart, in the power of God's Spirit, then, implies an increasing resembling Christ himself. This is of great importance, for this concerns God's eternal counsel with respect to the Ekklesia: "[T]hose whom he foreknew he also predestined to be conformed to the image of his Son, in order that he might be the firstborn among many brothers" (Rom. 8:29); "[H]e chose us in him before the foundation of the world, that we should be holy and blameless before him. In love he predestined us for adoption as sons through Jesus Christ, according to the purpose of his will, to the praise of his glorious grace, with which he has blessed us in the Beloved" (Eph. 1:4-6).

Where the veil has been taken away from the Torah, and the heart is directed to Christ, there transformation has occurred: the believer, "beholding [or, reflecting, Greek *katoptrizomenoi*] the glory of the Lord," is "being transformed [*metamorphoumetha*] into the same image [i.e., of Christ] from one degree of glory to another. For this comes from the Lord who is the Spirit" (2 Cor. 3:18). By observing the Torah of Christ, Christ himself is "formed" (*morphōtēi*, Gal. 4:19; cf. 6:2) in believers. As Jesus said himself, "It is enough for the disciple to be like his teacher, and the servant like his master" (Matt. 10:25). And Paul wrote, "put on the Lord Jesus Christ" (Rom. 13:14; cf. Gal. 3:27, "as many of you as were baptized into Christ have put on Christ").

In a positive sense, although the Torah does not literally lead the godly to Christ (see §6.4), at least it presents the picture of Christ. It is not the fact of someone's standing under the Mosaic Torah as such that turns that person into a slave.

---

19. Perhaps in a similar way Jesus *is* the covenant (Isa. 42:6; 49:8).

Could Moses, Joshua, Phinehas, David, Elijah, Elisha, Isaiah, Jeremiah, and also Zechariah and Elizabeth (see §6.3.2), Joseph and Mary, Simeon and Anna, etc., ever be called "slaves"? No, standing under the Mosaic Torah with too much self-assurance *and* being at the same time powerless through sin— *that* makes slaves of people: "[E]veryone who practices sin is a slave to sin. The slave does not remain in the house forever; the son remains forever. So if the Son sets you free, you will be free indeed" (John 8:34–36). "But thanks be to God, that you who were once slaves of sin have become obedient from the heart to the standard of teaching to which you were committed" (Rom. 6:17).

The negative meaning of *each* Torah, from the Adamic Torah to the Millennial Torah, is that it makes slaves of all those who, though perhaps (at least outwardly) belonging to God's people, are wicked trespassers or "decent" hypocrites, inflated legalists or arrogant ethnocentrists. But the true, positive meaning of *each* Torah, from the Adamic Torah to the Millennial Torah, is that it is the rule of life for those who, by grace and through faith, stand on the foundation of atonement and forgiveness, possess life with God, and walk in the power of the Holy Spirit. "For the *nomos* [i.e., principle] of the Spirit of life has set you free in Christ Jesus from the *nomos* [i.e., principle] of sin and death. . . . By sending his own Son in the likeness of sinful flesh and for sin, he condemned sin in the flesh, in order that the righteous requirement of the *nomos* [i.e., Torah] might be fulfilled in us, who walk not according to the flesh but according to the Spirit" (Rom. 8:2–4).

### 6.3.2 Passages in Luke's Writings

The priest Zechariah and his wife, Elizabeth, "were both righteous before God, walking blamelessly in all the commandments and statutes of the Lord" (Luke 1:6; cf. vv. 74–77). This is the best conceivable proof that, also according to the New Testament, a person can definitely be righteous through works of the Torah—but only by way of believing in God, living out of his strength and mercy (cf. Luke 1:72, 78), in true humility and repentance, in the power of the Holy Spirit (cf. vv. 41, 67). Since Jesus' death and resurrection, we should add: on the basis of the atoning work of Christ, and by the power of the Holy Spirit. This is what Paul expresses as a general, and in itself perfectly true, principle: "[T]he doers of the Torah will be justified" (Rom. 2:13). I refer here to both the first volume of this series, on the Torah, and the third volume, on righteousness and justification.

In his prophecy, Zechariah expresses his joy concerning the fact that God, in the imminent coming of the Messiah, will remember his covenant with Abraham (vv. 72-73; cf. Mary's words in vv. 54-55, without using the term "covenant"). This covenant was full of promises, anchored in Abraham's offspring, which ultimately is none other than the Messiah himself (cf. Gal. 3:16): "Blessed be the Lord God of Israel, for he has visited and redeemed his people and has raised up a horn of salvation for us in the house of his servant David; . . . to show the mercy promised to our fathers and to remember his holy covenant, the oath that he swore to our father Abraham, to grant us that we, being delivered from the hand of our enemies, might serve him without fear, in holiness and righteousness before him all our days" (Luke 1:68-75).

As stated earlier, at the institution of the Lord's Supper, Jesus uses these words: "[T]his is my blood of the covenant, which is poured out for many for the forgiveness of sins" (Matt. 26:28; cf. Mark 14:24). "This cup that is poured out for you is the new covenant in my blood" (Luke 22:20; cf. 1 Cor. 11:25).[20] Not the blood of goats and calves, characteristic of the Old Covenant, but his own blood is the foundation of the one, true covenant between God and his people. Matthew and Mark leave out the word "new,"[21] whereas Luke 22:20 and 1 Corinthians 11:25 include this word. For the meaning of the

---

20. See Ouweneel (2010c, chapters 8–9).
21. At least according to the newer editions of the Greek New Testament; see Metzger (1975, 64, 113).

text, this does not make any difference. At best we might say that Matthew and Mark underscore that what matters is "the" one covenant: the New Covenant is nothing but the renewal of the Old Covenant.

Van der Waal rightly pointed out that "the gospel [in Acts] is so compelling because those addressed are *children of the covenant*,"[22] and took Acts 3:25-26 as an example. Peter says here, in his address to the Jewish people: "You are the sons of the prophets and of the covenant that God made with your fathers, saying to Abraham, 'And in your offspring shall all the families of the earth be blessed.' [Gen. 22:18; cf. Gal. 3:8] God, having raised up his servant, sent him to you first, to bless you by turning every one of you from your wickedness." He makes clear that, although in Abraham's offspring *all* people would be blessed (insofar as they would come to faith in Christ), the blessing came to Israel first, because they were Abraham's physical offspring. We will return to this when we deal with the way Paul speaks of the "promise" in Galatians 3 (see §6.4).

In Acts 7:8, Stephen uses the remarkable expression "covenant of circumcision," referring to the Abrahamic covenant of Genesis 17, of which circumcision was a sign (v. 11). The expression reminds us of the common Jewish expression for circumcision: *berit milah*, literally "covenant of circumcision." I may add that circumcision is also closely connected with the Sinaitic covenant (Lev. 12:3; Josh. 5:1-8), so that Jesus even could say, "Moses gave you circumcision (not that it is from Moses, but from the fathers)" (John 7:22), and the circumcision party in Jerusalem said, ". . . circumcised according to the custom of Moses" (Acts 15:1).

Circumcision is also mentioned in connection with the Messianic kingdom. First, Scripture speaks of the circumcision of the heart in this context: "And the LORD your God will bring you into the land that your fathers possessed, that you

---

22. Van der Waal (1990, 102).

may possess it. And he will make you more prosperous and numerous than your fathers. And the LORD your God will circumcise your heart and the heart of your offspring, so that you will love the LORD your God with all your heart and with all your soul, that you may live" (Deut. 30:5-6). Second, Scripture refers to the circumcision of the flesh, though in an indirect way: "O Jerusalem, the holy city . . . there shall no more come into you the uncircumcised and the unclean" (Isa. 52:1). "O house of Israel, enough of all your abominations, in admitting foreigners, uncircumcised in heart and flesh, to be in my sanctuary. . . . No foreigner, uncircumcised in heart and flesh . . . shall enter my sanctuary" (Ezek. 44:6-9) — apparently with the implication that circumcised foreigners will be allowed into the new temple of the Messianic kingdom.

### 6.3.3 Passages in Paul's Writings

In Romans 9:4-5, Paul gives a summary of eight privileges and blessings of the Israelites:

(1) adoption (i.e., as sons; see §4.5.3);

(2) glory (the *Shekhinah* in tabernacle and temple; Exod. 40:55; 2 Chron. 7:1-3);

(3) the covenants (see chapter 2);

(4) the Torah-giving (Exod. 19-31; the Torah belongs to Israel, cf. Rom. 3:2);

(5) worship (the ministry of God in tabernacle and temple; see especially Lev. 1-7);

(6) promises (to the patriarchs; see [7]);

(7) the patriarchs (Abraham, Isaac, and Jacob);

(8) "and from their race, according to the flesh, is the Messiah, who is God over all, blessed forever."

Regarding (3) above, the covenants are enumerated here; federalists, who like to speak of "the" covenant, should notice the plural. By definition, the covenants are *God's* covenants in the sense that they proceed from him and are shaped by him. The LORD speaks many times of "my covenant," from Genesis

6:18 to Malachi 2:5, and Israel speaks many times of "your covenant," from Deuteronomy 33:9 to Jeremiah 14:21. At the same time, it is of course perfectly true that the covenants belong to Israel. In Ezekiel 16:61, God speaks to Israel about "the covenant with you," that is literally, "your covenant." This not only holds for the three covenants that were made specifically with Israel (see §2.4), but also for the covenant with Noah, which begins with all humanity but soon focuses upon Israel: Japheth will dwell in the tents of Shem (Gen. 9:27). And of course, the covenants with Abr(ah)am, Levi and David (§2.3) are of primary importance for Israel. They are *God's* covenants, but because they were made with, or on behalf of, Israel, they are also Israel's covenants.

At the same time these covenants have significance for all humanity.

(a) The *Noahic* covenant has a focus on Israel, but was made with all humanity, and even with the animal kingdom (cf. Gen. 6:18–20; 8:1; 9:8–10).

(b) The *Abrahamic* covenant was made with Abraham and his (physical) offspring, that is Israel, but with blessing promised extending to all humanity (Gen. 12:3; 18:18; 22:18; 26:4).

(c) The *Sinaitic* covenant was made with Israel, but even this covenant has significance for all humanity: Israel was to be "a guide to the blind, a light to those who are in darkness, an instructor of the foolish, a teacher of children, having in the Torah the embodiment of knowledge and truth" (Rom. 2:19–20).

(d) The *New Covenant* is made with Israel ("the house of Israel and the house of Judah"), but in view of all humanity: "I will give you as a covenant for the people, a light for the nations" (Isa. 42:6). "And the foreigners who join themselves to the LORD, to minister to him, to love the name of the LORD, and to be his servants, everyone who keeps the Sabbath and does not profane it, and holds fast my covenant—these I will bring to my holy mountain, and make them joyful in my house of prayer; their burnt offerings and their sacrifices will be accepted on my altar; for my house shall be called a house of prayer for all peoples" (Isa. 56:6–7).

Israel is always in the picture, and usually in the foreground. In contrast with this, it is said of believers of Gentile origin: "Therefore remember that at one time you Gentiles in the flesh, called 'the uncircumcision' by what is called the circumcision, which is made in the flesh by hands—remember that you were at that time separated from Christ, alienated from the commonwealth of Israel and *strangers to the covenants of promise*, having no hope and without God in the world" (Eph. 2:11–12). Gentile believers have come under the blessings of the covenants, but originally the covenants did not belong to them. They belonged to Israel.

Romans 11:26–27, which deals with the future redemption of all Israel, quotes the Old Testament: "[I]n this way all Israel will be saved, as it is written, 'The Deliverer will come from Zion, he will banish ungodliness from Jacob'; 'and this will be my covenant with them when I take away their sins.'" Here Paul is linking up with both Isaiah 59:20–21 ("And a Redeemer will come to Zion, to those in Jacob who turn from transgression. . . . And as for me, this is my covenant with them . . .") and Isaiah 27:9 ("Therefore by this the guilt of Jacob will be atoned for"). In this way, the ultimate salvation of all Israel is placed with the broad context of the New Covenant. No wonder: the New Covenant *is* about (ethnical) Israel, which is soon to be restored to the LORD.

In the next §§, I will deal with the New Testament epistles that speak in the most extensive way about the covenant(s): Galatians 3 and 4 (see §§6.4 and 6.5), and especially Hebrews (§§6.6 and 6.7).

## 6.4    The Covenant in Galatians 3
### 6.4.1    No Annulment of the Promise

In Galatians 3 Paul speaks about, among other things, the relationship between Torah and promise. In verse 15 he says,

"[E]ven with a man-made covenant [or, testament, Greek *diathēkē*; see §1.4.2], no one annuls it or adds to it once it has been ratified." The apostle is saying that the Abrahamic covenant was not abolished by the Sinaitic covenant that came 430 years afterward (v. 17).[23] The Abrahamic covenant contained unconditional promises, even though these did not exclude human responsibility (§§2.3.1 and 3.7). The Sinaitic covenant contained the Mosaic Torah, which undeniably placed the people under conditions (see on this relationship between conditional and unconditional, §3.5). However, these conditions of the Sinaitic covenant could in no way annul the unconditional promises of the Abrahamic covenant. That is, whatever the actions of Israel under the Sinaitic covenant, God *will* fulfill his Abrahamic promises to "a remnant, chosen by grace" (Rom. 11:5).

What Paul is arguing in Galatians 3:15 is that a correct, officially ratified will (testament) of a person cannot be annulled by anyone, and cannot be changed by codicils from anyone other than the testator himself. The implication is that even God could not possibly alter a will (testament) once ratified by himself without getting into conflict with his own holiness and righteousness. According to Genesis 15:10–11 and 17, this ratification was based upon the shedding of blood, so that even in this respect the parallel with a human will is applicable: the execution of a will is based on death. From the moment of the testator's death, no one can make any change in the will. Death has intervened: the will has to be executed immediately, in its unaltered form.

In his argument in Galatians 3, Paul apparently wants to say that the Abrahamic covenant was ratified centuries before God established his covenant with Israel at Mount Sinai. Nothing that came after this once-ratified Abrahamic covenant can annul or abolish the promise contained in this covenant. The Torah, introducing the principle of righteousness

---

23. See Ouweneel (1997, 202–203, 206–208, 216).

by grace-produced Torah-works, cannot annul the promise, which is based on righteousness by faith. That is, also after the Torah-giving at Mount Sinai, true justification is and remains based on the principle of faith, not merely by Torah-works. In other words, also under the Sinaitic covenant no person has ever been saved purely on the basis of his good works, without a surrender in faith to God and his grace, on the basis of a vicarious sacrifice, and by the power of the Holy Spirit. "Grace reigned" (cf. Rom. 5:21), even under the Sinaitic covenant.

The fact that *diathēkē*, as said before (§1.4.2), means especially "will, testament," is underscored in Galatians by the term "inheritance": in God's *diathēkē* an inheritance has been promised to certain heirs (cf. 3:29; 4:1, 7). This inheritance is the "blessing of Abraham" in Christ (v. 14); this refers here primarily to justification by faith. On the basis of the testator's death—Christ's work of atonement—this promised blessing, this inheritance, is now effectively received and enjoyed by the heirs, that is, all Jesus-believers, Jewish and Gentile.

What Paul says here is that this inheritance has been promised unconditionally, and therefore cannot depend on human Torah-works, done apart from God. If the latter were the case, the inheritance would indeed have been bound to conditions, which people would have to accomplish in their own power. In effect, the promise would be gone. As a matter of fact, the inheritance is granted by God's sovereign grace, not on the basis of Torah-works or any other merit on the human side. The only condition is faith, but this faith has in no way the character of merit; being "saved through faith" is a "gift of God" (Eph. 2:8).[24] On the contrary, it is the very recognition that the inheritance cannot be granted because of any merit—for natural persons have no merits—but because of pure, unmerited grace. If everything is lost on the human side, the only thing one can still do is to throw oneself in the arms of

---

24. Expositors have always differed on the grammatical question whether it is "faith" or "salvation through faith" that is the "gift of God" here.

divine grace; this is the surrender of faith. (At the same time, I repeat that, of course, such a faith can never be separated from keeping the Messianic Torah in the power of the Spirit; see §3.6.)

If we take Galatians 3:16 and 18 together, we could say that the Judaizers who wished to seduce the Galatian Gentile believers were trying, as it were, to add a codicil to God's unalterable covenant with Abraham. They did accept that the promise was based on sovereign grace, but the codicil they wished to add implied that Gentile believers, in addition to living out of grace, also had to keep the Mosaic Torah in order to attain salvation. With this they meant especially the alleged necessity of circumcision for male believers. Or perhaps they even rejected the principle of grace altogether, in order to make believers depend exclusively on Torah-keeping. In the sense of verse 16, this would indeed imply an annulment of the promise or covenant (or testament). This cannot be. Neither a human, nor a divine will, once ratified, can be annulled or supplemented. Thus, the Mosaic Torah does not annul the Abrahamic covenant, nor does it constitute a kind of appendix or supplement to it. The Abrahamic promise is unconditional; let no one ruin it by coming up with one's own conditions.

### 6.4.2 The Torah as Guardian: Correct Approach

Of great importance in Galatians 3 is verses 23–26 about the Torah as a "guardian":[25] "Now before faith came, we were held captive under the Torah, imprisoned until the coming faith would be revealed. So then, the Torah was our guardian until Messiah came, in order that we might be justified by faith. But now that faith has come, we are no longer under a guardian, for in Messiah Jesus you are all sons of God, through faith."

Here, Paul places two dispensations (redemptive-historical eras) in juxtaposition, which correspond precisely with those of the Old and the New Covenants. They are referred

---

25. See Ouweneel (1997, 222–34).

to here as that of "faith" (vv. 23, 25) and that of "the Torah" (vv. 23–24). "Faith" is here really "*the* faith" (the Greek has the article); this suggests that what is meant here is not so much the heart's *act* of faith, but rather the *contents* of faith (like in the expression "the Christian faith"), or the *era* of Christian faith.[26] Paul says that the era of the Torah continues *until* the era of faith; believers were "imprisoned" under the Torah "*until* the coming faith would be revealed" (v. 23).

It is regrettable that commentators have repeatedly suggested that Paul's intention here is to tell us that the Torah leads us "to Christ."[27] This confusion is exhibited even in some translations: "the law was our tutor [to bring us] to Christ" (NKJV); "the Law has become our tutor [to lead us] to Christ" (NASB); "the Law was our schoolmaster [to bring us] to Christ" (GNV); "the law was our guardian leading us to Christ" (NCV).

The ESV has the correct translation: "the law was our guardian until Christ came" (see also NIV; similarly RSV, CEB, ERV, GNT, Darby, Phillips). That this is the correct rendering is obvious from the fact that, immediately before this, Paul had used the Greek preposition *eis* in a strictly temporal sense: "Now before faith came, we were held captive under the law, imprisoned until [*eis*] the coming faith would be revealed." *First*, there was the era of the Mosaic Torah, *then* came a new era, in which God revealed a new divine polity: that of New Testament faith and the Messianic Torah belonging to it. This is the era of "faith working through love" (Gal. 5:6). Of course, faith as such was not a new thing (cf. Gen. 15:6; Hab. 2:4); but the *polity* of faith, rooted in the work of Christ, following upon, and standing in opposition to, the *polity* of the Mosaic Torah, definitely *was* new.

Under the old polity, the Mosaic Torah functioned like a guardian or tutor, a governess (Phillips), a custodian (RSV, CEB, ERV), a jailor, or even a prosecutor. The sense of this

---

26. Cf. extensively Ouweneel (2010a, §5.3.1).
27. See, e.g., recently Estelle et al. (2009, 94, 309).

term is highlighted by the preceding verse, where we find expressions such as Greek *ephrouroumetha*, "we were held captive," and *synkleiomenoi*, "imprisoned." The guardian's task was to check natural persons by constantly reminding them of what they ought to have done and where they had failed miserably (cf. Rom. 3:19). However, this is not meant in a negative sense only: the Torah is a custodian who holds people captive in order to protect them against themselves, so that they do not get lost. The Torah guards or watches people in anticipation of the New Covenant, for which the door would soon be opened (see, e.g., the same Greek *phroureō* in Acts 9:24; 2 Cor. 11:32; Phil. 4:7; 1 Pet. 1:5).

In verses 24–25, this positive element in the term "imprisoned" is also expressed in the term *paidagōgos*, "guardian, custodian": "the Law was like a strict governess in charge of us until we went to the school of Christ and learned to be justified by faith in him" (Phillips). "The law was like those Greek tutors, with which you are familiar, who escort children to school and protect them from danger or distraction, making sure the children will really get to the place they set out for" (MSG). The Mosaic Torah has been the governess or tutor of Israel, as Paul explains in Galatians 4:1–2: "I mean that the heir, as long as he is a child, is no different from a slave, though he is the owner of everything, but he is under guardians and managers until the date set by his father." Israel was like a child needing a tutor as long as the Son of God, as well as the Spirit of God's Son, had not yet come: "But when the fullness of time had come, God sent forth his Son, born of woman, born under the Torah, to redeem those who were under the Torah, so that we might receive adoption as sons. And because you are sons, God has sent the Spirit of his Son into our hearts, crying, 'Abba! Father!' So you are no longer a slave, but a son, and if a son, then an heir through God" (4:4–7). The *paidagōgos* kept an eye on the lad, checked him, and helped him to bridle "the flesh with its passions and desires" (cf. 5:16–24).

### 6.4.3 The Torah as Guardian: Incorrect Approach

The *paidagōgos* is not at all a "pedagogue" in the modern sense of the term. He is no *didaskalos*, no teacher or educator proper; therefore, even the rendering "tutor" is less accurate. In fact, those who teach that the Torah was a "tutor," or even "schoolmaster," to take the young child by the hand and lead him to Christ, have definitely misunderstood the term. How could the Mosaic Torah ever do this? Of course, *in retrospect* we see Christ typologically everywhere in the Mosaic Torah, but that is something very different. The guardian does not educate believers until they reach Christ, on the contrary: she keeps the boy humble and small by constantly pointing out to him that apparently he cannot fulfill her demands. She reminds him continually of his desperate situation from which no escape is possible, *until from some other direction* the hope of the gospel dawns.

As stated earlier, the guardian here does not differ essentially from the jailor in verse 23, who holds captive and imprisons. Apart from typological applications of the Mosaic Torah, the latter is *not* a way to Christ or to the New Testament gospel. She shows sinful humanity its misery[28] — but she does not show humanity the way of the gospel, not even the way *to* the gospel. Strictly speaking, she refers only incorrigible sinners to eternal condemnation. By presenting to sinners God's just sentence, she keeps a check on them, so that they will not fancy anything positive about themselves, and hopefully the worst outbursts of evil are prevented. The commandments as such offer sinners no hope; at best, they only increase their misery and bring them into a state of despondency.

Of course, *indirectly* — through the power of God's Spirit — this does help people to become fully conscious of the fact that their justification before God cannot possibly come by Torah-works, that is, in their own power, but has to come from a very different direction. However, the Torah itself

---

28. Cf. Heidelberg Catechism Q&A 3: "Q. How do you come to know your misery? A. The law of God tells me."

does not indicate what this other direction might possibly be; to this end, a new *revelation* was needed. Already in the Old Testament, there was essentially no other way of redemption than the way of faith in—that is, faithful surrender to—God's grace, on the basis of a vicarious sacrifice. But only under the New Covenant, this faith receives its true object: Christ. At present, no jailor, no guardian, no custodian is needed anymore, because it has been fully revealed what sinful humanity must do: faithful surrender to God's grace as revealed in the dead, risen, and glorified Christ, in the power of the Holy Spirit.

In no way does Galatians 3:23–25 speak of some personal development in an individual's life. One is not first under the Torah, and then led by the Torah to Christ. The passage does not offer any justification for the well-known Lutheran scheme "first the law, then the gospel."[29] Paul refers here exclusively to the juxtaposition of two redemptive-historical eras: that of the Torah and that of faith, that is, that of the Old Covenant and that of the New Covenant. The old polity has been done away with. Once the child has grown up, the guardian no longer has any authority over the child. What Paul wants to say is that you cannot declare this young adult to be grown-up now and emancipated through the inner work of the Holy Spirit (cf. Gal. 4:6–7; 5:22–23), and at the same time place that young adult under the guardian (the Mosaic Torah) like an immature child. This was precisely what the Galatian Judaizers wanted: they tried to place the young adult under a guardian again. This is what Paul refutes and condemns here.

It goes without saying that the emancipated Christian also maintains reverence for the Mosaic Torah, for the Torah is "holy and righteous and good" (Rom. 7:12). Both social-economically and typologically, unspeakably many things can be learned from it. It is also self-evident that this Mosaic Torah in some other sense, namely, as an *inner* principle, in the form

---

29. See, e.g., Schlatter (1963a, 98–99).

of the Messianic Torah, inseparably linked with the Holy Spirit, retains its significance, for the mature Christian as well (cf. Gal. 5:14; 6:2). However, that is not at all the subject of Galatians 3:22–28.

## 6.5 The Covenant in Galatians 4
### 6.5.1 Introduction

In Galatians 4:21–26 we find another very important exposition by Paul with regard to the Old and the New Covenants.[30] He speaks of two women whose histories we find in the Torah — here this refers to the Pentateuch[31] — namely, Sarah and Hagar: "For it is written that Abraham had two sons, one by a slave woman and one by a free woman. But the son of the slave was born according to the flesh, while the son of the free woman was born through promise. Now this may be interpreted allegorically: these women are two covenants. One is from Mount Sinai, bearing children for slavery; she is Hagar. Now Hagar is Mount Sinai in Arabia; she corresponds to the present Jerusalem, for she is in slavery with her children. But the Jerusalem above is free, and she is our mother" (vv. 22–26).

Paul states here that Sarah and Hagar have a typological significance. He uses the Greek word *allēgoroumena*, which reminds us of "allegory" (see ESV). However, here he is not giving us an allegory in the sense of the modern literary sense, but rather what Christians call "typology." It exhibits certain similarities to what rabbis call *midrash*. In a Christian-typological exegesis of a text, a correspondence is pointed out between, on the one hand, a certain Old Testament story and, on the other hand, the New Testament story of Christ, his person and his redemptive work.

Please note that Paul emphatically does not wish to read some typological exegesis "into" the text. Rather, he argues

---

30. Ouweneel (1997, 292–97, 305–306).
31. In Paul's writings, *nomos* is (a) the whole of the Mosaic commandments (thus from Rom. 2:12–13 to Titus 3:9), (b) the Pentateuch (in Gal. 4:24–26 he appeals to Genesis), and (c) the entire Old Testament (in Rom. 3:10–19 *nomos* apparently also includes the prophetic books and the Psalms).

that "these things *are* symbolic" (v. 24 NKJV), or "are being taken figuratively" (NIV). The two women *are* two covenants. This is also the sense of the word "correspond" (Greek *systoicheō*) in verse 25. The challenge, "Tell me, you who desire to be under the Torah [i.e., Mosaic Law], do you not listen to the Torah [i.e., the Pentateuch]?" (v. 21), unmistakably implies the challenge that the readers should themselves have thought of this typological exegesis. In other words, this really is indeed *exegesis*, not just some homiletical application. (Cf. Rom. 15:4, "[W]hatever was written in former days was written for our instruction"). After a typological exegesis of Israel's wilderness journey, Paul writes, "Now these things happened to them as an example, but[32] they were written down for our instruction, on whom the end of the ages has come" (1 Cor. 10:11). This even seems to suggest that the typological exegesis precedes the common historical exegesis.

### 6.5.2 The Two Women

The one woman, Hagar, represents the Sinaitic covenant, as is made clear through the term "slavery." Hagar is a slave, who "bears for slavery"; that is, despite what Abraham may have personally wished with respect to Ishmael, Hagar's son could never really be freed from servitude. He could not change his slave origin. Likewise, Mount Sinai, that is, the covenant that is founded upon the Mosaic Torah, is one "bearing for slavery"; that is, all those who fall under the covenant of the Sinaitic Torah, are slaves of that polity. (We may note here a certain tension in this typological interpretation of Hagar in that, of course, Hagar's literal descendants were never under the Sinaitic covenant, whereas Sarah's literal descendants were.)

The two women, Hagar and Sarah, represent two covenants: the Old and the New Covenants. The former is mentioned in verses 24–26, the latter in verse 26. The Old Cov-

---

32. The Greek *de* has here the sense of "moreover" rather than of "but," and is usually translated "and."

enant is associated with the *nun Ierousalēm*, Greek for the "now-Jerusalem," the earthly city with its temple and Sinaitic ministry. This stands in opposition to the *anō Ierousalēm*, the "above-Jerusalem," with its heavenly temple (cf. Rev. 7:15; 11:19) and heavenly ministry (Heb. 7:25; 10:19). Paul's parallels are quite accurate, as may be seen in the following summary (in which I have supplied only two elements myself):

| | Old Covenant | New Covenant |
|---|---|---|
| (1) | Old Covenant | New Covenant |
| (2) | Ishmael | Isaac |
| (3) | Hagar | [Sarah] |
| (4) | slavery | freedom |
| (5) | flesh | promise/spirit |
| (6) | Mount Sinai | [Mount Zion] |
| (7) | earthly Jerusalem | heavenly Jerusalem |
| (8) | children of the slave | children of the free woman |

In this list the eight contrasts are enumerated that we find in verses 21-31. Two elements are only implicitly hinted at in Paul's argument: the name Sarah for Abraham's free wife (Isaac's mother), and Mount Zion, which stands in opposition to Mount Sinai and to which the quotation in verse 27 from Isaiah 54:1 refers (cf. Isa. 12:6; Zeph. 3:14; Zech. 2:10; 9:9).[33] In fact, the Abrahamic covenant is not being discussed here either, but Paul had already done so in chapter 3:15-18. On the basis of this passage, and actually the whole of Galatians 3:1-4:7, we may add the following contrasts to our summary:

| | | |
|---|---|---|
| (9) | law | promise |
| (10) | (works of the) law | (works of) faith |
| (11) | merit | grace |
| (12) | child under age | adoption as [mature] sons |

---

33. Also see Ouweneel (1982, II, 86–87).

(13) Greek *stoicheia*[34]     Christ

(14) children of Abraham [children of the devil; cf. John 8:39–44]

The Judaizers who endeavored to seduce the Galatian Christians held on, so to speak, to the Hagar–Sinai polity (the Old Covenant), and grasped too little the specific character of the Sarah–Zion polity (the New Covenant), which does not allow for any intermingling with Hagar–Sinai elements. Concretely speaking, one cannot make salvation depend on unconditional promises, faith, and grace, and yet intertwine this with certain Sinaitic conditions, Torah-works and human merit (works righteousness). No one can have two mothers: it is either the one or the other. It must have been quite irritating for the Galatian heretics that Paul in fact argued that the Gentiles who, by faith, shared in the polity of promise and grace were in fact closer to God than the Jews who still lived under the polity of the law.

A person who is under the Sinaitic covenant cannot merit salvation[35] but, because of his sinful flesh, stands under the slavery of the Torah. In this sense, the Jew who still stands on the foundation of the Sinaitic covenant resembles Hagar/Ishmael more than Sarah/Isaac. The Jew is a physical descendant of Isaac, the Gentile is not. But the Sinaitic Jew, as long he takes a legalistic position, falls spiritually under the Hagar-Ishmael polity, whereas the Jesus-believing Gentile falls under the Sarah-Isaac polity — this is Paul's audacious claim. In the physical sense, the Sinaitic Jew is closer to Sarah/Isaac; in the spiritual sense, the Jesus-believing Gentile is closer to Sarah/Isaac. The legalistic-Sinaitic Jew is a physical descendant of Isaac, but a spiritual descendant of Ishmael. Some (Arab) Jesus-believing Gentiles are physical descen-

---

34. Elementary principles, elemental spirits (spiritual forces).
35. Of course, this holds for every person, under whatever covenant; the godly under the Sinaitic covenant lived out of grace, just like Adam, Noah, Abraham, etc.

dants of Ishmael, but spiritual descendants of Isaac.

### 6.5.3 Application

In the typological language of Galatians 4, only two mothers are conceivable: any person serving the God of Israel is a child either of the one mother, Hagar-Sinai-earthly Jerusalem, or of the other mother: Sarah-Zion-heavenly Jerusalem. That is the same as saying: he belongs either to the polity of Torah-works, of slavery, of the flesh, of one's own righteousness, or to the polity of faith in Christ, of the freedom of the Spirit, of the promise of God, of the righteousness in Christ. Insofar as the Judaizers were children of God at all, they were "under age" (Gal. 4:1-3); in the typological language used here this means: they were children of the wrong mother, Hagar. The Jesus-believing Jews as well as Jesus-believing Gentiles were mature sons of God (vv. 6-7); in typological language: they were spiritual children of the right mother, Sarah.

Thus, the notion of mother corresponds here with the polity into which one was given birth and under which one has been educated. It was undeniable that the Judaizers, too, had a certain relationship to the God of Israel, just as Ishmael, too, could claim that he was a son of Abraham. However, to express it typologically, Ishmael did not have the right mother. That is the same as saying that the Judaizers' relationship with God was embedded in the wrong polity: a polity of slavery (works righteousness).

It is striking that Ishmael, just like Jacob, had twelve sons, who became twelve princes (Gen. 25:14-16). In this way, the Old Testament hints at a remarkable parallel between Ishmael and Israel. This makes it all the more obvious that, according to Paul, Ishmael is a type of "Israel after the flesh" (cf. 1 Cor. 10:18 NKJV), that is, the Israel of the Sinaitic polity. Ishmael was "a wild donkey of a man" (Gen. 16:12); if the donkey is not redeemed with the Lamb it is destined for death (Exod. 13:13).

Already in the history of Abraham, it comes to light that

Ishmael and Isaac cannot live together in one tent (Gen. 21:8-10). That is, the slavery of Sinaitic legalism and the freedom of the Spirit cannot exist together in one and the same house (Gal. 4:29-30).[36] That is a fundamental impossibility, but in practice it is even less possible because the slaves of Sinaitic legalism persecute those who have been set free in Christ. At God's command the former are put aside. God does not reject the Jews, but quite the contrary; he does, however, reject the Judaistic polity of self-justification through Torah-keeping in one's own strength. Jewish non-Jesus-believers, on the one hand, and Jewish or Gentile Jesus-believers, on the other hand, can and may at all times enter into a dialogue with each other, and this is always a conversation between equals. However, the former have to realize that no dialogue is possible on the basis of equality between a Pharisaic polity of self-righteous Torah-works and a polity of faith and grace. The two cannot exist together as equal ways to God. The former polity "shall not inherit" with the latter polity (Gal. 4:30); inheriting the blessing is possible only by way of promise, grace, and faith (as all godly Jews have always known, for that matter).

For absolute clarity, I remind the reader here of what was said in §3.5 about the nature of the Old Covenant. It has a double character, which is also precisely the case for the Mosaic Torah (§3.4.2). In terms of its positive side, the Mosaic or Sinaitic or Old Covenant is just as much a revelation of divine grace as the New Covenant. This is especially evident from the sacrifices through which the person who trespassed the Torah could be restored to communion with God and his people. But this positive side is not what Paul is referring to. He is speaking of the negative aspect of this covenant: under the Sinaitic or Old Covenant, the Mosaic Torah kept a check on Israel as long as Christ had not yet come. It revealed the misery of natural persons in that the latter turn out to be incapable of keeping the Torah in their own strength.

---

36. See Ouweneel (1997, 301-302).

Viewed in this light, the great difference between the Old and New Covenants is not that the Torah has been abolished—it has not been—but the great difference is *Christ* and the *Holy Spirit*. The Old Covenant could not be anything else than what it was as long as Christ had not yet come, and as long as the Holy Spirit had not yet been poured out. In itself, this covenant was good; how could it be otherwise since God had given it. But it was incomplete: Christ was lacking in it. Now that Christ has come, and the Holy Spirit has been poured out, the old polity has necessarily been fulfilled.

This is what Paul tries to make clear: it is both foolish and misleading to intermingle the old and the new polities. His objection against the old polity in the present era is that it lacks Christ.[37] This means: there is nothing wrong with the polity of the Mosaic Torah—the Sinaitic covenant or Old Covenant—as such. However, it lost its significance after Christ had come, who is the foundation, the core, and the fulfillment of the Torah. This was and is not grasped by those who reject Christ, or who wanted, and still want, to intermingle the new polity with the old polity. The Mosaic Torah is still a source of divine knowledge for those who wish to study salvation history, or wish to investigate the Torah's typological meaning. But it is no longer a proper way of serving God; this may become clearer in the following chapters.[38]

## 6.6 The New Covenant in Hebrews: Israel
### 6.6.1 Israel and the Messianic Kingdom

In Hebrews 8:8 ("For he finds fault with them . . .") it is suggested that the establishment of the New Covenant implied a kind of reproof with regard to Israel.[39] If the Israelites had fulfilled their duties under the Old Testament—which they were not capable of doing, for that matter—then a New Covenant would not have been needed. The Old Covenant had

---

37. Cf. Sanders (1977, 552).
38. Ouweneel (2015a, especially Appendix IV).
39. See Ouweneel (1982, I, 109–110).

failed, not because of its own nature but because of Israel's sins;[40] it had been "broken" (Ps. 119:126; Isa. 24:5; Jer. 11:10; 31:32). The word "broken" cannot always be taken in an absolute sense, for the individual Israelite could "break" the covenant without abolishing it (Gen. 17:14). Yet, in the case of the Old Covenant the situation was so serious that God had to establish a New Covenant with the Israelites if he still wanted to bless them. And this is exactly what he wanted and wants.

I have stressed, and will do this more extensively in chapter 7, that the idea of the church as the "spiritual Israel" is condemnable. That is, we may not argue that, because the Old Covenant with Israel failed, God therefore establishes a New Covenant with another party, some "spiritual Israel," which (a) for 99% contains no Israelites at all, but only Gentiles, and (b) does not resemble ancient Israel in any way, because of the mistaken idea that the Mosaic Torah has been abolished (see again the first volume of this series). Nowhere in Scripture do we find God making a covenant with the Ekklesia as such. The fact that the New Testament believers do profit from the *blessings* of the New Covenant, or are placed as it were under the *umbrella* or in the *domain* of the New Covenant, is a very different matter. The difference is especially that the *proper* character, position, and blessings of the Ekklesia do not fall under the New Covenant at all, but surpass it, as we will see (chapters 7 and 9).[41]

Where the Old Covenant with Israel has failed, God establishes a New Covenant with that very same Israel or, more precisely, with the united twelve tribes: "the house of Israel and the house of Judah" (Jer. 31:31; Heb. 8:8; cf. Ezek. 37:15–28). That is in effect with those among Israel who repent and return to the LORD: "A remnant will return"[42] (Isa. 10:20–22;

---

40. Cf. on the concomitant "failure" of the Mosaic Torah, Ouweneel (2015a, §4.3.3).
41. See extensively Ouweneel (2010b).
42. Hebrew *Shear-jashub*, also the name of one of Isaiah's sons (Isa. 7:3); *shub* refers both to physical returning and converting to God (cf. Deut. 30:1–5); cf.

cf. 11:11, 16; 28:6). The broader context of Jeremiah 31 makes this perfectly clear by explicitly referring to Israel's return to the promised land. Of course, there is a hint here of the return from the Babylonian exile. However, it is obvious that the prophecy has a much wider bearing in that it links the return and restoration of Israel with the following prophetic events.

(a) The fulfillment of the prophecy is located in "the latter days" (23:20; 30:24), which invariably refers to the days of the Messiah and the establishment of his kingdom (cf. Isa. 2:2; Ezek. 38:16; Dan. 2:28; Hos. 3:5; Micah 4:1).

(b) Israel is restored in its own land (Jer. 30:3; 31:23; 32:37, 41; 33:11, 15; 50:4-5; cf. Isa. 61:7; Ezek. 37:25-26). The detailed description is such that this cannot reasonably be spiritualized away (see Appendix IV).

(c) This restoration of Israel is preceded by the "great tribulation," from which the believing remnant of the people will be delivered (Jer. 30:7 NKJV, "time of Jacob's trouble"; cf. Dan. 12:1, "time of trouble"; Matt. 24:21; Rev. 3:10).

(d) The wicked part of the nation is judged (Jer. 30:11; 31:30); cf. Isaiah 17:6, "Gleanings will be left in it, as when an olive tree is beaten—two or three berries in the top of the highest bough, four or five on the branches of a fruit tree."

(e) All nations, especially those that have opposed Israel, are judged and subdued (Jer. 30:6-8, 11).

(f) He who triumphs over these enemies is the Messiah, the Son of David, who will bring about Israel's restoration and will be the center thereof (Jer. 30:9, 21; cf. Ezek. 34:23-24; 37:24; Hos. 3:4-5).

(g) Other than at the return from the Babylonian exile, the future restoration will involve a return of all twelve tribes to the land, not just from Babylon but from all nations of the earth (Jer. 30:3-4; 31:9, 15, 27, 31; cf. Isa. 11:11-16; Ezek. 37:15-28).

(h) Righteousness, joy, and peace will reign in Israel with-

---

the rabbinical term *teshubah* for the eschatological restoration of Israel.

out ever being disturbed again (Jer. 30:18-20; 31:4-7, 12-14, 24-25, 38-40; cf. Isa. 9:6-7; 32:14-18; 60:17-22); this can refer to the conditions in the future Messianic kingdom only.

### 6.6.2 Again: Supersessionism

For our entire subject, this matter of Israel's future restoration, as prophesied already by Moses (Deut. 30:1-10), is of primary significance. One cannot suppose that one has been freed of supersessionism — by believing in a national restoration of ethnic Israel in its own city and country — while at the same time retaining some notion of a spiritual Israel, in which those very prophecies are still spiritualized and related to the Ekklesia (see chapter 7). We have to make a choice. Either we declare the spiritualizing exegesis of the prophetic Bible passages to be the true exegesis — I am not talking about spiritual *applications* of these passages — but then there is no room for a national restoration of Israel in its land. Or we interpret these prophecies literally, but then we cannot spiritualize the term "Israel" to mean that the church is the Israel of God.

It is no wonder that, as the idea of a spiritual Israel arose, people saw no room anymore for a national restoration of ethnic Israel. This is perfectly consistent. Too many Reformed Christians today want to have it both ways: they see in what happens today in the State of Israel to be a work of God, *and* they keep speaking of the church as the "spiritual Israel." The same prophecies are used to prove both points, although these positions contradict each other. That does not work; the prophecies either refer to the restoration of ethnic Israel (but then we cannot smuggle the Gentile church into it), or they refer to some spiritual Israel (but then forget about Israel's national restoration). Some have been so embarrassed that they even suggested that there are *two* New Covenants in the New Testament, one with the Ekklesia and one with future Israel.[43]

This subject directly involves the question at what time the New Covenant is established. The book of Hebrews makes

---
43. Cf. Chafer (1983, IV, 325); Ryrie (1953, 105–125).

clear that, although this covenant is officially established only at the outset of the Messianic kingdom, the foundation of this covenant was laid already at the moment that Messiah shed his blood and brought his atoning sacrifice. Therefore, although the blessings of the New Covenant will come upon the reunited and restored Israel only at the return of Christ, these blessings can come upon the Hebrews (Jewish Jesus-believers) already now. These are believers who, in the present dispensation, join the Ekklesia of God, the Body of Christ, assembled from all nations. To put it even more strongly, *all members of Christ's Body, even all believers of all times*, also those from before Israel and from after Christ's return (i.e., those born during the Messianic kingdom; see, e.g., Isa. 65:20) will be able to stand before God on no other foundation than that of the blood of the New Covenant, the blood of Christ. *But that does not imply that all these kinds of believers constitute the actual covenant partners*. The Ekklesia shares in the blessings of a covenant, but this covenant is formally made only with Israel. These are two very different matters. The Ekklesia's proper destination lies elsewhere (see chapters 7 and 9).[44]

Frederick Grant explains that, "[I]f we have not the [new] covenant *made* with us [i.e., with the Gentile believers in the Ekklesia, and not even with the Ekklesia as such], it can yet, in all the blessings of which it speaks, be *ministered* to us."[45] And Dwight Pentecost says: "[T]he new covenant of Jeremiah 31:34–35 must and can be fulfilled only by the nation Israel and not by the church. Since this was a literal covenant made with the physical seed of Abraham, any relationship of the church to the blood required by that covenant can not change the essential promises of God in the covenant itself. Apart from any relationship of the church to this blood, the covenant stands as yet unfulfilled and awaits a future literal fulfillment."[46]

---

44. See again Ouweneel (2010b).
45. Grant (1902, 48).
46. Pentecost (1964, 124–25).

One may wonder how it is possible that most Reformed theologians have so easily given up the literal fulfillment of the prophecies regarding Israel, especially the land promise. The answer is: they declare the Sinaitic covenant to be fully conditional. Because Israel has thoroughly broken this covenant, there is no room anymore for the fulfillment of *conditional* promises. So, for example, Michael Horton claims "that the covenant with Israel as a national entity in league with God was conditional and that the nation had so thoroughly violated that covenant that its theocratic status was revoked. . . . [Dispensationalism fails] to recognize that the Hebrew Scriptures themselves qualify this national covenant in strictly conditional terms."[47] Now, first, I have tried to refute this idea of the conditionality of the Sinaitic covenant earlier in §3.5. Second, even if it were fully conditional, then God is still sovereignly entitled to bring a remnant of his people to repentance and fulfill the prophecies after all, not because the people deserved anything, but because of his sovereign electing grace. *This is exactly the picture of Deuteronomy 30:1–10.* In the end time, Israel *will* repent, and not only return to the LORD but also return to exactly the same land from where the Lord had once driven their fathers.

### 6.6.3 The Promises of the New Covenant

On the basis of the blood of the covenant, nothing remains for God other than to bless those involved, and therefore the announcement of this New Covenant does not contain any demand from God but only promises, as expressed by seven future tenses ("I will . . .", Jer. 31:31–34; Heb. 8:8–12). In terms of the text speaking of "laws" (Hebrew *torot*), these are placed, not as a yoke on the shoulders (cf. Acts 15:10), but in the hearts of the beneficiaries (Jer. 31:33; cf. 2 Cor. 3:3; Deut. 6:6; Ps. 40:8). In this way, God makes his intentions clear: these *torot* are to be kept not in one's own strength but from *within*, by the power of the Holy Spirit: "I will put my Spirit within

---

47. Horton (2006, 47).

you, and cause you to walk in my statutes and be careful to obey my rules" (Ezek. 36:27). Notice the connection between the two parts in this sentence: the people will be able to obey God's Torah *because of* his Spirit who dwells in them. Paul says precisely the same thing: "the righteous requirement of the Torah" is "fulfilled in us, who walk not according to the flesh but according to the Spirit" (Rom. 8:4).

I will give the seven verbs in both Greek and Hebrew, and then quote the translation from Hebrews 8:

(a) *Synteleso (w'karatti):* "I will establish (a new covenant)" (v. 8).

(b) *Diathēsomai (ekrôt):* "I will make (the covenant)" (v. 10).

(c) *Didous (natatti):*[48] "I will put (my laws into their minds)" (v. 10).

(d) *Epigrapsō (ektabennah):* "I will write (them on their hearts)" (v. 10).

(e) *Esomai (w'hayiti):* "I will be (their God)" (v. 10).

(f) *Esomai hileôs (eslach):* "I will be merciful (toward their iniquities)" [i.e., against those who committed them]" (v. 12).

(g) *Mē mnēsthō (lô ezkár):* "I will remember (their sins) no more" (v. 12).

Believers under the New Covenant are mature children of God, who have learned to know both themselves and God (cf. vv. 10b, 11b) because the Spirit of God's Son has been sent into their hearts (Gal. 4:6). They are not only children begotten by the Spirit (cf. John 3:5) but children filled with the Spirit (Rom. 8:14).[49] Now compare this with the situation at Mount Sinai. Three times Israel vowed that it would do all that the LORD had spoken (Exod. 19:8; 24:3, 7). Humanly speaking we might say that, because of this triple vow, God was almost obliged to give his Torah to the people as an answer to their vow, in order to prove to them that they would not at all be

---

48. In Heb. 8:10 this is actually a participle ("giving"), but in the Hebrew of Jer. 31:33 this is a future tense.
49. See Ouweneel (2010a, 112–16).

able to fulfill "all that the LORD had spoken." The people were not only sinful, they were also ignorant of their utter sinfulness. They were still immature, "under age" (cf. Gal. 4:1–7), which in Hebrews 8:9 is beautifully expressed in the words "I took them by the hand" (cf. ". . . in the wilderness, where you have seen how the LORD your God carried you, as a man carries his son, all the way that you went", Deut. 1:31; cf. 8:5).

Paul expressed the same truth by saying, "[I]f it had not been for the Torah, I would not have known sin. For I would not have known what it is to covet if the Torah had not said, 'You shall not covet'" (Rom. 7:7; cf. 3:20b). Put a yoke on the shoulders of a boy, and he will find out that he is not capable of bearing it. But let the boy grow up, have his heart changed, have it filled with God's Spirit, then lay that same Torah in his heart, and he will desire to, and be able to, and will gladly fulfill it. *That* is one of the beauties of the New Covenant.

In the "latter days" the time of Israel's dispersion and distress (Jer. 30:7) will be over, and the days of the Messianic kingdom will arrive. Then, and not earlier, the New Covenant is formally established with Israel. Literally it says, "fulfilled" (Heb. 8:8, Greek *synteleso*, from *telos*, "goal, purpose"): this New Covenant will both fulfill the ways of God with his people and will perfect the beneficiaries themselves.[50] This covenant, which *then* will be formally established, is—since the Day of Pentecost—*now* administered to believers who belong to the Ekklesia (cf. 2 Cor. 3:3, 6), so that the blessings of that covenant significantly precede the actual establishment thereof (see §6.8).

## 6.7 The New Covenant in Hebrews: the Church
### 6.7.1 No Spiritualizing the Covenant

Again, we wish to state that Scripture knows of no covenant that is directly established with the Ekklesia as such. This means that the New Covenant is not at all *the* specific description of the Christian position, as federalists believe (see

---

50. Delitzsch (1857, i.l.).

chapters 4 and 5). The blood of the New Covenant is the foundation on which *every* believer of *every* dispensation stands before God, from Adam until the end of the Messianic kingdom. Therefore, according to its moral, spiritual nature, such a standing is neither typically Jewish, nor typically Christian. The blood of the covenant is only the *foundation* for the relationships of the New Testament believers to God; it does not describe the highest characteristics of these relationships as such (see chapters 7 and 9). Moreover, this foundation is not the Ekklesia's foundation for another reason: the characteristics of the New Covenant, such as the forgiveness of sins as well as the writing of the Messianic *torot* in the hearts, are strictly individual, not collective, matters.

Precisely in the book of Hebrews, matters are mentioned that greatly surpass what was explicitly promised in the Old Testament as such. Believers entering into the sanctuary as priestly sons (Heb. 7:25; 10:19) is a matter that was *never* promised to the primary beneficiaries of the New Covenant. In the Messianic kingdom, such entering will remain the prerogative of the Aaronic family only (Ezek. 44:15–31). However, in the Ekklesia *each* member belongs to the priestly family, the "house" of the "great priest" (Heb. 3:6; 10:21). Moreover, equally important is that these members do not serve in an *earthly* sanctuary, as will be the case in the Messianic kingdom (Ezek. 40–44; Zech. 6:12–15), but in the *heavenly* sanctuary.

Please note that this difference is *not* a basis for spiritualizing Ezekiel 40–44, as if the earthly sanctuary in these chapters must be *interpreted* as referring to the heavenly sanctuary of Hebrews (see Appendix IV). There is no way that all the specific details (the building, the altars, the utensils, the priestly ministry, the sacrifices, the festivals, etc.) of the Millennial temple can be spiritualized. There is no way that the explicitly limited Aaronic family in Ezekiel can be interpreted as referring to the *entire* Ekklesia now being a priestly family (for instance, who is Zadok, according to this interpretation?). There is no way that all the fine details of the sacrificial ministry in these chapters can be spiritualized. In short: such a spiritualization has nothing to do with sound exegesis (see Appendix IV); all of this is nothing but reading into Ezekiel 40–44 one's own theological prejudices.

Members of God's Ekklesia have the privilege of entering into the heavenly sanctuary as a family of worshippers because the blood of the New Covenant—typologically speaking—has been sprinkled before and on the ark of the covenant (cf. Lev. 16:14–15). But in Hebrews this ark of the covenant is in *heaven* (cf. Rev. 11:19, "Then God's temple in heaven was opened, and the ark of his covenant was seen within his temple"). Both this heavenly ark and this entering into the heavenly sanctuary by *all* members of the Ekklesia, even the communion with divine persons in the heavenly sanctuary, greatly surpass the specific blessings of the New Covenant (see further §§9.6–9.8).

### 6.7.2 Characteristics of the New Covenant

Then what *is* specific of the New Covenant as far as its spiritual aspects are concerned (that is, apart from the physical aspects: land, city, throne, temple)? This is carefully indicated in Jeremiah 31:31–34; it involves a double work of God.

(a) A work *in* the beneficiaries, namely, "I will put my Torah within them, and I will write it on their hearts," with everything flowing from this: "I will be their God, and they shall be my people. And no longer shall each one teach his neighbor and each his brother, saying, 'Know the Lord,' for they shall all know me, from the least of them to the greatest." This clearly corresponds with what in 2 Corinthians 3:8 is called the *ministry of the Spirit*, for it is the Holy Spirit who, according to verse 3, writes the Torah on the "fleshly tables" of believers' hearts, which Torah is here summarized in one word: Christ ("you show that you are a letter from Christ delivered by us, written not with ink but with the Spirit of the living God, not on tablets of stone but on tablets of human hearts").

(b) A work *for* the beneficiaries, namely, the forgiveness

of their sins: "For I will forgive their iniquity, and I will remember their sin no more." This obviously corresponds with what in 2 Corinthians 3:9 is called the *ministry of righteousness*, which is further explained in 5:21, "For our sake he [i.e., God] made him [i.e., Jesus] to be sin who knew no sin, so that in him we might become the righteousness of God." God does not only take away the *un*righteousnesses of his people but he declares them to be righteous (cf. Isa. 53:11, "by his knowledge shall the righteous one, my servant, make many to be accounted righteous, and he shall bear their iniquities") (on this, see extensively the third volume in the present series).

Under the Old Covenant, the law had been imposed upon Israel as a heavy yoke, which the people could not bear the way God had intended (cf. Acts 15:10). Because of the wages of death that were the consequence of this failure (Rom. 6:23), this covenant is called a *ministry of death* (2 Cor. 3:7) and a *ministry of condemnation* (v. 9). This was a consequence embedded not in the nature of the Old Covenant as such, but in the sinful nature of the people. A *good* covenant brings death and condemnation upon *bad* people. Thank God, within the boundaries of the Old Covenant there *was* room for forgiveness and atonement on the basis of the sacrifices that God provided. The same covenant God who gave the Sinaitic Torah also gave the Sinaitic sacrifices: "For the life of the [animal] flesh is in the blood, and I have given it for you on the altar to make atonement for your souls, for it is the blood that makes atonement by the life" (Lev. 17:11; cf. Heb. 9:22, "without the shedding of blood there is no forgiveness of sins").

### 6.7.3 Jesus As Example and Essence

It was all there under the Old Covenant: the blood was supplied for atonement, and the Torah was written in the hearts of true believers (Deut. 6:6; Prov. 3:3; 7:3). But the great thing that was lacking was *Christ*. It is only his blood that can *truly* take away sins, and it is his Spirit that now writes Christ in believers' hearts. The New Covenant's beneficiaries have been inwardly cleansed and reconciled, and they have received a new nature that desires, and by God's Spirit is able, to fulfill the Messianic Torah. Even under the Old Covenant the commandment was not too hard for true believers, just as John can say that God's commandments are "not burdensome" (1 John 5:3). But the commandment now has a *content*: it is *Christ himself* who is this content and who is the One that is now written in believers' hearts.[51] He *is* (the essence of) the Eternal Torah. What the Holy Spirit administers through the apostles (2 Cor. 3:3, 6) to believers' hearts is the person of Christ himself (v. 3).

The New Covenant is administered to the Ekklesia not according to the letter, but according to the Spirit (2 Cor. 3:6; cf. Rom. 7:6). The word "letter" (Greek *gramma*) refers back to *engegrammenē*, "written," in verse 3.[52] We are dealing here not with a Torah literally written on tables of stone but with a Torah figuratively written by the Holy Spirit on hearts. In the Messianic kingdom, the Millennial Torah, which in its essence will be identical with the Mosaic Torah, will be written on the hearts of restored Israel.[53] On the hearts of the Ekklesia's members Christ is written, who is the spirit, tenor, and essence of the Messianic Torah.

In the Messianic kingdom, restored Israel will cherish the Torah in its heart; they will know it spiritually, in all its spiritual bearing as intended by God and as explained by Jesus in the Sermon of the Mount and by the apostles in their epistles. Then, Israel will know and love the Torah in close connection with knowing and loving the Messiah. And conversely, the Jesus whom the Ekklesia cherishes in her heart is the one who is the Lord, the Spirit of all the Old Testament, a Lord whom we do not know and love apart from knowing and loving his Torah: the "Torah of Christ" (1 Cor. 9:21; Gal. 6:2). The "righ-

---

51. Ouweneel (2010c, chapter 13; 2015a, especially chapter 3).
52. Cf. Barnett (1997, 176–77); *contra* Bernard (1979, 54), who sees in "letter" the Torah itself, not the writing of the Torah.
53. See Ouweneel (2010c, chapter 13; 2015a, §3.3.2).

teous requirement of the law" will be "fulfilled in us, who walk not according to the flesh but according to the Spirit" (Rom. 8:4), which is exactly the same as "putting on" Christ (Rom. 13:14), displaying Christ in believers' lives.

This Torah is "given" (put) in the mind of the believers, so that they perceive, grasp, and understand it, and it is written in their hearts, their deepest inward parts, the existential center of all their thinking, willing, and feeling, of all their considerations, decisions, emotions, and affections.[54] Thus, from the heart the relationship with God is restored: he is their God, and they are his people—an expression occurring frequently in the prophecies, and quoted several times in the New Testament (2 Cor. 6:16; Rev. 21:7; see, e.g., Exod. 29:45; Lev. 26:12; Ezek. 37:26; Zech. 8:8).

## 6.8 The Old and New Covenants Again
### 6.8.1 The Ark and Its Covering

Hebrews 8:13 says, "In speaking of a new covenant, he makes the first one obsolete. And what is becoming obsolete and growing old is ready to vanish away." This underscores again what was already touched upon in verse 7, "[I]f that first covenant had been faultless, there would have been no occasion to look for a second." Merely by announcing a "new" covenant, God already in Jeremiah's time implicitly declared the Sinaitic covenant to be "old," "obsolete," "vanishing away." For if the earlier covenant had still been sufficient, God would not have had to announce a new covenant. In other words, the former covenant does not grow old when the New Covenant will be formally established, that is, at the outset of the Messianic kingdom. Actually, it *was* already old, that is, obsolete, from the very first moment the people broke the covenant (Exod. 32). Therefore, since Jeremiah 31, we live in the situation that the former covenant has been declared obsolete for 2,600 years, during which time the New Covenant has not yet formally been effectuated.

---
54. Cf. Ouweneel (2008a, 117–21).

In Hebrews 9 the differences between the two covenants are explained in more detail.[55] The author speaks of the "ark of the covenant" (v. 4; cf. Num. 10:33; etc.), which is also called the ark of the testimony (Exod. 25:22; etc.), the ark of the LORD (Josh. 3:13; etc.), and the ark of God (1 Sam. 3:3; etc.). The name "ark of the covenant" is obvious here because the two covenants are placed in juxtaposition. The ark, that holy case covered with gold (Exod. 25:10–22), constituted the heart of the entire ministry of the Old Covenant. It contained the "tables of the covenant" (see below), on which the conditions of the covenant were stipulated. The ark was also the place of encounter between the covenant God and the covenant people, where the violations of Israel's covenant duties were propitiated by the blood of the sacrifices (Lev. 16:2, 13–16).

Over against this heart of the Old Covenant stands Jesus as the heart of the New Covenant, of whom the ark is a type. In his inward parts, just as in the ark, was the Torah (Ps. 40:8), and he was the perfect place of encounter between God and his people. One striking similarity is this: Jesus was put forward by God as a *hilastērion*, "propitiation" (Rom. 3:25), a word that in the Septuagint is used for the "mercy seat," the covering that was on the ark (Exod. 25:17). Jesus is the true ark of the New Covenant. The prophet said, "And when you have multiplied and been fruitful in the land, in those days, . . . they shall no more say, 'The ark of the covenant of the LORD.' It shall not come to mind or be remembered or missed; it shall not be made again" (Jer. 3:16). No wonder, there will be another ark: Messiah himself.

### 6.8.2 The Need for a New Polity

True redemption and forgiveness, the creation of a true worship ministry in the heavenly sanctuary—all these things demand a totally new polity, a new covenant (Heb. 9:15–17).[56] If therefore Jesus is Mediator, one who mediates between a

---

55. See Ouweneel (1982, II, 10).
56. Ibid., 19–20.

holy God and sinful humanity, he cannot serve as such within the framework of the Old Covenant, for within this polity there was no provision for cleansing and worship according to God's standards. The reason is that the blood of bulls and goats cannot genuinely take away sins (Heb. 10:4), and as far as the temple worship was concerned, the people were not allowed to proceed any further than the court, the priests no further than the sanctuary, and the high priest no further than the holy of holies *on earth*, and this only once a year. The *heavenly* sanctuary was not even part of the framework of the Old Covenant.

Therefore, Jesus has become Mediator on the basis of his own blood, for it is through his blood that he has blotted out the people's covenant breaking, and thus opened the way for God's blessings. What he opened especially was the entrance into the *heavenly* sanctuary, and this not just for the priests but for *all* God's people—or rather, *all* God's people are now priests. In the Old Testament, priests were anointed with the sacred oil (Exod. 28:41; 29:21; Lev. 8:30); there were only vague hints of an anointing with the Holy Spirit (Isa. 61:1; cf. 1 Sam. 16:13). Joel 2 prophesies about an outpouring of God's Spirit on all flesh, that is, on the entire people of God (vv. 28-29). Jesus was the first who is said to have been anointed with the Holy Spirit (Acts 10:38); his followers receive the same anointing (2 Cor. 1:21-22; 1 John 2:20, 27). In effect, this means that today all those who belong to the people of God have been anointed to be priests.

Being the Mediator implies, among other things, that Jesus is (a) the Executor of God's will (or testament), and (b) the Testator himself, who through his death opened the way for effectuating this will. Formally, the New Covenant has not yet been established, but the Mediator has already come, the blood of the New Covenant has already been shed, and the Mediator of the New Covenant has already entered into the heavenly sanctuary, as the Guarantor of the eternal inheritance for his own (Heb. 9:15).

In order to understand Hebrews 9:16–17 we have to remind ourselves that the actual meaning of the Greek word *diathēkē* is "testament, (last) will" (§1.4.2). Everywhere in the book of Hebrews the word can be translated as "covenant," but in chapter 9:16–17 this is more difficult. Here the actual meaning of "testament, (last) will" (an arrangement made in favor of some other party) comes to the fore: "For where a will [*diathēkē*] is involved, the death of the one who made it [one word: *diathemenos*, one making a *diathēkē*] must be established. For a will takes effect only at death, since it is not in force as long as the one who made it is alive." God is the testament maker, the death of the Testator (God the Son, who is also the Man Jesus Christ) has occurred – of course, so too has his resurrection, but that is not the point now – and thus the will can be effectuated. Formally this occurs only at the outset of the Messianic kingdom but, with retrospective effect, the blessings thereof already benefit Jesus-believers since the Day of Pentecost.

### 6.8.3 The Blood of the Covenant

The "blood of the covenant" (Exod. 24:8; Zech. 9:11; Matt. 26:28; Mark 14:24; Heb. 9:20; 10:29; 13:20; cf. Luke 22:20; 1 Cor. 11:25) has basically two different meanings.

(a) The meaning mentioned so far concerns the *atoning* blood of the sacrifice, through which the covenant trespasses of God's people are taken away. In the Old Testament this was the blood of bulls and goats but, as we know, this had no genuinely atoning value in itself.[57] Under the New Covenant, it is Christ himself who sheds his blood. The value of this blood is so great that it blots out the trespasses not only of the New Covenant's beneficiaries but also of the truly believing, Torah-loving beneficiaries of the Old Covenant.

(b) At the establishment of the Old Covenant in Exodus 24, the "blood of the covenant" is mentioned as well (v. 8), but this is not atoning blood. It is blood that is sprinkled on

---

57. See Ouweneel (2009, chapters 4–6) on the Old Testament sacrifices.

the people, and also on the altar, and on the Book of the Covenant, in order to bring the people under the menace of death. It is *threatening* blood, which forms a response to the people's vow to keep the covenant: "All the words that the LORD has spoken we will do.... All that the LORD has spoken we will do, and we will be obedient" (vv. 3, 7). Here, blood is life that is poured out in death, and this is what would happen to Israel's blood if it would trespass the words of the LORD God (v. 8). The blood of all the sacrifices reminds us of death: either the death of the sacrifices for those who find refuge behind them, or the (eternal) death that the sinner has to undergo personally. This blood of Exodus 24 reminds us of the "blood street" that we saw in Genesis 15:10, 17 (see §2.3.1).

Under the New Covenant the "blood of the covenant" is still threatening blood to all the Lord's enemies. But to the beneficiaries of the New Covenant it is atoning, blessing, life-giving blood, the blood of Christ, with which these beneficiaries have been sprinkled (1 Pet. 1:2). The "sprinkled blood speaks a better word than the blood of Abel" (Heb. 12:24);[58] "better" in the sense that Abel's blood called for revenge (Gen. 4:10; cf. Matt. 23:35; Luke 11:51), whereas Christ's blood calls for salvation. In the value of *that* blood, the beneficiaries of the New Covenant, who by nature are not any better than Israel under the Old Covenant, can now stand before God.

Hebrews 13:20–21 says, "Now may the God of peace who brought again from the dead our Lord Jesus, the great shepherd of the sheep, by [Greek *en*, 'in (the power of)'] the blood of the eternal covenant, equip you with everything good that you may do his will...." Apparently, the author has adopted this phraseology from Zechariah 9:11 ("because of the blood of my covenant with you"), where the Septuagint also says "in [the power of] the blood of the covenant." Other prophets had already referred to this as the "eternal [or everlasting] covenant" (Isa. 55:3; 61:8; Jer. 32:40; 50:5; Ezek. 37:26).[59]

---

58. See Ouweneel (1982, II, 89–90).
59. Ibid., 105–106.

The quotation from Zechariah 9 is remarkable because in this chapter the prophet is speaking of redeeming or releasing the faithful remnant of Israel from the "waterless pit" (i.e., Jerusalem; cf. vv. 12-13). Just as Jesus has been brought again from the dead "in [the power of] the blood of the eternal covenant" (Heb. 13:20), so too the believers are associated with him beyond death. In the power of his blood, Jesus rose from the dead and entered into the heavens (Heb. 9:11-12), where he is now the great shepherd of the sheep. In the power of this blood Jesus today brings his sheep out of the fold (Israel; John 10:4),[60] that is, he brings Jewish Jesus-believers out of "Jerusalem," the "camp" (Heb. 13:13), the "waterless pit" (Zech. 9:11).

Moses, the shepherd, brought his sheep — the people of Israel — up out of the waters of death (Isa. 63:11b) in the power of the blood of the Passover Lamb. Jesus brings his people up out of the waters of death in the power of his own blood. Therefore, Jesus is a greater shepherd than Moses (cf. Heb. 3:1-6). It is the blood of the eternal covenant because it is a durable covenant, under which the Old Covenant has been subsumed as well. It is a covenant that cannot, and does not need to, be replaced because it has a perfect foundation, whose value is everlasting. It extends, beyond the "unshakable kingdom" (12:28) during the "age to come" (6:5) in the "world to come" (2:5), to the new heavens and the new earth.[61] Today, God has communion with his people in terms of everlasting conditions (see further Heb. 7:22; 8:6-10; 9:15; 10:16, 29; 12:24).[62]

---

60. See Ouweneel (2010b, 67–68, 71).
61. See extensively Ouweneel (2012, chapter 14).
62. See my comments in Ouweneel (1982, i.l.).

# Chapter 7
# Israel and the Church

*Give no offense to Jews*
  *or to Greeks*
  *or to the church of God.*
                              1 Corinthians 10:32

*Therefore remember that at one time you Gentiles in the flesh,*
  *called "the uncircumcision" —*
*remember that you were at that time separated from Christ,*
  *alienated from the commonwealth of Israel*
*and strangers to the covenants of promise,*
  *having no hope and without God in the world.*
*But now in Christ Jesus you*
  *who once were far off*
*have been brought near*
  *by the blood of Christ.*
*For he himself is our peace,*
  *who has made us both one . . .*
*that he might create in himself*
  *one new man in place of the two,*
  *so making peace,*
*and might reconcile us both to God*

> *in one body through the cross.*
> Ephesians 2:11–16

**Summary:** *In federalism, it is common to speak of a "church since Adam (or, Abraham)," or "the church of all ages," that is, the totality of believers throughout all time. The New Testament uses the word "church" in a more limited sense: it is the totality of post-Pentecost Jesus-believers, the Body of Christ, unified with its glorified Head in heaven, and the Temple of the Holy Spirit. The Old Testament does not know a* **totality** *of all (Jewish and Gentile) believers. Dispensationalists often overlook the many* **similarities** *between Old and New Testament believers, just as federalists tend to overlook the many* **differences***. At any rate, the church is never called, or counted as, "Israel," not even in Romans 11. (Believing and unbelieving) Jews remain Israel, and (believing and unbelieving) Gentiles remain Gentiles. The real problem behind this "spiritual Israel" idea is supersessionism (the church has replaced Israel, and taken over its blessings, leaving the curses to Israel) and spiritualism (Old Testament prophecies are spiritualized to apply them to the church).*

## 7.1 Introductory Remarks
### 7.1.1 The Central Question

RECENTLY, BROWN AND KEELE WROTE: "[T]he new covenant is the fulfillment of the Abrahamic covenant. There are not two peoples of God, Israel and the church. Rather, God has only one people: the offspring of Abraham, that is, all believers of God's promise in Christ. God's promise to Abraham that he would be a blessing to the nations has been fulfilled, for Israel's boundaries have been expanded to include the nations."[1] Randy Booth also wrote: "God has had one people throughout all the ages. Although this one church has developed through various stages, she is still the same church from age to age."[2] One reason he strongly emphasizes this idea is to supply us with an argument for infant baptism: if

---
1. Brown and Keele (2012, 145).
2. Booth (1995, 73).

the church remained basically the same throughout the ages, and if this church always included believers with their children, then today, too, children are included in the church, and are entitled to the initiatory rite: formerly circumcision, now (allegedly) baptism.

Cornelis Van der Waal also emphasized the one people of God: "The church of the new covenant is the continuation of the old Israel and therefore is under the clear obligation of the covenant."[3] And: "The Jews are presently an *ethnos* [i.e., a Gentile nation] and no longer a *laos* [i.e., a people of God]. They can, however, become again a *laos*, a covenant people, if they will let themselves be grafted into the church."[4] Please note how Van der Waal moves from Gentiles being grafted into Israel (cf. §7.6) to Jews being grafted into the (almost entirely Gentile) church! The same happens in the Annotations of the Dutch States' Translation (1637; the Dutch equivalent to the King James Version), where we find both "incorporated into the church of God" and "the Israelite church."

Of course, I could easily add many more Reformed statements claiming that the olive tree is Israel, or is the church, which terms are viewed as identical. The question whether such statements are correct or not is the subject of this chapter. Or, to put it in more general terms, how does the (New Testament) church relate to (Old Testament) Israel?

In many cases I will use the original word Ekklesia for church, in order to avoid confusion. I will not be speaking about particular denominations, nor about particular buildings, nor of some "visible church" (the "mixed multitude" of Christendom), but about what the New Testament, especially Paul in the epistles to the Ephesians and to the Colossians, understands by Ekklesia, and which is well summarized in the Belgic Confession (Art. 27): "We believe and confess one

---

3. Van der Waal (1990, 103).
4. Ibid., 139. This distinction between *ethnos* and *laos* must be relativized: in Gen. 12:2, God promised to make Israel a "great nation [Heb. *goy*, Septuagint *ethnos*]."

single catholic or universal church—a holy congregation and gathering of true Christian believers, awaiting their entire salvation in Jesus Christ, being washed by his blood, and sanctified and sealed by the Holy Spirit."

I realize that a few times in the New Testament the word *ekklēsia* is used for other purposes. Thus, Stephen speaks of the "congregation in the wilderness" (Acts 7:38), where *ekklēsia* stands for Hebrew *'edah* (e.g., Exod. 12:3, 19, 47) or *qahal* (e.g., v. 6), the gathered Israelites in the desert.[5] Naturally, some have taken this as evidence that the Bible does acknowledge a "church" in the Old Testament.[6] They overlook the fact that the word *ekklēsia* occurs also in Acts 19:32, 39, and 41, where it refers to the "(popular) assembly" (city parliament) of that city. Nobody would suggest that this refers to the "church" of Ephesus. Likewise, there is no "church" in Acts 7. For the rest, in the New Testament the word usually refers to a local church (congregation), or to the church as a whole.

Elsewhere[7] I have argued extensively that the Ekklesia, as especially Paul speaks about it, did not yet exist in the Old Testament period. This does not mean that in this period there were no regenerate people, no believers. Of course there were (see, e.g., the enumeration of the heroes of faith in Heb. 11). What I am saying is that these believers did not belong to the Ekklesia. To start with, we are therefore dealing with something that, for a Christian who is thinking along Augustinian lines, seems to be almost inconceivable: we must surrender the idea that the church is simply the totality of all regenerate persons, from the Garden of Eden until the last day. For those who are not prepared to reconsider this, the idea that the Ekklesia exists only since Acts 2 is incomprehensible and preposterous.

---

5. Cf. Erickson (1998, 1058); he does suggest, though, that the Old Testament believers afterwards *were* admitted to the church (1058–59), so that one wonders what difference it makes to have the church begin in Gen. 3 or in Acts 2.
6. E.g., Ridderbos (1975, 328).
7. Ouweneel (2010b).

The Reformed dogmatician Herman Bavinck rendered the view of Roman Catholics and traditional Protestants concerning the extent of the Ekklesia as follows: "In its broadest sense it embraces all who have been saved by faith in Christ or will be saved thus. . . . Belonging to it, accordingly, are all the believers who lived on earth from the time of the paradisal promise to this very moment, and were taken up . . . into heaven ([Heb.] 12:23). Belonging to it are all the believers who still live on earth now. And belonging to it, in a sense, are also those who will later, even to the end of the ages, believe in Christ."[8] In short, the church includes all believers of all ages. In such a view, it is inconceivable that there could be regenerate persons who at any time or in any place would not belong to "the church."

### 7.1.2 Reformed Creeds and Catechisms

Bavinck's view is in general agreement with the Reformed creeds and catechisms. The Westminster Confession says (XXV.1): "The catholic or universal church, which is invisible, consists of the whole number of the elect, that have been, are, or shall be gathered into one, under Christ the Head thereof." This is often called "the church of all ages."[9] Likewise, Article 27 of the Belgic Confession, just quoted, continues: "This church has existed from the beginning of the world and will last until the end, as appears from the fact that Christ is eternal King who cannot be without subjects." The argument of the Belgic Confession for this is rather strange: "Christ is eternal King who cannot be without subjects." Our questions multiply here.

(a) Can we say that Christ has been King from Genesis 1, or even from eternity? In the Old Testament it is the (triune) *God* who is King from eternity to eternity (Exod. 15:18;

---

8. Bavinck (2008, 4. 300–301).
9. E.g., Berkouwer (1976, 23); in all of his chapter 7 he reasons from the "self-evidence," which is not further substantiated, that the church is of all ages (i.e., from Adam).

Ps. 10:16; 29:10; 146:10; Jer. 10:10; 1 Tim. 1:17), which of course is not the same. Christ has been sent into this world to become Man, and *as such* become King of the world. Within history, God has *set*[10] his King on Zion (Ps. 2:6), namely, by his anointing with the Holy Spirit (Acts 10:38) at the moment of his being baptized by John the Baptist. It is true that the wise men ask: "Where is he who has been born king of the Jews?" (Matt. 2:2), but is that any different from saying that *President* Obama was born in 1961, though he became president in 2008?

(b) If God was King from eternity, then he definitely had no subjects until he created angels and humans, the earth and its inhabitants.

(c) Most importantly, is the kingdom of God the same as the church? In other words, does the fact that God had subjects already in the Old Testament necessarily have anything to do with the Ekklesia? For that matter, are not *all* creatures God's subjects, not only the believers?

(d) Why did the Belgic Confession not try to adduce positive arguments for the claim that "the church" exists through all ages? Is that perhaps because such arguments are difficult to give? The only evidence for a church existing since Eden is the prejudice that all believers of all times necessarily belong to one and the same community—which is precisely what must be demonstrated.

(e) Does not the first part of the quotation ("We believe and confess one single catholic or universal church—a holy congregation and gathering of true Christian believers") contradict the second part ("This church has existed from the beginning of the world")? In other words, can we say that the Old Testament believers were "Christian believers," "awaiting their entire salvation in Jesus Christ, being washed by his blood, and sanctified and sealed by the Holy Spirit"? I certainly hold that all Old Testament believers in anticipation

---

10. Heb. *nasakti*, "I have installed"; some translations (Darby, DRA) render this "I have anointed."

have been washed by Christ's blood. But I also hold that only a few of them have consciously "awaited their salvation" in the Messiah, insofar as they could have any idea of what such a concept might involve (e.g., how many of them would have understood the import of Isa. 53?[11]). And the allegation that they were sealed with the Holy Spirit cannot be supported at all. The Holy Spirit was given only to a few (especially judges and prophets), and this is never called a "sealing" (cf. 2 Cor. 1:22; Eph. 1:13; 4:30). There is no sealing with the Spirit before the day of Pentecost (Acts 2). Such a view is nothing but reading New Testament truths back into the Old Testament.

### 7.1.3 An Old Testament Church?

In its description, the Belgic Confession seems to think primarily of the New Testament church, and then, as an afterthought, extends this description to Old Testament believers. The same happens in the Heidelberg Catechism. First, we read: "Q. Why the next words: 'and is seated at the right hand of God'? A. Because Christ ascended to heaven to show there that he is head of his church, the one through whom the Father rules all things" (Q&A 50). Here Christ is presented as the glorified Lord, the Head of his Body; how then could the Ekklesia have existed before Christ's glorification? Apparently, the idea is that Christ at his ascension was *shown* to be what he already had been throughout the ages: the head of his church. Thus, in Q&A 54 we read: "I believe that the Son of God through his Spirit and Word, out of the entire human race, from the beginning of the world to its end, gathers,[12] protects, and preserves for himself a community chosen for eternal life and united in true faith. And of this community I am and always will be a living member."

In support of the words, "from the beginning of the world

---

11. The eunuch's question, "About whom, I ask you, does the prophet say this, about himself or about someone else?" (Acts 8:34), is still relevant, asked today usually in this form: does the prophet say this about Israel or about the Messiah?
12. Cf. the approval of Moerkerken (2004, 297).

to its end," three biblical references are given: Psalm 17:17-18 (about youth and old age), Isaiah 59:21 (about the covenant), and 1 Corinthians 11:26 (about the Lord's Supper). I cannot even begin to presume how one would prove from these that the church exists from Adam to the last day. I would have understood better if the Catechism had referred to Romans 4:11, 16, and Galatians 3:7-9, 14, 29, and 4:28, where we find that the New Testament believers are blessed with, and are spiritual offspring ("sons") of, Abraham. This proves that both Old and New Testament believers come under the blessed promises of Abraham. However, this does not prove that the Old Testament saints also belong to what Paul calls the Ekklesia, just as it does not prove, conversely, that the church would belong to Israel.

In line with Augustine, the idea that the church has existed from Adam and Eve is still generally proclaimed by Roman Catholics as well as by traditional Protestants. In 1932-33, Dietrich Bonhoeffer in his course on Genesis 1-3 claimed that chapter 2:23 ("This at last is bone of my bones and flesh of my flesh") revealed the church in its original form.[13] The typologically interested Bible reader might think that Bonhoeffer is referring here to Eve as a type of the church,[14] but no: Bonhoeffer simply wants to say that for the first time Man is not alone anymore. Adam and Eve formed the first and simplest form of community, and thus the church was supposedly born. Apparently, the church did not arise for the first time after the fall; it is not just a community of redeemed people. No, according to Bonhoeffer she was there before the fall, namely, as soon as human fellowship originated, which is founded in God himself.

Of course, I could give many quotations from traditional Protestant theologians telling us that the New Testament

---

13. Bonhoeffer (1997, 99).
14. Already Origen saw in Eve, Sarah, Tamar, Rahab, the woman of Prov. 31, the Virgin Mary, and Mary Magdalene types of the church; see Dulles (1987, 19); Congar (1970, 44); Denham Smith (n.d.).

church is essentially identical with what is called the "church" of the old dispensation,[15] or the historical continuation of Old Testament Israel.[16] Yet, it seems to me that some Reformed theologians today handle the notion of the "church of all ages" a little more carefully. Thus, Reformed theologian Ab Noordegraaf makes a clear distinction between the people of Israel and the (New Testament) church of Christ.[17] He does speak of the "church of all times," but on the same page he speaks of the "new people of God from Jews, but particularly from Gentiles."[18] Elsewhere he says that "in the *ekklesia* the Messianic church of the end times has become manifest, rooted in Israel"[19] — a description that I can accept insofar as the immanent-historical (not the eternal-transcendent) aspect is concerned.

How different the Reformed theologian Willem Balke sounds, who wrote in the same collection of articles: "In the one church of Christ, church and Israel belong together."[20] A nonsensical statement: within these eleven words, the term "church" is used in two contradictory ways, first, in the sense of the alleged community of believers of all ages, second, in the sense of the New Testament Body of Christ.

The Reformed theologian Ben Wentsel does not want to speak of the church as some "spiritual Israel": "the name Israel [cannot], without further ado, be transferred to the church; Israel retains its name, and also its own identity."[21] Yet, he too sees the church going back all the way to Abraham, or even to Adam.[22] But he also says: "The outpouring of the Holy Spirit on this Pentecostal feast [of Acts 2] does have *fundamental* and

---

15. Berkhof (1979, 571).
16. J. I. Packer in Henry (1962, 242).
17. A. Noordegraaf in Van 't Spijker et al. (1990, 19–62).
18. Ibid., 29.
19. Ibid., 47.
20. W. Balke in Van 't Spijker et al. (1990, 264).
21. Wentsel (1998a, 223); cf., e.g., Stam (1999, 89): "The covenant that God makes with the spiritual Israel . . ."
22. Wentsel (1995, 368; 1998a, 25–27).

*redemptive-historical significance for the rise of the World Church,* consisting of believers from the Jews and believers from the Gentiles."[23]

## 7.2 The Church Born at Pentecost
### 7.2.1 The Unity of the Church

Let me summarize here in ten points why the church, the way the New Testament writes about it, necessarily exists only since the day of Pentecost (Acts 2).[24]

1. *No unity.* In the Old Testament, the "people of God" was an *ethnic* people, that is, Israel, consisting of regenerate and unregenerate people. At the same time, there were regenerate people outside Israel, such as Melchizedek (Gen. 14:18–20), Job (and some of his friends? Cf. the book of Job), Naaman (2 Kgs 5), some members of the Kenites (Judg. 4:11–17; 5:24) and of the Rechabites (Jer. 35; cf. 1 Chron. 2:55), and Ebed-melech (Jer. 38:7–13). There simply *was* no "holy congregation and gathering of true Christian believers" (Belgic Confession, Art. 27) in which all true believers had been united into one entity. There was not yet something like what we call the Ekklesia, an entity that is more than the addition of its constituent parts, an entity with very specific characteristics (see the following points). I have never come across a plausible federalist explanation of how Old Testament Israel could be "the church," while there were true believers who never joined this Israel/church. Either "the church" is *not* the totality of all believers throughout all time, or Israel was not the Old Testament church. I believe both of these phrases to be true, whereas federalists want to have it both ways.

2. *Future.* Jesus spoke of "his church" in the future tense: "[O]n this rock I *will* build my church" (Matt. 16:18), not "I *have* built," or "I *am* building."[25] Is "his" church another church

---
23. Wentsel (1998a, 25).
24. Cf. the summaries of Chafer (1983, IC, 45–46) and Demarest (1997, 338–39).
25. F. Hahn in Kertelge (1977, 552) rejects attempts to explain this future tense as a so-called voluntative ("I *want* to . . .").

than the (alleged) Old Testament church? He also spoke in the future tense of the "one flock, one shepherd" (John 10:16) and his gathering "into one the children of God who are scattered abroad" (11:52). (Please note, there were scattered "children of God," both inside and outside Israel [see point 1.], but so far they had never been united into one, well defined entity.) Until Pentecost, the New Testament never speaks about the church as a present reality, but it does so after Pentecost (from Acts 5:11). Luke, who uses the word *ekklēsia* frequently in the book of Acts, never uses it in his Gospel. This suggests that Luke did not view the church as being present until the period described in Acts (on Acts 7:38 see §7.1.1).

Reformed authors have sometimes tried to square the circle by arguing that we should not compare Old Testament Israel with the New Testament "holy gathering of true Christian believers," but with the New Testament "visible church," say, Christendom. The Westminster Confession of Faith has even turned the "visible church" into a theological concept (XXV.2): "The visible Church, which is also catholic or universal under the Gospel (not confined to one nation, as before under the law), consists of all those throughout the world that profess the true religion; and of their children: and is the kingdom of the Lord Jesus Christ, the house and family of God, out of which there is no ordinary possibility of salvation."[26] This is rather far-fetched: in the Bible, the House of God is "a pillar and buttress of the truth" (1 Tim. 3:15) and consists only of "living stones" (1 Pet. 2:5). Likewise, the Family of God consists of the true children of God, those who have believed in the name of Jesus (John 1:12; cf. 1 John 3:1), "blameless and innocent, children of God without blemish in the midst of a crooked and twisted generation, among whom you shine as lights in the world" (Phil. 2:15).

Some Reformed authors, such as John M. Otis,[27] refer to this "visible church" all the time, one reason being that it

---
26. Cf. Horton (2011, 852–53).
27. See, e.g., Otis (2005).

helps them to stress the similarity and continuity between Old Testament Israel and the New Testament church. The similarity is that both are "people of God" in some external sense, encompassing both true believers and outward (unregenerate) followers. Viewed from this angle, there allegedly could be no problem anymore calling Old Testament Israel "church," and calling the church "(spiritual) Israel." However, the argument does not work. First, it still does not explain how Melchizedek and Naaman, who did not belong to Israel, could be outside the "church" in the Old Testament days. Second, how could something that is a *sin* in the New Testament church (unregenerate people having crept in; cf. Acts 20:29-30; 2 Tim. 2:16-26; 4:3-4; 2 Pet. 2; 1 John 2:18-19; Jude; Rev. 2-3, 17-18) be used as an argument to assert that the New Testament church is a mixed people of God just like Old Testament Israel?

Federalists seem to forget that Israel was explicitly called as a *nation* in the natural, ethnic sense of the word, which inevitably includes parents and children, regenerate and unregenerate. But the (New Testament) church was definitely *not* called as a natural, ethnic nation, not even as a natural people from among the nations. It was called to be redeemed "from all lawlessness" and purified for Christ to be "a people for his own possession who are zealous for good works" (Titus 2:14). If Israel was called to be a "holy nation" (Exod. 19:6), this could only be in some outward sense, that is, separated from the other nations (Num. 23:9b), outwardly dedicated to God, with an outward circumcision, only a limited number of them having circumcised hearts. But if the church is called to be a "holy nation" (1 Pet. 2:9), she is supposed to be a gathering of people with circumcised hearts: "[Y]ou were washed, you were sanctified, you were justified in the name of the Lord Jesus Christ and by the Spirit of our God" (1 Cor. 6:11). In Israel, every member of the nation was called upon to love and serve the LORD; in the church every member *is* by definition loving and serving the Lord, though perhaps in weakness.

The terms "visible church" and "invisible church" are utterly contrary to Scripture. What should be *visible* of the true church is that she is the "light of the world," a city on a hill (Matt. 5:14), shining "as lights in the world" (Phil. 2:15), a "pillar and buttress of the truth" (1 Tim. 3:15). The idea of a "visible church" that includes believers and unbelievers, an idea so vital in Reformed ecclesiology, blurs the New Testament truth about the church. Certainly, in Revelation 2 and 3, the term "church" is used for congregations that apparently do include unregenerate members. It is therefore warranted to speak of local "churches," although we know that they hardly ever will include only regenerate members. Christendom is the kingdom of heaven in its present mixed state, containing both wheat and weeds (Matt. 13:24–30, 36–43). But Christendom is not the *Ekklesia*, which is the holy gathering of true Christian believers, the true Body of Christ, the true Temple of the Spirit (see below). That is the church that Jesus calls "my church": "[T]he gates of hell shall not prevail against it" (Matt. 16:18). *This* church is to be carefully distinguished from both Old and New Testament Israel, as will become clearer in the following points, I trust.

### 7.2.2 The Mystery of the Church

3. *Mystery*. In the past ages, the church has been a "mystery" (Greek *mystērion*), that is, a secret, something hidden: ". . . the mystery of Christ, which was not made known to the sons of men in other generations as it has now been revealed to his holy apostles and prophets by the Spirit. This mystery is that the Gentiles are fellow heirs, members of the same body,[28] and partakers of the promise in Christ Jesus through the gospel" (Eph. 3:3–9; cf. 5:32); ". . . his body, that is, the church, of which I became a minister . . . to make the word of God fully known, the mystery hidden for ages and generations but now revealed to his saints. To them God chose to make known

---

28. In Greek this entire expression is one word, *syssōma*, from *syn*, "with," and *sōma*, "body": "together one body."

how great among the Gentiles are the riches of the glory of this mystery, which is Christ in you, the hope of glory" (Col. 1:24-27; cf. Rom. 16:25; 1 Cor. 2:7).

The fact that the Ekklesia was something hidden in Old Testament times is sufficient reason to claim that the Ekklesia cannot have existed during that period, since Israel was not hidden, and the notion of a people of God was not hidden. The notions of life from God, of circumcision of the heart, of cleansing through the blood of the sacrifice, of justification by faith, were not hidden. Nothing of this was a mystery in those days. No wonder: *none of these things constitute the true nature of the Ekklesia* as the Body of the glorified Christ, the Bride of the Lamb, the Temple of the Holy Spirit. *This* church is, in my view, one of the "things into which angels long to look" (1 Pet. 1:12).

Please note, the fact that Gentile believers could join Israel as proselytes, and could be blessed in Abraham, was no secret at all: "[M]any nations shall join themselves to the LORD in that day, and shall be my people" (Zech. 2:11; cf. 8:22-23; Ps. 86:9; Isa. 11:10; 19:18-25; 56:6-7; Jer. 3:17; 4:2; Micah 4:1-5). The notion of the church does not imply that Gentile believers have joined Israel (see §7.6), but that believers *from* Israel and believers *from* the Gentiles have been unified into something altogether new, into an entity that no one could have imagined beforehand.

4. *Eternal purpose*. The Ekklesia is based upon the eternal purpose (Greek *prothesis tōn aiōnōn*, literally the "purpose of the ages [or, eternities]") of God in Christ (Eph. 3:11; cf. 1:4, "he chose us in him before the foundation of the world," though this refers rather to individual election). Concerning Israel we never read such a thing. We only hear about God's counsel "*since* the foundation of the world" (Matt. 13:35; 25:34). The church, then, is a greater project than Israel: she is from eternity to eternity, whereas Israel is embedded in historical time, existing from after the creation of the earth

until the new earth. On the new earth, there is no reference to Israel anymore;[29] Revelation 21:1-3 speaks only of the "new Jerusalem" (i.e., the Bride of the Lamb [vv. 9-10], that is the church) and of "the men" (*tōn anthrōpōn*), who will be his "people" (other manuscripts, "peoples"). There is no reference to Israel before the foundation of the world and after the present world has passed away; but there *is* reference to the church before the foundation of the world — in God's eternal counsel — and after the present world has passed way. The old Jerusalem is temporary, the New Jerusalem is everlasting.

5. *The place of John the Baptist*. Although only implicitly, two New Testament passages show that John the Baptist never belonged to the new dispensation of the Ekklesia. In Matthew 11:11, Jesus says that "among those born of women there has arisen no one greater than John the Baptist. Yet the one who is least in the kingdom of heaven is greater than he." This is not a moral statement — as if everyone in the kingdom of God would morally stand above John — but a redemptive-historical statement: John did not yet have a part in the kingdom of God (in the limited sense of the kingdom as being subject to God's Man), which would arrive only after Jesus' resurrection and glorification.

In John 3:29, the Baptist himself says: "The one who has the bride is the bridegroom. The friend of the bridegroom, who stands and hears him, rejoices greatly at the bridegroom's voice." Apparently, John was conscious of the fact that he personally did not belong to the Bride (bridal church). Just like all the great heroes of the Old Testament, he merely belonged to the friends (groomsmen) of the Bridegroom. Revelation 19:7-9 ties in with this by making a distinction between the Lamb's wife, that is, the church, and "those who are

---

29. The term "new earth" is adopted from Isa. 65:17, but *there* it does not reach any further than the Messianic kingdom (vv. 17–25), when sin will still be found (v. 20). On the "new earth" in the New Testament sense, righteousness will not just "reign" (cf. Isa. 32:1), but "dwell" (2 Pet. 3:13); sin will be "taken away" (John 1:29).

invited to the marriage supper of the Lamb," whom I take to be all believers from all dispensations who do not belong to the Ekklesia.

6. *Jesus' death.* The Ekklesia could come into existence only after Jesus through his death had broken down the "dividing wall of hostility," so that believing Jews and believing Gentiles could be "reconciled in one body through the cross" (Eph. 2:14-16). The mystery concerning the Ekklesia involves the fact that, in her, Jewish and Gentile believers were to be joined together on equal footing (vv. 11-22; 3:1-12). The unique Pauline term "body" in regard to the Ekklesia, a term not occurring in this sense in the Old Testament or in the Gospels, brings to light the Ekklesia's unique character in the clearest way.[30]

It is important to understand this correctly. There are many blessings that, in anticipation of and founded upon Jesus' death, were known already in the Old Testament (cf. §7.3). Each Old Testament believer possessed forgiveness of sins through the blood of Christ, even though this was shed only much later. However, what did *not* exist during the Old Testament period was the abolition of the hostility between Israel and the Gentiles by breaking down the dividing wall that separated the two.

### 7.2.3 The Church and the Spirit

7. *Jesus' glorification.* At his ascension to and glorification in heaven, Christ was given as "head of all things" to the Ekklesia, "which is his body, the fullness of him who fills all in all" (Eph. 1:19-23; cf. 4:15; 5:23). As the "firstborn from the dead," he is the "head of the body, the church" (Col. 1:18; cf. 2:19). The Ekklesia, then, is inconceivable apart from the risen and glorified Lord. Essential for understanding the nature of the Ekklesia is that she be viewed as "seated with him in the heavenly places in Christ Jesus" (Eph. 2:6). This is often little understood by those who think that Jesus returned

---

30. Cf. Ridderbos (1975, 362, and chapter IX in its entirety).

to heaven more or less as he had descended, that is, to resume his former position. However, when Jesus descended, the Word became flesh (John 1:14), in order to remain flesh (i.e., a Man) forever. At his ascension, it was not simply the Son returning to the Father, although this too occurred (John 16:28). It was a Man who with his glorified body was given to sit at the right hand of God. There is a *Man* in glory. Even today it can be said of him: "[I]n him the whole fullness of deity dwells [present tense!] *bodily*" (Col. 2:9), that is, in his glorified body (cf. Phil. 3:21), and it will be as the *Son of Man* that he will descend on the clouds of heaven (Matt. 24:30; 26:64; cf. Dan. 7:13).

In the Old Testament, there could be no people of God who in Christ were seated in the "heavenly places" before Christ, since the Logos who had become flesh, and the Man who had died, was raised and glorified, did not yet sit there himself. Or to put it more broadly, there could be no Ekklesia as long as the Son had not become Man, had died, and was raised and glorified. The "new man" (4:22–24; Col. 3:9–11) involves participation in the humanity of Christ.[31] The Ekklesia is not just connected with God—however important that is in itself—but *unified* (made one) with the *Man* in glory, united as much as a head and a body are united. It would be theologically unacceptable to speak of a union between God and (redeemed) humanity; humans are not deified. But a union is definitely possible between God-who-has-become-human and (redeemed) humanity. I suppose Jesus could not tell his disciples: "You are in the Father." But he *could* say: "I am in the Father, and you [are] in me" (John 14:20), that is, believers are in the Man Christ, who at the same time, as the Son, is in the Father. In short: in Paul's presentation, the Ekklesia is something inseparable from the Man in glory.

8. *Foundation*. The "mystery of Christ" (the union of the glorified Head and his Body), which in earlier ages had not

---

31. See Ouweneel (2010b, §4.3.1).

been made known to people, "has now been revealed to his holy apostles and prophets by the Spirit" (Eph. 3:4–5). Just as in Ephesians 2:20, this text is undoubtedly referring to New Testament prophets (different than, e.g., in 2 Peter 3:2, where the prophets precede the apostles, and where apparently the Old Testament prophets are meant). This implies that the Ekklesia is built upon a foundation that did not exist before it was laid by the apostles and the (New Testament) prophets (2:20), and this was impossible before the day of Pentecost (see the next point). It is impossible that a building exists before its foundation has been laid. Therefore, there could be no Ekklesia before the apostles and the (New Testament) prophets had established its foundation.[32]

9. *Outpouring of the Spirit.* The Ekklesia is the Temple of the Holy Spirit (1 Cor. 3:16; Eph. 2:20–22), and she can be this only since the Holy Spirit has been poured out (Acts 2). For Jews it is common to say that God dwells in heaven, and that humans live on earth (cf. Ps. 115:16). But Christians can say that, since and because of Christ's ascension, there is a glorified *Man* in heaven at God's right hand,[33] and since Acts 2, *God* the Holy Spirit dwells in the Ekklesia on earth.[34] Craig Van Gelder, speaking about the essence of the Ekklesia, even calls her a "community created by the Spirit,"[35] and says that the Ekklesia is God's personal presence in the world through the Spirit.[36] Of course, the Holy Spirit *was working* in this world already long before Acts 2; actually, since Genesis 1:2. But we could in no way say that the Holy Spirit *dwelt* on the earth. Reformed theologian Johan Heyns calls the church the "residence" of the Holy Spirit.[37] John 7:39 literally says, "[T]he Holy Spirit was not yet," that is, did not yet dwell on the earth (cf. Acts 19:2 literally, "we have not even heard that the Holy

---

32. Ibid., §2.1.3.
33. See Ouweneel (2007b, 431–33).
34. See Ouweneel (2007a, chapter 7).
35. Van Gelder (2000, title, 24–25, 112–13).
36. Ibid., 25.
37. Heyns (1988, 362).

Spirit is," i.e., has come). In short: the existence of the Ekklesia is inseparably linked with the Spirit's dwelling on earth; the Ekklesia was never an empty dwelling place, and the Spirit never dwelt on earth without a house. The outpouring of the Spirit and the origin of the Ekklesia coincided.

10. The Body of Christ is the totality of all those who have been baptized in the Holy Spirit: "For in one Spirit we were all baptized into one body" (1 Cor. 12:13), that is, all believers have been baptized in one and the same Spirit, and have thus become members of the same Body. In my view, the expression "in one Spirit" (Greek *en heni pneumati*, just like *en pneumati* [Matt. 3:11]: baptized "in the Spirit") refers to Spirit baptism. Baptists usually see water baptism in this verse, and derive from it that one becomes a member of a local church through water baptism. However, I do not see how someone can receive water baptism "by" (or "through") the Holy Spirit. Even less can we read *en* here as if it meant *hypo* ("by") in the sense that the Spirit would be here the one who baptizes. Scripture does not know a baptism in which the Holy Spirit is the agent (*contra*, e.g., CEV: "God's Spirit baptized each of us").

In short, the Ekklesia is the community of those who have been baptized "in" the Spirit—like a body is baptized "in" (not "with") water—and thus have become members of the Body of Christ. This baptism occurred for the first time in Acts 2. Even in Acts 1:5, this baptism was still a future thing, though at that time the waiting was to last only a few more days. On the day of Pentecost, the hundred and twenty followers of Jesus Christ were baptized in the Holy Spirit, and as a consequence, the Ekklesia came into being, as people realized afterwards. From the beginning of its existence, the Ekklesia was the Temple in which the Holy Spirit dwelt. Before the fall of Jerusalem in 586 BC, the glory (*Shekinah*) of God had dwelt in the physical temple at Jerusalem; since AD 30 the Holy Spirit dwells in the spiritual Temple, that is, the Ekklesia.

In summary, we have seen that the church (a) could not exist before the death of Christ, (b) could not exist before the resurrection of Christ, (c) could not exist before the glorification of Christ, and (d) could not exist before the outpouring of the Holy Spirit. We can claim that the church is some "spiritual Israel," the continuation of God's Old Testament people, only by ignoring or denying all that is specific of the Ekklesia.

## 7.3 Similarities Between Old and New Testament Saints

### 7.3.1 Chafer's "Contrasts"

Dispensationalist Lewis Sperry Chafer mentions a number of contrasts between Israel and the church that are instead partial similarities; for instance:[38]

1. *The posterity of Abraham.* There is indeed a contrast between Abraham's natural and spiritual offspring (Rom. 4:11–12): the former involves ethnic Israel, the latter comprises all true believers who have lived or will live on earth since Abraham. However, the contrast is definitely not absolute: the "Israel of God" (Gal. 6:16) includes those who are both the natural and the spiritual offspring of Abraham. One day, in the Messianic kingdom, all Israelites will be both natural and spiritual progeny of Abraham (Isa. 45:25; 60:21).

2. *The ministry of both Israel and the church.* Both have received the commandment of God to make him known to the nations—a task in which both have equally failed to a large extent (Rom. 2:19–21; 16:26). Yet, Jesus-believers will manage to bring the gospel of the kingdom to the ends of the earth (Matt. 24:14; 28:18–19), and in the Messianic kingdom the prophet's words will become true: "[T]he time is coming to gather all nations and tongues. And they shall come and shall see my glory, and I will set a sign among them. And from them I will send survivors to the nations, to Tarshish, Pul, and Lud, who draw the bow, to Tubal and Javan, to the coastlands far away, that have not heard my fame or seen my glory. And they shall

---

38. Chafer (1983, IV, 47–53).

declare my glory among the nations. And they shall bring all your brothers from all the nations as an offering to the Lord, on horses and in chariots and in litters and on mules and on dromedaries, to my holy mountain Jerusalem" (Isa. 66:18-20).

3. *Law versus grace.* The governing principle in Israel and the church is allegedly law and grace, respectively; this was not the idea of Chafer alone, but of many theologians before and after him. However, there is no genuine contrast here. As I argue elsewhere in this book, as well as in the first volume in the present series, in the final analysis Israel, too, lived by pure grace (Exod. 34:6-7), while the Ekklesia has everything to do with the "law of Christ" (1 Cor. 9:21; Gal. 6:2; cf. Rom. 8:4; 13:8-10; James 1:25; 2:8, 12). There never was or will be any living under any form of Torah apart from the grace of God, and there never was or will be any living under God's grace apart from living under some form of Torah.

4. *Slaves versus sons.* This is not a real contrast either: the Old Testament Israelites were called sons of God just as the New Testament Jesus-believers are (Deut. 14:1), and the Jesus-believers are called slaves of God just as the Israelites were (Rom. 6:22). The only difference is that Old Testament believers were *natural* and *immature* sons of God as long as Christ and the Spirit had not yet come, whereas Jesus-believers are *spiritual* and *mature* sons of God (Gal. 3:22-4:7; see further §7.3.3).

5. *The priesthood.* Chafer says, "The nation Israel *had* a priesthood. The church *is* a priesthood."[39] However, Israel was a "kingdom of priests" (Exod. 19:6), just as the church is a "royal priesthood" (1 Pet. 2:9). This is just a reversal of noun and adjective, from which no drastic conclusions can be drawn. It is obvious that Peter is referring to Exodus 19. Both expressions amount to the same thing: a priestly kingdom or a royal priesthood. The real difference is gradual: Israel had one (Aaronic) family of priests and one (Davidic) king,

---

39. Ibid., 52.

whereas in the Ekklesia *all* members in principle are kings and priests (1 Pet. 2:5, 9; Rev. 1:6; 5:10; 20:4, 6; 22:5) — distinct from Jesus' special kingship and priesthood of course: believers are kings, Jesus is the King of kings (Rev. 19:16); believers are priests, Jesus is the High Priest (many times in Heb.).

6. *Future judgment*. Chafer: "It is clearly predicted that Israel must come into judgment . . . but it is as clearly declared that the church will not come into judgment." However, the church, as a responsible witness to God on earth, will come into judgment just the same (1 Pet. 4:17; Rev. 2-3, 17-18), apart from the fact that Paul states that *all* individuals, including those of the church, will one day appear before the judgment seat of God/Christ (Rom. 14:10; 2 Cor. 5:10; cf. 1 Cor. 3:12-15; 4:4-5).

In conclusion, we find that there are more similarities between Israel and the church than classical dispensationalists seem willing to accept.

### 7.3.2 More Similarities

We can elaborate on this subject a little more; Old and New Testament believers have many things in common, and in connection with our subject, we must add that in all these points *we are dealing with covenant blessings*. That is, what the two groups have in common is always of a covenantal nature, whereas blessings in which the New Testament believers surpass the Old Testament believers are *never* of a covenantal nature. There is no doubt that the latter blessings for the Ekklesia are the most lofty and interesting ones. As far as the former blessings are concerned, we may think of the following.[40]

7. Both Old and New Testament believers are born of the same Spirit (John 3:5-8), that is, have life from God, have a new nature that cannot sin (1 John 3:9), are godly (Heb. *hasidim*) or righteous (*tsaddiqim*), that is, faithful and devoted to God and his Torah, which today is the law of Christ (see point

---

40. See Ouweneel (2010a, §§3.5, 8.1–8.2), and cf. Clowney (1995, chapters 2–3).

## Israel and the Church

[3.]). Please note the great difference between being *born* of the Spirit and *receiving* the Spirit indwelling within oneself. We see this distinction, for instance, in Ezekiel 36:25, "I will sprinkle clean water on you, and you shall be clean from all your uncleannesses"; this corresponds with John 3:5, "born of water and *of the Spirit*." But Ezekiel 36:27 adds as a separate action: "I will put my Spirit within you." In the former case, the Spirit is the power of regeneration; but in the latter case, the Spirit comes to dwell *in person* in the believer: "[Y]our body is a temple of the Holy Spirit within you" (1 Cor. 6:19). A contractor may build a house, but he is not necessarily the one who is going to live in that house. The Spirit is the *power* that regenerates the Jesus-believer *and* is the *person* who subsequently comes to live within him.

8. Both groups are washed, prospectively or retrospectively, by the same blood of Christ, and therefore share in the same universal propitiatory sacrifice of Christ, the true Lamb of God: ". . . the redemption that is in Christ Jesus, whom God put forward as a propitiation by his blood, to be received by faith. This was to show God's righteousness, because in his divine forbearance he had passed over *former* sins [i.e., committed pre-Easter]. It was to show his righteousness at the present time [i.e., post-Pentecost], so that he might be just and the justifier of the one who has faith in Jesus" (Rom. 3:24–26). The term "passed over" is conspicuous here: in looking forward to the cross, God could "pass over" the sins of the Old Testament believers. Genuine atonement was accomplished only on the cross of Calvary. The way in which God "passed over" the sins of Old Testament believers is seen in a striking way in the case of David, of whom the prophet said afterwards: ". . . my servant David, who kept my commandments and followed me with all his heart, doing only that which was right in my eyes" (1 Kgs 14:8). In anticipation, David's sins were already under the blood of Calvary!

9. Both groups are justified, that is, declared (shown to be, or made, or accounted) righteous—in Old Testament lan-

guage: made *tsaddiq*—namely, by faith, without works. That is, their position before God is not rooted in the achievements of believers but in God himself and in his justifying grace, to which people entrust themselves in faith. For both groups, it is true that this faith has no relation to good works, but then, works that are the fruit of salvation, not the condition for it. Zechariah and Elizabeth, who still belonged to the old dispensation, are *the* example of this: "And they were both righteous before God, walking blamelessly in all the commandments and statutes of the Lord" (Luke 1:6). If understood properly, such a description essentially holds for *all* Old and New Testament believers. An example is what Solomon said about his father David: "[H]e walked before you in faithfulness, in righteousness, and in uprightness of heart toward you" (1 Kgs 3:6). "The righteous shall live by his faith" (Hab. 2:4).

10. The preceding points also imply that the blessings of the New Covenant, to which all previous covenants lead and open up, are shared not only by Old Testament believers, but also by New Testament believers (Luke 22:20; 1 Cor. 11:25; 2 Cor. 3:6; Gal. 3:15–18; 4:21–31; Heb. 7:22; 8:6; 9:15; 12:24; 13:20). As shown elsewhere in this book, these are basically two of these blessings: (a) placing the Torah in the hearts of God's people (Jer. 31:33); this is what Paul calls the "ministry of the Spirit" (2 Cor. 3:8); and (b) forgiving their iniquities (Jer. 31:35); this is what Paul calls the "ministry of righteousness" (2 Cor. 3:9). Administering the blessings of the New Covenant basically contains these two elements: the ministry of the Spirit and the ministry of righteousness.

11. Israel is *people* of God (Exod. 5:1; etc.), the church is too (Acts 15:14; Titus 2:14; 1 Pet. 2:9–10). However, the way Titus 2:14 speaks about God's "people" ("... to purify for himself a people for his own possession") suggests that Paul is speaking here of a *new* people that at the time of the cross was still a *future* people. In Acts 15:14 ("God first visited the Gentiles, to take from them a people for his name") this is even clearer

because James is referring to a *Gentile* people (see §7.4.1).⁴¹

12. Israel and the church each began with *twelve men:* the patriarchs (twelve sons of Jacob, ancestors of the twelve tribes) and the twelve apostles, respectively. Jesus underscores the deeper connection between the two by telling his disciples: "[I]n the new world, when the Son of Man will sit on his glorious throne, you who have followed me will also sit on twelve thrones, judging the twelve tribes of Israel" (Matt. 19:28). The New Jerusalem is described as having twelve gates as well as twelve foundations, on which the names of the twelve tribes and those of the twelve apostles are written, respectively (Rev. 21:12, 14).

13. Israel and the church each begin with a *Torah.* Israel is characterized by the Mosaic Torah, the church is characterized by the Messianic Torah. Moses is the great lawgiver of his people, Christ is the *novus Moses,* the "new Moses," the new lawgiver of his people, the church.⁴² On the subject of the Torah see extensively the first volume of this series.

14. Israel and the church each begin on a *mountain.* The Mosaic Torah was given at Mount Sinai; according to Jewish tradition, this happened at *Shavu'ot* (The Feast of Weeks, or Pentecost).⁴³ It was the occasion of the establishment of the Sinaitic covenant; therefore, *Shavu'ot* is a covenant feast (cf. 2 Chron. 15:9-14). The Jewish book of Jubilees (second century BC) links Pentecost with the covenants, especially the Noahic covenant.⁴⁴ The Essene sect of Qumran (first century AD) speaks of the feast of the New Covenant, very probably referring to Pentecost.⁴⁵

It is the more striking that at this very feast, *Shavu'ot,* the church was founded on another mountain, Mount Zion, thus

---

41. Bruce (1988, 293).
42. See Davies (1969, 10–16); for a Jewish view, see Schoeps (1949, 87–116).
43. Talmud: Shabbat 88a; see more extensively Ouweneel (2001, 120–25) for the many similarities between the Torah and the Spirit.
44. Jub. VI.15–22; XLIV.1–5.
45. E.g., 4QDa [4Q266] 11, 17; 1QS II.19–26; V.20–24; VI.

making of *Shavu'ot* the feast of the New Covenant as well (cf. Jer. 50:4-5), closely linked, by the way, with *Sukkot*, the Feast of Booths, *the* eschatological feast of the Messianic kingdom (cf. Zech. 14:16-19). Interestingly, on both occasions, at Mount Sinai (Exod. 19-20) and on Mount Zion (Acts 2), "many voices" were heard (Exod. 19:16, "thunders," Heb. *qôlôt*, lit. "voices"; Acts 2:4, Greek *glōssais*, "tongues"), and fire was seen (Exod. 19:18; Acts 2:3). The Torah/Logos is compared to fire (Jer. 23:29), and also to water (Eph. 5:26), just as the Spirit is compared to "fire" and "water."[46] Of course, there are also *contrasts* between Sinai and Zion, as we know from Galatians 4:24-27 and Hebrews 12:18-24 (see §§6.4-6.7).[47]

### 7.3.3 Metaphors

Often, the same or similar metaphors are applied to Israel and the church.[48]

1. Since Isaac, Abraham's son, all true believers, both in the Old and in the New Testament, are, as we saw, spiritual offspring, *children*, sons of Abraham (Rom. 4:11, 16; Gal. 3:7-9, 14, 29; 4:28; cf. Matt. 3:9; Luke 13:16; 19:9; John 8:39-40).[49] Beyond that, Israelites are also physical descendants of Abraham, but that is a different matter. To both circumcised and uncircumcised descendants comes the same question: Are they walking in the faith of their (natural and/or spiritual) father Abraham? If we wish, we could say: all true believers since Abraham belong to the one great faith-family of Abraham (something very different from the "family" of Abrahamic religions: Judaism, Christianity, Islam!). Jesus did recognize Israel's spiritual leaders as Abraham's "offspring" (John 8:37), but not as "children" of Abraham because they resisted the truth: "If you were Abraham's children, you would

---

46. See Ouweneel (2007a, 206-207; 2015a, §3.3.2).
47. Ouweneel (1982, II, 83-90; 1997, 292-98); cf. Pop (1999, 335).
48. Clowney (1995, 29-30).
49. Wentsel (1995, 367; cf. 1998a, 81-83): "Abraham, the representative of all believers, remains for Israel and the church the historical common patriarch and promise bearer, who links the two together."

be doing the works Abraham did, but now you seek to kill me, a man who has told you the truth that I heard from God. This is not what Abraham did" (vv. 39–40). He also denied that they were children of God (cf. Deut. 14:1), and called them children of the devil (vv. 41–44). Being "sons of Abraham" coincides with being "sons of God" (Gal. 3:7, 26): in order to be a son of God it is necessary to walk in the same faith as Abraham.

2. Israel is the *bride* of God, or of the Messiah (Isa. 49:18; 61:10; 62:5; Hos. 2:18–19), the church is the Bride of the Lamb (Rev. 21:2, 9). As to the former metaphor, we should also think of the image of the divorced and re-accepted wife (Isa. 50:1; 54:6–8; Jer. 2; Ezek. 16). If we wish, we could also say: Christ has two brides, Israel and the church, just as Jacob had two wives: Rachel and Leah, respectively: though he worked for Rachel, he initially received Leah, but in the end he will also have Rachel. Likewise, Jesus came for Israel (Matt. 10:5–6; 15:24; Rom. 15:8), what he received was the church (cf. Acts 13:46), but in the end he will also have Israel (Rom. 11:26).

3. Israel is compared to a *vine* (Ps. 80:8; Hos. 10:1), Christ (the actual vine) and his followers (the branches) are too (John 15:1–8). Incidentally, Israel is sometimes also compared to a vineyard (Isa. 5:1–7; Matt. 21:33–45), and sometimes Jerusalem is compared to a vine (Jer. 2:21; Ezek. 15:6). In all these cases, the point of the metaphor is that of bearing fruit to please the Owner.

4. Israel is the *flock* of God (Num. 27:17; 2 Sam. 24:17; Ps. 80:1; Isa. 40:11; 63:11; etc.), the church is too (John 10:16; 21:15–17; Acts 20:28–29; 1 Pet. 5:2–3). The point of this metaphor is that of God or Christ caring for his own, tending them, feeding them, leading them.

5. Both Israel and the church began with a figurative *rock*.[50] God says to Israel: "[L]ook to the rock from which you were hewn, and to the quarry from which you were dug. Look to

---

50. Pop (1999, 402).

Abraham your father and to Sarah who bore you" (Isa. 51:1–2). Jesus says of the church: "[Y]ou are Peter, and on this rock I will build my church" (Matt. 16:18). Both "peoples of God" started with a rock on which the further development of the respective "people" depended. God placed Abraham as a rock at the start of Israel's history, and Jesus placed Peter as a rock at the start of the church's history.

6. The histories of both Israel and the church began with an *exodus*.[51] The one experienced by Israel we know from the name that in the Septuagint was given to the second book of the Bible (the word occurs in this Greek translation in Exod. 19:1; Num. 33:38; Ps. 114:1). In the New Testament the word occurs in Luke 9:30–31 ("... Moses and Elijah, who appeared in glory and spoke of his *exodus* [departure, cf. 2 Pet. 1:15], which he was about to accomplish at Jerusalem").[52] In the church, the *exodus* character is even clearer: it is the "Exodus church,"[53] a people of pilgrims, who are repeatedly called to leave the world of sin and travel to the promised fatherland, which is not heaven but the kingdom of God as it will one day be established in power and majesty (cf. 1 Cor. 10:1–6; 2 Cor. 6:17–18; Eph. 1:13–14; Phil. 3:20; Heb. 11:13–16; 13:14; 1 Pet. 2:11–12; Rev. 18:4–5; cf. Isa. 48:20; 52:11; Jer. 51:6, 45).[54] That which the church proclaims is even called "the Way" (Acts 9:2; 19:9, 23; 22:4; 24:14, 22). The Israelites were called "strangers and sojourners" (Lev. 25:23; 1 Chron. 29:15), and the New Testament believers are called similarly (Heb. 11:13, "strangers and exiles"; 1 Pet. 2:11, "sojourners and exiles"). The *New Delhi Report on Witness* speaks of the "pilgrim church," which, like Abraham of old, boldly moves on to its unknown future, living in a tent of continual adaptation, looking forward to the

---

51. Cf. Wright (2011, 63–66).
52. Cf. Heitink (2007, 26): "In [Jesus'] life the new exodus from the bonds of sin and death takes place."
53. Cf. Moltmann (1975, 102–105).
54. Heyns (1988, 360); cf. Rahner (1966 title: *The Pilgrim Church*); Küng (1967, 108, 120, 144, 151–52, 172, 378, 558); Bijlsma (1981, 39); Verkuyl (1992, 378); Wright (2011, 144–45).

*Israel and the Church*

city whose designer and builder is God (Heb. 11:10).[55]

Again, I emphasize that the Old and New Testament believers in fact have much more in common than classical dispensationalists often seem to notice. Both groups share in the same salvation, the same justification, the same cleansing, the same Messiah, the same sacrifice, the same spiritual father Abraham, the same New Covenant. Some statements referring to ethnic Israel are even freely applied to the church in the New Testament, such as Exodus 19:5 (see 1 Pet. 2:9), Hosea 1:10 and 2:22 (see Rom. 9:24-25 and 1 Pet. 2:10), and Joel 2:28-32 (see Acts 2:17-21). These are such important connections and similarities that, in *this* (immanent-historical!) sense, we might speak of one "people of God" (*not* in the eternal-transcendent sense). This becomes problematic only if we call this people either "Israel" or "the church," for in that case although we do recognize the similarities, we do not sufficiently honor the differences between the Old and New Testament believers. It is not a heresy if one sees the church as beginning with Adam and Abraham, but it *is* an error. To see this, we now have to pay some more attention to the elementary differences between the pre-Easter believers and the post-Pentecost believers.

## 7.4 Differences Between Old and New Testament Saints
### 7.4.1 The People of God

Although the true Israel—the "Israel of God" (Gal. 6:16)—certainly is a spiritual people, Israel is first and foremost a natural people, a member of which one becomes through physical birth. In contrast to this, the church is a spiritual people, a member of which one becomes through rebirth.[56] As German Protestant theologian Wolfhart Pannenberg put it: "The church does not, like Israel, form a birth community through the generational coherence of its members, but is essentially

---

55. Quoted in Visser 't Hooft (1962, 90).
56. Cf. Wellum (2006, 97-98 [incl. note 3], 111-19).

a community of individuals reborn through faith and baptism."[57] The not-yet-believing children are certainly part of the community—they are holy in their believing parent(s) (1 Cor. 7:14)—but in the proper sense, the church is the "gathering of Christian believers"—old and young—not of the "children of Christian believers." (In Appendix I, I explain the significance of this point in my evaluation of the Abrahamic covenant and the New Covenant, and of baptism.)

It is a basic mistake to apply what holds for a *natural* people—with natural parents and children—to a *spiritual* people, where there are at best spiritual "parents" and "children" (cf. 1 Cor. 4:14-15; 1 Thess. 2:7, 11; 1 John 2:1, 28), or "fathers," "young men," and "children" (1 John 2:12-14), all in the purely spiritual sense. I wish to stress this time and again: one becomes a member of Israel through *birth*, and a member of the church through *rebirth*. In the former case, natural parent-child relationships are of vital importance; in the latter case, spiritual parent-child relationships are of vital importance. The two are never to be confused. A person is Jewish by being born of a Jewish mother. A person is a (regenerate) Christian by being born of a heavenly mother (Gal. 4:26).

As far as Israel is concerned, spiritually speaking it has been called *out of* the nations (Exod. 19:5; 33:16; Lev. 20:24; Deut. 7:6; 10:15; 2 Sam. 7:23; 1 Kgs 8:53), but at the same time it is a nation among the nations, a people like all other peoples, a *goy* (Gen. 12:2) among the *goyyim*. This is emphasized especially when Israel falls into apostasy. Then it lowers itself to the level of the other nations (1 Sam. 8:5, 20), or the prophet gives it this place: in Amos 1-2, the judgments over Judah and Israel are dealt with just as those over the (other) *goyyim* (cf. 9:7), and in Jeremiah 1:5 and 10, Judah seems to be included among the *goyyim*.

In addition to this, the point I am making is that Israel is an ethnic nation, whereas the church is a spiritual nation. The

---

57. Pannenberg (1993, 116).

latter consists of reborn persons gathered from all the nations to become a people of God, without this nation ever becoming a nation among the nations, a people like all other peoples.

When it is a question of the place of children among this people, we often encounter a major logical flaw in federalist thinking. This is due to the ambiguous meaning of the word "child," being either a descendent of two parents, irrespective of age, or a person that both physically and spiritually is still immature. When you are fifty, if your parents are still alive, you are still their child, though you are not immature anymore. Now the mistake often made is this: the fact that a covenant is also for the children, that is, descendants, does not necessarily mean that *young* (immature) children have a part in it.

For instance, Peter says on the day of Pentecost: "[T]he promise is for you and for your children and for all who are far off, everyone whom the Lord our God calls to himself" (Acts 2:39). In addition to noting that Peter is not speaking here of the Abrahamic promise—as is sometimes asserted (see §8.4.3)—but of the "promise of the Holy Spirit," note also the word "children" here. It should be obvious that the meaning of this word here is "descendants," not infants. When God promises the Spirit, he does so not only for those to whom the promise literally came, but also for their descendants. But *not* for infants, since the condition for factually *receiving* the Spirit is *repentance* and *faith*, as is made clear in the preceding verse: "Repent and be baptized every one of you in the name of Jesus Christ for the forgiveness of your sins, and you will receive the gift of the Holy Spirit" (v. 38). "In him [i.e., Christ] you also, when you heard the word of truth, the gospel of your salvation, and believed in him, were sealed with the promised Holy Spirit" (Eph. 1:13).

It is the same in connection with the New Covenant. God told Jeremiah: "And they shall be my people, and I will be their God. I will give them one heart and one way, that they may fear me forever, for their own good and the good of their children after them. I will make with them an everlasting covenant, that I will not turn away from doing good to them" (Jer. 32:38–40). And he told Isaiah: "And as for me, this is my covenant with them . . .: My Spirit that is upon you, and my words that I have put in your mouth, shall not depart out of your mouth, or out of the mouth of your offspring, or out of the mouth of your children's offspring, . . . from this time forth and forevermore" (Isa. 59:21).

Such passages have been used as an argument that infants are included in the New Covenant as well as adults, and that *therefore* the sign of covenant can be applied to the infants of the believers.[58] This is a threefold mistake: (1) the passages speak about descendants, not about infants; (2) the passages do not speak of any sign of the covenant; and (3) baptism is not a, or the, sign of the New Covenant anyway (see especially Appendix I).

### 7.4.2 The Family of God

The family of God is the totality of the children (or "sons") of God the Father. The Israelites were children of God (Deut. 14:1) simply by being born of Jewish mothers. The members of the Ekklesia, however, are children of God by being born *of God himself* (John 1:12–13). A Jew is a Jew if he or she has Jewish blood flowing through their veins. A member of the Ekklesia possesses not only natural life but has been "made alive together with Christ" (Eph. 2:5). That is, the life that one possesses is the "life of Jesus" (2 Cor. 4:10–11); the resurrected Christ is the life of the believers (Col. 3:4), that is, life that has passed through death: "I came that they may have life and have it abundantly. I am the good shepherd. The good shepherd lays down his life for the sheep" (John 10:10–11).

In the writings of John, the abundance of this life is expressed in the term "eternal life." This is not primarily a quantitative term (cf. the somewhat misleading term "ever-

---

58. See, e.g., Stam (1999, 152–54).

lasting life"), but a qualitative term: it is fellowship with the Father and the Son (John 17:3; 1 John 1:1–4), and as such is life belonging to eternity.

For pre-Easter believers, "eternal (or everlasting) life" referred unambiguously to the blessings of the Messianic kingdom, as we see in the prophetic Psalm 133 (v. 3, in Zion "the LORD has commanded the blessing, life for evermore"), in Daniel 12:2 ("many of those who sleep in the dust of the earth shall awake, some to everlasting life"), and the question in the Gospels addressed to Jesus: "Teacher, what good deed must I do to have eternal life?" (Matt. 19:16, cf. v. 29), or: "Teacher, what shall I do to inherit eternal life?" (Luke 10:25). The wicked "will go away into eternal punishment, but the righteous into eternal life," that is not heaven but "the kingdom prepared for you from the foundation of the world" (Matt. 25:34).

For the apostle Paul, eternal life apparently is a future blessing as well—although less clearly connected with the Messianic kingdom—on which one can lay hold already today (Rom. 5:21; 6:22–23; Gal. 6:8; 1 Tim. 1:6; 6:12; Titus 1:2; 3:7). The ministry of the apostle John, too, points to eternal life in the sense of blessings that believers can already possess and enjoy today. For the pre-Easter group, eternal life was purely a thing of the future, connected with the Messianic kingdom. For the post-Pentecost group, it is usually a present possession, especially in John's writings: whoever believes, *has* eternal life (John 3:16, 36; 5:24; 6:47, 54).

Pre-Easter believers had life from God, but Jesus has come in order that his sheep have divine life in its richest form, in that they have received *Jesus himself* as their life: "And this is the testimony, that God gave us eternal life, and this life is in his Son. Whoever has the Son has life; whoever does not have the Son of God does not have life" (1 John 5:11–12). Verse 20 even tells us: "Jesus Christ . . . is the true God and eternal life." Believers have and enjoy this life through the working of the indwelling Holy Spirit: "The water [of the Spirit] that

I will give him will become in him a spring of water welling up to eternal life" (John 4:14). "'Whoever believes in me, . . . [o]ut of his heart will flow rivers of living water.' Now this he said about the Spirit, whom those who believed in him were to receive, for as yet the Spirit had not been given, because Jesus was not yet glorified" (7:38-39). None of these blessings were, or could possibly have been, known to Old Testament believers.[59]

### 7.4.3 The Body of Christ

The church as the Body of Christ involved the great fact that post-Pentecost believers have been unified with their glorified Head in heaven. There was no Body of Christ in the Old Testament because there was no glorified Man at the right hand of God. There was no Body of Christ in the Gospels because, again, there was no glorified Man at the right hand of God. The truth of the Ekklesia is inseparably linked with the truth of the ascension and glorification of Jesus. Since his ascension, Jesus is in heaven what he had been since eternity: the beloved Son of the Father in his bosom (John 1:18). However, this fact is not enough to understand the truth of the Body of Christ. In heaven, Jesus is *also* what he had never been before: the glorified *Man* Christ Jesus at the right hand of God. In the fullness of time, the Word became what it had never been before: human (Gal. 4:4; John 1:14). God became Man, remained God, and will forever remain both God and Man. Jesus *is* the Father's Son (2 John 1:3), but as Man he can even be *distinguished* from God: the One who cried, "My God, my God . . ." (Matt. 27:46), is the One who is now seated at the right hand of *God* (Mark 16:19; Luke 22:69; Acts 2:33; 5:31; 7:55-56; Rom. 8:34; Col. 3:1; Heb. 1:3; 10:12; 12:2; 1 Pet. 3:22).

There is a *Man* in glory, who is God the Son, but at the same time will forever be the Man Christ Jesus. Ekklesia members are *associated* with the Son in the family of God, and they are *unified* with the glorified Man in the Body of Christ.

---

59. See extensively Ouweneel (2010a, §§4.1–4.2).

The Man in glory is as much one with his Ekklesia as a head is one with its body. The two are inseparable. What the Head has received, he shares with his Body, which "in him" is seated in the heavenly places (Eph. 2:6). Jesus is blessed with every spiritual blessing in these heavenly places—the believers are too (Eph. 1:3). Jesus is "the heir of all things" (Heb. 1:2)—the believers are "heirs of God and fellow heirs with Christ" (Rom. 8:17; cf. Gal. 4:7). As Jesus said himself, "The glory that you have given me I have given them" (John 17:22). "When Christ who is your life appears, then you also will appear with him in glory" (Col. 3:4; cf. 2 Thess. 1:10). Jesus is the King of kings, the Ekklesia members are kings with him. Jesus is the High Priest, the Ekklesia members are priests with him.

In addition to this, believers know this glorified Jesus, dwelling above in heaven, in many other qualities. Jesus is:

(a) Their Advocate, Helper, Intercessor with the Father (Rom. 8:34; cf. Luke 22:31–32; Heb. 7:25; 1 John 2:1).

(b) The Head of the Body, who coordinates all its members, and grants gifts and ministries to the Body (Eph. 1:19–23; 4:7–11, 15–16; Col. 2:19).

(c) The One who triumphed over the spiritual powers (Eph. 1:19–21; Col. 2:15; 1 Pet. 2:21–22; cf. Heb. 1:3, 13; 10:12–13), which is of great practical significance for their own spiritual battle (Eph. 6:12).

(d) The center of the true Christian life, which is hidden in God (Col. 3:1–3).

(e) The "minister in the holy places [or, sanctuary]" (Heb. 8:1–2), that is, the leader of believers' worship (cf. 2:11–12; 7:25; 10:19–22; 13:15).

(f) The example and the end goal of the Christian race (Phil. 3:12–14; Heb. 12:1–3; cf. 1 Cor. 9:24, 26; Gal. 2:2; 5:7; Phil. 2:16; 2 Tim. 4:7).

(g) The One who, together with his Ekklesia, waits for the day that "his enemies should be made a footstool for his feet" (Heb. 10:12–13).

Please note that *none* of these blessings could have been possibly known to, or even presumed by, pre-Easter believers. Post-Pentecost Ekklesia members differ essentially from them in that they have a *heavenly position*, being seated "in" the glorified Christ in heaven (Eph. 1:6). Abraham could look forward to a "heavenly country" and "city" (Heb. 11:10, 16). But he could have had no idea of what it is to be seated *right now* in heaven, in that the Man with whom Ekklesia members have been united is now for the first time seated there in glory.

## 7.4.4 The House or Temple of God

The Ekklesia is the Body of Christ, and as such there is a link with the Holy Spirit, since the Ekklesia members have become members of the Body through being baptized in the Spirit (1 Cor. 12:12-13; cf. Acts 1:5; 11:16-17). Post-Pentecost believers have been sealed (2 Cor. 1:21-22; Eph. 1:13; 4:30), and anointed with (2 Cor. 1:21-22; 1 John 2:20, 27), and—hopefully—filled with the Holy Spirit (Eph. 5:18; cf. Acts 2:4; 4:8, 31; 13:9). We do hear about a pre-Easter anointing (Isa. 61:1) and a being filled with the Spirit (e.g., Luke 1:15, 41, 67), but not about a baptism in the Holy Spirit, because the latter occurred only at and after Pentecost (Acts 1:5; cf. 2:4).[60] As we saw, the Holy Spirit *worked* in this world already since Genesis 1:2, but strictly speaking he never *dwelt* here because there was never an appropriate house for him—except Jesus himself, who called his own body a temple (John 2:19-21) after having received the Holy Spirit at his baptism.

Since the day of Pentecost, a new house or temple of God exists in this world: "the house of God, which is the church of the living God, the pillar and ground of the truth" (1 Tim. 3:15 NKJV). "Do you not know that you are God's temple and that God's Spirit dwells in you?" (1 Cor. 3:16). "[Y]ou are fellow citizens with the saints and members of the household of God, built on the foundation of the apostles and proph-

---

60. Ouweneel (2007a, 170–87).

ets, Christ Jesus himself being the cornerstone, in whom the whole structure, being joined together, grows into a holy temple in the Lord. In him you also are being built together into a dwelling place for God by [or, in] the Spirit" (Eph. 2:19–22).

In the Old Testament, the gift of the Holy Spirit was limited to specific individuals, tasks, and times. This was true as well for the pre-Easter period in the Gospels (Luke 1:15, 41, 67). However, according to the promise of Joel 2:28–32, one day the Spirit would be given to *all* "flesh" (i.e., all God's people). This occurred on the day of Pentecost (Acts 2:16–21), and this not just for a limited amount of time, but forever: "I will ask the Father, and he will give you another Helper, to be with you forever, even the Spirit of truth" (John 14:16–17). What had before been limited to kings, priests, and prophets, now became available to all Ekklesia members. This does not imply a degradation of the gift—first for an elite, now for all the people—on the contrary: all post-Pentecost believers have been upgraded: they are all anointed kings, priests, and prophets.

Due to the gift (Greek *dōrea*)—the being given—of the Spirit, the Jesus-believer knows the gifts (*charismata*, lit. "portions of grace") of the Spirit, that is, worked by the Spirit: "To each is given the manifestation of the Spirit for the common good. . . . All these [charismata] are empowered by one and the same Spirit, who apportions to each one individually as he wills" (1 Cor. 12:7, 11).

Misjudging the specific characteristics of post-Pentecost believers, that is, ignoring the fundamental differences between pre-Easter and post-Pentecost believers, has the practical effect that New Testament believers are too little aware of their New Testament privileges and blessings, and thus will all the more easily identify with the position and the experiences of Old Testament believers (see §8.6.3).

## 7.5 The "Spiritual Israel"
### 7.5.1 An Old Testament "Church"?

The idea that the church is some "spiritual Israel" is widespread in traditional Christianity, notwithstanding the fact that *not a single* Bible passage says anything of the kind, as we will see. Thus, Reformed theologian Louis Berkhof claimed that the New Testament church is essentially one with the church (!) of the old dispensation.[61] Reformed writer G. H. Kersten asserted: "The church was not founded first at the day of Pentecost. With the outpouring of the Holy Spirit she was freed from the bonds of the law but she existed long before that, even from the beginning of the world."[62] Interestingly, he considers the "assembly of the holy ones" (Ps. 89:6) to be the church,[63] whereas the verse does not even refer to Israel but to the angels. Reformed theologian Gordon Spykman denied that the church was born at Pentecost—he claimed she was "reborn"—and spoke of an "updating" of the church at Pentecost.[64]

To mention some other Christian traditions: Roman Catholic Hans Küng said that Jesus' disciples gradually considered themselves to be "not only the *true* but also the *new* Israel."[65] Baptist Millard Erickson called the church the "new Israel," and claimed that in the New Covenant it took the place that Israel had under the Old Covenant.[66] In the immanent-historical sense, as God's witness on earth, there is of course truth in the latter phrase. But it goes way too far to call the church therefore the "new Israel." At least, the New Testament never does so, as I intend to show.

Reformed writer Jan van Genderen formulated a special argument: the church was not born at Pentecost because she

---

61. Berkhof (1979, 571).
62. Kersten (1947, II, 116).
63. Ibid., 108.
64. Spykman (1992, 422).
65. Küng (1967, 126; cf. 132, 134, 138).
66. Erickson (1998, 1053).

existed already as the church of Christ that had come together (Acts 1:14–15).[67] This betrays a deep lack of insight into what the church is—as if she were nothing more than assembled Jesus-believers. These assembled saints in Acts 1 are not called "church" at all, and my point is that they *could* not yet be called "church." Luke starts using the term "church" only after Pentecost (Acts 5:11; 8:1, 3; 9:31; etc.). Pentecost was essential because only through the baptism in the Holy Spirit did it become possible to speak of the Body of Christ (Acts 1:5; 2:4; 1 Cor. 12:13). There is no church before this Spirit baptism; therefore, Jesus spoke about her in the future tense, as we saw (Matt. 16:18).

On the other side of the spectrum, we have someone like Charles C. Ryrie, who rightly wrote that the church differs from Israel, began first at Pentecost, and did not exist during the Old Testament period.[68] And David L. Smith wrote that neither linguistically, nor theologically, can we speak of an Old Testament church.[69] He recognized that both Israel and the church are called "people of God," and that both have their place in the kingdom of God, yet rightly claimed that they are not the same. To be sure, at present the church occupies the center of God's plan with the world, but this is only until the moment when God's plan for the Gentiles has been fulfilled. At that time, Israel will again take its place as his people, and as the center of God's dealings with the world.

According to George E. Ladd, in Old and New Testaments there is but one people of God.[70] However, in his view, this does not mean that the Old Testament believers belonged to the church, nor that we could speak of the church in the Old Testament. The church could not have existed before Pentecost, for she consists of all those who, in one Spirit, have been baptized into one Body (1 Cor. 12:13), and this Spirit baptism

---

67. Van Genderen (2008, 683).
68. Ryrie (1986, 399).
69. Smith (1996, 314).
70. Ladd (1959, 117).

began at Pentecost. In a laudable way, Ladd seeks a middle way here between, on the one hand, the Augustinian view of a "church since Adam" and, on the other hand, the dispensationalist view, which separates Israel and the church all too drastically. He does so by arguing that Old Testament Israel was not "church," but that it is correct to call Israel and the church the one people of God.[71] Along this line, Edmund Clowney could say that, at Pentecost, the people of God were not created but renewed.[72] And Paul Minear said that God's people did not come into existence somewhere between Jesus' birth and Pentecost, but with the Abrahamic covenant.[73]

This seems to me to be the limit: God's people began already with Adam, or Abraham. Gilbert Bilezikian went just a bit beyond the limit by arguing that with Abraham God began a universal new community, which in the New Testament is called "church."[74] N. T. Wright went quite a bit further beyond the limit by claiming that the church is the single multi-ethnic family that God promised to Abraham.[75] The problem is not that Bilezikian and Wright speak of one large community or family, but that they call it the church. This is the problem that we encounter all the time: either Old Testament believers are referred to as "church," or the New Testament church is called "Israel," or a community incorporated into Israel.

Let me illustrate the underlying mistake by a simple metaphor. Marriage may merge husband and wife together, but the husband does not become the wife, and vice versa. Believing that Old Testament Israel and the New Testament church to a certain (immanent-historical) extent form one faith community is fine, as long as we do not read any form of church

---

71. This viewpoint is sometimes called "revised dispensationalism"; cf. Wellum (2012, 46–50, 685–86), and references: C. A. Blaising in Blaising and Bock (2000, 10–13); E. E. Johnson in Bateman (1999, 121–68).
72. Clowney (1995, 53).
73. Minear (1960, 70–71).
74. Bilezikian (2001, 32–33).
75. Wright (2011, 220-28).

into Old Testament Israel, or any form of Israel into the New Testament church.

Quite a few theologians have groped for some middle road in their own fashion. David Watson called Israel the "shadow" of the church.[76] Roelof Bijlsma called "the Christian church the complementing and completing counter-image of Israel as people of faith. They reflect each other, and need each other."[77] Johan Heyns spoke of "the embryonic origins of the church in its Old Testament pre-history."[78] In all these cases, the authors see a strong continuity between the Old and New Testament people of God, but they seem to avoid, at least in the quotations given, calling Israel "church," and the church "Israel."

### 7.5.2 Supersessionism

In its most extreme form, the traditional view that the church is the spiritual Israel, or that Israel was the Old Testament church, has led to *supersessionism*, the belief that the church has superseded Israel. In this view, all Old Testament eschatological promises with regard to Israel are spiritualized (see Appendix IV). This holds true especially for the land promise: the eschatological restoration of a converted and blessed Israel in its own land, Canaan of old. That is, in supersessionism these promises are given a figurative sense and applied to the church. This view is also called "replacement theology," or "substitution theology," because in the ways of God upon earth, the church (for more than 99% Gentile) has replaced ethnic Israel. This implies that all Old Testament eschatological blessings are claimed by the church, whereas the curses are left to Israel.[79] I have discussed this view more extensively elsewhere.[80]

In the Old Testament prophetic books, the headings above

---

76. Watson (1978, 66).
77. Bijlsma (1981, 47).
78. Heyns (1988, 355).
79. See extensively Wentsel (1995, 365–71; 1998a, 122–32).
80. Ouweneel (2012, especially §4.5).

the chapters as well as the Annotations of the Dutch States' Translation abound with references to the church, whereas the text speaks of Israel, Judah, or Jerusalem. I limit myself to some conspicuous examples in the first part of Isaiah. For instance, at Isaiah 8:8: Immanuel is Christ, "who is the Head of his church, which at that time was in the land of Judah." At Isaiah 9:3, this alternative translation is given: "LORD, Thou hast multiplied the joy of the nation (speaking of the status of the church of the New Testament) in that they (consisting of Israelites and Gentiles) together of one accord will praise Thee because of the great benefits bestowed upon them in *Christ*." In connection with the word "assemble" in Isaiah 11:12 we read: "That is, in *Christ*, who assembles his church from the four corners of the world. In Him, then, it is spiritually fulfilled what God has promised."

Isaiah 11:14 (KJV) says that Judah and Ephraim "shall fly upon the shoulders of the Philistines." In the text, this is clearly a reference to judgment; compare the parallelism with the next lines: ". . . and together they shall plunder the people of the east. They shall put out their hand against Edom and Moab, and the Ammonites shall obey them. And the LORD will utterly destroy the tongue of the Sea of Egypt, and will wave his hand over the River with his scorching breath, and strike it into seven channels, and he will lead people across in sandals" (vv. 13b–14). Now listen to what the Annotations of the Dutch States' Translation have to say: "This must be understood spiritually, in this sense, namely, that the believing Israelites shall fly upon the shoulders of the Gentiles through preaching the holy *Gospel*, attacking and overcoming them in that they will bring some of them to the Christian faith, and will convince the others that they have no excuse before God. For through this similitude (taken from a raptor or a fox, who leaps upon the chicken), the prophet makes known the victory that the LORD would grant to his church against its enemies, as this has been fulfilled through the apostles and other teachers." I cannot see how it is possible to call this serious exegesis at all.

When Isaiah 11:16 (KJV) says, "there shall be an highway for the remnant of his people, which shall be left, from Assyria," the Notes say, "The sense is: All will be smoothed and without hindrances, when *Christ* will gather his church by the preaching of the holy *Gospel*." Of course, there is not the slightest basis in the text for such an exegesis. It is pure speculation, dictated by theological prejudice.

Such a method is followed unceasingly in the Annotations on the Old Testament biblical prophecies. Those who wish to investigate what damage supersessionism has caused among Reformed Christians in the Netherlands, need only study these Annotations. Fortunately, Reformed theologian Johan Verkuyl could write: supersessionism "is a theory and a life attitude that is entirely in conflict with the Bible, and especially with what Paulus writes in Romans 9–11.... The red thread running through Romans 9–11 is that God's promises indeed are for the entire Gentile world, but that his promises to the people of Israel have not been cancelled or withdrawn."[81] In this way, new light is breaking through in the Reformed world.

Likewise, with respect to Roman Catholicism, the Second Vatican Council carefully avoided explicitly equating the people of God with the Roman Catholic Church, or saying that, in some way or another, the church had taken the place of Israel as people of God.[82] The Council described the church as "the new people of God," building upon Israel. The election of the church as people of God does not imply the rejection of Israel but rather an extension of God's kingdom (broadly taken here as God's rule in the world, not the kingdom of the risen and glorified Christ). The point is well taken: Israel has not (necessarily) been rejected (forever), and the church is not (necessarily) some spiritual Israel. In the Reformed world as a whole, this insight is penetrating in only a small and limited way, I

---

81. Verkuyl (1992, 369).
82. Cf. McGrath (1997, 431).

am afraid. The reason is that the entire fabric of Reformed theology is so strongly interlaced with supersessionist thinking.

### 7.5.3 Incorporated into Israel?

Scripture nowhere says that the church is the spiritual Israel, or is a part of Israel. This insight is breaking through here and there. Thus, Reformed theologian Jan van Genderen does say that those who confess Jesus as the Messiah are the new Israel,[83] but he also says: "It cannot be inferred from the New Testament, not even from the image of the olive tree in Romans 11 . . . that those who believe must be incorporated into Israel in order to be the people of God."[84] Let us look at the evidence that is often adduced by those who think otherwise.

(a) In the Dutch rhymed version of *Psalm 87* it is said that Gentile believers are "incorporated into Israel." First, it is questionable whether this is a correct rendering of the text, which speaks only of a being recorded as born in Zion. Second, the text has nothing to do with the Ekklesia, which in the Old Testament was unknown (see §7.2.2). Psalm 87 is rather a glorious description of the Messianic kingdom, when Zion will be the "world center," "the capital of the kingdom of God,"[85] just as we find elsewhere: "It shall come to pass in the latter days that the mountain of the house of the LORD shall be established as the highest of the mountains, and shall be lifted up above the hills; and all the nations shall flow to it, and many peoples shall come, and say: 'Come, let us go up to the mountain of the LORD, to the house of the God of Jacob, that he may teach us his ways and that we may walk in his paths.' For out of Zion shall go the law, and the word of the LORD from Jerusalem. He shall judge between the nations, and shall decide disputes for many peoples; and they shall beat their swords into plowshares, and their spears into pruning hooks; nation shall not lift up sword against nation, neither shall they learn

---

83. Van Genderen (2008, 681).
84. Ibid., 698.
85. Cohen (1985, 283–84).

war anymore" (Isa. 2:2-4; cf. Micah 4:1-3; Isa. 56:6-7; Jer. 3:17; Zech. 2:10-11). All these future phenomena have very little to do with the Ekklesia because when these prophecies will be fulfilled the Ekklesia will be in glory with Christ.[86] This can be grasped, however, only if one is prepared to question the idea that all believers of all times necessarily belong to the church.

(b) From *Ephesians 2:11-22* and *3:3-11* I have concluded earlier that the New Testament Gentile believers did not join Israel, but that the Ekklesia consists of Jewish believers taken *out of* Israel, and Gentile believers taken *out of* the nations, in order to form together something entirely new, in which the distinction between the two has been abolished: the Ekklesia of God, which is neither some kind of Israel, nor was pre-Easter Israel some kind of church. From the fact that the Gentiles formerly were "alienated from the commonwealth of Israel" (Eph. 2:12), it does not logically follow that now they do belong to Israel. Paul's thought apparently is this: formerly the Gentiles did not have privilege P, but now they have privilege Q, which is much greater than P.

(c) In *John 10* we found the same for the flock of the Good Shepherd. He *brings out* all his own sheep from the fold (Israel), unites them with his other sheep (from the Gentiles), which are not of the fold of Israel. He puts all these sheep together, *not* in order to return to the old fold (Israel), not necessarily even to form a new fold — there is no new fold in John 10 — but to form the one flock of the one Shepherd.

(d) In *1 Corinthians 10:32* Israel and the church are clearly distinguished; how then could the church ever be called "Israel" (taken in whatever sense), if the term "Israel" remains reserved for ethnic Israel? In Acts, too, nowhere is the impression given that the church now factually is Israel. On the contrary, throughout the book, the two remain clearly distinguished. The non-Jesus-confessing Jews are viewed as err-

---

86. See extensively Ouweneel (2012).

ing, but nowhere are they considered as now being non-Jews; and conversely, the Jesus-confessing Gentiles are viewed as being on the right track, but nowhere are they considered as Jews-in-a-certain-sense. Israel is and remains Israel, Jews are and remain Jews, the church is and remains the church.

(e) It is striking that *Romans 2:28-29* is sometimes adduced as an argument: "For no one is a Jew who is merely one outwardly, nor is circumcision outward and physical. But a Jew is one inwardly, and circumcision is a matter of the heart, by the Spirit, not by the letter. His praise is not from man but from God." This passage is read as if it were saying that each person having a "circumcised heart" would be a "Jew" (in a spiritual or whatever sense).[87] But the text does not say so; it would not fit into the context, either. Paul is speaking here about the difference between a true Jew and a false Jew. The latter has been circumcised in the flesh, but not in his heart (cf. Deut. 10:16; 30:6; Jer. 4:4; 9:25-26). The true Jew is not only circumcised in the flesh but also in his heart. Of course, believing Gentiles are circumcised in their hearts, too, but that is not the point here. Paul is not speaking here at all about Gentiles.[88] The logical flaw is this: if A is P, and B is P, it does not follow that A is B.

(f) *Galatians 6:16*, too, belongs to the basic evidence that supposedly proves that the church is the spiritual Israel: "And as for all who walk by this rule, peace and mercy be upon them, and upon the Israel of God." Some take it that the church is this "Israel of God."[89] Hans Küng says that the church is "the new God-people," and adds: "[O]nly this can be meant by the expression 'the Israel of God' (Gal. 6:16)."[90] He and others overlook the fact that *two* groups are distin-

---

87. See, e.g., Moo (1996, 175).
88. See Ridderbos (1959, 69); Juster (1995, 104-105); Stern (1999, 336-40, 571-76); Ouweneel (2015a).
89. See, e.g., Clowney (1995, 42-44, caption: "Christ's church is the Israel of God").
90. Küng (1967, 134).

guished here: "all who walk by this rule," and "the Israel of God." The former group apparently includes the Gentile believers, who did not have to submit themselves to the Sinaitic Torah but only to the "rule" belonging to the "new creation" (cf. v. 15). The latter group is not simply Israel, but that part of Israel that had believingly accepted the Messiah: the true Israel.[91]

The only hope for seeing the church as part of the "Israel of God" in this text is to assert that we are dealing here with an epexegetical *kai*, so that we would have to read: "Peace and mercy to all who follow this rule—to the Israel of God" (NIV), or: "Peace and mercy be upon all who walk by this rule, upon the Israel of God" (RSV).[92] Now, of course, such a rendering is precisely what must be demonstrated: must this translation prove the premise (church = Israel), while at the same time the premise must prove the translation? That is not very convincing. Moreover, it is not obvious to assume in the text an epexegetical *kai*. The Greek text says, *eirēnē ep' autous kai eleos, kai epi ton Israēl tou theou*. Please note, first, that *autous* and *Israēl* are too far apart to warrant the assumption that they would refer to the same people. Second, the preposition *epi* is repeated before *Israēl tou theou*, which makes it virtually impossible to render *kai* here as "namely." Third, it is hard to find convincing examples of an epexegetical *kai* in Paul's writings at all.

(g) It is amazing that a verse like *1 Corinthians 10:18*, which speaks about "Israel according to the flesh," is viewed as evidence that there must also be an "Israel according to the Spirit," which then supposedly would be the church.[93] Does "forefather according to the flesh" (Rom. 4:1) prove that

---

91. See Ouweneel (1991, 34, 50; 1997, 400–402).
92. Thus also J. B. Lightfoot, M. Zerwick, W. Gutbrod; see references in Fung (1988, 310n61).
93. See, e.g., Küng (1967, 141); see Findlay (1979, 857, 863) on this verse and on v. 1, "our fathers," a phrase that supposedly proves that the church is Israel. Cf. Stern (1999, 471–72).

there must also be a "forefather according to the Spirit," or "masters according to the flesh" (Eph. 6:5; Col. 3:22) that there must be "masters according to the Spirit"? Paul speaks of his "kinsmen according to the flesh" (Rom. 9:3; 11:14); these were the non-Jesus-believing Jews. The Jesus-confessing fellow believers had become, so to speak, his "kinsmen according to the Spirit," whether from the Jews or from the Gentiles. But that does not make "Israelites" of the latter. Gentile believers have not become citizens of Israel, just as Jewish non-Jesus-believers have not stopped being Israelites. Gentile and Jewish Jesus-believers have become citizens of the totally new "commonwealth of the Ekklesia."

(h) *Romans 9:6* ("not all who are descended from Israel belong to Israel") has sometimes been explained as though an *extension* is intended here with regard to the term "Israel," in this sense: there are those who are "of [the new, true] Israel," though by nature not belonging to Israel.[94] However, the context makes clear that precisely the opposite is intended: Paul is envisioning a *restriction* of the term. There are those who are descended from Israel, that is, born of the patriarchs, yet who fall outside the patriarchal blessings, such as Abraham's son Ishmael, and Isaac's son Esau (vv. 7-13). Paul's argument is that likewise the unbelievers in Israel fell outside the patriarchal blessings, although they had descended from the patriarchs.

### 7.5.4 God's People, Abraham's Offspring, New Covenant

(i) In *Romans 9:25-26*, Paul quotes Hosea 2:23 and 1:10: "Those who were not my people I will call 'my people,' and her who was not beloved I will call 'beloved.'" "And in the very place where it was said to them, 'You are not my people,' there they will be called 'sons of the living God.'" In Hosea 1-2 these verses clearly refer to ethnic Israel, but in Romans 9 the meaning is extended, so that they also comprise the believing Gentiles. Something similar we find in *2 Corinthians 6:16b* ("I will

---

94. Fung (1988, 311n67).

make my dwelling among them and walk among them, and I will be their God, and they shall be my people"), which goes back to Leviticus 26:12 ("I will walk among you and will be your God, and you shall be my people"; cf. Ezek. 37:27).

Such quotations do not necessarily imply that Paul is thereby elevating believing Gentiles to being a part of ethnic Israel. On the contrary, in Romans 9:27-29 he quotes prophecies that do not refer to some broad Israel — to which also Gentile believers might belong — but only to Israel's believing remnant (cf. Isa. 10:20-22; 11:11, 16). The people of God under the New Covenant (cf. Acts 15:14; Titus 2:14) include the believing *remnant* of Israel (cf. Rom. 11:5) just as much as they include, so to speak, the believing *remnant* of the Gentiles, without Israel ever becoming church, or the church ever becoming Israel. Conversely, in Romans 9:31 Israel is not the people as a whole, but the unbelieving majority of the people. In no case does Israel in this chapter mean some spiritual Israel to which both Jesus-believing Jews and Jesus-believing Gentiles supposedly belong.

In 1 Peter 2:10 we find Hosea 2:23 quoted again, but here the situation is different because Peter presumably addresses his letter (mainly) to the believing remnant of Israel, given the prologue (1:1): "Peter, an apostle of Jesus Christ, to those who are elect exiles of the Dispersion."[95] What is said to *Jewish* Jesus-believers does not always automatically apply to Gentile Jesus-believers. For instance, when Paul says that "what God promised to the fathers, this he has fulfilled to us their children" (Acts 13:32-33), it does *not* follow that "[t]he covenant promise given to Israel of old is applied without question to the people of the New Testament time,"[96] because Paul was speaking here exclusively to *Jews*.

(j) The fact that New Testament believers are children or

---

95. Cf. Grant (1902, 142); Kelly (1923, I, iii–viii, 1–7); more recent expositors understand these addressees to be Gentile Christians instead; see, e.g., Davids (1990, 7–9).
96. Thus Stam (1999, 88).

sons of Abraham (*Gal. 3:7, 29; cf. 4:22-23, 28*) does not mean the same as being incorporated into Israel. Abraham's very name is "father of a multitude" (Gen. 17:5) because various groups, of which Israel is only one, may see him as their (physical and/or spiritual) father. In Romans 4:11-12 he is called both the father of the uncircumcised and the father of the circumcised. He is the father of the uncircumcised, that is, the Gentiles, insofar as they walk in the same faith as Abraham. He is also the father of the circumcised: as far as the non-Jesus-believers are concerned, he is only physically their father, and as far as the Jesus-believers among them are concerned, he is both physically and spiritually their father. In no way is the suggestion being made here that circumcised believers and uncircumcised believers would in fact form one Israel. From a spiritual point of view, *all* Jesus-believers are circumcised (Phil. 3:3; Col. 2:11), but that does not give us the right to conclude that they are Israel (see §7.5.3 point [e]).

(k) In *Jeremiah 31:31-34*, quoted in Hebrews 8:8-12, the establishment of the New Covenant is described. We are explicitly told that it is made with "the house of Israel and the house of Judah." Since the New Testament believers, too, come under the blessings of the New Covenant (see the next chapter), many have presumed that the Gentile believers under the New Covenant are included with Israel as well.[97] However, this is not the only possible conclusion. We could just as easily assume that non-Jews do not belong to Israel, and subsequently ask ourselves how it is possible that they do share in the blessings of the New Covenant? In Psalm 86:9 we read: "All the nations you have made shall come and worship before you, O Lord, and shall glorify your name." In Isaiah 56:6 there are foreigners who join themselves to the Lord "to minister to him, to love the name of the Lord, and to be his servants, everyone who keeps the Sabbath and does not profane it, and holds fast my covenant." And Jeremiah 4:2 says, "[N]ations shall bless themselves in him [i.e., the Lord], and

---

97. Thus, e.g., Poythress (1987, 106).

in him shall they glory." However, none of these and similar passages ever suggest that in this way these Gentiles have now become Jews. On the contrary, they continue to be called *goyyim*, even if they share in the covenant blessing of Israel. If even these Gentiles in the Messianic kingdom are not viewed as having been incorporated into Israel, then surely not the Ekklesia with its own very special character and calling.

## 7.6 The Olive Tree of Romans 11
### 7.6.1 Not Israel

In Romans 9–11, Paul continually maintains the distinction between (ethnic) Israel and the church (even if the latter is not explicitly mentioned here). There cannot be any doubt that in these chapters, the term "Israel" always and exclusively means ethnic Israel, Paul's "kinsmen according to the flesh" (9:3; 11:14). He distinguishes between the unbelieving part (11:7, 25) and the "remnant according to the election of grace" (v. 5 NKJV). The entire nation was chosen for a special position and calling on earth, but only a part of this chosen nation obtains salvation; "the rest were hardened" (v. 7). This involves two different types of divine election: Israel as such was a chosen nation, in the sense of having a separate position and calling on earth (cf. Deut. 7:6; 14:2; 18:5); but only part of them was elected for eternal bliss in the sense of Ephesians 1:3-5 ("he chose us in him [i.e., Christ] before the foundation of the world, that we should be holy and blameless before him. In love he predestined us for adoption as sons"). There are, then, two parts of Israel, a Jesus-confessing part and a non-Jesus-confessing part. However, not for a moment does Paul give the impression either that the latter part would not be Israel anymore, or that the Gentile believers now *are* Israel. The former are still, and always will be, Israel; the latter are not, and never will be, Israel.

It is therefore exegetically untenable, and even wholly arbitrary, when John Calvin suddenly discovers the church (of believing Jews and believing Gentiles) in the midst of Paul's argument in verse 26 ("all Israel will be saved"): "Many understand [these words] as referring to the Jewish people, as if Paul said that in them the ministry of God would again be restored in its former state. However, I extend the name *'Israel'* to the whole people of God, in this sense: When the Gentiles have come in [v. 25], the Jews too will return from the apostasy to the obedience of faith, and thus the salvation of the whole Israel of God, which had to be assembled from both groups, will be completed."[98] But the text does not contain any necessity for such an extension (apparently inspired only by Calvin's prejudice). When Paul says that one day Israel too will be saved, he does not include any reference here to the eternal destiny of Gentiles. However, prejudices here are powerful. Thus, James Dunn recognizes that "all Israel" in verse 26 can mean only the historical, ethnic Israel, yet he wishes to see the Gentile believers included within this "all Israel."[99]

In order to understand the meaning of verse 26 more profoundly, we have to consider the entire passage from verse 16. The cause of the confusion is that many have suggested that the olive tree mentioned here refers to Israel.[100] The Gentile believers, who by nature are branches of a wild olive tree, are grafted into the good olive tree (v. 17). And this would amount to saying that they have been incorporated into Israel.[101] For supersessionists, nothing seems to be more obvious. The big question, however, is whether the starting point of this reasoning is correct. Is the olive tree really Israel? The answer cannot be anything else than an emphatic No! Israel is here explicitly called the natural branches on the tree

---

98. Calvin (1950, 362–63).
99. Dunn (1998, 526–29).
100. E.g., Heyns (1988, 358); Wentsel (1995, 369); Moo (1996, 702); Stam (1999, 132–33); see Fruchtenbaum (1992, 94–97, 198–201, 290–95) for an extensive treatise on this view.
101. Van der Waal (1990, 139) even speaks of Jewish branches grafted into the *church* because, to him, Israel and church are identical.

(vv. 21, 24), *not* the tree itself. The two are distinguished so clearly that the natural branches can even be broken off the tree (v. 17), while the tree still remains the tree. It is the same here as with the vine in John 15:1-8: the believers are the branches of the vine, but they are not the vine itself.

"But if some of the branches were broken off, and you, although a wild olive shoot, were grafted in among the others . . . do not be arrogant toward the branches. . . . Then you will say, 'Branches were broken off so that I might be grafted in.' That is true. They were broken off because of their unbelief, but you stand fast through faith. So do not become proud, but fear. For if God did not spare the natural branches, neither will he spare you. . . . And even they, if they do not continue in their unbelief, will be grafted in, for God has the power to graft them in again. For if you were cut from what is by nature a wild olive tree, and grafted, contrary to nature, into a cultivated olive tree, how much more will these, the natural branches, be grafted back into their own olive tree" (Romans 11:17-24).

Apparently, the course of Paul's thought is this: he presents the image of an olive tree, whose precise meaning we still have to discuss. It is a cultivated olive tree, on which there are natural branches, representing Israel. The Jews who have refused to accept Jesus are the natural branches that are broken off this tree. The natural branches that remain on this tree are the Jesus-believing Jews. Other branches, coming from a wild olive tree, that is, Gentile believers, have been cut from that tree and grafted into this cultivated olive tree, thus taking the place as it were of the branches that were broken off. Paul argues that it is possible that, in the future, those wild branches, which had been grafted into the cultivated olive tree, will be broken off again because of their apostasy, and in his view it is equally conceivable that the natural branches, once they do come to believe in Jesus, will be grafted again into their own tree.

Interestingly, what is being described in verses 22-23 as a possibility becomes certainty immediately afterward (vv. 24-27). Thus, the text describes both the present situation—natural branches broken off, wild branches grafted in—and the future situation—wild branches broken off again (this is God's judgment on nominal Christians), and natural branches grafted in again. This is Israel's restoration to the extent that it will ultimately accept its Messiah, and will return to the olive tree under Messiah's blessings.[102]

The point I am trying to make right now is that the olive tree and the natural branches cannot be identical. Non-Jesus-believing Jews are cut off the tree, Jews who later do repent after all are grafted in again. If for some reason—for instance, because Paul would apply his metaphors in a sloppy way—the olive tree does have to be Israel, this would imply that the branches that are cut from the olive tree would cease being Jews,[103] and this would be fully contrary to Paul's views. He could not address unbelieving Jews as "Men of Israel" (Acts 13:16) if he believed in fact that they were no longer "men of Israel." To federalists we say that non-Jesus-believing Jews do remain Jews, and Jesus-believing Gentiles never become Jews. This is just as true as the fact that Jesus-believing Jews do not stop being Jews, even after having been accepted into the Ekklesia (Acts 21:39; 22:3; Rom. 11:1).

## 7.6.2 The Covenant Tree

So what *does* the olive tree represent? Not many options are left, even if there may still be nuances in the way we describe the tree. For instance, we may define the tree as the totality of the Abrahamic blessings that apply to all Abraham's progeny, both physical and spiritual, but in which only his believing descendants in effect receive a share. The Annotations of the Dutch States' Translation say that both the "firstfruits" and

---

102. See more extensively, Ouweneel (2012, §7.4).
103. Cf. Stam (1999, 133): "Unbelieving Jews are cut away from the people of Israel."

the "root" refer to Abraham and the patriarchs, from whom the Jews have originated. "Broken off" is not explained as broken from Israel, but as "repudiated from the covenant."

In the words of Hebrew Christian Arnold Fruchtenbaum: the olive tree is a place of blessing rooted in the Abrahamic covenant rather than Israel as such.[104] A little less accurately, Reformed writer Johan Verkuyl calls the olive tree "the people of God."[105] It is also inaccurate to say that the olive tree, or the root of it, represents Christ.[106] The natural branches cannot be said to have been broken off Christ because they were never "in" him.

In verse 16 Paul's starting point is this: "If the dough offered as firstfruits is holy, so is the whole lump, and if the root is holy, so are the branches." The first image is derived from the Sinaitic laws concerning the grain offerings (Num. 15:17–21). The second image forms the introduction to the entire similitude of the cultivated olive tree. It is no wonder, then, that people have considered the "root" to be Abraham, or possibly the patriarchs.[107] For Paul says, "To them [i.e., Israel] belong the patriarchs [lit., fathers]" (Rom. 9:5), and "as regards election, they are beloved for the sake of their forefathers [lit., fathers]" (11:28), that is, Abraham, Isaac, and Jacob. This explanation is supported by the fact that some Jewish texts call the patriarchs a "root" as well.[108]

All covenant promises and blessings for Israel, in which not only the Jesus-believing Jews but also the Jesus-believing Gentiles share, begin with the patriarchs. In the Old Testament, God granted these blessings to Israel, but in the patri-

---

104. Fruchtenbaum (1992, 97, 175; cf. 744).
105. Verkuyl (1992, 370).
106. E.g., Ellison (1976, i.l.); cf. Barrett (1957, i.l.).
107. E.g., Chrysostom, Grant (1901, 270); Murray (1968, II, 85); Cranfield (1981, i.l.); Fitzmyer (1993, i.l.); Moo (1996, 699); Smith (1996, 205); Godet (1998, i.l.).
108. E.g., 1 Enoch 93:5, 8; Philo, *Heir* 279 (Abraham); *Jubilees* 21:24 (Isaac); referred to by Moo (1996, 699n13).

archs he promised them to the Gentiles as well (Gen. 12:3; 18:18; 22:18; 26:4; 28:14). Peter said to the Jews, "You are the sons of the prophets and of the covenant that God made with your fathers, saying to Abraham, 'And in your offspring shall all the families of the earth be blessed'" (Acts 3:25). And Paul wrote to Gentile believers: "And the Scripture, foreseeing that God would justify the Gentiles by faith, preached the gospel beforehand to Abraham, saying, 'In you shall all the nations be blessed.' So then, those who are of faith are blessed along with Abraham, the man of faith" (Gal. 3:8–9).

All the branches on the cultivated olive tree, both the natural and those engrafted from elsewhere, are sons/children of Abraham. The severed branches are (physical) offspring of Abraham, but not children in the spiritual sense of the word. They are sometimes even called "children of the devil" (cf. Matt. 3:9, and the contrast mentioned earlier between John 8:33, 37, and vv. 39–44). All the branches, natural and engrafted, are supported by the root (v. 18), that is, they are spiritual sons and heirs of Abraham (4:11, 16; 9:8; Gal. 3:7, 29; 4:28), "children of the promise," through which they have received justification and life from God (Gal. 3:6, 11–12, 21, 24). Being grafted into the olive tree by faith is exactly the same as becoming a son/child of Abraham, that is, sharing in the Abrahamic blessings[109] — or at least making a *confession* of faith. I add the latter phrase because Paul also refers to apostate Christians (Rom. 11:22).

In the end, "all Israel will be saved" (v. 26), that is, all Jews who will believe in their Messiah will remain branches in the olive tree, or will have returned as branches grafted again into the olive tree. Together with them, all the branches that have come from the wild olive tree — the Gentile Jesus-believers — will be saved as well. To a certain extent we may call them altogether the "people of God," since all of them are branches on the same tree of the Abrahamic promises. However, in no

---

109. Shulam (1998, 363, 370, 387) notes that Heb. *b-r-k* means both "to bless" and "to graft" (see Talmud: Yevamot 63a).

way whatsoever does Romans 11 teach that Gentile Jesus-believers have been incorporated into Israel. Christians are *not* Jewish proselytes.

# Chapter 8
# Some Recent Developments in Covenant Theology

*Behold, I am making a covenant.*
  *Before all your people I will do marvels,*
*such as have not been created*
  *in all the earth or in any nation.*
*And all the people among whom you are*
  *shall see the work of the LORD,*
*for it is an awesome thing*
  *that I will do with you. . . .*
*Take care, lest you make a covenant*
  *with the inhabitants of the land to which you go,*
  *lest it become a snare in your midst.*
*You shall tear down their altars*
  *and break their pillars and cut down their Asherim*
  *(for you shall worship no other god,*
*for the LORD, whose name is Jealous,*
  *is a jealous God).*
Exodus 34:10–14

**Summary:** *In this chapter we take a closer look at some newer federalist theories concerning the "covenant of redemption," the "cov-*

enant of works," and the one "covenant of grace," and intra-federalist conflicts about these and many other matters. It is also shown how covenant theories are eventually imposed on ordinary church members as divine truths; sometimes they even found a place in Reformed confessions. One of the greatest federalist problems is the precise relationship between covenant and election: is the covenant governed by election, or by faith? Another great problem is supersessionism – the doctrine that the church is the spiritual Israel, and that for ethnic Israel as such there is no future, since the Old Testament prophecies are spiritualized. Many other problems are linked with this, such as the alleged relationship between circumcision and baptism, but also very practical problems, such as the assurance of salvation.

## 8.1 Newer Covenant Theories
### 8.1.1 One Covenant of Grace?

IN CHAPTERS 4 AND 5, I HAVE mentioned the South African Reformed dogmatician Willie Jonker. I referred to him as a fascinating example of authors who, in their description of the covenant doctrine and its development, implicitly and unintentionally indicate very clearly the actual logical-analytical status of covenant doctrine. I now continue this analysis, focusing on the notion of the covenant of grace. Of course, it is not the person of Jonker—with whom I have had excellent contacts—as such that matters in my analysis, but the illustrative character of his covenant view.

Jonker states: "According to general conviction, the covenant with Abraham is nothing but a confirmation and elaboration of God's revelation of grace directly after the fall" (a reference to Gen. 3:15, the so-called "mother promise" or *protevangelium*).[1] In Jonker's opinion, and that of most Reformed theologians, there must be an "encompassing *covenant of grace*," which came into force immediately after the fall. In Jonker's view, these thoughts would be "simply common knowledge." The question is: *whose* "general conviction"

---

1. Jonker (1988, 83).

is this, and *whose* "common knowledge"? Of course, it is only the conviction and common knowledge among Reformed Christians, that is, among those who have *a priori* accepted the covenant paradigm.

Clarence Stam has put it this way: "[T]here is only one covenant, which has existed from the beginning of time. There are in the course of history various *dispensations* in this one covenant, but the covenant itself does not change. . . . The word dispensation refers to the manner in which God's gifts are handed out ('dispensed') during a certain period. That manner may indeed differ from time to time, but the covenant itself is not altered thereby."[2] Incidentally, this citation shows that the use of the term "dispensation" is not limited to dispensationalists. The term can be used within different paradigms to refer to a specific redemptive-historical epoch in the sense of Ephesians 1:10 (NKJV): ". . . the dispensation of the fullness of the times."

Let us face it, at first sight no theologian would necessarily speak of just one covenant in the Bible, or, more specifically, make an immediate connection between the *protevangelium* of Genesis 3:15 (about the battle between Christ and Satan) and the Abrahamic covenant (about a promised progeny and land), or accept it as self-evident that *all* biblical covenants since the fall (the Noahic, the Abrahamic, the Levitical, the Davidic, the Sinaitic, the Palestinian, and the New Covenant) would be distinct forms of one and the same covenant, called the "covenant of grace." Such a connection is certainly not immediately obvious, and actually I do not believe it, and thousands of other theologians do not believe it either.

Of course, in all these covenants the grace of God is revealed in some special form, but that does not mean that they are all one and the same covenant. One has only to look at the very different covenant partners (creation, humanity, Israel, the house of Levi, the house of David) to understand that they

---

2. Stam (1999, 35; also see his chapters 13–14).

simply *cannot* be forms of one and the same covenant. This is why, for instance, the New Testament never speaks in an unqualified way of "the" covenant, but often of "the covenants": "They are Israelites, and to them belong the adoption, the glory, the covenants . . ." (Rom. 9:4). "[T]hese women [i.e., Hagar and Sarah] are two covenants" (Gal. 4:24). "[R]emember that you were at that time separated from Christ, alienated from the commonwealth of Israel and strangers to the covenants of promise" (Eph. 2:12). Hebrews 8:7–13 speaks of a "first" and a "second," an "old" and a "new" covenant.

Baptist Stephen Wellum, when dealing with the problem of infant baptism *versus* believers' baptism, views the essence of this problem to be the inability of paedobaptists to properly grasp the actual relationship between the biblical covenants.[3] There definitely is a certain continuity between the successive covenants, but there are also many differences as to covenant partners, the specific form of the Torah, the covenantal sign, the promised blessings, and the eschatological significance (see chapter 2). A Reformed theologian will always emphasize particularly the *continuity* of the covenants; a Baptist like Wellum will preferentially emphasize the *differences*. A middle road would be to underscore both the similarities and the differences, that is, both the continuity and the discontinuity between the covenants.

I repeat, the evidence for the one covenant of grace exists only within the paradigm of federalism; it is evident for those who already believe it. See, for instance, the Westminster Confession of Faith (VII.6): "There are not . . . two covenants of grace, differing in substance [namely, the Old and the New Covenants], but one and the same, under various dispensations." Even if this is true, however—and to a certain extent it *is* true—neither this Confession nor the majority of Reformed theologians distinguishes that both the Old and the New Covenants were made, and will be made respectively,

---

3. Wellum (2006, 160).

with *Israel*, not with the Ekklesia as such.

Jonker wrote for his own constituency, just like so many Reformed theologians who take the self-evidence of the covenant doctrine for granted (just like, of course, so many *other* theologians do who start from their *own* paradigm). The supposed "one and only" covenant of grace does not emerge from Scripture; it is a theoretical-theological construct. It is not only dispensationalists who have difficulty with this fact that alleged biblical ideas are often nothing but theological models.

### 8.1.2 A Covenant of Redemption?

According to federalism, the covenant of grace is rooted in God's eternal plan of salvation. Jonker says that, in view of this, Reformed thinkers make use of a "theological auxiliary construction, which is called the *pactum salutis* or *covenant of redemption*."[4] This refers to the idea that the Father and the Son allegedly made a covenant together in which the Son was constituted Guarantor and Head of the new humanity in view of the redemption of the elect.

Is this a correct idea? Of course, Scripture speaks of God's eternal plan of redemption, of the Father sending his Son, and of the Son's obedience to his Father. However, this is never referred to as a covenant. Jonker therefore correctly speaks of a "theological auxiliary construction," which intends to give to the covenant concept its universal theological meaning: federalists see covenants everywhere, even within the Trinity. Jonker argues: "As the basic relationship between God and his people has the character of a covenant, it was obvious to think that the relationship between God and the covenantal Mediator itself must be a covenantal relationship too."[5]

Of course, for a non-federalist this is not obvious at all. Logic has flown the coop here. If mom and dad have a parent–child relationship with their kids, is it "obvious to think

---
4. Jonker (1988, 83).
5. Ibid., 84.

that the relationship between mom and dad is also a parent-child relationship"? What is so obvious here? Moreover, what are we talking about? A "horizontal" covenant between the Father and the Son, or rather, between the three persons within the Godhead? *Or* a "vertical" covenant between God (the triune God!) and the *Man* Jesus, who is the covenantal Mediator? Unfortunately, such careful distinctions are seldom made. But apart from this, why would it be obvious that, if God makes covenants with his people, there must also be a covenant between God and the Mediator, or even between the Father and the Son (and the Spirit)?

Here we have another clear example of how a paradigm operates. New ideas are being developed, which have not been directly inspired by the observable data but which follow — or are thought to follow, or are *wished* to follow — from the inner logic of the paradigm itself. As soon as, *within the framework of the paradigm*, an idea is considered to be plausible, that is, logically consistent within that paradigm, it irresistibly becomes part of it. Of course, this is pure speculation. Even Reformed theologian Herman Bavinck had to admit: "The development of the doctrine of the *pactum salutis* [the intertrinitarian pact of salvation] among the Reformed was not free of scholastic subtlety."[6] Nevertheless, the idea of a "covenant of redemption" was elaborated by Caspar Olevianus, Robert Rollock, William Ames, John Preston, and Johannes Cloppenburg, and henceforth would remain "a fixed part of Reformed covenantal doctrine."[7] Others would not hesitate to identify it as *divine truth*.

By the time we come to Louis Berkhof (1873–1957), the *pactum salutis* within the Trinity has not only reached the level of unassailable truth but has also become the model for all other covenants: ". . . This does not mean, however, that the covenant idea originated with man and was then borrowed by God as an appropriate form for the description of the mu-

---

6. Bavinck (2006, 3.213).
7. Jonker (1988, 84).

tual relationship between Himself and man. Quite the opposite is true; the archetype of all covenant life is found in the Trinitarian being of God, and what is seen among men is but a faint copy of this."[8] How does Berkhof know this? As happens so often with scholarship, a certain thought is simply too beautiful not to be true. Here, theology itself has become a source of divine revelation. In reality, there is more Platonic idealism than biblical realism in Berkhof's view that the one heavenly covenant allegedly forms a prototype for all earthly covenants.

Even a staunch federalist like Michael Horton has to admit: "After all, each person [within the Trinity] is equally divine: there are no lords and servants in the eternal trinitarian relationship. Furthermore, there is no formal treaty structure to this [alleged] covenant in Scripture—no historical prologue, stipulations, sanctions, and so forth.... Only an overly restrictive definition of covenant would seem to justify the claim that the covenant of redemption is speculative rather than biblical."[9] My response is this: no, *not* "an overly restrictive definition of covenant," but a common one: a covenant is a formal agreement that possesses legal validity. First, the covenant of redemption is not found in Scripture; second, it does not satisfy common definitions of covenant, unless one declares all agreements and relationships between parties to be covenants.

Recently, the idea of an eternal covenant between Father, Son, and Holy Spirit has been defended again by Brown and Keele who, in line with Louis Berkhof, call the *pactum salutis* "that covenant from which all other biblical covenants flow."[10] They take great pains to show that there was an eternal plan of redemption, and quote well-known verses for that, the most important being Psalm 40:7-8 (cf. Heb. 10:7); 110:4 (cf. Heb. 5:6; 6:20; 7:17); John 17:4-5, 24; Ephesians 1:3–

---

8. Berkhof (1979, 263).
9. Horton (2006, 81–82).
10. Brown and Keele (2012, 23).

14 (amazingly, they do not mention 1 Pet. 1:19-20, "... a lamb without blemish or spot ... foreknown before the foundation of the world"). However, the errors of Brown and Keele are obvious.

(a) They do not prove that any of the Bible passages they quote is dealing with a divine counsel *from before the foundation of the world*, such as Psalm 110:4, Isaiah 53:10, and Zechariah 6:12-13.

(b) They never distinguish between God sending the Man Jesus *in time* (e.g., Zech. 6), and the *eternal* counsel of the Father and the Son (e.g., John 17). Thus, the "counsel of peace" (Zech. 6:13) does not at all refer to the eternal relationship between the Father and the Son. It does not even refer to the temporal relationship between God and Jesus, but it refers to that between the king and the priest on the throne (cf. the rendering in NKJV: the Messiah is both).

(c) The authors never prove that the eternal plan of redemption was rooted in a real *covenant* between the divine persons. Their only argument is that all relationships are covenantal, therefore the one between Father, Son, and Spirit must be covenantal, too. However, because the major premise of this syllogism is false, the conclusion is false, too.

Personally, I find it almost irreverent to describe the *familial* relationship between the divine persons as "covenantal," given the explicit legal connotations of this term. It is nothing but the speculative power of the covenant paradigm that makes the authors (and many of their predecessors) "see" the covenant even within the Trinity. Scripture says nothing of the kind; but if enough illustrious divines say so, who are we to doubt the *pactum salutis*?

### 8.1.3 Internal Speculations

Within federalism, discussions inevitably arise that are understandable and meaningful only for those who move within the paradigm concerned, but that are irrelevant for outsiders. In this way, the question arose as to how many covenants there are, not in the sense of the Old Testament (chapter 2) but of federalism. Is there only the one covenant of grace? Or are there two covenants: a covenant of works and a covenant of grace? Or are there three covenants: a covenant of works, a covenant of redemption, and a covenant of grace? Perhaps there are even four covenants, as R. Scott Clark suggests: "The God of the Bible relates to his creatures covenantally from eternity (*pactum salutis*), in creation (covenant of works), in providence (covenant of preservation [that is, the Noahic covenant]) and in redemption (covenant of grace)"[11] (cf. §5.5.1).

If we are to go that far, then why not distinguish five covenants? Is there not sufficient warrant to distinguish within the covenant of grace between the Abrahamic and the New Covenants, on the one hand, and the Old Covenant, on the other? Why not six covenants? Is there not sufficient warrant to distinguish between the Abrahamic and the New Covenants? Why not seven covenants? Is there not sufficient warrant to distinguish the Davidic covenant from all other biblical covenants?

As we saw, these question are closely related to the questions whether:

(a) there are two kinds of covenant members, namely, elect and non-elect,[12] or,

(b) there is only one kind of covenant member, namely, all those to whom, at infant baptism, the covenant promises have been made,[13] or,

(c) there is only one kind of covenant member, namely, the elect (Comrie, and in his wake, Kersten; see §5.3.3).

Here again, a rather sizeable number of possibilities are available. If there are two kinds of covenant members, namely, elect and non-elect, could it make sense to distinguish be-

---

11. http://rscottclark.org/2012/09/theses-on-covenant-theology/
12. Thus, e.g., T. Brienen in Hagoort (1999, 112–14).
13. Schilder (1946); see also Jongeleen (1927); Woelderink (1974); Van Genderen (2008, 542–44); cf. the fierce condemnation of this view by Kersten (1947, I, 311, etc.).

tween their infants? I bring this up because, as we know, some of these children will turn out to be elect in that they come to faith, while others will turn out to be non-elect in that they die in their unbelief. This yields four groups (all baptized): (1) elect members with elect children, (2) elect members with non-elect children, (3) non-elect members with elect children, and (4) non-elect members with non-elect children. We also have to reckon with the fact that these same four groups exist even among those who have not undergone infant baptism. In total, that makes eight different groups. I am quite serious about this matter; I simply want to show where further speculations might arise at any time within the federalist paradigm.

For Christian outsiders, this entire discussion, often fought on the razor's edge, is largely irrelevant, simply because these outsiders are not federalists. They feel that federalists take burdens upon themselves that would be unnecessary if only the latter would have the courage to question the very foundations of their paradigm. What outsiders can understand even less is that federalists are prepared to fight among themselves over their many different sub-models, as their numerous church divisions demonstrate (see, e.g., §8.4.1).

### 8.1.4 A Prelapsarian Covenant?

More federalist issues may be mentioned, which flow from the inner coherence of the covenant paradigm, and have played a role in the history of Reformed federalism. Jonker argued, on the basis of the *a priori* of the covenant paradigm, that it was considered "inconceivable that the relationship in which humanity stood to God before the fall would not have been a covenant relationship as well."[14] Even though there is hardly any scriptural evidence—we already saw that the reference to Hosea 6:7 is very doubtful—such a conclusion nevertheless seemed legitimate because of the inner logic of the covenant paradigm.[15] In this way, the doctrine of the *foedus naturale* or

---

14. Jonker (1988, 84).
15. Heyns (1988, 207) mentions these and other terms, though he himself prefers

*naturae* ("covenant of nature"[16]), or *foedus creationis* ("covenant of creation"), or *foedus operum* ("covenant of works") — or *foedus vitae* ("covenant of life"), or *foedus legalis* ("covenant of law"), or "Paradise covenant"[17] — and of the *foedus gratiae* or *gratuitum* ("covenant of grace"), or *foedus promissi* ("covenant of promise"), was developed (by Zacharias Ursinus, Caspar Olevianusus, Amandus Polanus, and others).

The most saddening result was that these theological speculations also made their way into the Westminster Standards of Presbyterian denominations and theology, and thus received an ecclesiastical — if not "divine" — authority that they never deserved. There are hundreds of scriptural references in these Standards, but that does not mean that the claims in the Standards are biblical. To many Christians, they are not. Thus, we read in the Westminster Confession of Faith (Art. VII.2): "The first covenant made with man was a covenant of works, wherein life was promised to Adam; and in him to his posterity, upon condition of perfect and personal obedience." And in Article VII.3: "Man, by his fall, having made himself incapable of life by that covenant, the Lord was pleased to make a second, commonly called the covenant of grace; wherein He freely offers unto sinners life and salvation by Jesus Christ."

The Westminster Larger Catechism speaks of "the first covenant, commonly [!] called the covenant of works . . . the second covenant, commonly [!] called the covenant of grace" (Q&A 30). And Q&A 97 claims: "Although they that are regenerate, and believe in Christ, be delivered from the moral law as a covenant of works, so as thereby they are neither justified nor condemned; yet, besides the general uses thereof common to them with all men, . . . ." Where do we read in

---

"creation covenant"; he calls the assumption of an Adamic covenant "theologically necessary"—given his standpoint, understandably so.

16. On the basis of the scholastic nature–grace dualism; confusingly, also the Noahic covenant was sometimes called a "covenant of nature," for that matter.
17. Heyns (1988, 207).

Scripture that believers have been delivered from some "moral law" or from a "covenant of works"? Again, this is nothing but vain speculation. Reformed Christians who hold only to the Three Forms of Unity may be thankful that these Forms are much freer from this kind of theologisms.

Compare the certainties of the Westminster Standards with the certainty with which Reformed writer G. H. Kersten asserted: "The establishment of this covenant [namely, the covenant of works] cannot be denied on good grounds by anyone."[18] He is so entangled in the covenant paradigm that he can no longer conceive of a person who would think otherwise and still consider himself to be an orthodox Christian. Actually, I am afraid that the latter judgment—"if you do not believe in a covenant of works, you are not orthodox"—is exactly what some federalists unashamedly assert. This is the consequence of theological theories that, after having been adopted in ecclesiastical confessional documents, have become sacrosanct. If the Westminster Standards are "the" standard of orthodoxy, then I am not orthodox—nor are those two billion other non-federalists either.

Jonker himself admitted that no direct scriptural evidence could be produced for the notion of the covenant of works[19] As a consequence, not all federalists accept the notion of a covenant of works.[20] Nevertheless, without any restraint the doctrine of the covenant of works led to other speculations, like the claim that Adam is the covenant head of fallen humanity, with its parallel claim that Christ is covenant Head of the New Covenant.[21] And so we can go on. The creativity of scholars working within a certain paradigm is often inexhaustible, both within the natural sciences and within the hu-

---

18. Kersten (1947, I, 266).
19. Jonker (1988, 85).
20. See, e.g., Robertson (1980, 54–57); Dumbrell (1984, 44–46); Van der Waal (1990, 53–56); Stam (1999, 47–53).
21. Thus, e.g., Kersten (1947, I, 325); cf. the critical questions by Van Genderen (2008, 555–58).

manities, and not least of all, within theology.

## 8.2 Further Developments
### 8.2.1 Theology and Truth

Within federalism, the process of logical inferences has continued inexorably. The only immediate basis for all new ideas (*pactum salutis*, covenant of works, covenant of grace, Adam as covenant head) was the inner logic of the covenant paradigm. See, for instance, how Reformed theologian Jan Hoek expresses this: "Once we have taken notice of God's covenantal relationship with Noah and with Abraham, we cannot help thinking that God's relationship with Adam and Eve already exhibited the characteristics of a covenant."[22] Willie Jonker tells us that all these ideas enjoy a "broad consensus."[23] But of course, this holds for only a part of the Reformed world, which itself is a tiny part of international Christianity. Moreover, from the viewpoint of the philosophy of science, such a statement means nothing. Many scholarly models that enjoyed a "broad consensus" in the past have perished over time. The only question that matters is whether the Reformed paradigm is capable of explaining more scriptural data, and leaves us with fewer unsolved problems, than, say, Roman Catholic ecclesiasticalism or Evangelical dispensationalism or epangelicalism, or whatever theological paradigm is in vogue.

There is one element in Jonker's argument that gives me some special concern because it is found so often in theology. He does acknowledge the *theological* character of the discussion surrounding the covenant and of the formation of certain federalist teachings. Yet, almost insensibly Jonker's reasoning changes the covenant paradigm into a (pre-theoretical) Reformed belief. I already gave some examples of this in Jonker's book,[24] and now add his conclusion: "The Reformed form of Christianity is inextricably connected with the confession of

---
22. J. Hoek in Hoek and Verboom (2010, 23).
23. Jonker (1988, 86).
24. Ibid., 82.

the truth of the covenant."[25]

According to the preceding sentences, Jonker explicitly refers here to the (theological) covenant *doctrine*, not just the biblical notion of the covenant, since *all* (thinking) Christians confess "the truth of the covenant," that is, they hold some view of the biblical covenant(s). However, because Jonker expresses himself in such a careless way, it is less obvious that here he is suddenly moving from the arena of theology to the arena of "confession" and "truth," or from theoretical reason to existential faith. At first, it was a theological theory, with many elements that could not be found in "direct scriptural evidence," and even with "theological auxiliary constructions." In itself there is nothing wrong with that; this is the way scholarly models work. But now, suddenly, this theory, or at least the kernel of it, is part of the (pre-theoretical) Reformed *confession* of faith, and is called "truth." What began as a theological theory eventually became unassailable divine truth.

Such a way of arguing is wrong, both logically and theologically. It is even misleading, because it suggests to people that you are not a good Christian if you do not accept the "divine truth" of Reformed covenant doctrine. Such a suggestion is quite blameworthy. What characterizes the "Reformed form of Christianity" is an elaborate covenant *theology*, which can never be called "truth." This is demonstrated by the fact that literally billions of Christians[26] do *not* accept covenant theology in one of its Reformed or Presbyterian forms — unless one would wish to call all these other Christians heretics.

Even worse is when typical covenant-theological notions (covenant of works, covenant of life, covenants of promise) find a place in ecclesiastical confessions, as has happened in

---

25. Ibid., 87.
26. There are perhaps 2.5 billion Christians in the world, of whom about 55–85 million may be counted as Reformed Christians (Calvinists, including Presbyterian Christians) (en.wikipedia.org/wiki/List_of_Christian_denominations_by_number_of_members).

the Westminster Standards. All Christians believe in the biblical notion of the covenant, but that does not make them federalists. In a similar sense, all believers accept the notion of church, but that does not make them adherents of Catholic ecclesiasticalism. On the contrary, the *Catechism of the Catholic Church* is full of references to "the Church," which always means the Roman Catholic Church, *not* the "one holy catholic and apostolic church" of, for instance, the Nicene Creed. No Protestant could ever accept this.

Likewise, all believers accept the notion of dispensation, if only because the word occurs in Ephesians 1:10 (according to the [N]KJV, ASV, DRA, and others): ". . . that in the dispensation of the fullness of the times He might gather together in one all things in Christ." But that does not make such believers adherents of Evangelical dispensationalism in whatever form. Theological theories are never "truths"; at best, they are fallible, deficient logical-analytical *attempts* to *approximate* the existential-transcendent truth of God—nothing less, but certainly nothing more than that.[27]

## 8.2.2 Theology and Church Divisions

Jonker's mode of argument, which is so characteristic for traditional scholastic federalist theologizing, does not distinguish between, on the one hand, our practical faith and our confession of faith, and on the other hand, our theological positions concerning matters of faith.[28] There is a tremendous danger in this type of thinking. It is true that too strong a separation between faith and theology may lead to the attitude of downgrading serious matters of faith to simply matters of theological debate. However, the reverse is just as serious. This occurs when merely theological differences of opinion are elevated to the level of tests for the faith and orthodoxy of ordinary church members.

Unfortunately, the consequences of this mental attitude

---

27. See extensively Ouweneel (2014a, 2014b).
28. See previous note.

have all too often come to light: polarization within denominations, serious conflicts, in the end even church divisions.[29] There are theological views concerning which it has sometimes been acknowledged that they are not rooted in "direct scriptural evidence" (see above), or where it is claimed that such alleged "evidence" should be thoroughly weighed. Yet, others have unashamedly claimed these theological theories to be "truth," and have subsequently elevated them to conditions for church communion. For instance, Reformed writer G. H. Kersten continually referred to masses of "scriptural proofs," which were no proofs at all, even for those who already believed in his theories.[30]

There certainly *are* theological conflicts that really do touch upon the foundations of the Christian faith and life. My criterion for this is as follows. If someone doubts those matters that are really foundational (especially concerning the person and the work of Christ), we have to wonder whether such a person could really be saved. But there is nothing in all of covenant theology that makes me wonder whether adherents of this theology can be saved or not. Likewise, conversely, there is nothing in anti-federalist theology that makes me wonder whether adherents of this anti-federalism can be saved or not, as long as anti-federalists honestly subscribe to, say, the Apostles' Creed. Non-fundamental theological conflicts should never lead to church conflicts, and even less to church divisions. If it does happen, this is nothing but sectarianism in its purest form, if we take this term in its biblical sense.[31]

There is a gaping chasm between federalism—the Reformed world—and non-federalism, that is, *all* other movements and denominations within Christianity. But what is worse: there is a gaping chasm *within* the Reformed world, which has taken on sectarian forms. Think of the insistence on accepting the following as litmus tests of orthodoxy: a cove-

---

29. Cf. ibid., §3.3; cf. the warnings by Troost (1983, 44–45).
30. Kersten (1947).
31. See extensively Ouweneel (2010b, chapters 13–14).

nant of works; or the idea of the Sinaitic covenant as in some sense a republication of the covenant of works; or whether there are one, two, three, or four covenants (or the relationship between the alleged "covenant of redemption" and the alleged "covenant of grace"); or whether there are one or two (or more) kinds of covenant members; or the relationship between election and covenant; etc. On top of all of this, there is endless quarrelling about what John Calvin exactly thought and taught about each of these topics.

### 8.2.3 Examples

To show that covenant matters sometimes create real denominational chasms, I already pointed to the discussions between the Netherlands Reformed Congregations and the Christian Reformed Churches in the Netherlands (1919). These were broken off because of a difference of opinion about the number of covenants.[32] Here, theoretical-theological differences were abused in order to legitimize what I think is an unnecessary ecclesiastical dissension.

Herman Bavinck pointed to another striking example, namely, with respect to the idea that infant baptism and regeneration are not automatically linked: "This view won the day when the church [i.e., the Reformed Church in the Netherlands], by its neglect of discipline, fell into decay. Election and church, the internal and external side of the covenant, concepts formerly held together as much as possible but increasingly differentiated since the days of Gomarus [i.e., Francis Gomarus, 1563–1641], moved ever farther apart. In the church (*ecclesia*) one saw the formation of the conventicle (*ecclesiola*). Gradually, therefore, baptism was totally separated from regeneration . . . ."[33] What Bavinck presumably is trying to say is this: the more faithful a church is, the more it approximates the ideal that it truly is a gathering of regenerate people, and

---

32. kerkgeschiedenis.web-log.nl/kerkgeschiedenis/2009/05/gereformeerde-g.html.
33. Bavinck (2008, 4.511).

the more self-evident it is to assume the baptized infants to be born again as well.

Elsewhere Bavinck wrote more or less the same thing in different words: "But when, since the middle of the seventeenth century, the Reformed churches in the Netherlands fell into decline, and the boundary of the covenant of grace was almost completely wiped out as a result of the neglect of discipline, the scriptural [!] view gradually gave way to the pietistic and Methodist [read: hyper-Calvinish] position. Although infant baptism was continued as a custom, faith in its sacramental power and value had vanished. Children were considered unregenerate and unconverted and therefore sinners and children of wrath [Eph. 2:3]."[34]

Many Reformed Christians, also today, would actually consider this to be a favorable development, simply because the ideal church does not exist, and because not all baptized children come to faith. However, in Bavinck's view the development he described was a disaster because, as he believed, the unity of the covenant was lost, and the covenant came increasingly to be viewed through the lens of election:[35] the covenant is only for the elect children, who are born again only when God converts them. Bavinck abhorred this: "The children of believers are to be regarded and treated as heirs of the promise until the contrary is clearly demonstrated by their 'talk' and 'walk'."[36] This does not necessarily exclude the need of some later conversion, although a typical Kuyperian federalist will emphasize instead the graduality of Christian life, whereas a typical hyper-Calvinist will emphasize instead a person's radical conversion and regeneration.[37]

Be this as it may, my point at this moment is especially the radical attitude with which Bavinck presented his view. He refused to see in this entire discussion a collision of two

---

34. Bavinck (2008, 4.154).
35. Cf. Van der Zwaag (2003, 150–54): "Covenant: the bed of election."
36. Bavinck (2008, 4.155).
37. Van der Zwaag (2003, 500–501).

theological models, each of which had its scholarly place under the sun. No, *his* (Bavinck's) view was the original one, and bad influences subsequently arose (Gomarus, first half seventeenth century!), the church began to decline, pietist and methodist influences (pejorative terms!) arose, hyper-Calvinism made progress. For Bavinck, it was a matter of truth over against the falsehood that was creeping in. Incidentally, the hyper-Calvinists felt precisely the same way with respect to Kuyper and Bavinck. (In honor to the former, it should be added—*contra* Bavinck—that hyper-Calvinist church discipline was never less strict than that of the Kuyperians, so that *this* cannot have been the historical origin of their views.)

No wonder that the attitude of Bavinck and so many others eventually contributed to a division within the Reformed Churches of the Netherlands in 1944 between those who maintained the close link between infant baptism and presupposed regeneration (*veronderstelde wedergeboorte*), and those who doubted or even rejected this.[38] It was not so much this doctrine as such that created the division, but the fact that the 1944 Synod presented this doctrine of presupposed regeneration as the only acceptable exegesis—in other words, as "divine truth." Here again, a purely theological theory was imposed upon ordinary church members, with all the dramatic consequences that resulted.

On the whole, we find that the two poles of Reformed thinking, predestination and covenant, have never been related well to each other. It was inevitable that two broad currents would develop: one in which predestination (election) became the leading principle, to which covenant was made subservient, and another one in which the covenant became the leading principle, to which predestination was made subservient. Let us have a closer look at these developments from

---

38. Cf. Stam (1999, 160): "This [Kuyperian] theory is clearly unbiblical. The Word of God teaches that baptism is to be administered not on the basis of a presumption but on the basis of a promise, namely that God makes his covenant with believers and their seed."

a little different angle: the covenant governed by election, that is, by the principle of divine sovereign grace, and the covenant governed by faith, that is, by the principle of human responsibility (although in fact faith is a gift of divine sovereign grace as well, Eph. 2:8).

## 8.3 The Covenant Governed by Election
### 8.3.1 Baptized Children

The further back one goes into Reformed history, the more unproblematic the covenant seems to be. In the Canons of Dort (from 1618-19) it is written with joyful freshness (I.17): "Since we must make judgments about God's will from his Word, which testifies that the children of believers are holy, not by nature but by virtue of the gracious covenant in which they together with their parents are included, godly parents ought not to doubt the election and salvation of their children whom God calls out of this life in infancy" (with references to Gen. 17:7; Acts 2:39; 1 Cor. 7:14). This point of view is the more interesting because the main subject of the Canons is predestination.

In the Reformed liturgical form for baptism (last edition: 1639) we read equally boldly in the final prayer: "Almighty God and merciful Father, we thank and praise thee, that thou hast forgiven us and our children all our sins, through the blood of thy Son Jesus Christ, and received us through thy Holy Spirit, as members of thine only begotten Son, and adopted us to be thy children and sealed and confirmed the same unto us by holy baptism." Where do we find here any distinction between elect and non-elect babies?[39]

Insofar as I can look into the future, I believe that federalism will survive only if it manages to free itself from the deadly grip of the disastrous doctrine of double predestination, including every debate about two or three covenants. However, this seems to be hardly conceivable nowadays.

(1) The entire conflict surrounding two covenants and

---
39. See Van der Zwaag (2003, 502–505).

three covenants is governed by one's view of election because those who teach three covenants make a distinction between the covenant of redemption, made with the elect only, and the covenant of grace, made with all baptized church members.

(2) The entire conflict regarding one or two kinds of covenant members is governed by one's view of election as well, leading to three options:

(a) There are two kinds of covenant members, namely, the elect and the non-elect, the latter referring to those who have been baptized but do not come to faith.

(b) There is only one kind of covenant member, namely, the elect only (children and adults).

(c) There is only one kind of covenant member, namely, all baptized church members (elect or non-elect), that is, all church members with their children.

To make things even more complicated, some have distinguished between the children of elect, and children of non-elect parents.

Group (2c) appears to avoid the predestination problem, but that is not really the case. If the well-meant promises of the covenant of grace come equally to all baptized children, how does this relate to the doctrine of predestination, which is accepted by group (2c), too, and according to which the covenantal promises become effective only in the elect? By definition, Reformed theologians will never be able to solve this problem because the starting points—federalism and predestination—are being commingled. Whether one argues that the covenant is for all baptized children, or only for elect baptized children, theologically one always runs into internal contradictions. This reality should be recognized as a firm proof that something is wrong with the very premises of Reformed theology.

## 8.3.2 A Well-Meant Offer

In the seventeenth century, several Reformed theologians,

such as Jacobus Koelman, attempted to approach the problem from a different angle by distinguishing between an *internal* and an *external* covenant.[40] The external covenant is made with all baptized church members, that is, believers and their children, and the internal covenant is made with the elect among them. But of course, for both group (2a) and group (2c) (see §8.3.2) this is unacceptable. Both of them could easily adduce the argument that Scripture does not know of such an internal and external covenant (forgetting, of course, that Scripture does not know of the one covenant of grace either). Both parties eliminate the problem by emphasizing either one of these two solutions: group (2a) accepts only what Koelman called the internal covenant, and group (2b) only accepts what Koelman called the external covenant.

In 1931, the General Synod of the Netherlands Reformed Congregations adopted "six solemn statements," in which the bond between covenant and election was rigidly strengthened.[41] The most important of these six statements is the first one: The Synod stated "that the covenant of grace stands under the domination of the election that is in view of redemption, [and] that therefore the essence of the covenant is valid only for the elect, and can never be valid for the natural offspring. That nature and essence of the covenant of redemption and the covenant of grace are one, and not two. In essence, it is one covenant."

In Statement 2 the Synod stated "that Holy Scripture speaks only of two covenants in relation to Man's eternal state, namely, the covenant of works and the covenant of grace." Is this not amazing? The only times that Scripture speaks of "two covenants" is in Galatians 4 and in Hebrews, and there these phrases are referring to the Old and the New Covenants. Scripture knows nothing of a covenant of works or a covenant of grace, and even less does it *speak* of them in any sense whatsoever. This manner of reading theologisms

---

40. See, e.g., J. Hoek in Hoek and Verboom (2010, 55–56).
41. See Moerkerken (1979, 47–48).

into the Bible is basically a lack of reverence for Holy Scripture. If "the covenant of grace stands under the domination of the election," we see here how the exegesis of Scripture stands under the domination of the theology of Scottish, English, and Dutch divines of the seventeenth and eighteenth centuries.

Now what is Statement 1 exactly trying to say? If "only the elect of God are essentially included in the covenant" (Statement 5), what is the implication of this for baptism? If not only the elect babies, but *all* babies of church members are baptized—which, of course, in practice could not be otherwise—for whom then are the covenant promises, since at the same time there is a universal and well-meant offer of grace to all those baptized (in fact even to all people) (cf., e.g., John 3:16; Rom. 3:22–24; 5:18; 1 Tim. 2:6; Titus 2:11; Heb. 2:9; 2 Pet. 3:9; 1 John 2:2)? As, according to the Netherlands Reformed Congregations, pastor Reinier Kok (1890–1982) did not sufficiently distinguish between the covenant promises—which are for the elect only—and the offer of grace—which is for all hearers—he was suspended from office (1950); with his congregation in Veenendaal (the Netherlands) he went over to the Christian Reformed Churches of the Netherlands.

The next ironclad consistency was already lurking in the shadows, but this time on the other side of the spectrum. In 1953, a church division arose involving pastor Cornelis Steenblok (1894–1966), who with his followers founded a new denomination, the Reformed Congregations in the Netherlands (perhaps the most extreme hyper-Calvinist denomination in the world). You can imagine what happened here: Kok was too broad in his thinking, Steenblok was too narrow. First, Steenblok denied the universal offer of grace; understandably so, for how can God with genuine intentions *offer* his grace to all people, and only *promise* it to the elect? Second, Steenblok claimed that those babies who have been reprobated from eternity are baptized only for the sake of the babies that have been elected from eternity. The reason was simple: at

God's command, the latter must be baptized, but they cannot possibly be distinguished from the non-elect babies. For the elect babies, their baptism signifies and seals divine blessing; for the non-elect babies, their baptism signifies and seals divine curse. Such reasoning, rooted in ironclad consistency, seems to me an absolute low point in the development of the Reformed covenant doctrine.

## 8.4 The Covenant Governed by Faith
### 8.4.1 Federal Vision

Things look very different if one does not begin with divine election but with human faith — as long as this starting point is understood in a correct way. Within federalism, when it comes to the role of faith, things often go wrong immediately. Some argue that baptized people who do not come to faith, though apparently non-elect, are not false covenant members, but just as much covenant members as those who do come to faith. In this case, the line of demarcation runs not between elect and non-elect, but between those who come to faith and those who remain unbelieving. This seems to amount to the same thing, but that is a mistake: in the former distinction, there are true and false covenant members. In the latter case, there are among the baptized only true covenant members, although some are "covenant breakers": by their unbelief they have robbed the covenant of its force. This was the position of not only the Kuyperian Klaas Schilder (1890–1952), but also of Dutch Reformed Jan Gerrit Woelderink (1886–1956), each with his own viewpoint and formulation.[42]

At this point a new question arises, however. How can it be argued plausibly that, viewed from the standpoint of the covenant, there is *no* distinction between true and false covenant members? Apparently, this can be done in only one way: by claiming that *all* those baptized have been (inwardly) sanctified in Christ, share in the redemption by his blood, and have been renewed by the Holy Spirit. But of course, this can-

---
42. Schilder (1946, 1957); Woelderink (1974).

not be right: baptized people who never come to faith have never been (inwardly) cleansed and sanctified. Therefore, this "solution" of the covenant problem is doomed to fail—although it hardly ever leads people to question the confused premises of federalism as such. Whatever form is given to Reformed covenant theology, controversy repeatedly arises as a consequence of the inner inconsistencies of federalism as such.

Take the rather recent Federal Vision controversy in North America. In 2002, a conference was held in Monroe, Louisiana, entitled: "The Federal Vision: An Examination of Reformed Covenantalism." The main speakers were afterwards called "Federal Visionists," or "Auburn Avenue Theologians," because the conference was held at Auburn Avenue Presbyterian Church. Their teaching reminds us of Jacobus Koelman's distinction between an internal and an external covenant (§8.3.2). Federal Visionists have been accused of teaching that the covenant is objective, and that all its members are "covenantally elect," that is, they have all been predestined to follow Jesus for a time (i.e., since infant baptism). Federal Visionists have given occasion for such an allegation by speaking of "covenant members who are not elect in the decretal sense" and of the "decretally elect," which seems to suggest that there are also covenant members who are elect in some covenantal but not decretal sense.[43] That is, among covenant members we would have to distinguish between the "decreed elect," that is, those who are *also* predestined to persevere in faith, and thus become saved, and those who are not, that is, who fall away.

Whether Federal Visionists explicitly teach this or not, there is not the slightest biblical ground, of course, for such a "covenantal election"; again, it is nothing but a form of inferentialism. One ground the Federal Visionists did appeal

---

43. See "A Joint Federal Vision Profession," 2007 (www.federal-vision.com/resources/ joint_FV_Statement.pdf); see further, e.g., Smith (2003); Wilkins and Garner (2004); Leithart (2007); Sandlin (2007).

to for their view is that Israel's (outward) election was a corporate one—there were elect and non-elect Israelites within this "chosen" nation (Rom. 11:7)—and "therefore" that of the church (the believers and their children) must also be a corporate one. The error is obvious: Israel's election as a nation is corporate, natural, temporal, and earthly; the New Testament believer's election is individual,[44] spiritual, eternal, and heavenly (just like that of the *individual* Old Testament believers, for that matter).

Like every Reformed covenant view, Federal Vision has been heavily criticized.[45] Again, terms like "heresy" fly through the air, indicating that combatants are willing to create new church divisions over these matters (why otherwise speak of "heresies"?). John M. Otis, a pastor in the Orthodox (!) Presbyterian Church, has spoken and written many times about the "heresies" of the Federal Visionists.[46] He and others, such as pastor Brian Schwertley of the Westminster Presbyterian Church in the United States (one of numerous micro Reformed splinter groups in North America), have insisted on disciplining these heretics.

In part, the discussion involves the doctrine of justification—for instance, whether believing in the imputation of Christ's active obedience, or not—and discussing this part must wait until the next volume in the present series.

The possibility of new church divisions is clearly demonstrated by the fact that even entire denominations have condemned Federal Vision in part or in totality. I mention the Reformed Presbyterian Church in the United States (2002), the Orthodox Presbyterian Church (2006), the Presbyterian

---

44. There is, of course, such a thing as a collective decree concerning the Ekklesia (Eph. 3:10–11), but election and predestination are almost exclusively mentioned in passages that deal with the individual blessings of believers (Acts 13:48; Rom. 8:29–30, 33; Eph. 1:4–5, 11; Col. 3:12; 1 Thess. 1:4; 2 Tim. 2:10; Titus 1:1; 1 Pet. 1:1; 2:9; 2 Pet. 1:10).
45. See, e.g., Beisner (2004); Otis (2005); Waters (2006); Clark (2007); Engelsma (2012).
46. See especially Otis (2005).

Church in America (2007), the Reformed Church in the United States (2009), and the United Reformed Churches in North America (2010). No formal ecclesiastical judgments have been rendered by the Christian Reformed Church in North America, the Canadian Reformed Churches, the American Reformed Churches, the Free Reformed Churches of North America, the Heritage Reformed Congregations, the Netherlands Reformed Congregations, or the Protestant Reformed Churches in America, although in some cases, leaders in some of these denominations have expressed their opinions.

Of course, all the denominations just mentioned form only a limited part of the Reformed and Presbyterian world in North America. I count far more than fifty Presbyterian and Reformed denominations,[47] which—apart from personality clashes and modern controversies (creationism, worship, women in office, homosexuality)—are for the most part divided over *the* Reformed controversies: covenant, election, and justification. Nobody seems to wonder why there are so many different views on these matters; nobody wants to ask whether this might not point to some internal weakness of the covenant–election paradigm as such. To mention this possibility is enough to be accused of heresy.

### 8.4.2 Disappointment

It is not just I, as an Evangelical outsider, who wonders about this inner dividedness within the Reformed camp, perhaps especially in the camp loyal to the Westminster Standards. I find it quite remarkable that a genuine Reformed theologian like Cornelis Graafland overtly expressed his disappointment about the vicissitudes of the Reformed covenant doctrine: "Surveying the entire story, we cannot escape the impression that the development of the Reformed covenant doctrine has followed a sad course. . . . For us [i.e., Graafland], this means a disappointment. For we began this investigation with the expectation, also raised in us by others, that salvation, which in

---

47. See Bauswein and Vischer (1999).

the Reformed doctrine of election had come to land in a narrowed path, had maintained its breadth within the Reformed doctrine of the covenant. That expectation was not fulfilled. On the contrary. The fact that election [i.e., the election *doctrine*] has swallowed up the covenant [i.e., the covenant *doctrine*] had as a consequence that in the doctrine and practice of the covenant the same narrowing occurred. And because this concerns the covenant, this narrowing receives an even heavier accent because we had expected quite differently in connection with the covenant."[48]

My question to Graafland would be how such an entanglement could ever have been avoided as long as Reformed theologians maintained the erroneous teaching of double predestination. The covenant doctrine stumbled over that of election, and subsequently imploded. Instead of starting with election—God's side—it would seem to be more fruitful to start with faith—the human side—or even better, with the balance between God's sovereign grace and human responsibility. However, federalism has never developed a responsible view of these two matters. This is due in part to history: the clash of 1618-19 (Synod of Dort) between Arminians and anti-Arminians has made Reformed Christians forever afraid of anything that smacks of a free will, or even human responsibility as distinguished from God's sovereign grace. Reformed theology has never overcome this Arminian trauma.

Even worse is the Roman Catholic trauma. In opposition to the (alleged) teaching of the Roman Catholic Church, those loyal to the Westminster Standards insist that justification is by faith alone (*sola fide*). Of course, Scripture never adds this word "alone" (*sola*). It is a product of the Roman Catholic trauma. To be sure, no Protestant would ever assert that a person is justified by works alone—but no informed Roman Catholic would ever claim that either. No justification exists apart from genuine faith. The point I am now making is that some people

---

48. Graafland (1996, 402).

loyal to the Westminster Standards already become nervous if one says, Yes, we are justified by faith alone, but then a faith "working through love" (Gal. 5:6). They see that as adding to the "pure" teaching of the Westminster Standards. I will enter extensively into this matter in the third volume of the present series. But already at this point, I am emphasizing that any theology that is traumatized—in a Roman Catholic, or an Arminian, or any other way—will necessarily develop in a one-sided, and therefore unbiblical direction. If in addition loyalists go around shouting "heresy" and "discipline," they risk great danger of falling into the purest sectarianism.

### 8.4.3 Confusion

An essential example of the mess in which federalist theology has landed is the way the (temporal-earthly!) election of Israel as an ethnic nation is sometimes confused with the (eternal-heavenly!) election of all believers, in both the Old and the New Testaments. To this is added the error of seeing the church as the new Israel. Taken together, these lead to a third error: the assertion that there is also a temporal-earthly election of the church (collectively!), that is, of New Testament believers *and* their children, sometimes called the "visible church."

A fourth error is added to this, namely, that New Testament baptism has taken the place of Old Testament circumcision (see extensively Appendix I). This leads to a fifth error: election involves the entire church (which coincides with the New Covenant), and this church—just like Old Testament Israel—also includes the children. *Therefore, all* baptized are elect, even the baptized children who never come to faith. Thus, a new error is invented: there is not only a decretal election (think of Koelman's internal covenant) but also a covenantal election (think of Koelman's external covenant), and thus the Federal Visionists' house of cards reaches its completion.

My central point is, however, not at all to attack Federal

Visionists, as if I would wish to take part in this intra-federalist discussion. I merely wish to use them as an example, realizing that their adversaries have their own federalist houses of cards, which do not fare any better.

The reality is that circumcision in Genesis 17 is a physical mark of an—at that time still future—*ethnic* nation, Israel, to distinguish it from all other nations, *entirely apart from the question of each Israelite's personal faith and salvation*. However, baptism is a physical mark of a *spiritual* nation, consisting of true (regenerate) Jesus-believers. The church is the "holy congregation and gathering of true Christian believers" (Belgic Confession, Art. 27), *not* a gathering of outward confessors, whether regenerate or unregenerate. People became part of ethnic Israel through birth (if I may leave proselytism aside), and people become part of the church through rebirth and faith. *There is not a single Abrahamic or New Covenant blessing in which one shares in any way other than through rebirth and faith.* The New Covenant consists of people who have received forgiveness of sins, and who have God's Torah written in their hearts (Jer. 31:33-34; Heb. 8:10-12), *and no other people*—no infants who have not yet received forgiveness of sins, and who do not yet have God's Torah written in their hearts, simply because they are too young to be converted. Including infants under the New Covenant is the result of pervasive covenantalizing by federalists, and is not found in Scripture.

Of course, I do not deny that children have a special place in the congregations of the saints. I am aware of their outward sanctification (1 Cor. 7:14).[49] But they are never reckoned to the church as such, for they are not (yet) "true Christian believers." Scripture never applies the term "election" to these infants as such; and as long as they have not come to personal true faith, they have not yet received forgiveness of sins, and God's Torah has not yet been written in their hearts. Imagine how many of the problems mentioned—about the number

---

49. Ouweneel (2010a, §11.2.1; 2011, passim).

of covenants, or the number of kinds of covenant members, or about the election of children—dissolve and disappear as soon as we discover the biblical truth that the New Covenant consists of regenerate believers.

One drastic consequence of this is that most Evangelicals baptize not infants but believers, or rather, those who confess to be willing to follow Christ. For almost all federalists this is totally unacceptable, and understandably so, because both historically and theologically, infant baptism is the cornerstone of federalism.

In Genesis 17 circumcision was instituted for all *natural* sons of Abraham, and even for the male members of his household. However, the New Covenant consists only of believers. I have shown this from Jeremiah 31, and I now add Paul's statements: "Know then that it is those of faith who are the sons of Abraham" (Gal. 3:7), *not* the baptized children of believers. "For as many of you as were baptized into Christ have put on Christ . . . you are all one in Christ Jesus. And if you are Christ's, then you are Abraham's offspring, heirs according to promise" (vv. 27–29). Believers only are children of Abraham! John the Baptist warned unbelievers in Israel not to appeal to their being "children of Abraham," merely on the basis of their birth and circumcision (Matt. 3:9), for, in order to truly call oneself a "child of Abraham," regeneration and faith as well as the works of faith are required (cf. Jesus in John 8:39, "If you were Abraham's children, you would be doing the works Abraham did").

In what biblical sense, then, could the not-yet-believing children of believers be called "children of Abraham"? The answer is: they *cannot*, for at least two reasons.

1. In Genesis 17, the command of circumcision involved *only* the physical descendants of Abraham. The fact that in him, and in his offspring, all nations of the earth would be blessed, does not mean that all these nations would have to be circumcised too, or, if infant baptism has replaced circumci-

sion (which we do not grant), would have to become children of Abraham through infant baptism.

2. If already in the Gospels, and also with the apostles, nobody, *not even Abraham's physical descendants*, was to be called a child of Abraham purely on the basis of physical descent (being a child of believing parents), then Christians are not excluded from this. The ongoing line in the New Testament is that someone is a child/son of Abraham through personal regeneration and personal faith.

In such cases Reformed theologians love to quote Acts 2:39, "For the promise is for you and for your children" — erroneously assuming that (a) this refers to the Abrahamic promise (immediately before [v. 33], Peter had referred to the "promise of the Holy Spirit"), and (b) infants are meant, whereas the context speaks of *believing* children: "Your sons and your daughters shall prophesy, and your young men shall see visions" (v. 17; see Joel 2:28).

### 8.4.4 Karl Barth

A totally new and quite creative approach was taken by Karl Barth on the basis of his peculiar view of election. It is striking that his covenant view was embedded in his creation doctrine. The section dealing with this subject[50] is divided into three parts, of which the second deals with creation as the external ground of the covenant, and the third with the covenant as the internal ground of creation. Through this alleged bond between, on the one hand, "the" covenant, and on the other hand, the whole of creation (rather than the elect or believers), Barth adopts a new approach, one rooted entirely in his deviating doctrine of election.[51]

According to Barth, Jesus is both the electing God and the

---

50. Barth (1986, §41: Creation and Covenant).
51. Barth (1957); cf. Graafland (1987a, chapters VII, IX), and the summaries by, e.g., L. Berkhof (1979, 111); Woelderink (1951, chapter VI); Wentsel (1982, 192–95); Heyns (1988, 93–96); Van Genderen (2008, 222–24); Pannenberg (1993, 490–91); Erickson (1998, 934–36); McGrath (2010, 470-72).

one elected Man, as well as the only real reprobate. However, as I have argued elsewhere, none of these three can be biblically defended.[52] We cannot properly speak of election and reprobation this way. First, Jesus is not the electing God, but (the triune) God elects humans in the Man Christ Jesus, who is himself the Son of God. These things must not be confused or intermingled.

Second, Christ is the elect Servant of God, the "Chosen One" (Luke 9:35; 23:35; cf. 1 Pet. 2:4, 6), but this has little to do with the way the Bible speaks of the election of those who believe and are predestined for eternal salvation. Christ is not the only elect one; all believers have been elected by God *in Christ* (Eph. 1:4).[53]

Third, Jesus is never called the Reprobate One; it seems to me also far-fetched to equate his being forsaken by God on the cross with reprobation in the traditional Protestant sense of the term. And even if one says that Jesus was reprobated on the cross for the sake of the elect, we should not forget that Jesus was accepted again in the resurrection, whereas at the end of history, the lost are and remain reprobate forever.

As far as this last point is concerned, Barth's approach implied that in the end there could not be any reprobation anymore. He saw creation and the covenant of redemption (or the covenant of grace) as coinciding. What God in Christ has brought about for all humanity could not be abolished by any human resistance. Thus, Barth's doctrine of predestination seemed to devolve into universal reconciliation: according to him, all people would ultimately share in election. In effect this implied that there is no *e*-lection (Greek *EK-logē*) at all. In this way, not much remained of biblical election, nor of human responsibility (without repentance there is no salvation), nor of eternal judgment. Likewise, in the end nothing remains of the New Covenant, which is explicitly a covenant with a redeemed people, alongside which we find the irrevocable

---
52. See Ouweneel (2008b, 307–308).
53. Ibid., §11.3.2.

"but" of Revelation 21:5–8: all things will be renewed, *but* the portion of the wicked is the lake of fire.[54] Jan Hoek rightly says, "Barth's design is genially one-sided, but fundamentally fails the biblical revelation."[55]

## 8.5 Different Views
### 8.5.1 A "Static" View

The doctrine of the so-called covenant of grace rests on, among other things, the presupposition that all divine covenants established with postlapsarian humanity by and large amount to the same thing. Thus, the Old Covenant would merely be a supplement to the Abrahamic covenant, and the New Covenant would in large part be one and the same with the Abrahamic covenant. The latter claim is of vital importance for federalism, because it is used as an argument for the claim that the New Covenant is made also with believers *and* their children.[56] The main difference would be that the initiatory rite has been changed: baptism has taken the place of circumcision. In reality, infants are never mentioned under the New Covenant: *all* the members of this covenant possess forgiveness of sins and have the Torah written in their (circumcised) hearts, which excludes infants (see Appendix I).

This is not a complaint made only by a non-federalist outsider. It is fascinating to see that a Reformed theologian like South African dogmatician Adrio König has altogether seen through this unnuanced identification of the covenants.[57] He turns against what he calls a static covenantal view, with its main elements being the *pactum salutis* (covenant of redemp-

---

54. See about universal reconciliation Ouweneel (2009, §12.2.1; 2012, §14.4).
55. J. Hoek in Hoek and Verboom (2010, 59); also see J. Hoek in Hagoort (1999, 93–101); Van Genderen (1995, 38–39, 100–101).
56. See already Calvin, *Institutes* 2.10.2: "The covenant made with all the patriarchs is so much like ours [i.e., the New Covenant] in substance and reality that the two are actually one and the same." Cf. Brown and Keele (2012, 137): "First, *the new covenant is new in relation to the Mosaic covenant, but not the Abrahamic*." Also see Berkhof (1979, 632–33), and many others (cf. Wellum [2012, 69–71]).
57. König (2006, 438–47).

tion), the covenant of works, and the covenant of grace. By contrast, he proposes a dynamic and historical covenant view: "In the course of history, radical changes occur in the way God is involved with people."[58] Therefore, he makes a clear-cut distinction between the successive covenants, and thus, without mentioning it, comes close to dispensationalism.

I do realize that dispensationalists have often separated the covenants far too much, by asserting, for instance, that the New Covenant is exclusively intended for a future restored Israel, and that the Ekklessia has nothing to do with that New Covenant. However, between dispensationalism and federalism there are many possible intermediate positions; recently, Gentry and Wellum have posited such an intermediate position.[59] At any rate, there is *not* one covenant of grace that appears in many successive forms. This is nothing but a federalist invention. All the covenants differ in terms of the partners involved, the form of Torah involved, their covenantal signs, the promised blessings involved, and the aspects of eschatological meaning involved (see chapter 2).

Of course, there is a certain continuity, which dispensationalists have hardly acknowledged: believers under both the Old and the New Covenants are sons of Abraham (Gal. 3:29), and have been saved by the same blood of Christ (see §7.3). However, the differences are that much more important (see §7.4 and chapter 9). In their turn, the federalists have hardly acknowledged them, as becomes apparent in several ways (see this and subsequent §§). Let us look again at some of these differences.

### 8.5.2 Nationalistic Supersessionism

Federalists do not honor the essential difference between a *natural* people, like Israel, and a *spiritual* people, like the Ekklesia. Federalists speak and write as if under the New Covenant God's people are a natural people, too, that is, including the

---

58. Ibid., 440.
59. Gentry and Wellum (2012).

infants of the believers and including the non-converted — but baptized — members. This error seems to be supported by the fact that the New Covenant is made with Israel (Jer. 31:31-34; Heb. 8:8-12), which *is* a natural people.

Arguing on the basis of such ideas easily leads to a view like that of the Reformed theologian Philippus J. Hoedemaker (1839-1910) in the Netherlands, who propagated the idea of the "nation church" (*volkskerk*, a church encompassing a whole nation) and of a "baptized nation." This is specifically a Reformed idea: the Reformed church and the (largely) Reformed nation coincide, just as in ancient Israel the religious community and the nation coincided. In this view, the royal house played a major role: the Protestant royal house in the Netherlands (stadholders from 1572 until 1795, kings/queens from 1813 until today), and the Protestant monarchs in England, and sometimes Scotland (Henry VIII, Elizabeth I, James I, William III of Orange — though these cannot all be called Reformed/Presbyterian).

The Netherlands as a New Israel! Think of the (obsolete) Dutch slogan "God, Netherlands, and Orange," in which the (Reformed) Netherlands was viewed as a spiritual Israel, and the house of Orange as a kind of present-day "house of David." In the Dutch national anthem (the *Wilhelmus*) the following words are placed on the lips of William of Orange (William the Silent): "Just as David had to fly before Saul the tyrant, I had to sigh as a nobleman. But God exalted him, . . . and gave him a great kingdom in Israel." Moreover, the Dutch fight for freedom against Spain (1568-1648) was compared with Israel's deliverance from Egypt. William the Silent was not only a new David, but also a new Moses.[60]

Similar ideas were found among Protestant communities in other countries: the Puritans who arrived in 1620 in New England identified themselves with the ancient Hebrews, and were convinced they were establishing God's New Israel. The

---

60. See, e.g., Meijer (1898); Huisman (1983).

settlers in Virginia were "a peculiar people, marked and chosen by the finger of God," as early settler John Rolfe put it. This self-image of being God's New Israel became especially important during the revolutionary period. In 1776, Benjamin Franklin and Thomas Jefferson (though not very Reformed themselves) wanted Promised Land images for the new nation's Great Seal. Franklin proposed Moses dividing the Red Sea with Pharaoh's army being overwhelmed by the waters, and Jefferson preferred a picture of the Israelites being led in the wilderness by the pillar of cloud.

George Washington was the American Joshua: "Never was the possession of arms used with more glory, or in a better cause, since the days of Joshua and the son of Nun," claimed pastor Ezra Stiles (president of Yale College) in 1783. "We cannot but acknowledge that God hath graciously patronized our cause and taken us under his special care, as he did his ancient covenant people," proclaimed pastor Samuel Langdon (president of Harvard University) in 1788. In 1805, Thomas Jefferson said in a public address: "I shall need . . . the favor of that Being in whose hands we are, who led our fathers, as Israel of old, from their native land and planted them in a country flowing with all the necessities and comforts of life."[61] (Incidentally, these leaders were nationalistic Protestants, but certainly not all Reformed/Presbyterians!)

The story of the Boers (Reformed farmers from the Netherlands) in South Africa was quite similar. Just as the American Protestants had done, the Boers compared their battle against the British oppressors with Israel's fight against its enemies. In 1836, the Boers abandoned the Cape area, and started their Great Trek to Transvaal to establish their own republic. This movement "forms the national epic—formal proof of God's election of the Afrikaner people and His special destiny for them."[62] As they set out in their wagons, they "were followed by the British army, like that of Pharaoh, and everywhere

---

61. See extensively Cherry (1971) and May (1997) and references there.
62. Moodie (1975, 3).

were beset by the unbelieving black 'Canaanites.' Yet because God's people acted according to His will, He delivered them out of the hands of their enemies and gave them their freedom in the promised land."[63]

The Boers attributed their victory over the Zulus at Blood River—in which 3,000 Zulus died, but no Boer—to God's covenant with them. Pastor Jacobus D. du Toit (or, Totius) said in a poem: "How the handful of trekkers suffer, the freedom seekers, creators of a People. Just like another Israel, by enemies surrounded, lost in the field, but for another Canaan elected, led forward by God's plan."[64] The indigenous Africans were viewed as Canaanites destined to be the servants of the Boers.[65] Such ideas, rooted in Israel's biblical history, lived on until the end of apartheid (around 1992).

Another example is the Huguenots (Reformed Protestants in France), who either compared themselves with the Israelites who were slaves under the Pharaoh of Egypt (the Catholic king of France), or, after they had fled, with the Israelites who were exiles in Babylon. During the religious wars in France (sixteenth/seventeenth centuries), the Reformed rebels fought against the French army like David against Goliath, often under the loud singing of Psalms in which Israel's battles were described.[66]

A last example is the Protestants, specifically the Presbyterians, in Ulster (Northern Ireland).[67] In 1795, the Orange Order was founded in Ulster by Protestants who felt surrounded by Roman Catholics, just as the Israelites in Canaan had been surrounded by hostile nations. These Protestants constantly made comparisons between themselves and ancient Israel. Men like Edward Carson and James Craig (Ulster nationalists) were compared to Moses, Gideon, Samuel, and Saul of

---

63. Ibid., 5.
64. Quoted in Akenson (1992, 74); cf. Du Toit (1985).
65. Akenson (1992, 75, 94).
66. Trim (2011).
67. See Craith (2002, 64–71), and references there.

Tarsus. Pastor Ian Paisley even compared *himself* to Moses, who brought his people out of tyranny. "Metaphorically, the implication of any of these Biblical stories is that Northern Irish Protestants are God's People and the Region can be compared with Israel or Judah."[68] Some of them even believe that the Ulster Protestants are the true lost tribe of Israel, a holy priesthood, destined to build a New Jerusalem in Ulster.

All such nationalistic ideas were and are necessarily embedded in supersessionism, the unfortunate idea of a spiritual Israel, which sometimes was even identified more or less with a certain (usually Reformed/Presbyterian) nation. Such an Israel was of course stripped of all its Jewish features (except for the staunch Psalm singing). The great leaders here were especially pastors, who sometimes were also politicians, embodying in their persons the identity of the state and the New Israel. Fascinating examples were pastor John Knox Witherspoon (signatory of the United States Declaration of Independence as a representative of New Jersey, 1776), pastor Abraham Kuyper (prime minister of the Netherlands, 1901-1905), pastor Daniel F. Malan (prime minister of South Africa, 1948-1954), and pastor Ian Paisley (first minister of Ulster, 2007-2008). Apparently, God had several New Israels, in the Netherlands, in North America, in France, in Ulster, and in South Africa, but at least they were all (mainly) Reformed/Presbyterian.

### 8.5.3 Natural *Versus* Spiritual

This nationalistic supersessionism, which is repulsive to most modern Christians, overlooks the essential fact that under the New Covenant we are dealing with a spiritual nation, to which access is granted not by birth but by rebirth, not by a kind of "circumcision" (infant baptism) but by personal faith. It is said of Israel in the Messianic kingdom: "In the LORD all the offspring of Israel shall be justified [or, shall be righteous people] and shall glory" (Isa. 45:25), and: "Your people shall

---
68. Ibid., 67.

all be righteous; they shall possess the land forever" (60:21). Please note: this is not a justified people *plus their* (elect or non-elect) *children*; no, *all the offspring of Israel shall be justified*. They will *all* have circumcised hearts, they will *all* have God's Torah written on their hearts, and they will *all* have forgiveness of sins on the basis of repentance, confession and faith (Jer. 31:33-34).[69]

Of course, the babies of Israel will belong to the New Covenant. That is why the Jewish boys will still be circumcised: uncircumcised males will have no place in the new Zion (Isa. 52:1; Ezek. 44:6-9). (Please note: this is one of the many arguments that baptism has *not* replaced circumcision because physical circumcision will remain valid as long as the present earth will last; see Appendix I.) But this cannot simply be applied to Gentiles coming under the umbrella of the New Covenant. They are exempt from the Mosaic Torah, including circumcision (Acts 15). In 2 Corinthians 3, where Paul calls the apostles "ministers of a New Covenant" (v. 6), he substitutes "Christ" for "law" (v. 3). This means that the New Covenant *exclusively* comprises regenerate people, that is, those who have Christ written on their hearts.

In many church denominations, there may be a few, or many, unconverted opportunists. If one so wishes, one might say that they, as well as the infants, are in the "courtyard" of the New Covenant. But actually, that is more a metaphor linked with the kingdom of God than with the New Covenant.[70] It is the company of those that "have tasted the heavenly gift, and have shared in the Holy Spirit, and have tasted the goodness of the word of God and the powers of the age to come" (Heb. 6:4-5), without necessarily having been born again. They were there where the Holy Spirit was working; they tasted, but they did not necessarily eat.

---

69. I leave aside here another way of reading Isa. 45:25, "In the LORD justice will be done to all the offspring of Israel" (NET: "All the descendants of Israel will be vindicated by the LORD"); see the third volume of this series.
70. Cf. Ouweneel (2011, §12.10); also see chapter 9 in the present book.

Those belonging to the New Covenant share in it only through personal faith, as Paul emphasizes: "Know then that it is those of faith who are the sons of Abraham. . . . So then, those who are of faith are blessed along with Abraham, the man of faith" (Gal. 3:7, 9). Notice the distinction again: one comes under the Abrahamic covenant—involving a *natural* people—(a) through birth into Abraham's physical offspring, and (b) (if male) through circumcision. It is quite different in the New Covenant, which involves a *spiritual* people. One comes under this covenant (a) through rebirth into a spiritual family, and (b) through spiritual circumcision, that is, inner cleansing through faith in Christ. The introductory rite of the Old Covenant (circumcision) was performed on sons of *Israel* on the basis of their *birth*. The introductory rite of the New Covenant (baptism) is performed on children of *God* on the basis of their *rebirth* (see again Appendix I).

The reply that federalists usually give is more or less as follows.

(a) *The Abrahamic covenant is basically identical with the New Covenant.* Already John Calvin claimed this, and many in his wake. Not a single biblical argument is given, except for the (in turn mistaken) answer that, whereas the Old Covenant allegedly is a law covenant, both the Abrahamic and the New Covenants are promise covenants—as if there might not be very different promise covenants.

In reality, the two covenants are indeed quite different: the *partners* are different (Abraham and all his progeny *versus* the houses of Israel and Judah), the forms of *Torah* are different (the Abrahamic Torah *versus* the Messianic/Millennial Torah), the *covenantal signs* are different (circumcision *versus* Christ himself [possibly, the Lord's Supper]), even the *present blessings* are different (justification by faith only *versus* justification by faith plus Christ written in the hearts and the gift of the Holy Spirit). This last point is very important and was taken up in chapter 7 (also cf. chapter 9).

(b) *The New Covenant also comprises infants*, for at its announcement, the "offspring of Israel" is referred to (Jer. 31:36-37; cf. 30:10; Deut. 30:6; Isa. 43:5; 44:3; 54:3; 59:21; 61:9; 65:22-23; Ezek. 37:24-27; and prophetic Psalms: Ps. 22:31-32; 25:13; 102:29; 103:17-18; 112:2). There are at least two replies to this. First, "offspring" simply means "descendants"; the term does not at all necessarily refer primarily or exclusively to babies (see extensively §7.4.1 for the important difference between children in the sense of "descendants" and in the sense of "infants"). Second, we must consider that all the passages mentioned above refer exclusively to the *ethnic* people of Israel in the Messianic kingdom.

Here again, we encounter ancient supersessionism, in which things that refer to ethnic Israel are applied to, and confused with, the (almost entirely Gentile) Ekklesia.[71] The New Covenant is explicitly made with the "house of Israel and the house of Judah" (Jer. 31:31, 33); in chapter 7 I have tried to show that there is not the slightest biblical basis for applying this to the (almost exclusively Gentile) Ekklesia as such. The latter's individual members do come under the umbrella of the blessings of the New Covenant, but she is not the actual covenant partner. It may help here to think of Noah's sons: Japheth dwells in the tents of Shem (Gen. 9:27), but *Japheth never becomes Shem*.

In this connection, the Reformed theologian Jakob van Bruggen exhibited remarkable insight when he wrote: "The Jewish people do retain a separate place as offspring of Abram and as mother people of the World Redeemer and his apostles. Their place and circumcision have not been blotted out. However, together with the uncircumcised they may have themselves blessed by the Promised One, who unifies all on the trail of faith and baptism. Thus, they attain the real goal of

---

71. Cf. Niell (2003, 131), who claims that the Church of the present era of the New Covenant (in Jer. 31:31–34) is referred to as Israel and Judah, the people of God. His whole chapter about what is new in the New Covenant is based on this error.

God with Abraham and with circumcision."[72]

(c) *The New Covenant is also definitely a "mixed multitude" of true believers, opportunists, and hypocrites.*[73] Those who argue this way confuse the New Covenant with what is called the "visible church," which indeed is such a mixed multitude (see, e.g., Acts 20:30; 2 Tim. 2:16-21; 3:1-9; Heb. 10:26-31; 2 Pet. 2; 1 John 2:18-19; Jude). From the *sad* fact of such a mixture of true and false Christians, something *never* desired nor intended by God, people derive the *right*, or even the *duty*, allegedly desired and intended by God, to baptize the children of the believers, or even of unregenerate church members, even though people know that many of them will never come to faith (see §7.2.1). From the *deplorable* fact that there are unbelievers in the church it is concluded that infants may be baptized, some of whom will never become believers. Thus, an allegedly biblical principle is partly based on a deplorable state of abuse.

The true argument is often of a purely intuitive nature: we hear it said that babies are also included. But included in what?

(1) *Not* in the Church, which is the holy gathering of true Christian believers (Belgic Confession, Art. 27).

(2) *Not* in the Abrahamic covenant, for that is made with Abraham's *physical* offspring, even though this covenant does imply blessing for all humanity (Gen. 12:3; etc.) in that, through faith, present-day believers (not their not-yet-believing babies!) are "sons of Abraham" (Gal. 3:7).

(3) *Not* in some vague "people of God." The Ekklesia *is* called "people of God," but then one that is "zealous for good works," "called out of darkness into his marvelous light" (Acts 15:13; Titus 2:14; 1 Pet. 2:9-10); these descriptions show that this is a people of *believers*.

(4) And finally, *not* in the New Covenant, which compris-

---
72. Van Bruggen (1997, 58).
73. See, e.g., Strawbridge (2003, 3–5, 156–74).

es only the truly righteous, those who know the Lord, those who have Christ written on their hearts.

(5) As far as I can tell, there is only one category remaining: infants *are* included, but then, very clearly in the kingdom of God: "Let the children come to me, and do not hinder them, for to such belongs the kingdom of God" (Luke 18:16). However, that is a very different matter, on which I will not dwell here.

### 8.5.4 Circumcision

In this context, let us look for a moment at circumcision in Genesis 17 again (see more extensively Appendix I). In its allegedly altered form, namely, infant baptism, it is applied to children under the New Covenant. But in doing so, at least four essential things are overlooked.[74]

(1) In Genesis 17, circumcision was performed not only on Abraham and his sons but on *all* male members of Abraham's household—believing or unbelieving—merely because they belonged to his household (vv. 13, 23). What is the practical application of this under the New Covenant (which allegedly is identical with the Abrahamic covenant)? Does it mean that, when an employer gets saved and is baptized, all his personnel are to be baptized as well? The answer is, *only if they believe.* Lydia was baptized "with her house," not because the members thereof were her servants but—how could it be otherwise?—because they had come to faith too (Acts 16:15).

(2) In Genesis 17, circumcision is a physical characteristic of a future *ethnic* people, Israel. Baptism, however, is a physical characteristic of a *spiritual* people, consisting of true Christian believers. People enter ethnic Israel through birth, people enter the Ekklesia through rebirth and faith. In the old days, it was enough to be circumcised when a boy was born into Israel. Today, as one becomes a child of Abraham *through faith*, millions of Christians baptize people when they have come to faith.

---

74. Cf. Wright (2006, 238).

(3) In Genesis 17, circumcision is performed on men only. Why did God not give a ritual that held for both boys and girls, as is the case in infant baptism? Why precisely *this* (rather radical) ritual? Why not already in the Old Testament an infant baptism (*mikveh*) for boys as well as for girls? This is related to the nature of circumcision, namely, the link with procreation: the circumcision of the "flesh"[75] reminds a man of the fact that he, as a "carnal" man ("man in the flesh" — now in the figurative sense) can beget only "carnal" children: "That which is born of the flesh is flesh" (John 3:6). "It is the Spirit who gives life; the flesh is no help at all" (6:63). Abraham fathered Ishmael while he was yet uncircumcised, but Isaac after he had been circumcised; therefore, only the latter could be a child of divinely gracious promises: "[T]he son of the slave [i.e., Hagar] was born according to the flesh, while the son of the free woman [i.e., Sarah] was born through promise . . . just as at that time he who was born according to the flesh [i.e., Ishmael] persecuted him who was born according to the Spirit [i.e., Isaac], so also it is now" (Gal. 4:23, 29).

It is striking that federalists never seem to pay much attention to this meaning of circumcision, and therefore cannot explain why God gave circumcision to Israel, that is, a rite for boys only in relation to procreation, whereas baptism does not have such a meaning at all, and is administered to women as well as men.[76] This simply underscores the fact that circumcision and baptism are totally different things (see Appendix I).

(4) In Genesis 17, circumcision was instituted for all the *natural* sons of Abraham. But under the New Covenant, only the believers are children of Abraham in the true sense of

---

75. Heb. *basar*, "flesh," is sometimes a euphemism for the male sexual organ (Lev. 15:2–3, 7; Ezek. 23:20).
76. As far as the women were concerned, the notion that the "flesh" can produce only "flesh" was brought out in a different way, namely, not at conception but at birth: after childbirth, she was unclean for a certain length of time, after which a burnt and a sin offering had to follow (Lev. 12; cf. Luke 2:22–24); see Ouweneel (2009, 128–29).

the word. In the present dispensation, children of believing parents are never called children of Abraham purely on the basis of their physical descent. They are holy in some outward sense (1 Cor. 7:14), to them belongs the kingdom of God (Mark 10:14), they are under the blessings of the Holy Spirit and taste the Word of God (Heb. 6:4-5) — but they will only become children of Abraham by personally coming to faith.

## 8.6  Final Questions
### 8.6.1  Practical Aspects

Federalism is not limited to the theologian's office; it pervades the life of Reformed Christians in many practical ways. Here are four examples.

(1) It is no wonder that in their church services federalists often read the Ten Commandments, that is, the essence of the Mosaic Torah. It illustrates how much they are still attached to the Old Covenant, with all the confusion such attachment entails, also concerning baptism. In their worship services, federalists should instead read the "Torah of Christ" (1 Cor. 9:21; Gal. 6:2), that is, the *new* commandment, or the Love Command (John 13:34; 1 John 2:8-11), or parts from the Sermon on the Mount (Matt. 5-7), or from the New Testament Epistles (e.g., Eph. 4:17-32), that is, passages fitting in with the New Covenant. Their preference for the Ten Commandments flows from the misunderstanding that, for Gentile Jesus-believers, God would have abolished the civil and ceremonial part of the Mosaic Torah, but not the moral part of it. That is a double error: first, no part of the Mosaic Torah has ever been abolished; and second, Gentile Jesus-believers never were, nor will be, under the Mosaic Torah or under any part of it. They are under the Messianic Torah (see the previous volume in this series).

(2) One consequence of observing the Ten Commandments is that federalists also maintain the Fourth Commandment: "Remember the Sabbath day, to keep it holy" (Exod. 20:8). In reading this to the congregation, one either places a curse

on the church members because of the way they spent their Saturday, or one must prove to them from the Bible that the Sabbath is observed not on Saturday anymore, but on Sunday (see on this the previous volume in the present series). The Bible considers Sunday a special day (the "Lord's Day"), but never an obligatory day of rest. It knows nothing of Sabbath observance shifting to another day. It is all a consequence of not keeping the Old and the New Covenants, or the Mosaic Torah and the Messianic Torah, sufficiently distinct. The Ten Commandments are part of the covenant of slavery, of Mount Sinai, of the "law of slavery," and *not* of the covenant of freedom, of Mount Zion, of the "law of freedom," that is, the Messianic Torah (Gal. 4:24-26; cf. James 1:25; 2:12). This Messianic Torah acknowledges the Lord's Day as a day of joy, but contains no Sabbath commandment whatsoever.

(3) Under the Old Covenant, sacrifices had to be repeated all the time; it was not yet possible to rest in the finished work of Christ, something that *is* possible under the New Covenant. Under this covenant, God's people "no longer have any consciousness of sins" (Heb. 10:2). For some federalists, who often argue that they remain "poor sinners" until their death (in spite of, e.g., Rom. 5:8), this is an incomprehensible statement. Because they are truly locked in the Old Covenant, they have no true assurance of salvation, and even if they have it, they seem to believe—unconsciously and unintentionally—that they have to retain God's favor through a sacred walk, which actually means: through good law-works (cf. the third volume in the present series). This means that, every time such believers fall into serious sin, they begin doubting their eternal salvation again. Insofar as they have (a certain measure of) assurance of their salvation, one hears them declaring that they cling to God's "baptismal promises"; in their terminology, the latter form a "basis for pleading." This is typical federalist parlance, totally foreign to the New Testament. Why don't these believers say: We cling to the finished work of Christ and to the promises of God's Word? Incidentally,

these benefits are valid not only for baptized people but for all people, and these benefits become their portion concretely and subjectively not through baptism, but through faith.

(4) Typical for many federalists is also that during their church services they sing exclusively or mainly psalms, those marvelous songs of the *Old* Covenant. For some of them this is such a matter of life and death that they really believe that in Ephesians 5:19 and Colossians 3:16 ("psalms and hymns and spiritual songs") Paul is referring to three kinds of Old Testament *psalms!*[77] This is strange for at least two reasons. First, all quintessential truths of Christianity (the Fatherhood of God, the person of the Son, the atoning work of Christ, the Ekklesia) are largely or entirely absent in the Psalms. Second, these psalms contain statements that Christians could hardly sing, such as: "[T]ake not your Holy Spirit from me" (Ps. 51:11b), since the Spirit will be with us forever (John 14:16). Precisely such words as Psalm 51:11b increase the burden that many people experience with the assurance of salvation. Singing psalms is lovely, consoling, and encouraging—but to limit ourselves to them is to rob ourselves of New Testament hymns, in which the full truth of God can be expressed.

Reformed psalters have sometimes added to the confusion. Dutch federalists love to sing at an infant baptism ceremony the line from Psalm 105: *'t verbond met Abraham, zijn vrind, bevestigt Hij van kind tot kind* ("The covenant made with his friend Abraham he confirms from child to child"). However, they do not realize (a) that this is not a faithful rendering of the original Psalm but a case of Reformed *eisegesis*, and (b) that the Abrahamic covenant among Gentiles is confirmed only to those who are *spiritual* offspring of Abraham, namely, his children through personal faith (Rom. 4:11-12; Gal. 3:7; cf. v. 29).

---

77. Greijdanus (1925, 118) tends to this view by mentioning biblical *psalms* as examples of "hymns" and "spiritual songs."

### 8.6.2 Covenant and Torah

Taking a closer look at the totality of federalism, I must say that it is not easy to become familiar with a doctrine about which the adherents themselves are so divided. One easily becomes entangled in the terminology employed. For instance, has the Old Covenant—often described as partly being a covenant of works—been abolished, yes or no? Formally yes, essentially no? What is the exact relationship between the alleged covenant of works aspect and the alleged covenant of grace aspect of the Old Covenant? What is the exact relationship between the alleged covenant of redemption and the covenant of grace? What is the exact relationship between the Abrahamic and the Sinaitic covenants? What is the exact nature of the grace involved in the alleged covenant of grace? Only saving grace for the elect? Or not just saving grace but also common grace? Or eventually the totality of all God's favors to humanity?

In the heat of many federalist controversies, sometimes chasms have been created that, at a closer look, were much less wide and deep than people had originally thought. At any rate, it is impossible to have much respect for people who have created church divisions over any component of federalist theology. They have ripped apart God's people over theological theories, which moreover were usually wrong. Paul says, "Now the works of the flesh are evident: . . . strife, jealousy, fits of anger, rivalries, dissensions, divisions, envy, . . . and things like these. I warn you . . . that those who do such things will not inherit the kingdom of God" (Gal. 5:19–21).

Let me say this about the relationship between the various covenants. There is definitely discontinuity, as dispensationalism claims: the Mosaic Torah is replaced by the Messianic Torah, the Old Covenant is replaced by the New Covenant. At the same time, there is definitely continuity, as is claimed by federalists and many Messianic Jews: the Mosaic Torah merges into, and is renewed in, the Messianic Torah, just as the Old Covenant merges into, and is renewed in, the New Covenant. In the previous volume of the present series I have given the following reason for this: both are forms of the one, Eternal Torah.

To make a comparison: it is like the age-old question whether the resurrection body will be the same body as the present one, or another body, or whether the new earth will be the same earth as the present one, or another earth. Of course, to a certain extent both statements are true. There is continuity, for it is *this* mortal body that will be given life at the resurrection (Rom. 8:11), and likewise it is *this* earth that will be renewed, not replaced, and it is the Old Covenant that will be renewed, not replaced. However, there is also discontinuity, for the resurrection body will differ from the present body just as much as the head of grain differs from the seed, or as the imperishable, glorious, powerful, and spiritual differs from the perishable, dishonorable, weak, and natural (1 Cor. 15:37, 42–44). *Mutatis mutandis* the same holds for the new earth—and also for the New Covenant, and the Messianic Torah.

The New Covenant was not a replacement, but a renewal of the Old Covenant—yet, it was really *new*. This is precisely the argument of Hebrews 8:13. And if new, then the Torah of the New Covenant will also be new. Not in the sense of replacement, but of renewal—yet, genuinely *new*. Therefore, what David Stern says is inaccurate, "[The Torah under the New Covenant] is not some new *Torah*, different from Old Testament *Torah*."[78] The weakness of Stern's viewpoint becomes clear from what follows: "Christian theology all too often tries to escape or water down the plain sense of what is said here [in Heb. 8], so that what is required [of believers] is very little, usually a vague 'sensitivity to God's will' that becomes impossible to pin down." Stern should not need to resort to such a caricature of his average opponent, for he is

---

78. Stern (1999, 686).

thereby implicitly judging the latter's motives, which is forbidden in the Messianic Torah (Matt. 7:1-2). We can definitely claim that the Jesus-believer ought to keep all the commands of the Messianic Torah, which comprise perhaps more than a thousand, if we include all the New Testament imperatives, and yet emphasize that this is a Torah manifestation that differs from the Mosaic Torah. Likewise, the Millennial Torah will be fundamentally new, for "the coastlands wait for his [i.e., Messiah's] Torah" (Isa. 42:4).[79]

As a matter of principle, one must always ask the question here what theological interest—I do not speak of mental motives—drives a certain type of theology to emphasize either the being the same or being different. The answer is obvious. Dispensationalists, such as Hebrew Christian Arnold Fruchtenbaum, are all interested in heavily underscoring the differences between the Abrahamic, the Sinaitic, and the New Covenants (with their various forms of Torah), because they believe in strongly distinct dispensations. Federalists and such Messianic Jews as David Stern are all interested in strongly emphasizing the basic parity of the three, because they believe that Jesus-believers are under the Mosaic Torah, whether under its moral essence, or under the Torah as a whole.

A virtually impossible intermediate position can be found by emphasizing both the oneness and the threeness (as with the Trinity).[80] This third way is extremely important, because the idea of oneness is a strong weapon against the view that the Mosaic Torah would have been abolished. And the idea of the threeness is a strong weapon against the view that Gentile Jesus-believers would be under the circumcision command or the Sabbath command, for example, or under the *kashrut* (food laws). Gentile believers are not under these commands, strictly speaking not even under the moral part of the Mosaic Torah; they live joyfully under the commands of the Messian-

---

79. Cf. a good example of this in John 13:34 and 1 John 2:7-8; see Ouweneel (2015a, §4.3.3).
80. Ibid.

ic Torah (see again the previous volume in this series).

# Chapter 9
# An Evangelical Covenant Theology

*To the eunuchs who keep my Sabbaths,*
    *who choose the things that please me*
    *and hold fast my covenant,*
*I will give in my house and within my walls*
    *a monument and a name*
    *better than sons and daughters;*
*I will give them an everlasting name*
    *that shall not be cut off.*
*And the foreigners who join themselves to the* L ORD,
    *to minister to him,*
*to love the name of the* L ORD,
    *and to be his servants,*
*everyone who keeps the Sabbath and does not profane it,*
    *and holds fast my covenant —*
*these I will bring to my holy mountain,*
    *and make them joyful in my house of prayer;*
*their burnt offerings and their sacrifices*
    *will be accepted on my altar;*
*for my house shall be called*
    *a house of prayer for all peoples.*
                                    Isaiah 56:4–7

*Summary:* Negatively, Evangelical covenant theology exposes the errors of Reformed covenant theology such as theologism, electionism, remissionism, supersessionism, and spiritualism. Especially the latter has had disastrous effects on biblical thinking. Positively, Evangelical covenant theology underscores all the great Christian blessings that surpass forgiveness of sins and justification, that is, surpass all the promised covenant blessings. On this point, the pervasive covenantalizing of federalism is utterly mistaken. Not only the continuity between the Abrahamic covenant and the New Covenant must be emphasized, but also the discontinuity. There is no room in the covenants for the Body of Christ, for the Ekklesia as the Temple of the Spirit, and for the fullness of God (Paul), for "eternal life" as John understands it, for becoming partakers of the divine nature (Peter), in short: for anything that is quintessentially and exclusively Christian, and as such surpasses the covenantal promises.

## 9.1  Federalism Evaluated
### 9.1.1  Misunderstandings

BY NOW IT MAY BE CLEAR WHY, although I attach great value to the biblical notion of the covenant, I am not a federalist. I consider federalism to be a theological theory in which there is too little genuinely biblical argument, and too much speculation. I view federalism as a form of inferentialism, a jumping from one theological idea to the next one, resulting to a large extent in nothing more than a house of cards. Let me be very clear: I consider federalism in no respect to be heretical. On the contrary, generally speaking, Reformed and Presbyterian Christians are fully orthodox, measured by the standards of, say, the Apostles' and Nicene Creeds. A theological error is something very different from a heresy. No fundamental Christian truth is at stake in federalism. Nevertheless, I see a number of errors, some of them with consequences that can damage someone's spiritual life.

Let me summarize a number of its main mistakes.

(a) Federalism has a limited concept of grace, insisting that divine grace always presupposes sin. Grace is not the opposite of sin or guilt, but of merit. Every divine blessing that is not earned — and no divine blessing *is* ever earned by any human being (except by Christ) — is a pure gift of God's grace. Thus, the alleged covenant of works — if there were any covenant at all with prelapsarian Adam — was primarily a covenant of grace, a covenant of divine favor, just like any covenant made with postlapsarian humanity. This has nothing to do with the seriousness of the fall and the necessity of redemption as such; it has to do only with a proper biblical understanding of divine grace.

(b) Federalism puts too much emphasis on the gospel of "repentance and forgiveness of sins" (Luke 24:47), and too little emphasis on the "gospel of the kingdom" (Matt. 4:23; 9:35; 24:14; cf. 28:18-19, and see next §). Forgiveness and redemption from sin are not at all the *goal* of God's redemptive plan; these are only the — in themselves very important — *means* to the actual goal: the kingdom of God. Reformed theology is a theology of election and covenant; historically, it has hardly been kingdom theology (except in the very broad sense of the kingdom as God's universal, providential rule). I personally find the kingdom a more central biblical notion than the covenant. It is more precise to say that the New Covenant is a *kingdom* covenant than a form of the covenant of *grace*. This subject is so important that §§9.1.4 and 9.2 are devoted to it.

(c) Federalism mainly sees the Mosaic Torah, on the one hand, as underlying the Sinaitic covenant and, on the other hand, as a "path to Christ" (often based on a false interpretation of Gal. 3:24). Too little attention is paid to the inner riches of the Mosaic Torah as such, which are much more than just the Ten Commandments. These riches will never be lost, and only in the Messianic kingdom will come to their full blossoming (see previous volume).

(d) On the one hand, federalists falsely preach that the Mosaic Torah has been in large part abolished in or by Christ, and on the other hand, they place the core of it, the Ten Commandments, on the shoulders of Gentile Christians (see previous volume). If anything should be read in public worship, it should be not the Ten Commandments, but the Messianic Torah, for instance, portions from Matthew 5–7, John 14–16, or Ephesians 4–5.

(e) Federalists have often considered themselves to be the champions of the sovereignty of God. In fact, they have often unintentionally belittled this sovereignty by not properly grasping its balance with human responsibility (which, unfortunately, is partly due to the "Arminian trauma"). The unbiblical claim that all things that occur have been decreed before the foundation of the world is not at all a defense of God's sovereignty, but rather a belittling of it (cf. Appendix III).

(f) Federalism has adopted the Augustinian and Medieval error of supersessionism, by (1) speaking of a church as existing since Adam (or since Abraham) (thus belittling the specific nature of the Ekklesia; see below and chapter 7), and (2) having adopted the blessings of Israel (leaving the curses to them), considering itself to be some "new" or "spiritual Israel," at the same time claiming that all *Jewish* aspects of this "Israel" have been abolished.

(g) Along with this, federalists committed the error of spiritualism, that is, ignoring the literal meaning of hundreds of Old Testament prophecies, and applying them to the church according to their alleged "spiritual sense" (see Appendix IV). In this way it has eliminated any hope for ethnic Israel, a hope to be realized—after repentance and restoration—in Israel's own land, in its own city, and in its own temple, under a Messiah not just sitting on a heavenly throne but on the throne of David in Jerusalem.

(h) By lumping together all the covenants, federalism has lost sight of the essential differences between, especially, the Abrahamic, the Sinaitic, and the New Covenants. The first and the third of these three covenants were considered to be identical in order to find a theological basis for infant baptism. (Historically, infant baptism was not based upon covenant doctrine, but a theological covenant doctrine was developed as a support for infant baptism; see further, Appendix I.)

(i) One of the main errors of federalism is its pervasive covenantalizing. By and by, it began to "discover" covenants everywhere, even within the Trinity. I consider this idea of a covenant relationship between the Father and the Son, thus belittling their true relationship, to be one of the low points in federalist development.

### 9.1.2 Goal and Means

Reformed theologian Seakle Greijdanus once wrote: "By God's covenant of grace we understand: God's gracious decree concerning, for, and with man, who fell and became a sinner, with a view to his restitution and restoration in a state of eternal blessedness, by granting and sending his only-begotten Son in our nature and in the state of our guilt and the condition of our misery; . . . ."[1] Reformed theologian Cornelis van der Waal once wrote: "[T]his book will seek to prove that the gospel is covenant-oriented from A to Z."[2] Clarence Stam wrote "that the covenant is the way in which God realizes his work of salvation."[3] And recently, Reformed pastors Brown and Keele wrote: "The covenant of grace is the one covenant through which all believers are saved."[4]

The idea that covenants are for humanity's salvation (redemption from sin) is a key idea of federalism. But unfortunately, it is simply wrong. To be sure, it is a tremendous thing that, from Adam until today, millions of people have been saved for eternity by surrendering themselves in faith to God (since Jesus, this includes faith in Jesus), by repenting from and confessing their sins and by receiving forgiveness of sins

---

1. Our translation from the original; see Kamphuis (1985, 73-74).
2. Van der Waal (1990, 3; cf. chapter 8: "The Covenantal Structure of the New Testament Gospel").
3. Stam (1999, 169).
4. Brown and Keele (2012, 58).

on the basis of a vicarious sacrifice (since Jesus, we know that this is *his own* sacrifice). All these people were in the mind of God from eternity; they were the objects of election and predestination from before the foundation of the world. This is all wonderful. *But this involves biblical covenants only to a limited extent.*

This may sound shocking to federalists' ears. To them, "the" covenant is everything, and redemption is everything, so the two must belong closely together. But please, let the federalist reader hear me out. I hope to show that the main purpose of the covenants was not the eternal salvation of souls — no matter how precious this is in itself — but the main purpose was and is *the establishment of the Messianic kingdom on earth* (see §9.2). Of course, everything is related with everything. What would the kingdom be without the eternal redemption of its subjects? But we should not confuse things. The theme and thrust of the covenants is not the gospel of God's grace for poor sinners, but the *gospel of the kingdom*. The reason why federalists have difficulty seeing this is because of the enormous preponderance, since Augustine, of the subject of God's redemptive grace for sinners. Individual redemption of sins and going to heaven are seen as God's ultimate *goal* instead of a *means* to a goal. However, in Scripture, the real goal is a collective goal: the "kingdom of our Lord and of his Christ" (cf. Rev. 11:15).

Six times in the New Testament the gospel is called the gospel of God, once the gospel of the glory of the blessed God (1 Tim. 1:11), nine times the gospel of (Jesus) Christ, once the gospel of God's Son (Rom. 1:9), once the gospel of the glory of Christ (2 Cor. 4:4), once the gospel of our Lord Jesus (2 Thess. 1:8), three times the gospel of the kingdom, once the gospel of peace (Eph. 6:15, which goes much further than peace for the human conscience), once the gospel of the grace of God (Acts 20:24, in v. 25 linked with preaching the kingdom), and only once the "gospel of your salvation" (Eph. 1:13; but cf. 1 Cor. 15:1–2). The gospel is *not* primarily about our needs as sinners; how anthropocentric to think that it is. The gospel is primarily theocentric: it is about (the glory of) God himself, and about (the glory) of his Christ (Messiah), and about "the mystery of his will, according to his purpose, which he set forth in Christ as a plan for the fullness of time, to unite all things in him, things in heaven and things on earth" (Eph. 1:9–10), in short: the kingdom. God's plan entails not primarily bringing saved sinners to heaven, but rescuing this world out of the bonds of Satan, sin, and death, and restoring it to his own glory in Christ. The forgiveness of our sins, no matter how important, is subservient to this; it is not the goal but a means.

Now look at the covenants again. Which of them is about bringing saved sinners to heaven? None whatsoever. "Going to heaven" is not even mentioned in any of the covenants. The only explicit reference to the problem of sin within the context of any covenant is in the New Covenant: "I will forgive their iniquity, and I will remember their sin no more" (Jer. 31:34). But even here, this forgiveness is not the goal of the New Covenant; it is only part of the means to the goal. The true goal is a redeemed nation of Israel, back in the promised land, under the glorious blessing of God; as Jeremiah says in the same context: "Again I will build you, and you shall be built, O virgin Israel! Again you shall adorn yourself with tambourines and shall go forth in the dance of the merrymakers. Again you shall plant vineyards on the mountains of Samaria; the planters shall plant and shall enjoy the fruit. For there shall be a day when watchmen will call in the hill country of Ephraim: 'Arise, and let us go up to Zion, to the LORD our God'" (vv. 4–6). One should simply read all of Jeremiah 31 (or 30–31) to get the complete picture.

## 9.2     Covenant and Kingdom
### 9.2.1  The Earlier Covenants and the Kingdom
First, look at the alleged *covenant with postlapsarian Adam*. Is it about the salvation of sinners? Of course, that is included.

But the *protevangelium* of Genesis 3:15 is not about that, but explicitly about the offspring of the first woman who one day would bruise the head of the serpent (cf. Rev. 12:9; 20:2). The implication is that, one day, this Seed thus destroys the kingdom of Satan and establishes his own kingdom. The Lamb in the book of Revelation is certainly there to free believers from their sins (1:5; 5:9), but the main message of the book is the wondrous story of a Lamb defeating a dragon (12:1-11; 17:14; 19:11-21), and establishing his own empire: "The kingdom of the world has become the kingdom of our Lord and of his Christ, and he shall reign forever and ever" (11:15), and: "Now the salvation and the power and the kingdom of our God and the authority of his Christ have come, for the accuser of our brothers has been thrown down, who accuses them day and night before our God" (12:10).

Forgiveness of sins is not the goal, but a means to a goal: he "made us a kingdom" (1:6; cf. 5:10). The point is not "going to heaven" but reigning triumphantly with Christ: "Then I saw an angel coming down from heaven, holding in his hand the key to the bottomless pit and a great chain. And he seized the dragon, that ancient serpent, who is the devil and Satan, and bound him for a thousand years. . . . [The martyrs] came to life and reigned with Christ for a thousand years . . . they will be priests of God and of Christ, and they will reign with him for a thousand years" (20:1-6).

Second, was the *Noahic covenant* about the salvation of sinners and bringing them to heaven? Not at all. Is it about the kingdom? Implicitly most emphatically. The Noahic covenant is not just about "common grace" (whatever that may be), but is based on a sacrifice prefiguring the sacrifice of Christ. Through the flood, Noah and his family reached a "new world," which was placed on the basis of the sacrifice, thus anticipating the new world that once will be inaugurated on the basis of Christ's work on the cross (cf. 1 Pet. 3:18-22). Jesus not only bore our sins: he "overcame the world" (John 16:33), thus paving the way for a new world: the kingdom of the Son of Man (Matt. 13:41; 16:27-28; 19:28; 24:30-31; 25:31; 26:64).

The rainbow of Genesis 9 reappears in the book of Revelation as a token of God's glory preparing the kingdom (4:3): there is a "mighty angel coming down from heaven, wrapped in a cloud, with a rainbow over his head, and his face was like the sun, and his legs like pillars of fire . . . he set his right foot on the sea, and his left foot on the land" (10:1). This is quite suggestive of King Jesus, conquering the world. It is the Messianic kingdom that will bring the final fulfillment of Genesis 9:27 (part of the Noahic polity), "May God enlarge Japheth, and let him dwell in the tents of Shem." Compare: "many peoples shall come, and say: 'Come, let us go up to the mountain of the LORD, to the house of the God of Jacob, that he may teach us his ways and that we may walk in his paths'" (Isa. 2:3). "Many peoples and strong nations shall come to seek the LORD of hosts in Jerusalem and to entreat the favor of the LORD. Thus says the LORD of hosts: 'In those days ten men from the nations of every tongue shall take hold of the robe of a Jew, saying, "Let us go with you, for we have heard that God is with you"'" (Zech. 8:22-23).

Third, was the *Abrahamic covenant* about the salvation of sinners and bringing them to heaven? Not at all. Of course, Abram "believed the LORD, and he counted it to him as righteousness" (Gen. 15:6), and in the New Testament this is related to justification by faith (Rom. 4:3, 9, 18, 22; Gal. 3:6; James 2:23). But this does not pertain to the *content* of the Abrahamic covenant as such. Of course, Abraham "was looking forward to the city that has foundations, whose designer and builder is God" (Heb. 11:10). But again, this does not pertain to the *content* of the Abrahamic covenant as such. This content involved two things, and nothing else (see Gen. 15): (a) a large (physical!) posterity, and (b) a wonderful land where this posterity would live under God's blessing. As a confirmation, God gave Abraham the sign of circumcision (Gen. 17). But tell me, what more does the Abrahamic covenant *as such* contain, beside these two things: a progeny and a land?

To be sure, in Abraham and in his offspring, respectively, all the nations would be blessed (Gen. 12:3; 18:18; 22:18; 26:4; cf. Acts 3:25; Gal. 3:8). However, this blessing is not primarily the salvation of sinners and bringing them to heaven, but the Messianic kingdom, where all nations will be blessed through the people of Israel restored in its land: "The nations shall see and be ashamed of all their [i.e., Israel's] might . . . they shall come trembling out of their strongholds; they shall turn in dread to the LORD our God, and they shall be in fear of you [i.e., Israel]. . . . You [i.e., God] will show faithfulness to Jacob and steadfast love to Abraham, as you have sworn to our fathers from the days of old" (Micah 7:16-17, 20; cf. 4:1-5; Ps. 72; Isa. 11:10; 25:6-8; 56:3-7; 60:1-22; Jer. 3:17; Zeph. 3:9; Zech. 8:20-23; 14:16; Mal. 1:11).

### 9.2.2 The Later Covenants and the Kingdom

Fourth, was the *Sinaitic covenant* about the salvation of sinners and bringing them to heaven? Not at all. Its primary significance was not even that of leading Israel to Christ (although God used it as a means to this goal). No, the purpose of the Old Covenant was this: "[I]f you will . . . obey my voice and keep my covenant, you shall be my treasured possession among all peoples, for all the earth is mine; and you shall be to me a kingdom of priests and a holy nation" (Exod. 19:5-6). God's purpose was a kingdom whose core would be Israel. They had already sung of this: "The LORD will reign [or, will be King] forever and ever" (Exod. 15:18). And Balaam said, "The shout of a king [or, the King] is among them" (Num. 23:21). "Thus the LORD became King in Jeshurun [i.e., Israel], when the heads of the people were gathered, all the tribes of Israel together" (Deut. 33:5). The Sinaitic covenant has in view as its goal the Messianic kingdom, not bringing saved sinners to heaven.

Fifth, was the *Palestinian covenant* about the salvation of sinners and bringing them to heaven? Not at all. It was about bringing Israel into the promised land, nothing else. Even if Israel were to backslide, God would never forget his primary and unshakable goal: "And when[5] all these things come upon you, the blessing and the curse, which I have set before you, and you . . . return to the LORD your God, you and your children, and obey his voice in all that I command you today, with all your heart and with all your soul, then the LORD your God will restore your fortunes and have mercy on you, and he will gather you again from all the peoples where the LORD your God has scattered you. . . . And the LORD your God *will bring you into the land that your fathers possessed, that you may possess it*. And he will make you more prosperous and numerous than your fathers. And the LORD your God will circumcise your heart and the heart of your offspring, so that you will love the LORD your God with all your heart and with all your soul, that you may live. . . . The LORD your God will make you abundantly prosperous in all the work of your hand, in the fruit of your womb and in the fruit of your cattle and in the fruit of your ground. For the LORD will again take delight in prospering you, as he took delight in your fathers" (Deut. 30:1–9).

To be sure, this restoration of Israel includes the forgiveness of their sins and the circumcision of their hearts. However, (a) this is not the goal, but a means to the goal: Israel's full (spiritual as well as physical) restoration; and (b) this is not about going to heaven at all, or even about going to the new heavens and the new earth, but about returning to the land that Israel's fathers had possessed, and out of which they had been driven.

Sixth, was the *Levitical covenant* about the salvation of sinners and bringing them to heaven? Not at all. Its purpose was to contribute to "a kingdom of priests and a holy nation" (Exod. 19:6). Its highest goal will be that the descendants of Levi, more specifically, of the priest Zadok, living in David's

---

5. Heb. *ki*, not *im* ("if"); temporal, not conditional.

lifetime, will minister in the temple of Jerusalem in the Messianic kingdom (Ezek. 40:46; 43:19; 44:15; 48:11; cf. 2 Sam. 8:17; 15:24-36).

Seventh, was the *Davidic covenant* about the salvation of sinners and bringing them to heaven? Not at all. It contained the promise that David would always have a descendant sitting on his throne, and ruling over Israel. His greatest son would be the Messiah, who would receive the throne of his father David (Luke 1:32). "The LORD swore to David a sure oath from which he will not turn back: 'One of the sons of your body I will set on your throne....' For the LORD has chosen Zion; he has desired it for his dwelling place: 'This is my resting place forever; here I will dwell, for I have desired it.... There I will make a horn to sprout for David; I have prepared a lamp for my anointed. His enemies I will clothe with shame, but on him his crown will shine'" (Ps. 132:11-18). "For to us a child is born, to us a son is given; and the government shall be upon his shoulder, and his name shall be called Wonderful Counselor, Mighty God, Everlasting Father, Prince of Peace. Of the increase of his government and of peace there will be no end, on the throne of David and over his kingdom, to establish it and to uphold it with justice and with righteousness from this time forth and forevermore" (Isa. 9:6-7).

Eighth, is the *New Covenant* about the salvation of sinners and bringing them to heaven? Not primarily. The book of Hebrews speaks extensively about the blotting out of sins, but points primarily to the kingdom: "Therefore he [i.e., Jesus] is the mediator of a new covenant, so that those who are called may receive the promised eternal inheritance" (9:15). This "eternal inheritance" is not a place in heaven, nor even a place in the new heavens and the new earth, but a share in the "world to come" (2:5), in the "age to come" (6:5); it is about "receiving a kingdom that cannot be shaken" (12:28). Even the "heavenly country" (11:16) is not about "going to heaven" the way Christians have traditionally viewed this, but it is, so to speak, the heavenly side ("upper story") of the coming kingdom, of which the "city to come" (13:14; cf. 11:10, 16; 12:22) will be, as it were, the heavenly capital (cf. the "Jerusalem above," Gal. 4:26).

To be sure, the blood of the New Covenant is for the forgiveness of sins (cf. Matt. 26:28), and that is an unspeakably great blessing. However, I repeat: forgiveness is not the goal, but the means to the actual goal. The goal is eventually to bring forgiven and redeemed sinners into the Messianic kingdom. The goal is not *our* redemption but *God's* glory: "Blessed be his glorious name forever; may the whole earth be filled with his glory!" (Ps. 72:19). "For the earth will be filled with the knowledge of the glory of the LORD as the waters cover the sea" (Hab. 2:14; cf. Isa. 11:9). After all, the gospel is "the gospel of the glory of the blessed God" (1 Tim. 1:11); Paul speaks of "the light of the gospel of the glory of Christ, who is the image of God" (2 Cor. 4:4), and says: "[H]e called you through our gospel, so that you may obtain the glory of our Lord Jesus Christ" (2 Thess. 2:14).

## 9.3 Christianity Is Not Federalist
### 9.3.1 Problems of Federalism

From all that has been said so far, it may have become clear what characterizes an Evangelical view of the covenant, as I see it. I will first summarize this in an antithetical (negative) way, and thereafter in a positive way, limiting myself to the meaning the covenant might have for Jesus-believers in the present dispensation:

(a) Scripture speaks neither explicitly nor implicitly of a covenant with Adam, whether with the prelapsarian Adam (the alleged covenant of works), or the postlapsarian Adam (the alleged covenant of grace). Hosea 6:7 is highly insufficient evidence.

(b) Scripture speaks neither explicitly nor implicitly of one single covenant of which all postlapsarian covenants would be varieties, a covenant that is commonly referred to as the "covenant of grace." To Israel belong "the covenants" (plural)

(Rom. 9:4; Eph. 2:12). The New Testament clearly distinguishes between the Abrahamic covenant (Gal. 3) and the New Covenant (especially Heb. 8-9). Each version of covenant theology has to discern very clearly what partners are involved in each covenant, and not lump the covenants together. This condition is not fulfilled by simplistically identifying Abraham's progeny, Israel, with the church as some "spiritual Israel," that is, by not distinguishing between Israel and the Ekklesia in God's redemptive plan.[6]

(c) Those who make a fundamental distinction between a covenant of works and a covenant of grace overlook the fact that the alleged covenant of works is full of grace—not incidentally, but essentially—while the alleged covenant of grace can never be in force apart from the responsibility of the covenant members to perform works: both a surrender in faith to God (Gen. 15:6) and "walking blamelessly in all the commandments and statutes of the Lord" (cf. Luke 1:6) are indispensable. There is no alleged covenant of works without an abundance of divine grace, and there is no alleged covenant of grace without the moral obligation of works that are the fruit of faith (Rom. 2:13; James 2:14-16). No matter how strongly it is emphasized that under the New Covenant, believers' works are accomplished through the grace of God and the power of his Spirit—which is perfectly true—this does not change the principle: no covenant of grace exists without works. This being so, we must conclude that both phrases, the "covenant of works" and the "covenant of grace," are misnomers. We will come back to this important matter in the third volume of the present series, which will discuss the issue of whether we are justified by faith and/or works.

Please note that two errors add to the confusion. First, in Reformed theology "grace" is usually restricted too much to "saving grace." It is a weakness of Western theology—including Roman Catholic, Lutheran, Anglican, and Evangeli-

---

6. See extensively Ouweneel (2010b).

cal thinking—that the problem of sin and its solution are so prominent. Therefore, some theologians can no longer think of "grace" apart from the problem of sin. Second, Reformed theology still suffers from "the Arminian trauma," evident in its fear of leaving too much room for human responsibility.[7] We have seen that every attempt to create such room invariably calls forth protests from those who complain that God's sovereignty is being attacked (see §5.6 and Appendix III).

(d) Apart from the Noahic covenant, the biblical covenants primarily involve Israel. To be sure, in the Abrahamic covenant and the New Covenant, blessing is promised for Gentiles outside the actual sphere of these covenants. However, the Sinaitic, Palestinian, Levitical, and Davidic covenants involve Israel exclusively. Federalism does not distinguish between those who are the factual covenant partners (Abraham, Isaac, and Jacob, and their physical descendants) and those who do profit by a covenant but who themselves are, strictly speaking, not covenant partners. If a king makes a covenant with his vassals, all their subjects profit thereby, even if they themselves are not covenant partners. When Jacob and Laban made a covenant (Gen. 31:22–55), their families benefited from it, even though the family members were not the actual covenant partners. Earlier, I argued that the Ekklesia has come under the umbrella or into the courtyard of the New Covenant, without itself becoming Israel. Japheth dwells in the tents of Shem without becoming Shem (Gen. 9:27).

(e) Federalism relates the biblical covenants, which all involve Israel—even to a certain extent the Noahic covenant (Gen. 9:27)—to the church (see chapter 7). As we have seen, this is possible only by asserting that the church is some "spiritual Israel." This doctrine commits two errors: it not only ignores the true character of the Ekklesia (see §9.8.2 and chapter 7), but it also robs ethnic Israel of its unique position and blessings. Those who believe they have freed themselves of

---

7. See extensively Ouweneel (2008b).

supersessionism because they accept the literal future national restoration of ethnic Israel, but who still believe that that restored Israel will find a place within the church—freed from anything that is typically Jewish!—are utterly mistaken. For instance, Reformed theologian Jan Hoek believes in the future national restoration of ethnic Israel, but still identifies the "all Israel" of Romans 11:26 with "the one church of Christ."[8] His co-author, Willem Verboom, calls the olive tree of verses 16–24 "Israel."[9] *Extra ecclesiam nulla salus*, "Outside the church there is no salvation." For supersessionists this also holds for ethnic Israel: its future is within the "de-jewishified" church.[10]

(f) Federalism has the character of a theoretical-theological paradigm, which through the inner dynamics of its own logic both removes itself ever further from biblical parlance, and gets more and more entangled within itself, given the many, mutually exclusive views within the Reformed world. This paradigm is so powerful that only those Reformed theologians who develop an ever-broader ecumenical-Christian horizon, such as Hendrikus Berkhof, find the inner strength to rise about this paradigm (naturally without necessarily throwing overboard *all* its elements, as I myself would not like to do either).

(g) Since Reformed theology has claimed many times that the doctrine of infant baptism rests in covenantal theology, the conclusion is painful: according to its own testimony, without covenantal theology, in whatever Reformed form, the foundation under infant baptism collapses. I venture the thesis that every theologian who, on the basis of covenantal theology, adheres to infant baptism, is and remains a supersessionist at heart (see further Appendix I for references).

---

8. J. Hoek in Hoek and Verboom (2010, 39).
9. W. Verboom in Hoek and Verboom (2010, 71).
10. This is also the standpoint of Gentry and Wellum (2012); on this, see Ouweneel (2009, 48–49).

### 9.3.2 Six "-isms"

In summary, as far as I can see, federalism suffers from at least six insurmountable problems, caused by six "-isms".

(1) *Theologism*. In Reformed federalism, we are dealing with the introduction of a theological construct, which was not directly derived from Scripture, and therefore *a priori* brings serious risks with it. Moreover, this construct has been elevated to *the* hermeneutical key for all theology. This cannot be reconciled with Scripture's overall language. By reading everything in Scripture through covenantal glasses, two subjects will especially suffer from this. First, the theologically highly important subject of the kingdom of God will suffer. Second, a proper view of the quintessentially Christian blessings of the Ekklesia is lost, as I hope to show below. Federalism is like a fishing net, which is sized to catch every covenant fish from the sea of the Word, while allowing many of the fish that are essentially Christian though non-covenantal to slip through.

(2) *Confessionalism*. Unfortunately, a number of federalist speculations have found a place in the Westminster Standards (thank God, far fewer are enshrined in the Three Forms of Unity). This has made the controversy all the more severe, because it is no longer a fight against certain theological theories but against confessional and catechism statements that for many have become non-negotiable, even sacrosanct. It is one thing to disagree with, say, Perkins and Witsius, but it is a very different thing to disagree with official Presbyterian church documents. In the eyes of many, to differ from Ursinus or Owen is serious enough; to differ from the Westminster Standards is outright heresy, which renders the suspected heretic liable to church discipline, if we may believe men like John M. Otis and Brian Schwertley. A discussion with such Westminster loyalists is impossible because they are not willing to question even the smallest detail in the Westminster Standards. This is strange, because even they should re-

alize that all creeds, confessions, and catechisms are necessarily fallible documents. If these function on the same level as Scripture itself, we are no better than Roman Catholics with their strong emphasis on tradition.

(3) *Electionism*. Federalism suffers under the pervasively confusing influence of the doctrine of double predestination. Apparently, Reformed theologians do not *dare* to begin with repentance and faith, that is, with human responsibility, out of sheer dread of being accused of being an Anabaptist or an Arminian. I myself am not an Arminian—I believe in God's sovereign predestination of believers—but I am not afraid to emphasize human responsibility. Faith is a gift of God (Eph. 2:8), so beginning with faith does not necessarily endanger God's sovereignty at all (cf. Appendix III). What I mean to say is that every covenant doctrine that is governed by the doctrine of double predestination gets lost amid insuperable problems.

(4) *Remissionism*. Federalists declare God's forgiveness ("remission") of sins, his redemptive grace for poor sinners, and getting them to heaven, to be the core of "the" (biblical) gospel. However, as we saw, the redemption of sinners is never an end in itself, but always only a means to an end. That end or goal is not some place in heaven, but the kingdom of God on earth. Federalism even goes so far as to claim that all postlapsarian covenants are just varieties of the *one* covenant of grace, which is specifically God's redemptive grace for sinners. In reality, *none* of those covenants is about God's redemptive grace as such.

(5) *Supersessionism*. This is *the* fundamental problem of federalism: the doctrine that the church has been incorporated into Israel, and is now factually the "true Israel," the "spiritual Israel," the "Israel of God." Conversely, this means that the Jew who wishes to receive God's eternal blessings must surrender everything about himself that is typically Jewish, and must join the church, 99% of which is Gentile, governed

## An Evangelical Covenant Theology

by Gentile Christians, and a strongly Gentile (Greek-Roman oriented) theology. This is both a misjudgment of Israel and a misjudgment of the Ekklesia. I repeat: Israel is a *natural*, ethnic people; one joins it through birth and circumcision. The Ekklesia is a *spiritual* people; one joins it through rebirth and personal faith. On the one hand, federalism makes the Ekklesia too Jewish ("we are the true Israel"), thus missing out on the specific nature and blessings of the Ekklesia (chapter 7 and §§9.6–9.8 below). On the other hand, federalism makes Israel too un-Jewish by falsely claiming that the civil and ceremonial parts of the Mosaic Torah have been abolished.

(6) *Spiritualism*. From a hermeneutical point of view, this is certainly the greatest problem with federalism (see Appendix IV). To me, the way in which dozens of Old Testament prophecies, often with many geographical details, are spiritualized, that is, are robbed of their literal meaning, is quite disturbing. God tells us that Israel is driven out of its land because of its sins, but after repentance will *return* to *precisely the same* land he had given to their fathers, a return that occurs not only after the Babylonian captivity, but in the *eschaton*. However, federalists tell us that the people returning to this land in the end time is not Israel but the church, and that this land is not Canaan but some heavenly country. I do realize that this approach has been followed generally from the fourth century onward, but that does not make it correct. It is a shocking violation of genuine hermeneutical principles of exegesis.

### 9.4 Again, the Abrahamic Covenant
### 9.4.1 Two Promises

The believers belonging to the Ekklesia are referred to as spiritual progeny of Abraham: he is the "father of all who believe without being circumcised, so that righteousness would be counted to them as well" (Rom. 4:11); he is "the father of us all" (v. 16). "Know then that it is those of faith who are the sons of Abraham. And the Scripture, foreseeing that God would justify the Gentiles by faith, preached the gospel beforehand to Abraham, saying, 'In you shall all the nations be blessed.' So then, those who are of faith are blessed along with Abraham, the man of faith" (Gal. 3:7-9). "And if you are Christ's, then you are Abraham's offspring, heirs according to promise" (v. 29).

The New Testament nowhere says that the Abrahamic covenant, let alone the covenant in a general sense, has been made with the Gentile believers of the Ekklesia as well. Rather they seem to belong to the "families" or "nations" of the earth who "in" the patriarchs receive the divine blessing (Gen. 12:3; 18:18; 22:18; 26:4; 28:4). Strictly speaking, the Gentile believers are not covenant partners at all, but they do receive blessings together with the actual (Jewish) covenant partners.

It is striking to see in what sense Paul seems to suggest a connection between the Abrahamic promises and the Holy Spirit: "... so that in Christ Jesus the blessing of Abraham might come to the Gentiles, so that we might receive the promised Spirit through faith" (Gal. 3:14). This verse offers us a typical example of the fact that, whereas for Reformed Christians the covenant blessing is the highest conceivable blessing, this is apparently *not* the case for Paul.[11] The first subordinate clause is a summary of verses 6-13: Jews as well as Gentiles receive "the" blessing exclusively through faith (see v. 14b), not through works of the law. Through this faith, they become sons of Abraham in the spiritual sense of the word, and thus are entitled to the "blessing of Abraham."

This blessing is actually a rather broad concept, but in the present context it apparently refers primarily to justification by faith. This blessing accrues to the believers through Christ, who himself is *the* Son of Abraham (v. 16). He is the One who for them has undergone the curse of God at the cross. In Romans 3:24-25, Paul shows precisely what elements are involved in this justification of those who come to faith:

(a) *tē autou chariti* ("by his grace"; a dative without a prep-

---

11. See Ouweneel (1997, 192–95).

osition); this is *God's* side: he is the One who bestows this grace upon Man;

(b) *dia tēs apolytrōseōs* ("through the redemption"); this is *Christ's* side: he is the One who has brought about this redemption for Man;

(c) *dia (tēs) pisteōs* ("through faith"); this is the *human* side: people are the ones who must believe, that is, entrust themselves to God, to Christ, and to the work of Christ;

(d) *en tōi autou haimati* ("in [the power of] his blood"); this is again *Christ's* side: he is the One who gave his blood for Man.

According to the context in Galatians 3, the second subordinate clause ("so that we might receive the promised Spirit through faith") does not depend on the first one, but in its own way refers back to Paul's preceding words, especially verses 1–5. This promise of the Spirit did not belong whatsoever to the things that had been promised to Abraham, or "in" Abraham to the nations. It does not belong to the actual "blessing of Abraham" in any sense whatsoever. Abraham believed God, and because of this fact he was justified, that is, declared righteous. He believed that God was going to fulfill all his promises in the "son of promise," who for him was Isaac (cf. Rom. 9:9; Gal. 4:23). Likewise, all those who put their trust in God, who fulfills all his promises in the "Son of promise," who for them is Jesus (cf. 2 Cor. 1:20), are sons of Abraham, that is, are blessed in and with Abraham.

However, one thing Abraham did not receive, and this was the Holy Spirit. At least Scripture is silent on this. I am not saying that the Holy Spirit did not *work* in Abraham; how else could he have been born again and put his trust in God, and how else could he have "seen" the "day of Christ" (John 8:56) and the heavenly city (Heb. 11:10, 16)? What I am saying is that the Holy Spirit never came to dwell in him (cf. John 14:17; Rom. 8:9, 11); his body could not be called a temple of God in which God's Spirit dwelt (1 Cor. 6:19). This indwelling is the prerogative of those who have believed on and after the day of Pentecost (Acts 2). Abraham did not even receive a *promise* concerning the Spirit with a view to his posterity. Since Acts 2 and 10, Jews and Gentiles who, in view of their salvation, entrust themselves to God and to Christ and his work, are declared righteous *and* they receive the Holy Spirit. But this emphatically surpasses the terms of the Abrahamic covenant as such. This is a first example of a blessing that surpasses the promised covenant blessings.

## 9.4.2 Continuity and Discontinuity

At the end of the previous section, we found a clear example of *discontinuity*: Old Testament believers did not receive the Holy Spirit, apart from some special ministers (especially judges and prophets), and this never in the sense of a permanent indwelling (cf. Ps. 51:11b with John 14:17 and 1 Cor. 6:19).[12] However, post-Pentecost believers did and do receive the Holy Spirit permanently dwelling in them, not because they are better but because they live in the present redemptive-historical era.

Likewise, all believers since Abraham, in both the Old and the New Testaments, are children of Abraham. That is *continuity*. However, Old Testament believers were not "sons of God" in the sense of Galatians 3:26 and 4:6, but the New Testament believers are.[13] That is *discontinuity*. These two matters, Spirit-indwelling and sonship, are closely related: no adoption as sons of God without the Spirit of adoption (Rom. 8:15; Gal. 4:6). Exodus 4:22 is no counter-proof, for that verse refers to *ethnic* Israel collectively, while Deuteronomy 14:1 ("You are the sons of the LORD your God") refers to the distinct members of ethnic Israel, *regenerate or not*. (God is Father of Israel in the sense of Creator; see, e.g., Isa. 64:8; Mal. 2:10.) Hosea 1:10 is no counter-proof either, for this verse involves a prophecy that is fulfilled only under the New Covenant,

---

12. See Ouweneel (2007a, 129–36).
13. Ouweneel, (1997, 198n18).

when the people of Israel will entirely consist of righteous members (Isa. 45:25; 60:21; cf. 33:24b).

The "promise of the Spirit," that is, the "promise from the Father" (Acts 1:4; 2:33), is *not* an Abrahamic promise,[14] but surpasses it. It is a promise linked with (a) the glorified Lord at God's right hand (Eph. 1:20-21), (b) the Ekklesia that "in him" is seated in the heavenly places (2:6), and (c) the Holy Spirit living on earth in the Ekklesia (1 Cor. 3:16; 2 Cor. 6:16; Eph. 2:20-22) and in the bodies of the individual believers (1 Cor. 6:19). These three elements belong to the essence of Christianity (see below and chapter 7), and at the same time all three surpass the Old Testament covenant promises. Therefore, "the" covenant does *not* constitute the essence of Christianity at all but at best belongs to the Old Testament foundations thereof.

First, there is what is called the Abrahamic blessing: apart from the promised posterity and the promised land, believers of the Old as well as of the New Testaments have been justified by basically the same faith, that is, confidence in God's promises, as anchored in the "Son of promise," and they have received the same life of God through regeneration. This is Old/New Testament *continuity*.

Second, there is that which surpasses the Abrahamic blessing: Old Testament believers did not have the Holy Spirit permanently dwelling in them, and New Testament believers (since Acts 2) do. Therefore, the former have not been adopted as sons because they never received the Spirit of adoption, but the latter have. This is Old/New Testament *discontinuity*.[15]

It is no wonder that Reformed theology, which thinks in such an Old Testament fashion and is not tired of stressing that the blessings of Christians are "covenant" blessings, traditionally has had little room for the Holy Spirit (except when it comes to regeneration and biblical inspiration).[16] If they had,

---

14. *Contra*, e.g., paedobaptist Vander Zee (2004, 125).
15. Cf. Ouweneel (1997, 251–54).
16. See extensively Ouweneel (2007a, especially chapter 2).

they would have developed a clearer view of those Christian blessings that surpass any promised covenant blessing.

## 9.5 Again, the New Covenant
### 9.5.1 Hebrews 7-12

In Jeremiah 31:31-34, the New Covenant is explicitly made with the house of Israel and the house of Judah. For those who are not supersessionists or spiritualists, and who do not believe that the church is some "spiritual Israel" (see chapter 7), this fact is of the greatest importance. The entire context of Jeremiah 30-34 is thoroughly Israelite: these chapters are about the restoration of literal Israel in the literal Holy Land, around the literal city of Jerusalem, with a literal throne of David, with a literal Messiah sitting thereon. Nowhere in either the Old or the New Testaments is it said that this covenant is made with still other groups, namely, with the church, or the Gentile part of the church. The fact that Gentiles receive a share in the blessings of this covenant is evident, but that is a very different matter.

I must settle a score here with classical dispensationalism as well. *Contra* this school, I maintain that the Ekklesia definitely does involve the New Covenant. As we saw, Jesus speaks about it at the institution of the last supper (Luke 22:20; 1 Cor. 11:25): the "blood of the covenant" (cf. Exod. 24:8; Matt. 26:28; Heb. 9:20; 10:29; 13:20) is for the forgiveness of the sins "for many," which includes Gentile believers.[17] The book of Hebrews often speaks of the Old and the New Covenants (7:22; 8:6-10; 9:1, 4, 15-20; 10:16, 29; 12:24; 13:20). To be sure, this always refers to "Hebrews," that is here, Jesus-believing Jews, yet who emphatically are part of the Ekklesia (12:23; cf. 2:12).

The concrete blessings of the New Covenant are for both Jewish and Gentile believers: salvation (Heb. 7:22-25), the promise of the eternal inheritance (9:15), forgiveness of sins

---

17. For ultra-dispensationalists, as represented by Bullinger (1972), this argument is not valid because they astonishingly believe that the Lord's Supper was not intended for the Ekklesia.

(vv. 19–20; 10:16–18; cf. 12:24), sanctification (10:29). These are precious blessings, but none of them are quintessentially *Christian* blessings. In other words, these are blessings that New Testament believers have in common with Old Testament believers, *not* blessings that New Testament believers possess but Old Testament believers do not possess (see next §§).

What seems to come closest to the quintessentially Christian blessings is the promise of the eternal inheritance. However, this is only superficially the case. Such expressions in Hebrews are always connected with the Messianic kingdom.[18] Israel was the object of an earthly calling, in view of an earthly land and material blessings, but it had lost these through breaking the covenant. Soon, at the start of the Messianic kingdom, a reconciled Israel will yet see its earthly calling fulfilled, and receive its earthly inheritance in the age to come. However, the Hebrews who in the present age had come to faith would not receive this earthly inheritance. When Israel receives it, the (Jewish and Gentile) Jesus-believers, belonging to the Ekklesia will be with Christ in the glory (Heb. 2:10), and will see their *heavenly* calling (cf. 3:1) fulfilled *there*, and will receive a heavenly inheritance. Together with the patriarchs they look forward to a *heavenly* city and a *heavenly* land (Heb. 11:10, 16).

This is not simply "going to heaven" as traditional Christianity (Catholic and Protestant) usually speaks of it—a notion hardly known in the New Testament.[19] The author refers to the Hebrews' glorious inheritance *in the Messianic kingdom*: they will reign with Christ forever (cf. Rev. 22:5). This concerns an eternal inheritance, just as the book of Hebrews

---

18. Ouweneel (1982, II, 19 and passim).
19. Luke 16:22–26; 23:43 (cf. 2 Cor. 12:3; Rev. 2:7); 2 Cor. 5:1–9 and Phil. 1:23 refer—in metaphorical language—only to the intermediate state (between death and resurrection); John 14:1–3 refers to the coming of Christ and the heavenly temple (cf. 2:16; Rev. 11:19; 14:15, 17; 16:1, 17), which is always in connection with the kingdom of God. See extensively Ouweneel (2012, chapters 1–2).

speaks of an "eternal salvation" (5:9), an "eternal judgment" (6:2), "eternal redemption" (9:12) and an "eternal covenant" (13:20). This inheritance is reserved for the Ekklesia, but also for the Old Testament believers, because at the second coming *all* the "dead in Christ" will be caught up to meet the Lord (1 Thess. 4:16-17). Thus, the eternal inheritance, just like reigning with Christ, does not involve specific Christian blessings either.

## 9.5.2 Second Corinthians 3

In 2 Corinthians 3:6, Paul calls the apostles "ministers of the new covenant," that is, God's servants who administer the New Covenant to the believers of the present age. Paul seems to relativize this to some extent by adding: "not of the letter but of the Spirit." Several explanations of this phrase have been given,[20] but one valid exegesis appears to be: "not literally," for there cannot be a New Covenant for Gentile Jesus-believers if there had never been an Old Covenant for them. However, the New Covenant *is* "of the Spirit," in the sense of verses 2-3: "You yourselves are our letter of recommendation, written on our hearts, to be known and read by all. And you show that you are a letter from Christ delivered by us, written not with ink but with the Spirit of the living God, not on tablets of stone but on tablets of human hearts."

The parallel with Jeremiah 31:31-34 is obvious, but at the same time Paul surpasses Jeremiah's prophecy.

(a) Under the Old Covenant, God wrote on tablets of *stone*. Under the New Covenant the Spirit of God writes on "tablets of *flesh*" (as it says literally), that is, on the hearts of the regenerate and justified Israel, and of all those who come under the umbrella of the New Covenant.

(b) Under the Old Covenant, it was the (Mosaic) Torah that was written down. Under the New Covenant it is the (Messianic) Torah, more specifically, *Christ himself*, that is written down, and in the age to come the (Millennial) Torah.

---
20. See, e.g., Hughes (1962, i.l.); Bernard (1979, i.l.); Barnett (1997, i.l.).

For the rest, the ministry of the New Covenant is described in 2 Corinthians 3 as a "ministry of the Spirit" (v. 8) and as a "ministry of righteousness" (v. 9). We have seen, first, that the "ministry of the Spirit" ties in with what was quoted from verses 2-3: the Spirit writes Christ on the hearts of those who believe in him. At the end of the chapter, this is explained in more detail: "Now the Lord is the Spirit, and where the Spirit of the Lord is, there is freedom. And we all, with unveiled face, beholding the glory of the Lord, are being transformed into the same image from one degree of glory to another. For this comes from the Lord who is the Spirit" (vv. 17-18).

Second, the "ministry of righteousness" ties in with the close of the passage in Jeremiah 31: "I will forgive their iniquity, and I will remember their sin no more" (v. 34b). This is a ministry of righteousness because God shows himself to be righteous in declaring the Jesus-believer to be righteous (Rom. 3:25-26; cf. 1:16-17; 1 John 1:9).

God is *righteous* in justifying the penitent sinner because God owes this—reverently speaking—to the redemptive work of Christ. But he is *loving* and *gracious* if he, in addition to this, writes Christ in the believers' hearts, that is, transforms them into Christ's image. This is the New Covenant for all Jesus-believers, Jewish and Gentile: it contains God's justifying work and his writing his Torah in the believers' hearts, transforming them into the image of Christ. We have to do here exclusively with blessings that Jesus-believers share with *all* those who will have, or receive, a part in the blessings of the New Covenant, *not* the specifically Christian blessings, which neither the Old Testament believers will receive, nor the believers on earth during the Messianic kingdom.

Time and again, this has been the core of my argument: *as long as we remain in the sphere of the New Covenant as such, we will never arrive at the quintessentially Christian blessings.* Federalism is in danger of closing its own eyes, and our eyes, to anything *specifically* Christian. Its thinking is thoroughly along Old Testament lines, and along New Testament lines only insofar as these tie in with the former. Federalism has little or no room for that in which the New Testament essentially differs from the Old Testament. Of course, this essential difference does not at all "contradict" the Old Testament, but rather "supplements" it.

## 9.6 More Than Justification
### 9.6.1 Quintessentially Christian

The following sections contain a summary of what I have dealt with in previous publications, especially in my Evangelical Dogmatic Series.[21] This is — or ought to be — a central element in Evangelical theology: what is quintessentially Christian in Christianity is not covenantal at all but rather *what surpasses the covenantal*. If I understand the New Testament correctly, Christianity contains at least three elements that belong to its essence. *None of them is covenantal*, or to put it more strongly, they surpass both the Abrahamic and the New Covenants. These are:

(1) In connection with *God the Father*: the revelation of the Trinity, and along with this, the relationship between God the Father — who is explicitly the eternal Father of the eternal Son — and the individual New Testament believers as his children and sons. This is not the Father of the Old Testament, who is no more than the Creator of his people (cf. Deut. 32:6; Ps. 68:5; 103:13; Prov. 3:12; Isa. 63:16; 64:8; Jer. 3:4, 19; 31:9; Mal. 1:6; 2:10). The New Testament point is that, if the Son is a regenerate person's life, no one less than the eternal Father of the eternal Son has become that person's Father (cf. John 6:57; 17:21-23; 20:17; 1 John 5:11-12; see §9.8.1). *No covenant contains, or refers to, this blessing*. We see the Ekklesia here as the *Family of God*.

(2) In connection with *God the Son*: the union of the New Testament believers of the Ekklesia with Christ as the glorified *Man* at God's right hand in heaven, and as such the Head

---
21. See especially Ouweneel (2007a; 2008b; 2010a–c).

of his Body (Eph. 1:22-23; 2:6; 4:15-16; Col. 1:18; 2:19). *No covenant contains, or refers to, this blessing.* We see the Ekklesia here as the *Body of Christ*; this precious truth was fully unknown and unpredicted in past ages.

(3) In connection with *God the Spirit:* the permanent dwelling of the Holy Spirit in New Testament believers, both individually (John 14:16-17; 1 Cor. 6:19) and collectively (3:16; 2 Cor. 6:16; Eph. 2:20-22). *No covenant contains, or refers to, this blessing.* We see the Ekklesia here as the *House* or the *Temple of God.*

It is of the greatest importance to get this straight. Conversion, regeneration, forgiveness of sins, eternal salvation, justification by faith, are wonderful blessings, for which Christians cannot praise God enough. But they are the portion of all believers of all times, from postlapsarian Adam until the end of the Messianic kingdom. They are in no way the quintessentially Christian blessings, that is, those blessings that only believers of the Ekklesia receive, and no believers outside the Ekklesia, blessings that surpass all the covenants.

The danger of a thoroughly covenantal theology is that it loses sight of the essence of Christianity. I know of no Reformed confessional document that presents these great truths in their essential meaning: eternal life in the Johannine sense, the Ekklesia in its union with its glorified Head, both the Ekklesia and the individual believer as temples of the Holy Spirit, and the meaning of being baptized in, filled, anointed, and sealed with the Holy Spirit.

## 9.6.2 Justification

Let me mention a striking example of what I see as the imbalance in Reformed theology. In the third volume of the present series, I hope to show how central the doctrine of justification is in Lutheran and Reformed theology, and how in other Christian traditions this is not the case at all.[22] This is not to belittle the meaning of justification—on the contrary—but to

---

22. See Ouweneel (2010a, 168–71).

assign justification its proper place within the whole of Christian thinking.

According to the Lutheran and Reformed traditions, with the doctrine of justification we touch "the center of the Pauline message," "the main pillar on which religion rests," "not the preliminary matter, but the highest matter," the "cornerstone of Christian theology and the church." It is "the essence of the New Testament, the proper matter of the gospel," "the heart of the gospel," "the foundation and the core of the salvation of sinners who were lost by their fault"; "there is no more comforting facet of the entire Gospel than that of justification." Luther therefore called "justification by faith alone" *articulus stantis et cadentis ecclesiae*: the "article by which the church stands or falls."[23]

To the degree that the doctrine of justification is central in Reformed theology, to the same degree Reformed theologians are suspicious toward every theology claiming there is something more than justification by faith.[24] The German theologian Kurt Hutten characterized most sects that arose after the Reformation as going "a step beyond justification."[25] He viewed this as being unsatisfied with the *sola gratia* (by grace alone) and the *sola fide* (by faith alone) of the Reformation. The idea that there is more than what the Reformation has brought us seems to have been sacrilege to him, and to many other Protestant theologians with him.

For Reformed theologian Jan Hoek in the Netherlands, too, spirituality is nothing but "the justification of the wicked by faith in Christ only." He wondered, therefore, with respect to what he called the "Evangelical spirituality": "Is, in the latter, justification not too much a transitory phase in a process of growth?"[26] This is exactly what it is; it could not have been said in a clearer way. But for Hoek such a view is condem-

---

23. See for all these and other quotations, ibid., 168.
24. See Ouweneel (2007a, 235).
25. Hutten (1957).
26. Hoek (2006).

nable.

Already with the apostle Paul, we see how many things surpass justification by faith. To begin with, justification is followed by peace with God and the hope of the glory of God (Rom. 5:1-2). This is not only a future aim, for he says later in this epistle that believers have been "predestined to be conformed to the image of his Son, in order that he might be the firstborn among many brothers. And those whom he predestined he also called, and those whom he called he also justified, and those whom he justified he also glorified" (Rom. 8:29-30). Being conformed to the image of God's Son seems to coincide here more or less with being glorified. Both are prospective in their full sense (cf. Phil. 3:20-21), but at the same time they are matters to be realized already in the present life of the believers. This can take place only in the power of the Holy Spirit, of which Paul says, "[H]ope does not put us to shame, because God's love has been poured into our hearts through the Holy Spirit who has been given to us" (Rom. 5:5).

Even within Paul's epistle to the Romans we find things that surpass justification as such: peace with God, being glorified, that is, being conformed to the image of God's Son, having become children of God, having received the Spirit of adoption as sons (Rom. 8:14-16), etc. Must we assume that Paul is a sectarian, too, if he takes "steps beyond justification"? We have been regenerated, forgiven, and justified by the power of the Holy Spirit—but *receiving* the Spirit, who is the Spirit of adoption as sons and who comes to *dwell* in the New Testament believers, already surpasses justification as such. In §7.3.2, I explained the difference between being reborn by the power of the Spirit and receiving the Spirit in person, who comes to dwell within the believer.

So where is the difficulty for Reformed Christians? Why this fear of speaking about things that *surpass* justification, as if in this way the Christian blessings are belittled? Lutherans may have different reasons, perhaps historical ones, since

Luther's own practical experiences have become the standard for Lutheran believers as a whole. As far as Reformed Christians are concerned, federalism seems to explain at least part of their fear: it is the Reformed fear of anything that threatens to go beyond the confines of the Abrahamic and the New Covenants. A Reformed theologian is by definition limited to what the covenants have to offer him. A non-Reformed theologian is free to go beyond them, and thus to discover the surpassing blessings of Christianity.

## 9.7  Theosis
### 9.7.1  Conform to the Image

Whoever wishes to and is able to see it, will understand that 2 Peter 1:4 is one of those things that greatly surpass justification: becoming "partakers of the divine nature" (Greek *theias koinōnoi physeōs*).[27] This is not contained in justification as such. Being declared, or accounted, or made, to be righteous, is marvelous. But there is nothing therein that points to any partaking of the divine nature. Adam was created in the image of God; as such, he was a "son" of God (Luke 3:38). But that is something very different from being a "partaker of the divine nature."

This passage is one of the key verses for what Eastern Christians have called *theosis*.[28] Literally, this means "deification," but this is never meant to imply that Christians in any way become "gods." Rather, it means that they are (supposed to be) always getting nearer to God, always becoming more like him, until, by the power of the Holy Spirit, they are transformed into the image of Christ; that is, this image comes to full blossoming in them. They "become" Christ, so to speak, and Christ is the incarnated God the Son (John 1:14, 18). This

---

27. See on this verse, apart from the commentaries, also Wolters (1990; a covenantal viewpoint); Starr (2003); S. Finlan in Finlan and Kharlamov (2006, 32–50).
28. See Ouweneel (2007a, 234–36; 2010a, chapter 14); rather recent theologians who have built their entire theology on this *theosis* are Lossky (1974; 1998), Nellas (1987), and Stavropoulos (2003).

comes very near to deification, but it stops just short of this since we are not allowed to say that believers become God the Son.

Western theology certainly knows of this as well. Thomas Aquinas wrote: *theosis* is "full participation in the divinity, which is humanity's true bliss and the destination of human life."[29] Also in Calvin's writings, *theosis* is a common thought (even if the word does not occur).[30] He sees this being "partakers of the divine nature" as something that is realized when believers will be with Christ in glory, with reference to 1 John 3:2 ("when he appears, we shall be like him") and 2 Thessalonians 1:10 ("he comes on that day to be glorified in his saints"). My own impression is that this "partaking" is no more future than Romans 8:30 ("those whom he justified he also glorified").

I repeat, *theosis* does not mean that the chasm between Creator and creature has been removed, and that human beings would merge into the essence of God (this would employ the Greek term *apotheosis*, not *theosis*). Rather it means that people are brought into intimate communion with God, and that God's image becomes more and more visible in them.[31] In the person of Jesus, God has assumed human nature (John 1:14; Rom. 8:3; Heb. 2:14), so that humans could partake in the divine nature. The Son of God became Man, in order that humans can become sons of God. The glorification of their bodies is indeed in the future (cf. Phil. 3:20–21; Col. 3:4), but God's glory manifesting itself more and more through their human spirits is present tense: "For God, who said, 'Let light shine out of darkness,' has shone in our hearts to give the light of the knowledge of the glory of God in the face of Jesus Christ" (2 Cor. 4:6).

---

29. Summa Theologiae III.1.2.
30. M. Habets in Finlan and Kharlamov (2006, 146–67), referring to Calvin's *Institutes* 1.13.14, 2.7.1, 3.2.24, 3.11.10; 3.25.10; 4.17.2, 4, 11, and especially Calvin's commentary on 2 Peter (1:4).
31. So John Damascenus; but also, e.g., Calvin, *Institutes* 3.3.9.

For many Reformed Christians, salvation seems essentially to be nothing more than the restoration of the status that humanity had in the Garden of Eden before the fall. For instance, the Heidelberg Catechism tells us that the prelapsarian Adam had been created "in true righteousness and holiness" (Q&A 6), and the Westminster Confession of Faith says (IV.2): "He created man, male and female, with reasonable and immortal souls, endued with knowledge, righteousness, and true holiness" (also see Westminster Larger Catechism, Q&A 17). In both cases this is a reference to Ephesians 4:24, which speaks of the "new man."[32] In other words, according to the Catechism and the Confession mentioned, the "new man" is nothing more than what Adam was before the fall. However, the Greek fathers explicitly — and rightly — taught that through *theosis* it is possible for the believer to have a deeper communion with God than what Adam and Eve had ever been, or would ever have been, capable of having.

This is the core of the matter: through his redemptive work, Christ has *acquired for us, and shared with us, unspeakably more than Adam and Eve had ever lost*.[33] Only in this way can we understand why God allowed the fall at all. Our corrupted and weakened existence has to be transformed more and more into the image of Christ (2 Cor. 3:18; Col. 3:10; cf. Rom. 12:2; Eph. 3:16-17), who himself is the image of God (2 Cor. 4:4; Col. 1:15).[34] Of course, this situation evokes many questions concerning the relationship between God's decree and humanity's fall, but that is not our subject right now.[35]

### 9.7.2 Two Central Questions

On the one hand, since Augustine, Western theology — and Reformed theology forms an excellent example of this — has

---

32. Cf. Stam (1999, 41): "The Bible tells us that man was created in true righteousness and holiness (Eph. 4:24)." A strange mistake: Paul is saying this about the "new man"! See extensively Ouweneel (2008a, 145–46, 163–64).
33. See extensively Ouweneel (2009).
34. Stavropoulos (2003, 184, 188).
35. Cf. extensively Ouweneel (2008a, chapters 10–14; 2008b, chapters 2–5).

focused on the question: "How can man be righteous before God?" (Job 25:4 NKJV). It is about solving the problem of sin. According to federalism, the covenant of grace is all about God's grace for poor sinners. On the other hand, since Athanasius, Eastern theology has focused on the question: How can the image of God be realized in human persons? And in line with this: how can human persons be "filled with the Spirit" (Eph. 5:18)? Neither question plays any prominent role in Reformed theology as far as I know it. The two questions are closely related: the image of God is realized in Man by the power of the Holy Spirit.

One might put it as follows: Western theology begins at Genesis 3, so to speak, whereas Eastern theology begins at Genesis 1. Or, in the words of Protestant theologian Jean-Jacques Suurmond, "The West begins from the Augustinian starting point of the sinful individual, who, judged by the Word of God, has to be justified and sanctified through Christ. Thus arose the strong emphasis on humanity's guilt and unworthiness, and not seldom faith degenerated into a joyless, moral code. The East, by contrast, has always beaten the feast drum far more because it better retained the early Christian emphasis on the Spirit."[36]

Of course, Western theology knows about the "feast drum" of God's grace. But it hardly seems capable of distinguishing this from the problem of sin. It views God's grace as referring to forgiveness of *sins* and redemption from the power of *sin*. Likewise, it views the Christian life as a constant fight against *sin*: ". . . my sinful nature which I need to struggle against all my life" (Heidelberg Catechism, Q&A 56); ". . . to be renewed more and more after God's image, until after this life [!] we reach our goal: perfection [which is here, sinlessness]" (Q&A 115); ". . . our sworn enemies — the devil, the world, and our own flesh — never stop attacking us. And so, Lord, uphold us and make us strong with the strength of

---

36. Suurmond (1994, 80); cf. Ouweneel (2007a, 26).

your Holy Spirit so that we may not go down to defeat in this spiritual struggle, but may firmly resist our enemies until we finally win the complete victory" (Q&A 127). Even where the Catechism refers to the role of the Spirit in Christian life, it is always in view of sin and victory over it. A positive exception is Q&A 86 ("Christ, having redeemed us by his blood, is also restoring us by his Spirit into his image"), where no reference to sin is made.[37]

If one criticizes such a view of God's grace and of the Christian's spiritual struggle, invariably the critic hears the reproach that he is belittling the problem of sin or the significance of the fight against sin. But that is not the issue at all. It is a logical flaw to assert that one who argues that there is *more* than the problem of sin and its solution, is thereby belittling these matters. If I say that gold is more precious than silver, I do not see how anyone could take this as belittling silver. Eastern theology, along with a good part of Evangelical theology, claims that there is *more* than the justification of the ungodly (cf. Rom. 4:5). Such a claim does not at all detract from the tremendous value of justification. If P is better than Q, this is not to deny that Q could be very good. I will return to this matter extensively in the third volume of this series.

Or, to use another metaphor, Reformed Christians, especially hyper-Calvinists, are very much concerned with the question how one, so to speak, as a spiritual fetus can become a spiritual baby. "Spiritual growth" is often confused with attaining full assurance of salvation. Eastern Christians and many Evangelical Christians are more concerned with the question how a spiritual baby can become a spiritual adult, which was Paul's aim: ". . . that we may present everyone mature in Christ" (Col. 1:28; cf. 4:12; 1 Cor. 2:6; 14:20; Eph. 4:13; Phil. 3:15; Heb. 5:14). But it would be absurd to assume that, therefore, Eastern and Evangelical Christians are less interested in spiritual birth as such. The emphasis on maturation

---

37. On sanctification, see also the Westminster Confession (chapter XIII) and the Westminster Larger Catechism (Q&A 75–79).

*An Evangelical Covenant Theology*

does not imply a belittling of rebirth. Without having been born there can never be an adult in the first place. What Eastern and Evangelical Christians do wish to emphasize is this: Look beyond rebirth; there is more than that.

### 9.7.3 The Eastern Approach

In the Eastern view, not just receiving the Holy Spirit but being filled with the Spirit (Acts 2:4; 4:8, 31; 9:17; 13:9, 52; Eph. 5:18) is of essential importance. Unfortunately, this is a matter that the Western tradition has badly neglected (since the twentieth century partly due to some charismatic excesses).[38] What the Reformed tradition has always carefully understood is the role of the Spirit in regeneration, but that is not what we are speaking about right now. I am speaking of the role of the Spirit *after* regeneration (spiritual growth, sanctification, being transformed to the image of Christ, worship, testimony, preaching "in the Spirit" [1 Cor. 2:4], "praying in the Spirit" [Eph. 6:18; Jude 1:20], the gifts of the Spirit [1 Cor. 12:4–11]). In Reformed soteriology, the events of regeneration and justification occupy the central place. *Theosis* has to do with all the quintessentially Christian blessings *that surpass regeneration and justification*. In some Reformed ears this sounds like sacrilege—and that is sad, to say the least.

We can also put it this way. In Reformed theology, regeneration and justification are central because they give sufficient access to heaven. In *theosis* theology, the emphasis is more on what lies between regeneration and entering into heaven (or rather, entering into the kingdom of God). It is a dramatic error of Western theology, anyway, that the gospel would simply be about the question: How do I get to heaven? One could hardly think of a question that is more central in Western Christianity, and less supported by Scripture, than this one. To put it more strongly: in fact, *the question simply does not occur in Scripture*. N. T. Wright has strongly empha-

---

38. See Ouweneel (2007a, especially chapter 11).

sized how mistaken this Medieval notion is.³⁹ In his words, what matters is not the question of how you can make sure that you end at the right side of Michelangelo's painting of the Last Judgment in the Sistene Chapel. Rather, the core of the gospel is that through following Jesus, we can discover the grandeur of the kingdom of God, enjoy it as a place of justice, spirituality, relationships, and beauty, and not only passively wait for it, but work to help realize it, not in heaven, but here on earth.⁴⁰

*Theosis* is about becoming a grown-up person *on earth* (1 Cor. 2:6; 14:20; Eph. 4:13; Phil. 3:15; Heb. 5:14; 6:1), a "man in Christ" (2 Cor. 12:2), a "man of God" (1 Tim. 6:11; 2 Tim. 3:17), a father in Christ (1 John 2:13-14). Paul's goal was not "leading people to Jesus," as the common view of the gospel has it—also for many Evangelicals!—but: "Him [i.e., Christ] we proclaim, warning everyone and teaching everyone with all wisdom, that we may present everyone mature in Christ" (Col. 1:28). Paul was not satisfied at all with people who had simply been regenerated and justified; he wanted to train believers to become mature people in Christ, devoted followers of Christ, who were exhibiting more and more the image of Christ, walking in the power of the Spirit (cf. Rom. 8:4-14; Gal. 5:16-18; Eph. 5:17-20). *All of that surpasses justification as such.* And it also surpasses all the blessings that had been promised in the series of biblical covenants.

Being conformed to the image of Christ is so much more that reparation or restoration of what Adam had lost (see §9.7.1). The "light of the knowledge of the glory of God," which here on earth shone "in the face of Jesus Christ" (2 Cor. 4:6), may now shine in the face of the believer in a way that

---

39. N. T. Wright (2011). Medieval indeed: Dante Alighieri (*Divina Comedia*) and Thomas à Kempis (*The Imitation of Christ*) are good examples, but also the more recent John Bunyan (*The Pilgrim's Progress*). See, e.g., how with Bunyan the believer's life is followed by death and subsequently the New Jerusalem, whereas in Scripture, this city (a) arrives only after the *resurrection*, and (b) is not a picture of heaven but of the Lamb's Bride (Rev. 21:9-10).
40. See extensively Ouweneel (2011, chapters 9-14).

prelapsarian Adam could not know, let alone understand, and even less experience. The *natural* way that prelapsarian Adam exhibited the image of God at his best was far inferior to the *supernatural* way — the way of the Holy Spirit — in which the image of God, as it shone in the face of Christ, may now be reflected in the face of God's children.

### 9.7.4 Some Highlights in the Epistles

There are many elements in a *theosis* theology that, even if the term *theosis* is not used, immediately tie in with the preceding thoughts. These are far above the poor-sinner faith that so strongly paralyzes and discourages certain parts of the Reformed world. Take Paul's statement that believers have been filled (brought to fullness, Greek *peplērōmenoi*) in him in whom dwells the whole fullness (*plēroma*) of deity (Col. 2:9-10); this is *theosis*. Traditional expositors often shift this to the future, when believers will be with Christ, thus denying its present fundamental reality. The passage just mentioned says: We *have* been brought to this fullness. *Our* fullness is — already now — in the One in whom is *God's* fullness. Christ is our foundation and example: "[B]e imitators of God, as beloved children. And walk in love, as Christ loved us and gave himself up for us, a fragrant offering and sacrifice to God" (Eph. 5:1-2).

Also note this most exalted prayer of Paul, that "according to the riches of his glory he [i.e., the Father] may grant you to be strengthened with power through his Spirit in your inner being, so that ... you ... may have strength to comprehend ... what is the breadth and length and height and depth [of God's mystery[41]], and to know the love of Christ that surpasses knowledge, that you may be *filled* (Greek *plērōthēte*) with all the *fullness* (*plēroma*) of God" (Eph. 3:16-19). This being filled with the fullness of God that is in Christ is possible only by being filled with the Holy Spirit (*plērousthe en pneuma-*

---

41. Cf. Zerwick (1969, 93); Bruce (1984, 327–28); or, "of love," wherein "and" is to be viewed as explicative. Cf. Grosheide (1960, 58–59).

*ti*, Eph. 5:18). The two are inseparable.[42]

John says, "[W]hoever keeps his word, in him truly the love of God is perfected.[43] By this we may know that we are in him[44]" (1 John 2:5). Even after having reached the level of fatherhood (vv. 13-17), there is a fullness remaining: "Beloved, we are God's children now, and what we will be has not yet appeared; but we know that when he [i.e., God/Christ] appears we shall be like [Greek *homoioi*] him, because we shall see him as he is" (3:2). Therefore, John too is convinced that believers will share in the life and nature of the triune God without becoming gods (cf. John 17:21-23, "[Y]ou, Father, are in me, and I in you . . . I in them and you in me"). That is the future. But he is also convinced of the present reality of these things: there are those who have been brought to perfection (which does not mean sinlessness). As Paul puts it: "[O]ne thing I do: forgetting what lies behind and straining forward to what lies ahead, I press on toward the goal for the prize of the upward call of God in Christ Jesus. Let *those of us who are mature* think this way" (Phil. 3:13-15). This is here and now: ". . .until we all attain to the unity of the faith and of the knowledge of the Son of God, to mature manhood, to the measure of the stature of the fullness of Christ" (Eph. 4:13).

John expresses this through a term that is so often ignored or misunderstood: "eternal life," that is, knowledge of (in the sense of relationship, intimacy, with) the Father and the Son (John 17:3), fellowship with the Father and the Son (1 John 1:1-4), the life of the Son himself (5:11-13, 20) (see further §9.8.1). And where is *theosis* expressed in more lofty terms than here: "In that day you will know that I am in my Father, and you in me, and I in you" (John 14:20); that is, you are "in

---

42. Cf. Ouweneel (2007a, 37–41).
43. Greek *teteleiōtai*; concerning "perfection" see also Matt. 5:48; Luke 6:36. Also note that "mature" in the passages mentioned in §9.7.2 is the Greek word *teleios*, at other places translated as "perfect."
44. As more often in 1 John (cf. 2:28–29), it is intentionally unclear whether God or Christ is meant; Marshall (1978, 172 incl. note 29); Smith (1979, 183).

me," in the One who himself is "in the Father." It would probably go too far to say that believers (creatures!) are "in the Father," but the wording comes as close as is possible: believers are "in him," the *Man* Jesus Christ, who as the *eternal Son* is "in the Father," and the Father is in *his Son*, who as the risen *Man* is the life of believers. The Father has life in himself, and he has granted the Son to have life in himself (John 5:26) — and this life is now in believers: "God gave us eternal life, and this life is in his Son. Whoever has the Son has life; whoever does not have the Son of God does not have life" (1 John 5:11-12).

Through the Spirit, we are being filled to the whole fullness of God (Paul). We have become partakers of the divine nature (Peter). We are in him who is in the Father, and will become like the Son (John). This is *theosis*. Higher things can hardly be said as to the bliss that Christ has prepared for us, and that is being practically realized in us already today through the Holy Spirit. I cannot understand how someone does not see how much this surpasses the — in itself wonderful — fact that we have been declared righteous by faith. Theosis refers to:

(a) All that surpasses what Adam had lost, and therefore also surpasses regeneration and justification.

(b) The things that no Old Testament prophet had revealed, or even known (Rom. 16:25-26; 1 Cor. 2:6-10; Eph. 3:3-5, 9; Col. 1:25-27), yes, "things in which angels long to look" (1 Pet. 1:12): "[B]lessed are your eyes, for they see, and your ears, for they hear. For truly, I say to you, many prophets and righteous people longed to see what you see, and did not see it, and to hear what you hear, and did not hear it" (Matt. 13:16-17).

(c) The things that Jesus himself, the heavenly Man, and subsequently his ambassadors, have revealed: the full import of the gospel — with eternal life (John), the divine nature (Peter) and the fullness of God (Paul) as highlights — the full glory of the humble as well as glorified Lord, the full truth concerning the Ekklesia as the Body of Christ — unified with its glorified Head—the House of God, the Bride of the Lamb (see §9.8).

### 9.7.5 Conclusion

*Theosis* is the route to the ultimate pure bliss. Therefore, 1 Timothy 1:11 speaks of "the glory of the blessed [Greek *makarios*][45] God," which refers to the ultimate goal of the gospel: divine glory and bliss (in common language: happiness). Clark Pinnock is one of several Evangelical authors who have understood and appreciated how Eastern Orthodoxy has grasped this: our identity is found in our relationship with God.[46] The aim of the gospel is to be immersed in the riches of divine life. We are not only forgiven and justified, but there is far more: we are transformed to, and elevated to, the divine. Christ is being formed in us (Gal. 4:19). Justification is not the goal, but a means to the actual goal: the bliss of God—not as a description of what tradition understands by "going to heaven," but as a blessing in which believers are destined to share already now by the power of the Holy Spirit.

The core of my argument is this: justification by faith and life from God seem to be *the* quintessential Abrahamic covenant blessings that Jesus-believers have received, as Paul argues in Galatians 3. However, *theosis* contains everything that is more than justification, *and therefore everything that surpasses "the" covenant*. Everything that is exclusively Christian, as comes to expression in, among other things, the term *theosis*, transcends any form of covenant blessing. According to Reformed theology, the covenant contains and entails our Christian blessings. According to the type of Evangelical theology I consider to be more biblical, our Christian blessings comprise all those elements that surpass any and all covenant blessings.

Perhaps this is the most important point where Reformed

---

45. The normal word for "blessed" is *eulogētos*. Greek *makarios* is not so much "blessed" but rather "blissful"; one could say "happy" (cf. Matt. 5:3–11 CEB, GNT, NLV, Phillips; or "fortunate" TLB).
46. Pinnock (1996, 151; including note 4 with many references).

and Evangelical theology unfortunately must differ for the time being. Let us beware that God will one day point to a heap of presents he had in store for us, but which he could never share with us, because we were content with our covenant blessings, namely, forgiveness, justification, and sanctification. Or worse: because we accuse those who do wish to receive all those things that God has in store for us of being heretics or sectarians.

## 9.8  Quintessential Christian Blessings
### 9.8.1  Individual Blessings

An example of a genuine covenant blessing is eternal life, but then explicitly in its Old Testament meaning. This always involves life in the Messianic kingdom, that is, life under the New Covenant: there where "brothers dwell in unity . . . the LORD has commanded the blessing, life forevermore," or "life until the age [to come]" (Heb. *chayyim ʿad-hâʿôlâm*) (Ps. 133:1, 3). Within the framework of all the songs of ascents (Ps. 120–134), I cannot doubt that this prophetic psalm points to the age to come, the age of the Messianic kingdom.[47] In that age, the Genesis brothers will finally dwell in unity: Isaac and Ishmael (representing Jews and [ex-]Muslims), Jacob and Esau (representing Israel and Christendom),[48] Joseph and his brothers (representing Jesus and his Jewish people).

Daniel 12:1–2, too, speaks of the future restoration of Israel: "And many of those who sleep in the dust of the earth shall awake, some to everlasting life, and some to shame and everlasting contempt." Here "everlasting life" is *chayyē ʿôlâm*, literally "life of eternity," or "life of the age [to come]." This corresponds with Matthew 25:31–46, where Jesus explains how the sheep will enter into the kingdom (v. 34), which apparently corresponds with "eternal life" (v. 46). The goats go

---

47. See Ouweneel (2010a, 102–105).
48. In rabbinic literature, "Edom" is the common expression for the Roman Empire, also for the Christianized Roman Empire, and hence for (European) Christendom; see extensively Ouweneel (2015b).

into the "eternal fire" (v. 41), that is, "eternal punishment" (v. 46; see further Luke 10:25; 18:18, 29-30; cf. 23:42; John 3:3-8).

Now compare this with the writings of the apostle John. Here, eternal life is elevated to a spiritual level way beyond any covenant blessing.[49] Having eternal life does not mean being entitled to eternal life, nor possessing an admission ticket to eternal life; believers *have* the thing itself (3:15-16, 36; 5:24; 6:40, 47, 53-54; 10:28). This is very different from Q&A 58 in the Heidelberg Catechism about "life everlasting": ". . . after this life I will have perfect blessedness such as no eye has seen, no ear has heard, no human heart has ever imagined: a blessedness in which to praise God forever."[50]

Possessing eternal life *now* is similar to Ephesians 2:6, "seated with him in the heavenly places in Christ Jesus," that is, *now*. This is much stronger than what some translations want us to read: "he has given us a place beside Christ in heaven" (CEV). Just as the believer in Christ really *is* already in heaven, so too he really *has* eternal life. 1 John 3:15 is very clear about this: the believer has eternal life *abiding* in him, that is, in Christ: Jesus himself *is* (the personification of) eternal life (cf. John 11:25; 14:6; 1 John 1:2; 5:11-12, 20; 2 Cor. 4:10-11; Col. 3:3-4). The Word, which is life, eternal life, and which was with the Father in the person of the Son, was made manifest to us in the person of the incarnate Son by descending from the Father (1 John 1:1-2). By revealing the name of the Father here on earth, Jesus can say, "[T]his is eternal life, that they know you the only true God, and Jesus Christ whom you have sent" (John 17:3), that is, know God as Jesus knew him, namely, as the Father of the Son, and know Jesus as God knew Jesus, namely, as the Son of the Father.

Eternal life is the life (intimacy, fellowship) of the divine

---

49. See Ouweneel (2010a, 105–112).
50. Cf. Westminster Confession of Faith, XXXIII.2: "For then shall the righteous go into everlasting life, and receive that fullness of joy and refreshing, which shall come from the presence of the Lord."

persons, to which believing creatures have been admitted, already now, by faith and through the power of the Holy Spirit. About what *covenant* blessing are we talking here? In what covenant was this blessing—unity and fellowship with divine persons (vv. 20-23)—promised to us? "[O]ur fellowship is with the Father and with his Son Jesus Christ" (1 John 1:3b). This surpasses all covenant blessings.

Of course, the Old Testament also knows about intimacy with God, such as the friendship or intimacy (NASB mg.; Heb. *sôd*) of Psalm 25:14, which is directly related to the covenant: "The friendship of the LORD is for those who fear him, and he makes known to them his covenant."[51] Abraham was the (covenant) friend of God (2 Chron. 20:7; Isa. 41:8; James 2:23); to Moses, the mediator of the Sinaitic covenant, the LORD spoke "as a man speaks to his friend" (Exod. 33:11). But what a distance there is between this Old Testament friendship and the New Testament admission into the intertrinitarian fellowship.[52]

The difference has to do with the Fatherhood of God. God as Father in the Old Testament sense of Creator or Maker is a quintessential covenant blessing (I provided the references earlier). However, there is a fundamental difference between God's Fatherhood in the Old and in the New Testaments, and therefore also between the believers' sonship in the Old and in the New Testaments. In the New Testament, God is Father not primarily as the Creator of humans but as the eternal Father of the eternal Son.[53] To the *natural* people of Israel belongs a *natural* sonship, that is, the unregenerate Israelites were God's children as well, for they belonged to his chosen people. In this creaturely sense, also angels are referred to as "sons of God" (Gen. 6:2, 4; Job 1:6; 2:1; 38:7). And if Adam in Luke 3:28 is called "son of God," *all* humans are "children/sons of God" in the sense that God is Creator of them all

---

51. Stam (1999, 32) speaks of "covenantal intimacy."
52. See Ouweneel (2010a, 358).
53. See Ouweneel (2007b, §8.3).

(cf. Eph. 3:14-15; 4:6). Israel is "son" or "sons" of God in a special way because of the covenant relationship with God (Exod. 4:22; Deut. 14:1; Hos. 1:10; 11:1).

In the New Testament, however, the situation is very different. Here, a person becomes a child of God not through birth into a chosen people, but only through rebirth into the family of God (John 1:12-13). This is because here we are dealing not with a natural (ethnic) but with a spiritual (reborn) people of God (Acts 15:14; Titus 2:14; 1 Pet. 2:9-10). God is not only the Father of the Jesus-believer because the latter is his creature, but God has become his Father because the eternal Son of that Father has become the believer's life (1 John 5:11-13). The very Father *of the Son* has become the Father of the believer. Therefore Jesus says, "I am ascending to my Father and your Father" (John 20:17), that is, to my Father who through faith is now your Father as well — not just as your Creator, but your Father in the same way he is *my* Father.

In what covenant was this blessing — intertrinitarian fellowship, sonship — promised to believers? Please note, I am not belittling the divine covenants. I am protesting against those who do the very opposite: belittle the quintessentially Christian blessings in either ignoring them, or reducing them to covenant blessings.

### 9.8.2 Collective Blessings

Ephesians 2:11-22 shows that Jews and Gentiles, if they believe in Jesus as Messiah, Redeemer and Lord, are no longer enemies of God and enemies of each other, but they have been brought together in one new community, namely, the Ekklesia (see chapter 7), which is:

(a) The one "new man" (v. 15; cf. 4:24; Col. 3:9-11), that is, Christ as he is displayed morally in believers.[54]

(b) The one Body of Christ (v. 16; cf. 1:23; 4:4, 12, 16; 5:23, 30; Col. 1:18, 24; 2:19; 3:15), that is, the Ekklesia as united with

---

54. See Ouweneel (2010a, §3.2.3; 2010b, §4.3.1).

## An Evangelical Covenant Theology

its glorified Head in heaven.

(c) The one family of God (v. 18; cf. 1:5; 4:6), that is, the whole of Jewish and Gentile children of God, or children of the one Father.

(d) The one *politeia* (see v. 19, *sympolitai*; cf. v. 12, *politeia*, "commonwealth"), that is, no longer Israel but the totality of all New Testament saints.

(e) The one House of God (v. 19), a building whose stones are believers (1 Pet. 2:5), but also the one in which they commune with God (1 Tim. 3:15).

(f) The one Temple in the Lord (v. 20), a place where God dwells (1 Cor. 3:16; 2 Cor. 6:16), and where he is honored.

(g) The one dwelling place of God in the Spirit, that is, where his Spirit is active (v. 21).

Being fellow citizens (*sympolitai*) and household members (*oikeioi*) involves enjoying together—Jewish and Gentile Jesus-believers—all the privileges of God's new people (Eph. 2:19). The new *politeia* and the new House are not Israel, not some spiritual Israel, but the Body of Christ, which contains believers *from* Israel and believers *from* the Gentiles (Acts 2:40; 15:14; Rom. 11:5). In what covenant was such a peculiar community ever promised? At the proclamation of the New Covenant, the Ekklesia was not yet known. In the past ages, she was a "mystery," that is, something hidden from God's people (Eph. 3:3-9; Col. 1:25-27; cf. Rom. 16:25-26; 1 Cor. 2:6-8). Therefore, it could not be part of the New Covenant—which was not made with the Ekklesia but with ethnic Israel.

It is striking that the Ekklesia was a subject of God's eternal counsel, that it involves a divine project that develops in the present age and extends into eternity, but that remained concealed during many centuries, until it was revealed to the New Testament apostles and prophets, especially Paul. The most important reasons for this concealment were (see again chapter 7):

(a) The Ekklesia, as the Body of the glorified Man at God's

right hand, could not be revealed as long as Jesus was not glorified. Before the ascension of Christ, there could be no Ekklesia in the New Testament sense. In what covenant was union with a glorified Christ, and sharing his heavenly position, promised?

(b) The Ekklesia, as the Temple of the Holy Spirit, could not exist before the Holy Spirit was poured out, and this could occur only after Jesus was glorified (John 7:38-39). Compare Acts 19:2 (ASV; cf. DLNT): ". . .we did not so much as hear whether the Holy Spirit was [given]" (Darby: ". . . if [the] Holy Spirit was [come]").[55] The Spirit *worked* on earth during the Old Testament, but he *dwells* on earth only since Jesus' ascension and glorification. There was no Ekklesia of God before Acts 2. Therefore, Matthew 16:18,[56] John 10:16 and 11:52 speak of the Ekklesia, explicitly or implicitly, only in the future tense, and Luke uses the term Ekklesia (in the present meaning) only in Acts 5:11, 8:1, 3, etc., that is, after Pentecost.

The existence of the Ekklesia is inextricably linked with these two great redemptive facts, which did not yet exist in the Old Testament and which presuppose the death and resurrection of Christ: the glorification of Christ at his ascension, and the outpouring of the Holy Spirit at Pentecost (Acts 1-2). Under the New Covenant, the restored Israel will be the center of the Messianic kingdom on earth. But of the Ekklesia it is said, "[O]ur citizenship [or, commonwealth, Greek *politeuma*] is in heaven" (Phil. 3:20). This never has, and could have, been said of ethnic Israel. Israel's fatherland is Canaan of old, entirely according to the conditions of the New Covenant (Jer. 30-34). The Ekklesia's fatherland is heaven, not in the sense of the "intermediate state" (between a person's death and resurrection) but, so to speak, in the sense of the heavenly side of the Messianic kingdom on earth. In what covenant was such

---

55. The common translation, "whether there is a Holy Spirit," is mistaken; it cannot reasonably be assumed that disciples of John the Baptist had never heard of the Holy Spirit (cf. Matt. 3:11, 16).
56. Matthew 18:17 ("tell it to the church") is clearly anticipative.

a heavenly position ever promised?

The covenants with all their blessings are marvelous things that God has prepared for his own. But he prepared even far greater things than that. Many Evangelical Christians have little appreciation for the covenant. Many Reformed Christians have little appreciation for those greater things God has prepared for them. This book has endeavored to highlight both sides.

# Appendix 1
# Infant Baptism and "the" Covenant

## 1 Exegesis of Colossians 2:11–12
### 1.1 Figurative Circumcision

IN §4.2, I POINTED TO THE close historical link between infant baptism and federalism. The two seem to be inseparable, a fact about which Baptists, including Reformed Baptists—a name that is a *contradictio in terminis*[1]—often have little understanding. In this Appendix, it is not my intention to make a case for believers' baptism as such. I leave that matter to the reader, with this note, that I actually believe the real issue to be not whether to baptize infants or mature believers, but what baptism as such stands for. In this respect, I take issue with some of the federalist arguments as well as with some of the Baptist arguments. However, my intention right now is not to give a full treatise on baptism,[2] but to investigate the federalists' argument for the supposed links between infant baptism and "the" covenant.

Let us start with the most prominent "proof text" of fed-

---

1. Yet, in North America many Baptists defend a theology with strongly Reformed overtones; see recently, e.g., Nichols (2011), Gentry and Wellum (2012, especially 694–703).
2. See for this extensively Ouweneel (2011, chapters 5–8, in connection with the covenant [chapters 1–4] and with the kingdom [chapters 9–14]).

eralists: "In him also you were circumcised with a circumcision made without hands, by putting off the body of the flesh, by the circumcision of Christ, having been buried with him in baptism, in which you were also raised with him through faith in the powerful working of God, who raised him from the dead" (Col. 2:11-12).

The exegesis of these verses is of essential importance for federalists. For example, Horton wrote: "Baptism, in fact, is now the true circumcision (Col 2:11-12)."[3] And Brown and Keele wrote rather recently: "Because he [i.e., Christ] was our bloody circumcision on the cross, the covenant sign of inclusion [into the covenant] changed from circumcision to baptism. Paul makes this equation in Colossians 2:11-12."[4] Notice two things here. First, the authors use the strong word "equation"; in their view, Paul makes clear in these verses that baptism (as "a one-time, initiatory sign and seal of God's covenant promise"[5]) equals circumcision in that both allegedly are signs of "the" covenant of God. Second, the authors also claim to know *why* circumcision was replaced by baptism. Because Christ — in figurative language — was "bloodily circumcised" on the cross, it was appropriate that no more blood would flow, so that another initiatory covenant sign was desirable (at least, this is the way I understand the authors). Of course, this is pure speculation. I hope to argue that *(infant) baptism has not replaced circumcision at all*, and has nothing to do with the bloody character of the latter.

The word "circumcised" in verse 11 is Greek *perietmēthēte* (from *peritemnō*, "to circumcise"). The tense is aorist, which points to a concrete, momentary event, in this case, in the past. Verse 11 does not speak of a literal circumcision, "made with hands" (*cheiropoiētos*, cf. Eph. 2:11); we may assume that the pagan Colossians had never been literally circumcised. Instead, the text refers to a spiritual circumcision, namely, at

---

3. Horton (2011, 790).
4. Brown and Keele (2012, 96).
5. Ibid, 97.

the moment of their conversion. At that moment, what had objectively occurred on the cross—God's judgment on the flesh—became reality to them subjectively: they had died with Christ on the cross (Rom. 6:6; 2 Cor. 5:15; Gal. 2:20). This "circumcision" was an internal matter, that "of the heart, by the Spirit" (Rom. 2:29; cf. Phil. 3:3), which ties in with certain Old Testament statements: "uncircumcised heart" (Lev. 26:41); "[c]ircumcise . . . the foreskin of your heart" (Deut. 10:16); "circumcise your heart" (30:6). "Circumcise yourselves to the LORD; remove the foreskin of your hearts" (Jer. 4:4); "their ears are uncircumcised" (6:10); "foreskins of the heart" (lit. in 9:25); "uncircumcised in heart and flesh" (Ezek. 44:7, 9; also cf. "uncircumcised in heart and ears," Acts 7:51).

## 1.2 The "Circumcision of Christ"

The inward circumcision of the heart is called the "circumcision of Christ." Of course, this is not a reference to the literal circumcision ("made with hands") that Jesus underwent on the eighth day of his earthly life (Luke 2:21), for in this the Jesus-believers have no share. Even the circumcision that Jesus-believing Jews today perform on their little boys is not the "circumcision of Christ"; it is the boys' own circumcision. The expression also goes further than a "circumcision effectuated by Christ,"[6] or a "circumcision belonging to Christ," or a "circumcision that is possible only in Christ,"[7] or a circumcision "done by Christ, . . . demanded by Christ and also given by him."[8] I believe the "circumcision of Christ" is the circumcision that Christ personally *underwent*, namely, in his death on the cross.[9] Just as physical circumcision involved God's judgment on the flesh, Christ's death involved God's judgment coming upon him because of our sinful flesh. This

---

6. Thus, e.g., Ridderbos (1960, 179); Schweizer (1976, i.l.); Versteeg (1983, 109); Bruce (1984, 104); Loonstra (2008, 84).
7. De Ru (1968, 203–204).
8. Stam (1999, 154).
9. Thus, e.g., Peake (1979, 525); O'Brien (1982, 117); Schreiner (2006, 76, 95); Wright (2007, 19).

explanation is supported by the fact that Paul subsequently speaks of Christ's burial and resurrection. Believers have been circumcised with the circumcision of Christ in that by faith they share in his death on the cross (and in his resurrection).

Paul adds, "by putting off the body of the flesh." Apparently, this clause ties in with "circumcised": "In him also you were circumcised with a circumcision consisting in putting off the body of the flesh." That is, spiritual circumcision consists of the judgment that God has brought upon the entire "body of the flesh" (Greek *sōma tēs sarkos*), in which *sōma* stands here for the whole machinery of the sinful flesh (cf. Rom. 6:6, "body of sin," *sōma tēs hamartias*).[10] In physical circumcision, a part of literal flesh is taken away; in spiritual circumcision, "flesh" in the spiritual sense is judged.

When the Colossians were converted, they realized in their hearts, by faith, that they underwent the "circumcision of Christ," that is, that the propitiatory death of Christ was imputed to them. In other words, they became aware that they had died *with* Christ on the cross. Subsequently, this had become visible externally in their baptism: "having been buried with him in baptism." Baptism, too, refers to the death of Christ: "Do you not know that all of us who have been baptized into Christ Jesus were baptized into his death? We were buried therefore with him by baptism into death" (Rom. 6:3-4). Jesus himself called his physical death a "baptism": "I have a baptism to be baptized with, and how great is my distress until it is accomplished!" (Luke 12:50; cf. Mark 10:38-39). Both circumcision and baptism, then, speak, each in its own way, of the death of Christ: the former in its application to the inner parts, the "circumcision of the heart" (Deut. 10:16; Jer. 4:4), the latter in its application to our outward position on earth as disciples of the kingdom (cf. Matt. 28:18-19). In baptism, they had crossed death as the boundary marking the

---

10. Ridderbos (1960, 179): "'Body' refers here . . . to the way human beings exist, and thus to human beings themselves"; the "body of the flesh" is then the "sinful, corrupt way of existing."

outside and inside of the kingdom.

Thus, in Colossians 2:11-12, as in so many other passages, conversion (i.e., spiritual "circumcision") and baptism are two sides of the same coin: in conversion, people lay off their sinful existence inwardly through faith, whereas through baptism they do so outwardly. See the close connection in Acts 22: "[B]e baptized and wash away your sins" (v. 16). Sins are washed away inwardly through faith, and outwardly through baptism. As Curtis Vaughan put it: "The context suggests that Christian baptism is the outward counterpart of that experience [i.e., spiritual circumcision] and as such is the means by which it is openly declared."[11] This death side of both circumcision (inwardly) and baptism (outwardly) is the negative side of conversion.

The positive side is that the believer, inwardly at rebirth and outwardly at baptism, puts on (the risen) Christ ("as many of you as were baptized into Christ have put on Christ," Gal. 3:27). In this sense, baptism is *more* than the outward counterpart of spiritual circumcision, for the latter refers only to our having part in Christ's death as the judgment on our sins, but baptism also refers to our having part in Christ's resurrection: ". . . having been buried with him in baptism, in which you were also raised with him." Or as Paul says in Romans 6:4, "We were buried therefore with him by baptism into death, in order that, just as Christ was raised from the dead by the glory of the Father, we too might walk in newness of life." Baptism does not effectuate this *ex opere operato*; that is, this rite has no quasi-magical power in itself, but, as Colossians 2:12 says, it is effectuated "through faith in the powerful working of God, who raised him from the dead."

The "in which" in verse 12, Greek *en hōi*, may refer back to the immediately preceding *en tōi baptismōi*: ". . . in baptism, in [or, through] which you were also raised."[12] It may also

---

11. Vaughan (1978, 200); Ferguson (2009, 159) goes too far in saying that the spiritual circumcision is "received" in baptism.
12. Thus, Calvin, and most commentaries and translations.

refer back to Christ in verse 11,[13] especially because of the parallel with the beginning of verse 11 (twice *en hōi*, i.e., "in whom," that is in Christ). Ultimately, it does not make much difference for the exegesis:[14] baptism is here an image of both the burial and the resurrection of Christ. A person who is submerged in water is figuratively buried, and when he is raised from the water he is figuratively raised with Christ. For the alleged parallel with circumcision it does make a difference: the "circumcision of Christ" can refer only to his death, but baptism refers here also to the burial and resurrection of Christ.[15]

## 2 How Some Federalists Handle Colossians 2
## 2.1 A Parallel?

Paedobaptists read things in Colossians 2:11-12 that are not there but that do fit within their covenant theories. A rather shocking example is Reformed theologian Johannes P. Versteeg, who claimed in regard to this passage: "Paul says that circumcision does not have to take place anymore, appealing to the baptism that everyone in the congregation had received."[16] Clarence Stam said something similar: ". . . What is this circumcision? Paul continues his argument [in Col. 2:11-12] with the words: 'having been buried with him in baptism.' The believer's circumcision took place when baptism was administered. . . . The important underlying point is that circumcision is no longer necessary in the new covenant."[17]

Of course, Paul says nothing of the kind. He is not even speaking here about the circumcision of the flesh—which allegedly was replaced by baptism—but about the spiritual circumcision of the heart. The text does not say that *physical* circumcision is no longer necessary (because it allegedly has been *replaced* by baptism), but rather that the *spiritual* circum-

---

13. Thus already John Chrysostom, followed by Luther, F. B. Meyer, and many others.
14. Ridderbos (1960, 182).
15. Schreiner (2006, 77).
16. Versteeg (1983, 32; see more accurately 105–112).
17. Stam (1999, 154).

cision (in Christ) finds its outward counterpart in baptism. This is something totally different. If there is any question of replacement here, Paul's argument is that (a) *physical* circumcision has been replaced by *spiritual* circumcision, and (b) this spiritual circumcision *is* not the same as baptism, but finds its *outward* counterpart in baptism, spiritual circumcision itself being an *inward* matter.

Others do recognize that physical circumcision is not in view here, yet still wish to link baptism to Old Testament physical circumcision, for instance, by claiming that baptism is a "divine circumcision," which "cuts the sins out of your life."[18] However, this "divine circumcision" is not baptism but the "circumcision of Christ." There is no logical reason why the clause "having been buried with him in baptism" would make baptism identical with this "circumcision of Christ." If someone undergoes A, and at the same time B, this does not mean that A and B are identical.

Usually, paedobaptists pay little attention to the important addition in Colossians 2:12: in baptism, a person is buried and raised with Christ *through faith* in the powerful working of God. Without this faith, baptism is meaningless. Scripture nowhere says that the faith of the parents is sufficient. In other words, no person can ever be called buried and raised with Christ without having *personal* faith in Christ. For physical circumcision, a newborn son did not need any faith; it was enough simply to have Jewish parents (and even *their* faith was not a condition). But for the spiritual circumcision of the heart and the baptism that is its counterpart, faith is indispensable.[19] Again: to enter the Old Covenant, birth was needed; to enter the New Covenant, rebirth (faith) is needed. In summary, Colossians 2:11–12 says exactly the reverse of what paedobaptists read in it: *not* that baptism has *replaced* physical circumcision, but rather that neither spiritual circumcision

---

18. Voorberg (2007, 341); cf. Van Genderen (2008, 788): baptism is the "Christian circumcision."
19. Cf. Versteeg (1983, 111); Wright (2006, 239).

nor baptism can be separated from faith.

I hasten to add here that undoubtedly there is a parallel between (physical) circumcision and baptism. Just as *literal* circumcision gave access to the Old Covenant, *spiritual* circumcision (rebirth, faith, inner cleansing) gives access to the New Covenant; baptism is the outward counterpart of this, as we just saw. The same chapter that tells us about the covenant with Abraham (Gal. 3:17), and assures believers that they are sons and heirs of Abraham through faith (vv. 7, 29), also tells us that through baptism we have put on Christ (v. 27). If the blood of the New Covenant is "for the forgiveness of sins" (Matt. 26:28; Luke 22:20), and baptism is "for the forgiveness of sins" (Acts 2:38; cf. 22:16; Mark 1:4), it is hard to deny a connection between baptism and covenant. Evangelicals are not afraid to accept a connection between circumcision and baptism because such a connection does not necessarily point to infant baptism at all, as it is often thought.[20] Three considerations may support this.

(1) Circumcision was the initiation into a *natural* people of God, with *natural* promises—a geographical land, many material blessings[21]—and therefore could be performed on newborn boys. However, baptism is the initiation into a *spiritual* people, with *spiritual* promises—a heavenly "country" (Heb. 11:14, 16), "every spiritual blessing in the heavenly places" (Eph. 1:3)—and therefore can be performed only after someone has come to faith. Again: circumcision presupposed only (Jewish) *birth*, baptism presupposes *rebirth*.

(2) Colossians 2:11–12 deals not with literal circumcision at all but with spiritual circumcision—not the circumcision of the flesh but the circumcision of the heart—whereas baptism

---

20. See, e.g., the title of Schreiner and Wright (2006): *Believer's Baptism: Sign of the New Covenant in Christ*.
21. See, e.g., the title of Schreiner and Wright (2006): *Believer's Baptism: Sign of the New Covenant in Christ*, especially chapter 4 (S. J. Wellum): "Baptism and the Relationships between the Covenants." Federalists reduce the meaning of Old Testament circumcision to its spiritual aspects; cf. Jewett (1978, 89–137).

is an outward matter. We therefore cannot say that we underwent spiritual circumcision *in that* we were baptized. The two are not identical; rather we should say that the two are one another's counterpart; they are two sides—the inward side and the outward side—of the same matter.

(3) There is not the slightest logic in arguing that Colossians 2:11-12 teaches that baptism has replaced circumcision. I enter into this matter a little further in the following section.

## 2.2 Reformed Arguments

Reformed theologian Jacobus A. C. van Leeuwen wrote without any further arguments (a pattern followed by so many Reformed authors): "Circumcision was for Israel sign and seal of the covenant of God; for the church of the New Covenant this is baptism."[22] Reformed theologian Herman Ridderbos is far more careful in his formulation: "As to, lastly, the question whether in Colossians 2:11-12 baptism is put into the place of circumcision, the answer will have to be: not intentionally and directly. In the place of [physical] circumcision comes 'the circumcision-without-hands,' which consists of the being baptized with Christ through baptism. There is therefore more reason to say that the being buried with Christ has come in the place of circumcision. However, this takes place in, and is brought about through, baptism. In our view, then, no direct connection is made between circumcision and baptism, even if a partial correspondence cannot be denied (namely, insofar as through baptism the thing is brought about to which circumcision referred)."[23]

Reformed theologian Johannes P. Versteeg was more careful, too: Paul "does not simply put (Old Testament) circumcision in juxtaposition with (New Testament) baptism. The juxtaposition is first and foremost between [on the one hand]

---

22. Van Leeuwen (1953, 39); cf. Stam (1999, 150).
23. Ridderbos (1960, 182); unfortunately not quoted by Wentsel (1995, 229–31), who draws the unwarranted conclusion: "In baptism, circumcision comes to its profound meaning and fulfillment."

(Old Testament) circumcision as a circumcision that is a work of human hands and [on the other hand] the circumcision in Christ that consists in sharing in his redemptive work of cross and resurrection, and therefore is not a work of human hands. ... There is, then, no direct line that connects circumcision and baptism."[24]

Reformed theologian Jakob van Bruggen followed a nuanced reasoning as well: "According to some Christians living later, that revolution [which the gospel implied for Jewish Jesus-believers] can be characterized very briefly: as the incorporating rite, circumcision was replaced by baptism. Did not this baptism come in the place of that circumcision? Strikingly enough, we find this reasoning nowhere in the New Testament."[25] On the contrary, Van Bruggen points to the significant fact that for a long time baptized Jews continued the practice of circumcising their newborn boys. Timothy, too, was not only baptized but also circumcised (Acts 16:3) — apparently because for Paul these were two very different things. Van Bruggen continued: the conclusion that according to Colossians 2:11-12 baptism has replaced circumcision "seems plausible at first sight, but it is drawn a little too fast, because Christian water baptism is, just like Jewish circumcision, a 'work of human hands'. . . . [The circumcision of Christ] itself is therefore something different from that baptism: it is 'proven' through it, but it does not coincide with it."[26]

Neither does Reformed theologian Abraham van de Beek see in the New Testament any basis for the idea that baptism is intertwined with the covenant.[27] Baptism and covenant each have their own eschatological meaning. Insofar as the covenant has any link with the sacraments, he sees the link with the Lord's Supper rather than with baptism. Van de Beek does remain an adherent of infant baptism, but for different

---

24. Versteeg (1983, 107–108).
25. Van Bruggen (1997, 53).
26. Ibid., 56–57; also see 67–68; cf. Loonstra (2008, 86–87).
27. Van de Beek (2008).

reasons; he no longer bases it upon the covenant.

All these Reformed views are in line with what the church father Cyprian (third century) already claimed: baptism is not the sign that one belongs to God's covenant, but that one has died to the old world, and has been raised in and with Christ.[28] Today, we are happy to find Reformed authors who see far more clearly the connection between baptism and the kingdom rather than between baptism and the covenant; they speak of a "kingdom baptism."[29] To be sure, the New Covenant is realized within the Messianic kingdom, but that does not mean that covenant and kingdom are identical. There are three gates here: circumcision is the entrance gate to the Old Covenant people of Israel, faith is the entrance gate to the church, baptism is the entrance gate to the kingdom of God. It does not really help to confuse these things.

I repeat, *insofar as* Colossians 2:11–12 would imply at all that "something" has come in the place of "something else," one would have to conclude that under the New Covenant the spiritual circumcision has taken the place of the outward circumcision. In this case, the only issue about which one could still differ is whether this spiritual circumcision is identical with baptism (so, e.g., Ridderbos), or whether the former is an *inward* circumcision—a circumcision of the *heart*—and baptism only the *outward* counterpart thereof (so, e.g., Vaughan). The latter seems to me a far more accurate description of what the text is saying.

Historical investigation has made it plausible that in the early church in the fourth century, the idea first emerged of assuming a relationship between Colossians 2:11–12 and infant baptism.[30] Only after infant baptism had become customary on the basis of different arguments, and had become a kind of initiatory rite for babies into Christianity, as circum-

---

28. A. van de Beek in Bakker et al. (2009, 143–64).
29. Graafland (1979, 33–36); Loonstra (2008, 88); cf. extensively Ouweneel (2011, §11.3.1, and more broadly chapters 5–14).
30. Hunt (1988; 1990).

cision was in Israel, as an afterthought people began to appeal to Colossians 2:11-12 as evidence for this idea.

## 3   The Context of Colossians 2
### 3.1   Credobaptism

Incidentally, credobaptists have to take care as well not to read things into Colossians 2:11-12 that are not there. Sometimes, they suggest that Paul intends some temporal order here: *after* someone has been inwardly circumcised—that is, has repented and come to faith—he *then* has to express this by undergoing baptism. But that is not Paul's point at all. He does not refer here to two subsequent events, but to two aspects of the same event, namely, the application of Christ's death to a person, both inwardly (the spiritual circumcision of the heart) and outwardly (someone's position on earth, as expressed in baptism). In the New Testament, the two are always closely connected: "Whosoever believes and is baptized . . ." (Mark 16:16). "Repent and be baptized" (Acts 2:38); "when they believed . . . they were baptized" (8:12). "Rise and be baptized and wash away your sins, calling on his name" (22:16).

This temporal order—first conversion, then baptism—is a typical credobaptist mistake. It is as if one were to say, "If you have died and risen with Christ through faith, you now have to be buried in baptism"—as if we should bury *living* persons. Credobaptists say, as it were: If your sins are washed away, you must be baptized. But Acts 22:16 says, "[B]e baptized and wash away your sins." Credobaptists say: If you have put on Christ, you must be baptized. But Galatians 3:27 says that those who are baptized put on Christ. Credobaptists say: If your conscience is cleansed, you must be baptized. But 1 Peter 3:21 says that baptism is "an appeal to God for a good conscience." Credobaptists say, as it were: If (and when and because) you have received A, you must undergo B (i.e., baptism). Scripture says: In undergoing B (which is an outward thing), you receive A (which is an inward thing). You do not undergo B *because of* A, but you receive A inwardly and B outwardly *in view of* living a Christian life.

Paedobaptists baptize *before* faith; that is too early. Credobaptists baptize *because of* faith; that is equally wrong. Of course, when one baptizes a person because he or she professes Christ, this person has to become a believer first. But we do not perform baptism on that person *because* of what *has* happened to such a person, but as a counterpart of their conversion, that is, *in view of* their further life as a follower of Christ. Baptism is not a testimony or celebration of someone's conversion, but an *initiatory* rite into the kingdom of God. Inward faith and outward baptism are the two sides of this initiation; as a matter of principle, they are viewed as happening at the same time.

Because some credobaptists do not see this clearly, they sometimes baptize people too late, whereas paedobaptists baptize them too early. The kingdom of God is for the *infants* of believers (Luke 18:15-17). Children of believers should be brought up "in the discipline and instruction of the Lord" (Eph. 6:4); that is, they should be treated as disciples of Christ. That presupposes baptism, because baptism is the entrance gate to the kingdom of God. Baptizing people as *babies* is too early; baptizing people as young adults, who were raised in Christian families and made an early confession of faith, is usually too late.

## 3.2   Leaving the World Behind

The Colossian believers were in danger of not holding fast to the Head, that is Christ (2:19), and their hearts went out to all kinds of teachings in the ideological and religious world that drew them away from Christ (2:8). However, they should consider that all the good, all the beautiful, all the divine, all the perfect, were exclusively to be found in Christ: "For in him the whole fullness of deity dwells bodily, and you have been filled in him, who is the head of all rule and authority" (2:9-10). A beautiful wordplay: in him in whom God's fullness dwelt they themselves had been brought to fullness;

what, then, could they desire outside him?

Now the point is this: *how* had they been brought into this relationship with Christ? It is of this that the apostle reminds them in the following verses. The answer was: by the application of Christ's *death* to their former existence, both inwardly (spiritual circumcision) and outwardly (baptism), and these two belonged inseparably together. I repeat: these are viewed as if they had occurred at the very same moment. The illusions that the Colossian Christians were tempted to pursue belonged to an existence to which they had definitively said farewell, both inwardly (through rebirth and faith) and outwardly (by separating from the world in baptism, and entering into the "world" of Christ).

It is fascinating to pay attention here to the various nuances.

(a) *Sin*. In Romans 6, Paul says as it were: In baptism you made an end to a life in the *debauchery* of sin (cf. 1:23-32; 13:13-14)—how, then, could you ever begin living in sin again? Immediately after Peter had mentioned baptism (1 Pet. 3:21), he describes a similar world from which the believers had been delivered: "Since therefore Christ suffered in the flesh, arm yourselves with the same way of thinking, for whoever has suffered in the flesh has ceased from sin, so as to live for the rest of the time in the flesh no longer for human passions but for the will of God. For the time that is past suffices for doing what the Gentiles want to do, living in sensuality, passions, drunkenness, orgies, drinking parties, and lawless idolatry" (4:1-3).

(b) *Satan*. In Galatians 3, the core of Paul's argument is this: in baptism you made an end to a life under the *elementary principles* (or, *elemental spirits*; Greek *stoicheia*, here referring to idolatry, which is worship of Satan and his demons)—how, then, could you ever return under them (*stoicheia*, here referring to legalism and ritualism)?[31] Believers are viewed as

---

31. See Ouweneel (1997, i.l.).

freed from the domain of the spirits.

(c) *World*. In Colossians 2:8, Paul argues: "See to it that no one takes you captive by philosophy and empty deceit, according to human tradition, according to the elemental spirits of the world, and not according to Christ" (v. 8). In baptism you broke with the *ideologies* and *religious institutions* of the evil world—how, then, could you ever return to them? You stood back from them, inwardly through your spiritual circumcision, and outwardly through your baptism: "If with Christ you died to the elemental spirits of the world, why, as if you were still alive in the world, do you submit to regulations—'Do not handle, Do not taste, Do not touch' (referring to things that all perish as they are used)—according to human precepts and teachings?" (vv. 20–22).

So radical is the effect of the death of Christ on our existence, and so important is baptism. It figuratively separates us from the domain of sin, Satan, and world through the death of Christ. It is through baptism that one is turned to Christ, symbolically, yet very really and overtly, before the world and all the earthly and spiritual powers, and is withdrawn from this evil world (cf. 1 John 2:15–17), from the demons, and from the power of sin. The purpose of this is to live in, with, and for Christ on the "other side" of death, represented by the water of death, prefigured in baptism.

## 4  Further Arguments
### 4.1  No Replacement of Circumcision

Here I will add a number of considerations in regard to the alleged connection between the covenant and (infant) baptism, without at this point entering too deeply into these matters.

(a) If baptism had replaced circumcision, why did male proselytes (converts to Judaism) have to undergo both baptism (the *mikweh*) as well as circumcision? Does it not follow from this that, to the Jewish mind, baptism and circumcision have always referred to two different spiritual realities?

(b) If baptism had replaced circumcision, why did the

Jesus-believing Jews in the early church administer both baptism and circumcision? In the first volume of the present series, I have argued that these Jewish believers had the fullest right—if not duty—to do so, simply because they had never stopped being Jews. We read of Paul that he circumcised the half-Jewish Timothy, whom he undoubtedly also baptized (Acts 16:3). According to Versteeg this would be totally wrong: "Therefore where there is baptism . . . there is no place for circumcision anymore."[32] Yet Paul did administer both to the same person! He also made the important remark to Jewish leaders: "I had done nothing against our people or the customs of our fathers," which customs necessarily included circumcision (Acts 28:17). Apparently, Paul and the other Jesus-believing Jews never entertained the thought that baptism has replaced circumcision. They administered baptism to new converts (Jewish or Gentile), and continued the practice of circumcising their newborn boys.

(c) If baptism had replaced circumcision, why did this not form a strong argument against the Judaizers, who tried to introduce circumcision among the Gentile Jesus-believers (Acts 15)? Why did Paul not use the same argument as a powerful argument over against the Galatian believers? He warned many times that Gentile believers should not have themselves circumcised, for legalistic or other reasons. If one important reason why this was no longer necessary or desirable was that circumcision had been replaced by baptism, why did Paul never use this strong and obvious argument? Those who have been baptized do not have to be circumcised anymore, do they? (We have seen that this is exactly what some Reformed theologians want to read into Col. 2:11–12, and also why this does not work.)

(d) If Paul turned so fiercely against those who wanted to introduce circumcision among the Gentile Jesus-believers, would he not have had reason to criticize also those who

---

32. Versteeg, 1983:32–33.

wanted to introduce figurative circumcision, that is, circumcision in its allegedly new form: infant baptism? If the former were wrong, why not the latter?

(e) If, as is assumed in Reformed federalism, there is such a strong continuity between the Old and the New Covenants, being forms of the one covenant of grace, why did circumcision have to be replaced by a new sign in the first place? The argument by Brown and Keele that circumcision is a bloody sign, which after Jesus' bloody "circumcision" on the cross was no longer appropriate,[33] is pure speculation. Jelle Horjus rightly asked the question whether the alleged "replacement" does not indicate that baptism has a meaning very different from that of circumcision.[34] Circumcision concerned the male reproductive organ and therefore *must* involve reproduction. The explanation seems to be that the judgment that God brought upon Christ on the cross (his "circumcision") had been figuratively brought upon Abraham and his house already, and since then upon every Jewish boy, to remind them of the fact that "the flesh profits nothing" (John 6:63 NKJV) and "nothing good dwells in me, that is, in my flesh" (Rom. 7:18). The significance of this was that every male should realize that he could father only sinful children (cf. John 3:6), who needed salvation. *Nothing of this deeper meaning is retained in infant baptism.* Every link with reproduction has been cut. How could this be, if baptism had really replaced circumcision?

(f) If baptism has replaced circumcision, why did so many other elements have to be changed as well? Why was it first a sign for men only, but now also for women? ("[T]hey were baptized, both men and women," Acts 8:12.) Why was the command not given that baptism had to be administered on the eighth day? Why so many changes if at the same time the continuity of the Old and the New Covenants is so strongly emphasized?

---

33. Brown and Keele (2012, 96).
34. Horjus (2009, 53).

To me, only one conclusion can be drawn: baptism and circumcision (physical or spiritual) are quite different things. It is the simple truth that nowhere in Scripture is baptism ever linked with "the" covenant, no matter how the latter is understood. As a consequence, Willem Verboom must depend entirely on secondary and tertiary evidence to be able to maintain: "When we consider all this, we become more and more convinced that there is no reason to claim that in the New Testament there would be no connection between covenant and baptism."[35] Not only is this a very weak way to put it, but I am also afraid that this conviction was already fixed in his federalist mind beforehand.

## 4.2 Natural and Spiritual Progeny

One of the basic errors that federalists commit in this respect is the confusion between Abraham's natural progeny and his spiritual progeny (Rom. 4:11–12), as I pointed out in chapter 7. For this natural progeny there was physical circumcision, but for this spiritual progeny—which, of course, partly overlaps with the natural progeny—there was and is spiritual circumcision. Federalists make the category mistake of applying what was meant for Abraham's *natural* progeny—parents with their natural children—to his *spiritual* progeny as well, as if this also involved parents with their *natural* children. Insofar as baptism exhibits any parallel with circumcision, it is this: physical circumcision is for those who have become *natural* (male) children of Abraham, that is, through *birth*, whereas spiritual circumcision, with baptism as its outward counterpart, is for those who have become *spiritual* children of Abraham, that is, through *rebirth*.[36]

In the covenant community of the New Covenant—differently than under the Abrahamic and Sinaitic covenants—there is no place for unreborn persons and for those who

---

35. W. Verboom in Hoek and Verboom (2010, 71).
36. Cf. Wellum (2006, 132–37).

perhaps will never be reborn, young or old.[37] That does not mean that the children of believers would not have a special position and special privileges in some *outward* sense (cf. 1 Cor. 7:14). But these things belong far more to the sphere of the kingdom of God (Matt. 19:14). In the present dispensation the kingdom is a wider sphere than the covenant. The church is the "holy congregation and gathering of true Christian believers" (Belgic Confession, Art. 27); they are the people who are under the umbrella of the New Covenant. The kingdom of God, however, contains all those who stand in some outward relationship to the King (see for this mixed character of the kingdom, e.g., Matt. 13:24-30, 36-43, 47-50; 21:33-45; 22:1-14). This includes the children of Christians. The church, and thus the New Covenant, involves individuals, while the kingdom of God involves families.[38]

Nowhere in the New Testament are the young children of believers called "children of Abraham"; on the contrary: "Know then that it is *those of faith* who are the sons of Abraham" (Gal. 3:7)—not the children of believers, or those who have received infant baptism. "So then, *those who are of faith* are blessed along with Abraham, the man of faith" (v. 9); "so that in Christ Jesus the blessing of Abraham might come to the Gentiles, so that we might receive the promised Spirit *through faith*" (v. 14). "But the Scripture imprisoned everything under sin, so that the promise *by faith* in Jesus Christ might be given to *those who believe*" (v. 22). One can apply this to the little children of believers only by confusing the natural and the spiritual descendants of Abraham, which the New Testament never does. As happens pervasively throughout the New Testament, Galatians 3 links baptism with faith: "[I]n Christ Jesus you are all sons of God, *through faith*. For as many of you as were baptized into Christ have put on Christ" (vv. 26-27).

In Reformed thinking, the link between the Abrahamic promise and (infant) baptism is so strong that Willem

---
37. Ibid. (140–41); Carson (1987, 152).
38. See more extensively, Ouweneel (2011, chapters 9–14).

Van 't Spijker can assert, as an argument against Baptists: "For most of them baptism is not an underscoring of God's gracious promise, but the making public of their own internal decision. In baptism it is [for Baptists] not so much a matter of God's promise, but our commitment."[39] However, here Van 't Spijker is beginning with precisely what must be demonstrated. In the Bible, baptism is *nowhere* "an underscoring of God's gracious promise." Van 't Spijker must identify one Bible verse where God promises something to the one who is baptized. It cannot be found. It is rather the one baptized who requests something of God: baptism is "an appeal to God for a good conscience" (1 Pet. 3:21). I am not a Baptist, but I cannot see how Van 't Spijker could ever convince one single Baptist with such a promise-argument. Actually, such arguments are not given for that purpose at all; they are designed only for congenial Reformed Christians, who have already accepted the long reasoning by which one travels from the Abrahamic promise to Christian baptism. The New Testament never makes this link.

The last resort for paedobaptists are the "households" in the New Testament that were baptized in their entirety (Acts 16:15, 31, 34; 18:8; 1 Cor. 1:16). However, in some cases it is clearly stated that all the members of such a household had come to faith (16:31, 34 NIV; 18:8), or it can be easily inferred (16:15). In cases where this may be unclear, no reference whatsoever is made to any little children. Infant baptism is simply unknown in the New Testament. Where such children might have easily been mentioned ("both men and women," Acts 8:12), they were not. Actually, that is not my primary concern; there are more things that we infer from Scripture although they are not explicitly mentioned. My main concern at present is that baptism *as such* is misunderstood by federalists because they link it with "the" covenant, something Scripture never does.

---

39. Van 't Spijker (1985, 25).

# Appendix 2
# Traveling and Destination

## 1 The Traveling Concept
### 1.1 Traveling in the Covenants

IT IS AMAZING THAT IN several covenants the establishment of a covenant was linked with the command to travel, to undertake a journey. If we can indeed speak of an Adamic covenant, it is of interest that the reiteration of this covenant after the fall was coupled with the command to leave Paradise: "Then the LORD God said, 'Behold, the man has become like one of us in knowing good and evil. Now, lest he reach out his hand and take also of the tree of life and eat, and live forever—' therefore the LORD God sent him out from the garden of Eden to work the ground from which he was taken. He drove out the man, and at the east of the garden of Eden he placed the cherubim and a flaming sword that turned every way to guard the way to the tree of life" (Gen. 3:22-24). This was a journey with mainly a negative meaning: Humanity had no access to the tree of life anymore. It was not a journey *to* a certain place but *away from* a certain place.

If in Genesis 6:18 and 9:9 we must indeed read that God *confirmed* his covenant with Noah (see §§2.2.2 and 2.2.3), then God had entered into a covenantal relationship with Noah in Genesis 6:8 ("Noah found favor in the eyes of the LORD"). Again, this was linked with the command to travel: "Make yourself an ark of gopher wood. . . . For behold, I will bring a flood of waters upon the earth to destroy all flesh in which is the breath of life under heaven. Everything that is on the earth shall die. But I will establish [or, confirm] my covenant with you, and you shall come into the ark, you, your sons, your wife, and your sons' wives with you" (6:14-18). This was a journey with a negative as well as a positive meaning: it meant leaving the "old world," which was judged because of the wicked, and travelling to a "new world," which was to be placed on the foundation of the sacrifice, pointing forward to the true sacrifice of Christ.

The Abrahamic covenant formally began in Genesis 15 and 17, but in its preliminary form God's covenant relationship with him had already begun in chapter 12, and it clearly began with a command to travel: "Go from your country and your kindred and your father's house to the land that I will show you. And I will make of you a great nation, and I will bless you and make your name great, so that you will be a blessing. I will bless those who bless you, and him who dishonors you I will curse, and in you all the families of the earth shall be blessed" (vv. 1-3). Because the patriarchal promises involved a promised posterity as well as a promised land, Abram had to leave his land of birth, and travel to the land that God would point out to him, and that his descendants would inherit.

Of course, the Sinaitic covenant also entailed traveling. Although it formally began in Exodus 19-24, in its preliminary form God's covenantal relationship with Israel already began in chapters 3-4 with the calling of Moses. Already then, God revealed to Moses the true covenant meaning of his name (YHWH; 3:14-15; 6:2-4). In chapters 13-14, Israel was led out of Egypt, and in chapter 15 they sang about the goal toward which they were traveling: the promised land (v. 17). In Exodus 20, at the beginning of the Ten Commandments, this travelling is underlined as the basis for God's covenant dealings with his people: "I am the LORD your God, who brought you out of the land of Egypt, out of the house of slavery" (v. 2; see many other such references, given already in §2.4.1).

As we have seen, the Palestinian covenant was the renewal of the Sinaitic covenant, now especially in view of the promised land, Canaan, to which Israel was traveling (Deut. 29:1, 9, 12, 14). Deuteronomy 30 describes the ultimate fulfillment of this covenant in the promised land, to which the people always—that is, after every exile anew—would be "on their way," in the Messianic age for the last time: "And the LORD your God will bring you into the land that your fathers possessed, that you may possess it. And he will make you more prosperous and numerous than your fathers" (v. 5; cf. vv. 16, 20).

Finally, the New Covenant (Jer. 31:31–34) implies the return of the children of Israel from all the countries in the world to the promised land: "Behold, I will bring them from the north country and gather them from the farthest parts of the earth, among them the blind and the lame, the pregnant woman and she who is in labor, together; a great company, they shall return here. With weeping they shall come, and with pleas for mercy I will lead them back, I will make them walk by brooks of water, in a straight path in which they shall not stumble, for I am a father to Israel, and Ephraim is my firstborn. . . . They shall come and sing aloud on the height of Zion, and they shall be radiant over the goodness of the LORD, over the grain, the wine, and the oil, and over the young of the flock and the herd; their life shall be like a watered garden, and they shall languish no more . . . your children shall come back to their own country" (vv. 8–9, 12, 17).

## 1.2 Traveling in Luke

If we may believe the present-day editions of the Greek New Testament, Luke is the only Gospel writer who uses the term "New Covenant" (Luke 22:20; the Textus Receptus also has the word "new" in Matt. 26:28 and Mark 14:24). In this Gospel traveling plays a great role: " In those days Mary arose and went with haste into the hill country . . ." (1:39); "And Joseph also went up from Galilee, from the town of Nazareth, to Judea, to the city of David, which is called Bethlehem" (2:4). "And when the time came for their purification according to the Law of Moses, they brought him up to Jerusalem to present him to the Lord" (v. 22). "Now his parents went to Jerusalem every year at the Feast of the Passover. And when he was twelve years old, they went up according to custom" (vv. 41-42). "Soon afterward he [i.e., Jesus] went on through cities and villages, proclaiming and bringing the good news of the kingdom of God" (8:1).

The most remarkable thing in Luke, when it comes to traveling, is that Jesus begins his way to the cross as early as chapter 9:51, "When the days drew near for him to be taken up [i.e., in heaven], he set his face to go to Jerusalem." "As they were going along the road . . ." (v. 57). "Now as they went on their way . . .' (10:38). "He went on his way through towns and villages, teaching and journeying toward Jerusalem" (13:22). "On the way to Jerusalem he was passing along between Samaria and Galilee" (17:11). This is quite amazing. Noah had to travel to a "new world" before the Noahic covenant could be made. Abram had to travel to the promised land before the Abrahamic covenant could be made. Israel had to travel to Mount Sinai before the Sinaitic covenant could be made. They had to travel through the wilderness before the Palestinian covenant could be made. David had to roam around as "a partridge in the mountains" (1 Sam. 26:20) before the Davidic covenant could be made. And Jesus had to travel to Jerusalem before the New Covenant could be made.

Not only that: even in Jesus' parables, as recorded in Luke, people seem to be traveling all the time: the good Samaritan is "journeying" (10:33), as the robbed man had been "going down from Jerusalem to Jericho" (v. 30), as well as the priest and the Levite (vv. 31-32). The "friend" in Luke 11:6 "has arrived on a journey," the prodigal son "took a journey into a far country" (15:13), and the nobleman likewise "went into a far country" (19:12).

This traveling aspect comes to light also in living under God's covenant. Luke tells about Zechariah and Elizabeth that "they were both righteous before God, walking blamelessly in all the commandments and statutes of the Lord" (1:6). Joel Green says about this "walking": "The image of living lives that conform to God's will as a journey is an important one for Luke, who develops it further in the central 'journey' section of his Gospel [from Luke 9:51] and in the label he uses for the Jesus movement in Acts, 'the Way'" [9:2; 19:9, 23; 24:14, 22]."[1] Living in a (pre-)covenant relationship with God is described as a "walking": "Enoch walked with God" (Gen. 5:22, 24). "Noah was a righteous man . . . [he] walked with God" (Gen. 6:9). God told Abram, "Arise, walk through the length and the breadth of the land, for I will give it to you" (13:17). "When Abram was ninety-nine years old the LORD appeared to Abram and said to him, "I am God Almighty; walk before me, and be blameless, that I may make my covenant between me and you, and may multiply you greatly" (17:1-2). Abraham himself spoke of "[t]he LORD, before whom I have walked" (24:40). And Jacob spoke of "[t]he God before whom my fathers Abraham and Isaac walked, the God who has been my shepherd all my life long to this day" (48:15).

Notice this latter phrase: shepherding is traveling: "The LORD is my shepherd. . . . He leads me in paths of righteousness for his name's sake. Even though I walk through the valley of the shadow of death, I will fear no evil" (Ps. 23:1-4). "The sheep hear his voice, and he calls his own sheep by name and leads them out. When he has brought out all his own, he goes before them, and the sheep follow him, for they know his voice" (John 10:3-4).

Living under the covenant is never a static, timeless event; covenant members are always "on the move." In this way, every covenant knows its own "pathway" through history. God told Israel, "You shall follow my rules and keep my statutes

---

1. Green (1997, 65 nt 10).

and walk in them" (Lev. 18:4; cf. 26:3; Deut. 8:6; 10:12). "You shall walk in all the way that the LORD your God has commanded you, that you may live, and that it may go well with you, and that you may live long in the land that you shall possess" (Deut. 5:33). "You shall walk after the LORD your God and fear him and keep his commandments and obey his voice, and you shall serve him and hold fast to him" (13:4; cf. 19:9; 26:17; 28:9; 30:16).

## 2 The Altar Concept
## 2.1 The Destination of Traveling

If we spoke of traveling in the previous sections, we may now add that usually, at the end of each journey, there is an *altar* waiting. This means that the traveling usually is a pilgrimage, that is, a journey to a sacred place.[2] This may be a temple, but sometimes it is just an altar. In biblical theology the notion of the altar is of greater importance than is often realized. Jesus even seems to suggest that it is more significant than the sacrifice lying on it: "You blind men! For which is greater, the gift or the altar that makes the gift sacred?" (Matt. 23:19). In the words of Michael Horton: "[T]he Bible identifies God's covenant people as *pilgrims*. Neither having arrived nor merely carried along by arbitrary whim, we are travelers who 'seek the city that is to come' (Heb 13:14)."[3]

Of course, traveling to just any city does not make someone a pilgrim. A pilgrim is traveling to some *holy place*, in this case, a "holy city" (cf. Neh. 11:1, 18; Isa. 48:2; 52:1; Dan. 9:24; Matt. 4:5; 27:53; Rev. 11:2; 21:2, 10; 22:19). This always implies a city with a "holy temple" (see for the heavenly city, Ps. 11:4; 138:2; Micah 1:2; Hab. 2:20; cf. Rev. 3:12; 7:15; 11:19; 14:15; 16:1, 17; also see 21:22, where God himself is the temple of the New Jerusalem). And a temple implies an altar in whatever form or sense. A *hadj* is a Muslim pilgrim to Mekka; this Ara-

---

2. Cf. Horton (2011, subtitle: "A Systematic Theology for Pilgrims On the Way").
3. Horton (2011, 47).

bic word *hadj* is related to the Hebrew word *hag*, which refers to any of the three pilgrim festivals in Jerusalem. Three times a year all the male Israelites were obliged to travel, that is, to undertake the pilgrimage journey to Jerusalem: for *Pesach* (Passover), *Shavuot* (Pentecost), and *Sukkoth* (Feast of Booths) (Exod. 23:14, 17; 34:23-24; Deut. 16:16). Each of these pilgrimages was a miniature replica of Israel's great pilgrimage to the Messianic kingdom.

Even before the history of Israel began, covenants entailed traveling, as we saw. The first altar mentioned in the Bible is the one Noah built after the flood: "Then Noah built an altar to the Lord and took some of every clean animal and some of every clean bird and offered burnt offerings on the altar" (Gen. 8:20). His long journey of almost a year ended so to speak on a "new," that is, cleansed earth, which Noah through his sacrifice on the altar dedicated to the Lord.

Abram's journey to "the land that I will show you," as God said, ended when he was certain that he indeed had reached this land: "Then the Lord appeared to Abram and said, 'To your offspring I will give *this land.*' So he built there an altar to the Lord, who had appeared to him. From there he moved to the hill country on the east of Bethel and pitched his tent, with Bethel on the west and Ai on the east. And there he built an altar to the Lord and called upon the name of the Lord" (Gen. 12:7-8). Just like Noah, Abram made a journey that ended, so to speak, at an altar. It was a holy place—of which the name of Bethel ("house of God") was a reminder—where he could meet with the Lord (cf. 13:4). In this sense, Abram's journey, too, was a pilgrimage.

This was also the case with Israel in quite an amazing way. As soon as they had left Egypt and had passed through the Red Sea, they spoke of the great goal of their journey: "You will bring them in and plant them on your own mountain, the place, O Lord, which you have made for your abode, the sanctuary, O Lord, which your hands have established" (Exod.

15:17). They did not refer to the milk and the honey, and all the other blessings they would receive in the promised land, but they spoke of the coming "sanctuary." However, the people did not have to wait that long. Already in Exodus 17:15, after the triumph over Amalek, Moses built an altar in the desert. As soon as the Ten Commandments had been given, God spoke of an altar: "An altar of earth you shall make for me and sacrifice on it your burnt offerings and your peace offerings, your sheep and your oxen. In every place where I cause my name to be remembered I will come to you and bless you" (Exod. 20:24).

## 2.2   The Altar of the Old Covenant

When the Sinaitic covenant was established, we read again of an altar: "And Moses . . . rose early in the morning and built an altar at the foot of the mountain, and twelve pillars, according to the twelve tribes of Israel. And he sent young men of the people of Israel, who offered burnt offerings and sacrificed peace offerings of oxen to the LORD. And Moses took half of the blood and put it in basins, and half of the blood he threw against the altar. Then he took the Book of the Covenant and read it in the hearing of the people. And they said, 'All that the LORD has spoken we will do, and we will be obedient.' And Moses took the blood and threw it on the people and said, 'Behold the blood of the covenant that the LORD has made with you in accordance with all these words'" (24:4–8). Subsequently, in Exodus 27–31 we read of the bronze altar and the golden altar that was built for the tabernacle.

Yet, of course, Mount Sinai was no destination. When the people had reached the "fields of Moab," Moses repeatedly reminded them that they were on their way to "the place that the LORD your God will choose, to make his name dwell there, there you shall bring all that I command you: your burnt offerings and your sacrifices, your tithes and the contribution that you present, and all your finest vow offerings that you vow to the LORD" (Deut. 12:11; see further 14:23; 16:2, 6, 11;

26:2). Similarly, the Palestinian covenant reminded Israel of the fact that, after forty years of traveling, they still had not reached the destination of their pilgrimage: the true sanctuary (in spite of the tabernacle that they carried with them).

In fact, after they had entered into the land, there seems to have been no one who sought this place. This is indeed what the LORD had said: "[Y]ou shall *seek* the place that the LORD your God will choose out of all your tribes to put his name and make his habitation there. There you shall go, and there you shall bring your burnt offerings and your sacrifices, your tithes and the contribution that you present, your vow offerings, your freewill offerings, and the firstborn of your herd and of your flock" (Deut. 12:5-6). It took about four hundred years before a man appeared who really sought this place with all his heart; this was king David. That is, he sought—and found—the place where the ark of the covenant would find its final rest, after centuries of traveling: "[H]e [i.e., David] swore to the LORD and vowed to the Mighty One of Jacob, 'I will not enter my house or get into my bed, I will not give sleep to my eyes or slumber to my eyelids, until I *find* a place for the LORD, a dwelling place for the Mighty One of Jacob.' Behold, we heard of it [i.e., the ark] in Ephrathah [i.e., the land of Ephraim]; we found it in the fields of Jaar [i.e., Kiriath-jearim, 1 Sam. 7:1-2]. 'Let us go to his [i.e., God's] dwelling place; let us worship at his footstool [i.e., the ark, 1 Chron. 28:2]! Arise, O LORD, and go to your resting place, you and the ark of your might" (Ps. 132:2-8).

In fact, the ark of the covenant, which played such an important role under the Sinaitic covenant, had never come to a permanent rest from the moment of its construction (Exod. 25:10-22) until it found its final place in the temple of Solomon; as David said, "Hear me, my brothers and my people. I had it in my heart to build a *house of rest* for the ark of the covenant of the LORD and for the footstool of our God . . ." (1 Chron. 28:2). He was not allowed to build that house, but at least he was allowed to build an altar at the spot where the temple would arise: the threshing floor of Ornan the Jebusite: "And David built there an altar to the LORD and presented burnt offerings and peace offerings and called on the LORD, and the LORD answered him with fire from heaven upon the altar of burnt offering" (1 Chron. 21:26). Even before the ark found its final rest, an altar, which was acknowledged by the LORD with fire from heaven, marked its future. Henceforth, the house of David (his offspring) and the house of God (the temple) would be linked forever.[4]

## 2.3 The Altar of the New Covenant

As we have seen, the New Covenant will be formally established with the restored houses of Israel and Judah in the "world to come" and the "age to come": the Messianic kingdom. But we have also seen that the Ekklesia, though distinguished from restored Israel in the future, has found a place of blessing under the umbrella of the New Covenant. Both future Israel and the present Ekklesia have their own temple and their own altar.

The Ekklesia does not just *have* a temple, she *is* the temple of God in the spiritual sense: "Do you not know that you are God's temple and that God's Spirit dwells in you?" (1 Cor. 3:16). "[W]e are the temple of the living God" (2 Cor. 6:16). "Christ Jesus himself" is "the cornerstone, in whom the whole structure, being joined together, grows into a holy temple in the Lord. In him you also are being built together into a dwelling place for God by the Spirit" (Eph. 2:20–22). The Ekklesia has also its own altar: "We have an altar from which those who serve the tent [i.e., Israel's physical sanctuary] have no right to eat" (Heb. 13:10). Presumably, this is a reference to the whole of the Ekklesia's priestly service. More specifically, Paul speaks of an altar in referring to the spiritual place where the Lord's Supper is celebrated: "Consider the people of

---

4. Cf. Brown and Keele (2012, 124): "[I]n 2 Samuel 7, there are three main uses for house: temple, dynasty, and people/kingdom." More correctly: palace, temple, and dynasty. The latter two are forever inseparably connected.

Israel: are not those who eat the sacrifices participants in the altar? What do I imply then? That . . . what pagans sacrifice they offer to demons and not to God. I do not want you to be participants with demons. You cannot drink the cup of the Lord and the cup of demons. You cannot partake of the table of the Lord and the table of demons" (1 Cor. 10:18-21).

It is clear that when speaking of the "table of the Lord," Paul is referring to the "altar" in some spiritual sense. This is obvious because four times in the Old Testament the altar in the temple is referred to as "table of the Lord": "[I]n front of the Holy Place was something resembling an altar [i.e., the altar of burnt offering] of wood, three cubits high, two cubits long, and two cubits broad. Its corners, its base, and its walls were of wood. He said to me, 'This is the *table* that is before the LORD'" (Ezek. 41:20-21). "They shall enter my sanctuary, and they shall approach *my table* [i.e., the altar of incense], to minister to me, and they shall keep my charge" (44:16). "But you say, 'How have we despised your name?' By offering polluted food upon my altar [i.e., the altar of burnt offering]. But you say, 'How have we polluted you?' By saying that the LORD's *table* may be despised" (Mal. 1:6-7). "For my name will be great among the nations. . . . But you profane it when you say that the LORD's *table* [i.e., the altar of burnt offering] is polluted, and its fruit, that is, its food may be despised" (vv. 11-12).

The New Covenant, as it will be established with the houses of Israel and Judah at the beginning of the "world to come" and the "age to come," will entail for Israel that all its travels, all its exiles, have finally come to an end, as we saw. At the end, they will find in the restored city of Jerusalem a rebuilt temple, which is described by Ezekiel in the finest detail, and which again will have both a bronze and a golden altar, that is, an altar of burnt offering and an altar of incense (see Ezek. 41 and 44, as just quoted).

Other prophets speak of this altar too: "And the foreigners who join themselves to the LORD, to minister to him, to love the name of the LORD, and to be his servants, everyone who keeps the Sabbath and does not profane it, and holds fast my covenant—these I will bring to my holy mountain, and make them joyful in my house of prayer; their burnt offerings and their sacrifices will be accepted on my altar; for my house shall be called a house of prayer for all peoples" (Isa. 56:6-7). "All the flocks of Kedar shall be gathered to you; the rams of Nebaioth shall minister to you; they shall come up with acceptance on my altar, and I will beautify my beautiful house" (60:7). "And on that day there shall be inscribed on the bells of the horses, 'Holy to the LORD.' And the pots in the house of the LORD shall be as the bowls before the altar" (Zech. 14:20).

Elsewhere in this book, we have seen how impossible and erroneous it is to try to spiritualize all such passages (see Appendix IV). It is a mark of supersessionism, which claims all the promises of Israel for the Ekklesia, but leaves all the curses for Israel. Supersessionism is one of the saddest features of federalism.

# Appendix 3
# Some Notes on the Sovereignty of God

## 1   Theological Imagination

AMONG MANY OTHER THINGS, God is the sovereign God who is both perfectly powerful and perfectly free in the way he exercises that power. In the words of Job, "He is wise in heart and mighty in strength—who has hardened himself against him, and succeeded?" (Job 9:4). This divine sovereignty includes God's will: "[H]e does according to his will among the host of heaven and among the inhabitants of the earth; and none can stay his hand or say to him, 'What have you done?'" (Dan. 4:35). "Am I not allowed to do what I choose with what belongs to me?" asks the master in the parable (Matt. 20:15), thus representing God's own feelings. God does with his creation *what he wants*.

This will of God is the foundation of his counsel (Rom. 9:22-23; Eph. 1:5, 9, 11), his creation (Rev. 4:11; James 1:18), his dominion (Ps. 115:3; Prov. 21:1), his work of redemption (Matt. 26:42; Rom. 9:15-18; Phil. 2:13), his providence (Acts 18:21; Rom. 15:32; 1 Cor. 4:19; Heb. 6:3; James 4:15; 1 Pet. 3:17), the charismata in the church (1 Cor. 12:11), etc. God's sovereignty implies that he is responsible to no human (Job 33:13, "he will answer none of man's words"). People are in his hands like clay in the potter's hands (Job 10:9; Isa. 29:16; 30:14; 45:9; 64:8; Jer. 18:6; Rom. 9:21). Human beings are only instruments in God's hand, who cannot resist their Maker: "Shall the axe boast over him who hews with it, or the saw magnify itself against him who wields it? As if a rod should wield him who lifts it, or as if a staff should lift him who is not wood!" (Isa. 10:15). "If one wished to contend with him, one could not answer him once in a thousand times" (Job 9:3). "If he passes through and imprisons and summons the court, who can turn him back?" (11:10).

In describing the precise content of the idea of divine sovereignty, the danger exists that the theologians' common sense determines what it does and does not entail. Thus, it has often been argued that this or that would affect God's sovereignty because it allegedly would be "unworthy of him."[1] For instance, it has been claimed that it would be inappropriate — according to Williams Perkins, even "very wicked"[2] — to assume that *not* everything that ever happens was determined by God from eternity. Why is this wicked? Because it does not fit Perkins' sense of logic? At any rate, although this is a rather central Reformed doctrine, Scripture nowhere teaches that everything that happens was determined by God from eternity.

Apparently the only criterion for such a statement is what we can *imagine*, or not, that God's sovereignty entails. Of course, the quality of being "unworthy" is a very subjective notion. One might just as well argue that it is unworthy of God to create people of whom he knows — or even, has determined — beforehand that they will land in hell forever. Or one might argue that it is unworthy of God to enter into a history whose every detail he has already determined beforehand, so that there is no leeway for humans, in spite of the fact that he himself created them with responsibility and options.

---

1. Thus, e.g., Boyd (2000, 14–15, 130–31).
2. Quoted in Kersten (1947, I, 285n1; see extensively 285–88). Cf. Arminius on Perkins: Verboom (2005, 29–36).

What does more justice to God's sovereignty? The view in which all world events, including all human actions, are fixed beforehand in a divine blueprint, which God only has to carry out; a chess match whose moves have been written down beforehand, which God only has to re-enact? *Or* the view in which he does not need to determine everything beforehand, but in which God trusts his own power and wisdom so strongly that he is prepared to allow humanity a certain freedom, and yet realizes his purposes with absolute certainty?[3]

## 2  God's Counsel and God's Ways

In the distinction between God's (eternal) counsel and God's (temporal) ways through which he realizes his counsel in history,[4] God's sovereignty is not endangered at all. The simple reason for this is that God himself apparently has decided sovereignly to make himself to a certain extent dependent on the free choices of people. God is "sovereign over his sovereignty,"[5] that is to say, he decides himself—and not the theologians—how his sovereignty must be defined. Thus, apparently it was his own sovereign choice to make free creatures who would voluntarily follow his will but would also be able to withstand his will. It was his own sovereign choice to enter into history with humanity in a continual interaction with the latter's choices and decisions. And at the same time, God confirms his sovereignty in that, despite what people may choose or decide, he ultimately always realizes his own purposes. In the establishment of his *counsel* God always acts absolutely alone—but he chooses the *ways* through which he realizes his counsel in continual interaction with the choices and decisions of people.

Therefore, what Calvinist R. C. Sproul asserts is not only very one-sided but even emphatically wrong.[6] He claims

---
3. Boyd (2000, 68); cf. Pinnock (2001, 49).
4. See extensively Ouweneel (2008b, chapters 2–5).
5. Pinnock (2001, 92).
6. Sproul (1986, 43).

that if God's sovereignty is restricted by human beings, then God is not sovereign; then human beings are sovereign. I pass by the logical flaw in this assertion, which could be indicated as follows: if a human being's sovereignty in turn is restricted by God, then human beings are not sovereign either. However, what is more important is that Sproul's allegation would have an appearance of truth only if God's power would be restricted *against his will* by some other power, in this case, human freedom. Apparently Sproul overlooks the possibility that God has, *according to his own will*, that is, sovereignly, restricted his sovereignty by human freedom (in such a way, for that matter, that this human freedom can never obstruct God's *counsel*; it can only influence his ways[7]).

In this connection, Greg Boyd uses a striking parallel, which I wish to elaborate a bit.[8] We may compare God with a chess grandmaster who condescends to play against a moderately skilled player. This grandmaster has voluntarily chosen to be obliged to respond to awkward, foolish moves, which are an affront to his genius. In every position on the chessboard the grandmaster oversees *all* possible combinations, and also the opponent's most *probable* moves. But especially if his opponent is a rather weak player, the grandmaster can never exactly predict what move the other player will make. Therefore, he constantly has to adapt his moves to those of his weak, clumsy opponent, and sometimes this will lead to disappointment and irritation. However, he does have the enormous likelihood of gaining the victory, in whatever way this might be.

The grandmaster does not prove his greatness by determining the opponent's moves, as hyper-Calvinism claims with respect to God and his sovereignty. In other words, the grandmaster is not enacting a match that has been determined beforehand. No, he wins by anticipating the opponent's possible moves in an optimal way, and at any rate by continually

---

7. In Ouweneel (2008b, chapters 2–5), I give many biblical examples for this.
8. Boyd (2000, 127–28; 2001, 112–13); cf. Pinnock (2001, 52, 139).

responding to them in an adequate and sovereign way. The grandmaster's ultimate victory is just as certain as the counsel of God. But the way through which this victory is reached is just as uncertain—because it depends on the opponent—just like the ways through which God realizes his counsel, in that he has made himself dependent on his "opponents."

If Reformed theology could be healed of its "Arminian trauma," if it would work on attaining a better balance between God's sovereign grace and human responsibility, it could also reach a healthier view of God's sovereignty. This would have consequences for both its predestination doctrine—think of the error of eternal reprobation—and its covenant doctrine. That is, the false distinction between the alleged "covenant of works" and the alleged "covenant of grace" would be overcome, because all covenants would be viewed as a fine harmony of grace and responsibility, of promises and commands. There is no covenant without a certain form of the Torah. That is, there are no covenant promises without a certain form of Torah works, and there is no Torah without a certain manifestation of God's sovereign redemptive grace. This is worked out elsewhere in this study, especially in chapter 3.

# Appendix 4
# Spiritualization

## 1   Spiritualizing Prophecy Away
### 1.1   Romans 9–11

IN THE COURSE OF THIS STUDY, I have pointed several times to the error of spiritualization, a hermeneutical approach to prophecy that is not governed by Scripture's own guidelines but by those of federalism. The principle behind this spiritualizing is this: if Old Testament prophecies speak of some material blessing P, and the New Testament speaks in similar terms of some spiritual blessing Q, then (a) not only is Q typologically represented by P, *but (b) Q is also the fulfillment of P.* The logical flaw is obvious: (a) is valid, but (b) is a *non sequitur*. For the spiritualizer, it does not matter whether P is prophesied in the finest details—all those details are irrelevant, for he "knows" P is not literally fulfilled, but is fulfilled in Q. To support this view, such spiritualizing has to pay a high hermeneutical price.

To be sure, the New Testament sometimes makes a typological *application* of certain Old Testament prophecies, without suggesting, however, that this application is the "fulfillment." The model for this is Romans 10:18b, "Their voice has gone out to all the earth, and their words to the ends of the world," in which Psalm 19:4 (about the celestial bodies) is very freely *applied* to the preaching of the gospel. No one would suggest that Romans 10 describes the "fulfillment" of Psalm 19.

However, in the same vein, one chapter earlier (Rom. 9:25-26), Paul makes an unconstrained *application* of Hosea 1:10b ("in the place where it was said to them, 'You are not my people,' it shall be said to them, 'Children of the living God'") and 2:23b ("I will have mercy on No Mercy, and I will say to Not My People, 'You are my people'"). To claim that Paul is hereby indicating the true *exegesis* of Hosea 1 and 2 is simply absurd.[1] The passages in Hosea unequivocally deal with a people who, because of their sins, had been rejected for a while, and will be accepted again if and when they repent. The general *principle* behind this — accepting those who before were not accepted — is *applied* by Paul to the Gentile believers, without saying that the Hosea texts about Israel's restoration do not apply to ethnic Israel anymore but only to the Gentile church. On the contrary, in Romans 11:26 Paul tells us that "all Israel will be saved," and all of Romans 9-11 proves that this is referring to *ethnic* Israel. Moreover, Paul also localizes this salvation: "The Deliverer will come from *Zion*," an allusion to Psalm 14:7 ("Oh, that salvation for Israel would come out of Zion!") and Isaiah 59:20 ("And a Redeemer will come to Zion"). In both passages, the authors could not have thought of any other "Zion" than literal Jerusalem. If in verse 26 Israel is literal, then so too is Zion.

## 1.2 Matthew 24

Likewise, Jesus himself shows in Matthew 24 that in the end time, just before his return (the "coming of the Son of Man," vv. 27-30, 39), Israel will again be found in its own land.[2] The parallel passage, Luke 21, clearly refers to the fall of Jerusalem in AD 70, but in Matthew 24 it is different.

First of all, note that the whole chapter is a reply to the disciples' question (v. 3): "[W]hen will these things [i.e., the fall

---

1. Cf. the discussion by Moo (1996, 612–14) and references.
2. See on this exegesis extensively Ouweneel (2012, §7.1).

of city and temple] be, and what will be *the sign of your coming and of the end of the age?*" In the first part of his reply, Jesus speaks very generally about what is often called "the signs of the times" (cf. 16:3). This part ends with the clear statement: "... and then the end will come" (24:14). Indeed, from verse 15 to verse 31 Jesus clearly speaks of "the end of the age," that is, the end of the present age (Gal. 1:4; 1 Tim. 6:17; Titus 2:12; Heb. 9:9), contrasted with the "age to come," the age of the Messianic kingdom (Matt. 12:32; Mark 10:30; Luke 18:30; Eph. 1:21; Heb. 6:5). If this is correct, Jesus is *not* speaking here of the events around AD 70, but of what we call the "end time."

This conclusion is supported by the fact that the whole context of verses 15–31 is eschatological. This is so, first, because of the several references to the coming [again] of the Son of Man (cf. Dan. 7:13) but, second, because of the reference to the "great tribulation" (v. 21; cf. Rev. 2:22; 7:14; Jer. 30:7; Dan. 12:1). This is the final stage of Israel's (and all the believers') sufferings, just before the second coming (cf. v. 29, "Immediately after the tribulation . . ."). Also, in Revelation 7:14, Jeremiah 30:7 and Daniel 12:1, this tribulation is followed by the restoration of Israel and the beginning of the Messianic kingdom.

Now, if verse 14 refers to "the end," and verses 21–30 clearly refer to the end of the present age, what are verses 15–20 all about? I would suggest that they are about the end of the present age as well. Notice the introductory word "for" in verse 21, which shows that the following verses are an explanation of the preceding verses. Several Reformed expositors have at least discerned that verses 15–20 have eschatological significance.[3] I myself would like to go one step further: verses 15–20 *cannot* refer to AD 70 because *there was no "abomination of desolation" in the temple of that time*. This is the "abomination" of which Daniel has spoken, in a clearly eschatological context (Dan. 9:27; 11:31; 12:11). Several attempts have been

---

3. Grosheide (1954, 363); Ridderbos (1987, 442); Hill (1972, i.l.).

made to relate this "abomination of desolation" to the events of AD 70, but Reformed theologian Herman Ridderbos admitted that such interpretations are inadmissible,[4] even though he in his own way also tried to read AD 70 into the text.

The great difficulty for many expositors is that they cannot, or will not, accept that there will be a people of Israel in the Holy Land at the end of the present age, a people who will have their own "holy place" and who will celebrate the Sabbath (v. 20). If one does accept this, many exegetical difficulties disappear.[5] Then Jesus is describing events, just before his return, in the "end time" to which also Revelation 6–19 refers.

## 2    Examples of Spiritualization
### 2.1   Israel: Physical Aspects

What exactly are some examples of unwarranted spiritualization? I mention a few cases in which a certain prophecy will be literally fulfilled in future Israel—in the Messianic "world to come"—while the New Testament makes a typological application of these same cases, without claiming that this *application* is the *fulfillment* of the prophecies concerned. I limit myself to eight examples.

(a) *Israel*. Romans 11:26 says, "[I]n this way all Israel will be saved." Many Reformers wanted to understand "Israel" here as the church: Martin Luther, John Calvin, Martin Bucer, Philipp Melanchton, Johannes Oecolampadius, John Lightfoot.[6] However, there have always been Reformed expositors who saw this verse to be referring to ethnic Israel: for the seventeenth century we may mention in the Netherlands, Gisbertus Voetius and the Voetians Franciscus Ridderus (with hesitation), Jacobus Koelman, Wilhelmus à Brakel, Herman Witsius, Theodorus van der Groe, and Johannes

---

4. Ridderbos (1987, 442–44).
5. Thus, e.g., Schuyler English (1935, i.l.); Lagrange (1948, i.l.); Schniewind (1956, i.l.); Schlatter (1963b, i.l.); Walvoord (1974, i.l.).
6. See Van Campen (2007, 436) for references.

Hoornbeeck.[7] And of the Cocceians:[8] (not Cocceius himself but) Jacobus Alting, Henricus Groenewegen, David Flud van Giffen, Campegius Vitringa, Friedrich Adolph Lampe, Joachim Mobachius, and Franciscus Burman Sr. Also in our present time, several Reformed expositors have argued that, since in Romans 9–11, Israel *always* refers to ethnic Israel, one cannot suddenly interpret Israel to be referring to the church in chapter 11:26.[9]

(b) *The land.* The New Testament knows of "a better country, that is, a heavenly one" (Heb. 11:16). It is better because it is heavenly and because the patriarchs never possessed the promised land. It is *not* better because this heavenly country allegedly has now replaced the promised land of Canaan. As argued earlier (§7.6.2), it is good old Canaan to which the future restored Israel will *return*. You cannot return to a land where you have never been before — the heavenly country — but you *can* return to a land that your fathers once possessed, and from which they were driven because of their sins.

(c) *The city.* The New Testament does indeed speak of a "Jerusalem above" (Gal. 4:26), the "city that has foundations" (Heb. 11:10; cf. v. 16), the "city of the living God" (12:22), the "city that is to come" (13:14), and the "new Jerusalem" (Rev. 3:12; 21:2; 21:10).[10] However, the existence of this spiritual "city" does not at all contradict the Old Testament prophecies concerning Israel's return to the promised land, which also involves the return to and restoration of the earthly Jerusalem (e.g., Ps. 69:35; 102:13-14; 147:2; Isa. 51:3; 58:12; 60:10; 61:4; Jer. 33:4-6).

(d) *The throne.* The New Testament depicts Jesus as sitting

---

7. Ibid., 42–44, 152, 166, 192–93, 206, 225, 241–43, 267.
8. Ibid., 318–20, 324–25, 328, 410–13, 428, 471, 503, 515, 541.
9. Roozemeijer (1911, 313); Matter (1951, 67); Ridderbos (1959, 265); Van Genderen (2008, 854–55).
10. They are not always necessarily the same city. I understand the "city" in Hebrews to be what could be called the heavenly capital of the "world to come," whereas the "New Jerusalem" is identical with the Bride of the Lamb (Rev. 21:9–10).

at present "at the right hand of the throne" of God (Heb. 8:1; 12:2; cf. Matt. 26:64; Acts 2:33-34; 5:31; Rom. 8:34; Eph. 1:20; Col. 3:1; Heb. 1:3, 13; 10:12; 1 Pet. 3:22). But that is not *Jesus'* throne. He himself clearly makes the distinction: "The one who conquers, I will grant him to sit with me on my throne, as I also conquered and sat down with my Father on his throne" (Rev. 3:21). One is the past (and present): Jesus sat down, and sits, with his Father on *the Father's* throne, but in the future (the Messianic kingdom) he will sit on *his own* throne. Jesus confirmed this in other statements: ". . . in the new world, when the Son of Man will sit on his glorious throne . . ." (Matt. 19:28). "When the Son of Man comes in his glory, and all the angels with him, then he will sit on his glorious throne" (25:31).

This is nothing other than the throne of David: "And the Lord God will give to him the throne of his father David, and he will reign over the house of Jacob forever, and of his kingdom there will be no end" (Luke 1:32-33). "Of the increase of his [i.e. Messiah's] government and of peace there will be no end, on the throne of David and over his kingdom, to establish it and to uphold it with justice and with righteousness from this time forth and forevermore" (Isa. 9:7). There is no throne of David either in heaven or in the Ekklesia. The throne of David will be where it always was: in Jerusalem (e.g., 1 Kgs 2:12, 24, 45; 3:6; Jer. 13:13; 17:25; 22:2, 4, 30). It is also called the "throne of Israel" (1 Kgs 8:25; 9:5; 2 Chron. 6:16), and the (earthly) "throne of the LORD" (1 Chron. 29:23).[11]

## 2.2   Israel: Spiritual Aspects

(a) *Circumcision.* The New Testament speaks of circumcision in a spiritual sense (Acts 7:51; Rom. 2:28-29; Phil. 3:3; Col. 2:11), though it must be added that the Old Testament knew of such an application as well (Exod. 6:12, 30; Lev. 26:41; Deut. 10:16; 30:6; Jer. 4:4; 9:26; Ezek. 44:7; 44:6-9). The spiritual ap-

---

11. In Exod. 17:16 it is the heavenly throne of the LORD; in the "world to come," Jerusalem as such will be called the "throne of the LORD" (Jer. 3:17).

plication of circumcision does not deny the fact that Israel in the Messianic kingdom will be a literally circumcised nation: "Awake, awake, put on your strength, O Zion; put on your beautiful garments, O Jerusalem, the holy city; for there shall no more come into you the uncircumcised and the unclean" (Isa. 52:1). "No foreigner, uncircumcised in heart and flesh, of all the foreigners who are among the people of Israel, shall enter my sanctuary" (Ezek. 44:9).

(b) *The temple.* In the New Testament, the Ekklesia is figuratively called a "temple" (1 Cor. 3:16; 2 Cor. 6:16; Eph. 2:20-22), but this never suggests that such is the fulfillment of Old Testament prophecy concerning the future temple. Prophecy teaches that the Messiah will build a temple, which in Zechariah's days could refer only to Jerusalem: "Behold, the man whose name is the Branch: for he shall branch out from his place, and he shall build the temple of the LORD. It is he who shall build the temple of the LORD and shall bear royal honor, and shall sit and rule on his throne. And there shall be [NKJV: So He shall be] a priest on his throne, and the counsel of peace shall be between them both" (Zech. 6:12-13). The Branch is generally taken to be the Messiah. It is not Zerubbabel, for the Branch will sit on the throne of David, and Zerubbabel did not (cf. 2.1 point [d]). NKJV and other translations make clear that the Messiah is both King and Priest.

This temple of the Messianic "world to come" is extensively described in Ezekiel 40-43, in such detail that any spiritualization simply renders these chapters meaningless. Compare Jesus' declaration to Jerusalem: "See, your house [i.e., the temple; cf. 21:13; Micah 3:12] is left to you desolate. For I tell you, you will not see me again, until you say, 'Blessed is he who comes in the name of the Lord'" (Matt. 23:38-39; cf. Ps. 118:26). The temple in Jerusalem will not remain desolate forever; one day Messiah himself will rebuild it (see further Isa. 56:7; 60:7-13; 62:9).

(c) *The altar.* The New Testament speaks of an "altar" in a figurative sense (1 Cor. 10:18-21; Heb. 13:10). However, this does not change the fact that in the temple of Ezekiel, there will be both an altar for burnt offerings and an altar of incense (40:46-47; 41:22; 43:13-27; 45:19; 47:1; cf. "table" in 44:16), both of which will be literal altars (see §2.5.3).

## 3 The Kingdom of God
### 3.1 Passages

In the light of the New Testament, it is easy enough to spiritualize away the Messianic kingdom altogether: "My kingdom is not of this world. If my kingdom were of this world, my servants would have been fighting, that I might not be delivered over to the Jews. But my kingdom is not from the world" (John 18:36; cf. Rom. 14:17; Col. 1:13). It is indeed a "kingdom of heavens" (a heavenly kingdom; thus almost always in Matthew), but emphatically on this earth. Even in the New Testament the reign of Christ is geographically defined: we saw that he will receive the throne of David, and will reign over Israel (Luke 1:32-33). The coming of the Son of Man is connected with the "holy place" (in Jerusalem) and with Judea (Matt. 24:15-30). In Acts 1, the words of the angels ("This Jesus, who was taken up from you into heaven, will come *in the same way* as you saw him go into heaven," v. 11) remind us of Zechariah 14:4-5 ("On that day his feet shall stand on the Mount of Olives.... Then the LORD my God will come, and all the holy ones with him").

In the Old Testament, it is clearly stated that "heaven rules" (Dan. 4:26), but that nevertheless God's kingdom is on earth, in a very tangible way. Out of dozens of possible references I choose only these: "[T]he LORD of hosts reigns on Mount Zion and in Jerusalem, and his glory will be before his elders.... On this mountain the LORD of hosts will make for all peoples a feast of rich food, a feast of well-aged wine, of rich food full of marrow, of aged wine well refined. And he will swallow up on this mountain the covering that is cast over all peoples, the veil that is spread over all nations. He will swallow up death forever; and the Lord God will wipe away tears from all faces, and the reproach of his people he will take away from all the earth, for the Lord has spoken. For the hand of the Lord will rest on this mountain, and Moab shall be trampled down in his place" (Isa. 24:23; 25:6-8, 10).

"It shall come to pass in the latter days that the mountain of the house of the Lord shall be established as the highest of the mountains, and it shall be lifted up above the hills; and peoples shall flow to it, and many nations shall come, and say: 'Come, let us go up to the mountain of the Lord, to the house of the God of Jacob, that he may teach us his ways and that we may walk in his paths.' For out of Zion shall go forth the Torah, and the word of the Lord from Jerusalem. He shall judge between many peoples, and shall decide for strong nations far away; and they shall beat their swords into plowshares, and their spears into pruning hooks; nation shall not lift up sword against nation, neither shall they learn war anymore; but they shall sit every man under his vine and under his fig tree, and no one shall make them afraid, for the mouth of the Lord of hosts has spoken" (Micah 4:1-4).

"And the Lord will be king over all the earth. On that day the Lord will be one and his name one. The whole land shall be turned into a plain from Geba to Rimmon south of Jerusalem. But Jerusalem shall remain aloft on its site from the Gate of Benjamin to the place of the former gate, to the Corner Gate, and from the Tower of Hananel to the king's winepresses. And it shall be inhabited, for there shall never again be a decree of utter destruction. Jerusalem shall dwell in security. . . . And the wealth of all the surrounding nations shall be collected, gold, silver, and garments in great abundance. . . . Then everyone who survives of all the nations that have come against Jerusalem shall go up year after year to worship the King, the Lord of hosts, and to keep the Feast of Booths. And if any of the families of the earth do not go up to Jerusalem to worship the King, the Lord of hosts, there will be no rain on them. And if the family of Egypt does not go up and present themselves, then on them there shall be no rain; there shall be the plague with which the LORD afflicts the nations that do not go up to keep the Feast of Booths. This shall be the punishment to Egypt and the punishment to all the nations that do not go up to keep the Feast of Booths" (Zech. 14:9–19).

## 3.2 Approaches

In principle, there are four ways to approach the prophecies just mentioned and many similar ones. They are seen as fulfilled ... :

1. *Shortly after the Babylonian captivity.* However, Zechariah prophesied *after* this captivity, yet speaks of events in the future. He even speaks of a *future* return of Israel to the promised land after a new exile (Zech. 10:8–9 NKJV; notice v. 9a in a literal translation, "I will sow them among the peoples"; see 4.2 below). Moreover, also in the pre-exilic prophecies, the restoration promises are invariably linked with the establishment of the Messianic kingdom in power and glory. No return prophecy, then, can be considered to be completely fulfilled; the ultimate fulfillment involves the return of the King himself.

2. *In the present age*, in a spiritualized form. I have already indicated why I think this to be unwarranted and impossible: it robs prophecy of its obvious literal interpretation, and cannot do any justice to the many details of prophecy. It even *falsifies* prophecy: if God's Word tells us that Israel will return to the land from which their forefathers had been driven, this can in no way be applied to some land, physical or spiritual, other than Canaan. Such an approach is a typical example of a (rather common) hermeneutical error: allowing dogmatics (in this case, the federalist prejudice) to govern exegesis instead of the other way around.

3. *In the new heavens and the new earth.* This does not work either, because the prophecies all presuppose very present-earthly conditions, and even sin and judgment. In the eternal state, there will be no more sin; but Zechariah 14, for

example, speaks of the sin of those who will refuse to go up to Jerusalem for the Feast of Booths. Likewise, Isaiah tells us about the Messianic kingdom: "No more shall there be in it an infant who lives but a few days, or an old man who does not fill out his days, for the young man shall die a hundred years old, and the sinner a hundred years old shall be accursed" (65:20).[12]

4. Only one plausible interpretation remains: the prophecies quoted, and many others like them, refer to the Messianic kingdom in the "world to come." Isaiah and the other prophets clearly spoke of an age *after* the present age (and beginning with the coming of Messiah in power and glory), and *before* what Peter and John call the "new heavens and the new earth."

Please note carefully here the difference between *typology* and *spiritualizing*. In typology the historical significance of the events described — either in the past or in the future — is *undisputed*. Typology searches for a deeper, spiritual meaning, but leaves the historical character of the events untouched. In spiritualizing, however, the historical significance of the Old and New Testament prophecies is *replaced by* the spiritual significance. Typology claims that prophetic events must be honored in their historical character, although they may have a typological meaning for the church. Spiritualizing *robs* prophecies of their literal meaning and accepts only their (alleged) spiritual meaning. We have seen that the apostle Paul made several typological applications of certain Old Testament prophecies, though always honoring the literal fulfillment of these prophecies.

---

12. The expression "new heavens and a new earth" in Isa. 65:17 should not confuse us. Isaiah's horizon does not reach any further than the future Messianic kingdom *before* the end of the present creation (which is yet a "world to come"), whereas "the new heavens and the new earth" in 2 Pet. 3:13 and Rev. 21:1 clearly reach *beyond* the present creation.

## 4 Federalism and Spiritualism
### 4.1 The Promised Land and the Covenant of Grace

In the present study, I have pointed repeatedly to the distinction between a natural people, such as Israel, and a spiritual people, such as the Ekklesia. Federalists seem to have little sensitivity for this distinction, and for some other distinctions as well. For instance, someone who wishes to view all Old Testament covenants as forms of the one (alleged) "covenant of grace" *and* wishes to view Gentile Christians as included in them, can do so only by spiritualizing all typically Israelite aspects.[13] That is, they are entirely separated from natural, ethnic Israel—for *that* Israel there is no place anymore in their thinking—and they are robbed of their literal meaning.

Take an obvious example. Both the Abrahamic and the Palestinian covenants contain an explicit land promise and very material blessings: Israel would possess the land "from the river of Egypt to the great river, the river Euphrates" (Gen. 15:18). "And the LORD your God will bring you into the land that your fathers possessed, that you may possess it. And he will make you more prosperous and numerous than your fathers. And the LORD your God will circumcise your heart and the heart of your offspring, so that you will love the LORD your God with all your heart and with all your soul, that you may live. . . . The LORD your God will make you abundantly prosperous in all the work of your hand, in the fruit of your womb and in the fruit of your cattle and in the fruit of your ground. For the LORD will again take delight in prospering you, as he took delight in your fathers" (Deut. 30:5-9).

Jeremiah 31, *the* chapter about the institution of the New Covenant (vv. 31-34), also says, "Sing aloud with gladness for Jacob, and raise shouts for the chief of the nations; proclaim, give praise, and say, 'O LORD, save your people, the remnant of Israel.' Behold, I will bring them from the north country

---

13. Berkhof (1979, 632) recognizes both the national and spiritual aspects of the Abrahamic covenant, but in practice he does not seem to know what to do with the former.

and gather them from the farthest parts of the earth, among them the blind and the lame, the pregnant woman and she who is in labor, together; a great company, they shall return here. . . . Once more they shall use these words in the land of Judah and in its cities, when I restore their fortunes: 'The LORD bless you, O habitation of righteousness, O holy hill!'" (vv. 7–8, 23–24).

What is *in concreto* left of this in all federalist views of the one, universal "covenant of grace"?[14] The genuine, consistent federalist has only one way out here, and that is to spiritualize under the New Covenant all that is written about Abraham's physical offspring and about the promised land.[15] If this is done in a consistent way, *physical* Israel, Jerusalem, the promised land (Canaan), the Davidic throne and kingdom, the temple and altar of Ezekiel, and circumcision, are all robbed of their literal meaning. That is, they become a *spiritual* Israel, a heavenly city, a heavenly land, a heavenly throne and kingdom, the Ekklesia as God's Temple, a spiritual altar, and spiritual circumcision (see above).[16]

I acknowledge that, of course, according to the New Testament there *is* a heavenly city, a heavenly land, a heavenly throne, a spiritual temple, a spiritual altar, and spiritual circumcision. *But nowhere in Scripture is it taught that these matters have **replaced** the promised land, the earthly Jerusalem, throne, and temple.* This is the fundamental logical flaw in supersessionism. It overlooks the fact that the presence of these New Testament spiritual matters does not alter in the least God's eternal promise of an earthly land, city, throne, and temple to *Israel*. To say otherwise is not simply a federalist invention, but an outright distortion of Scripture. It is emphatically about God's promises to *ethnic Israel* that Paul says, "[T]he

---

14. Cf. the similar question by Wellum (2006, 109–110).
15. A shocking example is still Kuyper (see, e.g., 2014, 451–89), whose supersessionism even exhibits anti-Semitic traits. Regarding this, see Van Klinken (1996, 38–53).
16. See, e.g., Robertson (2000).

gifts and the calling of God are irrevocable" (Rom. 11:29).

## 4.2 Irrevocable Promises

Imagine, *God* says to Israel many times: If you depart from me, I will drive you out of your land. But if you repent and return to *me*, I will make you return to your land as well. Then the federalist comes and says to the Jew: If you repent, you will have to give up everything that is Jewish about you, you have to join the (almost entirely Gentile) church, that is, factually you have to become "one of us" — a Gentile. And in the end God will give you your land — which turns out to be, not Canaan, but some heavenly land. Now what kind of exegesis is this? What kind of message is this to Israel? It almost looks as if God is deceiving his people. He tells them exactly what land he is going to give them — please notice, not after the Babylonian exile but in the Messianic kingdom — namely, *their land of old*, with many geographical details (e.g., Jer. 31:6, 12; Ezek. 47:13-23; Joel 3:12, 16-18; Zech. 14:10-11; etc.). No, says the federalist, all these details have to be spiritualized.[17]

Let us carefully take notice of what is happening here. God says: Israel will return to *their own* land, the *same* land in which their fathers had lived and from which they were driven. No, says the federalist, since Christ, that "land" means heaven. God says: Israel will *rebuild* its city, Jerusalem of old (Jer. 30:18). No, says the federalist, since Christ, that city is the new, heavenly Jerusalem. *How* does the federalist know this? He has no proof for it — except that the New Testament turns out to know also of a heavenly land, a heavenly city, and a heavenly sanctuary — apart from his federalist prejudices.

"I will give to you and to your offspring after you the land of your sojournings, all the land of Canaan, for an everlasting possession" (Gen. 17:8; cf. 48:4). Foreseeing that Israel would be driven out because of their sins, Moses says, "And the LORD your God will bring you into the land that your fathers possessed, that you may possess it" (Deut. 30:5), *no other land*.

---

17. A recent Baptist example is Wellum (2012, 707–16).

"They shall dwell in the land *that I gave to my servant Jacob, where your fathers lived*. They and their children and their children's children shall dwell there forever, and David my servant [i.e., Messiah] shall be their prince forever. I will make a covenant of peace with them. It shall be an everlasting covenant with them. And I will set them in their land and multiply them, and will set my sanctuary in their midst forevermore" (Ezek. 37:25–26). Please note: no other land than Canaan; the land that your fathers possessed, the land that God gave to Jacob; and this as an *everlasting* covenant.

Moreover, the fulfillment of such prophecies is *not* limited to the return from the Babylonian captivity, as federalists have often claimed. First, Israel's physical and spiritual restoration in its own land is invariably connected with the Messianic kingdom as it will be established in peace and righteousness, power and majesty, at the coming of Messiah.

Second, the prophecies do not speak of a return from Babylon only (as in Isa. 43:14; Jer. 3:17), but a return from the Diaspora: Israel's dispersion throughout *all* the nations: "He will raise a signal for the nations and will assemble the banished of Israel, and gather the dispersed of Judah from the *four corners of the earth*" (Isa. 11:12). "Behold, I will bring them from the north country and gather them from the *farthest parts of the earth*" (Jer. 31:8). "I will take you from the nations and gather you from *all the countries* and bring you into your own land" (Ezek. 36:24).

Third, also the *post-exilic* books, written after Judah's return from Babylon, speak of a *future* return of Israel: "I will bring them back because I have compassion on them, and they shall be as though I had not rejected them. . . . Though I scattered them among the nations,[18] yet in far countries they shall remember me, and with their children they shall live

---

18. This is a prejudiced rendering; literally, the text says, "I will sow them among the peoples, and they shall remember Me in far countries" (NKJV). *After* the return from Babylon, then, this prophecy speaks of a future, worldwide Diaspora *and* a return from there.

and return. I will bring them home from the land of Egypt, and gather them from Assyria, and I will bring them to the land of Gilead and to Lebanon, till there is no room for them" (Zech. 10:6, 9–10).

Today, there are Reformed theologians who have emphatically denounced any form of supersessionism and spiritualizing.[19] But I wonder whether they have really thought through their standpoint. Baptist Jelle Horjus rightly says, "[T]he statement, 'baptism has replaced circumcision,' sounds suspiciously much like that other one, 'the church has replaced Israel.'"[20] In other words, one may reject supersessionism, which has caused so much misery to Israel, and yet maintain the notion of some "spiritual Israel," and the idea that baptism has replaced circumcision. When someone rejects supersessionism, he will also believe again in a redemptive future for ethnic Israel, in its own land, under the blessed dominion of the Messiah. *In that nation, all men will be circumcised* (Isa. 52:1; Ezek. 44:6–9). Circumcision has not been done away with, and therefore cannot have been replaced by baptism (see further, Appendix I).

With a variation on 1 Kings 18:21 (NIV), I would like to say to those federalists who tell us they reject supersessionism — and I take them seriously: "How long will you waver between two opinions?" As long as they keep baptizing infants with an appeal to the one "covenant of grace," they have not really shaken off supersessionism, even if they think they have done so. For how could there be any literal land promise remaining for ethnic Israel within that one "covenant of grace"? How can there be room for Messianic (i.e., Jesus-confessing) Jews who circumcise their little boys *and* baptize them after they have come to faith? How, in the *eschaton*, can that one "covenant of grace" have any room for a distinct position of *circumcised* Israel on earth, distinguished — though not

---

19. A beautiful example is the Reformed Wentsel (1998a, 122–32).
20. Horjus (2009, 53).

separated—from the glorified Ekklesia?[21]

---

21. See chapter 7 above, and extensively Ouweneel (2012).

# Bibliography

Aalders, G. C. 1939. *Het verbond Gods: Een hoofdstuk uit de geschiedenis der openbaring.* Kampen: Kok.

Akenson, D. H. 1992. *God's Peoples: Covenant and Land in South Africa, Israel and Ulster.* Ithaca, NY: Cornell University Press.

Bakker, H., P. Van Geest, and H. Van Loon, eds. 2009. *Cyprian of Carthage: Studies on His Life, Language, and Thought.* Leuven: Peeters.

Balke, W., J. Klok and W. Van 't Spijker. 2008. *Johannes Calvijn: Zijn leven, zijn werk.* Kampen: Kok.

Barker, K. L. 1985. *Zechariah.* Expositor's Bible Commentary VII. Grand Rapids, MI: Zondervan.

Barnett, P. 1997. *The Second Epistle to the Corinthians.* New International Commentary on the New Testament. Grand Rapids, MI: Eerdmans.

Barnouw, P. J. 1963. *Philippus van Limborch.* Den Haag: Mouton and Co.

Barrett, C. K. 1957. *A Commentary on the Epistle to the Romans.* Harpers New Testament Commentary. San Francisco: Harper and Row.

Barth, K. 1957. *Church Dogmatics.* Vol. II/2. Edinburgh: T. & T. Clark.

― ― ―. 1986. *Church Dogmatics*. Vol. III/1. Edinburgh: T. & T. Clark.

Bateman, H. W. IV, ed. 1999. *Three Central Issues in Contemporary Dispensationalism: A Comparison of Traditional and Progressive Views*. Grand Rapids, MI: Kregel.

Bauswein, J.-J. and L. Vischer, eds. 1999. *The Reformed Family Worldwide: A Survey of Reformed Churches, Theological Schools, and International Organizations*. Grand Rapids, MI: Eerdmans.

Bavinck, H. 2002–2008. *Reformed Dogmatics*. Edited by J. Bolt. Translated by J. Vriend. 4 vols. Grand Rapids, MI: Baker Academic.

Becking, B. E. J. H. 1986. *Blijf bij uw Bevrijder! In de leer van de Tien Geboden*. Kampen: Kok.

Beisner, E. C., ed. 2004. *The Auburn Avenue Theology: Pros and Cons*. Fort Lauderdale: Knox Theological Seminary.

Berkhof, H. 1966. *Om het verbond*. Bijlage Maandblad *Kerk en Israël*. 20(10). 's-Gravenhage: Boekencentrum.

― ― ―. 1991. *Christian Faith: An Introduction to the Study of the Faith*. Translated by S. Woudstra. Grand Rapids, MI: Eerdmans.

Berkhof, L. 1979. *Systematic Theology*. 4th ed. Grand Rapids, MI: Eerdmans.

Berkouwer, G. C. 1976. *The Church*. Translated by J. E. Davison. Grand Rapids, MI: Eerdmans.

Berkowitz, A. and D. 1999. *Take Hold: Embracing Our Divine Inheritance with Israel*. 2nd ed. Littleton, CO: First Fruits of Zion.

Bernard, J. H. 1979. *The Second Epistle to the Corinthians*. The Expositor's Greek Testament. Vol. 3. Grand Rapids, MI: Eerdmans.

Bierma, L. D., C. D. Gunnoe Jr., K. Maag, and P. W. Fields. 2005. *An Introduction to the Heidelberg Catechism: Sources, History, and Theology*. Grand Rapids, MI: Baker Academic.

Bijlsma, R. 1981. *Toch gemeente*. Kampen: Kok.

Bilezikian, G. 2001. *De kerk als gemeenschap*. Translated by P. Geertse. Hoornaar: Gideon. (Orig. Eng. ed.: *Community 101*. 1997. Grand Rapids, MI: Zondervan)

Blaauwendraad, J. 2000. *De leer tegen het licht: Belofte en verbond in Woord en Reformatie*. Heerenveen: Groen.

Blaising, C. A. and D. L. Bock. 1993. *Progressive Dispensationalism*. Grand Rapids, MI: Baker Academic.

Bonhoeffer, D. 1997. *Creation and Fall: A Theological Exposition of Genesis 1–3*, Vol. 3. Minneapolis: Fortress.

Booth, R. R. 1995. *Children of the Promise: The Biblical Case for Infant Baptism*. Phillipsburg, NJ: P&R Publishing.

Boston, T. 1741 (repr. 2013). *A View of the Covenant of Grace*. N.p.: Book on Demand Ltd.

Boyd, G. A. 2000. *God of the Possible: A Biblical Introduction to the Open View of God*. Grand Rapids, MI: Baker.

– – –. 2001. *Satan and the Problem of Evil: Constructing a Trinitarian Warfare Theodicy*. Downers Grove, IL: InterVarsity Press Academic.

Brienen, T., K. Exalto, K., J. Van Genderen, C. Graafland, and W. Van 't Spijker, eds. 1986. *De Nadere Reformatie: Beschrijving van haar voornaamste vertegenwoordigers*. 's-Gravenhage: Boekencentrum.

Brown, C., ed. 1976 (repr. 1992). *The New International Dictionary of New Testament Theology*, 4 vols. Carlisle: Paternoster.

Brown, M. G. and Z. Keele. 2012. *Sacred Bond: Covenant Theology Explored*. Grandville, MI: Reformed Fellowship.

Bruce, F. F. 1984. *The Epistles to the Colossians, to Philemon, and to the Ephesians*. New International Commentary on the New Testament. Grand Rapids, MI: Eerdmans.

– – –. 1988. *The Book of the Acts*. Rev. ed. New International Commentary on the New Testament. Grand Rapids, MI: Eerdmans.

Bullinger, E. W. 1972 (repr.). *The Foundations of Dispensational Truth*. London: Samuel Bagster and Sons.

Bullinger, H. 1534 (repr. 1991). *A Brief Exposition of the One and Eternal Testament or Covenant of God*, in *Fountainhead of Federalism: Heinrich Bullinger and the Covenantal Tradition*, translated by C. S. McCoy and J. W. Baker (Louisville, KY: Westminster/John Knox).

— — —. 1537 (repr. 1844). *The Old Faith*. In *Writings and Translations of Miles Coverdale, Bishop of Exeter*. Edited by G. Pearson. Cambridge: The University Press.

Calvin, J. 1960. *The Institutes of the Christian Religion*. Translated by Ford Lewis Battles. Edited by John T. McNeill. The Library of Christian Classics. Vol. 20. Philadelphia: Westminster Press.

— — —. 1973 (repr.). *The Epistles of Paul The Apostle to the Romans and to the Thessalonians*. Translated by R. Mackenzie. Edited by D. W. Torrance and T. F. Torrance. Grand Rapids: Eerdmans.

— — —. 1989. *The First and Second Epistles of St. Peter*. Translated by W. B. Johnston. Edited by D. W. Torrance and T. F. Torrance. Grand Rapids: Eerdmans.

Carson, D. A. 1987. *Showing the Spirit: A Theological Exposition of 1 Corinthians 12–14*. Grand Rapids, MI: Baker.

Chafer, L. S. 1983. *Systematic Theology* 15th ed. 8 vols. Dallas: Dallas Seminary Press.

Cherry, C., ed. 1971. *God's New Israel: Religious Interpretations of American destiny*. Englewood Cliffs: Prentice Hall.

Christiansen, E. J. 1995. *The Covenant in Judaism and Paul: A Study of Ritual Boundaries as Identity Markers*. Leiden: Brill.

Clark, R. S., ed. 2007. *Covenant, Justification, and Pastoral Ministry: Essays by the Faculty of Westminster Seminary California*. Phillipsburg, NJ: P&R Publishing.

Clowney, E. P. 1995. *The Church*. Contours of Christian Theology, Downers Grove, IL: InterVarsity Press.

Cocceius, J. 1660 (repr. 2015). *The Doctrine of the Covenant and Testament of God*. Translated by C. Carmichael. Grand Rapids, MI: Reformation Heritage Books.

Cohen, A. 1983. *The Soncino Chumash*. The Soncino Books of the Bible. London: Soncino.

— — —, ed. 1985 (repr.). *The Psalms*. The Soncino Books of the Bible. London: Soncino.

Congar, Y. 1970. *L'Église de S. Augustin à l'époque moderne*. Paris: Cerf.

Craith, M. N. 2002. *Plural Identities – Singular Narratives: The Case of Northern Ireland*. New York: Berghahn Books.

Cranfield, C. E. B. 1981. *Romans*. International Critical Commentary. Vol. 2. Edinburgh: T. and T. Clark.

Darby, J. N. n.d.-a. *The Collected Writings of J. N. Darby*. Kingston-on-Thames: Stow Hill Bible and Tract Depot.

— — —. n.d.-b. *Letters of J. N. Darby*. 3 vols. Kingston-on-Thames: Stow Hill Bible and Tract Depot.

Davids, P. H. 1990. *The First Epistle of Peter*. New International Commentary on the New Testament. Grand Rapids, MI: Eerdmans.

Davies, W. D. 1969. *The Sermon on the Mount*. Cambridge: Cambridge University Press.

De Graaf, S. G. 1940. *Hoofdlijnen in de dogmatiek*. Kampen: Kok.

— — —. 1977. *Promise and Deliverance*. Translated by H. E. and E. Runner. 4 vols. St. Catharines, Ont.: Paideia Press.

De Kroon, M. 1996. *De eer van God en het heil van de mens: Bijdrage tot het verstaan van de theologie van Johannes Calvijn naar zijn Institutie*. Leiden: J. J. Groen and Zoon.

Delitzsch, F. 1874. *Commentary on the Epistle to the Hebrews*. Translated by T. L. Kingsbury. Edinburgh: T. and T. Clark.

Demarest, B. 1997. *The Cross and Salvation: The Doctrine of Salvation*. Wheaton, IL: Crossway Books.

De Moor, R. 2001. *Reformed: What It Means, Why It Matters*. Grand Rapids, MI: CRC Publications.

Den Boer, W. 2008. *Duplex Amor Dei: Contextuele karakteristiek van de theologie van Jacobus Arminius (1559-1609)*. Apeldoorn: Instituut voor Reformatieonderzoek.

Denham Smith, J. n.d. *The Brides of Scripture, or, Foreshadows of the Coming Glory*. Glasgow: Pickering and Inglis.

De Ru, G. 1968. *De kinderdoop en het Nieuwe Testament*. 3rd ed.Wageningen: Veenman and Zonen.

De Vries, P. 2001. *Een vast verbond: De visie van de puriteinen op het verbond*. Houten: Den Hertog.

Diemer, N. 1933. *Het scheppingsverbond met Adam*. Kampen: Kok.

Dods, M. 1979 (repr.). *The Epistle to the Hebrews*. Expositor's Greek Testament. Vol. 4. Grand Rapids, MI: Eerdmans.

Douma, J. 1976. *Algemene genade: Uiteenzetting, vergelijking en beoordeling van de opvattingen van A. Kuyper, K. Schilder en Joh. Calvijn over 'algemene genade'*. 2nd ed. Goes: Oosterbaan and LeCointre.

Dulles, A. R. 1987. *Models of the Church*. Garden City, NY: Image Books.

Dumbrell, W. J. 1984 (repr. 1997). *Covenant and Creation: A Theology of the Old Testament Covenants*. Carlisle: Paternoster.

Duncan, J. L. 1998. "The Covenant Idea in Irenaeus of Lyons: An Introduction and Survey." Paper given at the North American Patristic Society. Greenville, SC: Reformed Academic Press.

Dunn, J. D. G. 1998. *The Theology of Paul the Apostle*. Edinburgh: T. and T. Clark.

Du Toit, A. 1985. "Puritans in Africa? Afrikaner 'Calvinism' and Kuyperian Neo-Calvinism in the Late Nineteenth-Century." *Comparative Studies in Society and History* 27.2 (April 1985): 209-40.

Elam, A. E., R. C. Van Kooten, and R. A. Bergquist. 2014. *Merit and Moses: A Critique of the Klinean Doctrine of Republication*. Eugene, OR: Wipf and Stock.

Ellison, H. L. 1976. *The Mystery of Israel*. Rev. ed. Carlisle: Paternoster Press.

Engelsma, D. J. 2012. *Federal Vision: Heresy at the Root*. Jenison, MI: Reformed Free Publishing.

Engle, P. E. and J. H. Armstrong, eds. 2007. *Understanding Four Views on Baptism*. Grand Rapids, MI: Zondervan.

Erickson, M. J. 1998. *Christian Theology*. Rev. ed. Grand Rapids, MI: Baker Book House.

Estelle, B. D., J. V. Fesko, and D. VanDrunen, eds. 2009. *The Law Is Not of Faith: Essays on Works and Grace in the Mosaic Covenant*. Phillipsburg, NJ: P&R Publishing.

Faulenbach, H. 1973. *Weg und Ziel der Erkenntnis Christi: Eine Untersuchtung zur Theologie des Johannes Coccejus*. Neukirchen/Vluyn: Neukirchener Verlag.

Fensham, F. C. 1967. "Covenant, Promise and Expectation in the Bible." *Theologische Zeitschrift* 23: 305–22.

Ferguson, E. 2003. *Backgrounds of Early Christianity*. 3rd ed. Grand Rapids, MI: Eerdmans.

— — —. 2009. *Baptism in the Early Church: History, Theology, and Liturgy in the First Five Centuries*. Grand Rapids, MI: Eerdmans.

Finlan, S. and V. Kharlamov. 2006. *Theosis: Deification in Christian Theology*. Princeton Theological Monograph. Vol. 1. Eugene, OR: Pickwick Publications.

Fitzmyer, J. A. 1993. *Romans: A New Translation with Introduction and Commentary*. New Haven, CT: Yale University Press.

Flesseman-van Leer, E. 1974. "Om de tweezijdigheid van het verbond." In *Weerwoord: Reacties op dr. H. Berkhof's "Christelijk geloof"*, 33–43. Nijkerk: Callenbach.

Frame, J. M. 2011. *The Escondido Theology: A Reformed Response to Two Kingdom Theology*. N.p.: Whitefield Media Productions.

Freeman, H. 1962. "The Problem of Efficacy of Old Testament Sacrifices." *Bulletin of the Evangelical Theological Society* 5:73–79.

Friedman, R. E. 1987. "The Hiding of the Face: An Essay on the Literary Unity of Biblical Narrative." In *Judaic Perspectives on Ancient Israel*, edited by J. Neusner, B. A. Levine and E. S. Frerichs, 207–22. Philadelphia: Fortress.

Fruchtenbaum, A. G. 1992. *Israelology: The Missing Link in Systematic Theology*. San Antonio, TX: Ariel Ministries Press.

Fung, R. Y. K. 1988. *The Epistle to the Galatians*. New International Commentary on the New Testament. Grand Rapids, MI: Eerdmans.

Geisler, N. L. 1979. "Philosophical Presuppositions of Biblical Errancy." In *Inerrancy*, edited by N. L. Geisler, 305–34. Grand Rapids: Zondervan.

– – –, ed. 1981. *Biblical Errancy: An Analysis of Its Philosophical Roots*. Grand Rapids, MI: Zondervan.

Gentry, P. J. and S. J. Wellum. 2012. *Kingdom through Covenant: A Biblical-Theological Understanding of the Covenants*. Wheaton, IL: Crossway Books.

Ginzberg, L. 1968. *The Legends of the Jews*. Vol. 3. Philadelphia: Jewish Publication Society of America.

Glueck, N. 1967. *Hesed in the Bible*. Cincinnati: Hebrew Union College Press.

Godet, F. L. 1998. *Commentary on Romans*. Grand Rapids, MI: Kregel.

Golding, P. 2004. *Covenant Theology: The Key of Theology in Reformed Thought and Tradition*. Fearn: Mentor.

Graafland, C. 1978. *Het vaste verbond: Israel en het Oude Testament bij Calvijn en het gereformeerd protestantisme*. Amsterdam: Bolland.

– – –. 1979. *Volwassendoop, kinderdoop, herdoop: Een bijbelse verkenning*. 2nd ed. Amersfoort: Echo.

– – –. 1987a. *Van Calvijn tot Barth: Oorsprong en ontwikkeling* van de leer der verkiezing in het gereformeerd protestantisme. 's-Gravenhage: Boekencentrum.

———. 1987b. "Gereformeerde Scholastiek, V. De invloed van de scholastiek op de Gereformeerde Orthodoxie." *Theologia Reformata* 30:4–25.

———. 1987c. "Gereformeerde Scholastiek, VI. De invloed van de scholastiek op de Nadere Reformatie (1, 2)." *Theologia Reformata* 30:109–31, 313–40.

———. 1992–1996. *Van Calvijn tot Comrie: Oorsprong en ontwikkeling van de leer van het verbond in het Gereformeerd Protestantisme*. 3 vols. Zoetermeer: Boekencentrum.

Gräbe, P. J. 2006. *New Covenant, New Community: The Significance of Biblical and Patristic Covenant Theology for Contemporary Understanding*. Milton Keynes: Paternoster.

Grant, F. W. 1901. *The Numerical Bible: Acts to II Corinthians*. New York: Loizeaux Brothers.

———. 1902. *The Numerical Bible: Hebrews to Revelation*. New York: Loizeaux Brothers.

———. n.d. *Reasons for my Faith as to Baptism*. New York: Loizeaux Brothers.

Grant, J. A. and A. I. Wilson, eds. 2005. *The God of Covenant: Biblical, Theological and Contemporary Perspectives*. Leicester: InterVarsity Press.

Green, J. B. 1997. *The Gospel of Luke*. New International Commentary on the New Testament. Grand Rapids, MI: Eerdmans.

Greijdanus, S. 1925. *De brief van den apostel Paulus aan de Epheziërs*. Korte Verklaring. Kampen: Kok.

Grogan, G. W. 1986. *Isaiah*. Expositor's Bible Commentary. Vol. 6. Grand Rapids, MI: Zondervan.

Grosheide, F. W. 1954. *Het heilig evangelie volgens Mattheüs*. 2nd ed. Commentaar op het Nieuwe Testament. Kampen: Kok.

———. 1955. *De brief aan de Hebreeën en de brief van Jakobus*. Commentaar op het Nieuwe Testament.. Kampen: Kok.

———. 1962. *De Handelingen der Apostelen* (1). Korte Verklaring. Kampen: Kok.

———. 1960. *De brief van Paulus aan de Efeziërs*. Commentaar op het Nieuwe Testament.. Kampen: Kok.

Grotius, H. 1646. *Annotationes in N. T.* Vol. 2. Paris: Gulielmus Pelé.

Guthrie, D. 1983. *Hebrews*. Tyndale New Testament Commentaries. Leicester: InterVarsity Press.

Hagoort, H., ed. 1999. *Het verbond van God met mensen*. Heerenveen: Groen.

Hahn, S. W. 2009. *Kinship by Covenant: A Canonical Approach to the Fulfillment of God's Saving Purposes*. New Haven, CT: Yale University Press.

Harinck, C. 1986. *De Schotse Verbondsleer: Van Robert Rollock tot Thomas Boston*. Utrecht: De Banier.

Harinck, C. 2002. *De prediking van het Evangelie: Het aanbod van genade*. Houten: Den Hertog.

Harris, R. L., G. L. Archer Jr., and B. K. Waltke. 1980. *Theological Wordbook of the Old Testament*. Chicago: Moody Publishers.

Hays, J. D., J. S. Duvall, and C. M. Pate. 2007. *Dictionary of Biblical Prophecy and End Times*. Grand Rapids, MI: Zondervan.

Heerma, W. 1951. *Van Gods verbond en woorden*. Haarlem: Ds. H. Janssen-Fonds.

Heitink, G. 2007. *Een kerk met karakter: Tijd voor heroriëntatie*. Kampen: Kok.

Helm, P. 1983. "Calvin and the Covenant: Unity and Continuity." *The Evangelical Quarterly* 55:65–81.

Henry, C. F. H., ed. 1962. *Basic Christian Doctrines*. Grand Rapids, MI: Baker.

Henry, M. 1691 (repr. 2003). *Unpublished Sermons on the Cove-*

nant of Grace. Fearn, UK: Christian Focus Publications.

Heppe, H. L. J. 1861 (repr. 2008). *Reformed Dogmatics*. Eugene, OR: Wipf and Stock.

Heyns, J. A. 1988. *Dogmatiek*. Pretoria: NG Kerkboekhandel.

Hicks, J. M. 1985. *The Theology of Grace in the Thought of Jacobus Arminius and Philip van Limborch: A Study in the Development of Seventeenth-Century Dutch Arminianism*. Ann Arbor, MI: UMI.

Hill, D. 1972. *The Gospel of Matthew*. Grand Rapids, MI: Eerdmans.

Hillers, D. R. 1969. *Covenant: The History of a Biblical Idea*. Baltimore: Johns Hopkins Press.

Hodge, C. 1859 (repr. 1998). *A Commentary on I and II Corinthians*. Edinburgh: Banner of Truth.

Hoek, J. 2006. "Terug naar het midden en zo vooruit." *Ellips* 268:8.

Hoek, J. and W. Verboom. 2010. *Eeuwige vriendschap: Om de waarde van Gods verbond*. Zoetermeer: Boekencentrum.

Hoekema, A. A. 1967. "The Covenant of Grace in Calvin's Teaching." *Calvin Theological Journal* 2:133–61.

Honig, A. G. 1892 (repr. 1991). *Alexander Comrie*. Leiden: J. J. Groen and Zoon.

Horjus, J. 2009. *Dopen wat mondig is*. N.p.: Unie van Baptisten Gemeenten in Nederland.

Horton, M. S. 2002. *Covenant and Eschatology: The Divine Drama*. Louisville, KY: Westminster John Knox Press.

– – –. 2006. *God of Promise: Introducing Covenant Theology*. Grand Rapids, MI: Baker Books.

– – –. 2007. *Covenant and Salvation: Union with Christ*. Louisville, KY: Westminster John Knox Press.

– – –. 2009. *Introducing Covenant Theology*. Grand Rapids, MI: Baker Books.

– – –. 2011. *The Christian Faith: A Systematic Theology for Pilgrims On the Way*. Grand Rapids, MI: Zondervan.

Hugenberger, G. 1994. *Marriage as a Covenant: A Study of Biblical Law and Ethics Governing Marriage Developed from the Perspective of Malachi.* Supplements to Vetus Testamentum 52. Leiden: Brill.

Hughes, P. E. 1962. *Paul's Second Epistle to the Corinthians.* New International Commentary on the New Testament. Grand Rapids, MI: Eerdmans.

— — —. 1977. *A Commentary on the Epistle to the Hebrews.* Grand Rapids, MI: Eerdmans.

Huisman, C. 1983. *Neerlands Israel: Het natiebesef der traditioneel-gereformeerden in de achttiende eeuw.* Dordrecht: J. P. van den Tol.

Hunt, J. P. T. 1988. "The History of the Interpretation of Colossians 2:11–12 up to the Council of Chalcedon, with Particular Reference to the Uses of these Verses as an Argument for Infant Baptism." MA thesis, Durham University.

— — —. 1990. "Colossians 2:11–12, the Circumcision/Baptism Analogy, and Infant Baptism." *Tyndale Bulletin* 41:227–44.

Hutten, K. 1957. *Geloof en sekte: Het sektarisme als anti-reformatorisch geloofsverschijnsel, zijn doelstelling en zijn tragiek.* Franeker: T. Wever.

Jeon, Jeong Koo. 2009. *Calvin's Covenant Theology in Light of Contemporary Discussion.* Eugene, OR: Wipf and Stock.

Jewett, P. K. 1978. *Infant Baptism and the Covenant of Grace.* Grand Rapids, MI: Eerdmans.

Jongeleen, J. 1927. *Lesboek over de gereformeerde geloofsleer.* Woerden: Grootendorst.

Jonker, W. D. 1988. *Uit vrye guns alleen: Oor uitverkiesing en verbond.* Pretoria: NG Kerkboekhandel.

Juster, D. 1995. *Jewish Roots: A Foundation of Biblical Theology.* Shippensburg, PA: Destiny Image Publishers.

Kac, A. W., ed. 1986. *The Messiahship of Jesus: Are Jews Changing Their Attitude Toward Jesus?* 2nd ed. Grand Rapids, MI: Baker Book House.

Kaiser Jr., W. C. 1970. "The Eschatological Hermeneutics of 'Epangelicalism': Promise Theology." *Journal of the Evangelical Theological Society* 13:2 (Spring 1970): 92-99.

———. 1978. *Toward an Old Testament Theology*. Grand Rapids, MI: Academie Books.

———. 1987. *Toward Rediscovering the Old Testament*. Grand Rapids, MI: Zondervan.

Kamphuis, J. 1985. *An Everlasting Covenant*. Translated by G. van Rongen. Launceston, Tas.: Publication Organization of the Free Reformed Churches of Australia.

Kaufmann, Y. 1988. *Christianity and Judaism: Two Covenants*. Jerusalem: Magness Press.

Kelly, W. 1923. *The Epistles of Peter*. London: C. A. Hammond.

Kersten, G. H. 1947. *De gereformeerde dogmatiek voor de gemeenten toegelicht*. 2 vols. Utrecht: De Banier.

Kertelge, K., ed. 1977. *Das kirchliche Amt im Neuen Testament*. Darmstadt: Wissenschaftliche Buchgesellschaft.

Kittel, G. et al., eds. 1964-76. *Theological Dictionary of the New Testament*. Translated by G. W. Bromiley. 10 vols. Grand Rapids, MI: Eerdmans.

Kline, M. G. 1963. *Treaty of the Great King*. Grand Rapids, MI: Eerdmans.

———. 1967. *By Oath Consigned*. Grand Rapids, MI: Eerdmans.

———. 2006a. *God, Heaven and Har Magedon: A Covenantal Tale of Cosmos and Telos*. Eugene, OR: Wipf and Stock.

———. 2006b. *Kingdom Prologue: Genesis Foundations for a Covenantal Worldview*. Eugene, OR: Wipf and Stock.

König, A. 2006. *Die Groot Geloofswoordeboek*. Vereeniging: Christelike Uitgewersmaatskappy.

Kuhn, T. S. 1962. *The Structure of Scientific Revolutions*. Chicago: University of Chicago Press.

Küng, H. 2001. *The Church*. London: Bloomsbury Academic.

Kuyper, A. 1965. *Principles of Sacred Theology*. Translated by J. H. DeVries. Grand Rapids, MI: Eerdmans.

———. 2011. *Wisdom and Wonder: Common Grace in Science and Art*. Edited by J. J. Ballor and S. J. Grabill. Translated by N. D. Kloosterman. Grand Rapids, MI: Christian's Library Press.

———. 2013. *Common Grace*. Vol. 1, Part 1: *Noah–Adam*. Edited by J. J. Ballor and S. J. Grabill. Translated by E. van der Maas and N. D. Kloosterman. Grand Rapids, MI: Christian's Library Press.

———. 2014. *Common Grace*. Vol. 1, Part 3: *Abraham–Parousia*. Edited by J. J. Ballor and S. J. Grabill. Translated by E. van der Maas and N. D. Kloosterman. Grand Rapids, MI: Christian's Library Press.

Ladd, G. E. 1959. *The Gospel of the Kingdom: Scriptural Studies in the Kingdom of God*. Grand Rapids, MI: Eerdmans.

Lagrange, M.-J. 1948. Évangelile *selon Saint-Matthieu*. Paris: Lecoffre.

Lane, W. L. 1991. *Hebrews 9–13*. Word Biblical Commentary. Vol. 47b. Waco, TX: Word.

Lang, A. 1907 (repr. 1967). *Der Heidelberger Katechismus und vier verwandte Katechismen*. Leipzig: A. Deichert (repr.: Darmstadt: Wissenschaftliche Buchgesellschaft).

Lapide, P. 1983. *Hij leerde in hun synagogen: Een joodse uitleg van de evangeliën*. Baarn: Ten Have.

———. 1984. *Uit de Bijbel leren leven: Op joodse wijze de Schriften lezen*. Baarn: Ten Have.

Lehne, S. 1990. *The New Covenant in Hebrews*. Journal for the Study of the NT, Suppl. Ser. 44. Sheffield: JSOT Press.

Leithart, P. 2007. *The Baptized Body*. Moscow, ID: Canon Press.

Leurdijk, G. H. and A. Moerkerken. 1986. *Twee pastorale brieven van Alexander Comrie: voorafgegaan door een overzicht van Comrie's theologische inzichten*. Veenendaal: Kool.

Lillback, P. A. 2001. *The Binding of God: Calvin's Role in the*

*Development of Covenant Theology.* Grand Rapids, MI: Baker.

Locher, G. W. 1979. *Die Zwinglische Reformation im Rahmen der europäischen Kirchengeschichte.* Göttingen: Vandenhoeck and Ruprecht.

Lohfink, N. 1991. *The Covenant Never Revoked: Biblical Reflections on Christian-Jewish Dialogue.* New York: Paulist Press.

Loonstra, B. 1987. "De historische wortels van de leer aangaande het verbond." *Theologia Reformata* 30,1:46–63.

Loonstra, B. 1990. *Verkiezing – Verzoening – Verbond: Beschrijving en beoordeling van de leer van het pactum salutis in de gereformeerde theologie.* 's-Gravenhage: Boekencentrum.

Loonstra, B. 2008. *Het badwater en de kinderen: Gedachten over de doop.* Zoetermeer: Boekencentrum.

Los, S. O. et al. 1943. *Verklaring van gevoelen: Met enkele bijlagen.* Pamflet (proregno.files.wordpress.com/2010/06/verklaring-van-gevoelen1.pdf).

Lossky, V. 1974. *In the Image and Likeness of God.* Crestwoord, NY: St. Vladimir's Seminary Press.

Lossky, V. 1976 (repr. 1998). *The Mystical Theology of the Eastern Church.* Crestwoord, NY: St. Vladimir's Seminary Press.

McCarthy, D. J. 1972. *Old Testament Covenant: A Survey of Current Opinions.* Oxford: Blackwell.

— — —. 1978. *Treaty and Covenant: A Study in Form in the Ancient Oriental Documents and in the Old Testament.* 2nd ed. Rome: Biblical Institute Press.

McGrath, A. 2010, *Christian Theology: An Introduction.* 5th ed. Hoboken, NJ: Wiley-Blackwell.

McGraw, R. M. 2012. *By Good and Necessary Consequence.* Grand Rapids, MI: Reformation Heritage Books.

McKay, D. 2001. *The Bond of Love: God's Covenantal Relationship with His Church.* Geanies House: Christian Focus Publications.

Marcel, P. 1958. *The Biblical Doctrine of Infant Baptism: Sacrament of the Covenant of Grace*. Cambridge: James Clarke and Co.

Marshall, I. H. 1978. *The Epistles of John*. New International Commentary on the New Testament. Grand Rapids, MI: Eerdmans.

Matter, H. M. 1951. "'Aldus zal geheel Israël behouden worden.' Waarheid en verdichting rondom Rom. 11:26a." In *Arcana Revelata* (feestbundel F.W. Grosheide), 59–68. Edited by N. J. Hommes et al. Kampen: Kok.

May, R. H. 1997. *Joshua and the Promised Land*. N.p.: United Methodist Church.

Medema, H. P. 1994. *De heerlijkheid en de verbonden: De openbaring van God in het oude en het nieuwe verbond: Een evangelische visie*. Vaassen: Medema.

Meijer, W. 1898. "Oranje en Israël." In *Oranje-album: Feestbundel ter gelegenheid van het aanvaarden der regeering door H.M. Koningin Wilhelmina op 31 Augustus 1898*. 434–52 Edited by A. J. Servaas van Rooijen. 's-Gravenhage: Mouton and Co.

Mendenhall, G. E. 1955. *Law and Covenant in Israel and the Ancient Near East*. Pittsburg: Biblical Colloquium.

Metzger, B. M. 1975. *A Textual Commentary on the Greek New Testament*. 2nd ed. London/New York: United Bible Societies.

Minear, P. S. 1960. *Images of the Church in the New Testament*. Philadephia: Westminster Press.

Moerkerken, A. 1979. *Genadeleven en genadeverbond*. Texel: Stark.

― ― ―. 2004. *Ons troostboek: Verklaring van de Heidelbergse Catechismus*. Houten: Den Hertog.

Moltmann, J. 1977. *The Church in the Power of the Spirit: A Contribution to Messianic Ecclesiology*. London: SCM Press.

Moo, D. J. 1996. *The Epistle to the Romans*. New International Commentary on the New Testament. Grand Rapids, MI:

Eerdmans.

Moodie, T. D. 1975. *The Rise of Afrikanerdom: Power, Apartheid, and the Afrikaner Civil Religion*. Berkeley, CA: University of California Press.

Moulton, J. H. and G. Milligan. 1930. *The Vocabulary of the Greek Testament*. Grand Rapids, MI: Eerdmans.

Murray, J. 1954. *Covenant of Grace: A Biblico-Theological Study*. London: Tyndale.

— — —. 1968. *The Epistle to the Romans*. New International Commentary on the New Testament. Grand Rapids, MI: Eerdmans.

— — —. 1977. *The Collected Writings of John Murray*. Vol. 2. Edinburgh: Banner of Truth.

Nellas, P. 1987. *Deification in Christ: Orthodox Perspectives on the Nature of the Human Person*. Crestwoord, NY: St. Vladimir's Seminary Press.

Nichols, G. 2011. *Covenant Theology: A Reformed and Baptistic Perspective on God's Covenants*. New Haven, CT: Yale University Press.

Nicholson, E. W. 1986. *God and His People: Covenant and Theology in the Old Testament*. Oxford: Clarendon.

Niehaus, J. J. 2009. "Covenant: An Idea in the Mind of God." *Journal of the Evangelical Theological Society* 52.2: 225–46.

Niell, J. D. 2003. "The Newness of the New Covenant." In *The Case for Covenantal Infant Baptism*, 127–55. Edited by G. Strawbridge. Phillipsburg, NJ: P&R Publishing.

Noort, E., P. Beentjes, and F. Van Dijk-Hemmes, eds. 1989. *Sleutelen aan het verbond: Bijbelse en theologische essays*. Boxtel/Brugge: KBS/Tabor.

O'Brien, P. T. 1982. *Colossians, Philemon*. Word Biblical Commentary. Waco, TX: Word.

Olevianus, C. 1995. *A Firm Foundation: An Aid to Interpreting the Heidelberg Catechism*. Grand Rapids, MI: Baker Academic.

Osterhaven, M. E. 1984. "Calvin on the Covenant." In *Readings in Calvin's Theology*. Edited by D. K. McKim. Grand Rapids, MI: Baker Book House.

Oswalt, J. N. 1986. *The Book of Isaiah Chapters 1–39*. New International Commentary on the Old Testament. Grand Rapids, MI: Eerdmans.

Otis, J. M. 2005. *Danger in the Camp: An Analysis and Refutation of the Heresies of the Federal Vision*. Corpus Christi, TX: Triumphant Publications.

Ouweneel, W. J. 1982. *'Wij zien Jezus': Bijbelstudies over de brief aan de Hebreeën*. 2 vols. Vaassen: Medema.

– – –. 1991. *Israël en de Kerk, oftewel: Eén of twee volken van God?: Confrontatie van de verbondsleer en de bedelingenleer*. Vaassen: Medema.

– – –. 1997. *De vrijheid van de Geest: Bijbelstudies bij de Brief van Paulus aan de Galaten*. Vaassen: Medema.

– – –. 2001. *Hoogtijden voor Hem: De bijbelse feesten en hun betekenis voor Joden en christenen*. Vaassen: Medema.

– – –. 2007a. *De Geest van God: Ontwerp van een pneumatologie*. Evangelisch Dogmatische Reeks. Vol. 1. Vaassen: Medema.

– – –. 2007b. *De Christus van God: Ontwerp van een christologie*. Evangelisch Dogmatische Reeks. Vol. 2. Vaassen: Medema.

– – –. 2008a. *De schepping van God: Ontwerp van een scheppings-, mens- en zondeleer*. Evangelisch Dogmatische Reeks. Vol. 3. Vaassen: Medema.

– – –. 2008b. *Het plan van God: Ontwerp van een voorbeschikkingsleer*. Evangelisch Dogmatische Reeks. Vol. 4. Vaassen: Medema.

– – –. 2009. *Het zoenoffer van God: Ontwerp van een verzoeningsleer*. Evangelisch Dogmatische Reeks. Vol. 5. Vaassen: Medema.

– – –. 2010a. *Het heil van God: Ontwerp van een soteriologie*.

Evangelisch Dogmatische Reeks. Vol. 6. Heerenveen: Medema.

———. 2010b. *De Kerk van God (I): Ontwerp van een elementaire ecclesiologie.* Evangelisch Dogmatische Reeks. Vol. 7. Heerenveen: Medema.

———. 2010c. *De kerk van God (II): Ontwerp van een historische en praktische ecclesiologie.* Evangelisch Dogmatische Reeks. Vol. 8. Heerenveen: Medema.

———. 2011. *Het verbond en het koninkrijk van God: Ontwerp van een verbonds-, doop- en koninkrijksleer.* Evangelisch Dogmatische Reeks. Vol. 9. Heerenveen: Medema.

———. 2012a. *De toekomst van God: Ontwerp van een eschatologie.* Evangelisch Dogmatische Reeks. Vol. 10. Heerenveen: Medema.

———. 2012b. *Het Woord van God: Ontwerp van een openbarings- en schriftleer.* Evangelisch Dogmatische Reeks. Vol. 11. Heerenveen: Medema.

———. 2013. *De glorie van God: Ontwerp van een godsleer en van een theologische vakfilosofie.* Evangelisch Dogmatische Reeks. Vol. 12. Heerenveen: Medema.

———. 2014a. *Wisdom for Thinkers: An Introduction to Christian Philosophy.* St. Catharines: Paideia Press.

———. 2014b. *What Then Is Theology? An Introduction to Christian Theology.* St. Catharines: Paideia Press.

———. 2015a (forthcoming). *The Eternal Torah: An Evangelical Theology of Living Under God.* St. Catharines: Paideia Press.

———. 2015b (forthcoming). *The Ninth King: The Last of the Celestial Empires: The Triumph of Christ over the Powers.* St. Catharines: Paideia Press.

Owen, J. 1991 (repr.). *Works.* Vol. 22: *An Exposition of the Epistle to the Hebrews.* Edinburgh: Banner of Truth.

Pannenberg, W. 2009. *Systematic Theology.* Vol. 3. Grand Rapids, MI: Eerdmans.

Peake, A. S. 1979 (repr.). *The Epistle to the Colossians.* Expositor's Greek Testament. Vol 3. Grand Rapids, MI: Eerdmans.

Peirce, J. 1727. *A Paraphrase and Notes on the Epistles of St. Paul to the Colossians, Philippians, and Hebrews.* London: J. Noon and J. Chandler.

Pentecost, J. D. 1958 (repr. 1964). *Things to Come: A Study in Biblical Eschatology.* Grand Rapids, MI: Academie Books.

Pinnock, C. 1996. *Flame of Love: A Theology of the Holy Spirit.* Downers Grove, Ill.: InterVarsity Press.

————. 2001. *Most Moved Mover: A Theology of God's Openness.* Grand Rapids, MI: Baker.

Plantinga, C. 2001. *A Sure Thing: What We Believe and Why.* Grand Rapids, MI: CRC Publications.

Pop, F. J. (1951) 1999. *Bijbelse woorden en hun geheim.* 10th ed. Zoetermeer: Boekencentrum.

Popper, K. R. 1972. *Conjectures and Refutations.* 4th ed. London: Routledge and Kegan Paul.

Poythress, V. S. 1987. *Understanding Dispensationalists.* Grand Rapids, MI: Academie Books.

Rahner, K. 1967: *The Pilgrim Church.* New York: Herder.

Ridderbos, J. 1935. *De kleine profeten.* Vol. 3: *Haggai, Zacharia, Maleachi.* Korte Verklaring. Kampen: Kok.

Ridderbos, H. N. 1962: *The Coming of the Kingdom.* Trans. H. de Jongste. Edited by R. O. Zorn. Philadelphia: Presbyterian and Reformed Publishing.

————. 1959. *Aan de Romeinen.* Commentaar op het Nieuwe Testament. Kampen: Kok.

————. 1960. *Aan de Kolossenzen.* Commentaar op het Nieuwe Testament. Kampen: Kok.

————. 1975. *Paul: An Outline of His Theology.* Translated by J. R. DeWitt. Grand Rapids, MI: Eerdmans).

————. 1987. *Matthew.* Translated by Ray Togtman. Bible Student's Commentary. Grand Rapids: Zondervan.

Robertson, O. P. 1980. *The Christ of the Covenants.* Phillipsburg, NJ: P&R Publishing.

———. 2000. *The Israel of God: Yesterday, Today, and Tomorrow.* Phillipsburg, NJ: P&R Publishing.

Roozemeijer, J. H. L. 1911. *De brief van Paulus aan de Romeinen.* Arnhem: G.W. van der Wiel and Co.

Rosner, B. S., Alexander, T. D., G. Goldsworthy, and D. A. Carson, eds. 2000. *New Dictionary of Biblical Theology: Exploring the Unity and Diversity of Scripture.* Downers Grove, IL: InterVarsity Press Academic.

Ryrie, C. C. 1953. *The Basis of the Premillennial Faith.* Neptune, NJ: Loizeaux Brothers.

———. 1986. *Basic Theology.* Wheaton, IL: Victor Books.

Sanders, E. P. 1977. *Paul and Palestinian Judaism: A Comparison of Patterns of Religion.* Philadelphia: Fortress Press.

Sandlin, P. A., ed. 2007. *A Faith That Is Never Alone: A Response to Westminster Seminary California.* LaGrange, CA: Kerygma Press.

Saucy, R. L. 1993. *The Case for Progressive Dispensationalism: The Interface Between Dispensational and Non-Dispensational Theology.* Grand Rapids, MI: Zondervan.

Schilder, K. 1946. *Looze kalk: Een wederwoord over de (zedelijke) crisis in de „Gereformeerde Kerken in Nederland".* Groningen: Erven A. de Jager.

———. 1957. *Schriftoverdenkingen.* Vol. 2. Verzamelde werken, Part II. Edited by C. Veenhof. Goes: Oosterbaan and Le Cointre.

———. n.d. *Het verbond in de gereformeerde symbolen.* Kampen: Van den Berg.

Schlatter, A. 1963a. *Die Briefe an die Galater, Epheser, Kolosser und Philemon.* Stuttgart: Calwer Verlag.

———. 1963b. *Der Evangelist Matthäus: Seine Sprache, sein Ziel, seine Selbständigkeit.* 6th ed. Stuttgart: Calwer Verlag.

Schniewind, J. 1956. *Das Evangelium nach Matthäus*. Göttingen: Vandenhoeck and Ruprecht.

Schoeps, H. J. 1949. *Theologie und Geschichte des Judenchristentums*. Tübingen: Mohr (Siebeck).

Schouls, C. A. 1996. *The Covenant of Grace: Its Scriptural Origins and Development in Continental Reformed Theology*. spindleworks.com.

Schreiner, T. R. 2006. "Baptism in the Epistles: An Initiation Rite for Believers." In *Believer's Baptism: Sign of the New Covenant in Christ*, 67–96. Edited by T. R. Schreiner and S. D. Wright. Nashville, TN: B and H Academic.

Schreiner, T. R. and S. D. Wright, eds. 2006. *Believer's Baptism: Sign of the New Covenant in Christ*. Nashville, TN: B and H Academic.

Schreiner, T. R. 2008. *New Testament Theology: Magnifying God in Christ*. Grand Rapids, MI: Baker Academic.

Schrenk, G. 1923 (repr. 1967). *Gottesreich und Bund im älteren Protestantismus, vornehmlich bei Johannes Coccejus*. Darmstadt: Wissenschaftliche Buchgesellschaft.

Schuyler English, E. 1935. *Studies in the Gospel According to Matthew*. New York: Revell.

Schweizer, E. 1976. *Der Brief an die Kolosser*. Evangelisch Katholischer Kommentar. Zürich: Benziger.

Scofield, C. I. 1909 (repr. 1967). *The New Scofield Reference Bible*. New York: Oxford University Press.

Shepherd, N. 2000. *The Call of Grace: How the Covenant Illuminates Salvation and Evangelism*. Phillipsburg, NJ: P&R Publishing.

Shulam, J. and H. Le Cornu. 1998. *A Commentary on the Jewish Roots of Romans*. Baltimore: Messianic Jewish Publishers.

Slotki, I. W. 1949 (rev. 1983). *Isaiah: Hebrew Text and English Translation with an Introduction and Commentary*. Rev. by A. J. Rosenberg. London/New York: Soncino Press.

Smith, D. 1979. *The Epistles of John*. Expositor's Greek Testament. Vol. 5. Grand Rapids, MI: Eerdmans.

Smith, D. L. 1996. *All God's People: A Theology of the Church.* Wheaton, IL: Bridgepoint Books.

Smith, R. A. 2003. *The Eternal Covenant: How the Trinity Reshapes Covenant Theology.* Moscow, ID: Canon Press.

Söding, T. 1995. *Das Liebesgebot bei Paulus: Die Mahnung zur Agape im Rahmen der paulinischen Ethik.* Münster: Aschendorff.

Sproul, R. C. 1986. *Chosen by God.* Wheaton, IL: Tyndale House Publishers.

Spykman, G. J. 1992. *Reformational Theology: A New Paradigm for Doing Dogmatics.* Grand Rapids, MI: Eerdmans.

Stam, C. 1999. *The Covenant of Love: Exploring Our Relationship with God.* Winnipeg, MB: Premier Printing.

Starr, J. M. 2003. *Sharers in Divine Nature: 2 Peter 1:4 in its Hellenistic Context.* Stockholm: Almqvist and Wiksell.

Stavropoulos, C. 1976 (repr. 2003). "Partakers of Divine Nature." In *Eastern Orthodox Theology: A Contemporary Reader.* Edited by D. B. Clendenin. 2nd ed. Grand Rapids, MI: Baker.

Stern, D. 1989. *Jewish New Testament: A Translation of the New Testament that Expresses its Jewishness.* Clarksville, MD: Jewish New Testament Publications.

— — — . 1999. *Jewish New Testament Commentary.* 6th ed. Clarksville, MD: Jewish New Testament Publications.

Strawbridge, G., ed. 2003. *The Case for Covenantal Infant Baptism.* Phillipsburg, NJ: P&R Publishing.

Strehle, S. 1988. *Calvinism, Federalism, and Scholasticism.* Bern: Peter Lang.

Suurmond, J.-J. 1994. *Het spel van Woord en Geest: Aanzet tot een charismatische theologie.* Baarn: Ten Have.

Trim, D. J. B., ed. 2011. *The Huguenots: History and Memory in Transnational Context: Essays in Honour and Memory of Walter C. Utt.* Leiden: Koninklijke Brill.

Troost, A. 1983. "Theologische misverstanden inzake een reformatorische wijsbegeerte (III)." *Philosophia Reformata* 48:19–49.

Turretin, F. 1994. *Institutes of Elenctic Theology*. 3 vols. Phillipsburg, NJ: P&R Publishing.

Van Asselt, W. J. 1997. *Johannes Coccejus: Portret van een zeventiende-eeuwse theoloog op oude en nieuwe wegen*. Heerenveen: Groen.

— — —. 2008. *Coccejus: Een inleiding met kernteksten*. Kampen: De Groot Goudriaan.

Van Bruggen, J. 1997. *Het diepe water van de doop*. Kampen: Kok.

Van Campen, M. 1988. *Leven uit Gods beloften: Een centraal thema bij Johannes Calvijn*. Kampen: Kok.

— — —. 2007. *Gans Israël: Voetiaanse en coccejaanse visies op joden gedurende de zeventiende en achttiende eeuw*. 2nd ed. Zoetermeer: Boekencentrum.

Van de Beek, A. 2008. *God doet recht: Eschatologie als christologie*. Zoetermeer: Meinema.

Van den Bergh, W. 1879. *Calvijn en het Genadeverbond*. 's-Gravenhage: Beschoor.

Van der Ploeg, A. 1990. *Messiasbelijdende joden: Vergeten eerstelingen: Philippus van Ronkel*. Leiden: J. J. Groen and Zoon.

Van der Schuit, J. J. 1982. *Het verbond der verlossing: Antwoord op de vraag: Twee of drie verbonden?* 2nd ed. Kampen: Kok.

Van der Vegt, W. H. 1938. *Het verbond der genade bij Calvijn*. Aalten: De Graafschap.

— — —. n.d. *Verbond en verkiezing bij Calvijn*. Aalten: De Graafschap.

Van der Waal, C. 1990. *The Covenantal Gospel*. Neerlandia, AB: Inheritance Publications.

Vander Zee, L. J. 2004. *Christ, Baptism and the Lord's Supper: Recovering the Sacraments for Evangelical Worship*. Downers Grove, IL: InterVarsity Press.

Van der Zwaag, K. 2003. *Afwachten of verwachten? De toe-eigening des heils in historisch en theologisch perspectief.* Heerenveen: Groen.

Van Gelder, C. 2000. *The Essence of the Church: A Community Created by the Spirit.* Grand Rapids, MI: Baker Books.

VanGemeren, W. A., ed. 1996. *New International Dictionary of Old Testament Theology and Exegesis.* Grand Rapids, MI: Zondervan.

Van Genderen, J. 1995. *Covenant and Election.* Translated by C. Pronk. Neerlandia, AB: Inheritance.

Van Genderen, J. and W. H. Velema. 2008. *Concise Reformed Dogmatics.* Translated by G. Bilkes and E. van der Maas. Phillipsburg, NJ: P&R Publishing.

Van Klinken, G. J. 1996. *Opvattingen in de Gereformeerde Kerken over het Jodendom, 1896–1970.* Kampen: Kok.

Van Leeuwen, J. A. C. 1953. *De brief aan de Colossenzen. – De brieven aan de Thessalonicensen.* Korte Verklaring. Kampen: Kok.

Van Rongen, G. 1966. *Zijn vast verbond: Studies over de bijbelse verbonden in het licht van buiten-bijbelse verbondsteksten.* Goes: Oosterbaan and Le Cointre.

Van Ronkel, Ph. S. 1886. *Uit het jodendom tot den Christus.* Amsterdam: J. A. Wormser.

Van Til, C. 1977. *Common Grace and the Gospel.* Nutley, NJ: Presbyterian and Reformed.

Van 't Spijker, W. 1985. *Doop in plaats van besnijdenis.* Kampen: De Groot Goudriaan.

— — —. 1986. *Gereformeerden en dopers: Gesprek onderweg.* Kampen: Kok.

— — —, W. Balke, K. Exalto, and L van Driel, eds. 1983. *Rondom de doopvont: Leer en gebruik van de heilige doop in het Nieuwe Testament en in de geschiedenis van de westerse kerk.* Kampen: De Groot Goudriaan.

― ― ―, W. Balke, K. Exalto, and L.van Driel, eds. 1990. *De kerk: Wezen, weg en werk van de kerk naar reformatorische opvatting*. Kampen: De Groot Goudriaan.

Van Unnik, W. C. 1960. "La conception paulinienne de la nouvelle alliance." In *Littérature et théologie pauliniennes (Recherches bibliques* V). Paris: Desclee de Brouwer.

Vaughan, C. 1978. *Colossians*. Expositor's Bible Commentary. Vol. 11. Grand Rapids, MI: Zondervan.

Venema, C. P. 2003. "Covenant Theology and Baptism." In *The Case for Covenantal Infant Baptism*, 201–29. Edited by G. Strawbridge. Phillipsburg, NJ: P&R Publishing.

Veninga, J. F. 1974. "Covenant Theology and Ethics in the Thought of John Calvin and John Preston." 3 vols. PhD diss., Rice University. Ann Arbor, MI: University Microfilms.

Verboom, W. 2005. *De belijdenis van een gebroken kerk: De Dordtse Leerregels, voorgeschiedenis en theologie*. Zoetermeer: Boekencentrum.

― ― ―. 2009. "Calvijn en het verbond." In *Calvijn spreekt: De actualiteit van een hervormer na 500 jaar*, 35–54. Edited by J. Hoek. Heerenveen: Groen.

Verkuyl, J. 1992. *De kern van het christelijk geloof*. Kampen: Kok.

Versteeg, J. P. 1983. "De doop volgens het Nieuwe Testament." In *Rondom de doopvont: Leer en gebruik van de heilige doop in het Nieuwe Testament en in de geschiedenis van de westerse kerk*, 9–133. Edited by W. van 't Spijker et al. Kampen: De Groot Goudriaan.

Visser 't Hooft, W. A., ed. 1962. *The New Delhi Report: The Third Assembly of the World Council of Churches*. London: SCM.

Voorberg, P. L. 2007. *Doop en Kerk: De erkenning, door kerkelijke gemeenschappen, van de elders bediende doop*. Heerenveen: Groen.

Vos, G. 1939 (repr. 2001). "The Doctrine of the Covenant in Reformed Theology." In *Redemptive Histgory and Biblical*

*Interpretation: The Shorter Writings of Geerhardus Vos*. Phillipsburg, NJ: P&R Publishing.

Walvoord, J. F. 1974. *Matthew: Thy Kingdom Come*. Chicago: Moody Press.

— — —. 1999. *The Church in Prophecy: Exploring God's Purpose for the Present Age*. Grand Rapids, MI: Kregel.

Warfield, B. B. 1932 (repr. 1981). "The Polemics of Infant Baptism." *Studies in Theology* 9. Grand Rapids, MI: Baker.

Waters, G. P. 2006. *The Federal Vision and Covenant Theology: A Comparative Analysis*. Phillipsburg, NJ: P&R Publishing.

Watson, D. 1978. *I Believe in the Church*. London: Hodder and Stoughton.

Weinfeld, M. 1970. "The Covenant of Grant in the Old Testament and in the Ancient Near East." *Journal of the American Oriental Society* 9:184–203.

Weir, D. A. 1990. *The Origins of the Federal Theology in Sixteenth-Century Reformation Thought*. Oxford: Oxford University Press.

Wellum, S. J. 2006. "Baptism and the Relationships between the Covenants." In *Believer's Baptism: Sign of the New Covenant in Christ*, 97–161. Edited by T. Schreiner and S. D. Wright. Nashville, TN: B and H Academic.

Wentsel, B. 1982. *Dogmatiek*. Vol. 2: *De openbaring, het verbond en de apriori's*. Kampen: Kok.

— — —. 1987. *Dogmatiek*. Vol. 3a: *God en mens verzoend: Godsleer, mensleer en zondeleer*. Kampen: Kok.

— — —. 1995. *Dogmatiek*. Vol. 4a: *De Heilige Geest, de kerk en de laatste dingen: De persoon en het werk van de Heilige Geest*. Kampen: Kok.

— — —. 1998a. *Dogmatiek*. Vol. 4b: *De Heilige Geest, de kerk en de laatste dingen: De kerk als het saamhorige volk Gods*. Kampen: Kok.

— — —. 1998b. *Dogmatiek*. Vol. 4c: De *Heilige Geest, de kerk en de laatste dingen: De genademiddelen, het gemenebest en het eschaton*. Kampen: Kok.

White, A. B. 2012. *What Is New Covenant Theology? An Introduction*. Frederick, MD: New Covenant Media.

Wilkins, S. and D. Garner, eds. 2004. *The Federal Vision*. Monroe, LA: Athanasius Press.

Williamson, P. R. 2007. *Sealed with an Oath: Covenant in God's Unfolding Purpose*. Downers Grove, IL: InterVarsity Press Academic.

Witsius, H. 1693 (trans. 1822; repr. 1990). *The Economy of the Covenants between God and Man*. Escondido: Den Dulk Foundation.

Woelderink, J. G. 1951. *De uitverkiezing*. Delft: Van Keulen.

– – –. 1974. *Verbond en bevinding*. Amsterdam: Bolland.

Wolf, H. H. 1958. *Die Einheit des Bundes: Das Verhältnis von Altem und Neuem Testament bei Calvin*. Neukirchen: Moers Verlag.

Wolters, A. 1990. "'Partners of the Deity': A Covenantal Reading of 2 Peter 1:4." *Calvin Theological Journal* 26:418-20.

Wright, D. F. 2007. *Infant Baptism in Historical Perspective: Collective Studies*. Milton Keynes, UK/Waynesboro, GA: Paternoster.

Wright, N. T. 1991. *The Climax of the Covenant: Christ and the Law in Pauline Theology*. Edinburgh: T. and T. Clark.

– – –. 2011. *Simply Jesus: A New Vision of Who He Was, What He Did, and Why He Matters*. New York: HarperCollins Publishers.

Wright, S. D. 2006. "Baptism and the Logic of Reformed Paedobaptists." In *Believer's Baptism: Sign of the New Covenant in Christ*, 207-55. Edited by T. Schreiner and S. D. Wright. Nashville, TN: B and H Academic.

Zerwick, M. 1969. *The Epistle to the Ephesians*. London: Burns and Oates.

# Scripture Index

**OLD TESTAMENT**

**Genesis**

| | | | | | |
|---|---|---|---|---|---|
| 1 | 57, 309, 449 | 5:22 | 489 | 9:9 | 35, 64, 485 |
| 1–3 | 61, 312 | 5:24 | 489 | 9:9–15 | 11, 25 |
| 1–5 | 60 | 6 | 60, 64 | 9:9–17 | 64 |
| 1:2 | 57, 322, 340 | 6:2 | 459 | 9:11 | 35 |
| 1:3–29 | 138 | 6:3 | 66 | 9:12–13 | 67 |
| 1:14 | 59 | 6:4 | 459 | 9:14–15 | 67 |
| 1:26–28 | 22 | 6:5 | 66, 153 | 9:16 | 64, 145 |
| 1:28 | 62, 63 | 6:8 | 66, 485 | 9:20 | 67 |
| 1:29 | 62 | 6:8–9 | 64 | 9:22 | 117 |
| 2:4 | 60 | 6:9 | 20, 147, 489 | 9:23 | 117 |
| 2:7 | 165 | 6:14–18 | 486 | 9:25 | 67 |
| 2:8–10 | 63 | 6:18 | 11, 25, 35, 60, 61, 64, 270-271, 485 | 9:25–27 | 117 |
| 2:9 | 135 | | | 9:27 | 67, 271, 404, 423, 429 |
| 2:15 | 62, 63 | 6:18–20 | 271 | 11:1–9 | 71 |
| 2:16–17 | 62 | 8:1 | 271 | 11:30 | 71 |
| 2:23 | 312 | 8:20 | 491 | 12 | 486 |
| 3 | 22, 65, 210, 308, 449 | 8:20–21 | 66 | 12:1–3 | 486 |
| | | 8:20–9:17 | 31 | 12:2 | 307, 334, |
| 3:6 | 65 | 8:21 | 66, 153 | 12:3 | 8, 71, 271, 360, 405, 424, 434 |
| 3:8 | 63, 77 | 9 | 18, 64, 423 | | |
| 3:15 | 61, 63, 206, 364, 365, 422 | 9:1 | 66 | | |
| | | 9:1–17 | 65 | 12:7–8 | 491 |
| | | 9:2 | 67 | 13:4 | 491 |
| 3:15–16 | 67 | 9:3–4 | 67 | 13:10 | 73 |
| 3:21 | 62 | 9:5–6 | 67 | 13:15 | 90 |
| 3:22 | 63 | 9:5–6 | 65 | 13:17 | 489 |
| 3:22–24 | 485 | 9:7 | 66 | 14 | 11, 117 |
| 4:10 | 302 | 9:8–10 | 271 | 14:13 | 28 |

| | | | | | |
|---|---|---|---|---|---|
| 14:17-18 | 77 | 18:19 | 20, 72, 147 | 31:53 | 54 |
| 14:18 | 78 | 20:13 | 108 | 31:54 | 54 |
| 14:18-20 | 314 | 21 | 11 | 32:5 | 130 |
| 15 | 69, 70, 257, 423, 486 | 21:8-10 | 285 | 32:10 | 108 |
| | | 21:22-33 | 28, 53 | 33:18 | 54 |
| 15:1 | 70 | 21:23 | 27, 53 | 34 | 30, 54 |
| 15:6 | 8, 20, 69, 276, 423, 428 | 21:27 | 53 | 34:8-9 | 30 |
| | | 21:28-32 | 49 | 34:9 | 54 |
| 15:7-21 | 31 | 21:31 | 12, 53 | 34:21 | 54 |
| 15:9-11 | 72 | 22:16-18 | 70 | 34:25-30 | 76 |
| 15:10 | 302 | 22:18 | 4, 8, 71, 96, 269, 271, 360, 424, 434 | 35:11 | 69, 70 |
| 15:10-11 | 273 | | | 35:14 | 24 |
| 15:13-16 | 71 | | | 43:9 | 31 |
| 15:17 | 72, 273, 302 | 24:27 | 108 | 47:29 | 130 |
| 15:17-21 | 72 | 24:40 | 489 | 47:29-30 | 202 |
| 15:18 | 24, 69, 514 | 24:49 | 108, 203 | 48:4 | 69, 90, 516 |
| 16:12 | 117, 284 | 25:14-16 | 284 | 48:15 | 489 |
| 17 | 18, 69, 70, 72, 73, 147, 257, 269, 392, 393, 406, 407, 423, 486 | 26 | 11 | 49:5-7 | 76 |
| | | 26:3 | 12, 70 | 50:4 | 130 |
| | | 26:4 | 8, 71, 271, 360, 424, 434 | **Exodus** | |
| | | | | 1 | 84 |
| | | 26:4-5 | 147 | 2:24 | 25, 69, 86 |
| 17:1 | 70, 72 | 26:5 | 20, 72 | 2:25 | 84 |
| 17:1-2 | 147, 489 | 26:26-30 | 28, 49, 53 | 3-4 | 486 |
| 17:1-21 | 69 | 26:28 | 23 | 3:6 | 70 |
| 17:2-21 | 11, 25, 35 | 26:28-29 | 53, 117 | 3:7 | 84, 210 |
| 17:5 | 354 | 26:30 | 53 | 3:7-9 | 86 |
| 17:7 | 64, 104, 145, 176, 177, 227 | 26:31 | 53 | 3:10 | 84, 210 |
| | | 28:3 | 69 | 3:13-15 | 138 |
| 17:7-9 | 205 | 28:4 | 434 | 3:14 | 70 |
| 17:8 | 90, 516 | 28:13 | 70, 146 | 3:14-15 | 486 |
| 17:10-11 | 72 | 28:14 | 8, 71, 360 | 4:22 | 11, 101, 199, 436, 460 |
| 17:11 | 73, 227, 269 | 28:18 | 24 | | |
| 17:12-14 | 72 | 29:22 | 24 | 4:22-23 | 88 |
| 17:13 | 104, 145, 406 | 30:27 | 130 | 5:1 | 84, 210, 328 |
| 17:13-14 | 227 | 31 | 11 | 6:2 | 70, 85 |
| 17:14 | 12, 18, 73, 176, 287 | 31:22-55 | 28, 53, 429 | 6:2-4 | 486 |
| | | 31:43-53 | 49 | 6:3-4 | 69 |
| 17:17 | 19, 382 | 31:44 | 49 | 6:4-5 | 11, 25 |
| 17:19 | 104, 145 | 31:44-47 | 24 | 6:6-7 | 85 |
| 17:23 | 406 | 31:44-50 | 47 | 6:6-8 | 70, 85 |
| 18 | 147 | 31:44-54 | 199 | 6:8 | 83, 85 |
| 18:1-15 | 73 | 31:45 | 54 | 6:12 | 508 |
| 18:18 | 8, 71, 271, 360, 424, 434 | 31:46 | 54 | 6:29 | 70 |
| | | 31:51-54 | 49 | | |

| | | | | | |
|---|---|---|---|---|---|
| 6:30 | 508 | 19:16-17 | 113 | 25:22 | 36, 299 |
| 7:4 | 84, 210 | 19:18 | 330 | 25:31-36 | 77 |
| 7:5 | 70 | 20 | 486 | 26:33-34 | 36 |
| 7:16 | 84, 210 | 20:1-17 | 86 | 27-31 | 492 |
| 12:3 | 308 | 20:2 | 35, 70, 85, 125, 138, 232, 486 | 28:41 | 300 |
| 12:6 | 308 | | | 29 | 76 |
| 12:19 | 308 | | | 29:21 | 300 |
| 12:47 | 308 | 20:5 | 120 | 29:22 | 76 |
| 13-14 | 486 | 20:6 | 120 | 29:26 | 76 |
| 13-17 | 138 | 20:8 | 408 | 29:26-33 | 77 |
| 13:2 | 75 | 20:8-11 | 87 | 29:27 | 76 |
| 13:3 | 232 | 20:11 | 166 | 29:31 | 76 |
| 13:5 | 83 | 20:18 | 36 | 29:38-46 | 90, 126 |
| 13:9 | 232 | 20:24 | 88, 492 | 29:45 | 298 |
| 13:11 | 83 | 22:21-22 | 109 | 29:46 | 70, 85 |
| 13:13 | 284 | 22:25 | 109 | 31:13-16 | 87, 166 |
| 13:14 | 232 | 22:29 | 75 | 31:13-17 | 87 |
| 13:16 | 232 | 23:6 | 109 | 31:16 | 83, 104, 145 |
| 15 | 486 | 23:9 | 109 | 31:18 | 36, 253 |
| 15:17 | 88, 89, 486, 492 | 23:11 | 109 | 32 | 298 |
| | | 23:14 | 491 | 32-34 | 125 |
| 15:18 | 22, 138, 309, 424 | 23:17 | 491 | 32:13 | 83, 90 |
| | | 23:25 | 124 | 32:15 | 36 |
| 16:23-29 | 87, 166 | 23:32 | 54 | 32:16 | 262 |
| 16:35 | 86 | 24 | 4, 72, 301, 302 | 32:26 | 75 |
| 17:7 | 75 | | | 32:26-29 | 75 |
| 17:15 | 492 | 24:1-11 | 31 | 33:1 | 83 |
| 17:16 | 508 | 24:3 | 84, 101, 114, 138, 292, 302 | 33:11 | 459 |
| 19 | 325 | | | 33:16 | 334 |
| 19-20 | 330 | 24:4 | 24, 114 | 33:32-33 | 143 |
| 19-24 | 19, 84, 486 | 24:4-8 | 86, 492 | 34:1 | 253 |
| 19-31 | 270 | 24:5 | 72, 88 | 34:6 | 86, 108 |
| 19:1 | 111, 332 | 24:6-8 | 72 | 34:6-7 | 231, 232, 325 |
| 19:4 | 86 | 24:7 | 24, 84, 101, 114, 138, 292, 302 | 34:10 | 83 |
| 19:4-6 | 139 | | | 34:10-14 | 363 |
| 19:5 | 333, 334 | | | 34:12 | 54 |
| 19:5-6 | 83, 142, 264, 424 | 24:7-8 | 83 | 34:14 | 54 |
| | | 24:8 | 32, 113, 136, 301, 302, 438 | 34:19 | 75 |
| 19:6 | 29, 316, 325, 425 | | | 34:22 | 111 |
| | | 24:8-11 | 87 | 34:23-24 | 491 |
| 19:8 | 84, 100, 114, 138, 292 | 24:9-11 | 114 | 34:27-28 | 83 |
| | | 24:15-16 | 113 | 34:28 | 35 |
| 19:9 | 113 | 25-27 | 126 | 34:29 | 36 |
| 19:10 | 113 | 25:10-22 | 299, 493 | 35:2-3 | 87, 166 |
| 19:16 | 330 | 25:17 | 299 | 37:17-22 | 77 |

| | | | | | |
|---|---|---|---|---|---|
| 38:21 | 36 | 22:33 | 85 | 14:4 | 233 |
| 40:55 | 270 | 22:43 | 85 | 14:18 | 86, 233 |
| | | 23:3 | 87, 166 | 14:29 | 89 |
| **Leviticus** | | 23:16–22 | 111 | 15:17–21 | 359 |
| 1–7 | 270 | 23:17 | 111 | 15:22 | 18 |
| 3:11 | 88 | 23:20 | 111 | 15:30 | 120 |
| 3:16 | 88 | 23:22 | 109 | 15:32–36 | 87 |
| 4–5 | 126 | 24:8 | 83, 104, 145 | 15:41 | 85 |
| 4:20 | 136 | 25:23 | 332 | 17:7–8 | 36 |
| 4:26 | 136 | 25:38 | 85 | 18 | 77 |
| 4:31 | 136 | 25:55 | 85 | 18:2 | 36 |
| 4:35 | 136 | 26 | 14, 35, 117 | 18:19 | 24 |
| 7:14 | 88 | 26:2 | 87, 166 | 23:9 | 316 |
| 7:19 | 88 | 26:3 | 490 | 23:21 | 138, 424 |
| 7:32–35 | 88 | 26:3–13 | 16, 142 | 25:11–13 | 75 |
| 8–9 | 76 | 26:9 | 64 | 25:12 | 30, 223 |
| 8:29–32 | 77 | 26:12 | 298, 353 | 27:17 | 331 |
| 8:30 | 300 | 26:13 | 85 | 30 | 103 |
| 11:45 | 85, 138, 232 | 26:14–39 | 86 | 30:6 | 103 |
| 12 | 407 | 26:15 | 11, 18, 25 | 30:3–4 | 103 |
| 12:3 | 269 | 26:41 | 233, 265, 467, 508 | 30:6–7 | 103 |
| 15:2–3 | 407 | | | 30:9 | 103 |
| 15:7 | 407 | 26:42 | 69 | 30:10–11 | 103 |
| 16 | 90, 126 | 26:42–44 | 11, 25 | 30:14 | 103 |
| 16:2 | 299 | 26:44 | 18 | 32:11 | 89 |
| 16:13–16 | 299 | 26:45 | 85 | 33:38 | 332 |
| 16:14–15 | 295 | | | | |
| 16:15–16 | 126 | **Numbers** | | **Deuteronomy** | |
| 17:11 | 296 | 1:50 | 36 | 1:31 | 88, 101, 199, 293 |
| 18:1–3 | 139 | 1:50–53 | 76 | | |
| 18:4 | 490 | 1:53 | 36 | 4:8 | 118 |
| 18:5 | 123, 139, 232 | 3:11–13 | 86 | 4:12–13 | 1 |
| 18:15 | 139 | 3:12 | 75 | 4:13 | 35 |
| 19:3 | 166 | 3:13 | 75 | 4:20 | 71, 85 |
| 19:10 | 109 | 3:15–51 | 75 | 4:23–24 | 1 |
| 19:14 | 109 | 3:40–51 | 86 | 4:30 | 255 |
| 19:15 | 109 | 8:5–26 | 76 | 4:31 | 1, 69 |
| 19:18 | 262 | 8:15–18 | 75 | 4:34 | 85 |
| 19:30 | 87, 166 | 8:17 | 75 | 4:37 | 58 |
| 19:33 | 109 | 8:19 | 76 | 4:40 | 139 |
| 19:34 | 109 | 9:15 | 36 | 5:2–3 | 83 |
| 19:36 | 85, 232 | 10:11 | 36 | 5:6 | 35, 85, 125, 138 |
| 20:24 | 334 | 10:33 | 299 | | |
| 21:1–22:16 | 77 | 10:35 | 120 | 5:6–21 | 90 |
| 22:32–33 | 138 | 12:5 | 36 | 5:9 | 120 |

| | | | | | |
|---|---|---|---|---|---|
| 5:10 | 120 | 10:16 | 129, 233, 265, | 25:15 | 139 |
| 5:12–15 | 87 | | 350, 467, 468, | 26:2 | 493 |
| 5:15 | 85, 166 | | 508 | 26:6 | 85 |
| 5:27–29 | 101 | 10:19 | 85 | 26:12–13 | 109 |
| 5:33 | 139, 490 | 11:1 | 120 | 26:17 | 490 |
| 6:5 | 262 | 11:9 | 139 | 27 | 12 |
| 6:5–6 | 129 | 11:13 | 120 | 27:11 | 117 |
| 6:6 | 291, 296 | 11:13–15 | 16 | 27:18 | 109 |
| 6:12 | 85 | 11:22 | 120 | 27:19 | 109 |
| 6:21–22 | 85 | 11:26–27 | 100 | 28 | 14 |
| 6:24–25 | 123 | 11:26–28 | 117 | 28–29 | 35 |
| 7 | 203 | 12:5–6 | 493 | 28:1–14 | 16, 83, 100, 142 |
| 7:2 | 28 | 12:11 | 492 | 28:9 | 490 |
| 7:6 | 334, 355 | 13:3 | 120 | 28:15–68 | 83, 90 |
| 7:6–10 | 16 | 13:4 | 490 | 28:45–47 | 119 |
| 7:6–11 | 142 | 13:5 | 85 | 28:48 | 119 |
| 7:7–8 | 58, 86, 230 | 13:10 | 85 | 28:68 | 117 |
| 7:7–9 | 106 | 13:15 | 85 | 29:1 | 89, 487 |
| 7:8 | 12, 85, 109 | 14:1 | 101, 199, 325, 331, 336, 436, 460 | 29:2 | 124 |
| 7:9 | 107, 120, 195 | | | 29:8 | 124 |
| 7:10–11 | 120, 231 | | | 29:9 | 89, 487 |
| 7:11–20 | 100 | 14:1–2 | 88, 142 | 29:12 | 89, 124, 487 |
| 7:12 | 69, 107, 124 | 14:2 | 355 | 29:12–14 | 23 |
| 7:12–13 | 109 | 14:21 | 142 | 29:14 | 89, 487 |
| 7:12–24 | 16 | 14:23 | 492 | 30 | 487 |
| 7:13 | 106 | 14:29 | 109 | 30:1–5 | 287 |
| 7:15 | 85 | 15:7–11 | 109 | 30:1–6 | 92 |
| 8:1 | 139 | 15:45 | 100 | 30:1–9 | 425 |
| 8:2–5 | 90 | 16:2 | 492 | 30:1–10 | 127, 289, 291 |
| 8:4–5 | 88 | 16:6 | 492 | 30:5 | 487, 516 |
| 8:5 | 101, 199, 293 | 16:11 | 109, 492 | 30:5–6 | 270 |
| 8:6 | 490 | 16:12 | 85 | 30:5–9 | 514 |
| 8:14 | 85 | 16:14 | 109 | 30:6 | 120, 129, 231, 233, 265, 350, 404, 467, 508 |
| 8:18 | 69 | 16:16 | 491 | | |
| 9:9 | 36 | 16:20 | 139 | | |
| 9:11 | 36 | 17:2 | 25 | 30:11 | 15, 119 |
| 9:15 | 36 | 17:14–20 | 80 | 30:14 | 129 |
| 10:2 | 253 | 18:5 | 355 | 30:15–16 | 100 |
| 10:4 | 35 | 19:9 | 120, 490 | 30:16 | 120, 139, 487, 490 |
| 10:5 | 35 | 20:10–12 | 30 | | |
| 10:12 | 490 | 21:15–17 | 115 | 30:18 | 139 |
| 10:12–13 | 120 | 23:6 | 55 | 30:19–20 | 118 |
| 10:12–22 | 142 | 24:14 | 109 | 30:20 | 120, 487 |
| 10:15 | 58, 334 | 24:17–21 | 109 | 31:16 | 18 |
| 10:15–19 | 110 | 24:22 | 85 | | |

| | | | | | |
|---|---|---|---|---|---|
| 31:20 | 18 | 8 | 79 | 7:13 | 80 |
| 32:6 | 442 | 8:5 | 334 | 7:13–14 | 81 |
| 32:40–43 | 120 | 8:20 | 334 | 7:14 | 14, 80 |
| 32:47 | 118 | 11 | 11 | 7:16 | 80 |
| 33:3 | 69 | 11:1–2 | 29, 55 | 7:23 | 334 |
| 33:5 | 424 | 11:7 | 55 | 8:17 | 78, 426 |
| 33:8–9 | 75 | 12 | 50 | 9 | 54 |
| 33:8–11 | 75 | 13:14 | 79 | 9:3 | 203 |
| 33:9 | 271 | 14:39 | 12, 13 | 10:2 | 28, 54 |
| 33:10 | 76 | 14:45 | 12, 13 | 10:19 | 28, 30 |
| 33:11 | 120 | 16:6–13 | 79 | 12 | 81 |
| | | 16:13 | 300 | 12:17 | 23 |
| **Joshua** | | 17:8 | 23 | 12:24–25 | 81 |
| 2:14 | 203 | 18:3 | 28, 54 | 13:6 | 23 |
| 3:13 | 299 | 18:3–4 | 27, 111 | 13:10 | 23 |
| 4:3 | 24 | 19:6 | 12 | 15:20 | 108 |
| 4:8–9 | 24 | 20:8 | 27, 28, 54, 108 | 15:24–36 | 78, 426 |
| 4:20 | 24 | | | 16:5–13 | 13 |
| 5:1–8 | 269 | 20:14–15 | 27, 54, 108 | 16:17 | 202 |
| 8:30–34 | 12 | 20:16 | 28, 54 | 19:13 | 12 |
| 8:30–35 | 35 | 20:16–17 | 111 | 21:7 | 28, 54 |
| 9 | 11, 28, 55 | 22:8 | 28, 54 | 22:44 | 209 |
| 9:14 | 55 | 23:18 | 28, 54 | 23:5 | 78, 104 |
| 9:15 | 30, 55 | 26:20 | 488 | 24:17 | 331 |
| 10:6 | 55 | 31 | 79 | 24:24–25 | 31, 80 |
| 14:9 | 90 | | | 24:25 | 78 |
| 24:16–17 | 103 | **2 Samuel** | | | |
| 24:21 | 103 | 1:23 | 111 | **1 Kings** | |
| 24:25–27 | 49, 50 | 1:26 | 111 | 2:12 | 508 |
| 24:26 | 24 | 2:6 | 108 | 2:23 | 12 |
| 24:26–27 | 24 | 3:8 | 108 | 2:24 | 508 |
| | | 3:35 | 12 | 2:45 | 508 |
| **Judges** | | 5:1–5 | 80 | 3:4 | 78 |
| 2:1 | 18, 104, 145 | 5:4 | 80 | 3:6 | 20, 328, 508 |
| 4:11–17 | 314 | 5:7 | 80 | 3:15 | 78 |
| 5:24 | 314 | 5:9 | 80 | 5 | 11 |
| 14:10 | 24 | 6:10 | 80 | 5:10–12 | 30 |
| | | 6:12 | 80 | 5:12 | 54 |
| **Ruth** | | 6:16 | 80 | 6:18 | 77 |
| 1:17 | 12 | 6:17 | 31, 80 | 6:29 | 77 |
| 3:13 | 12 | 6:17–18 | 78 | 6:32 | 77 |
| | | 6:19 | 81 | 6:35 | 77 |
| **1 Samuel** | | 7 | 494 | 7:18 | 77 |
| 3:3 | 299 | 7:10 | 88 | 7:20 | 77 |
| 7:1–2 | 493 | 7:12 | 78 | 7:22 | 77 |

| Reference | Page |
|---|---|
| 7:24 | 77 |
| 8:9 | 35 |
| 8:21 | 69 |
| 8:23 | 107 |
| 8:25 | 78, 508 |
| 8:51 | 71 |
| 8:53 | 334 |
| 8:62–63 | 78 |
| 8:62–64 | 80 |
| 9:4 | 21 |
| 9:5 | 80, 508 |
| 9:13 | 28, 200 |
| 9:16 | 24 |
| 9:25 | 78 |
| 14:8 | 102, 327 |
| 15:19 | 28, 55 |
| 18:21 | 518 |
| 18:25 | 23 |
| 20 | 11 |
| 20:10 | 12 |
| 20:31 | 108, 203 |
| 20:32 | 200 |
| 20:32–33 | 28, 55 |
| 20:33 | 200 |
| 20:34 | 28, 55, 200 |
| 22:4 | 209 |

## 2 Kings
| Reference | Page |
|---|---|
| 3:7 | 209 |
| 5 | 314 |
| 6:31 | 12 |
| 11:4 | 12, 23 |
| 11:17 | 104 |
| 13:23 | 25, 69, 104 |
| 17:15 | 69 |
| 23:2–3 | 52 |
| 23:3 | 103, 104 |

## 1 Chronicles
| Reference | Page |
|---|---|
| 2:55 | 314 |
| 6:48 | 76 |
| 11:3 | 51 |
| 16:14–18 | 145 |
| 16:15–18 | 104 |
| 16:16 | 23, 69 |
| 16:17 | 69 |
| 17:12 | 80 |
| 17:14 | 80 |
| 21:26 | 494 |
| 22:10 | 80 |
| 28:2 | 209, 493 |
| 28:8 | 90 |
| 29:14 | 209 |
| 29:15 | 332 |
| 29:23 | 81, 508 |

## 2 Chronicles
| Reference | Page |
|---|---|
| 6:14 | 107 |
| 6:16 | 78, 80, 508 |
| 7:1–3 | 270 |
| 9:8 | 80 |
| 13:5 | 24 |
| 15:9–14 | 329 |
| 15:9–15 | 51 |
| 15:12 | 104 |
| 15:12–13 | 103 |
| 15:12–14 | 12 |
| 20:7 | 459 |
| 20:35 | 28 |
| 21:7 | 78 |
| 23:3 | 51 |
| 29:10 | 104 |
| 29:10–11 | 51 |
| 33:8 | 143 |
| 36:13 | 11 |

## Ezra
| Reference | Page |
|---|---|
| 10 | 53 |
| 10:2–5 | 53 |
| 10:3 | 104 |

## Nehemiah
| Reference | Page |
|---|---|
| 1:5 | 107, 195 |
| 9:17 | 233 |
| 9:29 | 123 |
| 9:30–31 | 93 |
| 9:31 | 233 |
| 9:32 | 107 |
| 9:38 | 24, 52 |
| 11:1 | 490 |
| 11:18 | 490 |

## Esther
| Reference | Page |
|---|---|
| 2:9 | 203 |
| 2:17 | 130 |
| 5:8 | 130 |

## Job
| Reference | Page |
|---|---|
| 1:6 | 459 |
| 2:1 | 459 |
| 5:23 | 59 |
| 6:14 | 202–203 |
| 9:3 | 498 |
| 9:4 | 497 |
| 9:7 | 57 |
| 10:9 | 498 |
| 11:10 | 498 |
| 12:4 | 147 |
| 15:14–16 | 153 |
| 25:4 | 449 |
| 31:1 | 59 |
| 33:13 | 497 |
| 38:7 | 459 |
| 41:4 | 59 |

## Psalms
| Reference | Page |
|---|---|
| 1:1–2 | 106 |
| 1:2 | 259 |
| 2:6 | 310 |
| 10:16 | 310 |
| 11:4 | 490 |
| 14:1 | 22 |
| 14:7 | 504 |
| 15 | 128 |
| 16:10 | 107 |
| 17:17–18 | 312 |
| 19 | 504 |
| 19:4 | 503 |
| 19:5 | 113 |
| 19:8 | 259 |
| 22:10 | 176 |
| 22:31–32 | 404 |
| 23:1–4 | 489 |
| 24:7–10 | 22 |
| 25:10 | 25 |

| | | | | | |
|---|---|---|---|---|---|
| 25:13 | 404 | 105:7–11 | 146 | 3:19–20 | 58 |
| 25:14 | 25, 459 | 105:8–11 | 69, 70, 83, 104 | 4:1–2 | 101 |
| 29:10 | 310 | | | 6:20 | 101 |
| 30:4 | 107 | 105:9 | 23, 69 | 7:1–2 | 101 |
| 30:5 | 107 | 110:4 | 77, 369, 370 | 7:3 | 296 |
| 32:1–2 | 21 | 111:5 | 104 | 11:5 | 147 |
| 32:11 | 21 | 111:9 | 104 | 11:17 | 203 |
| 36:7–9 | 77 | 112:2 | 404 | 11:20 | 147 |
| 37:18 | 90, 147 | 114:1 | 332 | 14:2 | 108 |
| 40:6–8 | 121 | 115:3 | 497 | 16:4 | 157 |
| 40:7–8 | 369 | 115:16 | 322 | 16:6 | 108 |
| 40:8 | 291, 299 | 118:26 | 509 | 20:38 | 108 |
| 44:2 | 88 | 119:1 | 147 | 21:1 | 497 |
| 51:11 | 410, 436 | 119:14 | 259 | 28:7 | 101 |
| 68:5 | 442 | 119:16 | 259 | 28:10 | 147 |
| 68:19 | 92 | 119:24 | 259 | 31 | 312 |
| 69:29 | 143 | 119:35 | 259 | 31:26 | 203 |
| 69:35 | 507 | 119:47 | 259 | | |
| 72 | 424 | 119:70 | 259 | **Isaiah** | |
| 72:19 | 427 | 119:77 | 259 | 1:11 | 121 |
| 78:10 | 19 | 119:92 | 259 | 1:13 | 121 |
| 78:67–71 | 79 | 119:97 | 106 | 2:1–4 | 5 |
| 80:1 | 331 | 119:126 | 287 | 2:2 | 255, 288 |
| 80:8 | 88, 331 | 119:142 | 19 | 2:2–4 | 349 |
| 80:15 | 88 | 119:143 | 259 | 2:2–5 | 96 |
| 81:10 | 85 | 119:174 | 259 | 2:3 | 423 |
| 86:9 | 318, 354 | 120–134 | 457 | 4:5 | 113 |
| 87 | 348 | 132:2–8 | 493 | 5:1–2 | 88 |
| 89:3–4 | 56, 78 | 132:11–12 | 80 | 5:1–7 | 331 |
| 89:4 | 80 | 132:11–18 | 82, 426 | 5:2 | 88 |
| 89:6 | 342 | 133 | 337 | 5:7 | 88 |
| 89:26 | 81 | 133:1 | 457 | 7:3 | 287 |
| 89:29 | 80 | 133:3 | 143, 337, 457 | 8:8 | 346 |
| 89:30–32 | 80 | 138:2 | 490 | 9:3 | 346 |
| 89:36 | 80 | 141:5 | 203 | 9:6–7 | 5, 82, 94, 289, 426 |
| 89:36–37 | 56 | 146:10 | 310 | | |
| 95:10 | 118 | 147:2 | 507 | 9:7 | 80, 508 |
| 101:6 | 147 | | | 10:15 | 498 |
| 102:13–14 | 507 | **Proverbs** | | 10:20–22 | 32, 287, 353 |
| 102:29 | 404 | 2:16–17 | 54 | 10:20–23 | 104 |
| 103:7–10 | 233 | 2:17 | 24, 101, 203 | 11:9 | 427 |
| 103:13 | 442 | 2:21 | 147 | 11:10 | 318, 424 |
| 103:17–18 | 404 | 3:1 | 101 | 11:11 | 32, 288, 353 |
| 105 | 230, 410 | 3:3 | 108, 296 | 11:11–16 | 288 |
| 105:6 | 234 | 3:12 | 90, 442 | 11:12 | 346, 517 |

## Scripture Index

| | | | | | |
|---|---|---|---|---|---|
| 11:13–14 | 346 | 45:25 | 21, 324, 401, 402, 437 | 59:20–21 | 272 |
| 11:14 | 346 | | | 59:21 | 3, 91, 112, 148, 256, 312, 336, 404 |
| 11:16 | 32, 288, 347, 353 | 48:2 | 490 | | |
| | | 48:20 | 198, 332 | | |
| 12:6 | 282 | 49:3 | 198 | 60:1–22 | 424 |
| 17:6 | 288 | 49:8 | 92, 148, 256, 266 | 60:7 | 496 |
| 17:11 | 88 | | | 60:7–13 | 509 |
| 19:18–25 | 318 | 49:18 | 112, 331 | 60:10 | 507 |
| 24:5 | 18, 19, 61, 64, 83, 104, 145, 148, 287 | 50:1 | 103, 112, 331 | 60:12 | 88 |
| | | 51:1–2 | 332 | 60:13 | 95 |
| | | 51:2 | 71 | 60:17–22 | 289 |
| 24:23 | 511 | 51:3 | 73, 95, 507 | 60:21 | 21, 90, 324, 402, 437 |
| 25:6–8 | 424, 511 | 51:7 | 21 | | |
| 25:6–9 | 95 | 51:8 | 19 | 61:1 | 300, 340 |
| 25:10 | 511 | 52:1 | 94, 265, 270, 402, 490, 509, 518 | 61:3 | 89 |
| 27:9 | 272 | | | 61:4 | 507 |
| 28 | 55 | | | 61:7 | 288 |
| 28:6 | 288 | 52:11 | 332 | 61:7–9 | 148 |
| 28:15 | 34, 55 | 53 | 311 | 61:8 | 17, 112, 256, 302 |
| 28:18 | 34, 55 | 53:10 | 370 | | |
| 29:16 | 498 | 53:11 | 21, 296 | 61:8–9 | 91 |
| 30:1 | 25 | 54:1 | 30, 282 | 61:9 | 404 |
| 30:1–7 | 55 | 54:3 | 404 | 61:10 | 112, 331 |
| 30:14 | 498 | 54:4–8 | 103, 104 | 62:4–5 | 112 |
| 32:1 | 319 | 54:5–8 | 102, 112 | 62:5 | 102, 331 |
| 32:14–18 | 289 | 54:6–8 | 331 | 62:9 | 509 |
| 33:14–16 | 128 | 54:6–10 | 203 | 63:11 | 303, 331 |
| 33:24 | 437 | 54:9–10 | 91 | 63:16 | 442 |
| 36:6–9 | 55 | 54:10 | 30, 75, 223, 256 | 64:8 | 436, 442, 498 |
| 40:11 | 331 | | | 65:17 | 319, 513 |
| 41:8 | 198, 459 | 55:1–5 | 91 | 65:17–25 | 319 |
| 41:19–20 | 95 | 55:3 | 17, 78, 79, 112, 148, 256, 302 | 65:20 | 290, 319, 513 |
| 42:4 | 413 | | | 65:22–23 | 404 |
| 42:6 | 92, 148, 251, 256, 266, 271 | | | 66:3 | 121 |
| | | 55:12–13 | 95 | 66:18–20 | 325 |
| 43:5 | 404 | 56:1–7 | 94 | 66:23 | 94 |
| 43:14 | 517 | 56:3–7 | 424 | | |
| 44:1–2 | 198 | 56:4 | 148 | **Jeremiah** | |
| 44:1–3 | 176 | 56:4–7 | 91, 112, 415 | 1:5 | 334 |
| 44:3 | 404 | 56:6 | 195, 354 | 1:10 | 334 |
| 44:21 | 198 | 56:6–7 | 93, 251, 272, 318, 349, 496 | 2 | 331 |
| 45:4 | 198 | | | 2:2 | 102, 105, 108, 120 |
| 45:8 | 128 | 56:7 | 509 | | |
| 45:9 | 498 | 58:12 | 507 | 2:2–3 | 111 |
| 45:18 | 57 | 59:20 | 504 | 2:21 | 88, 331 |

| | | | | | |
|---|---|---|---|---|---|
| 2:32 | 112 | 30:18–20 | 289 | 32:27 | 70 |
| 3:4 | 442 | 30:20–21 | 255 | 32:36–41 | 91 |
| 3:16 | 299 | 30:21 | 288 | 32:37 | 288 |
| 3:17 | 81, 318, 349, 424, 508, 517 | 30:21–22 | 256 | 32:37–41 | 148 |
| | | 30:24 | 255, 288 | 32:38–40 | 336 |
| 3:19 | 442 | 30:36–41 | 3 | 32:39 | 233 |
| 4:2 | 318, 354 | 31 | 250, 254, 255, 288, 298, 393, 421, 441, 514 | 32:40 | 17, 302 |
| 4:4 | 233, 265, 350, 467, 468, 508 | | | 32:41 | 88, 288 |
| | | | | 33:4–6 | 507 |
| 4:19 | 122 | 31:3–4 | 93 | 33:9 | 251 |
| 4:23 | 57 | 31:4–6 | 421 | 33:11 | 288 |
| 6:10 | 265, 467 | 31:4–7 | 289 | 33:15 | 288 |
| 6:20 | 121 | 31:6 | 255, 516 | 33:15–22 | 94 |
| 9:25 | 265, 467 | 31:7–8 | 515 | 33:17 | 80 |
| 9:25–26 | 350 | 31:8 | 517 | 33:20–21 | 56, 80 |
| 9:26 | 508 | 31:8–9 | 487 | 33:21 | 78 |
| 10:10 | 310 | 31:9 | 288, 442 | 33:22 | 78 |
| 11:4 | 71 | 31:10 | 251 | 33:25–26 | 56, 78 |
| 11:10 | 18, 69, 287 | 31:12 | 17, 487, 516 | 34:8–9 | 29 |
| 11:17 | 88 | 31:12–14 | 289 | 34:8–10 | 52 |
| 13:13 | 508 | 31:15 | 255, 288 | 34:11 | 52 |
| 14:21 | 18, 271 | 31:17 | 487 | 34:12–22 | 52 |
| 16:7 | 115 | 31:23 | 288 | 34:13 | 85 |
| 17:13 | 77 | 31:23–24 | 515 | 34:18 | 24 |
| 17:25 | 508 | 31:24–25 | 289 | 34:18–20 | 72 |
| 18:6 | 498 | 31:27 | 288 | 35 | 314 |
| 22:2 | 508 | 31:30 | 288 | 38:7–13 | 314 |
| 22:4 | 508 | 31:31 | 214, 236, 250, 287, 288, 404 | 42:10 | 88 |
| 22:30 | 508 | | | 46:27–28 | 198 |
| 23:20 | 288 | 31:31–32 | 84, 104 | 50:2–5 | 91 |
| 23:29 | 330 | 31:31–34 | 4, 91, 122, 291, 295, 354, 398, 404, 438, 440, 487, 514 | 50:4–5 | 148, 288, 330 |
| 24:6 | 88 | | | 50:5 | 17, 302 |
| 29:11 | 30 | | | 51:6 | 332 |
| 30 | 255 | | | 51:45 | 332 |
| 30–31 | 254, 256, 421 | 31:32 | 69, 287 | | |
| 30–34 | 438, 462 | 31:32–33 | 104 | **Lamentations** | |
| 30:3 | 288 | 31:33 | 19, 105, 128, 253, 291, 292, 328, 404 | 3:22 | 89 |
| 30:3–4 | 288 | | | | |
| 30:6–8 | 288 | | | **Ezekiel** | |
| 30:7 | 288, 293, 505 | 31:33–34 | 17, 392, 402 | 1:28 | 67, 94 |
| 30:9 | 78, 79, 94, 255, 256, 288 | 31:34 | 421, 441 | 11:19 | 233 |
| | | 31:34–35 | 290 | 15:6 | 331 |
| 30:10 | 198, 404 | 31:35 | 328 | 16 | 110, 112, 331 |
| 30:11 | 255, 288 | 31:36–37 | 404 | 16:7 | 88 |
| 30:18 | 255, 516 | 31:38–40 | 255, 289 | 16:7–8 | 110 |

## Scripture Index

| | | | | | |
|---|---|---|---|---|---|
| 16:8 | 24, 54, 102, 112, 195, 203 | 40–43 | 509 | 11:31 | 505 |
| 16:8–14 | 99 | 40–44 | 97, 294, 295 | 12:1 | 288, 505 |
| 16:59 | 12, 18, 23 | 40:46 | 78, 426 | 12:1–2 | 457 |
| 16:59–63 | 54, 91, 110, 112 | 40:46–47 | 510 | 12:2 | 143, 337 |
| | | 41 | 495 | 12:11 | 505 |
| 16:60 | 105 | 41:18–20 | 77 | | |
| 16:61 | 271 | 41:20–21 | 495 | **Hosea** | |
| 17:13 | 23 | 41:22 | 510 | 1 | 504 |
| 17:13–15 | 34 | 43:13–27 | 510 | 1–2 | 352 |
| 17:13–16 | 11 | 43:19 | 78, 426 | 1–3 | 203 |
| 17:16–19 | 12, 23 | 44 | 77, 495 | 1:6–10 | 116 |
| 17:18 | 24 | 44–46 | 93 | 1:10 | 95, 199, 333, 352, 436, 460, 504 |
| 18:9 | 123 | 44:6–9 | 270, 402, 508, 518 | | |
| 20:11–13 | 123 | | | 2 | 504 |
| 20:12 | 87 | 44:7 | 18, 265, 467, 508 | 2:14–23 | 116 |
| 20:20 | 87 | | | 2:18 | 59, 65 |
| 23 | 112 | 44:9 | 94, 265, 467, 509 | 2:18–19 | 331 |
| 23:20 | 407 | | | 2:19–20 | 102, 112 |
| 28:25 | 198 | 44:15 | 78, 426 | 2:22 | 333 |
| 34:20–31 | 91 | 44:15–31 | 294 | 2:23 | 352, 353, 504 |
| 34:23–24 | 78, 79, 94, 288 | 44:16 | 495, 510 | 3:4–5 | 288 |
| | | 44:24 | 94 | 3:5 | 79, 94, 255, 288 |
| 34:25 | 30, 65, 75, 223 | 45:19 | 510 | | |
| | | 45:25 | 59 | 4:1 | 202 |
| 36:24 | 517 | 46:1 | 94 | 6:6–7 | 121 |
| 36:24–31 | 127 | 46:3–4 | 94 | 6:7 | 18, 60, 372, 427 |
| 36:25 | 327 | 46:6 | 94 | | |
| 36:25–27 | 129 | 47:1 | 510 | 8:1 | 19 |
| 36:26 | 233 | 47:1–12 | 77 | 8:12–13 | 121 |
| 36:27 | 292, 327 | 47:13–23 | 516 | 9:4 | 121 |
| 36:35 | 73, 95 | 48:11 | 78, 426 | 10:1 | 88, 331 |
| 37 | 256 | | | 11:1 | 11, 88, 101, 199, 460 |
| 37:15–28 | 91, 287, 288 | **Daniel** | | | |
| 37:24 | 288 | 1:9 | 203 | 12:1 | 55 |
| 37:24–25 | 78, 79, 94 | 2:28 | 288 | 12:2 | 34 |
| 37:24–26 | 256 | 4:26 | 510 | | |
| 37:24–27 | 404 | 4:35 | 497 | **Joel** | |
| 37:24–28 | 149 | 7:13 | 321, 505 | 2 | 300 |
| 37:25 | 78, 198, | 9:4 | 107, 195 | 2:16 | 113 |
| 37:25–26 | 288, 517 | 9:24 | 19, 56, 490 | 2:28 | 394 |
| 37:26 | 17, 30, 75, 223, 298, 302 | 9:24–27 | 55 | 2:28–29 | 300 |
| | | 9:25–26 | 56 | 2:28–32 | 333, 341 |
| 37:27 | 353 | 9:26 | 56 | 3:12 | 516 |
| 38:16 | 255, 288 | 9:27 | 55, 56, 505 | 3:16–18 | 516 |
| | | 11:6 | 25 | | |

559

| | | | | | |
|---|---|---|---|---|---|
| 3:18 | 17 | 6 | 370 | **NEW TESTAMENT** | |
| | | 6:12–13 | 370, 509 | **Matthew** | |
| **Amos** | | 6:12–15 | 294 | 1:1 | 73, 79 |
| 1–2 | 334 | 6:13 | 78, 94, 223, 370 | 2:2 | 310 |
| 1:9 | 28 | | | 3 | 234 |
| 5:4 | 123 | 7:9 | 202 | 3:9 | 234, 330, 360, 393 |
| 5:6 | 123 | 8:8 | 298 | | |
| 5:14 | 123 | 8:20–23 | 424 | 3:11 | 323, 462 |
| 5:21–24 | 121 | 8:22–23 | 318, 423 | 3:16 | 462 |
| 6:12 | 128 | 9 | 303 | 4:5 | 490 |
| 9:7 | 334 | 9:9 | 282 | 4:23 | 417 |
| 9:11 | 94 | 9:11 | 301, 302, 303 | 5–7 | 93, 408, 418 |
| 9:13 | 17 | 9:12–13 | 303 | 5:3–11 | 456 |
| 9:15 | 89 | 10:6 | 518 | 5:7 | 130 |
| | | 10:8–9 | 512 | 5:14 | 317 |
| **Micah** | | 10:9 | 512 | 5:17 | 123 |
| 1:2 | 490 | 10:9–10 | 518 | 5:45 | 57, 58, 66 |
| 3:12 | 509 | 11:10 | 59, 65 | 5:48 | 454 |
| 4:1 | 288 | 14 | 5, 512 | 6:2 | 120, 121 |
| 4:1–3 | 349 | 14:4–5 | 510 | 6:5 | 120, 121 |
| 4:1–4 | 511 | 14:9–19 | 512 | 6:16 | 120, 121 |
| 4:1–5 | 96, 318, 424 | 14:10–11 | 516 | 7:1–2 | 413 |
| 4:4 | 16 | 14:16 | 424 | 7:5 | 120 |
| 6:6–8 | 121 | 14:16–19 | 330 | 7:13 | 252 |
| 7:16–17 | 424 | 14:20 | 496 | 7:22 | 252 |
| 7:19–20 | 74 | | | 8:11–12 | 252 |
| 7:20 | 69, 424 | **Malachi** | | 9:13 | 121 |
| | | 1:2–3 | 118 | 9:27 | 79, 130 |
| **Habakkuk** | | 1:6 | 198, 442 | 9:35 | 417 |
| 2:4 | 276, 328 | 1:6–7 | 495 | 10:5–6 | 331 |
| 2:14 | 427 | 1:10 | 121 | 10:25 | 266 |
| 2:20 | 490 | 1:11 | 424 | 11:11 | 319 |
| | | 1:11–12 | 495 | 11:30 | 119 |
| **Zephaniah** | | 1:13 | 121 | 12:7 | 121 |
| 3:9 | 424 | 2 | 111 | 12:8 | 266 |
| 3:14 | 282 | 2:4–5 | 75 | 12:23 | 79 |
| | | 2:5 | 271 | 12:28 | 23 |
| **Haggai** | | 2:8 | 75 | 12:32 | 505 |
| 2:4–5 | 3 | 2:10 | 111, 436, 442 | 13:16–17 | 455 |
| | | 2:13 | 121 | 13:24–30 | 317, 483 |
| **Zechariah** | | 2:14 | 24, 54, 102, 112, 195, 203 | 13:35 | 318 |
| 2:10 | 282 | | | 13:36–43 | 317, 483 |
| 2:10–11 | 349 | | | 13:38 | 252 |
| 2:11 | 318 | | | 13:41 | 423 |
| 3:10 | 16 | | | 13:47–50 | 483 |

| | | | | | |
|---|---|---|---|---|---|
| 15:7 | 120 | 24:22 | 144 | 1:32–33 | 78, 508, 510 |
| 15:22 | 79, 82, 130 | 24:27–30 | 504 | 1:39 | 487 |
| 15:24 | 331 | 24:29 | 505 | 1:41 | 268, 340, 341 |
| 16:3 | 505 | 24:30 | 321 | 1:54–55 | 268 |
| 16:18 | 314, 317, 332, 343, 462 | 24:30–31 | 423 | 1:55 | 69 |
| | | 24:31 | 505 | 1:67 | 268, 340, 341 |
| 16:27–28 | 423 | 24:39 | 504 | 1:68–73 | 251 |
| 17:15 | 130 | 24:51 | 120 | 1:68–75 | 268 |
| 18:17 | 462 | 25:31 | 423, 508 | 1:69 | 78 |
| 19:14 | 176, 483 | 25:31–46 | 457 | 1:72 | 25, 268 |
| 19:16 | 337 | 25:34 | 318, 337, 457 | 1:72–73 | 69, 268 |
| 19:17 | 143 | 25:41 | 458 | 1:74–77 | 267 |
| 19:28 | 329, 423, 508 | 25:46 | 457, 458 | 1:78 | 268 |
| 19:29 | 337 | 26:28 | 4, 15, 26, 32, 91, 94, 136, 193, 252, 268, 301, 427, 438, 472, 487 | 2:4 | 80, 488 |
| 20:15 | 497 | | | 2:11 | 80 |
| 20:28 | 252 | | | 2:21 | 467 |
| 20:30 | 130 | | | 2:22 | 488 |
| 20:30–31 | 79 | | | 2:22–24 | 407 |
| 21:9 | 79 | 26:42 | 497 | 2:40 | 131 |
| 21:13 | 509 | 26:64 | 321, 423, 508 | 2:41–42 | 488 |
| 21:15 | 79 | 27:46 | 338 | 2:51 | 266 |
| 21:33–45 | 331, 483 | 27:53 | 252, 490 | 3 | 63 |
| 22:1–14 | 483 | 28:18 | 3 | 3:8 | 234 |
| 22:14 | 252 | 28:18–19 | 3, 94, 324, 417, 468 | 3:23 | 63 |
| 22:18 | 120 | | | 3:28 | 459 |
| 22:37–40 | 262 | 28:19 | 252, 258 | 3:38 | 63, 446 |
| 23:13–29 | 120 | | | 6:35 | 95 |
| 23:19 | 490 | **Mark** | | 6:36 | 454 |
| 23:27 | 121 | 1:4 | 472 | 8:1 | 488 |
| 23:35 | 20, 117, 302 | 10:14 | 408 | 9:2 | 489 |
| 23:38–39 | 509 | 10:30 | 505 | 9:30–31 | 332 |
| 24 | 504 | 10:38–39 | 468 | 9:34–35 | 113 |
| 24:3 | 504 | 10:45 | 252 | 9:35 | 395 |
| 24:5 | 252 | 14:24 | 136, 252, 268, 301, 487 | 9:51 | 488, 489 |
| 24:10 | 252 | | | 9:57 | 488 |
| 24:12 | 106, 252 | 14:25 | 4 | 10:25 | 337, 458 |
| 24:14 | 252, 324, 417, 505 | 16:16 | 476 | 10:28 | 123 |
| | | 16:19 | 338 | 10:30 | 488 |
| 24:15 | 505 | | | 10:31–32 | 488 |
| 24:15–20 | 505 | **Luke** | | 10:33 | 488 |
| 24:15–30 | 510 | 1:6 | 21, 119, 232, 267, 328, 428, 489 | 10:38 | 488 |
| 24:15–31 | 505 | | | 11:6 | 488 |
| 24:20 | 506 | | | 11:51 | 302 |
| 24:21 | 288, 505 | 1:15 | 176, 340, 341 | 12:50 | 468 |
| 24:21–30 | 505 | 1:32 | 82, 426 | 13:16 | 330 |

561

| | | | | | |
|---|---|---|---|---|---|
| 13:22 | 488 | 3:6 | 153, 407, 481 | 11:52 | 315, 462 |
| 13:29 | 252 | 3:15–16 | 458 | 13:1 | 266 |
| 15:13 | 488 | 3:16 | 337, 385 | 13:34 | 408, 413 |
| 16:22–26 | 439 | 3:29 | 113, 319 | 13:34–35 | 262 |
| 17:11 | 488 | 3:35 | 213 | 14–16 | 418 |
| 18:11–12 | 122 | 3:36 | 337, 458 | 14:1–3 | 439 |
| 18:15–17 | 477 | 4:14 | 338 | 14:6 | 458 |
| 18:16 | 406 | 4:22 | 4, 81 | 14:15 | 106, 114 |
| 18:18 | 458 | 5:20 | 213 | 14:16 | 410 |
| 18:29–30 | 458 | 5:24 | 337, 458 | 14:16–17 | 13, 341, 443 |
| 18:30 | 505 | 5:26 | 455 | 14:17 | 435, 436 |
| 19:9 | 330, 489 | 6:40 | 458 | 14:20 | 321, 454 |
| 19:12 | 488 | 6:44 | 144, 154 | 14:21 | 106 |
| 19:23 | 489 | 6:47 | 337, 458 | 14:23–24 | 106 |
| 20:36 | 95 | 6:53–54 | 458 | 14:26 | 13 |
| 21 | 504 | 6:54 | 337 | 15:1–8 | 331, 357 |
| 22:18–20 | 256 | 6:57 | 442 | 15:9–10 | 213 |
| 22:19 | 115, 264 | 6:63 | 407, 481 | 15:10 | 107, 114 |
| 22:19–20 | 249 | 6:70 | 234 | 16:28 | 321 |
| 22:20 | 7, 94, 122, 136, 252, 255, 268, 301, 328, 438, 472, 487 | 7:22 | 269 | 16:33 | 422 |
| | | 7:38–39 | 338, 462 | 17 | 370 |
| | | 7:39 | 322 | 17:3 | 14, 337, 454, 458 |
| | | 8 | 74, 235 | | |
| 22:31–32 | 339 | 8:33 | 235, 360 | 17:4–5 | 369 |
| 22:69 | 338 | 8:34–36 | 267 | 17:20–23 | 459 |
| 23:35 | 395 | 8:37 | 235, 330, 360 | 17:21–23 | 442, 454 |
| 23:42 | 458 | 8:39 | 393 | 17:22 | 339 |
| 23:43 | 439 | 8:39–40 | 330, 331 | 17:24 | 213, 369 |
| 24:14 | 489 | 8:39–41 | 235 | 17:26 | 213 |
| 24:22 | 489 | 8:39–44 | 283, 360 | 18:36 | 510 |
| 24:47 | 258, 417 | 8:41–44 | 331 | 18:37 | 266 |
| | | 8:44 | 235 | 20:17 | 201, 442, 460 |
| | | 8:51 | 143 | 21:15–17 | 331 |
| **John** | | 8:56 | 74, 435 | | |
| 1:12 | 315 | 10 | 349 | **Acts** | |
| 1:12–13 | 336, 460 | 10:3–4 | 489 | 1 | 510 |
| 1:14 | 321, 338, 446, 447 | 10:4 | 303 | 1–2 | 462 |
| | | 10:10–11 | 336 | 1:4 | 437 |
| 1:18 | 338, 446 | 10:16 | 252, 315, 331, 462 | 1:5 | 323, 340, 343 |
| 1:29 | 319 | | | 1:6–8 | 23 |
| 2:16 | 439 | 10:17 | 213 | 1:11 | 510 |
| 2:19–21 | 340 | 10:27–28 | 258 | 1:14–15 | 343 |
| 3:3–8 | 458 | 10:27–29 | 154 | 2 | 177, 308, 311, 313, 314, 322, 323, 330, 436, |
| 3:5 | 160, 172, 292, 327 | 10:28 | 458 | | |
| 3:5–8 | 326 | 11:25 | 458 | | |

## Scripture Index

|   |   |   |   |   |   |
|---|---|---|---|---|---|
|        | 437, 462              | 9:24      | 277            | 22:16     | 469, 472, 476 |
| 2:3    | 330                   | 9:31      | 343            | 23:12     | 13 |
| 2:4    | 330, 340, 343, 451    | 10        | 436            | 23:14     | 13 |
|        |                       | 10:38     | 300, 310       | 23:21     | 13 |
| 2:16–21 | 341                  | 10:47     | 176            | 24:14     | 332 |
| 2:17   | 394                   | 11:16–17  | 340            | 24:22     | 332 |
| 2:17–21 | 333                  | 13:9      | 340, 451       | 26:6      | 69 |
| 2:33   | 13, 14, 338, 394, 437 | 13:16     | 358            | 28:17     | 480 |
|        |                       | 13:21     | 79, 80         |           |    |
| 2:33–34 | 508                  | 13:32     | 69             | **Romans** |   |
| 2:38–39 | 176                  | 13:32–33  | 353            | 1:5       | 130 |
| 2:38   | 335, 472, 476         | 13:34     | 80             | 1:9       | 420 |
| 2:39   | 14, 177, 227, 335, 382, 394 | 13:46 | 331            | 1:16–17   | 441 |
|        |                       | 13:48     | 388            | 1:18–32   | 65 |
| 2:40   | 461                   | 13:52     | 451            | 1:23–32   | 478 |
| 2:42   | 264                   | 14:16–17  | 57, 58         | 1:30      | 120 |
| 2:46   | 264                   | 14:17     | 66             | 2:4       | 144 |
| 3:13   | 69                    | 15        | 402, 480       | 2:11–16   | 65 |
| 3:19   | 96                    | 15:1      | 269            | 2:12–13   | 280 |
| 3:21   | 96                    | 15:10     | 106, 119, 263, 291, 296 | 2:13 | 21, 260, 268, 428 |
| 3:25   | 69, 73, 227, 251, 360, 424 | 15:13 | 405            | 2:14      | 165 |
|        |                       | 15:14     | 328, 353, 460, 461 | 2:14–15 | 163 |
| 3:25–26 | 269                  |           |                | 2:19–20   | 198, 271 |
| 4–8    | 4                     | 16:3      | 474, 480       | 2:19–21   | 324 |
| 4:8    | 340, 451              | 16:15     | 406, 484       | 2:28–29   | 211, 265, 350, 508 |
| 4:31   | 340, 451              | 16:31     | 176, 484       |           |    |
| 5:11   | 315, 343, 462         | 16:34     | 484            | 2:29      | 467 |
| 5:31   | 338, 508              | 18:8      | 484            | 3:2       | 270 |
| 7      | 308                   | 18:21     | 497            | 3:10–19   | 280 |
| 7:8    | 19, 31, 73, 269       | 19:2      | 322, 462       | 3:19      | 277 |
| 7:23   | 86                    | 19:9      | 332            | 3:19–20   | 153 |
| 7:32   | 69                    | 19:23     | 332            | 3:20      | 293 |
| 7:38   | 36, 177, 308, 315     | 19:32     | 177, 308       | 3:22–24   | 385 |
|        |                       | 19:39     | 177, 308       | 3:23      | 153 |
| 7:51   | 265, 467, 508         | 19:41     | 177, 308       | 3:24–25   | 434 |
| 7:53   | 36                    | 20:24     | 420            | 3:24–26   | 327 |
| 7:55–56 | 338                  | 20:25     | 420            | 3:25      | 137, 299 |
| 8      | 4                     | 20:28–29  | 331            | 3:25–26   | 441 |
| 8:1    | 343, 462              | 20:29–30  | 316            | 3:27      | 260 |
| 8:3    | 343, 462              | 20:30     | 405            | 3:30      | 265 |
| 8:12   | 476, 481, 484         | 21:39     | 358            | 4         | 73, 235 |
| 8:34   | 311                   | 22        | 469            | 4:1       | 351 |
| 9:2    | 332                   | 22:3      | 358            | 4:3       | 8, 423 |
| 9:17   | 451                   | 22:4      | 332            | 4:3–22    | 20 |

| Ref | Pages | Ref | Pages | Ref | Pages |
|---|---|---|---|---|---|
| 4:5 | 450 | 8:14–15 | 95 | 11:14 | 352, 355 |
| 4:9 | 423 | 8:14–16 | 445 | 11:16 | 356. 359 |
| 4:11 | 8, 312, 330, 360, 433 | 8:15 | 436 | 11:16–24 | 430 |
| | | 8:17 | 339 | 11:17 | 356, 357 |
| 4:11–12 | 69, 235, 324, 354, 410, 482 | 8:19 | 95 | 11:18 | 360 |
| | | 8:23 | 95 | 11:17–24 | 357 |
| 4:12 | 265 | 8:29 | 153, 201, 266 | 11:21 | 357 |
| 4:16 | 312, 330, 360, 433 | 8:29–30 | 388, 445 | 11:22 | 360 |
| | | 8:30 | 447 | 11:22–23 | 358 |
| 4:18 | 423 | 8:33 | 388 | 11:24 | 357 |
| 4:22 | 423 | 8:34 | 338, 339, 508 | 11:24–27 | 358 |
| 5:1–2 | 445 | 9 | 235, 352 | 11:25 | 355, 356 |
| 5:5 | 445 | 9–11 | 347, 355, 503, 504, 507 | 11:26 | 356, 360, 430, 504, 506, 507 |
| 5:8 | 409 | | | | |
| 5:12–19 | 61 | 9:3 | 352, 355 | 11:26–27 | 272 |
| 5:12–21 | 28, 173 | 9:4 | 4, 366, 428 | 11:28 | 69, 359 |
| 5:18 | 241, 385 | 9:4–5 | 270 | 11:29 | 257, 516 |
| 5:21 | 274, 337 | 9:5 | 69, 359 | 12:1 | 265 |
| 6 | 478 | 9:6 | 352 | 12:2 | 448 |
| 6:1–4 | 173 | 9:6–7 | 235 | 13:8–10 | 259, 263, 325 |
| 6:3–4 | 468 | 9:7–13 | 352 | 13:13–14 | 478 |
| 6:4 | 469 | 9:8 | 360 | 13:14 | 266, 298 |
| 6:6 | 467, 468 | 9:9 | 435 | 14:10 | 326 |
| 6:17 | 267 | 9:13 | 118 | 14:17 | 510 |
| 6:19–22 | 198 | 9:15–18 | 497 | 14:17–18 | 81 |
| 6:22 | 325 | 9:21 | 498 | 15:4 | 281 |
| 6:22–23 | 337 | 9:22–23 | 157, 497 | 15:8 | 69, 331 |
| 6:23 | 296 | 9:23 | 153 | 15:30 | 213 |
| 7:2 | 104 | 9:24–25 | 333 | 15:32 | 497 |
| 7:6 | 297 | 9:25–26 | 352, 504 | 16:25 | 318 |
| 7:7 | 293 | 9:27–29 | 353 | 16:25–26 | 455, 461 |
| 7:12 | 118, 260, 279 | 9:31 | 260, 353 | 16:26 | 324 |
| 7:14 | 260 | 10 | 504 | | |
| 7:16 | 260 | 10:5 | 123, 139 | **1 Corinthians** | |
| 7:18 | 481 | 10:6 | 261 | 1:16 | 484 |
| 8:2–4 | 267 | 10:18 | 503 | 1:30 | 92 |
| 8:3 | 447 | 11 | 306, 348, 355, 361 | 2:4 | 451 |
| 8:4 | 16, 143, 150, 260, 292, 298, 325 | | | 2:6 | 450, 452 |
| | | 11:1 | 358 | 2:6–8 | 461 |
| | | 11:5 | 14, 32, 104, 142, 273, 353, 355, 461 | 2:6–10 | 455 |
| 8:4–14 | 452 | | | 2:7 | 318 |
| 8:9 | 435 | | | 3:12–15 | 326 |
| 8:11 | 412, 435 | 11:7 | 119, 220, 234, 355, 388 | 3:16 | 3, 322, 340, 437, 443, 461, 494, 509 |
| 8:13 | 150 | | | | |
| 8:14 | 292 | 11:9 | 13 | | |

## Scripture Index

| | | | | | |
|---|---|---|---|---|---|
| 4:4–5 | 326 | 15:45–47 | 22 | **Galatians** | |
| 4:14–15 | 334 | 15:45–49 | 3, 61 | 1:4 | 154, 505 |
| 4:19 | 497 | 15:46 | 79 | 2:1 | 260 |
| 4:20 | 23 | 15:53 | 165 | 2:2 | 339 |
| 6:11 | 316 | | | 2:20 | 467 |
| 6:19 | 327, 435, 436, 437, 443 | **2 Corinthians** | | 3 | 73, 74, 230, 250, 269, 272, 273, 275, 428, 435, 456, 478 |
| | | 1:20 | 13, 435 | | |
| 7:14 | 176, 177, 334, 382, 392, 408, 483 | 1:21–22 | 300, 340 | | |
| | | 1:22 | 311 | | |
| | | 3 | 253, 402, 440, 441 | 3:1–5 | 435 |
| 7:19 | 265 | | | 3:1–4:7 | 282 |
| 8:37 | 265 | 3:2–3 | 440, 441 | 3:6 | 8, 20, 360, 423 |
| 9:21 | 260, 297, 325, 408 | 3:3 | 253, 291, 293, 295, 297, 402 | 3:6–9 | 73 |
| | | 3:4–6 | 250 | 3:6–13 | 434 |
| 9:24 | 339 | 3:6 | 3, 7, 26, 91, 193, 210, 293, 297, 328, 402, 440 | 3:7 | 73, 235, 257, 331, 354, 360, 393, 403, 405, 410, 472, 483 |
| 9:26 | 339 | | | | |
| 10:1–5 | 118, 139 | | | | |
| 10:1–6 | 332 | | | | |
| 10:6–12 | 139 | | | | |
| 10:11 | 281 | 3:7 | 296 | 3:7–9 | 312, 330, 434 |
| 10:16–17 | 4, 114 | 3:8 | 295, 328, 441 | 3:8 | 71, 257, 269, 424 |
| 10:18 | 284, 351 | 3:9 | 296, 328, 441 | | |
| 10:18–21 | 495, 510 | 3:14 | 26, 38, 84, 100, 122 | 3:8–9 | 73, 360 |
| 10:31 | 265 | | | 3:9 | 235, 403, 483 |
| 10:32 | 305, 349 | 3:17–18 | 441 | 3:11–12 | 261, 360 |
| 11:17–32 | 4 | 3:18 | 266, 448 | 3:12 | 123, 139 |
| 11:24 | 115 | 4:3–6 | 57 | 3:14 | 73, 74, 227, 257, 274, 312, 330, 434, 483 |
| 11:24–25 | 264 | 4:4 | 420, 427, 448 | | |
| 11:24–26 | 257 | 4:6 | 447, 452 | | |
| 11:25 | 7, 91, 94, 136, 210, 252, 255, 268, 301, 328, 438 | 4:10–11 | 336, 458 | 3:15 | 25, 31, 273 |
| | | 5:1–9 | 439 | 3:15–18 | 282, 328 |
| | | 5:10 | 326 | 3:15–4:7 | 257 |
| | | 5:14–15 | 241 | 3:16 | 268, 275, 434 |
| 11:26 | 4, 312 | 5:15 | 467 | 3:17 | 25, 31, 273, 472 |
| 12:4–11 | 451 | 5:21 | 154, 296 | | |
| 12:7 | 341 | 6:16 | 298, 352, 437, 443, 461, 494, 509 | 3:18 | 31, 275 |
| 12:11 | 341, 497 | | | 3:18–19 | 10 |
| 12:12–13 | 3, 160, 340 | | | 3:19 | 36, 114 |
| 12:13 | 323, 343 | 6:17–18 | 332 | 3:21 | 260, 360 |
| 14:20 | 450, 452 | 6:18 | 95 | 3:22 | 483 |
| 15:1–2 | 420 | 11:2 | 3, 114, 115 | 3:22–28 | 280 |
| 15:3 | 154 | 11:32 | 277 | 3:22–4:7 | 325 |
| 15:21–22 | 61 | 12:2 | 452 | 3:23 | 276, 278 |
| 15:37 | 412 | 12:3 | 439 | 3:23–24 | 276 |
| 15:42–44 | 412 | | | 3:23–25 | 279 |

565

| | | | | | |
|---|---|---|---|---|---|
| 3:23–26 | 275 | 5:1 | 263 | 2:5 | 336 |
| 3:24 | 360, 417 | 5:6 | 144, 149, 243, | 2:6 | 320, 339, 437, |
| 3:24–25 | 277 | | 265, 276, 391 | | 443, 458 |
| 3:25 | 276 | 5:7 | 339 | 2:8 | 274, 382, 432 |
| 3:26 | 73, 95, 331, | 5:13 | 154 | 2:8–10 | 143 |
| | 436 | 5:13–14 | 263 | 2:11 | 466 |
| 3:26–27 | 483 | 5:14 | 280 | 2:11–12 | 272 |
| 3:27 | 266, 469, 472, | 5:16 | 150 | 2:11–16 | 306 |
| | 476 | 5:16–18 | 452 | 2:11–22 | 212, 252, 320, |
| 3:27–29 | 393 | 5:16–24 | 277 | | 349, 460 |
| 3:29 | 227, 235, 257, | 5:19–21 | 411 | 2:12 | 349, 366, 428, |
| | 274, 312, 330, | 5:22–23 | 279 | | 461 |
| | 354, 360, 397, | 6:2 | 259, 262, 266, | 2:14 | 92 |
| | 410, 434, 472 | | 280, 297, 325, | 2:14–16 | 320 |
| 4 | 272, 280, 284, | | 408 | 2:15 | 460 |
| | 384 | 6:8 | 337 | 2:16 | 460 |
| 4:1 | 274 | 6:15 | 265, 351 | 2:18 | 461 |
| 4:1–2 | 277 | 6:16 | 119, 212, 324, | 2:19 | 461 |
| 4:1–3 | 284 | | 350 | 2:19–22 | 341 |
| 4:1–7 | 293 | | | 2:20 | 5, 322, 461 |
| 4:4 | 338 | **Ephesians** | | 2:20–22 | 322, 437, 443, |
| 4:4–7 | 277 | 1:3 | 339, 472 | | 494, 509 |
| 4:5–6 | 95 | 1:3–5 | 153, 355 | 2:21 | 461 |
| 4:6 | 292, 436 | 1:3–14 | 369-370 | 2:22 | 3 |
| 4:6–7 | 279, 284 | 1:4 | 318, 395 | 3:1–12 | 320 |
| 4:7 | 274, 339 | 1:4–5 | 234, 388 | 3:3–5 | 455 |
| 4:19 | 266, 456 | 1:4–6 | 266 | 3:3–9 | 317, 461 |
| 4:21 | 281 | 1:5 | 95, 461 497 | 3:3–11 | 212, 349 |
| 4:21–26 | 280 | 1:6 | 340 | 3:4–5 | 322 |
| 4:21–31 | 282, 328 | 1:9 | 497 | 3:9 | 455 |
| 4:22–23 | 354 | 1:9–10 | 421 | 3:10–11 | 388 |
| 4:22–26 | 280 | 1:10 | 96, 179, 365, | 3:11 | 318 |
| 4:23 | 407, 435 | | 377 | 3:14–15 | 460 |
| 4:24 | 253, 281, 366 | 1:11 | 388, 497 | 3:16–17 | 448 |
| 4:24–26 | 280, 281, 409 | 1:13 | 311, 335, 340, | 3:16–19 | 453 |
| 4:24–27 | 330 | | 420 | 3:18 | 182 |
| 4:25 | 281 | 1:13–14 | 332 | 4–5 | 418 |
| 4:26 | 281, 334, 427, | 1:19–21 | 339 | 4:4 | 154, 460 |
| | 507 | 1:19–23 | 320, 339 | 4:6 | 460, 461 |
| 4:27 | 282 | 1:20 | 508 | 4:7–11 | 339 |
| 4:28 | 253, 312, 330, | 1:20–21 | 437 | 4:12 | 460 |
| | 354, 360 | 1:21 | 505 | 4:13 | 450, 452, 454 |
| 4:29 | 407 | 1:22–23 | 443 | 4:15 | 3, 320 |
| 4:29–30 | 285 | 1:23 | 460 | 4:15–16 | 339, 443 |
| 4:30 | 285 | 2:3 | 380 | 4:16 | 460 |

| | | | | | |
|---|---|---|---|---|---|
| 4:17–32 | 408 | 3:21 | 321 | **1 Thessalonians** | |
| 4:22–24 | 321 | 4:3 | 143 | 1:4 | 388 |
| 4:24 | 135, 165, 448, 460 | 4:7 | 277 | 2:7 | 334 |
| | | | | 2:11 | 334 |
| 4:30 | 311, 340 | **Colossians** | | 2:12 | 154 |
| 5:1–2 | 453 | 1:12–13 | 81 | 4:3–8 | 265 |
| 5:2 | 266 | 1:13 | 213, 510 | 4:16–17 | 440 |
| 5:17–20 | 452 | 1:15 | 448 | 5:18 | 264 |
| 5:18 | 340, 449, 451, 454 | 1:18 | 3, 320, 443, 460 | **2 Thessalonians** | |
| 5:19 | 410 | 1:24 | 460 | 1:8 | 420 |
| 5:20 | 264 | 1:24–27 | 318 | 1:10 | 339, 447 |
| 5:21–31 | 114 | 1:25–27 | 455, 461 | 2:14 | 427 |
| 5:23 | 3, 320, 460 | 1:28 | 450, 452 | 3:3 | 154 |
| 5:25 | 266 | 2 | 470, 476 | | |
| 5:25–26 | 113 | 2:8 | 477, 479 | **1 Timothy** | |
| 5:25–27 | 115 | 2:9 | 321 | 1:6 | 337 |
| 5:25–32 | 3 | 2:9–10 | 453, 477 | 1:11 | 420, 427, 456 |
| 5:26 | 330 | 2:10 | 3 | 1:17 | 310 |
| 5:28–33 | 115 | 2:11 | 211, 265, 354, 466, 470, 508 | 2:5 | 92 |
| 5:30 | 460 | | | 2:5–6 | 136 |
| 5:32 | 317 | 2:11–12 | 3, 465, 466, 469, 470, 471, 472, 473, 474, 475, 476, 480 | 2:6 | 241, 385 |
| 6:4 | 477 | | | 2:9 | 265 |
| 6:5 | 352 | | | 3:15 | 315, 317, 340, 461 |
| 6:12 | 339 | | | | |
| 6:15 | 420 | 2:11–13 | 176, 177, 178 | 6:11 | 452 |
| 6:18 | 451 | 2:12 | 469, 471 | 6:12 | 154, 337 |
| | | 2:15 | 339 | 6:16 | 165 |
| **Philippians** | | 2:19 | 3, 320, 339, 443, 460, 477 | 6:17 | 505 |
| 1:6 | 154 | | | | |
| 1:11 | 128 | 2:20–22 | 479 | **2 Timothy** | |
| 1:23 | 439 | 3:1 | 338, 508 | 1:9 | 129 |
| 2:9–11 | 3 | 3:1–3 | 339 | 1:12 | 154 |
| 2:12–13 | 132, 144 | 3:3 | 256 | 2:10 | 220, 388 |
| 2:13 | 497 | 3:3–4 | 458 | 2:16–21 | 405 |
| 2:15 | 198, 315, 317 | 3:4 | 336, 339, 447 | 2:16–26 | 316 |
| 2:16 | 339 | 3:9–11 | 321, 460 | 3:1–9 | 405 |
| 3:3 | 211, 265, 354, 467, 508 | 3:10 | 165, 448 | 3:17 | 452 |
| | | 3:11 | 265 | 4:3–4 | 316 |
| 3:6 | 122, 260 | 3:12 | 388 | 4:7 | 339 |
| 3:12–14 | 339 | 3:15 | 460 | | |
| 3:13–15 | 454 | 3:16 | 410 | **Titus** | |
| 3:15 | 450, 452 | 3:22 | 352 | 1:1 | 388 |
| 3:20 | 332, 462 | 4:2 | 264 | 1:2 | 13, 337 |
| 3:20–21 | 445, 447 | 4:12 | 450 | 2:11 | 241, 385 |

| | | | | | |
|---|---|---|---|---|---|
| 2:11–14 | 258 | 6:17 | 12 | 8:13 | 84, 100, 122, 298, 412 |
| 2:12 | 243, 505 | 6:17–18 | 33 | | |
| 2:14 | 144, 316, 328, 353, 405, 460 | 6:20 | 77, 369 | 9 | 31, 299 |
| | | 7 | 77 | 9:1 | 122, 438 |
| 3:4–8 | 143 | 7–12 | 438 | 9:4 | 35, 36, 299, 438 |
| 3:5 | 160, 172 | 7–13 | 193 | | |
| 3:7 | 337 | 7:1 | 77 | 9:9 | 505 |
| 3:9 | 280 | 7:1–3 | 77 | 9:11–12 | 303 |
| | | 7:10–11 | 77 | 9:11–14 | 77 |
| **Hebrews** | | 7:15 | 77 | 9:12 | 440 |
| 1:2 | 339 | 7:17 | 77, 369 | 9:13–14 | 137 |
| 1:3 | 338, 339, 508 | 7:19–25 | 33 | 9:14–15 | 136 |
| 1:5 | 81 | 7:20–21 | 23 | 9:15 | 3, 15, 17, 31, 32, 33, 92, 93, 94, 114, 122, 193, 300, 303, 328, 426, 438 |
| 1:13 | 339, 508 | 7:22 | 3, 26, 31, 94, 122, 136, 193, 303, 328, 438 | | |
| 2:2 | 36 | | | | |
| 2:5 | 17, 256, 303, 426 | | | | |
| | | 7:22–25 | 438 | | |
| 2:9 | 241, 385 | 7:23–28 | 77 | 9:15–17 | 299 |
| 2:10 | 439 | 7:25 | 77, 282, 294, 339 | 9:15–20 | 26, 151, 438 |
| 2:11 | 201 | | | 9:16–17 | 25, 26, 31, 301 |
| 2:11–12 | 339 | 7:28 | 23 | | |
| 2:12 | 438 | 8 | 33, 250, 292, 412 | 9:18 | 31, 122 |
| 2:14 | 447 | | | 9:19–20 | 439 |
| 2:17 | 32, 77 | 8–9 | 428 | 9:20 | 15, 32, 136, 301, 438 |
| 3:1 | 439 | 8:1 | 508 | | |
| 3:1–6 | 303 | 8:1–2 | 77, 339 | 9:22 | 137, 296 |
| 3:6 | 294 | 8:2 | 33 | 9:22–26 | 93 |
| 3:16–19 | 118 | 8:6 | 3, 33, 94, 114, 122, 136, 193, 255, 328 | 9:26–28 | 136 |
| 4:1 | 33 | | | 10:1 | 17 |
| 4:9 | 17, 33 | | | 10:2 | 409 |
| 4:14–16 | 77 | 8:6–10 | 303, 438 | 10:4 | 136, 300 |
| 4:15 | 77 | 8:7 | 100, 122, 298 | 10:5–10 | 121 |
| 5:6 | 77, 369 | 8:7–13 | 366 | 10:7 | 369 |
| 5:9 | 440 | 8:8 | 32, 122, 214, 236, 250, 254, 286, 287, 292, 293 | 10:10 | 136 |
| 5:10 | 77 | | | 10:12 | 338, 508 |
| 5:14 | 450, 452 | | | 10:12–13 | 339 |
| 6:1 | 452 | | | 10:14 | 136 |
| 6:2 | 440 | | | 10:16 | 19, 193, 303, 438 |
| 6:3 | 497 | 8:8–10 | 193 | | |
| 6:4–5 | 402, 408 | 8:8–12 | 291, 354, 398 | | |
| 6:5 | 17, 256, 303, 426, 505 | 8:9 | 293 | 10:16–18 | 439 |
| | | 8:10 | 19, 105, 214, 292 | 10:19 | 282, 294 |
| 6:11–12 | 33 | | | 10:19–22 | 33, 339 |
| 6:13–18 | 70 | 8:10–12 | 392 | 10:21 | 294 |
| 6:16–17 | 23 | 8:11 | 292 | 10:26–31 | 405 |
| | | 8:12 | 292 | 10:29 | 3, 15, 32, 136, |

|  |  |  |  |  |  |
|---|---|---|---|---|---|
|  | 193, 301, 303, 438, 439 | 2:8–12 | 263 | 2:1 | 157 |
| 11 | 308 | 2:12 | 262, 325, 409 | 2:5 | 20 |
| 11:4 | 20, 117 | 2:14 | 144 | 3:2 | 322 |
| 11:7 | 20 | 2:14–16 | 428 | 3:5–13 | 68 |
| 11:10 | 74, 333, 340, 423, 427, 435, 439, 507 | 2:14–26 | 143, 149 | 3:9 | 93, 385 |
|  |  | 2:17 | 144 | 3:13 | 319, 513 |
|  |  | 2:23 | 8, 20, 423, 459 | **1 John** | |
| 11:13 | 332 | 3:17–18 | 128 | 1:1–2 | 458 |
| 11:13–16 | 332 | 4:15 | 497 | 1:1–4 | 337, 454 |
| 11:14 | 472 |  |  | 1:2 | 458 |
| 11:16 | 340, 426, 427, 435, 439, 472, 507 | **1 Peter** | | 1:3 | 459 |
|  |  | 1:1 | 353, 388 | 1:9 | 441 |
|  |  | 1:2 | 302 | 2:1 | 334, 339 |
| 12:1–3 | 339 | 1:5 | 277 | 2:2 | 154, 241, 385 |
| 12:2 | 338, 508 | 1:12 | 318, 455 | 2:5 | 454 |
| 12:5–8 | 95 | 1:19–20 | 370 | 2:7–8 | 413 |
| 12:11 | 128 | 2:4 | 395 | 2:8–11 | 408 |
| 12:15–17 | 118 | 2:5 | 265, 315, 326, 461 | 2:12–14 | 334 |
| 12:18–24 | 330 |  |  | 2:13–14 | 452 |
| 12:22 | 427, 507 | 2:6 | 395 | 2:13–17 | 454 |
| 12:23 | 309, 438 | 2:9 | 264, 316, 325, 326, 333, 388 | 2:15–17 | 479 |
| 12:24 | 3, 32, 33, 92, 94, 114, 122, 136, 193, 255, 302, 303, 328, 438, 439 |  |  | 2:18–19 | 316, 405 |
|  |  | 2:9–10 | 328, 405, 460 | 2:20 | 300, 340 |
|  |  | 2:10 | 333, 353 | 2:25 | 13 |
|  |  | 2:11 | 332 | 2:27 | 300, 340 |
|  |  | 2:11–12 | 332 | 2:28 | 334 |
| 12:28 | 17, 303, 426 | 2:21–22 | 339 | 2:28–29 | 454 |
| 13:10 | 494, 510 | 2:24 | 154 | 3:1 | 315 |
| 13:13 | 303 | 3:3 | 265 | 3:2 | 447, 454 |
| 13:14 | 17, 332, 427, 490, 507 | 3:17 | 497 | 3:6 | 135 |
|  |  | 3:18 | 136 | 3:9 | 135, 326 |
| 13:14–16 | 265 | 3:18–22 | 422 | 3:12 | 117 |
| 13:15 | 339 | 3:21 | 476, 478, 484 | 3:15 | 458 |
| 13:20 | 15, 17, 32, 122, 136, 193, 301, 303, 328, 438, 440 | 3:22 | 338, 508 | 4:10 | 154 |
|  |  | 4:1–3 | 478 | 5:3 | 15, 114, 119, 297 |
|  |  | 4:17 | 326 |  |  |
|  |  | 4:18 | 144 | 5:11–12 | 337, 442, 455, 458 |
| 13:20–21 | 302 | 5:2–3 | 331 |  |  |
|  |  |  |  | 5:11–13 | 454, 460 |
| **James** |  | **2 Peter** |  | 5:18 | 135 |
| 1:18 | 497 | 1:4 | 446, 447 | 5:20 | 14, 337, 454, 458 |
| 1:25 | 262, 263, 325, 409 | 1:10 | 388 |  |  |
|  |  | 1:15 | 332 |  |  |
| 2:8 | 262, 325 | 2 | 316, 405 |  |  |

**2 John**
1:3          338

**Jude**
316, 405
11           117
20           451

**Revelation**
1:5          154, 422
1:6          326, 422
2            317
2–3          316, 326
2:7          64, 439
2:22         505
3            317
3:5          143
3:10         288
3:12         490, 507
3:21         81, 508
4:3          67, 94, 423
4:11         497
5:9          422
5:10         326, 422
6–19         506
7:14         505
7:15         282, 490
10:1         67, 94, 423
11:1         25-26
11:2         490
11:15        420, 422
11:19        26, 282, 295, 439, 490
12:1–11      422
12:9         61, 422
12:10        22, 422
13:8         143
14:15        439, 490
14:17        439
16:1         439, 490
16:17        439, 490
17–18        316, 326
17:1–3       115
17:8         143
17:14        422
18:4–5       332
19:6–9       114
19:7         115
19:7–9       3, 319
19:11–16     3
19:11–21     422
19:16        326
20:1–6       422
20:2         61, 422
20:4         326
20:6         326
20:15        143
21:1         513
21:1–3       319
21:2         114, 115, 331, 490, 507
21:5–8       396
21:7         95, 298
21:9         114, 115, 331
21:9–10      115, 319, 452, 507
21:10        490, 507
21:12        329
21:14        329
21:22        490
21:27        143
22:1         77
22:1–2       64
22:5         326, 439
22:17        114, 115
22:19        143, 490

# Subject Index

**A**
À Brakel, Wilhelmus 221, 506
Aalders, Gerhard C. 91, 230
Aaron 76, 87, 114, 126
Abel 20, 117, 302
Abihu 87, 114
Abimelech 11, 27, 28, 49, 53
Abraham 8, 9, 10, 11, 19, 20, 27, 28, 31, 53, 68, 69, 70, 71, 72, 73, 74, 78, 80, 83, 89, 90, 108, 118, 127, 138, 146, 147, 172, 174, 201, 230, 234, 235, 236, 251, 252, 253, 257, 268, 269, 270, 271, 274, 275, 280, 281, 283, 284, 290, 306, 312, 313, 318, 324, 330, 331, 332, 333, 340, 344, 354, 359, 360, 364, 375, 393, 394, 397, 403, 405, 406, 407, 408, 410, 418, 423, 424, 429, 433, 434, 435, 436, 459, 472, 481, 482, 483, 489
Abrahamic blessing 73, 437
Abrahamic covenant 4, 9, 18, 19, 43, 73, 74, 83, 94, 105, 117, 118, 145, 147, 171, 172, 230, 233, 242, 250, 257, 269, 271, 273, 275, 282, 306, 334, 344, 359, 365, 396, 403, 405, 406, 410, 416, 423, 428, 429, 433, 434, 436, 456, 486, 488, 514
Abrahamic promise 10, 14, 275, 335, 394, 437, 483, 484
Abrahamic promises 74, 257, 273, 360, 434

Abrahamic Torah
    18, 72,
    232, 403
Abram    11, 69, 70,
    71, 72, 90,
    154, 404,
    423, 486,
    488, 489,
    491
Adam    2, 3, 9, 18,
    20, 22, 28,
    59, 60, 61,
    62, 63, 67,
    68, 84,
    117, 123,
    130, 131,
    132, 133,
    135, 141,
    159, 162,
    164, 165,
    166, 169,
    173, 175,
    207, 229,
    230, 237,
    242, 253,
    257, 259,
    283, 294,
    306, 309,
    312, 313,
    333, 344,
    373, 374,
    375, 417,
    418, 419,
    421, 427,
    443, 446,
    448, 452,
    453, 455,
    459
Adamic covenant
    59, 60, 61,
    62, 132,
    373, 485
Adamic Torah
    18, 61, 62,
    131, 267

Africans    400
Ahab    11, 28, 55,
    200
Ahaziah    28, 51
Akenson, D. H.
    400
Alting, Jacobus
    507
Amalek    138, 492
American Reformed
    Churches
    389
Ames, William
    368
Amillennialists
    8
Ammonites
    346
Amorites    28, 71
Anabaptist theology
    183
Anabaptists
    152, 153,
    171, 179,
    183, 188,
    203, 216,
    221, 238
Ancient Near Eastern
    covenants
    27, 49
Aner    11, 28
Angels    10, 36, 73,
    310, 318,
    342, 455,
    459, 508,
    510
Anglicans    6, 153
Anna    267
Apostles    5, 7, 201,
    202, 250,
    253, 254,
    297, 317,
    322, 329,
    340, 346,
    394, 402,

    404, 440,
    461
Apostles' Creed
    378, 416
Apostolic Creed
    162
Appelius, Johannes
    Conradus
    221
Aquila    26
Aquinas, Thomas
    447
Araunah    80
Aristotle    164
Ark of the covenant
    35, 80,
    295, 299,
    493
Arminian trauma
    390, 418,
    429, 501
Arminianism
    144, 229,
    240, 243,
    244
Arminians    222, 224,
    229, 240,
    242, 390
Arminius, Jacob
    140, 225,
    240, 242,
    498
Armstrong, J. H.
    175
Asa    28, 29, 51,
    55, 103,
    104
Assyria    34, 55,
    347, 518
Athanasius    449
Atonement    15, 32, 75,
    76, 77,
    126, 127,
    136, 141,
    149, 154,

*Subject Index*

Augustine 140, 312, 156, 213, 225, 226, 241, 267, 274, 296, 327
420, 448

**B**
Babel 71
Babylon 288, 400, 517
Babylonian captivity 433, 512, 517
Babylonian exile 143, 288, 516
Baker, J. Wayne 220
Bakker, H. 221, 475
Balaam 424
Balke, Willem 218, 313
Baptists 3, 8, 41, 175, 239, 323, 465, 484
Barker, K. L. 65
Barnett, P. 297, 440
Barnouw, P. J. 242
Barrett, C. K. 359
Barth, Karl 182, 394
Bateman, H. W. IV, 344
Bathsheba 81
Bauswein, J.-J. 389
Bavinck, Herman 66, 133, 134, 183, 205, 207, 208, 210, 236, 237, 309, 368, 379, 380, 381
Baxter, Richard 221
Becking, B. E. J. H. 139
Beeke, Joel R. 14
Beisner 388
Belgic Confession 158, 159, 161, 171, 177, 238, 246, 307, 309, 310, 311, 314, 392, 405, 483
Believers' baptism 3, 152, 175, 176, 207, 366, 465
Ben-hadad 11, 28, 55, 200,
Benjamin 31, 51, 79, 511
Bergquist, R. A. 180
Berit 17, 19, 23, 24, 25, 26, 28, 30, 31, 54, 71, 107, 269
Berkhof, Hendrikus, 49, 84, 140, 194, 195, 246, 247, 430
Berkhof, Louis 57, 172, 229, 313, 342, 368, 369, 394, 396, 514
Berkouwer, G. C. 309
Berkowitz, A. 49
Bernard, J. H. 297, 440
Bethel 491
Bethlehem 80, 488
Beza, Theodore 186, 221, 240, 245
Bible 6, 7, 11, 14, 26, 27, 28, 29, 30, 36, 37, 38, 39, 40, 41, 42, 43, 44, 48, 52, 55, 69, 84, 94, 129, 152, 154, 155, 156, 157, 180, 184, 185, 186, 187, 189, 191, 193, 197, 199, 202, 208, 212, 213, 214, 215, 217, 218, 238, 289, 308, 312, 315, 332, 342, 347, 365, 370, 371, 385, 395, 409, 448, 484, 490, 491
Biblical covenants 6, 10, 11, 25, 34, 37,

40, 48, 49, 125, 146, 147, 184, 365, 366, 369, 371, 420, 429, 452
Biblicism 44, 45, 157, 218
Bierma, L. D. 162, 221
Bijlsma, Roelof 332, 345
Bilezikian, Gilbert 344
Blaising, C. A. 7, 344
Blood of Christ 17, 290, 302, 305, 320, 327, 397
Blood of the covenant 4, 15, 32, 86, 87, 136, 151, 252, 268, 291, 294, 301, 302, 438, 492
Bock, D. L. 7, 344
Body of Christ 2, 3, 4, 96, 114, 207, 209, 212, 213, 228, 290, 306, 313, 317, 323, 338, 340, 343, 416, 443, 455, 460, 461
Boers 399, 400

Bonar, Andrew A. 140
Bonhoeffer, Dietrich, 312
Book of the covenant, 24, 52, 114, 302, 492
Booth, Randy 173, 306
Boston, Thomas 185, 227, 228
Boyd, Greg 498, 499, 500
Bremen 224
Bride of the Lamb 96, 214, 318, 319, 331, 456, 507
Brienen, T. 222, 371
Brockhaus, Carl 176
Brown, C. 25, 32
Brown, Michael G. 10, 13, 40, 42, 60, 65, 66, 72, 74, 80, 94, 105, 129, 132, 135, 180, 191, 192, 196, 202, 206, 229, 254, 306, 369, 370, 396, 419, 466, 481, 494
Bruce 36, 329, 453, 467
Bruges 224
Bucer, Martin 506

Bullinger, E. W. 438,
Bullinger, Heinrich 178, 183, 221, 227
Bunyan, John 175, 452
Burman, Franciscus 507

C
Cain 20, 117
Calvin, John 152, 153, 159, 166, 171, 183, 206, 216, 218, 219, 220, 221, 227, 240, 241, 355, 379, 396, 403, 447, 469, 506
Calvinism 140, 144, 153, 184, 381, 500
Calvinists 153, 155, 157, 158, 222, 226, 376, 381, 450
Canaan 69, 73, 74, 82, 89, 90, 117, 146, 205, 345, 400, 433, 462, 487, 507, 512, 515, 516, 517
Canaanites 400
Canadian Reformed Churches 389

*Subject Index*

Canons of Dort
  33, 132,
  158, 177,
  382
Carson, D. A.
  483
Carson, Edward
  400
Catholics  6, 41, 187,
  194, 309,
  312, 400,
  432
Chafer, Lewis Sperry
  7, 97, 125,
  289, 314,
  324, 325,
  326
Chauncy, Isaac
  160
Cherry, C.  399
Children of Abraham
  234, 235,
  236, 283,
  330, 360,
  393, 394,
  407, 408,
  436, 482,
  483
Christendom
  236, 307,
  315, 317,
  457
Christian Reformed
  Church
  389
Christian Reformed
  Churches
  58, 225,
  228, 379,
  385
Christianity
  153, 157,
  182, 192,
  236, 330,
  342, 375,
  376, 378,
  410, 427,
  437, 439,
  442, 443,
  446, 451,
  475
Christiansen, E. J.
  10
Christology
  185
Chrysostom, John
  359, 470
Church of England
  158
Church of God
  3, 4, 305,
  307
Church of Scotland
  158
Church Order of Dort
  178
Circumcision of
  Christ
  466, 467,
  468, 470,
  471, 474
Circumcision of the
  heart
  129, 231,
  233, 269,
  318, 467,
  468, 470,
  471, 472,
  475, 476
Clark, R. Scott
  10, 184,
  242, 371,
  388
Cloppenburg,
  Johannes
  123, 368
Clowney, Edmund
  326, 330,
  344, 350
Cocceius, Johannes
  123, 185,
  191, 206,
  221, 222,
  223, 224,
  225, 507
Cohen, A.  86, 89,
  110, 348
Common grace
  57, 58, 66,
  411, 422
Commonwealth of
  Israel
  212, 272,
  305, 349,
  366
Comrie, Alexander
  123, 185,
  206, 221,
  222, 224,
  225, 226,
  227, 228,
  234, 237,
  242, 371
Confessionalism
  431
Congar, Y.  312
Continuity  2, 8, 83,
  105, 173,
  176, 183,
  184, 207,
  233, 257,
  316, 345,
  366, 397,
  411, 412,
  416, 436,
  437, 481
Conversion
  62, 127,
  380, 443,
  467, 469,
  476, 477
Coornhert, Dirk
  Volkertszoon
  240

575

Corner Gate
255, 511
Covenant breakers
150, 386
Covenant members
117, 150,
161, 227,
234, 236,
371, 379,
383, 386,
387, 393,
428, 489
Covenant of
circumcision
19, 269
Covenant of creation
130, 373
Covenant of God
3, 4, 149,
173, 179,
187, 242,
466, 473
Covenant of grace
9, 14, 30,
41, 48, 78,
83, 100,
123, 124,
125, 126,
129, 131,
140, 141,
145, 146,
157, 159,
160, 161,
163, 164,
172, 173,
174, 175,
178, 184,
189, 206,
207, 210,
213, 219,
223, 224,
225, 226,
227, 228,
229, 230,
233, 236,
237, 238,
239, 241,
242, 364,
365, 366,
367, 371,
373, 375,
379, 380,
383, 384,
385, 395,
396, 397,
411, 417,
419, 427,
428, 432,
449, 481,
501, 514,
515, 518
Covenant of life
22, 220,
373, 376
Covenant of love
105, 107,
231
Covenant of nature
130, 162,
373
Covenant of peace
30, 59, 75,
91, 149,
223, 225,
256, 517
Covenant of redemption
30, 41, 48,
157, 181,
225, 226,
229, 236,
237, 363,
367, 368,
369, 371,
379, 383,
384, 395,
411
Covenant of works
9, 30, 40,
41, 48, 60,
83, 100,
122, 123,
124, 125,
126, 128,
129, 131,
132, 133,
134, 135,
140, 141,
145, 146,
157, 159,
161, 162,
163, 164,
167, 168,
169, 170,
175, 181,
223, 224,
225, 228,
229, 230,
231, 232,
233, 237,
241, 371,
373, 374,
375, 376,
379, 384,
397, 411,
417, 427,
428, 501
Covenant paradigm
180, 183,
184, 187,
189, 192,
193, 200,
202, 205,
365, 370,
372, 374,
375
Covenant people
2, 83, 88,
187, 206,
214, 299,
307, 399,
475, 490
Covenant theology
2, 5, 7, 21,
39, 40, 41,

## Subject Index

42, 43,
151, 152,
153, 159,
170, 173,
175, 180,
184, 185,
190, 191,
193, 205,
206, 209,
216, 217,
222, 223,
363, 371,
376, 378,
387, 415,
416, 428

Covenantalism
   37, 387

Covenantalizing
   155, 156,
   197, 201,
   210, 392,
   416, 419

Craig, James
   400

Craith, M. N.
   400

Cranfield, C. E. B.
   359

Credobaptism
   3, 476

Credobaptists
   8, 174,
   476, 477

Cyprian   475

### D

Damascenus, John,
   447

Dante Alighieri
   452

Darby, John N.
   7, 8, 154,
   175, 276,
   310, 462

David   11, 20, 21,

22, 24, 27,
28, 29, 50,
51, 54, 56,
57, 59, 68,
78, 79, 80,
81, 82, 90,
97, 110,
111, 121,
148, 149,
154, 209,
255, 256,
267, 268,
271, 288,
327, 328,
365, 398,
400, 418,
426, 438,
488, 493,
494, 508,
509, 510,
517

Davidic covenant
   51, 80, 81,
   104, 371,
   426, 488

Davidic throne
   81, 515

Davids, P. H.
   353

Davies, W. D.
   329

De Bie, Hendrik J.
   26, 34, 71,
   141

De Graaf, Simon G.,
   134, 135,
   156

De Labadie, Jean
   206, 245,
   246

De Moor, Robert
   153

De Ru, G.   467

De Vries, P.
   141

Decalogue   138, 139

Delitzsch, F.
   293

Demarest, B.
   314

Demons   130, 478,
   479, 495

Den Boer, William
   242

Denham Smith, J.
   312

Denominations
   140, 226,
   236, 307,
   373, 376,
   378, 388,
   389, 402

Descartes, René
   166

Dewitz, L. R.
   259

Diathēkē   25, 26, 31,
   34, 100,
   257, 273,
   274, 301

Diemer, N.   162

Dinah   30

Discontinuity
   8, 183, 184,
   366, 411,
   412, 416,
   436, 437

Dispensationalism
   7, 8, 9, 41,
   42, 45, 175,
   179, 180,
   184, 192,
   193, 194,
   206, 217,
   218, 291,
   344, 375,
   377, 397,
   411, 438

Dispensationalists
   7, 8, 9, 41,

43, 179,
215, 257,
306, 326,
333, 365,
367, 397,
413, 438
Dispensations
10, 45, 137,
160, 207,
237, 254,
275, 320,
365, 366,
413
Divine covenants
11, 12, 27,
28, 29, 30,
36, 37, 48,
49, 53, 124,
129, 175,
396, 460
Doctrine of
justification
169, 170,
388, 443,
444
Doctrine of the
covenant
2, 6, 134,
152, 171,
172, 183,
185, 227,
238, 239,
374, 390
Dods, M.   33
Douma, J.   58
Du Toit, Jacobus D.,
400
Dulles, A. R.
312
Dumbrell, W. J.
10, 60, 61,
374
Duncan, J. L.
182

Dunn, James
261, 356
Dutch States'
Translation,
307, 346,
358

**E**
Eastern Christians,
446, 450
Eastern theology
449, 450
Ebed-melech
314
Ecclesiasticalism
41, 42, 180,
184, 192,
193, 206,
375, 377
Ecclesiology
8, 317
Eden   62, 63, 67,
73, 77, 95,
100, 129,
130, 135,
164, 224,
308, 310,
448, 485
Egypt   16, 34, 35,
55, 71, 85,
86, 88, 105,
109, 110,
116, 118,
125, 126,
138, 139,
166, 199,
231, 232,
233, 346,
398, 400,
486, 491,
511, 512,
514, 518
Egyptians   85, 86
Ekklesia   2, 74, 113,
114, 177,

228, 252,
255, 266,
287, 289,
290, 293,
294, 295,
297, 307,
308, 309,
310, 311,
312, 313,
314, 315,
317, 318,
319, 320,
321, 322,
323, 324,
325, 326,
336, 338,
339, 340,
341, 348,
349, 352,
355, 358,
367, 388,
397, 404,
405, 406,
410, 416,
418, 428,
429, 431,
433, 434,
437, 438,
439, 440,
442, 443,
455, 460,
461, 462,
494, 496,
508, 509,
514, 515,
519
Elam   52
Elam, A. E.   10, 168,
169, 180
Eleazar of Modin
18
Election   14, 71, 80,
86, 150,
153, 155,
156, 157,

# Subject Index

177, 190, 219, 220, 222, 234, 244, 318, 347, 355, 359, 364, 379, 380, 381, 382, 383, 384, 385, 386, 387, 388, 389, 390, 391, 392, 393, 394, 395, 399, 417, 420

Electionism 416, 432
Elijah 267, 332
Eliphaz 59
Elisha 267
Elizabeth 21, 119, 267, 328, 489
Elizabeth I 398
Ellison, H. L. 359
Elsinga, C. B. 72
Engelsma, D. J. 388
England 158, 398
Engle, P. E. 175
Enoch 60, 489
Epangelicalism 206, 215, 217, 218, 375
Ephesus 177, 308
Ephraim 79, 255, 346, 421, 487, 493
Ephrathah 493
Erasmus, Desiderius, 140, 240

Erickson, Millard 308, 342, 394
Erskine, Ebenezer, 160, 228
Erskine, Ralph 160, 228
Esau 118, 130, 235, 352, 457
Eschatology 5, 8
Eshcol 11, 28
Estelle, B. D. 10, 168, 169, 237, 276
Eternal covenant 17, 19, 32, 83, 145, 178, 250, 302, 303, 369, 440
Eternal life 13, 14, 96, 132, 133, 135, 139, 140, 143, 159, 162, 198, 232, 253, 254, 258, 311, 336, 337, 338, 416, 443, 454, 455, 457, 458
Eternal state 9, 384, 512
Eternal Torah 18, 19, 20, 61, 259, 297, 412
Ethnic Israel 8, 91, 148, 187, 207,

255, 289, 324, 333, 345, 349, 352, 353, 355, 356, 364, 392, 404, 406, 418, 429, 430, 436, 461, 462, 504, 506, 507, 514, 515, 518
Euphrates 514
Evangelical Christians 153, 154, 450, 451, 463
Evangelical theology, 42, 182, 224, 239, 241, 243, 442, 450, 456, 457
Evangelicalism 140, 179, 183, 184
Evangelicals 6, 39, 180, 181, 183, 187, 189, 193, 206, 238, 245, 246, 393, 452, 472
Eve 3, 20, 60, 62, 131, 132, 133, 165, 196, 312, 375, 448
Everlasting covenant 19, 64, 78, 83, 91, 104, 105, 112,

145, 146, 147, 148, 149, 205, 256, 302, 336, 517
Exclusive Brethren 8, 175
Exegesis 40, 41, 42, 182, 280, 281, 289, 295, 347, 381, 385, 433, 440, 465, 466, 470, 504, 512, 516

**F**
Faulenbach, H. 222
Feast of Booths 330, 491, 511, 512, 513
Feast of Weeks 111, 329
Federal Vision 386, 387, 388
Federal Visionists 387, 388, 391
Federalism 2, 5, 6, 7, 8, 9, 41, 42, 43, 45, 140, 146, 150, 152, 159, 172, 174, 175, 179, 180, 181, 184, 185, 189, 193, 203, 207, 209, 216, 217, 218, 228, 253, 306, 366, 367, 370, 371, 372, 375, 378, 382, 383, 386, 387, 390, 393, 396, 397, 408, 411, 416, 417, 418, 419, 427, 429, 430, 431, 432, 433, 441, 442, 446, 449, 465, 481, 496, 503, 514
Federalist paradigm 78, 179, 181, 193, 213, 372
Federalist theology 183, 391, 411
Federalists 8, 43, 45, 137, 177, 181, 194, 196, 197, 204, 206, 207, 210, 211, 215, 240, 253, 254, 270, 293, 306, 314, 316, 358, 367, 372, 374, 377, 392, 393, 397, 403, 407, 408, 409, 410, 411, 413, 417, 418, 420, 432, 433, 465, 466, 470, 472, 482, 484, 514, 517, 518
Fensham, F. C. 10
Ferguson, E. 182, 469
Findlay 351
Finlan, S. 446, 447
Fisher, James 160
Fitzmyer, J. A. 359
Flesseman-van Leer, Ellen 247
Frame, J. M. 10
France, 400, 401
Franklin, Benjamin 399
Free Reformed Churches 389
Freeman, H. 137
Friedman, Richard E. 18, 39
Friedrich, G. 25, 143
Fruchtenbaum, Arnold 5, 125, 356, 359, 413
Fung, R. Y. K. 351, 352

**G**
Galilee 488

## Subject Index

Garden of Eden
    62, 63, 67,
    77, 95,
    129, 164,
    224, 308,
    448, 485
Gareb   255
Garner   10, 387
Geba   511
Geisler, Norman L.
    44
Gentile believers
    212, 265,
    272, 275,
    290, 306,
    318, 320,
    348, 349,
    351, 352,
    353, 354,
    355, 356,
    357, 360,
    413, 434,
    438, 480,
    504
Gentile Christians
    211, 353,
    418, 433,
    514
Gentiles   67, 82, 92,
    120, 127,
    160, 163,
    211, 212,
    252, 253,
    254, 257,
    265, 272,
    283, 284,
    287, 305,
    306, 307,
    313, 314,
    317, 318,
    320, 328,
    343, 346,
    349, 350,
    352, 353,
    354, 355,
    356, 358,
    359, 360,
    402, 410,
    429, 433,
    434, 436,
    438, 460,
    461, 478,
    483
Gentry, Peter
    3, 10, 27,
    29, 39, 41,
    56, 59, 60,
    61, 66, 69,
    87, 202,
    397, 430,
    465
Gibeon   11, 12, 28,
    55
Gibeonites   28
Gideon   400
Gilead   518
Gill, John   254
Ginzberg, L.
    138
Glueck, N.   107
Goath   255
God's kingdom
    3, 22, 256,
    257, 347,
    510
God's love   48, 49, 58,
    62, 66, 71,
    76, 79, 86,
    89, 93,
    108, 109,
    110, 203,
    231, 445
God's people
    2, 5, 17,
    33, 84,
    172, 197,
    201, 210,
    267, 300,
    301, 328,
    341, 344,
    352, 397,
    400, 401,
    409, 411,
    461
God's promises
    13, 33, 59,
    62, 91,
    147, 347,
    437, 515
God's sovereignty
    247, 418,
    429, 432,
    497, 498,
    499, 500,
    501
God's temple
    295, 340,
    494, 515
God's Torah
    116, 142,
    261, 262,
    292, 392,
    402
God's Word
    40, 44,
    409, 512
Godet, F. L.
    359
Golding, P.   10
Goldsworthy, G.
    238
Gomarus, Franciscus
    140, 221,
    224, 379,
    381
Good Shepherd
    258, 336,
    349
Gospel   5, 38, 133,
    141, 154,
    159, 160,
    161, 167,
    169, 187,
    193, 226,
    241, 252,

253, 254, 269, 278, 279, 315, 317, 324, 335, 346, 347, 360, 417, 419, 420, 421, 427, 432, 433, 444, 451, 452, 455, 456, 474, 487, 489, 503
Gospel of the kingdom 252, 324, 417, 420
Gospels 23, 120, 204, 320, 337, 338, 341, 394
Graafland, Cornelis 123, 159, 161, 182, 183, 185, 186, 187, 188, 218, 219, 220, 221, 222, 224, 240, 241, 242, 243, 244, 245, 247, 389, 390, 394, 475
Gräbe, P. J. 10
Grant, Frederick W. 175, 290, 353, 359
Grant, J. A. 10, 194
Great tribulation 288, 505
Green, Joel 489

Greijdanus, Seakle 410, 419
Groenewegen, Henricus 507
Grogan, Geoffrey 65
Grosheide, F. W. 14, 32, 453, 505
Grotius, H. 33
Gutbrod, Walter 143, 351
Guthrie, D. 31

**H**
Habets, M. 447
Hadadezer 28
Hagar 250, 280, 281, 282, 283, 284, 366, 407
Hagoort, H. 26, 34, 36, 71, 72, 141, 159, 218, 221, 222, 224, 247, 371, 396
Hahn, F. 314
Hahn, S. W. 10, 199, 206
Ham 117, 201
Hamor 30, 54, 55
Hanun 54
Haran 201
Harinck, Cornelis 219, 220
Harris, R. L. 23
Harvard University 399
Hays, J. D. 125

Heaven 22, 33, 56, 57, 70, 77, 81, 87, 90, 93, 114, 118, 141, 147, 166, 237, 252, 254, 295, 306, 309, 311, 317, 319, 320, 321, 322, 332, 337, 338, 339, 340, 420, 421, 422, 423, 424, 425, 426, 432, 439, 442, 451, 452, 456, 458, 461, 462, 486, 488, 494, 497, 508, 510, 516
Hebron 50
Heerma, W. 225
Heidelberg Catechism 23, 135, 158, 161, 162, 163, 176, 221, 229, 253, 278, 311, 448, 449, 458
Heitink, G. 332
Hell 155, 317, 498
Helm, P. 218
Henry, C. F. H. 313

*Subject Index*

Henry VIII 398
Hepp, Valentijn 186
Heppe, H. L. J. 190
Heresy 58, 221, 333, 388, 389, 391, 416, 431
Heretics 283, 376, 388, 457
Heritage Reformed 389
Herod 36
Hesed 27, 54, 79, 89, 107, 108, 119, 120, 202, 203, 231
Heyns, Johan 34, 48, 60, 205, 212, 213, 214, 322, 332, 345, 356, 372, 373, 394
Hezekiah 29, 51, 104
Hicks, J. M. 242
High Priest 31, 32, 33, 77, 300, 326, 339
Hillers, D. R. 10, 23
Hiram 11, 30, 54, 200
Hodge, C. 123
Hoedemaker, Philippus J. 398
Hoek, Jan 13, 71, 73, 141, 174, 191, 194, 204, 205, 215, 218, 219, 222, 227, 238, 247, 375, 384, 396, 430, 444, 482
Hoekema, Anthony 218, 219
Holy Land 91, 148, 438, 506
Holy One of Israel 95, 104
Holy Spirit 2, 3, 8, 15, 16, 25, 32, 34, 106, 115, 127, 128, 131, 143, 147, 150, 159, 176, 220, 258, 261, 263, 267, 268, 274, 279, 280, 286, 291, 295, 297, 300, 306, 308, 310, 311, 313, 318, 322, 323, 324, 327, 335, 337, 340, 341, 342, 343, 369, 382, 386, 394, 402, 403, 408, 410, 434, 435, 436, 437, 443, 445, 446, 449, 450, 451, 453, 455, 456, 459, 462
Honig, A. G. 224
Hoornbeeck, Johannes 507
Horjus, Jelle 481, 518
Horse Gate 255
Horton, Michael 10, 14, 40, 74, 135, 149, 150, 173, 218, 291, 315, 369, 466, 490
House of Israel 4, 17, 19, 84, 91, 105, 236, 250, 270, 271, 287, 354, 404, 438
House of Judah 4, 84, 91, 236, 250, 271, 287, 354, 404, 438
Houtepen, A. 204
Hugenberger, Gordon 195
Hughes, P. E. 125, 440
Huguenots 400
Huisman, C. 398
Human responsibility 129, 132, 140, 141, 142, 144,

Humanity 12, 22, 28,
32, 33, 34,
57, 58, 59,
60, 61, 62,
63, 64, 66,
68, 71, 82,
105, 107,
122, 130,
131, 134,
141, 161,
190, 194,
212, 213,
223, 242,
244, 246,
265, 271,
278, 279,
300, 321,
365, 367,
372, 374,
395, 396,
405, 411,
417, 448,
485, 499
Humankind
131, 237,
242
Hunt, J. P. T.
475
Hutten, Kurt
444
Hyper-Calvinism
140, 381,
500
Hyper-Calvinists
222, 226,
146, 206,
224, 228,
229, 233,
236, 241,
243, 244,
247, 258,
273, 382,
390, 395,
418, 429,
432, 501

Hypocrites 100, 120,
121, 122,
267, 405

I
Ibn Ezra, Abraham
89
Infant baptism
3, 150,
152, 157,
158, 159,
160, 161,
163, 171,
172, 173,
174, 175,
176, 177,
188, 189,
206, 221,
306, 366,
371, 372,
379, 380,
381, 387,
393, 394,
401, 406,
407, 410,
419, 430,
465, 466,
472, 474,
475, 479,
481, 483,
484
Inferentialism
155, 156,
157, 174,
179, 210,
387, 416
*Institutes of the Christian Religion*
171, 219,
220, 396,
447
Irenaeus 182
Isaac 11, 28, 49,
381, 450

53, 69, 70,
72, 78, 80,
117, 118,
138, 145,
146, 147,
250, 252,
270, 282,
283, 284,
285, 330,
359, 407,
429, 435,
457, 489
Ishmael 117, 235,
250, 281,
282, 283,
284, 285,
352, 407,
457
Israel of God
119, 212,
253, 254,
289, 324,
333, 350,
351, 356,
432
Israelites 4, 7, 76,
84, 138,
199, 233,
270, 286,
287, 308,
324, 325,
330, 332,
336, 346,
352, 366,
388, 399,
400, 459,
491

J
Jabesh 11, 12, 29,
55
Jacob 5, 11, 24,
28, 47, 49,
53, 54, 56,
69, 70, 74,

584

*Subject Index*

|  |  |
|---|---|
|  | 75, 76, 78, 79, 83, 96, 104, 118, 130, 138, 146, 149, 198, 199, 202, 234, 252, 256, 270, 272, 284, 329, 331, 348, 359, 423, 424, 429, 457, 489, 493, 508, 511, 514, 517 |
| James I | 398 |
| Janssonius, Hillebrandus | 221 |
| Japheth | 117, 201, 271, 404, 423, 429 |
| Japhethites | 67 |
| Javan | 324 |
| Jedidiah | 81 |
| Jefferson, Thomas | 399 |
| Jehiel | 52 |
| Jehoshaphath | 28 |
| Jeon, Jeong Koo | 10, 218 |
| Jerome | 26 |
| Jerusalem | 5, 29, 51, 52, 54, 55, 74, 78, 80, 81, 94, 96, 97, 102, 250, 251, 255, 269, 270, 280, 282, 284, 303, 319, 323, 325, 329, 331, 332, 346, 348, 401, 418, 423, 426, 427, 438, 452, 488, 490, 491, 495, 504, 507, 508, 509, 510, 511, 513, 515, 516 |
| Jeshurun | 424 |
| Jesse | 79 |
| Jesus Christ | 3, 6, 15, 38, 43, 66, 92, 135, 137, 154, 159, 160, 173, 242, 258, 266, 301, 308, 310, 315, 316, 323, 335, 337, 353, 373, 382, 420, 427, 447, 452, 455, 458, 459, 483 |
| Jesus-believers | 73, 96, 201, 211, 236, 250, 257, 274, 285, 290, 301, 303, 306, 324, 325, 343, 352, 353, 354, 360, 361, 392, 408, 413, 427, 439, 440, 441, 456, 461, 467, 474, 480 |
| Jesus-believing Gentiles | 283, 284, 353, 358, 359 |
| Jesus-believing Jews | 284, 352, 353, 357, 358, 359, 438, 467, 480 |
| Jewett, P. K. | 10, 472 |
| Jews | 4, 5, 26, 81, 141, 159, 160, 211, 212, 251, 252, 253, 254, 255, 265, 283, 284, 285, 305, 306, 307, 310, 313, 314, 320, 322, 349, 350, 352, 353, 355, 356, 357, 358, 359, 360, 411, 413, 434, 436, 438, 457, 460, 467, 474, 480, 510, 518 |
| Joash | 29, 51, |

585

104, 209
John the Baptist
    119, 234,
    254, 310,
    319, 393,
    462
Johnson, E. E.
    344
Jonathan    13, 27, 28,
    54, 110,
    111
Jongeleen, J.
    371
Jonker, Willie
    183, 184,
    185, 190,
    191, 193,
    205, 216,
    364, 367,
    368, 372,
    374, 375,
    376
Joseph    22, 79,
    130, 202,
    457
Josephus, Flavius
    36
Josiah    29, 51,
    103, 104
Judah    4, 31, 50,
    51, 52, 79,
    84, 91,
    148, 209,
    236, 250,
    254, 255,
    271, 287,
    334, 346,
    354, 401,
    403, 404,
    438, 494,
    495, 515,
    517
Judaism    26, 66,
    330, 479
Judaizers    250, 275,

279, 283,
284, 480
Judea    488, 510
Judeans    52, 53
Judgment    10, 14, 65,
66, 68, 85,
118, 220,
326, 346,
358, 374,
395, 440,
452, 467,
468, 469,
481, 512
Juster, D.    350
Justification
    8, 19, 20,
    23, 73, 74,
    128, 142,
    164, 169,
    170, 219,
    241, 243,
    261, 268,
    274, 278,
    279, 285,
    318, 333,
    360, 388,
    389, 390,
    403, 416,
    423, 434,
    442, 443,
    444, 445,
    446, 450,
    451, 452,
    455, 456,
    457
Justification by faith
    8, 19, 23,
    73, 74,
    170, 243,
    274, 318,
    403, 423,
    434, 443,
    444, 445,
    456

**K**
Kac, A. W.  125, 259
Kaiser, Walter C.
    10, 140,
    215
Kamphuis, J.
    419
Kaufmann, Y.
    10
Kedar    496
Keele, Zach
    10, 13, 40,
    42, 60, 65,
    66, 72, 74,
    80, 94,
    105, 129,
    132, 135,
    180, 191,
    192, 196,
    202, 206,
    229, 254,
    306, 369,
    370, 396,
    419, 466,
    481, 494
Kelly, William
    176, 353
Kenites    314
Kersten, G. H.
    206, 224,
    226, 228,
    239, 342,
    371, 374,
    378, 498
Kertelge, K.
    314
Ketubah    100, 114
Kharlamov, V.
    446, 447
Kidron    255
Kingdom of God
    3, 4, 21,
    22, 23, 81,
    94, 127,
    178, 179,

*Subject Index*

207, 238, 243, 256, 262, 310, 319, 332, 343, 348, 402, 406, 408, 411, 417, 431, 432, 439, 451, 452, 475, 477, 483, 488, 510
Kiriath-jearim 493
Kish 79
Kittel, G. 25, 143
Kline, Meredith 10, 34, 168, 169, 170
Klineans 169
Koelman, Jacobus 221, 384, 506
Kok, Reinier 385
König, Adrio 191, 396
Kroneman 221
Kuhn, Thomas S. 40
Küng, Hans 332, 342, 350, 351
Kuyper, Abraham 57, 194, 205, 208, 234, 239, 381, 401, 515
Kuyperians 381

**L**
Labadists 245
Laban 11, 24, 28, 47, 49, 53, 130, 199, 429
Ladd, George E. 343, 344
Lagrange, M.-J. 506
Lampe, Friedrich Adolph 221, 507
Lane, W. L. 31
Lang, A. 162,
Langdon, Samuel 399
Lanning, Ray B. 14
Lapide, Pinchas 110 141
Latter days 5, 96, 255, 288, 293, 348, 511
Leah 115, 331
Lebanon 95, 518
Legalism 120, 285, 478
Lehne, S. 10
Leithart, P. 387
Leuner, H. D. 125
Leurdijk, G. H. 224
Levi 11, 28, 68, 74, 75, 76, 77, 154, 271, 365, 425
Levites 28, 51, 52, 53, 75, 76, 77
Levitical covenant 51, 75, 77,

425
Lightfoot, J. B. 351
Lightfoot, John 506
Lillback, Peter A. 10, 171, 183, 218, 220
Lohfink, N. 10
Loonstra, B. 218, 467, 474, 475
Lord's Supper 4, 7, 94, 114, 153, 160, 176, 178, 252, 256, 264, 268, 312, 403, 438, 474, 494
Los, S. O. 227
Lossky, V. 446
Louisiana 387
Lud 324
Luther, Martin 140, 153, 175, 221, 444, 446, 470, 506
Lutherans 6, 153, 445
Lydia 406

**M**
Mackintosh, Charles H. 176
Malan, Daniel F. 401
Mallan, Frans 239
Mamre 11, 28
Marcel, P. 173
Maris, J. W. 222, 224
Marriage 24, 30, 54,

587

100, 101,
102, 103,
104, 106,
108, 111,
112, 114,
154, 155,
195, 203,
208, 209,
320, 344
Marshall, I. H.
454
Mary 194, 267,
312, 487
Mary Magdalene
312
Matrimonial covenant
101, 106
Matter, H. M.
507
May, R. H. 399
McCarthy, D. J.
10, 23, 199
McGrath, Alister
176, 347,
394
McGraw, R. M.
156
McKay, D. 10
Mediator 2, 3, 33,
34, 92, 93,
94, 114,
136, 151,
236, 255,
299, 300,
367, 368,
426, 459
Meijer, W. 398
Melanchton, Philip,
162, 506
Melchizedek
77, 78, 314,
316
Mendenhall, G. E.
34

Mennonites
153, 238,
239
Messiah 56, 78, 81,
94, 97, 115,
160, 255,
256, 258,
259, 260,
262, 265,
268, 270,
275, 288,
290, 297,
299, 311,
331, 333,
348, 351,
358, 360,
370, 418,
421, 426,
438, 460,
509, 513,
517, 518
Messianic Jews
265, 411,
413
Messianic kingdom
8, 17, 33,
56, 59, 64,
74, 78, 79,
91, 94, 97,
105, 115,
116, 254,
255, 269,
270, 286,
289, 290,
293, 294,
297, 298,
301, 319,
324, 330,
337, 348,
355, 401,
404, 417,
420, 423,
424, 426,
427, 439,
441, 443,

457, 462,
475, 491,
494, 505,
508, 509,
510, 512,
513, 516,
517
Messianic Torah
15, 19, 33,
93, 114,
143, 243,
250, 259,
260, 261,
262, 264,
265, 275,
276, 280,
297, 329,
408, 409,
411, 412,
413, 418,
440
Metzger, B. M.
268
Meyer, F. B.
470
Miersma, Thomas
14
Millennial Torah
19, 93, 105,
233, 267,
297, 403,
413, 440
Milligan, G.
32
Minear, Paul
344
Moab 346, 492,
511
Mobachius, Joachim
507
Modernists 246
Moerkerken, Aart
189, 224,
226, 311,
384

## Subject Index

Moltmann, J. 332
Monroe 387
Moo, D. J. 260, 350, 356, 359, 504
Moodie, T. D. 399
Mosaic Law 65, 281
Mosaic Torah 9, 19, 76, 90, 105, 136, 149, 232, 250, 260, 262, 264, 266, 267, 273, 275, 276, 277, 278, 279, 281, 285, 286, 287, 297, 329, 402, 408, 409, 411, 413, 417, 433, 440
Moses 9, 22, 24, 75, 83, 85, 86, 87, 89, 101, 109, 113, 114, 118, 119, 123, 138, 143, 151, 232, 233, 267, 269, 289, 303, 329, 332, 398, 399, 400, 401, 459, 486, 488, 492, 516

Moulton, J. H. 32
Mount Sinai 76, 100, 105, 111, 112, 115, 116, 123, 162, 167, 169, 224, 230, 273, 274, 280, 281, 282, 292, 329, 330, 409, 488, 492
Mount Zion 79, 80, 81, 115, 282, 329, 330, 409, 510
Murray, John 130, 168, 169, 170, 186, 359

**N**

Naaman 314, 316
Nachmanides, Rabbi 86
Nadab 87, 114
Nahash 11, 12, 28, 29, 54, 55
Nahor 201
Nathan 81
Nation of Israel 8, 11, 81, 421
Natural sciences 40, 374
Natural theology 162, 163
Nazareth 488
Nebaioth 496
Nebuchadnezzar 11, 12, 34

Nellas, P. 446
Netherlands 176, 181, 183, 186, 193, 222, 224, 225, 226, 228, 239, 242, 347, 379, 380, 381, 384, 385, 389, 398, 399, 401, 444, 506
Netherlands Reformed 225, 226, 228, 239, 379, 384, 385, 389
New Covenant theologians 43
New Covenant Theology 42, 43
New Delhi Report on Witness 332
New earth 9, 68, 74, 90, 303, 319, 412, 425, 426, 512, 513
New England 398
New heavens 9, 68, 74, 303, 425, 426, 512, 513
New Jersey 401
Nicene Creed 182, 377, 416

589

Nichols, G. 10, 465
Nicholson, E. W. 10
Niehaus, J. J. 154
Niell, J. D. 125, 404
Noah 9, 20, 28, 60, 64, 65, 66, 67, 68, 117, 154, 230, 271, 283, 375, 422, 485, 488, 489, 491
Noahic covenant 9, 18, 43, 48, 59, 62, 64, 65, 67, 117, 145, 232, 271, 329, 371, 373, 422, 429, 488
Noahic Torah 18, 66, 232
Noordegraaf, Ab 313
Noort, E. 204
North America 186, 193, 239, 387, 388, 389, 401, 465
Northern Ireland 400
Nun 399

O
O'Brien 467
Oath 12, 13, 16, 23, 24, 51, 53, 54, 70, 82, 83, 84, 103, 109, 112, 195, 201, 231, 251, 268, 426
Oecolampadius, Johannes 183, 506
Olevianus, Caspar 161, 162, 163, 221, 224, 368
Olive tree 288, 307, 348, 355, 356, 357, 358, 359, 360, 430
Orange Order 400
Origen 312
Ornan the Jebusite 494
Orthodox Christians 154, 157, 194
Osterhaven, M. E. 218
Oswalt, John 65
Otis, John M. 315, 388, 431
Owen, J. 123, 431

P
Packer, J. I. 313
*Pactum salutis* 225, 367, 368, 369, 370, 371, 375, 396
Paedobaptism 3, 14
Paedobaptists 8, 174, 175, 190, 366, 470, 471, 477, 484
Pagans 165, 495
Paisley, Ian 401
Palestinian covenant 9, 50, 82, 89, 90, 91, 424, 487, 488, 493
Pannenberg, Wolfhart 333, 334, 394
Paradise 64, 73, 77, 129, 130, 133, 134, 141, 373, 485
Parity covenants 12, 28, 53, 54, 195
Passover 303, 488, 491
Patriarchs 58, 83, 84, 219, 270, 329, 352, 359, 396, 434, 439, 507
Paul 4, 8, 10, 13, 21, 74, 79, 115, 118, 122, 129, 130, 132, 135, 160, 163, 177, 210, 211, 232, 235, 250, 252, 253, 258, 259, 260, 262, 266, 268, 269, 270, 272, 273,

*Subject Index*

274, 275, 276, 277, 279, 280, 281, 282, 283, 284, 285, 286, 292, 293, 307, 308, 312, 326, 328, 337, 350, 352, 353, 355, 356, 357, 358, 359, 360, 402, 403, 410, 411, 416, 427, 434, 440, 445, 448, 452, 453, 454, 455, 456, 461, 466, 468, 469, 470, 473, 474, 476, 478, 479, 480, 494, 495, 504, 513, 515

Paul, Mart-Jan 36, 141
Peake, A. S. 467
Peirce, James 33
Pelagius 140
Pentateuch 120, 280, 281
Pentecost 8, 38, 111, 115, 116, 293, 301, 306, 311, 314, 315, 322, 323, 327, 329, 333, 335, 337, 338, 340, 341, 342, 343, 344, 436, 462, 491

Pentecost, Dwight 5, 6, 7, 10, 37, 48, 96, 97, 125, 290
Perkins, William 185, 221, 227, 241, 431, 498
Perth 224
Peter 20, 113, 251, 269, 325, 332, 335, 353, 360, 394, 416, 455, 478, 513
Pharaoh 16, 109, 130, 231, 399, 400
Pharisees 121
Philistines 346
Philosophy of science 186, 188, 223, 375
Phinehas 75, 77, 267
Piety 107, 190, 206, 215, 216, 217
Pinnock, Clark 456, 499, 500
Piscator, Johannes 123
Pisidian Antioch 79
Plantinga, Cornelius 153

Polanus, Amandus 373
Polman, Andries 220
Pop 330, 331
Popper, Karl 217
Post-Pentecost believers 333, 338, 340, 341, 436
Postlapsarian covenants 78, 242, 427, 432
Postmillennialists 8
Poythress, V. S. 354
Predestination 152, 155, 161, 181, 182, 206, 207, 219, 222, 223, 227, 229, 241, 246, 381, 382, 383, 388, 390, 395, 420, 432, 501
Premillennialists 8
Presbyterian Christians 157, 158, 167, 376, 416
Presbyterian Church in America 389

591

Presbyterian
  theologians
    158, 181
Presbyterian theology
    161, 171
Presbyterianism
    157, 158
Preston, John
    368
Priesthood 75, 264,
    325, 326,
    401
Priests    29, 51, 52,
    53, 76, 77,
    78, 86,
    142, 264,
    300, 325,
    326, 339,
    341, 422,
    424, 425
Princes    52, 284
Promised land
    8, 71, 73,
    74, 78, 82,
    88, 89, 90,
    91, 97,
    139, 255,
    288, 399,
    400, 421,
    425, 437,
    486, 487,
    488, 492,
    507, 512,
    514, 515
Prophets   5, 36, 52,
    93, 121,
    251, 262,
    269, 302,
    311, 317,
    322, 341,
    360, 436,
    455, 461,
    495, 513

Protestant Reformed
  Churches
    58, 389
Protestant
  theologians
    312, 444
Protestantism
    182, 183
*Protevangelium*
    63, 364,
    365, 422
Pul    324
Puritanism 158
Puritans   158, 166,
    221, 398

**R**
Rabbis     65, 113,
    142, 280
Rachel     115, 331
Rahab      312
Rahner, K. 332
Ramah      255
Rashi      65, 110,
    145
Rationalism
    166
Rechabites 314
Red Sea    399, 491
Redeemer   102, 138,
    139, 272,
    404, 460,
    504
Redemption
    30, 41, 48,
    92, 127,
    128, 130,
    131, 142,
    157, 181,
    225, 226,
    229, 232,
    236, 237,
    242, 272,
    279, 299,
    327, 363,
    367, 368,
    369, 370,
    371, 379,
    383, 384,
    386, 395,
    411, 417,
    419, 420,
    427, 432,
    435, 440,
    449, 497
Redemptive grace
    66, 161,
    169, 420,
    432, 501
Reformation
    153, 158,
    170, 184,
    191, 216,
    238, 444
Reformed Baptists
    8, 175, 465
Reformed Christians
    39, 154,
    158, 167,
    178, 182,
    214, 289,
    347, 365,
    374, 376,
    380, 390,
    408, 434,
    445, 446,
    448, 450,
    463, 484
Reformed Church in
  the US
    389
Reformed Churches in
  Netherlands
    225, 228,
    239, 379,
    380
Reformed Churches
  Liberated
    239

## Subject Index

Reformed covenant
 theology
 2, 151,
 152, 170,
 173, 190,
 205, 206,
 216, 217,
 222, 387,
 416
Reformed doctrine
 169, 170,
 239, 390,
 498
Reformed expositors
 14, 32, 81,
 505, 506,
 507
Reformed theologians
 6, 14, 17,
 27, 37, 42,
 48, 66,
 123, 124,
 130, 142,
 150, 155,
 168, 180,
 183, 186,
 187, 190,
 191, 192,
 195, 215,
 218, 224,
 226, 234,
 237, 240,
 244, 246,
 291, 313,
 364, 366,
 367, 383,
 390, 394,
 430, 432,
 444, 480,
 518
Reformed theology
 23, 40, 42,
 83, 152,
 175, 182,
 183, 186,
 187, 189,
 203, 207,
 222, 229,
 239, 348,
 383, 390,
 417, 428,
 429, 430,
 437, 443,
 444, 448,
 449, 451,
 456, 501
Reformed thinkers
 188, 205,
 222, 241,
 246, 367
Reformed tradition
 23, 451
Reformed world
 167, 226,
 347, 375,
 378, 430,
 453
Reformed worldview
 216
Regeneration
 144, 154,
 160, 172,
 177, 327,
 379, 380,
 381, 393,
 394, 437,
 443, 451,
 455
Remonstrants
 240
Repentance 14, 32, 66,
 93, 126,
 127, 137,
 144, 149,
 150, 237,
 253, 258,
 268, 291,
 335, 395,
 402, 417,
 418, 432,
 433
Replacement
 theology
 5, 187, 345
Reprobation
 155, 156,
 157, 241,
 244, 395,
 501
Restoration of Israel
 74, 231,
 288, 289,
 425, 457,
 505
Ridderbos, J.
 65
Ridderbos, Herman
 205, 210,
 211, 308,
 320, 350,
 467, 468,
 470, 473,
 475, 505,
 506, 507
Ridderus, Franciscus
 506
Righteousness
 2, 18, 19,
 20, 21, 68,
 72, 82, 88,
 92, 96,
 102, 104,
 116, 121,
 122, 128,
 135, 141,
 147, 149,
 150, 164,
 198, 229,
 235, 250,
 251, 259,
 260, 261,
 262, 268,
 273, 274,
 283, 284,
 288, 296,

319, 327, 328, 423, 426, 433, 441, 448, 489, 508, 515, 517
Rimmon 511
Ritualism 120, 478
Robertson, O. Palmer 10, 61, 130, 374, 515
Rolfe, John 399
Rollock, Robert 221, 368
Roman Catholic Church 186, 347, 377, 390
Roman Catholic theology 42, 182, 186, 187
Roman Catholicism 171, 187, 188, 347
Roman Empire 56, 457
Rome 170
Roozemeijer, J. H. L. 507
Rosner, B. S. 238
Ryrie, Charles C. 7, 289, 343

S
Sabbath 17, 33, 82, 85, 87, 93, 94, 166, 251, 266, 271, 354, 408, 409, 413, 415, 496, 506
Sabbaths 87, 415
Sacraments 49, 160, 163, 174, 245, 474
Sacred Text 42, 43
Saints 107, 154, 155, 157, 182, 312, 317, 324, 333, 340, 343, 392, 447, 461
Salem 77, 78
Salvation 4, 8, 43, 57, 92, 95, 132, 134, 144, 149, 150, 154, 156, 159, 160, 164, 166, 174, 177, 187, 188, 190, 200, 206, 211, 220, 222, 224, 226, 229, 236, 237, 241, 245, 247, 253, 258, 259, 268, 272, 274, 275, 283, 286, 302, 308, 310, 311, 315, 328, 333, 335, 355, 356, 364, 367, 368, 373, 382, 389, 392, 395, 409, 410, 419, 420, 421, 422, 423, 424, 425, 426, 430, 436, 438, 440, 443, 444, 448, 450, 481, 504
Samaria 421, 488
Samaritans 4
Samson 24
Sanctification 92, 137, 198, 243, 392, 439, 450, 451, 457
Sanders, E. P. 286
Sandlin, P. A. 387
Sarah 71, 145, 250, 280, 281, 282, 283, 284, 312, 332, 366, 407
Satan 196, 365, 421, 422, 478, 479
Saucy, R. L. 7
Saul 13, 55, 79, 80, 111, 398
Saul of Tarsus 400
Schilder, Klaas 72, 134, 226, 227, 239, 371, 386
Schlatter, A. 279, 506
Schniewind, J. 506

*Subject Index*

Schoeps, H. J. 329
Scholasticism 163, 185
Schouls, C. A. 10
Schreiner, T. R. 10, 238, 467, 470, 472
Schrenk, Gottlob 220, 222
Schuyler English, E. 506
Schweizer, E. 467
Schwertley, Brian 388, 431
Scofield, Cyrus 7, 42, 43, 101
*Scofield Reference Bible* 7, 42, 43
Scotland 158, 398
Scots Confession 163
Scripture 2, 5, 6, 7, 18, 38, 40, 41, 42, 43, 44, 48, 60, 83, 103, 123, 125, 132, 139, 140, 146, 152, 153, 155, 156, 157, 162, 165, 168, 169, 178, 179, 180, 183, 185, 188, 190, 191, 192, 193, 196, 197, 200, 208, 211, 214, 215, 217, 224, 229, 236, 237, 242, 244, 263, 269, 270, 287, 293, 317, 323, 348, 360, 367, 369, 370, 374, 384, 385, 390, 392, 420, 427, 431, 432, 433, 435, 451, 452, 471, 476, 482, 483, 484, 498, 515
Second Helvetic Confession 163, 178
Second Vatican Council 347
Sectarianism 378, 391
Septuagint 25, 26, 31, 299, 302, 307, 332
Shecaniah 52
Shechem 30, 50
Shem 67, 117, 201, 271, 404, 423, 429
Sheol 55
Shepherd, Norman 10, 168, 170
Shimei 13
Shishko, W. 168
Shulam, J. 360
Simons, Menno 238, 239
Sinaitic covenant 4, 9, 15, 19, 20, 24, 30, 35, 36, 43, 52, 70, 82, 83, 84, 85, 89, 101, 103, 104, 105, 109, 111, 118, 122, 123, 124, 140, 141, 145, 169, 228, 229, 230, 232, 233, 234, 237, 242, 250, 259, 269, 271, 273, 274, 281, 283, 286, 291, 298, 329, 379, 417, 424, 459, 486, 487, 488, 492, 493
Sinaitic Torah 10, 15, 65, 86, 87, 281, 296, 351
Slotki, I. W. 65
Smith, D. 454
Smith, David L. 343, 359
Smith, R. A. 10, 387

Snecanus, Gellius 240
Solomon 11, 21, 22, 24, 30, 54, 77, 78, 80, 81, 90, 121, 200, 328, 493
Son of David 68, 78, 79, 80, 82, 97, 288
Son of God 63, 73, 77, 81, 253, 277, 311, 331, 337, 395, 446, 447, 454, 455, 459
Sonship 48, 49, 59, 63, 67, 73, 77, 81, 88, 90, 95, 436, 459, 460
South Africa 193, 399, 401
Sovereign grace 57, 132, 134, 140, 142, 147, 206, 229, 233, 236, 241, 243, 274, 275, 382, 390, 501
Sovereignty of God 26, 153, 418, 497
Spain 398
Spirit baptism 160, 323, 343

Spiritual circumcision 71, 94, 177, 403, 466, 468, 469, 470, 471, 472, 473, 475, 476, 478, 479, 482, 515
Spiritual Israel 2, 7, 91, 115, 187, 207, 253, 254, 287, 289, 306, 313, 316, 324, 342, 345, 347, 348, 350, 353, 364, 398, 401, 418, 428, 429, 432, 438, 461, 515, 518
Spiritualism 41, 306, 416, 418, 433, 514
Spiritualization 250, 295, 503, 506, 509
Spiritualizing 289, 293, 294, 503, 513, 514, 518
Sproul, R. C. 499, 500
Spurgeon, Charles H. 175
Spykman, Gordon 194, 342

Stam, Clarence 10, 19, 20, 21, 22, 23, 37, 38, 39, 58, 71, 78, 86, 87, 105, 106, 133, 134, 135, 144, 196, 199, 313, 336, 353, 356, 358, 365, 374, 381, 419, 448, 459, 467, 470, 473
Stavropoulos, C. 446, 448
Steenblok, Cornelis 186, 228, 385
Stephen 31, 73, 269, 308
Stern, David 265, 350, 351, 412, 413
Stiles, Ezra 399
Strawbridge, G. 10, 173, 405
Strehle, S. 10
Substitutionalism 5, 187
Sunday 87, 264, 409
Supersessionism 5, 74, 187, 207, 250, 289, 306, 345, 347, 364, 397, 401, 404, 416, 418,

## Subject Index

430, 432, 496, 515, 518
Supersessionists 356, 430, 438
Suurmond, Jean-Jacques 449
Suzerainty covenants 12, 28, 55
Symmachus 26
Synod of Dort 390
Systematic theology 7, 41, 42, 152, 182, 490

## T

Tabernacle 36, 76, 77, 126, 270, 492, 493
Tabrimmon 55
Talmud 15, 18, 19, 110, 113, 121, 329, 360
Tamar 312
Tarshish 324
Temple of God 214, 340, 435, 443, 494
Temple of Solomon, 77, 81, 493
Temple of the Holy Spirit 2, 8, 306, 318, 322, 327, 462
Temple of the Spirit 317, 416

Ten Commandments 1, 35, 36, 85, 162, 164, 165, 166, 408, 409, 417, 418, 486, 492
Ten Words 35, 86, 90, 125, 126, 137, 138, 139, 262
Tertullian 182
Theological paradigms 152, 179, 180, 191, 206
Theologism 416, 431
Theosis 96, 156, 446, 447, 448, 451, 452, 453, 454, 455, 456
Thirty-Nine Articles 163
Thomas à Kempis 452
Three Forms of Unity 158, 163, 164, 167, 168, 170, 171, 374, 431
Throne of David 80, 82, 97, 418, 426, 438, 508, 509, 510
Torah of Christ 258, 260, 266, 297, 408

Torah of liberty 263
Torah of Messiah 258, 259, 260, 262
Torrance, James B. 220
Tower of Hananel 255, 511
Transvaal 399
Tree of life 63, 64, 139, 485
Trim, D. J. B. 400
Trinity 157, 223, 367, 368, 369, 370, 413, 419, 442
Trinterud, Leonard J. 220
Troost, A. 378
Tsaddiqim 117, 119, 128, 326
Tubal 324
Turretin, Francis 155
Twelve tribes of Israel 85, 89, 92, 250, 329, 492
Typology 136, 137, 280, 513
Tyre 200

## U

Ulster 400, 401
United Reformed Churches 389
Universal atonement 225, 226, 241
Ursinus, Zacharias 134, 161,

597

## V

Valley of Achor
116
Van 't Spijker, Willem
183, 220,
313, 484
Van Asselt, W. J.
222
Van Bruggen, Jakob
404, 405,
474
Van Campen, M.
218, 221,
506
Van de Beek,
Abraham
474, 475
Van den Bergh, W.
218
Van der Groe,
Theodorus
506
Van der Schuit, J. J.
225
Van der Vegt, W. H.
183, 218
Van der Waal,
Cornelis
10, 11, 38,
39, 53, 60,
64, 66, 107,
130, 162,
163, 166,
193, 200,
201, 230,
269, 307,
356, 374,
419
Van der Zwaag, K.
123, 185,
186, 218,
221, 225,
162, 221,
373, 431
Van Gelder, Craig
322
Van Genderen, Jan
14, 159,
171, 191,
206, 207,
221, 225,
246, 342,
343, 348,
371, 374,
394, 396,
471, 507
Van Giffen, David
507
Van Klinken, G. J.
515
Van Kooten, R. C.
180
Van Leeuwen, Jacobus
473
Van Limborch,
Philipp
206, 242,
243
Van Mastricht, Petrus
221
Van Ronkel,
Philippus
183, 185,
188
Van Til, C.  58
Van Unnik, W. C.
211
Vander Zee, L. J.
437
VanGemeren, W. A.
23
Vassals  28, 34, 35,
108, 198,
199, 429
Vaughan, Curtis
469, 475
241, 380,
382
Veenendaal
385
Veluanus, Joannes
Anastasius
240
Venema, Cornelis
149, 172,
174
Veninga, James
218, 219
Verboom, Willem
13, 71, 73,
141, 174,
191, 194,
199, 200,
201, 204,
205, 215,
218, 219,
220, 221,
222, 227,
238, 239,
247, 375,
384, 396,
430, 482,
498
Verkuyl, Johan
332, 347,
359
Versteeg, Johannes P.
177, 467,
470, 471,
473, 474,
480
Vetus Latina
26
Virgin Mary
194, 312
Virginia  399
Vischer, L.  389
Visser 't Hooft, W. A.
333
Vitringa, Campegius
507
Voetius, Gisbert
186, 506

598

## Subject Index

Voorberg, P. L. 173, 471
Voorhoeve, Herman 176
Vulgate 3, 219

## W

Walvoord, J. F. 7, 125, 506
Warfield, Benjamin 172
Washington, George 399
Water baptism 2, 160, 323, 474
Waters, G. P. 10, 388
Watson, David 345
Weinfeld, Moshe 29
Weir, D. A. 10, 222
Wellum, Stephen 3, 8, 10, 40, 41, 61, 64, 81, 125, 130, 146, 149, 152, 173, 175, 184, 190, 207, 238, 333, 344, 366, 396, 397, 430, 465, 472, 482, 515, 516
Wentsel, Ben 49, 173, 174, 177, 182, 205, 207, 214, 313, 314, 330, 345, 356, 394, 473, 518
Western theology 428, 447, 448, 449, 451
Westminster Assembly 158
Westminster Confession 42, 43, 137, 155, 156, 158, 159, 161, 164, 168, 229, 309, 315, 366, 373, 448, 450, 458
Westminster Larger Catechism 158, 160, 163, 164, 373, 448, 450
Westminster Seminary 167
Westminster Shorter Catechism 158, 160
Westminster Standards 43, 124, 157, 158, 159, 161, 164, 167, 168, 169, 170, 373, 374, 377, 389, 390, 391, 431
White, Blake 42
Wiggertszoon, Cornelis 240
Wilkins, S. 10, 387
William III of Orange 398
William the Silent 398
Williamson, Paul R. 39, 61, 69
Wilson, A. I. 10, 194
Wink, Adriaan 239
Witherspoon, John 401
Witsius, Herman 185, 221, 227, 431, 506
Woelderink, Jan Gerrit 192, 226, 371, 386, 394
Wolf, Hans H. 183, 220, 232
Wolters, A. 446
Wright, D. F. 467
Wright, N. T. 10, 73, 332, 344, 451, 452
Wright, S. D. 10, 406, 471, 472

## Y

Yale College 399
YHWH 60, 70, 73, 138, 486

Yitschaqi, Rabbi
    Shlomo
        110
Yom Kippur
    90, 126

## Z
Zadok    76, 77, 294, 425
Zanchius, Hieronymus
    186, 221, 245
Zechariah    21, 119, 251, 267, 268, 328, 489
Zedekiah    11, 12, 29, 34, 52
Zerubbabel 509
Zerwick, M.
    351, 453
Zion    5, 22, 78, 79, 80, 81, 82, 95, 96, 97, 115, 148, 250, 255, 272, 282, 283, 284, 310, 329, 330, 337, 348, 402, 409, 421, 426, 487, 504, 509, 510, 511
Zulus    400
Zwingli, Ulrich
    153, 171, 183, 188, 221
Zwinglians 153

www.ingramcontent.com/pod-product-compliance
Lightning Source LLC
Chambersburg PA
CBHW060646150426
42811CB00086B/2444/J